MY
DIARIES
Part
One

BOOKS BY WILFRID SCAWEN BLUNT

PROSE

THE FUTURE OF ISLAM 1882
IDEAS ABOUT INDIA 1885
THE SECRET HISTORY SERIES
   I THE SECRET HISTORY OF THE ENGLISH OCCU-
      PATION OF EGYPT 1907
  II INDIA UNDER RIPON 1909
 III GORDON AT KHARTOUM 1911
 IV THE LAND WAR IN IRELAND 1912
  V MY DIARIES PART I. [THE SCRAMBLE FOR
      AFRICA] 1919
 VI MY DIARIES PART II. [THE COALITION
      AGAINST GERMANY] 1920

POETRY

LOVE SONNETS OF PROTEUS 1880
THE WIND AND THE WHIRLWIND 1883
IN VINCULIS 1889
A NEW PILGRIMAGE 1889
ESTHER AND LOVE LYRICS 1892
GRISELDA 1893
SATAN ABSOLVED 1899
SEVEN GOLDEN ODES OF ARABIA 1903
POETICAL WORKS. A COMPLETE EDITION 1914
POEMS [SELECTION BY FLOYD DELL] 1923

PUBLISHER'S NOTE

This edition of MY DIARIES is a full and complete reprint of the much sought after London edition of 1919–1920. Mr. Blunt has himself passed the proofs as well as the Foreword by Lady Gregory.

I owe a special word of thanks to my friend, Osmond Kessler Fraenkel, Esq., for great assistance in seeing these volumes through the press. Mr. Fraenkel is also in a large part responsible for the indices.

A. A. K.

PREFACE WRITTEN FOR THIS EDITION BY LADY GREGORY

A few Sundays ago I was staying with Mr. Blunt at Newbuildings Place, that ancient and beautiful manor house which has been a best loved part of his inheritance, as I have been used to do perhaps once in a year when chance or business draws me from Ireland to London. We were out of doors all the morning, he in his pony chair, in the beautiful oak woods that cover some five hundred of his Sussex acres. Our midday meal was set out nearer the house yet still under blossoming trees. Peacocks came to be fed and among them a Spanish lamb, black-spotted, using its sprouting horns to butt at the watch dog in whose companionship it had been reared. And as we talked "the Squire," (for so he is known to his people) told me, and with pleasure in the telling, that these volumes of his "Diaries," being sold out in England were now being printed in America, an honour new to him, for his work is not yet so widely known there as at home. But he said, and he was a little troubled with regard to this, that a new preface had been asked of him that would give something more of a biography, even of a confession, than is to be found in the text of the "Diaries" and "I am not at present" he said "in a mood for writing this." I did not see him again, but after my return to Ireland not many days later, a homecoming hastened by news of troublesome events near by, a letter came from him reminding me of our talk and asking me to "do him a great kindness" and myself write the few needed words. I felt such a request from my friend of forty years an honour and not to be refused if I could but accomplish it, but there is much to say in a short space and it is sometimes harder to say less than more.

"I have lived my life in full" he said the other day and he had written, as I remembered, in the preface to the complete edition of his verse, "No life is perfect that has not been lived, youth in feeling, manhood in battle, old age in meditation," and that very same day someone said to me in London when I spoke of him "His life has been lived for freedom." That full life of his has, more happily than many, found its record not only in public action but in the intensity of lyrical expression — as an earlier poet has said "outward to man—inward to the Gods." He tells in these diaries

vii

in vigorous prose of the circumstances that have in the last 30 years surrounded him, of talks with friends, and the gossip of Parliaments, of gatherings for shooting or for tennis or for the sales of his famous Arab Stud. They were written in early mornings not only where Eastern travel accustomed him to rise with the rising of the sun but through London seasons, and visits to great country houses in fine society, for he was many sided; a man of fashion, rider to hounds at home; rider also on the camels of the desert; attaché at the court of a King of Greece, a Queen of Spain, an Emperor of the French at the time of that Emperor's supreme vain glory, translator from the Arabic; painter, architect and sculptor (as is shown in his greatest effort, the beautiful monument at Crawley, the recumbent figure of his brother); politician outside Parliament; revolutionist and helper of revolutions.

A brief summary of his earlier history, before I knew him, has been given me by a friend of his and mine:

"The English books of reference tell us that Mr. Wilfrid Scawen Blunt was born at Crabbet Park in Sussex in the year 1840. His father was a squire possessed of some four thousand acres mostly of forest land; a justice of the peace, a Deputy Lieutenant of that county, and master of the local foxhounds, who had served in the Peninsular campaign and had carried the colours of the Grenadier Guards under Sir John Moore at the battle of Corunna where he was wounded, and remained through life a follower of the Duke of Wellington, the object of his political devotion.

"Mr. Blunt's sole hereditary connection with letters, it is interesting to learn, was that the family estates in Sussex lay closely adjoining those of the Shelleys and that his great grandfather was fellow justice of the peace to Percy Shelley's father and that they sat as Magistrates on the same Bench at the County town of Horsham, also that his father was a contemporary at Harrow School of that other great poet Byron, and acted as "fag" to him there according to English public school fashion for a year, memories that are cherished in the family traditions.

"Left an orphan while yet a child, he had been brought up a Catholic and had received his education under the Jesuits at Stonyhurst and later at Oscott, but pursued his education no further. He was never at an university, but at the early age of eighteen was given, by one of his guardians connected with the Ministry of the day, a post in the Diplomatic Service and was sent abroad the same year as attaché to the British Legation at Athens and afterwards by way of Constantinople to Germany, where he went through a mental crisis connected with the Darwinian discussions of the day, allusions to which will be found in the diaries.

"From Frankfort he was transferred in 1863 to Madrid and in the following year to the Paris Embassy, just then at the full height of the short lived glory of the Second Napoleonic Empire. Here the romantic follies of his youth began and with them the first out-pourings of his poetic faculty followed by a diplomatic exile to the remoter posts in the service — to the Legations of Portugal and the River Plate. On his return to Europe he married Lady Anna-bella Noel, the only daughter of William Earl of Lovelace and of Ada Byron, that child of romance to whom the poet Byron addressed those pathetic lines: "Ada, sole daughter of my house and heart"; and the year after on the death of his elder brother he left the diplomatic service and settled down to a country life on his ancestral acres. There he and his highly gifted wife busied themselves for some half dozen years, she with painting, he with sculpture, and in secret with those verses which afterwards were to become so celebrated as "The Sonnets of Proteus," and both in the rebuilding of their family home, Crabbet Park, a work for which they were their own sole architects.

"In 1875 tiring of too inadventurous a life at home, a sudden impulse started them on a series of romantic horseback journeys in Spain, Algeria and Asia Minor, and eventually in that still wilder wandering in Mesopotamia, Persia and the as yet quite unvisited regions of Central Arabia."

It was in 1881 that my first meeting with him and Lady Anne took place, at Cairo, when they were living in the garden they had bought on the desert edge of Heliopolis; and at that meeting my husband had told us how some years before at a bull fight at Madrid he had been struck by the extraordinary good looks of the young matador awaiting the rush of the bull in the arena and asking who he was heard he was an attaché from the English Embassy, Wilfrid Blunt. That fine poem of his on the dying bull fighter Sancho Sanchez shows perhaps the hidden root of that adventure:

"Meaning was there in our courage and the calm of our demeanour,
For there stood a foe before us which had need of all our skill,
And our lives were as the programme, and the world was our arena,
And the wicked beast was death and the horns of death were Hell.

"And the boast of our profession was a bulwark against danger
With its fearless expectation of what good or ill may come,
For the very prince of darkness shall burst forth on us no stranger
When the doors of death fly open to the rolling of the drum. "

I will quote again from the summary: "At the time of his arrival at Cairo Mr. Blunt was still in the good books of the Foreign Office and in personal correspondence with Mr. Gladstone as an authority on Oriental matters and had just published his first prose work "The Future of Islam." But overborne by his strong natural sympathy for liberty he espoused the cause of Egyptian National-ism, and when the quarrel between England and the Egyptians came to hostilities at the bombardment of Alexandria he refused to abandon the cause that he had taken up, with the result that when after the defeat of Tel el Kebir the Egyptian leader Arabi found himself a prisoner of war threatened with death at the hands of a court martial, he succeeded in rousing popular feeling in England to shame at their betrayal of an honourable cause, the first of free-dom in the East, and secured his release and honourable exile.

"The public action taken by Mr. Blunt in opposition to the Foreign Office, his first appearence in English political life, brought him into close connection with the leading politicians of the day and amongst others Parnell and the other members of the Irish Party and he joined the new group of Tory Democrats founded by Lord Randolph Churchill at that time in opposition which eventually succeeded in over-throwing the Government at the election of 1885. His fearless action with regard to Egypt ended his friendly relations with the Foreign Office and resulted in his exile from Egypt and he was forbidden to enter that country for some three years; and came to be regarded as the *'enfant terrible'* in politics just as Samuel Butler was in art and literature."

I wrote to him a little while ago asking if he had any letters of mine written from or to Egypt at the time of Arabi's rebellion for, I said, it seemed to me I had made my education in politics there. And he an-swered "You talk of having made your political education in Egypt, and so too did I with you, for before that eventful year 1882 I had never played a public part of any kind or written so much as a letter to *The Times* with my name to it and we made our education together over it." All that story is told in his "Secret History of the Occupation of Egypt"; and he records that among his most important supporters there were Lord Houghton "who in early life had been an enthusi-astic advocate of freedom in the East, and Sir William Gregory, an old follower of Gladstone and well known Liberal and who sent more than one powerful letter to what was then the leading journal of Europe (*The Times*) giving the Nationalist side. . . It is hardly too much to say that Gregory's letters and mine, especially his, were largely the means of obtaining a respite for Egypt from the dangers that threatened her." But after the war had been formally declared and at London evening parties "everyone was rejoicing over the bombardment of

Alexandria " Wilfrid Blunt was almost alone in openly taking the part of the Egyptians; though Lord Houghton, while declaring himself for victory, characteristically told him that if he did go to Egypt he must bring back Arabi with him " and you must both come and dine with me." When after Tel el Kebir the short war was over, and Cairo had fallen and Arabi had surrendered, a rumor went round that he and his officers, prisoners of war in English hands, were to be put to death, and a private letter of Mr. Gladstone's confirmed this possibility, some men of honour and good feeling held up their hands in horror yet saw no way to compel the Ministry to abide by justice and custom and avoid this disgrace. But Mr. Blunt found a way and within two or three days he had engaged Counsel to act for the Egyptian rebels' defence. He wrote to me at the time, " I have taken the precaution of sending out a couple of lawyers to see what can be done. We are the rear guard of a beaten army where there are plenty of blows and no glory to be won. Egypt may get a certain share of financial ease but she will not get liberty, at least not in our time, and the bloodless revolution so nearly brought about has been drowned in blood."

When the expenses of the defence of the prisoner began to be very heavy some subscriptions were sent towards it by, amongst others, Lord Wentworth, Lord Wemyss, Frederic Harrison, Admiral Lord Mark Kerr, Lord Randolph Churchill A. W. Kinglake, George Meredith, and General Gordon (who wrote with his, " I suppose Government will not pay it. Arabi himself will repay it within a year's time "). But with a splendid generosity Mr. Blunt took the whole burden upon himself, paying if I remember aright a sum of £3,000. It was not his last service to Egypt, and that passionate denunciation of the Imperal Government in "The Wind and the Whirlwind," though it went past the ears closed to any but an official voice still stands as an indictment and a prophecy. Here are some of his lines:

> Oh insolence of strength! Oh boast of wisdom!
>   Oh poverty in all things truly wise!
> Thinkest thou, England, God can be outwitted
>   For ever thus by him who sells and buys?
>
> Thou sellest the sad nations to their ruin.
>   What hast thou bought? The child within the womb,
> The son of him thou slayest to thy hurting,
>   Shall answer thee "An Empire for thy tomb."
>
> Thou hast joined house to house for thy perdition.
>   Thou hast done evil in the name of right.
> Thou hast made bitter sweet and the sweet bitter,
>   And called light darkness and the darkness light.

Thou art become a by-word for dissembling,
  A beacon to thy neighbors for all fraud.
Thy deeds of violence men count and reckon.
  Who takes the sword shall perish by the sword.

The Empire thou didst build shall be divided.
  Thou shalt be weighed in thine own balances
Of usury to peoples and to princes,
  And be found wanting by the world and these.

Thy Empire shall be parted and thy Kingdom.
  At thy own doors a Kingdom shall arise,
Where freedom shall be preached and the wrong righted
  Which thy unwisdom wrought in days unwise.

Truth yet shall triumph in a world of justice.
  This is of faith. I swear it. East and West
The law of Man's progression shall accomplish
  Even this last great marvel with the rest.

Thou wouldst not further it, Thou canst not hinder.
  If thou shalt learn in time thou yet shalt live.
But God shall ease thy hand of its dominion,
  And give to these the rights thou wouldst not give.

The nations of the East have left their childhood.
  Thou art grown old.   Their manhood is to come;
And they shall carry on Earth's high tradition
  Through the long ages when thy lips are dumb.

The wisdom of the West is but a madness,
  The fret of shallow waters in their beds.
Yours is the flow, the fulness of Man's patience,
  The ocean of God's rest inherited.

I think when London fashion turned against him for his support
of the Egyptians who fought for freedom, his good looks were a positive
annoyance to his enemies. All had not the good humour of Lord
Houghton who said to me in his whimsical way "The fellow knows he
has a handsome head and he wants it to be seen on Temple Bar." Those
good looks on the other hand and perhaps his love of horses softened
the sternness of magistrates who visited him according to their duty
when he was picking oakum as a prisoner in a cell of Galway gaol. For
in the Land League days, turning from the East he had taken up the

cause of "the Westernmost of all European nations and the most Christian," and had held it an honour to be "the first Englishman put in prison for Ireland's sake." He was condemned to two months of that prison life for holding a meeting of protest "against the denial of the right universally claimed by our countrymen to speak where grievances exist." Lady Anne, devoted and heroic, Byron's granddaughter, Ada's daughter, lingered near the gaol until work on his behalf called her to England. He took his punishment with a gallant spirit. Bereft of books he found pleasure in watching the seagulls as they hovered overhead, and the jackdaws and sparrows on the look out for scraps of prison food; talking of horse flesh with the visiting justices, even finding a solace in the oakum-picking "the unravelling of an old tarred rope with a good healthy smell " — (I still possess a strand of this smuggled from the cell, and acting as a marker to my copy of his prison poems "In Vinculis") ; even hiding a bit of rope on Saturday to begile the tedium of the unoccupied Sabbath; but finding his chief hardship in those January nights, being given but scanty covering as he lay on the plank bed that he found harder than the naked ground of any of his Eastern encampments. But with a hidden scrap of pencil he wrote sonnets on the blank leaves of his prayer book, and some of these are a cry from one who feels real suffering:

> "God knows, 'twas not with a fore-reasoned plan
> I left the easeful dwellings of my peace
> And sought this conflict with ungodly Man
> And ceaseless still through years that do not cease
> Have warred with Powers and Principalities.
> My natural soul, ere yet these strifes began,
> Was as a sister, diligent to please
> And loving all, and most the human clan.
> God knows it. And He knows how the world's tears
> Touched me. And He is witness of my wrath,
> How it was kindled against murderers
> Who slew for gold, and how upon their path
> I met them. Since which day the World in arms
> Strikes at my life with angers and alarms."

An *"enfant terrible"* of politics indeed, he has kept to the resolve recorded in the first page of these Diaries of " pleading the cause of the backward nations of the world " in and out of season. He has never given up his right of protest against injustice in Egypt and elsewhere, denouncing the floggings and hangings of the villagers of Denshawai in 1905; calling out against the hanging of Dingra, the Hindoo political assassin, in 1909; against the Italian massacres of Arabs in Tripoli

in 1911; against the hanging of Roger Casement in 1914; and against
the "lawyers arguments" used in the British Cabinet to urge and
justify the late war. An unusual and gallant record for a Sussex
gentleman of many acres, of inherited wealth and ease.

The story told in these Diaries from year to year, sometimes from
day to day, the "humour, the charming good temper that flickers into
all corners of life" through its pages makes a richly woven background,
a tapestry of rich colour, for the adventure of that personal life, the
"life of love, the romance of travel, the delight in woods and fields and
skies, the pride of ancestry and race" ascribed to him by one who
knew him; the many gifts, the mastery of living, that seem to belong
to the heroic ages of the world, that show him out as one of Plutarch's
men.

JUNE 12, 1921.   A. GREGORY.

FOREWORD

In issuing this, the fifth volume of my " Secret History " series, at the present moment, I feel that, with much that is only too trivial in the diary (a thing not written for publication) here are certain passages in it for which apology is due from me for their too plain speaking in what will be thought by some an unpatriotic sense. The fault is perhaps not wholly mine, rather the change which has been wrought in the public mind and heart of England by the heroic efforts made by her sons unselfishly in the war.

The period the volume travels over in English public life — 1888 to 1900 — was in truth anything but a noble one, and judged by the high standards now professed in Downing Street and echoed by the universal popular voice, proclaiming international right and a respect for the weak nations of the world, may deserve the worst that I have said of it, and yet my telling be resented as an untimely reminder of lapses the country would wish to forget. It includes the Matabele and Boer wars, and the wars on the Nile, where England led the way in the white scramble for Africa. There is a special danger for me of displeasure in regard to Egypt, which forms so large a topic in the text, as it becomes more clear that among the many contributory causes leading to the final catastrophe of the great World War of 1914, our obstinacy in retaining Egypt, notwithstanding all our promises, must be counted as one of the foremost. It will be reproached to me that I have sought to excuse Germany by showing that there were others primarily guilty and not only the Central Empires. I regret this the more because I know how many of the noblest there are amongst us who are consoling their sore hearts, wounded in the war, with the thought that at least the quarrel was thrust on England by no fault of hers, and who cannot but be disturbed by my reminder of the broader truth which teaches that our own Imperial ambitions were also a reason of the quarrel. Yet the truth of history needs to be told, and not only in Blue Books, where the essential facts are travestied, but by individual testimony such as mine, recording the words of statesmen in out of office hours, when they have spoken their naked thought to me in very different language. I cannot believe but that it is a service rendered to my fellow countrymen to do this at a moment when we are endeavouring to reconstruct our ruined world on a basis sounder than before, to disabuse them of an illusion, even a happy one, obscuring their clear vision.

Nor must it be imagined that, because the period treated here shows England the chief sinner among the white Empires in their dealings with the weak nations of the African world, my sympathy is more with the others. As masters of alien races both France and Italy, to say nothing of Portugal and Belgium, have shown themselves far worse and less scrupulous oppressors than we have been, or in Asia than Russia was under the Czars, while, as for Germany, it was less the will than the opportunity of evil that limited its lawless ventures. I have no love for the German race or its ideals, having an ancient bone to pick with Prussia dating from as long ago as the Franco-Prussian War of 1870, when, young and enthusiastic, I made a vow of boycotting the whole Teutonic race (a vow which I have kept), but this does not blind me to the fact that as active aggressors in deed as well as word, it was not at Berlin that the first steps were taken in the direction of world-wide conquest. The will was there, theatrically displayed at intervals in Kaiser Wilhelm's not quite sane pronouncements, and to my knowledge had been there before his day; but Germany's plunder of the weak had been small in act compared to ours, or even to that of France, during the past half century, while in each and all of the great Empires there had been the same ominous growth of militarism and contempt for the old rules of international right where the defenceless peoples were concerned. The only difference between Berlin morality and ours in Downing Street had been that we had been careful to preserve our outward attitude of forbearance and respect for moral right, while Berlin had been shameless in its anti-human logic. Also that as an Empire we were already sated like a lion surrounded with the carcasses of its prey, while Germany was alert and hungry. Well might we want peace! Almost as well might Germany prepare for war!

These things, which need to be remembered, will be found more plainly indicated in Part II of the present issue, which will be published in the course of the summer, and complete my contribution of *Mémoires pour servir à l'histoire de mon temps,* and, as I think, discharge my true patriotic duty as a nineteenth century Englishman.

Xmas, 1918.   W. S. B.

P.S.— It has been suggested to me, as an appropriate addition to the value of the present volume, that I should place in the Appendix a transcript of a yet earlier diary kept by me during the first months of the Franco-Prussian War of 1870. There is so much in these that stands in close relation with the war just over, that I have agreed, and so I print them here.

CONTENTS

PART ONE

THE SCRAMBLE FOR AFRICA

PART I

1888 TO 1900

CHAPTER I

A VISIT TO GREECE IN 1888

The year 1888 saw the close of my activities in English public life. How this came about was described in my volume, " The Land War in Ireland." It told how, having fought my battle for Nationalism there and lost it (for my imprisonment had failed to win me the seat in Parliament which alone would have justified me in English eyes for the part I had played in the Celtic quarrel) I resolved to look no more to action at home but to seek in other ways what I still felt to be my mission in life, that of pleading the cause of the backward nations of the world, and especially those of Asia and Africa, from their slavery to Europe. I knew myself to be regarded as a beaten man, and for the moment my depression was extreme.

Socially, as well as politically, I needed rehabilitation. My " unpatriotic " vagaries, for such they were looked upon, had estranged me from most of my personal friends, my blood relations and those I loved best; nor could I content myself with my new political acquaintances or, with the strong instinct I had of the claims of kinship, shift my heart at once to a new hold and break permanently with the society in which I had been bred. All my relations and nearly all my intimate friends were in the Tory camp, and I had no natural footing in any other. With the exception of the Carlisles and the Harcourts, I was at home in none of the great Whig houses, and in my own county of Sussex I stood absolutely alone in my opinions. Nothing can be conceived more dispiriting than the attempts at social entertainment made that Spring in London by the few Liberal peers who had declared for Home Rule, unwilling followers of Gladstone. I went with my wife to one of these, at Spencer House, but we found ourselves among strangers and did not go to another. At Crabbet it mattered less, for I was Lord there of my own Manor, cock on my own dunghill, yet I had been shocked by the incongruity of being met at my door on

my return from Kilmainham by a deputation consisting of three Irish
M.P.'s and Langridge, our local cobbler and only Radical. It revealed
the full nakedness of the land for me at home, on any lines but those
of silence and abstention. And thus the summer passed. I occupied
myself once more with my Arab horse breeding, I wrote verses and
enjoyed my physical life in the green Sussex woods as in former days,
but with the sadness a sense of failure brings. I left off keeping my
journal, so little there was of happy interest to record, so much that
was unhappy. An unfortunate family quarrel about this time, in which
I was constrained, unwillingly, to take a part, added to my bitterness in
regard to the public situation, and a gap of four months occurs in the
entries. It was not till quite the end of the summer that I was able
to rouse myself into any more profitable line of thought than that of
vain regrets and hopes made void.

By the middle of autumn, however, tired of inaction, a longing
seized me once more to visit Egypt and those desert lands in which so
many of my winters had been spent. With the Arabs I had a second
home, less estranged from me than the other, and I should find myself,
I knew, in that " rut of centuries " which is so soothing to the Japhetic
soul troubled with Europe's ephemeral ills. Thus, on the 9th of
November my journal is resumed, and shows me on my way eastwards
with my wife and my daughter Judith, now taken for the first time
abroad with us, at Paris, enjoying, for a few days, something of my
old life with my cousin, Francis Currie, whom I had not for some
years seen.

" 10th Nov.— Bitters and I breakfasted together this morning and
took one of our familiar walks in the afternoon, visiting Richelieu's
tomb at the Sorbonne and the Panthéon and the Hôtel de Cluny. The
tomb is a fine thing in the best style of French sculpture. We also
stopped and looked at the new monument to Gambetta [by Aubé, then
an unknown name to me] which I like better than I could have thought
possible. It has good proportion and a certain movement and originality which have merit. We could not have produced anything half
so good in England. They are pulling down the sheds on the site of
the Tuileries, leaving the Carousel open to the garden. This has a
poor effect, but it leaves a fine opportunity of rebuilding to Boulanger,
or whoever else succeeds to the French throne.

" 11th Nov.— Hearing that Lady C. was in Paris, I called on her,
and through her persuasion was introduced to her friend Lacretelle,
the painter, whose brother, a prominent deputy, was intimate with
Boulanger, and he invited me to call upon the *brave général*. Lady C.
had already made Boulanger's acquaintance, and had spcken to me
about him when I had seen her in London. Her description of him
reminded me not a little of Napoleon III, ' very amiable, but rather

dull, not at all like a soldier, and with a hand the most disagreeable to touch of any she remembered. She could not explain in what the repulsion consisted.' Nevertheless, she seemed impressed with him. He is floated financially, she tells me, by Mrs. Mackay the American, and if war comes, he may yet achieve his fortune."

This resulted in my being taken (15th Nov.) by Lacretelle to see the General at his house near the Barrière de l'Etoile. The moment of our visit was that of the very height of his popularity, when it was believed in Paris that he was about to repeat the adventure of Prince Louis Napoleon in 1851, when France, tired of her constitutional *régime* and a Republic which had brought her no credit, was ready for "a Saviour of Society," who should restore to her something of her military glory. This might be effected either by a restoration of the monarchy, or by Boulanger's proclaiming himself Dictator. The thing seemed possible enough, especially in Paris, where the idea of a *guerre de revanche* against Germany had still many adherents. I, as member of the acting Committee of the Peace and Arbitration Society, was interested to find out how far the General, if he succeeded, was likely to prove a serious danger to the peace of the world, and it was with that view principally that I hailed the opportunity of an interview. Lacretelle, the deputy, though personally friends with the General, was a strict Republican of the Victor Hugo school, and opposed to ideas of war for any purpose, and he had assured me that the popular hero was in reality no swashbuckler, though he gave himself the airs of one for popularity's sake with his principal supporters, Royalists and Bonapartists, who affected to quarrel with the Republic for having agreed to a cession of the lost provinces when peace was made with Germany in 1871. England, however, was at that date regarded in France as the chief enemy, and Alsace-Lorraine was already beginning to be forgotten in favour of Egypt. The following is the account my diary gives of the visit, but I wrote a much fuller and better one to the " Times," which was published in it a few days later:

"15th Nov.— With Lacretelle at 10 o'clock to call on General Boulanger. He lives in one of the streets beyond the Barrière de l'Etoile, and we found the house crowded. Not only were the two anterooms full, but the staircase also, men of every rank of life, from the priest to the decayed soldier and the artisan, a few women, too. After waiting nearly an hour, we were let in by special favour, most of the suppliants (the mulatto button boy who did the honours of the waiting room told us) having no chance whatever of an audience. The General's reception room is on the second floor, a singular room, as you go down half-a-dozen steps to the level of the floor when the door to it is opened. It is a very large place with a single table at the far end of it and some Louis XIV chairs. The General, who was at

the far table in a snuff-coloured morning dress, not uniform, came
forward to receive us (Lacretelle has just been painting his portrait
for the Salon) and gave us each a hand, and when he heard who I
was, led me with some pomp and made me sit on a gigantic Louis XIV
chair beside him. Lacetelle began to compliment him as "l'homme
du destin," a bit of flattery which the General took very much as a
matter of course, saying that there were moments when people were
obliged to act, and that the wave was rising now, and that whether he
liked it or not it would carry him on to whatever was intended — just
the same words of pleasant fatalism I remember in Arabi's mouth
seven years ago at Cairo.

"The General is a man of about fifty, fair-haired, turning gray, a
fresh complexion, a good but not especially military figure, a very
pleasant voice, and a quite frank manner. He gave one the impression
at once of simplicity and sincerity and of a sort of manly self-reliance
which is doubtless his power. There was nothing of the *général de
café chantant* in what I saw of him. After a little desultory conversation I asked him to allow me to put him a serious question. ' It has
been much debated,' I said, ' in our Peace Societies, how the quarrel
between France and Germany could be settled without war. Is it
possible to arrange for the neutralization of the ceded Provinces?'
To this he replied, that such a solution might possibly be in the future,
but that he could not say now it was his own; the German Government
had made it impossible by their policy in Alsace-Lorraine for any
inhabitant of the Provinces to do otherwise than call himself a Frenchman; the only way one had of knowing the opinion of districts was
by the ballot, and the Provinces had universally elected deputies who
demanded restoration to France; while this was the case neutralization
was hardly a practical question; still he did not say it might not become one. As for war, he, Boulanger, knew war too well to take
the responsibility of rushing into it without absolute necessity. War
is so largely a matter of chance, *chose aléatoire,* that a man must be a
traitor who would risk the fortunes of his country on it; therefore I
must not doubt him when he told me he was a man of peace. Lacretelle
then explained to him my connection with Arabi and Egypt, and his
manner became extremely cordial, and he told me that he had English
or rather Welsh blood in his veins through his mother [her name,
Lacretelle told me, was Griffiths] and begged me when I returned to
Paris to come and see him again. I said I would do so and that I
might be able to influence public opinion in England somewhat in his
favour, at which he was much pleased and we parted the best of friends.
Lacretelle tells me that he has never heard him talk so well or so
amiably to a stranger, especially an Englishman, as he hates the English
in common now with all Frenchmen. My impression of the General

is that he is honest, that he is able, and that, the circumstances of
France being what they are, he will succeed."

I had called at the Embassy on arriving in Paris, hoping to find
Lytton, who had just been named Ambassador there, but he was
unfortunately away delivering his Rectorial Address at Glasgow.
"Bitters tells me that Lytton is doing very well here, having made
friends with the Press and leaving all real business to Austin Lee."

Another interesting new acquaintance whom I made during my few
days at Paris was Louise Michel, then so popular with the extreme
Socialists, almost as notoriously so as Boulanger with the army. This,
too, I owed to Lacretelle and his wife and to a certain Madame Dorrian
(*née* Princess Merstcherska), who took me with her to call upon
Louise, with whom she is great friends — a most interesting visit. This
is the account of it:

"*14th Nov.*— We drove to Neuilly where Louise lives in a miserable
house on the fifth floor. Her apartment consists of two very small
rooms only, without even an ante-room, and when we opened the door
I thought we must have come to the wrong place. It resembled a
concierge's box both in appearance and smell, crammed full with four
people, three dogs, five cats, a cage of monkeys and a parrot, all scream-
ing at the tops of their voices, and though the rest were silenced the
parrot continued its shrieking the whole time we were there. The
family party consisted of Louise and another woman, a young man
and a fourth person whose sex I forget. They were engaged as we
entered on a meal. A deal table, without cloth plates or utensil of
any kind but a bottle of wine and some glasses, was covered with roast
chestnuts which they were peeling and eating. Louise rose to receive
us, a gray-haired woman of about fifty with a wild but honest and
kindly face, dressed in a ragged gown of rusty black, guiltless of linen.
Her forehead is retreating, her features large, her face colourless, its
expression that of a 'believer.' It might have been a French country
priest's. She spoke hurriedly, with an excitement which was evidently
habitual and was not altogether coherent. She seemed not to hear the
fearful screams of the parrot or the yelping of the dogs, or perhaps
these excited her, as noise excites the hearing of some deaf people.
The Princess kissed her, calling her by her Christian name, and Louise
seemed pleased to see her. When Louise was in prison the Princess
used to visit and read to her. She tells me Louise is the best of
women, giving away everything she possesses to the poor, and serving
as midwife to the women of her quarter. She is certainly not a prophet
of the sort that goes clothed in purple and fine linen. The Princess
explained who I was and how I, too, had been in prison in Ireland,
and Louise began to talk about the prospects of Socialism. She said
a revolution was certain and near in Germany, and next year would

see one too at Paris. She was under the impression that England was mined with Socialism and when I told her how little that was true was visibly distressed. She then read us one of her poems and tore out of a book and gave me the manuscript of one beginning ' Nul souffle humain ne se trouve sur ces pages,' and invited us to go with her to a meeting to take place that evening at Belleville, which we promised to do, but later I made the Princess explain to her that it was impossible I should really go, as I have no mind to be mixed up in a free fight, or to be arrested by the Paris police. But it was difficult to make her understand. She imagined that as I had been in prison I must necessarily be ready for everything. ' Why should he hesitate,' she said. ' There will be no danger, we shall all have revolvers.' I like the woman, as she is evidently honest and of an unselfish kindly heart."

This is the programme she gave me of the meeting:

Grand Meeting Internationale
a l'occasion de l'anniversaire de l'execution des anarchistes de Chicago.
Ordre du Jour.
Primo Les Crimes de la Bourgeoisie &c. &c.
Avec Le Concours d'Orateurs Socialistes Révolutionnaires.
Et de la Citoyenne
Louise Michel.

Here is also the full text of her verse:

BOUCHE CLOSE

Nul souffle humain n'est sur ces pages,
Rien que celui des éléments,
Le cyclone hurlant sur les plages,
Les legendes des océans,
Les sapins verts sous les nuées
Tordant les branches remuées
Comme les harpes dans les vents.
Sous les coraux ou sous les sables
La nature parfois ouvrant
Dans les tourmentes formidables
Un cercueil, ville ou continent,
Et l'être ayant la bouche close,
Feuille de chène ou lien de rose
Tombant au gré de l'ouragan.

LOUISE MICHEL.

14 *Novembre* '88.
Souvenir à M. Wilfrid Blunt.

From Paris we travelled on by Marseilles to Greece, where my wife had a family interest through her grandfather Lord Byron's death there in 1827; how glorious in those romantic days! how disappointing

in its results to-day! We had interests, too, in a long promised visit
to her relations the Noels in Eubaea, and I was curious to see the
changes which should have come about in the thirty years which had
elapsed since I first knew Athens as a member of the English Legation
in the days of King Otho.

"*20th Nov.*— We arrived by night at the Piraeus and landed in the
early morning, Frank Noel having come from Achmetaga to meet us.
It is thirty years almost to a month since I first drove up the road to
Athens, and I find little change. The suburbs have extended somewhat, and the olive groves have shrunk, and the hills are even barer
than before, but nothing marks the progress of the age unless it be the
overthrow of the fine old Venetian walls of the Acropolis. I regret
these as much as if they had pulled down the Parthenon itself. I
wandered in the town for a couple of hours, looking for houses I used
to frequent, and for friends I used to know, but all of these last were
gone. Our diplomatic set at Athens in 1859 was certainly a distinguished one. At the Russian Legation we had Ozeroff for Minister
with Staal for First Secretary, now Ambassador in London, and Neli-
doff for attaché, now Ambassador at Constantinople. Haymerlé, afterwards Prime Minister at Vienna, was Austrian Secretary. At our own
Legation we had that good Irishman, Sir Thomas Wyse, with William
Eliot, afterwards Lord St. Germans, for First Secretary. Drummond,
Digby, and myself attachés. I was the youngest of all the Corps
diplomatique, only eighteen years old, and a favourite on account of my
youth. The Dufferins were spending the winter there of '59–60, he
little over thirty, his mother, with whom he had been travelling in
Egypt, the most delightful of women. We used all to ride out, a
merry party, twice a week, following a paper chase, of which I was
generally the leader on an old white horse, which, in memory of
Shelley's lines, I called Apocalypse." [1]

We used to gallop through the olive groves, armed with revolvers,
as robbers were still common in the mountains round, just as described
by Edmond About in his "Roi des Montagnes" and "La Grèce Con-
temporaine," while one met retired bandit chiefs in the best Athens
society. King Otho wore the Albanian *fustanelle,* and that and the
costume of the Islands, with its immense balloon-like calico nether garments and red cap, were the common dress of the young Greek bloods.
The king's footmen are the only wearers of the *fustanelle* to-day.

On the 22nd we paid our visit to Achmetaga, for me a romantic
spot, for I had spent some weeks in Eubaea in 1860 in merry company

---

[1] Next came Anarchy, he rode
On a white horse splashed with blood;
He was pale even to the lips,
Like Death in the Apocalypse.

in Frank Noel's father's time. Edward Noel had come to Greece soon
after the War of Independence in the year 1830, and had purchased a
good many thousand acres in the island, mostly mountain and forest
land, of a Turkish Aga, who was leaving the country on Eubaea being
made over to Greece. He had paid only £2,000 for the whole, and it
must be now worth, with its magnesia mines, ten times that price.
The value of land (Frank Noel tells me) is still rising, and agricultural
Greece is prospering. The peasants are everywhere purchasing their
holdings. They have few debts and are saving money. This is due
in part to the general advance of the country, in part to the abolition of
the land tithe for which a tax on yoke oxen has been substituted. The
peasantry round here are an excellent race, sober, hard-working, cheerful, with many pristine virtues. Such is Frank Noel's testimony.
Eubaea, unlike the rest of Greece, is well wooded with pines on the
hillsides, and plane trees by the river banks. " I measured the largest
of these last while I was there and found it 53 feet in girth, with a
circumference round the extreme circuit of its boughs of 170 yards,
the finest single tree I ever saw, as it is perfect without break or blemish
more than a few bare twigs on the extreme summit." Returning by
road to Athens on 2nd December we slept a night at Chalcis and another
at Thebes. The journey was made in lovely weather and along a
carriageable road. At Chalcis they were talking of widening the
channel between the island and the main land, and of making of it a
large naval station for warlike purposes. To do it they will destroy
the old Venetian tower which is now a chief ornament. We heard the
details of this plan from Admiral Mansell, a fossilized English naval
officer who has inhabited Chalcis for the last twenty-five years. Both
there and at Thebes we were entertained by Greek friends of the
Noels.

During the following days at Athens we enjoyed something of the
society of Edmund Monson, our Minister there, at the Legation, afterwards Ambassador at Paris, and of Rennell Rodd, afterwards Ambassador at Rome, the latter a budding diplomatist with a small talent
for verse, but no great originality, as to whom I shall have more to
say in the course of this volume. All that I need quote from my
journal is that on the 3rd December I had an hour's interesting talk
with the then Prime Minister, Tricoupi, on Greek politics, and the
ambitions developed later in the direction of territorial expansion at
the expense of Turkey.

" *3rd Dec.*— Tricoupi is a hard-headed man without any special
graces of manner, but he talks straightforwardly and to the point. We
discussed finance, agriculture, road making, free trade, peasant pro-
prietorship, debts public and private, the shipping trade, the Corinth
Canal, and, lastly, foreign politics and Greece's prospects in the Ot-

toman inheritance. On this last point he said that it was impossible
for any Greek politician not to look to an extension of territory, and
that if Greece did not go forwards she would go back and lose her
independence at the hands of either Austria or Russia. They were
quite content to let things alone as long as the Ottoman Empire survived, but they must prepare for the future. The Turks were no
longer an enemy, but the others were. I asked him where he would
draw the line of Greek claims northwards, and he said they could no
longer claim the line of the Balkans, but in Macedonia would ask for
a boundary as far north as Seres, beyond Salonika, and in Thrace as
far as Adrianople. The exact limit, however, could hardly, he thought,
be settled without a war with the Bulgarians. Then the conqueror
would fix his own limit.

" I asked him about Albania. He said that Southern Albania, which
was Christian, would revert to Greece, but Mohammedan Albania, on
the extinction of the Sultan's power, would find itself isolated and
might accept a personal union with Greece under the crown, after the
model of Hungary with Austria. I told him I doubted the possibility
of this. Otherwise I agreed with him in his view that it was necessary
Greece should put forward her claims or prepare to put them forward.
Also I am of opinion that if England is to have a policy of the future
it should be to help Greece rather than Bulgaria. Greece would be
always under the influence of pressure from a naval power in the Mediterranean, whereas Bulgaria must remain under pressure of the Continental powers.

" With regard to Greek progress there is no doubt things are improving, though slowly. The revenue has tripled since 1858, when the
financial Commission sat, and this without oppressing the peasantry.
On the contrary, Tricoupi has lately abolished the land tax, a really
great measure, and the peasants, in spite of recent bad harvests, have
money to buy their holdings whenever they are not already the owners.
He has had the sense to put heavy duties on manufactured imports;
and he gives no facilities to the peasantry for borrowing. The country
is certainly improving. Only the rascality of the officials remains unchanged. Tricoupi was silent on this head, though he hinted that all
was not quite satisfactory. Noel tells me the Constitution is worked
by a vast system of jobbery. If so, it differs little from other Constitu-
tions, notably those of France and Italy. On the whole, I find Tricoupi
a superior man. All give him a perfectly clean character.

" *4th Dec.*— To Corinth alone, to see the Canal. Good luck took me
in the train with Mme. Türr whom I had known an extraordinarily
pretty woman twenty-two years ago, when I was staying on Lago
Maggiore with the Usedoms at the Prussian Legation in Italy. Türr
was at that time negotiating co-operation between Bismarck and the

Hungarians, or had been doing so, but Bismarck, Mme. Türr tells me, threw them over. Now Türr is President of the Corinth Canal Company, and his wife, a fat good-natured woman, lives at Kallimaki on the Isthmus. She was daughter of Mme. Bonaparte Wyse, wife of my old chief at Athens whom she calls her father, but old Sir Thomas always repudiated the parentage of her and her brother, who were born after his separation from his Bonaparte wife. With her, in widow's weeds and looking the picture of woe, was a little Greek lady, Mme. P——, and we three are now in the Hotel at Isthmia, the General being away at Paris, and are having a very amusing time, Madame P. having recovered her spirits, and giving us her ideas about Socialism, Eastern politics, and Zola's novels. She was a Greek, born at Alexandria, but has lived most of her life at Paris. I was sent with an employé to see the Canal works. They are monumental.

"*5th Dec.*— On to Nauplia, having spent twenty-four hours very agreeably with these two women. Madame P. has given me a deal of political information. She says every serious person in Greece has been obliged to abandon the *grande idée* (that of inheriting Constantinople from the Turks). She herself does not think Salonika can be saved from Austria, which is making a successful propaganda there with the Jews and other non-Hellenic inhabitants. The Bulgarians must eventually join Russia, and the Servians too, seeing that they are Slavs. The Roumanians will not do so willingly, but the two great Empires will divide the spoils. The Albanians will be merged either in Greece or elsewhere and lose their nationality.

"*6th Dec.*— At Nauplia I find nothing changed since I was last here, not twenty new houses built. The plain, however, which is the richest in Greece, has become wonderfully well cultivated. I drove this morning early to Mycenae to see how much of the ruins Schleimann had left. He has made a sad hash of the town with his excavations, but the Gate of Lions and the Treasury still stand (with Agamemnon's coat of arms over the entrance). What was most interesting, however, in the place is gone, the ancient ruins virgin of all meddling for three thousand years. Back to Athens by train in the evening. The last time I was here we were travelling on horseback, there being no roads in the Morea except the mountain mule tracks."

This is all that is worth recording of our visit to Greece. On 8th December we went on by sea to Alexandria, travelling in company with Prince Osman Pasha on his way back from Constantinople, where he had been with his uncle the ex-Khedive Ismaïl, now practically a prisoner in his own palace on the Bosporus. "He gave me a deal of information about Constantinople affairs. There is much sympathy there for the Mahdists, the Sultan having refused to take part against them at Suakim. It is not believed now that the English occupation of

Egypt will be permanent. Osman Pasha is a most intelligent good
fellow, better worthy of his Khedivial rank than the rest of his race.
He narrated to me amongst other things his experience in educating
his daughters, which has only resulted in making them unhappy. It
was impossible, he said, to find them educated husbands; nearly everybody now at Constantinople has abandoned the practice of polygamy,
only half-a-dozen among the men of rank he knew having more than
one wife. He named the Grand Vizier, Kiamil Pasha, as one of the
few who continued it; the Sultan is of course an exception, but he does
what no other Sultan has done for generations; when his women are
with child he marries them. Among the common people of the Turks
all are monogamists. This may be in part from poverty."

During my stay that winter in Egypt I was obliged to be very careful
how I meddled with politics, even in conversation, for, though Lord
Salisbury had given me leave to return there notwithstanding Sir
Evelyn Baring's unwillingness, I was under a certain obligation to
avoid any kind of publicity in my sympathy with the National cause.
I did not therefore remain more than a few days at Cairo on arrival,
but went on to my country place at Sheykh Obeyd, ten miles outside
the town, where I got the little garden house ready for my wife and
daughter to inhabit, a beautiful retired place on the desert edge far
from European intrusion, standing on the old pilgrim camel-track where
it branches off to Syria, and little frequented except by the Arab horse
merchants, who bring their horses for sale each spring to Cairo. There
we lived in seclusion and very happily for the three winter months,
building and enlarging the house and recovering the garden from the
neglected state into which it had fallen through the roguery of those
left in charge. These, getting news of my imprisonment in Ireland,
had imagined that my career in life was over and that they might
treat the garden as their own, economising the cost of its watering and
using it as a run for their cattle. It was a labour of love for me
restoring its prosperity and arranging for its future better management.
It was only little by little that my peasant neighbours came to pay me
their polite visits of congratulation, and then I found that there was
much hidden sympathy with me among them, repressed only through
fear of the government, to which they knew I had been opposed. My
journal, however, of that winter contains little in it that is politically
worth transcribing. It is a record of conversations with my peasant
neighbours and, as they began to hear of my arrival, with the obscurer
members of the old National Party, which still looked to the possibility
of their old chief Arabi's recall to Egypt, and who came furtively to
see me under the guidance of Arabi's old body servant, Mohammed
Ahmed, the same who had faithfully preserved and delivered to those
who were defending him at his trial his master's political papers and

so saved his life. (See " Secret History of English Occupation of Egypt.") He had been the first to come to me now, and finding him out of employment I had put my garden under his charge, a fortunate inspiration, for he was a man of integrity and energy and speedily acquired great influence in the neighbourhood and so restored to working order 'the lands entrusted to him. To these Arabist visitors from Cairo were gradually added other sources of native information, the most important of whom were my old friends Aarif Bey and Mohammed Moelhi, nephew of my other friend Ibrahim Moelhi, both of whom were now much in the confidence of the Ottoman High Commissioner at Cairo, Mukhtar Pasha Gazi. We saw, too, something of Osman Pasha and his sister, Princess Nazli, both of them persons of the highest intelligence and knowledge of affairs, while from the Greeks we obtained much secondhand information of their view of things through Frank Noel, who had came on to Egypt with us. Nor were we wholly cut off from the English official world. We did not think it necessary to call on Baring, but I found my connection, Colonel Charles Wyndham, in command of a regiment of the army of occupation, and Anne her cousin Hugh Locke King. From all these sources, though I hardly stirred from the solitude of my country retreat during the winter, I was able to gather a sufficient knowledge of the situation to be able to piece it together now for the purposes of the present narrative. The political situation in Egypt at the time, as I came to under stand it during the four months that I was at Sheykh Obeyd in the winter of '88-'89, was briefly as follows :

The failure of the Drummond Wolff Convention at the last moment, after it had been already agreed to by its negotiators, through the refusal of the Sultan under French and Russian pressure to ratify their signatures, had left affairs in Egypt diplomatically " in the air." Not only had further negotiations for evacuating the English garrison been brought to a standstill, but every section of native opinion had been checked and disorganized. Instead of a new beginning having been frankly attempted on lines preparatory to Egypt's restoration to self-government, all had been left in precisely the same confusion from which the Convention had sought to rescue it. The Khedive Tewfik was still occupant of the Vice-regal throne, but commanding no respect in the country, and dependent for his maintenance on English support which might at any moment be withdrawn, leaving him to deal as he could with the Soudanese menace threatening his frontier at Wadi Halfa. Weak and discredited he was, without personal authority, and he enjoyed less consideration than Mukhtar the Sultan's Commissioner. Baring, in whom all real power was vested at Cairo, was for the moment without settled policy beyond that of waiting events, a kind of marking time with no definite instruction as to the future of England's connection with the Nile Valley, except that Lord Salisbury, feeling that he had done what honour required in fulfilment of English promises of evacuation, was resolved now to leave things where they were, including the garrison of occupation.

As to the National Party, whether represented by the former Arabists or by any other group, their condition was one of patriotic torpor; as a party they had ceased to exist, being without leaders and without organization. They were disappointed in the hopes raised at the commencement of the Wolff mission that Tewfik would be replaced as Khedive by Prince Halim, or some other member of the Khedivial family unconnected with the misfortunes of 1882, who should restore their lost constitution of that year, and make good Lord Dufferin's promises. In default of these and of Arabi's recall, impossible under Tewfik, what poor hopes they had turned mostly towards the Sultan. But undoubtedly the popular man among the Egyptian fellahin that winter was the Mahdi, or rather his successor the Khalifa Abdallah and. his fighting lieutenant, Osman Digna, who carried on a perpetual guerilla warfare in the neighbourhood of Suakim. The popular imagination amongst the fellahin credited these with heroic qualities, and it was confidently believed that the Dervish forces would before long overrun Upper Egypt, and that they were already driving the Belgian Congo Company out of their territory in Central Africa, that they would rid Senegal of the French, and, as the issue of a holy war against all infidel intruders, that they would even reconquer the northern shores of the Mediterranean. News came while I was there that Emin Pasha, to rescue whom Stanley had been sent by King Leopold on his filibustering expedition to the Nile sources, had made his submission to the Mahdists and that Stanley himself had been slain. From the Eastern desert, too, news reached me through the Bedouins of an interesting kind. It was to the effect that my former friend Mohammed Ibn Rashid, taking advantage of a quarrel between the two sons of Saoud Ibn Saoud with their uncle Abdallah, had marched with an army to Riad and made himself master of the whole of Nejd, an event of high importance in Peninsula Arabia. I listened to these stories and found my interest in the East once more supreme over the petty hopes and fears of Western politics, and recovered in this way and in the routine of my daily life in my garden, the peace of mind I had left behind me on leaving England. I find the following description in my diary of my life at Sheykh Obeyd.

" *3rd Jan.* 1889.— I left Cairo on the 27th, escaping like a bird out of the hand of the fowler and am established here at Sheykh Obeyd. It has been a blessed change, and though I have been here all these days alone, I have not for a moment felt otherwise than happy. I have been getting the place ready for habitation by the others, and it is quite com-

fortable already in an Oriental way. The house is merely the old
gardener's house with two rooms added, four in all, and an open
salamlik, which I use as sitting room. I have had the floors covered
with two inches of clean white sand after the Nejd fashion, and I
spread my carpet over it and sit there. For more furniture I have had
in a man from the village to make bedsteads, divans, and seats (*gufass*)
which he does out of our own palm branches newly cut at the rate of
four shillings, two shillings, and seven pence halfpenny a piece. The
village carpenter has put up a few screens for more privacy, and the
whole furnishing for the family will cost about two pounds. My room
is like a lantern with windows facing East, North, and West, and from
my bed I can see the first glimmer of the false dawn, which makes the
owls hoot and the jackals cry. Then, with the real dawn, crows begin
to pass overhead, and I get up and go outside the garden wall where
I sit at the desert's edge and wait for the sunrise. At this hour one
sees all the wild life of the place, foxes, ichneumons (*nims*), jackals,
and birds in great variety, kites, kestrels, doves, and occasionally a
woodcock at flight from the marshes to the garden where he would
spend the day. There are night ravens, too, which have their home
in the *lebbek* trees next the house, and now in winter time a flock of
rooks with their attendant jackdaws. This is a rarity in Egypt as
rooks are never seen south of Cairo. There are two foxes which live
inside the garden, and I see them most days; they sleep generally in
the day time behind some cactuses or at the foot of a palm tree, and
they often jump up as I walk round, and trot away. They come sometimes within a few yards of my feet, being accustomed to the work-
people, and not afraid of me because I wear an Arab dress. I have
given orders here that there shall be absolute *amân* even for wolves, and
the hyenas which sometimes make their way over the garden wall. I
superintend the labour now, mark out the work, and pay the wages,
pruning the trees with a pair of garden nippers. This is a delightful
occupation.

" *20th Jan.*— I don't know how sufficiently to describe the delight
of the life here. Anne and Judith and Cowie (their maid), have
joined me here, and we are idly busy all day long. The whole of the
garden (30 acres) has now been weeded and dug twice. The irrigation engine has been repaired, and watering will begin regularly next
week. Day has gone by like day, each full of interest. This morning
we began pulling down an outhouse to clear the land for a new building; thirty men and boys have been working at the job in high good
humour, and certainly they are neither lazy nor unintelligent. In the
midst of the demolition a large cobra jumped out and put up his hood
in the middle of them, but they knocked him over with their picks
before he could do any harm. He measured exactly six feet in length,

and by general advice he was cut up at once into four portions and thrust down the throat of a sick camel they had with them, for a cure.[1] Four other smaller snakes were also killed, but these were of a harmless kind. They tell me a horned viper was also seen in the garden, a fortnight before I came, but this is unusual except in the extreme heat of summer. Lizards, of course, are plentiful. I have seen one with rudimentary legs only, making its way along the ground as snakes do, its feet hardly helping it.

" *22nd Jan.*— We have begun a new wing to the house, building with the ordinary sun-dried bricks, contracted for at the rate of 8 piastres to the cubic metre. There will be three rooms upstairs and three downstairs, and the whole will cost about £80. Also I bought a new engine for irrigation, and I am restocking the garden with young orange plants, and in two or three years, if things go well, it will be a better property than when I bought it seven years ago. I could be quite content to spend the rest of my days in this pleasant work.

" *29th Jan.*— To-day two three-year-old colts and a filly arrived at the garden, which I have bought of Ali Pasha Sherif, all three of the Viceroy Abbas I's stock, one colt and a filly, a Jellabi, the other a Seglawi Ibn Soudan. This last ought to be valuable some day for our stud in England. [This was ' Mesaoud,' so celebrated afterwards as our most successful sire.] Ali Pasha's horses are the only ones of pure Arabian breed in Egypt, and there are certain points about them superior to all others, perhaps. He has an old one-eyed Seglawi named Ibn Nádir, which I consider the finest horse, taking him all round, I ever saw, white, with immense strength and breeding combined, long and low, with splendid legs and hocks, a fine head and neck, tail always carried. Our colts arrived as the noonday gun was being fired from the citadel at Cairo. They had been brought round by the desert entrance through Zeyd's precaution to avoid the evil eye. He also sacrificed a lamb on the threshold of the garden and sprinkled their foreheads with blood. I like these old Mosaic rites and superstitions. Similarly on Friday the first stone of our new house was laid, and another lamb was slaughtered on the corner-stone, and the blood made to flow over it with a *Bismillah errahman errahim.* It is possible that the blood of bulls and of goats do not wash away sin, but it must be pleasing still, at any rate more so than the godless rites of our own stone-laying with a champagne bottle. The work-people were then feasted, and a heavy shower of rain came down to bless the building. Zeyd is in the seventh heaven at all these high doings, and is encamped with the horses under the great fig tree. The work-people have a merry time here, men and women working together, and

---

[1] N.B.— The camel recovered.

there are one or two pretty girls among them who have a deal of attention paid them. They wear no veils while at work, but are quiet and
well behaved." Zeyd, here spoken of, was a Bedouin from Nejd, who
had attached himself to our service, a man of imagination, a poet and,
like all the Nejd Bedouins, an enthusiast about horses. He was a constant pleasure to us for this reason though repeatedly in trouble through
his little respect for persons and the inconsequence of his tongue. He
was also of value to us as a centre of Arabian gossip, including political
news, sometimes of importance.

"Zeyd tells me that when he was at Damascus in 1887 he learned
that the French Government had written a letter to Ibn Rashid and
had sent it to Haïl through Mohammed Ibn Abdul Kader, the Emir's
eldest son. It contained an offer of alliance, and to make Ibn Rashid
independent of the Sultan under French protection. Ibn Rashid, however, had forwarded the letter to Constantinople, and Ibn Abdul Kader
had been hauled over the coals by the Sultan, but had excused himself,
saying that as a French subject he could not disobey the order of his
government.

"*10th March.*— There is certainly just now a movement going on in
Egypt in favour of Arabi's recall, and I have received notices of it
from various quarters with a list of those who would act with Arabi
in forming a Nationalist Ministry. Also Ahmed Minshawi Pasha has
sent one of the principal Sheykhs of Tantah to consult me on the
matter, Sheykh Abdul Mejid, and a message has come from a number
of ex-officers from Arabi's army who wish to see me, but I have declined
this, as it could do no possible good and might make trouble; the
Egyptians have not spirit in them to revolt and if they did it would
not profit them. I am glad all the same to find that Arabi is not
forgotten."

One visit only I record that winter of any great interest now. This
was one I paid with Lady Anne to Zebehr Pasha, Gordon's old enemy
in the Soudan, now held a prisoner in Egypt. During the troubles at
Cairo which had followed Gordon's death he had been arrested by
Baring by an arbitrary act of authority and sent on board a man-of-war
to Gibraltar, and there detained at the Queen's pleasure for two years
on no legal charge, for none was brought against him, and there he
might have remained for the rest of his days had it not been for the
interest excited in his case by Lord Ribblesdale who had made friends
with him at Gibraltar and brought his case before the House of Lords.
In 1889 he was newly returned to Egypt, and was now once more a
State prisoner of the Khedive, occupying one of the minor palaces on
the banks of the Nile. It is thus that I describe our breakfast with
him.

"Zebehr Pasha is a really charming man who entertained us with the greatest honour at breakfast. He is lodged in the Ghizeh palace where he is a State prisoner, though allowed to go about to a certain extent in Cairo, under the charge of a certain Cashmiri Abderrahman Effendi. Zebehr is a tall, slight man, with long *effilé* hands, and a face of the profoundest melancholy. His complexion is brown, and his features show a cross between the Arab and the Berberi, the Arab predominating, and a smile of great beauty. He was dressed in Egyptian uniform loosely made, shivered much, though it was a bright sunny day, and complained of the cold. He has a bad cough, and I should think would not live long. State prisoners have a way of dying in Egypt. We talked on most political subjects, but he avoided giving an opinion on the actual position in the Soudan; perhaps he was afraid of the Cashmiri. 'It is the Government's affair not ours,' he said. Of Gordon he spoke with hearty respect, and of Sir John Adye, and of several other English officers he had known, but he had no good word for Baring, who was a financier, he had heard, not a politician. He told us Emin's history and Osman Digna's. He spoke highly of Arabi, said that he had been present at a conversation between him and Dervish Pasha in which Dervish had offered Arabi £250 a month if he would go to Constantinople, but Arabi had replied that even if he were willing, there were 10,000 men would stand between him and the sea. He said that he had been very much misrepresented about this conversation in the English papers, and had never spoken a word but what was honourable to Arabi. He could not advise Arabi to come back to Egypt except as Minister; this, however, Tewfik would never have. All our conversation was in Arabic, which he speaks purely, being easy to understand. When I told him the English Occupation would not last for ever he smiled incredulously.

"He took us round the garden, an uninteresting French garden laid out in pebbled walks and rockeries, and imitation lawns. It and the palace cost Ismaïl, they say, several millions, and the building is in ruins already. Then we had breakfast and Zebehr was delighted because I ate with my hands; he would have nothing to do himself with knives and forks. 'I am only a wild man,' he said, 'and use the instruments God gave me.' And he turned angrily upon the Cashmiri, who was pretending that he could not manage without European ways. Before going I asked him if I could do anything for him, and he said: 'No, we two are in the same position, the Government does not regard us favourably. We cannot help each other,' and he laid his hand affectionately on my arm. He complained, however, how badly he had been treated in money matters, and I said that the day might come when I could do something for him. Our visit was, I fancy, the

greatest pleasure, poor man, he has had for many months. He came
down to put us into our carriage and insisted upon paying the driver
his hire."

We left Sheykh Obeyd on the 8th of March and Alexandria on
the 10th.

Here ends our winter's stay in Egypt of that year.

" 13*th March.*— We are in the Gulf of Fiume, and our journey is
nearly over, on our way to Fiume to spend a fortnight with the Hoyos
family before returning home. The captain of our ship, the *Ceres,* is
a Dalmatian, and by his own account was much mixed up in past times
with revolutionary affairs. He tells me his two brothers emigrated to
America after 1848, and his son has recently been in prison for political
reasons. He talks of a social war as imminent in Europe, especially
in Germany, France, and Italy, and looks upon Bismarck as the deviser
of all evil, and on a revolt against him and military ideas as certain.
He believes, too, in the overthrow of the British Empire in India by
the Russians, who will be joined by the Indians. He has recently seen
Arabi in Ceylon. We touched at Corfu and Lissa, and the Ionian
Islands, terribly bare and scored with burnings. We saw them well,
coasting close under Zante, Ithaca, and Cephalonia. Corfu is a pretty
town, little changed since the British evacuation, though the people on
board say the place is in decline. Lissa we saw by moonlight. Admiral
Tegethoff, who won the battle there for Austria, did so against orders
and against rules. The Italian fleet was four times his strength, but
his action was fortunate and probably saved the Dalmatian coast to
Austria. There are three parties it seems in Dalmatia: a Philo-Rus-
sian, the most numerous; a Philo-Austrian, the most wealthy and
educated; and a Philo-Italian, confined to a few sea-coast towns. The
officers on board are all Catholic and Philo-Austrian but radicals, and
talk something very like socialism without disguise. They are bitterly
opposed to Russia. They are all Dalmatians. They resent the union
of Fiume to Hungary, but admit that there is no National party in
Dalmatia. The captain, Gelachich, is a capital fellow, a native of
Lessina."

At Lissa we received news of the discomfiture of the " Times " in
the Parnell case, by far the most important incident at home since the
overthrow of Gladstone in 1886.

" 18*th March, Villa Hoyos, Fiume.*— We have been a week here
staying with Count and Countess George Hoyos and their children,
governesses, and tutors, a large cheerful party of the kind I like. The
villa is like Paddockhurst (their place in Sussex) in miniature. The
Hoyos' are of ancient Spanish extraction, brought to Austria by Charles
Quint, and she is the daughter of Whitehead, the inventor of the
torpedo, who, beginning life as an engineer on board an Austrian

Lloyd steamer, has made a large fortune. He is an admirable sample
of the self-made man, quiet, unobstrusive, absorbed in his work, liberal
to his men, open-handed in all his ways. The Countess is a pretty
woman, mother of pretty daughters, he a well-bred man of much sense
and information, a first cousin of Hoyos the Ambassador at Paris and
of that younger Hoyos who was connected the other day with the
Austrian Crown Prince Rudolph's death. This is what they tell me,
or rather what she has told me about that tragedy.

" The Crown Prince Rudolph was a very charming man and had
had innumerable successes with women, but had never been in love
till at a party last year he met a girl of seventeen, Mademoiselle de
Wetschera, daughter of a certain Baroness of that name, of no very
honest reputation. The girl, however, was charming, and when the
Prince made love 'to her fell desperately too in love. Their liaison had
lasted four months, and though the Prince talked somewhat strangely,
nobody suspected there was anything so serious in the case. Hoyos
was a friend of the Prince, not in his service but very intimate and in
the habit of going with him on his shooting excursions. He went
down at the Prince's invitation to Meyerling, to shoot with him the
following day, and they passed the evening till nine o'clock very gaily,
when the Prince went to bed. Hoyos knew nothing of Mademoiselle
de Wetschera's being at the shooting lodge. In the morning, however,
he was called by the Prince's servant, who complained that his master's
door was locked, and they went together, and after knocking in vain,
broke it open, when they found the two bodies together in the Prince's
bed. The girl was then recognized by Hoyos, and seeing her to be ' a
member of society,' his first idea was to conceal her presence there.
He accordingly carried her with the servant's help into a distant room,
where they left her, undressed as she was, locked up, till her relations
should come. This was not till the evening, when her uncle arrived,
dressed the girl with his own hands, and placed her in his brougham,
upright, beside him, and so conveyed her home, and she was buried
with equal secrecy in the night. With regard to the Prince, Hoyos
also conveyed the news to the Emperor, and it was tried to hush up
the truth but in vain. The Crown Prince had previously written to
Sechenyi a letter, part of which only has been made public; the un-
published part contained these words: ' I am resolved to die, since I
am no longer worthy to wear the Imperial uniform.' The Countess
says she knew the Crown Prince well, she had also met the girl and
liked her. She could not condemn them for their death, poor things.

" Another topic of conversation has been King Milan's abdication
in Servia. According to the Hoyos', Queen Nathalie has long been
plotting against her husband, hoping to become Regent for her son.
She is a very pretty, charming woman, but ' a Russian, and therefore

an intriguer.' The first hint her husband had of her designs was on
his return from his lost battle of Slivnitza in Bulgaria. He was dis-
pirited and thought of abdicating, and, when he told her, she was for
his doing it at once. This shocked him. Now she has gained half
her object and the other half she will gain soon by returning as Regent
to Servia." The battle of Slivnitza here referred to was one of the
earliest of the Balkan internecine fightings after the independence of
Servia and Bulgaria had been enforced upon the Sultan by European
pressure. It ended disastrously for the Servians who, without much
cause of quarrel, had invaded Bulgaria and were routed with heavy
loss. The Austrian Empire at that time was believed to be in a very
unstable position, held together only by the personal popularity of the
aged Emperor. We stayed ten days with the Hoyos' and while there
were shown experiments in torpedo practice by Whitehead, who had
his factory adjoining the villa. I find, however, nothing in my diary
worth transcribing here, unless it be a list of persons whose acquaintance we made, belonging to Viennese society. This includes
Count Zichy, governor of the town, and his father, formerly Austrian
Ambassador at Constantinople; Prince and Princess Sanguscko, cousins
of our friends the Potockis in Poland, and joint owner with them of
their famous Arabian stud; Count and Countess Breuner, Countess
Palffy and others. From Fiume we went on by Vienna and the
Orient Express to Paris, and so home to England, arriving there on
the 5th of April.

Here there is a long gap in my diary and nothing of any public importance, except the record of a second interview I had with Boulanger,
who had come to London with the idea of making friends there, and
had made an appointment with me to see him at a house he had taken
in Portland Place. I write:

"*19th May.*— On Wednesday I saw General Boulanger by appointment at his house in Portland Place. He looks older and more worn
than when I saw him six months ago, but he talked cheerfully enough.
I told him I had been much taken to task by the leaders of the Liberal
Party for my avowal of sympathy with his cause (my letter to the
'Times' of last year), and asked him to inform me on certain points
which might strengthen my position. The first point I put was whether
he intended to destroy liberty in France, to shut up the Chambers and
make himself Dictator? intentions commonly attributed to him. To
this he said that the idea was ridiculous. The French could never get on
without talking, and a Parliament in some form they must have. What
he wanted was to do away with the personal politics of the Chamber,
which he could effect by reforming it (the Revision). Frenchmen
must be united into a National Party instead of broken up into small
groups. The power of the President must be strengthened, but within

limits. Those possessed by the President of the United States will probably suffice. There must be the Veto, but he would not say that in an old society like the French it would do to assimilate the American régime too closely. He had no intention at all of destroying liberty. Thus, in the matter of education he was for full liberty for all creeds, not as at present when religious education was persecuted. The French provinces did not want secular education and it should not be forced on them, but he was not for this a Clerical. He did not himself go to Mass, but he was determined everyone else should do so who liked. If a man chose to go about in fancy dress it was no concern of his neighbours. On my second point, peace and war, he repeated what he had said to me last autumn about the hazards of war, and his unwillingness to rush into hostilities. He could not ever propose to disarm till the question of Alsace-Lorraine was settled. No Government which did so could stand a fortnight. He believed, however, that the question could be settled without war if Frenchmen were united. He would then most gladly propose a disarmament. In this sense I might say of him that his ultimate end was to bring about a disbanding of the great ·armies of the Continent. This he authorized me to tell my Liberal friends. He invited me cordially to come again any Tuesday, Wednesday, or Thursday morning."

I fear I did little towards helping the General in this or any other way. Politics were at that moment repugnant to me, and I could not bring myself to start on any new campaign. I never saw the General again.

CHAPTER II

The summer of 1889 saw me occupied almost exclusively with literary work. It was then that I wrote my poem, "A New Pilgrimage," which with many other pieces of more or less the same date I published in the early autumn. This brought me once more into pleasant relations with my friends, even those who had been most angry with me for my doings in Ireland. Chief among these was my cousin, George Wyndham, who already the year before had sent me a pleasant word. "We have so many grounds," he wrote, "for friendship, our common love of sport and of poetry, and especially our common blood, that I think it would be very foolish to allow differences of politics and opinion to interfere with it in any way. I sincerely hope that you think so too." Now, on my return to England in 1889, I found him full of affectionate endeavour to make things pleasant for me on my re-emergence into social life. In this he showed himself no idle friend. I had hardly arrived in London when he arranged occasions of meeting for me at his house in Park Lane with our mutual friends, and eventually one with Arthur Balfour, at which we buried our political hatchet in mutual amiabilities, an attitude we have ever since preserved as often as we have met. Another friend, equally dear to me with George, whom I recovered at this time, was Lytton. He, too, had written me an affectionate letter, regretting that he had missed seeing me on my passage through Paris. As to my women friends, my prison adventures, I soon found, had done me no real discredit with them. The only one of them that had been seriously shocked at it was Princess Wagram, who, not being English, had made herself more English in the matter than were my own countrywomen, and now she, too, was reconciled. With the rest the episode was a title to romantic interest, which made it easy for me to resume my place and more than my place in society. Their kindness did me full amends, and for the next few years strewed my path with flowers to the extent that politics lost their hold over my mind, more than perhaps they should have done. My daughter Judith, too, now growing up, was a new interest of a very absorbing kind, and my diary, when it is resumed, I find dealing mainly with home occupations and the details of my private life.

Nor must I omit another influence which was an important one with me that summer in the direction of weaning me from home politics, that of an intimacy which I then for the first time enjoyed with William Morris. I had already for some years known the Morrises, my first acquaintance with them having been begun in 1883, when I met Mrs. Morris at Naworth, having been invited specially for the purpose by Mrs. Howard (Lady Carlisle), and had spent a week there in her company, and we had made friends, but of Morris himself I had as yet seen little except occasionally when I called on them in Hammersmith. This summer, however, of 1889 saw me for the first time at Kelmscott Manor, where I had an opportunity of intimate intercourse with him during the many pleasant days of gudgeon fishing we enjoyed together on the Upper Thames and the evenings when we argued the questions, artistic and political, which occupied his mind.

Morris was at that time in a mood of reaction from his socialistic fervour. He had quarrelled with Hyndman, and was disgusted at the personal jealousies of his fellow-workers in the cause and at their cowardice in action. He never got over the pusillanimity they had shown at the Trafalgar Square meeting two years before, when a few hundred policemen had dealt with thousands of them as though they had been schoolboys. Morris was too loyal and too obstinate to abjure his creed, but the heart of his devotion to the cause of the proletariat had gone. In some ways our two positions were the same. We had both of us sacrificed much socially to our principles, and our principles had failed to justify themselves by results, and we were both driven back on earlier loves, art, poetry, romance. Morris, with one who understood him and dared to argue with him boldly, was a delightful companion. He was intolerant of the conventional talk of society, and had little sympathy with ideas foreign to his own. He had little patience with fools, and the prettiest woman in the world could not seduce him into listening to nonsense if there was nothing of fact behind it. His time was too precious to waste on them; and the fine ladies who affected artistic tastes in his company without real knowledge put him straightway to flight. To such he was rude and repellent, but to anyone who could increase his stock of knowledge on any subject he lent a willing ear, whether artist or artisan, with absolute indifference as to his social position. In his domestic life Morris was too busy to be unhappy, and of too sanguine a temperament to worry himself much over past disappointments; yet disappointments cannot but have been his. He had a strong and affectionate heart, and had centred his home affections on his two children, and the younger, May, had just made an engagement he disapproved, while the elder, Jenny, who had been his pride as a child for her intellectual faculties, had overworked her brain and was now subject to epileptic fits. It was touching now at

Kelmscott to watch Morris's solicitude for this poor girl on whom his chief home love was bestowed.

Kelmscott Manor was a romantic house, and the life there extremely primitive. There were few of the conveniences of modern life. The rooms below and also on the upper floor were all passage rooms opening one into another, and in order to reach the tapestried chamber in which we sat in the evenings, it was necessary to pass to and fro through Morris's own bedroom, in which he lay at night in a great square Elizabethan four-post bed, an arrangement which would have been of extreme discomfort to anyone less tolerant of such things than he, and less indifferent to his personal convenience. It was the same thing in the day time. He worked at the designs he was making for his carpets, and at his drawings, and the corrections of his proofs in a room where he was liable every minute to disturbance. Such discomforts had been submitted to by our forefathers, and why not, he thought, by us. It was this insensitiveness to his surroundings that enabled him to deal with the prodigious volume of work which he daily assigned himself, both manual and intellectual.

Such was the house. Out of doors the river — an upper branch of the Thames — was a constant attraction, and there Morris each afternoon took complete holiday. He loved boating, as it reminded him of his Oxford days, and he loved sitting hour after hour in a punt with rod and line, capturing the local gudgeon, a sport requiring skill, on which he prided himself, not without modest reason. In all matters concerning the river he took a passionate and proprietary interest, cherishing a special grudge against the Thames Conservancy, a body which interfered with individual rights, and whose legitimate authority he denied. Against these he constantly inveighed. He loved, too, in memory of Oxford, to engage in wordy warfare with the bargees, and had a strong vocabulary of abuse for them which he did not spare. When on the river he affected a rough manner even with his fellows in the boat, and scorned to apologize if accidents through his fault occurred, all which was in keeping with his appearance, which was that of a Norwegian sea captain rather than a poet, and of this he was proud. He was very dogmatic, with violent likes and dislikes. He used to say that St. Peter's was the ugliest building in the world after St. Paul's, and of these things he would discourse when the fish were off their feed, for when they were biting he was too absorbed in his catch to have a thought for anything else.

Of poetry he affected to have little knowledge, and of the work of those he was averse to, he would pretend never to have read a word. I remember that on one boating excursion in which we all took part, we were compelled to take refuge from heavy rain in a little inn by the river side, and that we found in it a book of poetical extracts which we amused ourselves by reading, and that among the rest were those lines of Byron, perhaps his best and quite his best known:

There was a sound of revelry by night.

This he declared to be rubbish, and that he had not a notion whom they were by. Morris in these playful moods was very attractive, and of all the great men I have been in close relations with, I reckon him intellectually the strongest. He had an astonishingly firm grasp of things, and an immensely wide range of knowledge. I never knew him deceived by a false argument, and he was difficult to overcome in discussion even on subjects his adversary knew the best. One thing only, I think, he did not know, much as he had written about it, the love of women, and that he never cared to discuss. My talks with him that summer confirmed me in my resolution politically to retire into my shell, and I think my resolution had a corresponding influence on him.

"*13th Oct., 1889. Paris.*— I have left home once more for the winter, and with a lighter heart than I have lately had. My last act before leaving England was to write two letters severing the last links which bound me to political life. One was to the Kidderminister electors telling them that they must not depend on me to stand again for Parliament, the other to T. P. O'Connor resigning my directorship of the 'Star.' I have intended this for more than a year, but have taken time to reflect, and am sure now that the step is a wise one. As a matter of principle I cannot go on pretending to believe in the Liberal Party, with which I have not an idea in common, beyond Irish Home Rule. As a matter of personal ambition, politics have nothing more to give me. I will not be a parliamentary drudge, and I cannot aspire to lead a party.

"Of doing good in the world in any public way I also despair. I do not see clearly in what direction good lies. I do not love civilised humanity; and poor savage human nature seems a lost cause. I have done what I could for it. I have, I think, saved Egypt from absorption by Europe, and I have certainly, by stopping the Soudan war in 1885, put back the clock of African conquest for a generation, perhaps for a century. But the march of 'Progress' is irresistible in the end; and every year the old-fashioned idea of the rights of uncivilised man dies more completely out. Even in Ireland, the National cause is putting itself in line with nineteenth century thought. The moonlighters and cattle-houghers and rebels of all kinds are disappearing; and, instead, we see Parnell manœuvring and deceiving in Parliament neither more nor less than Gladstone himself, and declaring with Rosebery for Imperial Federation! In all this I have no real lot or part. Ireland will doubtless get something of what she wants, and she has all my good wishes still. But Imperial Federation is not worth going to prison for a second time nor even standing another contested election. I have done enough — possibly too much — and am sick and weary of the machinery of English public life.

"On the other hand stands the world of art and poetry. In this I can still hope to accomplish something, and with an advantage of experience not every poet has. I have a great deal to accomplish before old age takes me and little time. My poems, my memoirs, my book of maxims (the 'Wisdom of Merlyn),' my book of the Arab horse. These are work enough for all my remaining strength. Then, how delightful life is in perfect liberty! Never have I felt more capable of enjoyment, of the pleasures of friendship, of the casual incidents of romance, of the continuous happiness of life at home. These harmonize with a literary, not with a political ambition, and so it is best it should be. Am I not right?"

The three weeks that I spent at Paris on this occasion were delightful ones passed all in this mood. I found Lytton at the Embassy, and our old intimate intercourse was renewed. He, older than me by nine years, was already entering that valley of the shadow of old age from which he was never to emerge, and which ended in his death two years later. It was that in which his last volume of verse was written, and he made me the confidant of his sorrows, but this is not the place in which to give them more publicity than the volume itself gave them when it was published after his death. They served to accentuate my own mood of aversion from public affairs, and I spent most of my time with him at the Embassy, the same well-known house and garden where I had spent so much of my early youth officially as a member of it in the days of Lord Cowley and the Second Empire. I paid a visit, too, to the Wagrams at Gros Bois, where I mixed again in French society. The château was at that time undergoing repair of a substantial kind, an experience it had not had since 1830, and my hosts were living in the *dépendance,* an interesting suite of little rooms once the abode of Marshal Berthier's aides-de-camp, and possessed of a certain historic charm, with their Empire furniture and decorations. We shot each day in the great woods.

"Gros Bois, Wagram tells me, has been an oak wood ever since the time of the Druids. It was a royal domain, and had been given over and over again to different favourites of the kings of France. The last instance was when it was bestowed by Napoleon on the Prince's grandfather, as the inscription over the door records, his 'companion in arms.' The estate is of about 4,000 hectares, of which fully half are woodlands, 1,200 being inside the park wall, an ancient enclosure dating from 1650. I never saw so completely isolated a place, nor one quite so enjoyable. The woods are laid out formally (as French woods are) with straight rides or rather drives of grass cut through them, and though there is no old timber, all having been levelled with the ground in 1814, the oak trees grown up again from the stub are very beautiful, and the place is full of woodpeckers, jays, and magpies, besides game. There is a stone recording the death of the late Prince's first roebuck: *Ici mon fils a tué son premier chevreuil,* with the date 1826. This was Wagram's father, who went on till 1888, killing something every day in season and out of season, partridges on their nests if he could find no other, dogs, and sometimes beaters. All is recorded in a book; and he might have been the original of Carlyle's Baron: *qui centum mille perdices plumbo confecit et statim in stercore convertit.* (I am not sure of the Latinity.) He died at the beginning of last year, being about eighty years old, but shooting on to the last week of his life.

"I have received a nice letter from Kidderminster in answer to mine, and the 'Pall Mall Gazette' announces my retirement publicly from political life. The Princess is triumphant at this retirement, as she was always opposed to my politics."

All this was very demoralizing from a public point of view. On the 25th I was joined by my family at Paris, and on the 2nd November we moved on to Rome and Egypt. At Rome, where we spent a month, I found myself once more within the sphere of the serious life of two years before, having many friends among the Irish clergy, who formed so strong an element at the Vatican, and I find many entries in my diary connected with Irish politics, some of which are worth transcribing here.

"*4th Nov.*— To see Monsignore Stonor, who has inherited much of Cardinal Howard's position, being a sort of diplomatic go-between with the Papal court as well as having been made an archbishop. He tells me that Lintorn Simmons is coming here on an official mission to the Vatican. When he, Stonor, saw Lord Salisbury in London this summer, Lord Salisbury told him that diplomatic relations would have to be established with the Pope, but that there was such fear of opposition from the Non-conformists that it would have to be done cautiously. Rosebery had told him much the same thing. Now the pretext is a settlement of ecclesiastical disputes at Malta. This, Stonor says, is a pretext only, as the disputes were settled some time ago through himself. He also told me what happened between the Pope and the German Emperor. There was no rudeness intended by the Emperor nor offence taken by the Pope. An arrangement had been come to between the Emperor and Prince Henry, that Prince Henry and Herbert Bismarck should come to the Vatican half an hour after the Emperor, but owing to the slow pace of the Emperor's carriages Prince Henry arrived too soon by ten minutes. Herbert Bismarck thereupon made a scene, declaring that he and Prince Henry would leave the Vatican if not at once announced. They were consequently announced, although the Pope had given orders that he and the Emperor should be undisturbed for half an hour, ten minutes before the time, but the Emperor told them to wait. Stonor assures me that this was all. It has, however, I fancy been agreed to hush up whatever happened, and the Emperor has made whatever amends was required.

"*5th Nov.*— Made a round of visits with Stonor, among others to the Embassy. The Dufferins arrived last night, but we did not see them. With Dering [the first Secretary], however, we had some talk. Simmons is to arrive next week and with him as secretary, Ross of Bladensburg. This will make a storm in Ireland, where Ross is known to have had much to do with the Papal Rescript against the Plan of Campaign. [See my ' Land War in Ireland.']

"*6th Nov.*— We breakfasted at the Palazzo Caetani, and went on in the afternoon in a storm of thunder and lightning with the Duke and Duchess [of Sermoneta] and their daughter Giovanella to Fogliano. Fogliano, however, we were not destined to reach, for the rain was quite equatorial, and we stopped for the night at Cisterna, where the Duke has a half-deserted palace, and there we are camped. The floods on the Campagna were beyond belief, torrents of red water pouring over the edges of the railway cuttings, and in some places the train having to drive its way against a strong and deep current. Every water course was a raging flood and broad streams were forming themselves rapidly in the fields and still broader lakes. At Villetri we left the train and took carriage, but stopped here as it was thought dangerous to go farther. I never in Europe saw such continuous lightning or such rain over so long a space of time. It has been like the breaking of the monsoon in India. The torrent in one of the valleys gave one an idea of what the world may have been in the tropic age when the great valleys were first formed.

" This palace here at Cisterna has many remains of grandeur, fresco paintings by Zucchero, and fine marble chimney-pieces. The weather, too, in spite of the rain is warm, and we are lodged comfortably enough. We play dominoes in the evening on an old fire screen propped on two chairs to serve as table."

We went on next morning with the first light to Fogliano, just in time to get across the Pontine Marshes, for the floods were rising and in one place had already covered the road. Here we spent four days in this the most delightful country place in Italy. I have already described Fogliano in one of my previous volumes and need not repeat it here. We occupied our time pleasantly enough duck shooting on the lagoons, which lie between the great oak forest and the sea, in the early mornings, and riding in the afternoons to visit the Duchess's stud, which she has established very successfully here, and for which she had bought a couple of Arab stallions a year or two ago. The Duke much busied with public affairs, and the municipal elections now going on at Rome. He was on the committee of selection, and after much telephoning to and from headquarters ended by sending in his resignation. This was an early stage of his public career which led him later to the mayoralty of Rome, and later still to office in the Government. " The Duke," I write, 9th November, after much talk on these subjects, " is certainly a most distinguished man, not a man of genius but of very superior talents. He has read enormously, philosophy, science, history, and can talk well on most subjects. He is president of the Italian Geographical Society and the Italian Alpine Club, an honest man in public affairs, but disenchanted with knowledge and doubtful of the ends of life like all the rest of us. ' Neither the moral law nor the law of beauty,' he says, ' can be found in nature, and without these the world must be lacking in interest.' He is not religious, but supports religion as being the reason of these two ideas, at least so I gather from what he has told me."

It was in accordance with this view of religion, and out of politeness to us, that on Sunday the 10th it was arranged that mass should be said in a little movable hut on wheels like a bathing machine, evidently a new experiment, a talked-of chapel not being finished or apparently likely to be. " The Duke is clearly a latitudinarian though he attended mass, and the Duchess enjoys life too much to be very *dévote*. There were some thirty servants and peasant neighbours brought in and a sprinkling of dogs to make up the congregation, which was all out of doors in front of the house, the celebrant a mass priest brought in from a distance. Altogether a quaint admixture of mediæval simplicity with a nineteenth century lack of faith, but it is not for me to criticize." On our return to Rome the same afternoon, 10th November, I found letters and newspapers with news from Egypt. " The Stanley expedition has come to grief in Africa, and Wadelai was really captured by the Mahadists just as Osman Digna declared it to be more than a year ago. Stanley and Emin are now reported to be together endeavouring to get to the coast, but an end will have been put to their filibustering projects of re-conquest on the Upper Nile. The German, Peters, too, has been knocked on the head by the Somalis, and Islam triumphs all along the equatorial line. The German Emperor, meanwhile, is at Constantinople being fêted with all honour by Abdul Hamid."

The news inspired me with a fresh longing for the East, where my true heart lay, and hastened our departure for Egypt, the rest of our time at Rome being spent partly, as I have said, with my old friends the Irish priests in the various colleges and monasteries, partly with new artistic acquaintances, of whom there are so many resident in the ancient city. But I must not linger over these personal recollections, interesting as they are to me, for they would take up too much space. All I need notice is that, calling again at the Embassy, I found Lord Dufferin, to my pleasure, favourable to the pleading I made that he should help if possible in any decision there might be in the direction of re-establishing that free government at Cairo he had promised the Egyptians in 1883, and recalling Arabi. On my last day at Rome I attended a dinner at the Irish college, where I met the Maronite Archbishop of Damascus, and where good old Dr. Kirby, rector of the College, proposed my unworthy health, and where I was constrained to speak at length to the students on the prospects of Home Rule. It was my last public utterance about Ireland. On the morning of the 4th we left for Naples, and there took ship for Alexandria, and by the 12th found ourselves once more at Sheykh Obeyd, where we spent the rest of the winter in the purely Oriental surroundings I have more than once described.

On the occasion of this second visit to Egypt of 1889–90 I adopted a new attitude towards the British occupation and Baring, who represented it at Cairo as Consul-General and British Resident. When I had been there the previous year I had avoided all intercourse with the Anglo-official world, but now, on my return, influenced by the conversation I had had with Dufferin at Rome and thinking that I might perhaps thus help on the re-establishment of a more liberal *régime* at Cairo, I took occasion of an informal message sent me that he would be glad to see me to call on Baring, and from that time remained in friendly relations with the Residency, which were not without their advantage in a public way. In business matters I found Sir Evelyn a pleasant man to deal with. He was quick to understand a case, and straightforward in his replies, willing always to listen to arguments, however opposed to his own opinions, and with nothing of the conventional insincerities of diplomacy. It is to this, no doubt, that he owed his success in converting to his view the many English Radical M.P.'s who, arriving at Cairo with the idea of hastening on the evacuation, left it persuaded that the proposal was impossible or at least premature, and that the Occupation must be maintained.

" *12th Jan.*— Yesterday I called by appointment on Sir Evelyn Baring. I had not done so since our meeting in 1883, but it came about in this wise. When Prince Wagram (he had followed us to Egypt at the end of the year) was here a fortnight ago he gave me a kind of informal message from Baring to the effect that he would be pleased if I came to see him. At the time I was not quite sure how to respond to this, and I delayed taking any action, but last Sunday I received a visit from Mohammed el Moelhi, who gave me news of how things were going politically. He assured me that people were becoming more reconciled to the state of affairs, that Riaz was allowing rather more personal liberty, and that Tewfik had retired altogether from political action. Nearly all the exiles had been allowed to return, and Mohammed Abdu had been appointed judge at Benha. Under the circumstances he strongly advised me in Arabi's interest to respond to Baring's advance. He said it would increase my opportunities of influence, for now people were afraid to come to me for fear of Baring's displeasure. He did not think that Riaz was hostile, though the Khedive doubtless was. The Khedive, however, was malleable, and if he saw that Baring was friends with me he would think it safest to follow suit. I believed this to be sound advice, and I consequently wrote a note to Baring saying that I had received this informal message from Wagram and asking when I could see him. He replied very politely and so my visit was arranged.

" I found Baring at two in his study, and stayed with him for about half an hour. People say that he is stiff and ill-mannered. I did not find him so. On the contrary he was courteous and kindly. We spoke pretty frankly about things. I said I had not called before because I was not sure whether he would wish to see me. He replied that the only thing he had thought unfair in our political quarrel was Randolph Churchill's having accused him in the House of Commons of having attacked me through my property in Egypt; he had not been there to answer him, and he thought it unfair; as a fact he had entirely forgotten the existence of my property, and he certainly had had nothing to do with the proceedings taken against me concerning it. I answered that to the best of my recollection I had never supposed him to have intervened personally in the affair, and that it was doubtless the Khedive's doing. Randolph had, moreover, exceeded my instructions in pushing the case as far as he had done. We did not discuss this long. I told him the Khedive had had me spied upon, and he said it was natural his Highness should not be very friendly to me, and should want to know what I was doing in Egypt, but the Khedive had not spoken to him about me for a long while.

" We then went on to the state of the country, and I told him I thought things were going better now he had got rid of Nubar and was working with a Mohammedan Ministry. He said the Nubar Ministry was a mistake, but the difficulty is to get Mohammedans who are capable of the work. They are either of the old-fashioned sort who will hear of no improvement, or else young fellows who take some modern European plan, and wish to pitchfork it into Egypt whether it is suitable or not. I said that as to that it was just Arabi's merit that he stood between these two extremes. Arabi knew nothing of Europe, but wanted to improve on Oriental lines. I mentioned that I had heard Mohammed Abdu had returned and received an appointment, and he gave the Sheykh a high character, and said that nearly all the exiles were now recalled. I told him that I hoped the amnesty would be general and would include Arabi and the other exiles who are in Ceylon. To this he demurred, and said that Arabi, having made an unsuccessful revolution had to pay the penalty, 'not, however,' he added, 'that I have ever accepted the theory that his was a *military* revolt, but it was unsuccessful.' 'On the contrary,' I said, 'it was altogether successful, except for the British Army.' 'That,' he said, 'was one of the elements he should have reckoned with'; and I 'a British army of 20,000 men is too strong an element for any Oriental calculation.'

"He then went on to talk of practical improvements and said he was pleased that I had recognized these, but it would be necessary for many years to come to have some European guidance, and he believed English guidance to be better than French or any other. Lastly, we discussed agricultural methods and a school of agriculture which was being founded, and agreed that schools of this sort were a doubtful benefit. [*N.B.*— The school in question which had been started under a Scotchman proved a comical failure, the professors after several years of experiments having had to call in their fellah neighbours to show them how crops could be grown successfully.] We parted on cordial terms, and he invited Anne and me to luncheon for to-day. I declined as I do not wish to go into town again, but I accepted for Anne, and so she and Judith are to go in there this morning. I trust this may all be for the best.

"I have been reading Gordon's 'Letters to his Sister,' and find them very consoling in their resignation to Providence; his doctrine is entirely Mohammedan."

This extract has its importance as showing in connection with other extracts of a later date that the difficulty about recalling Arabi, which was the essential condition of any true intention of restoring the National Party in Egypt, resided not in the Khedive only but in Lord Cromer. The following, too, will have its interest as indicating perhaps the point of departure taken by him so markedly at a later date in Arabian affairs.

"*20th Feb.*— Sháhir Ibn Nassár, son of the chief Sheykh of the Dhaheri Harb tribe of Hedjaz came to Sheykh Obeyd on the 25th of January with his cousin Seyid and a friend, Ali, from Mecca. Sháhir is a pleasing young man and we invited him to stay with us, and he has been ever since at Sheykh Obeyd. He came to Cairo to claim a debt of £350 due to his tribe for the hire of camels supplied to the Haj last year, and was very angry because Riaz and the Khedive had refused to see him notwithstanding his having brought letters, also the money had been refused him, and the Khedive had refused his gift of a delul. After waiting in ante-rooms all this month he made up his mind to go back to his people, who have it in their power to block the pilgrim road, or at least to make things very uncomfortable for the pilgrims, but I proposed to him as a last resource to see Baring. This he did on Tuesday, I having spoken about him the day before to Baring when I lunched at the Residency. Baring received him, by Zeyd's account who went with him, with all honour and sent at once for Riaz and told him Sháhir was under his protection, and he must see justice done. Riaz then went to the Khedive, who already knew of Sháhir's being with me, and they sent Thábit Pasha to Sháhir and another Pasha Abderrahman, and all together went to the Emir el Haj and gave him a wigging and made him acknowledge the debt. Sháhir is to have his money in a few days, and is, of course, highly delighted. He has given me the delul, which is rather a white elephant as I shall have to give him a present in exchange."

This Sháhir was a most interesting man, being a quite wild Bedouin, and his father, the chief Sheykh of the most important tribe between Mecca and Medina, the hereditary occupants of the mountain passes through which the pilgrimage yearly has to pass. From very early times they have been subsidized by the Caliphs and Sultans who have been responsible for the safe conduct of the pilgrims to grant a free passage, but of late years the subsidy had remained unpaid through the dishonesty of the agents entrusted with its delivery, a neglect which brought about much trouble, and occasionally loss of life, through the hostility of the tribe. Sháhir had had little dealing with civilization, even that of Mecca, and found himself more at home with us than at Cairo, sharing Zeyd's tent on the desert edge outside our garden wall. He was a wonderful camel-rider, performing strange feats of agility with his delul, but was unable to ride a horse, for the Harb are not horse owners, at least not that section of the tribe which inhabits the Hedjaz. When he left us to return to his home by sea from Suez, his delul, an Udeyhah, remained with me, I giving him in exchange £50, a very full price, for the expense of his journey.

Another matter which I took up that winter with Lord Cromer was one that lay at the root of all sound progress in Egypt, as it does wherever a Mohammedan population finds itself subjected to a Christian government, that of its demoralization by drink. I am no fanatic on the question of drink in Europe, where the use of wine and strong drinks stands in no direct opposition, except by its abuse, to morals. But in Mohammedan lands the case is entirely different. There the abstention from wine is a fundamental principle of the moral code, and those who transgress on this point become reprobate in their own eyes, and lose all sense of decency and decorum. This was beginning to show itself markedly in Egypt as a consequence of the establishment of English rule. It had been against the spread of drink as much as anything that the revolution of 1881 had acquired its moral strength in public opinion and, with the suppression of the Nationalists after Tel-el-Kebir, and the reinstatement of European control, the evil had returned in double force. It is hardly too much to say that we had intervened in Egypt to reinstate the Greek drink sellers, who combined it with moneylending in the villages of the Delta. The country district where I had my home was a good instance of how the evil worked. The villages in our immediate neighbourhood at Sheykh Obeyd were inhabited entirely by Mohammedans; in the whole of them there were not half-a-dozen Copts or Christians of any sect and there was no demand whatever for drink in any of them. On my return there, however, in this year I found that a small local railway had been opened, joining these with Cairo, and that at each station on the line as the first sign of the coming civilization a drink shop had been established, kept by a Greek moneylender in the interest of his financial business. It was calculated that if the fellahin could be tempted inside his doors to taste the forbidden liquor the rest of his morality would soon give way, and with it his independence of borrowing. Against this coming evil the respectable heads of the villages were doing their best to make opposition, and one morning they called on me to advise what they should do. I advised them to make formal protest to the Government, and offered if they should fail in obtaining a favourable answer, to plead their cause with Baring, who alone had it in his power to put pressure not so much on the Khedivial officials as on the Greek Consulate. The Greek drink-sellers were most of them Hellenic subjects, and as such protected by the international agreements known as the Capitulations against interference in their trade by the Khedivial police, and the privileges thus enjoyed by them had been re-established in full force with the overthrow of the National Government, and it rested with Baring, who exercised all real power, to decide to what extent the privileges should be permitted to go. The whole question of the drink shops might, if he was willing, be treated as a police matter to be dealt with as a common nuisance, and it would not have been possible for the Greek Consul-General to make a serious question of it if Baring should insist. The secret reason, however, of the protection extended to them at the Consulate was, that they bought their immunity there in part with cash paid down, in part with threats of complaints laid against the Consul-General at Athens, a form of black-mailing much in vogue amongst the Greeks.

" *25th March.*— Saw Sir Evelyn Baring on the drink question, especially with regard to our being threatened here at Sheykh Obeyd. I told him of the deputation which had come to me from Merj and Kafr el Shórafa (in protest against the drink shops being open in those villages in connection with the new railway), and he expressed his general sympathy and desire to help in stopping the spread of drink in Egypt, but said it was a large question, and a question of law; he would see Riaz (the Prime Minister), and find out how the law was; Riaz was very hostile to the Greeks, and so would be likely to do what he could. He would let me know the result, and then, if there was a possibility, the inhabitants of Merj and the other villages should protest, and he would do all in his power to help them.

" *6th April.*— Called again on Baring to show him the petition against the drink shops. It had been signed by seventy-three of the principal Sheykhs and notables of Merj, Kafr el Jamus, Kafr el Shórafa, and Birket el Haj, also by Salaam Abu Shedid and Hassan Abu Tawil, Sheykhs from the Howeytat and Aiaideh tribes. He seemed pleased with it, and I left him a translation, and we discussed the question together and with Tigrane Pasha, who had come in and whom Baring sent off at once with the original to Riaz. Tigrane [he was the Armenian Under-Secretary for Foreign Affairs] declared that the case could be dealt with without infringing upon National rights. I argued strongly against its being treated fiscally, but rather as a matter of police and public morals. In this Tigrane agreed with me, and Baring said he would do all in his power to stop the spread of the drink shops, if according to the ruling of the International Courts, and if not, he would submit a modification of the law to the Powers. We discussed also several other cases, especially that of the Government salt tax, an imposition which pressed hardly upon the people, and that of certain Bedouins imprisoned at Ghizeh. He showed himself anxious to intervene in all these matters, sent for the persons responsible, and promised to see into the cases. A good morning's work."

The above will give some idea of the practical way in which Lord Cromer did the work of administration at Cairo, and of the kind of questions I was able to bring before him. That he had the reformation of abuses at that date, 1890, the period of his first and best practical energies, much at heart, is certain, nor did I then suspect him of working, as he did so flagrantly later, less for the good of Egypt than in English political and financial interests. It is, however, necessary to remark that, in spite of his promises of assistance and the undoubted good faith of Riaz Pasha on the drink question, nothing at all was ever done to protect these villages from the Greek intruders, who ply their trade in them unchecked to the present day. Their case was as strong a one as could well have been brought forward, for it was one where the demand for alcohol needed to be created in the midst of a totally abstaining population, and it worked the ill results we foresaw. The drink shops were put under regulations good enough in their way, but the sale was not suppressed, and like many another regulation in

Egypt where no advantage of revenue was concerned, they were not insisted on; energy in introducing them, however sincere at the outset, soon slackened, and the regulations became a dead letter.

I will add to this, because they are amusing, a couple of extracts from my diary, conversations I put down in it, with Zeyd, my Bedouin horse master, of the Muteyr tribe in Nejd, as I was riding with him on two occasions on the desert edge in the evening that winter. They have an interest worth preserving, as they show the way the Arabs of Arabia think in contrast to the Egyptian fellahin whom they come in contact with during their visits to Cairo, a contrast which has a significance in view of the political developments we have witnessed in these last years.

" *Zeyd*. The fellahin are a timid folk, if they see a cat cross their path after dark they think it an *afrit*, they believe in all manner of foolish things.

" *I*. What then? Are there no *afrits* in Nejd?

" *Zeyd*. Wallah! The belief in *afrits* is foolishness. There are no *afrits*, neither in Nejd nor here. But the fellahin have no heart. They are without blood. They are afraid.

" *I*. You are a philosopher. Do all in Nejd think like you?

" *Zeyd*. The men of Nejd have brave hearts. They are used to being alone. They journey alone through the desert, ten days, twenty days, forty days perhaps. They know nothing of *afrits*. There is none other but God.

" *I*. Truly none. But do they see nothing?

" *Zeyd*. They fear nothing. There is of course Shaitan, who sometimes appears to them in the likeness of a goat or a cow. But they are not afraid. He does not harm them.

" *I*. And do they speak to him?

" *Zeyd*. Shaitan will sometimes journey with them in disguise. There was once a man of Bereydah who was riding his delul alone in a storm. There was lightning amid the darkness. He heard a voice in front of him asking what he was doing there in such tempestuous weather, and if he was not afraid. A flash revealed to him the figure of a sheep set on the neck of his camel. It was Shaitan, who was speaking to frighten the man. The man, however, put out his hand and caught the sheep by the fleece, saying, ' I know you are a sheep by your wool.' But Shaitan answered, ' And you. I know you are a sheep by your wits!' and he slid down the camel's neck to the ground and disappeared.

" *I*. Yet you do not believe in *afrits*.

" *Zeyd*. No. That is a vulgar superstition.

         *   *   *   *

" *I*. What is this to the right of us? A tomb?

"*Zeyd.* Ay, verily. The tomb of a saint. The fellahin have a hundred thousand saints. They are a credulous people. They kill sheep for Abu Seriyeh still, though he has been dead a thousand years.

"*I.* And we, too, killed a sheep when we went on the pilgrimage to Abu Seriyeh three years ago.

"*Zeyd.* Yes, to bring a blessing on your camels. And one of your camels died within the year. How can a Sheykh, a holy man who has been dead so long, help any one, beast or man?

"*I.* This, too, is philosophy.

"*Zeyd.* No. It is truth. An uncle or a grandfather, I can understand that one should give them a sheep, but not to Abu Seriyeh. This land is full of the tombs of holy men. The fellahin are a credulous people.

*   *   *   *

"*Zeyd.* This road from Kafr el Shórafa to the bridge, how often I used to think of it when I was journeying from Syria with the Seglawi horse, the grey Seglawi, and the Jilfa mare. I used to ask of God that he would grant me this, that I might ride along the sand just here with them in safety. And see, I arrived with them and rode along this very road.

"*I.* Thank God.

"*Zeyd.* Yes, thank God. There is no word it does one more good to say than this, ' thank God,' when a danger is past. *El hamdu l'Illah; el hamdul l'Illah!* "

*   *   *   *

Another conversation of nearly the same date has the additional interest that it concerns a mission I had sent him on the year before, to purchase a stallion for me from the Anazeh in Northern Arabia.

"*Zeyd.* I will tell you how I bought the Seglawi [this was the stallion ' Azrek,' see General Stud Book]. I did not, of course, tell them the truth, that I was the servant of the Bey (meaning me). There is no shame in this. It is policy (*siasa*). I am a master of policy. I made a deceit. I said to them that I was of the Agheylat, looking for horses for India, horses from the north and tall ones, for those are the horses that bring most price in India. What did I want with the pure bred? I wanted to make money. And so I went to the Sebáa. I alighted at Ibn ed Derri's tent, as it were by accident. But I made a mistake. It was not the tent of Mishlab Ibn ed Derri, but of his brother Fulan (the name *Fulan* is used as we say So-and-So). There are four brothers. Fulan and Fulan and Fulan and Mishlab. Mishlab was the owner of the Seglawi. I stayed there for three days, without speaking of the Seglawi. The horse was at pasture and I did not see him. On the fourth day came Mishlab to breakfast with his brother, and they killed a lamb — and behold the Seglawi was with him — he did not bring him to sell, but, as the custom is with strangers, that I might see him. He stood tethered outside the tent, but I did not even turn his way. Only lifting up my eyes stealthily, I saw him, and the sight of his forehead and of his eyes gave me joy. For you know the Seglawi's face is of those which, if a man, a sorrowful man, sees, he needs must rejoice. Only it made my heart beat terribly, and I said to myself, 'Zeyd must never more return to the Bey — he must die — if he do not obtain that horse.' Then, after we had eaten, I arose as one who wishes to go outside for a private purpose; and I walked past the Seglawi with my face to the ground as though I did not see him, and hàrdly putting one foot before the other, like a thief. And when I returned Mishlab was alone with his son Sakr in the tent, and we talked of the buying of horses. And I told them of my desire of tall horses for the Indian market.

"And after a while I said to the father that I had something that I should wish to speak to him of in private — for I knew that his son would not consent to the sale, seeing that it was he who received the money of the Arabs when their mares were served, and I knew, too, that the father was displeased at this. All that is customary is that those who bring mares should also bring flour for the stallion, and it may be a *kiswah* (a complimentary robe), but not money. But Sakr had taken money, to his father's displeasure. So I said to the young man, when we had gone outside, 'On Salameh, stay you here on one side, for I have something to speak of with your father. And you may watch us, and, if you see me strike your father, then come to his assistance, but if I do not raise my hand to him, then wait till we have finished, for it is not necessary you should hear.' And to my friend who was with me, I told him to take his spear, and sent him on another errand to fetch my dromedary.

"Then when we were alone, I said to Mishlab: 'O Mishlab, it is time I went on my business, for I am engaged in the purchase of horses. But before I go I would see your horse. I cannot buy him, for I am looking only for horses from the North at a low price, but yours, the Seglawi, would I see. For I am of the Muteyr and you are of the Sebáa, and I am a master of fortune (*sáhib el bukht*), and you are a master of fortune, and it would be a shame that I did not name a price or put a value on him, for otherwise, you might think that I did not know his worth.' And Mishlab said, 'So be it.' And I named £100, as if it were a great price. And when I had named it, I saw that Mishlab put his hand under his kefiyeh to scratch his head and stroke his beard. And at last he spoke: 'Nay, it would be a sin.' And I pressed him, for I saw by his manner that he was in doubt, and I could hardly believe in my fortune that there should be a hope of his consenting. And again my heart beat so that you might hear it. And at last I said, as if rising to go, ' There shall be another ten added to the hundred.' And I gave him my hand, and he gave me his hand. And I said, ' O Mishlab, listen. The Seglawi is the Seglawi, and the men of the tribe send their mares to you on his account. But he is but flesh and blood, and a shot might destroy him, and then where would be the £110?' And he said, ' If it were not for my son's ill doing, I would not do it. And I do not want money, for God has blessed me with many camels and I have all I need. But I fear that Sakr will bring disgrace on me, for he takes money for the mares, which thing is forbidden; and I fear lest my good fortune should fail me.'

" And so it was settled in that one talking, and immediately I called for my delul, and having given him the advance money (*arbun*), I begged him to send his son with me to Aleppo to receive the full price. And I mounted in haste, fearing that the rest would return and would make him change his mind."

CHAPTER III

BRIGANDAGE IN EGYPT

The summer of 1890 I spent in large part at Paris with Lytton at the Embassy, and was one of the most delightful in my experience, but it contained little of a political nature or that can be repeated here. Our talks were mainly of literature, and more especially of dramatic literature, on which he was just then engaged, the detail of his official work being left principally to his staff, though I would not be understood to mean that he was a mere figurehead. As Ambassador, on the contrary, his political influence at Paris was greater than that of his predecessor, Lord Lyons. With all the latter's dignity and discretion and solid good sense, he had never succeeded in obtaining any kind of popularity, and in his time the relations between France and England had become the reverse of cordial. Lytton, however, by the very qualities which had proved his defects when in India, had obtained an immediate personal success at Paris, and had in large measure restored the international good feeling. His literary Bohemianism and lack of pomposity, his devotion to the stage, his ready patronage of artists, actors, and those *littérateurs* who count for so much in Paris journalism, had been a passport for him to favour with the Press, and through the Press to public opinion. Lytton was by taste a Bohemian, and Paris, which is also so largely Bohemian, recognized him as a brother artist. It was impossible to regard him as representative of the *morgue britannique,* of which not only Lord Lyons but Lord Cowley before him had been such notable examples. Treated with a light hand, many a difficult question was in his time easily circumvented, if not permanently solved, and this at the expense of no real dignity. It was felt that he wished well to Frenchmen and French views of life, and that was sufficient.

In the intervals of my Paris visits I find notices of my life in England, showing that I, too, had learned to take life more lightly than in previous years. I busied myself not at all with parliamentary politics, and even about Ireland I ceased to take any absorbing interest. The prospects of Home Rule were better assured just then in all appearance than they had been since Gladstone's defeat in 1886. The result of the great " Times " prosecution had been a notable victory for the National-

40

ists, and had re-established Parnell's character as a responsible statesman at a higher point than ever before in English eyes, so that it was
confidently expected that at the next general election Gladstone would
be returned to power with a majority sufficient to overcome the opposition of the House of Lords, and carry his Home Rule Bill into law.
It was, therefore, with a free conscience that I led an idle life at home,
writing my verses and enjoying social pleasures in the company of my
friends.   It was in that summer that the Crabbet Club, which was to
acquire a certain social celebrity, was established on a footing which
was to gain for it a character almost of importance.   It will not be
out of place, seeing that our memoir writers of the day have included
it, or rather have not left it unnoticed in their recollections, if I say a
few words here as to what it really was.

The Crabbet Club was in its origin a purely convivial gathering,
unambitious of any literary aim.   It began in this way: When George,
Lord Pembroke (the 13th Earl) came of age in 1871, having been a
very popular boy at Eton, with many school friends, and afterwards at
Oxford, he thought it would be amusing to continue in some measure
the life they had led by having them to stay with him once or twice
every summer at Wilton, for a day or two at a time, to play cricket,
and row on the river, and otherwise divert themselves, and they took
the name of the " Wilton," or " Wagger " Club, and it proved a great
success.   In 1876, though much older than the rest of the members, I
was asked to join it as one who had known the Herberts from their
school days.   Pembroke was staying with me at Crabbet, and his two
brothers and their sister Gladys (afterwards Lady Ripon), and several
of their friends, and several of mine, and I drove them all to Epsom
for the Derby (Silvio's year), and we had a cricket match and a lawn
tennis handicap (lawn tennis was in the process of being invented, and
we played on a court 20 feet longer than what afterwards became the
regulation length), and it was on this occasion that I joined the club.
The party at Crabbet had proved such a success that the next year it
was proposed that the club should make one of its regular meetings
there, and so it gradually came about that the members came to Crabbet
annually.   The members of the club were never more than a few, a
dozen to twenty, and consisted, besides the Herbert brothers, of Eddy
Hamilton, who was afterwards Gladstone's private secretary, Lord
Lewisham, Jocelyn Amherst, Granny Farquhar, Lionel Bathurst, with
Harry Brand (afterwards Lord Hampden), Nigel Kingscote, Godfrey
Webb, Button Bourke, Frank Lascelles, Mark Napier, and half-a-
dozen more of my own intimates, and these came regularly to Crabbet
every summer, and we gradually adopted the " Crabbet Club " as the
name of our branch.

Though we professed no kind of politics, and looked to amusement

only, nearly all the members of it were Tories, two or three of them in
Parliament, and when in 1882 I took the somewhat violent line I did
about Egypt and war ensued, several of the members taking offence
ceased their attendance, and the Club as far as the Crabbet meetings
were concerned became less popular, and this state of things was
aggravated when I stood for Parliament as a Home Ruler in 1885 and
1886, and it was all but submerged by my imprisonment at Galway.
Hardly any of the old Wilton members would answer the invitations
to it, and Pembroke himself, the most tolerant of men, as an Irish
landlord with large interests at stake in the county of Dublin, felt it
a grievance that I should have identified myself with the Land League
and the Plan of Campaign. All this was natural enough, and I could
not complain of the defection. The Club as the " Crabbet Club " was
still continued, but reconstructed on different lines with a number of
young men, Oxford undergraduates, most of them professing Home
Rule opinions. The chief of these were the two Peels, Willy and
George, sons of the Speaker, Arthur Pollen, Herbert Vivian, Leo
Maxse, Percy Wyndham (son of Sir Hugh), Theodore Fry, Theobald
Mathew, Artie Brand, and Loulou Harcourt, the only three of the old
set being Mark Napier, Eddy Hamilton, and Nigel Kingscote.

The young men thus got together, most of them fresh from the Uni-
versities, though also bent on amusement, had tastes more intellectual
than their predecessors, and besides our lawn tennis handicaps, we had
much after-dinner speaking, and a verse competition with the election
of a poet laureate for the year. The Club was in this condition when
in 1889 George Wyndham, becoming a member, took it in hand, and
seeing its intellectual capabilities brought new blood into it by introducing friends of his own, already holding a certain position in the
political world, and who have since no few of them climbed to fame.
Among these were George Curzon, Harry Cust, Houghton (now Lord
Crewe), Frederick Locker, Umphreville Swinburne, cousin of the poet,
St. George Lane Fox, Eddy Tennant, Laurence Currie, George Leveson
Gower, Esmé Howard, Elcho, Dick Grosvenor, Alfred Douglas, Charles
Gatty, Morpeth, and his brother Hubert Howard, and on a single occasion Oscar Wilde, and it was in the company of these that our meetings of the early nineties were held. They were really brilliant meetings, with post-prandial oratory of the most amusing kind, and were
productive of verse of a quite high order. The number of the members
was limited to twenty, and there was much competition when a vacancy
occurred. The poetry of the Crabbet Club has been preserved in print,
and is one of the curiosities of literature, deserving a place, I venture
to think, in company with the best verse of a not serious kind, including
even perhaps that of the Mermaid Tavern. My own part in these
meetings, which were essentially convivial, was that of Chairman and

President, an anomalous one seeing that I was a teetotaller, but which yet worked well.

The latter half of the summer of 1890 was darkened for me by the final illness and death of my cousin, Francis Currie. He had been my Mentor, not always in the ways of wisdom, during my youth at Paris, and had remained there a constant and very dear friend for close on thirty years. On my visit to Paris in the Spring I had found him ill with an ominous cough, and other symptoms of a decline, but his French doctor, whom I consulted about him, persisted in declaring that it was nothing more than the legacy of a fever he had long before contracted in India while serving in the campaign of the Mutiny, and encouraged him to go for change of air to the Alps, though to my eye, and to that of his faithful *bonne* Julienne he was already "*un homme frappé.*" Now, however, soon after my return to the Paris Embassy in July, I learned that he was at Aix les Bains, and, as it seemed, in an almost hopeless state. This broke short my stay at Paris, and took me first to Aix, and then moving him away from the great heat there to Glyon in Switzerland, where, a month later, in spite of our care, he died. The history of those few weeks, as of the rest of the summer of 1890, belongs, if ever I write it, to my most private memoirs.

On the 18th of October we again left England for Egypt, spending three more weeks on our way with the Lyttons at Paris, and then on by Marseilles to Alexandria and Sheykh Obeyd, where we once more spent the winter. The political position in Egypt at this time was as follows: Riaz Pasha was still in office under the Khedive Tewfik, and the provinces of Lower Egypt, laxly ruled, were much disturbed with brigandage, especially in our immediate neighbourhood. Riaz, who at that time was working with the Khedive in secret opposition to Baring and the British Occupation, allowed the brigandage to continue, with the idea that it would serve as a proof of the unpopularity of the English *régime* and its powerlessness to preserve order. Baring was occupied now almost exclusively with the struggle to make both ends of Egyptian finance meet, being convinced on his side that a prosperous balance sheet was the best argument he could use with the British public in favour of retaining Egypt as a permanent British dependency. In this he was supported by Lord Salisbury at the Foreign Office, who had made up his mind, now that the Wolff Convention for a withdrawal of the British garrison had failed, to stay on in military occupation without any legal settlement of England's position on the Nile. It was argued that the legal road to such a settlement had been barred by the Sultan, who, when the Convention had been agreed to, had withheld his signature of ratification. Though I did not know it at the time, our Queen (Victoria) had taken the Sultan's action as a personal slight, seeing that she had affixed her own royal signature in ratification before the Sultan's refusal, nor is it possible to say that she was without justification in feeling the matter strongly. In accordance with this, Baring was beginning those changes in the fiscal and administrative domain which were intended to transfer all real power in Egypt, little by little, from the Turco-Circassian class represented by Riaz which he had hitherto patronized, into his own. The new policy, however, was as yet only in embryo, and the intention of remaining in Egypt was not avowed. It was impossible to do so openly, not only through the fear of trouble with France, but also because Liberal opinion in England was not prepared for it, and unless it could be converted to the idea before the next general election, which was to take place in 1892, it was always possible that Gladstone, coming once more into power, might suddenly reverse the whole process of absorption, and without further waiting recall the troops from Cairo.

It was with this fear before his eyes that Baring had obtained the services in Egypt of Alfred Milner, a journalist of distinction, the same whom I had known in 1884 as sub-editor of the " Pall Mall Gazette " under Stead (see " Gordon at Khartoum "), and who, a year later, had been taken on by Goschen as his private secretary. It was through Goschen's recommendation that Baring gave him a place in Egypt of £1,000 a year at the Ministry of Finance, nominally for administrative work, but in reality with a mission of organizing a press campaign in London in favour of a continuance of the Egyptian occupation. For this work no man could have been better chosen. He was nominally a Liberal, and had stood as a supporter of Gladstone at the general election of 1885, while his experience in Northumberland Street had put him in touch with all the chief writers of the English Liberal press. No man better than he knew the length of the English electoral foot. At Cairo, without appearing personally in his journalistic character, he knew how to bring the case he had to argue forward by encouraging the various Englishmen officially employed there to write articles in the monthly magazines and elsewhere in praise, not of their own, but of their fellow-administrator's achievements in the way of reform, knowing well that if it could be proved that Egypt, instead of a burden on the British Exchequer, was becoming a paying concern, the battle would be won with the new government, should a Liberal one come into office, even with Mr. Gladstone. And so, in fact, it happened. The appearance of Milner's very able volume, " England in Egypt," in which he drew together all these threads of argument in lucid and attractive form, and which was published a few months before the general election of 1892, effected, as I will show later, exactly the object aimed at. Milner's reward for this service was not delayed. The same year he was relieved from his nominal functions in Egypt, and given the important place at home of Chairman of the Inland

Revenue Board. I saw him pretty frequently at Cairo during his stay
there, and liked him, as I had liked him when in his humbler position
as Stead's assistant editor. He did not display, at that time, anything
of that violent Imperialism which led him later to aspire to the sublime
heights of Tory officialdom which he now occupies.

This was the position in Egypt in the early spring of 1891. I was
now on excellent terms with Baring, whom I found willing to listen
to any suggestions I might make to him for improving the lot of the
fellahin, a matter which I understood, while he, shut up in his office
and seeing practically nothing of native Egypt beyond the tame officials
whom he had attracted to his camp, lived in comparative darkness, and
I was able in this way to effect a good deal in the direction that most
interested me, and I did not fail to bring before him once more the
case of Arabi's return; but he was still too strongly opposed to it,
though, he explained, if it was decided to occupy Egypt permanently
he should have no objection. Failing in this, as far as Arabi was
concerned, I now limited my pleading to an attempt to interest him in
other members of the former National Party, and at the suggestion of
my old friend, Sheykh Mohammed Abdu, who was now living in my
part of Egypt as judge of our chief country town, Benha, and whom
we now saw pretty frequently, I brought before him a plan that he
should take these old Nationalists into his councils and substitute for
the Circassian Pashas who had so far been the only class of Mohammedans permitted to hold office under the restored régime since Tel-el-
Kebir, an Egyptian fellah government. Neither Riaz, nor Nubar, nor
any other of the ministers who had held office during the past seven
years, though patriotic some of them to the extent of having it for their
aim to get rid of all foreign elements in the administration, had taken
any real interest in bettering the condition of the fellahin, and it seemed
to me a lack of intelligence on Baring's part that he had failed to understand the popularity he might have gained by the creation of a fellah
ministry, and the comparative ease with which he could have introduced
the reforms he professed to have at heart, and really at that time had.
I find this alluded to in my diary:

"*20th Feb.*— A few days ago, there being a ministerial crisis, I
wrote to Baring suggesting that he should take new men into the
ministry instead of Riaz and the Circassians, who, despising the fellahin, look only to their own class interests. He answered me favourably, and to-day I called on him, and after luncheon we discussed the
position. Riaz has already given in, so nothing is to be done at present;
but he expressed himself willing to make the acquaintance of any men
of the fellah class whose names I could suggest, and I am to write to
him again on the subject in a few days. He fully admitted that Riaz
was an obstructive; ' but where,' he said, ' is there anyone better?' It

was a doubtful question whether it was possible to put Mohammedans on any road of reform. I said: ' If you give up that hope you give up everything, but you have not tried the Liberal party to help you in reforms.' He said he ' was quite willing. If the National party in 1882 had not allied itself with the army it might have been supported.' ' That was the fault,' I said, ' of the Joint Note.' He agreed 'that ' the Joint Note was a mistake,' and, I think, was impressed with what I said, and we parted on the understanding that I was to give him the names of persons I thought able to afford him political help, but he enjoined on me complete secrecy. ' I will take some opportunity,' he said, ' of making their acquaintance, but there is a difficulty sometimes in my seeing the people.' I shall wait until Hassan Pasha Sherei returns from Upper Egypt, and then see if we cannot make out a fellah Cabinet together." I have a few letters which passed between me and Baring at this time. They are of importance as showing that the policy of introducing reforms through native Egyptians of the Mohommedan Reform Party was laid before Sir Evelyn Baring, and its advantages more or less acknowledged by him full fifteen years before he, as Lord Cromer, adopted it as the only one which could give a hope of making self-government in Egypt possible. (See his Reports for the year 1905.)

Our life at Sheykh Obeyd that Spring was not without incident, as our immediate neighbourhood was disturbed almost nightly by gangs of robbers, who visited the country houses round, breaking into them in the night time and coming in armed conflict with such of the owners as resisted them. The bands were composed principally of Bedouins, with whom were associated certain refugees from Upper Egypt and a few broken men escaped from the prisons at Toura, but the direction of them was in Bedouin hands. For this reason we, who were on good terms with the tribes, were left unmolested, though every one of our near neighbours suffered. This is from my diary:

" *7th March.*— Last night at half-past twelve I heard a great noise of dogs barking, and occasional shots. I went out on to the balcony and listened, and was about to go to bed again, for the guards have a habit of firing without reason in the night to show they are awake, when I heard cries, and I called to Deyf Allah, our head ghaffir, and asked him what it was. He answered, ' there are robbers at Selim Bey's.' I consequently dressed hastily and ran down, having first awakened Anne, and taking my Winchester rifle and a revolver sallied forth, followed by Deyf Allah and Mahmud the Berberin. It was a dark night and I held my rifle ready to fire as we went through the palm grove where I thought I saw one or two people moving. As we got near to Selim Faraj's house (a quarter of a mile from ours) the noise of the dogs increased and mixed with it there were groans, while occasional shots were still being fired at a distance. I went cautiously up to the house where I met an Arab with whom I exchanged greetings. He was probably one of Selim's guards. At the door lay a fellah groaning with his head cut open. There was a light at the window, and women began to scream. On my coming close they told me they had been robbed, and I found the window bars wrenched open. Presently Selim appeared at the door [he was a County Court Judge, a Syrian Christian] his face a coagulated mass of blood, and he let me in and told me the history of what had happened. There had been a noise of knocking at his door, and on his opening it, thinking it was the guard, he received a blow from a *nabout* (a quarter staff) on his shoulder, but managed to slip back inside and bar the door. Then a number of men attacked the house, calling on him to open, and on his refusal they broke through the windows, while he struck at them with a meat chopper, but they pushed him back and got through, six of them, and called for his money. He proposed to them to pay next day, but they declined to wait and broke open his chests of drawers and made search. While this was going on, he hid with his little girl in the scullery, but later issued out again to defend his property, and received three wounds on his head with some sharp instrument. Then the robbers, having found the money they were looking for in his pockets, £37, and hearing me coming, for there was a cry of ' *tarbush,*' their watchword for the police, decamped. The wounded fellah was a servant whom they had cut down outside with their *nabouts,* but nobody paid him the least attention, and I had great difficulty in getting him carried inside the house. The ladies begged me to stay on with them, but I refused, as I had my own people to look after, and so went back, and nothing further happened till daybreak. On my return in the morning I found Selim in bed, and heard his story again. The men, he said, were nearly naked, but had their faces masked. They spoke the Mogrebbin dialect. They were Arabs of the West. I then went with Sheykh Hassan Abu Tawil, the chief of our local Arabs and a tracker, and we followed the track of seven men, which was very distinct in the sand, running towards Matarieh. When within a quarter of a mile of the railway station there, they had sat down and then separated, one who had been wearing shoes going to the ostrich farm, the rest towards the tents of Prince Ahmed Pasha's guard. It is generally thought that they are local people, though Abu Tawil insists they are Mogrebbins, who once lived near the Obelisk (of Heliopolis), and come back every year to rob. One of them had enormous footprints, probably a Negro. I have taken Selim Bey into Cairo, first to Baring, who, however, was too busy to see him, and then on with a note from him to Baker Pasha,

the English Chief of Police, an old military fogey whom I worked up
into unwonted action by telling him that the state of the country was
worse than either Greece or Asia Minor."

The curious part of this episode, though I do not find it in my diary,
was Selim Bey's attitude in the affair. He was a native Christian
Judge, and had been a man of the law all his life, but it was with the
greatest difficulty that I could persuade him to report the attack made
on him to the police. " It would only put me on bad terms with the
neighbours," he said, worse than those he was already on, for he was
very unpopular, and it was only on my declaring that I would myself
report it that he consented to go in with me to Cairo.

" *14th March.*— The attack on Selim Bey has made a stir and his
house is guarded by the regular police. The Mudir has been there and
Baker Pasha. They have made nine or ten arrests, among them the
two Ghaffirs. Poor old Eid, our *bowab* (gatekeeper), being one of
them. I found him sitting disconsolately among the prisoners with his
little child he is so fond of. I am sorry I troubled myself in the
matter, for I do not believe one of the arrested men had anything to
do with the business, but this is the fourth serious case round about us
in eighteen months, and last time they killed a man, and a woman died
of fright. Selim Bey's wound is rather serious, and the servant may yet
die; he is in hospital. The Mudir took from me a deposition, but it
was very meagre, and I had a difficulty in preventing the insertion in it
of things quite untrue."

This affair put an end for the time to the night attacks. I came to
the conclusion later that the tolerance the bands had so long enjoyed
had been due to Riaz' tacit complicity joined to Baker's muddle-headed
incapacity (he was replaced soon afterwards). I took advantage of it
to draw a moral for Baring, and wrote a letter to him recapitulating my
arguments in favour of a fellah government, sending him a list of the
names of men of the fellah party who might make up a Reform Ministry. The list was drawn up in consultation with Sheykh Mohammed
Abdu and Mohammed Moelhi. These are the names:

Hassan Pasha Sherei of Minieh.
Baligh Bey.
Emin Bey Fikri.
Saïd Effendi Zaghloul.
Ahmed Effendi Mahmoud.
Ibrahim Effendi el Wakil.
Mahmud Bey Shukri.
Ahmed Bey Heshmet.
Yusuf Bey Shoki.
Sheykh Mohammed Abdu.

It is to be remarked that this list includes the name of Saad Zaghloul, whom fifteen years later Cromer made Minister of Public Instruction, as well as Sheykh Mohammed Abdu's, afterwards Grant Mufti, whom he declared to be the chief hope of Liberal Islam in Egypt. Baring, however, missed his real opportunity by neglecting my recommendation of Hassan Sherei, who politically was of far greater weight than any of them, and who had died before Baring could bring himself to accepting a fellah Ministry. " Baring, however, answers: 'I do not think there is a ghost of a chance of the Khedive forming a fellah Ministry.' Still Baring may come to it, as Riaz has been coquetting with the French, and has brought about a fine diplomatic storm. Our only policy is to wait the disappearance, one after the other, of the old ministers, and sooner or later they must come to us if they do not annex. Sherif is gone and Nubar, and now Riaz seems going.

" *4th April.*— To Cairo and saw Baring. I asked him first about the drink shops, and he said that though he still hoped to be able to issue his regulations, there was great opposition to these for political reasons from the French; the question of public security was much more important; it was a difficult job; he should put an end to it in time, but he hardly knew how; with regard to the native government it was impossible to get men capable and honest; things were going badly and were leading to a new smash-up; he had only to work on as he could. I asked him what he thought would happen if we evacuated. He said everything would go to smash, but we should not evacuate. I said we might be obliged to do so if there was a change of government at home. He said, 'I shall protest against it, and, if it is insisted on, I wash my hands of the consequences.' I said, 'It is impossible you should not be responsible if you do nothing to prepare for it.' He said, 'They are all alike (meaning the Egyptians). I know most of the men you wrote of.' 'And Hassan Sherei?' I asked. 'No, not Hassan Sherei, but they are all alike.' He said, 'The Khedive is in favour of reform.' 'Yes, as long as he thinks you stronger than the French, but if England were forced to evacuate, you would see how soon he would go over.' 'I daresay. My experience of Easterns is all that way, but we shall not evacuate; we shall have a war with France.' I reminded him of our conversation of 1883, when I told him he could make nothing of Tewfik and the Circassians. He said, 'Whom would you have had? There would only have been Halim, and it would have been the same thing. At any rate, it is too late now to change.' And so we parted."

All this is of interest now as showing how little reality there was in the excuse so commonly made for the breach of our declarations that we were going to leave Egypt, and that our remaining on there was thrust upon us against our will. It was only true in the sense that it was impossible to leave Egypt and at the same time remain its lords and masters politically; only one way was really possible, and that we always refused to take, to restore the National party with its liberal ideas, and thus earn its gratitude and confidence. Egypt might then have remained, not a dependency of the British Empire, but its very good friend and the faithful guardian of the route by the Suez Canal to India. The mistake made on this head by Baring was among the many causes that led, as I shall show, to England's being obliged to take part in the quarrel between France and Germany in the great war of 1914. Lord Cromer's obstinacy on this point was a misfortune. Another was the unlooked-for secession which occurred that spring of Lord Randolph Churchill from the counsels of the Tory party at home. Churchill had, ever since 1882, been a powerful advocate with Lord Salisbury of Egypt's claim to a restoration of her independence so unwisely taken from her in that year, and his quarrel now with his party left my advocacy of Egyptian liberty without support at the Foreign Office of effective Cabinet kind.

We left Sheykh Obeyd for Europe in April, taking Rome again on our way home and Paris.

"*23rd April* 1891.— Landed at Naples this morning, having finished a letter yesterday to Lord Salisbury about Egyptian affairs, and I hope he may pay the attention to it it deserves.

"Having seen our things through the custom house we drove to Agnano and the Grotto del Cane. The lake which used to be the beauty of the place has been dried up these twenty years by a French company, which thought to find the ancient Roman town but found nothing; their operations have left a desolation hideous to the eye. How horrible civilized man is. All day the spectacle of these Neapolitans in their modern slop clothes has been to me a nightmare; all nature is defiled by them. What countenances of filthy passions! what abominations to the senses! what foul rubbish heaps! what stenches! We looked into the Grotto del Cane where criminals they say were cast in the days of Nero. It must have been a merciful death; witness the custode's little dog which has 'died daily' there for sixteen years and still wags its tail at each new performance. A nightingale was singing, the only thing quite in harmony with the beauty of the sky and hills. Later we saw the young Duke, the heir to the Italian throne, a small timid-faced young man, very unlike the House of Savoy of which he is to be the head. The prince is physically unimposing, though on horseback he looks well enough.

"*At Rome, 24th April.*— To Monsignor Stonor's, who showed me a huge correspondence he has been having with O'Shea on the subject of a libel committed on him by Dr. McCormack, Bishop of Galway, O'Shea having appealed to the Pope. There was one specially interesting letter he gave me to read. It related to Parnell's doings with

Chamberlain in 1885, and his acceptance of a local government scheme, also to the part played by O'Shea, Dr. O'Dwyer, and Cardinal Manning in the appointment of Dr. Walsh to the Archbishopric of Dublin. They had all, according to the letter, guaranteed Dr. Walsh as a sound champion of law and order. 'Law and Order,' however, meant another thing in 1885 from what it has meant since. Monsignor Stonor says that Cardinal Moran was already appointed to Dublin and on his way from Australia to Rome, when his nomination was reversed and Dr. Walsh appointed instead. He laments now the ignorance of the Vatican, which sees in Ireland only a faithful Catholic land oppressed by a Foreign Government. I am staying on at the Minerva, Anne and Judith having gone home straight from Naples.

"*25th April.*— To the Irish College where I saw my old friend the Monsignore Rector, who spoke despondingly of Ireland, praying only that God's will might be done. Not so Prior Glyn and Archbishop Walsh whom I next saw. They are very confident of beating Parnell out of Ireland, and winning the English elections (next year) ; if not they agree that the cause of Home Rule is hopeless, for Irish America would not continue to support a parliamentary struggle, but would fall back on secret societies and assassination. Dr. Walsh estimates Parnell's party in Ireland after the elections at sixteen out of a total of eighty Home Rule Members. Prior Glyn's last words to me were 'We shall meet again at College Green when the Parliament is opened.'

"*28th April.*— Called on Dufferin at the Embassy, who showed me a number of drawings he had made in former times, including one of his mother, done at Athens in the year of our first acquaintance, 1859. He talked a good deal on Eastern subjects, but he skilfully avoided politics, making it clear that he wished the visit to be one of friendship only."

At Paris I stayed four days, principally with the Lyttons, the talk of the day being of the French failure at Tonkin.

"*30th April.*— To a coiffeur in the Rue de la Paix to be trimmed and washed and combed after the fashion of the country. The man who attended me was very voluble, having been a soldier in Tonkin and a blood-thirsty one to boot, by his own showing. 'Ah, Monsieur,' he exclaimed, 'quel gouvernement que le notre, un gouvernement qui ne sait rien faire marcher. Figurez vous qu'on vous envoie des civils pour gouverner la Colonie, des hommes de science qui s'imaginent que tous les hommes sont frères. Ce n'est pas cele qu'il faut à la Colonie, en agissant avec des brutes il faut être brutal. Si j'avais été nommé gouverneur pendant un mois seulement, j'aurais exterminé tout ce monde Tonquinois. Il faut les assommer, Monsieur, comme fait le gouvernement Anglais aux Indes.' Voilà un gouvernement qui a la main raide; c'est ce qu'il faudrait à nos colonies.' He asked me whether I was not of his opinion. I said, ' Perhaps not quite.' "

On my arrival a few days later in London I had a momentary hope about Egypt, seeing it announced in the " Times " (13th May) that the Riaz Ministry had resigned. I had heard the news the night before from Rivers Wilson, and was full of hope that the new men who, the " Times " said, were to take their place would be of the Fellah Party, but the hope was speedily dispelled, as it proved to be merely a shifting of places, no single member of the new Ministry being of the National Party or of the native fellah class. Also Lord Salisbury, 21st May, made a speech about Egypt, which seemed to exclude all thought of preparing for evacuation. It put an end for a while to my pleading for the Egyptian cause, except with my few political friends, Evelyn, Labouchere, Auberon Herbert, and Sir Wilfrid Lawson. Soon after this:

" *2nd June.*— I saw Sir William Gregory in London, who was interesting himself in the hoped-for return to Egypt of the Ceylon exiles. We agreed that Lord Salisbury was hopeless, and that we had better put Labouchere on our Egyptian business, so to Labouchere I went. He has moved into a delightful house in Old Palace Yard exactly opposite the Houses of Parliament. I met him on the doorstep just coming in from the House, in an old skull-cap which he wears instead of hat, and he took me in to luncheon. We talked about Egypt, as to which he has always been sounder than any other politician except Randolph. I was glad to find that he was not prepared to evacuate *unconditionally,* but intended, when the Liberals came into power, to get Egypt neutralised, and I think he will serve us better than anyone else can. ' If you have any influence with the French,' he said, ' get them to propose terms of neutralization.' I explained to him what the position in Egypt was. He was very amusing about the actual state of the Liberal party, ' Gladstone in his dotage pulled this way by one and that way by another. They don't expect a dissolution until next year, but hope to keep the old man alive like the Tycoon of Japan, even after he is dead.' All agree that there will be a general break up in the party when Gladstone dies. Labouchere is looking old, he tells me he is fifty-eight, but I trust he may last long enough some day to lead his party."

With Lawson I had a long talk, June the 4th, and " found him nearly as much a pessimist about the human race as I have become. In England he looks to the advent of a really democratic parliament as a last chance, beyond which, if it fails, there is nothing to hope." With Morris, too, whom I again saw much of, I found the same political despondency. He had just published his " News from Nowhere." " The picture he draws in it of social communism is pretty, but he, too, is not very hopeful of its ever coming true. I am determined now to get on with my ' Secret History of the Invasion of Egypt,' so as to have it ready for publication when Gladstone comes back to office. My old friend, too, Eddy Hamilton, I saw. I found him occupying the ground floor rooms of No. 10, Downing Street. His sitting room is that in which the Cabinet Councils have always been held, and many a scurvy decision been come to in the last hundred years." Hamilton was now permanent official head of the Treasury, and the rooms had been lent him by Lord Salisbury who did not occupy them. He was suffering, however, with the disease, creeping paralysis, of which some years later he died, and we did not talk much on Egypt or on politics.

In my disappointment about Egypt I turned with redoubled zest to my social pleasures of the year before, and at this time saw much of that interesting group of clever men and pretty women known as the " Souls," than whom no section of London Society was better worth frequenting, including as it did all that there was most intellectually amusing and least conventional. It was a group of men and women bent on pleasure, but pleasure of a superior kind, eschewing the vulgarities of racing and card-playing indulged in by the majority of the rich and noble, and looking for their excitement in romance and sentiment. But this is not the place in which to describe the life we led, though it well deserves being eternalized in print. It harmonized well with my literary work, and the verses I was preparing for a new edition of the " Sonnets and Songs of Proteus." This William Morris had proposed to print as one of the earliest volumes of the Kelmscott Press, and I was much with him in connection with it.

" 10th June.— There is a great turmoil in the papers about Lord Salisbury's Treaty or Agreement with Italy in 1887. It appears now that King Humbert told Prince Napoleon about it, and at last it has come out. This coincides with the change of policy in Egypt, and the determination to remain there." [This Agreement, which has never been officially admitted by our Foreign Office, related to an intended seizure by Italy of Tripoli, and a promise that England would help Italy if it led to a quarrel between her and France. The reality of the agreement, however, has since been acknowledged by Crispi in his Memoirs.]

To London in the evening and dined in Park Lane (a small dinner arranged by George Wyndham, in which I was to meet Arthur Balfour and bury the hatchet with him of our Irish quarrel). The party consisted of George and his wife, Lady Clifden's daughter, Miss Ellis, Mrs. Hardinge, Lord Edmund Talbot, Bo Grosvenor (Lord Ebury), Charles Gatty, with Balfour and me. It was a pleasant party, and after the ladies had left we stayed on talking till past one o'clock. I had not met Balfour since my Irish campaigning, and we did not talk

politics, discussing instead literature, and especially the influence of
Arabia on the Middle Ages. Balfour was agreeable and the conversation brilliant, and he showed especial amiability to me as if to make
up for past severities, offering me a place in his brougham to go home
in when we went away. Why, indeed, should we quarrel? He has
mitigated his prison rigours in Ireland and I am aloof from politics.

" 11*th July.*— Arabi's case has been brought forward in Parliament
by Labouchere, and the Foreign Office answer is fairly satisfactory.
Ferguson says that the Government has uttered no *non possumus* about
the exiles, and is seeing what can be done.

" All the world is agog just now about the visit of the German Emperor to London, and the Liberals are just as absurd (in their adula-
tion) as the Tories. I met Justin McCarthy to-day in the street with
his son Huntly, and walked some way with them. They were jubilant
about the Carlow election and Parnell's collapse, but Huntly told me
he did not intend to come forward again in Parliament, but would
stick to literature. His talk about Egypt was quite in the Imperialistic
vein, justifying what I have always predicted that the Irish, once free,
would be more English than the English in enslaving the weaker nations.

" 15*th July.*— To see Cardinal Manning, taking with me a basket of
roses from Crabbet for his birthday, of which I was reminded by
Hedgecock's remark in the morning that to-day was ' Swithums.' The
old man is less infirm, I thought, and we talked politics and literature.
He told me of two new poets, Symons and Mrs. King. He is satisfied
with the way things are going in Ireland, and asked me what I thought
of the Pope's Labour Encyclical. It is, in truth, a rather colourless
pronouncement, saying too little.

'" 6*th Aug.*— At Coombe, where I heard from Bertram Currie the
history of the Baring financial crisis, and the part he had played in
averting its being an absolute crash. The collapse was due to Revel-
stoke's having gambled outside the line of his ordinary business. He
had had his head turned by the million he had made over the Guinness
affair, and he had come to think that everything he touched must turn
to gold, and he went on to his ventures in South America, which let
him in. The House of Baring would have broken altogether if he,
Bertram, had not got the Bank of England to secure its liabilities for
a million and taken half a million himself and persuaded Lord Rothschild as late as six o'clock in the evening to take another. The prospects in South America are bad, as things there do not settle down and
Ned [Revelstoke] has only £500 a year settled income. [This was a
case that had made an immense sensation in the City. But the House
of Baring has happily survived it.]

" 7*th August.*— Lunched at Kelmscott House when Mrs. Morris took me to see the printing. Morris's own poems were being struck off, most beautiful they are with their rubrics. The sheet I saw being printed contained the Ballad of John a Wood."

This also of nearly the same date relates to the Kelmscott Press. " Had supper with Morris and his wife and her sister, Miss Burden, and a Mr. Walker [Emery Walker], who helps in the printing work. Morris was busy drawing a title-page for his ' Golden Legend ' and there were some sheets of his new volume of poems, which is to be uniform with the volume he is printing for me. He was immensely pleased when I told him that I had read his ' News from Nowhere,' and that Anne also had read it. He gave an amusing account of an old house ' that that fellow Watts (the painter) had been daubing over. But a coat of whitewash,' he said, ' would soon set that right.' I told him in return about George Wyndham's visit to Swinburne at Putney, a few months ago, when the other Watts, Theodore Watts-Dunton, had insisted on talking politics with him instead of literature, to George's disgust, and how it had ended in Watts reading out his own poems instead of letting Swinburne read his. Watts, George tells me, keeps Swinburne prisoner, as a keeper keeps a lunatic. He had explained to George that some years ago he had found Swinburne in bed, dying of what is called ' drunkard's diarrhœa,' and that having got him round, he now considers Swinburne as his own property, and treats him like a naughty boy, ' a case,' said George, ' for police interference.' Morris was greatly amused at this."

The month of September saw me in Scotland for a fortnight's grouse shooting at Castle Menzies, which had been rented for the season by my friends the Wagrams, where I had the advantage of meeting a number of French royalists who were staying there to pay their court to the Comte de Paris, who rented a moor close by, the Broglies, the Jaucourts, and the Hautpouls, as well as Count Mensdorff, afterwards Austrian Ambassador in London. With these I made friends, and also had more than one opportunity of seeing the Comte and Comtesse de Paris and their beautiful daughter, Princess Hélène, who was at one time so nearly marrying the heir to our own English throne, and who afterwards married the Duke of Aosta (I had already met her once before at the Wagrams'). My diary describes the life led by these most worthy Pretenders to the throne of France in their summer Highland home thus:

" 13*th Sept. Sunday.*— We drove over to Loch Kinnaird, a lovely place in a fir wood high up on the moors. The house is a wooden one without any kind of pretension. The inside of varnished deal, no upper story, no garden, and no attempt at beautifying inside or out. There we found the Comte de Paris, a lean, bent, grisly-bearded man, on the wrong side of middle age, undistinguished in appearance or manner, though courteous and amiable, difficult to recognize as the descendant of French kings or the representative of divine right in the world. His Queen, a masculine, plain woman.

"With them, the flower of their wilderness, Princesse Hélène de France et de Navarre, a tall, very tall, slight girl of immense charm and distinction, whom I taught to play lawn tennis at Castle Menzies three years ago. She remembered it well and was very nice to me in her greeting. She poured out tea for us, and we all sat down to it, a regular meal in the dining-room. The little conversation I had with the Comte de Paris was only about shooting." I saw them again on the 15th, when they came to Castle Menzies for a great *chasse* of blue hares on Shehallion. "It was close opposite Shehallion on the tops of the hills, and to these the hares were driven, poor timorous beasts of the blue mountain kind. We got four hundred of them, a terrible massacre. The party consisted of the Comte and Comtesse de Paris, with three French gentlemen of their suite, of Wagram, the Prince de Broglie, Lord Crawford and his son Balcarres, Algy Grosvenor, Godfrey Webb, Needham, and me. The Comtesse de Paris shoots well. I walked the last two miles across the moor with her and saw her kill a brace of strong flying driven grouse in excellent style. She marches over the heather like a grenadier, shouts at the beaters, and jokes in rough country fashion with those near her. The Comte is equally without pretence. They are addressed as Monseigneur and Madame — sometimes, but rarely, as Altesse — their conversation a long sequence of royal commonplace. They are full of *bonhomie*. Coming to the high road on our way home a gipsy woman stopped the Count, and he gave her two sixpences.

"*20th Sept.*— At 1, came the Comte and Comtesse de Paris, and the little Princess looking lovely in a hat with pink flowers. I was put next her at luncheon, and we talked all the time, Balcarres being on her right hand. We talked about the East, and she promised to come to Egypt and that I should be her dragoman and take her to Mount Sinai. She told me about her life at home at Stowe, where she rides and hunts with the Duke of Grafton's hounds, and at Loch Kinnaird where she walks about the hills alone each summer with her dogs. I asked her, 'Have you no governess with you?' 'I should like to see the governess,' she said, 'who would undertake to look after me.' And she looked proudly out of her blue eyes. In Spain, where they spend part of their winters near Seville, they hunt wild camels on horseback. We talked, too, about her brother, the Duc d'Orléans' imprisonment at Paris, and mine in Ireland."

On my way back south I paid a first visit to the Glen, where most of the Tennant family were assembled, though Margot was away. Lucy and Charty, however, were there, and I made great friends with old Lady Tennant, a quiet little old lady, very well dressed, active and alert, whom I found exceedingly pleasant and conversable, with a heart overflowing with kindness. She showed me a book about Souls, which gives diagrams of the various kinds of souls, the surface soul, the deep soul, and the mixed soul, half-clever, half-childish (the book had something to do, I think, with the name given to the set of which her daughters were such notable members).

"Talking about Gladstone, she tells me that Gladstone's grand-father lived in this neighbourhood at Peebles. He was a baker, spelling his name Gladstanes, but known locally as ' licht bap,' on account of his selling his bread at false weight, ' bap ' being the name of a kind of loaf. After luncheon we all drove to Traquhair, an interesting old house much fallen into decay, the present owner taking no interest in it. We were shown over the rooms by his brother, who might have been one of Scott's Osbaldistones. The family pedigrees were lying littered round the library, hardly legible for damp.

"*30th Sept.*— To Kelmscott Manor, to wish the Morrises good-bye for the winter. It was very perfect weather and we did our gudgeon fishing and took our walks as usual there. Jenny is better than she has been for several years. Her devotion to her father is most touch-ing and his to her. Morris in high feather. He read us out several of his poems of his best, including ' The Haystack in the Floods,' but his reading is without the graces of elocution. He did it as if he were throwing a bone to a dog, at the end of each piece breaking off with ' There, that's it,' as much as to say, ' You may take it or leave it, as you please.' He is to lecture on art at Birmingham on Friday. Politi-cally he is in much the same position as I am. He has found his Socialism impossible and uncongenial, and has thrown it wholly up for art and poetry, his earlier loves. I fancy I may have influenced him in this."

The early autumn saw me once more in Paris, where the unrest of the military party which had given Boulanger his chance two years before, a chance which he had failed to take, had given place to apathy. " Poor Boulanger," I write, 1st October, "·has blown his brains out over the grave of Madame Bonnemain. Politically he was ·already defunct, and this is a graceful and dramatic exit "; and a week later, " Parnell is dead."

Here I spent my time, as usual, mostly at the Embassy, where Lady Salisbury was staying with her daughter, Lady Gwendolen, and her sister-in-law, Lady Galloway, both very charming women. Lady Salis-bury, too, was clever with much dry wit. I find the following in my journal: " I sat between Lady Salisbury and Lady Galloway to-night at dinner, and during it she told us a story of a visit she had paid long ago to old Lady Palmerston, and how Lady Palmerston had said to

her, *à propos* of the bondage of social observances : ' My dear you will
some day be in my position (of Prime Minister's wife), and when you
are I advise you to pay no visits at all.' ' So I never pay any,' she said,
' except to the Foreign Ambassadresses. Of course,' she added, ' I
don't include those of the South American Republics or any others of
the people who live up trees.' "

The question of the evacuation of Egypt was being a good deal discussed at that time in Paris, as the French Government, suspecting Lord
Salisbury of the intention, he in fact had, of making the Occupation
there more permanent, was beginning to give trouble, and I found both
Lytton and Egerton, first Secretary of the Embassy, an old friend of
mine, who did much of the work of the Embassy, and had been acting
as Chargé d'Affaires during Lytton's absence on leave during the summer, anxious to hear what I had to say on the subject, and I discussed
it thoroughly with both. I had learned from my Egyptian friend,
Sanua, who had just been at Constantinople and had had an interview
with Sultan Abdul Hamid, that the Sultan had declared positively to
him that he would take action to enforce the evacuation. There was
a perfect understanding now between the Turkish Government and the
French, probably also the Russian Government, who had repented the
pressure they had put upon Abdul Hamid to prevent his ratifying the
Wolff Convention, and were pressing the Sultan to re-open the question. Lytton, poor .fellow, had returned to Paris from a cure he had
been taking in England, very seriously ill, and the doctors had enjoined
upon him complete idleness, a remedy which would involve his giving
up his Embassy, but he was interested in what I told him, and asked
me to write him a memorandum on the whole subject of Egypt, and
especially that I should discuss it with Egerton. This I did and found
Egerton strongly in favour of my views. " To my surprise he told
me that he was in favour of evacuating Egypt seeing the pledges that
had been given. ' We have managed,' he said, ' to set everybody there
against us except that stupid fool the Khedive who counts for nothing,'
and urged me strongly not only to write but to publish my memorandum,
if only anonymously in the ' Times.' " Later (the same day, 27th
October) I saw George Curzon who is staying in Paris with Condy
Stephens. He, Curzon, of course, talks all the other way, and says
the whole Conservative party will oppose evacuation tooth ᴀnd nail.
I breakfasted with him, Oscar Wilde, and Willy Peel, on which occasion Oscar told us he was writing a play in French to be acted in
the Français. He is ambitious of being a French Academician. We
promised to go to the first representation, George Curzon as Prime
Minister. A day or two later, with Lytton's approval and Egerton's,
I gave my memorandum to Blowitz (the " Times " correspondent), and
it appeared in due course in the " Times " without my name, and ac-

companied with a leading article. Lord Salisbury, however, had already made up his mind, and in a new speech reiterated his intention to remain in Egypt. "Lytton," I write, 11th November, "is delighted with Lord Salisbury's boldness in refusing to evacuate. Egerton says it is foolhardy."[1]

It is worth noting that, if Egerton's view had prevailed, and our quarrel with France had then been solved on the basis of our evacuating Egypt, it would in all probability have forestalled the mistake made twelve years later of effecting the reconciliation, through the fatal error of basing it on "compensating" France by encouraging her seizure of Morocco. The Entente with France, begun in 1904 by an act of aggression on a harmless neighbour, involved France necessarily in a quarrel with Germany, who had earmarked Morocco as her share of the plunder of North Africa; it revived at Paris the half-forgotten dream of a *guerre de revanche* for Alsace-Lorraine, and strengthened the war party on both sides the Rhine. England it involved in the Entente with Russia, cemented with the betrayal of a second weak Mohammedan state, Persia, and drove progressive Turkey, in fear of a third betrayal, into an alliance with Kaiser Wilhelm.

I left Paris a few days later for Rome and Cairo. During the fortnight that I had been at the Embassy, Lytton's condition had rapidly grown worse, and when, on the 13th of November, I was taken in to where he lay in bed to say good-bye, I felt that our farewell might be the last. "Give my love to Dufferin," were his last words, "when you are at Rome — *that* he always has — and tell him I am a wreck, but do not mean to make a vacancy yet." And so we said, God bless you and good-bye. It was less than a fortnight later (25th November, at Fogliano) that a telegram reached me, forwarded through Lord Dufferin at Rome, from Paris, telling me that my friend had died. His death was a loss I can hardly estimate, and to many more than me, for by the public in Paris it was looked on as a State calamity. He had managed to make himself beloved there as no English ambassador had been since Waterloo, and as Dufferin, who, as had been expected, succeeded him, with all his great social gifts was never able to achieve. It was not merely that Lytton was popular, but he was beloved. His death was a loss to the cause of our good understanding with France, and I think to Egypt too, for though too pronounced an Imperialist to wish to see England's hand over the Nile relaxed, no one could so well have settled the conditions of an evacuation as Lytton could have done had it been so decided. And he placed value on my opinion in the matter.

During the few days I spent at Rome that November I attended a

---

[1] For my memorandum, see Appendix II.

Peace Congress, to which as member of the acting committee of the Arbitration and Peace Society I had been invited, but I was very unfavourably impressed with the Italian tone in regard to international matters where the rights of non-European nationalities were at stake. The Italians, like the French and all the Latin races, seemed to me incapable of grasping the idea, which we in England at any rate admit in theory if seldom in practice, that the nations outside the community of Christian civilization have any rights at all. I did not speak on this occasion, but I left the meeting convinced that the establishment of international peace if it could be secured for Europe would bode no good for Africa or Asia, and that as far as these regions of the world were concerned the old proverb probably held good, " When thieves fall out honest men come by their own."

From Fogliano we went straight on without returning to Rome, and so by the first boat to Alexandria, reaching Sheykh Obeyd on 7th December, where we spent the rest of the winter.

About the close of the year 1891, I received the following letter from Sir William Harcourt in answer to one of mine from Paris, inclosing a copy of my Paris memorandum. As it is of great importance I give it textually here:

" Malwood, 16*th December* 1891.

" DEAR WILFRID BLUNT,

" I have not written before to thank you for your paper on Egypt, as you sent me at the time no address. I was greatly impressed by the ability and moderation of its views, and the fulness with which the question was discussed in every aspect. I forwarded it to John Morley, who entirely concurred with me, in the high opinion I had formed of its merits.

" The question is, no doubt, one of great complexity and cannot be rushed. At the same time I have never varied in my opinion of the mischief and danger of the continued occupation, as far as England is concerned, and though probably you will not agree with me I regard this as by far the most important consideration. It is quite impossible for the Government to take a high line as to occupation after the Drummond-Wolff negotiations. The whole thing is summed up in a nutshell by Wolff in his concluding despatch, after the ratification by the English Government of the Convention for the Evacuation in 1887, within the space of three years. He says, ' It has more than once been suggested that England should take permanent possession of Egypt. This would have been violation of the traditional policy of England, of her good faith to the Sultan, and of public law. In time of peace it would have exposed her to constant jealousy and danger. In time of war, it would have been a weak point, entailing a constant drain on her resources. Her Majesty's Government have disclaimed all idea of annexing Egypt or of establishing a Protectorate over it.'

"This language was approved by Salisbury, and was a deliberate renewal in the face of Europe of the pledges given in 1881. Salisbury undertook to 'guarantee the neutralization of Egypt as the mandatory of the other Powers, that duty being regarded as a burden rather than a privilege.' The great mischief, as you properly point out, is that since that period the policy of Evelyn Baring has been to administer the Government of Egypt in such a manner as to make it constantly less instead of more able to stand by itself, and so to make the task of fulfilling our obligation more rather than less difficult.

"I hope by this time you are enjoying your wild life in the desert. We are raising our rural tribes here, who are rallying round the Mahdi Schnadhorst — but I forgot you have sworn off British Politics, a wise determination to which I advise you to adhere.

"Yrs. sincerely,

"W. V. HARCOURT."

This is a very important letter, as it indicates doubtless what Mr. Gladstone's view at the time was, for Sir William Harcourt and he worked together on questions of foreign policy. It is also of importance as showing that John Morley then shared their opinion. It was a combination of Baring, and of Milner, acting under his direction on the London Press, with Rosebery, that prevented an honest solution of the Egyptian question when the Liberals, shortly afterwards, returned to power.

CHAPTER IV

THE YOUNG KHEDIVE ABBAS

1892 to 1893

The year 1892 opened with an event which was to prove a turning-point in Egyptian history, one where a new opportunity was given to our Government of making a fresh start in the direction of that National Government on constitutional lines, which Lord Dufferin had promised and which might have enabled England to withdraw her army of occupation in agreement with the Sultan, and the Powers of Europe, but which was once more unfortunately let slip, mainly through Sir Evelyn Baring's fault, who misjudged the character of those with whom he had to deal, and found in it only an opportunity of taking the reins of Government at Cairo more completely into his own hands. On the 7th of January of the new year the Khedive Tewfik, still comparatively a young man, suddenly and unexpectedly died. He had been ailing for a few days at his country palace at Helwan, and no one had at all foreseen what was to happen. In the common view of native Egypt he was supposed to have been poisoned, the memory of such doings for political reasons being still strong in the popular mind, though, in fact, it was a natural death hastened only by the mistake of the doctors called in to attend him.

"*9th Jan.* 1892.— Yesterday at eleven o'clock Mutlak (our Bedouin horse rider), came to me and told me that the Khedive was dead, and immediately afterwards Mohammed Nassr the Berberi porter repeated the news, ' It is Husseyn Pasha the Prince,' the latter said, ' who has done it, I was in his service, and he is a son of sin, *ibn el haram.*' On the roof, old Ali, the plasterer, who is a Halimist, and had just been to the station at Matarieh for gossip, remarked with a wink to me, ' Are you not going to the funeral? ' and he went through the pantomime of drinking a cup of coffee (meaning he had been poisoned). This morning he tells me about it more precisely. ' It is the Dowlah that did it (the Sultan's Government). Mukhtar had advised Tewfik many times to try a change of air, for the air of Egypt did not agree with him, but he would not listen.' I asked the old man whether he meant that Mukhtar had had it done. ' Oh, no,' he said, ' they have sent somebody on purpose from beyond the water ' (from Stamboul). It cer-

tainly looks suspicious. They hurried on the funeral with extravagant
haste. Tewfik died at 8 p.m. on Thursday, and was buried the next
afternoon, Friday. The palace physician gave his certificate that the
death was a natural one; no European doctor examined the body. It
takes us back to the good old times.

"For the interests of the Egyptians I cannot pretend to be sorry.
I was talking on Monday to Mohammed Moelhi, and we agreed that
it was hopeless to look for any improvement as long as Tewfik was on
the throne; he would never consent to a reconstruction of the National
Party or work with the Constitution; latterly he had gone over very
much to the French. Of the *prince héritier* Abbas, Mohammed said
he was very anti-English, though too young to have fixed opinions.
A Constitution might be possible with him if strongly supported for a
few years by England. Lord Salibury will have his hand forced, to
make a settlement of the Egyptian question, and I am glad of it, as the
English Liberals cannot be trusted to protect native interests here, and
would probably hand over the Protectorate in all but name to the
French. I have not seen any European yet, so do not know how Baring
takes the event."

"*10th Jan.*— Went in to Cairo to see Baring, and had a few minutes' conversation with him. I suggested that on the accession of the
new Khedive there might be a general pardon and amnesty. He said,
'Perhaps, but not for those in Ceylon.' 'Why not?' I asked. 'I
understood from you that it was Tewfik's personal unwillingness that
stood in the way.' He answered, 'Anyhow, it cannot be done. They
(the exiles) have got nothing the matter with them, and they only
want to go to Cyprus.' Again I asked, 'Why not to Cyprus?' But
he would not hear of it. We talked about the Khedive's death, and
he told me he had had an inflammation of the kidneys, and passed no
water for forty-eight hours; he blamed the doctors. 'The Khedive,'
he added, 'always had a very bad *entourage.*'

"Lunched with the Tennants. They had been to tea with us on
the last day of the old year, and Margot had been very charming and
very amusing.

"Then to Helwan to see Minshawi Pasha, and hear his version of
the news. 'Ah,' said Minshawi (he was living in a villa close by the
Khedivial palace), 'if you had only come to see me a week sooner,
we should have had the pleasure of making Tewfik angry.'

"*20th Jan.*— Dr. Abdel Razak Bey came to see me. He had been
with Salim Pasha a day or two ago, who was one of the late Khedive's
two doctors. Salim had told him that what the Khedive died of was
in reality a stricture. Abdel Razak speaks highly of the young Abbas
as well instructed and intelligent, and we discussed the new situation
Tewfik's death must cause for the Egyptian National Party."

Abdel Razak had been one of Arabi's personal friends, and one of his most level-headed advisers, knowing Europe well, and speaking English as well as French, a rare accomplishment at that time. By his advice and that of Sheykh Mohammed Abdu, who formed a favourable opinion of the young Khedive Abbas, who now succeeded his father, I decided that the time was now come for me to make my peace formally with the Egyptian Government. As long as Tewfik was alive it had been difficult for me to do this. I had taken too prominent a part in the revolution, and had denounced Tewfik too openly after it to make it possible for me to take any step towards a reconciliation or pay my respects to him by calling at the palace. But it was now thought by my friends that I should do well in asking an audience of his successor, and I consequently asked Baring to present me formally to Abbas, as was the custom in the case of other Englishmen visiting Egypt. In pursuance of this resolve I find in my diary:

"*1st Feb.*— Went into Cairo with Anne and lunched with the Barings, and was taken by Baring afterwards to call upon the Khedive Abbas at the Abdin Palace. It is rather more than eleven years since I had paid just such another visit to Tewfik with Malet. When we were shown in to-day we were met at the door of the room by a little young man in military undress whom I took to be an Aide-de-Camp, but who turned out to be Abbas himself, a quite unmilitary figure of proportions which made him look like a woman dressed up in man's clothes. He has, however, a very good manner in talking, and a pleasant smile, with brown eyes, and just a tinge of russet in his hair. He reminded me much of his grandfather, Ismaïl, and has just the same sort of French accent, talking French well but not perfectly. He showed no sign of shyness, and treated Baring with easy politeness, without any sign of special deference; me he treated with considerable amiability. We talked a little about the brigandage in the neighbourhood of his Koubbah Palace and Sheykh Obeyd (the two places are within three miles of each other), and then about petitions, and then about certain receptions and ceremonies, nothing at all interesting, but I thought he showed considerable intelligence, and there was a slight touch of sarcasm in his talk reminding me very especially of Ismaïl. I shall be surprised if he does not give Baring trouble. He is said about here to be very anti-English, but Baring will not hear a word of this, though I expect it is true." So far my journal. My recollection, however, goes further than this. It is that Baring's manner on this occasion was very abrupt, like that of a schoolmaster to a schoolboy, and that on our way back from the palace I remarked to him that I thought the Khedive would not bear driving with any but a very light rein, his answer being that it was necessary to treat Orientals firmly; also I warned him he would have trouble.

" I have written to Sir William Harcourt to tell him of Tewfik's death and my impressions of Abbas, and to urge him to push forward Constitutional Government in Egypt."

We left Egypt soon after this and were back in England by the middle of April.

The summer that followed, like the last, I devoted more to literature and society than to politics. My daughter Judith was now being brought out in society, and though I did not attend many of her balls and parties, it was a distraction for me from serious work. There is very little of my diary connected with politics until the middle of August, when the general elections took place, which resulted in a moderate triumph for the Liberal party, and Lord Salisbury's retirement from office in favour once more of Gladstone. In the meanwhile there are a few entries in my journal worth transcribing :

" 9*th May*.— Called on Lady Gregory, and found her sad in her widow's weeds. Sir William died during the winter.

" I have finished ' Griselda,' and the Arabic ballads, and ' The Stealing of the Mare,' and am publishing an article on Lytton as a Poet in the ' Nineteenth Century.'

" 18*th May*.— Riding in the park I was joined by Frederic Harrison, who told me he had been converted to Islam as a living religion, and offered to support my candidature if I would come forward as a Mohammedan at the elections.

" 19*th May*.— To lunch with Sir William Harcourt. The old man was very communicative both about Egypt and about Ireland. As to the former he is for evacuation, but is sound about not giving the country up to France. He asked me about the Soudan danger, about which I reassured him ; then as to whether it would not be possible to occupy the Suez Canal only. I said I thought it would be quite possible. He would not hear of allowing the Sultan to intervene. I told him that it would be easy to constitute a Liberal native Government and retire. He seemed surprised to hear that the land tax had not been reduced. ' As to justice,' he said, ' justice is only a question of personalities in any country.' Next we discussed Ireland. He said, ' I am afraid there is no doubt we shall be in office after the elections, and then our troubles will begin. The Irish are impossible ; they are split up into four sections, and there is no leader among them to treat with.' We went through the various prominent men in the Irish party, and he asked me about Dr. Walsh and Dr. Crook, also about Persico's mission, and the politics of the Vatican. I gather from him that the Home Rule Bill will be no simple matter, and that he is not personally much interested in it. He spoke severely of the individual Irish leaders.

" 20*th May*.— To the Frederic Harrisons. We had a long talk about Egypt, and agreed that the best chance of getting an honest policy of evacuation would be to prevent Rosebery's returning to the Foreign Office. Harrison thinks that Rosebery will either not join Gladstone's Ministry, or make it a condition that the *status quo* in Egypt should be continued. On Ireland he is quite pessimistic, considers Home Rule for the present a lost cause, and the G.O.M. destined to retire from public life discredited. Morley would follow him, and there would then be a reconstruction of the Liberal party under Rosebery, Chamberlain, Harcourt, and Randolph. He thinks, nevertheless, that Ireland would some day or other get its independence, while I maintained that the tendency of progress was towards the amalgamation of nations, not their separation. To this he said, ' You know we, the Positivists, believe that in the next century there will be one hundred and fifty separate States in Europe,' but Mrs. Harrison dissented, and I should fancy that his faith in the Comtist prediction is not very solid.

" *23rd May.*— I am staying at Babraham with the Adeanes, and went to-day, with Adeane, to Gogmagog to see the pictures of the Godolphin, and other Arabians, and the former's grave. The original portrait of the Godolphin, which is there, is of a second-rate Arab, with a heavy head, lop ears, and a drooping quarter. It is difficult to understand that race-horses should have sprung from his loins. The view from Gogmagog over the plain is grand, but the house is mean, though beloved of its ducal owner. In the afternoon to Audley End, a stately place, but unfortunately cleaned up, plate glassed, and adorned in recent years.

" *24th May.*— Dined with Philip Currie in Connaught Place, Mrs. Singleton doing the honours. I sat between Mrs. Algy Grosvenor and Oscar Wilde. Beyond Oscar Mrs. Singleton, then Godfrey Webb. There were also Lady Ducane and a daughter, Lady Sykes, Lady Baring, just made a peeress, O'Connor [1] and Trench, diplomats, and three or four more. Oscar was in good form, and he and I, Philip and O'Connor sat up till half-past twelve talking when the rest were gone.

" *25th May.*— To a meeting at Lord Cowper's, respecting a memorial for Lytton. Lord Salisbury was present, and made an inappropriate proposal (as I thought) that the monument should be placed in the India Office. Alfred Austin opposed this on literary grounds, and I seconded him, asking that the Committee should first try for a place, however small, in the Abbey. I am quite sure this would have been Lytton's own wish, for he cared far more for his position as a poet than for all the rest.

" *4th June.*— Took Judith to lunch at Hammersmith. Morris in

---

[1] Afterwards Ambassador at Constantinople.

good talk, told us he had never in all his life been owner of a dog, and did not care for pets — thought he might perhaps make friends with a horse, if he had the time and opportunity. He showed us round the printing press, where his Golden Legend sheets were hanging on strings to dry, the printers being away for their Whit Saturday afternoon.

"*5th June.*— Whit Sunday at Crabbet. Staal the Russian Ambassador came to lunch with his wife and daughter. He is of all foreigners the man with whom I can talk most intimately, for we were fast friends thirty-three years ago at Athens, he then thirty-seven, I eighteen. Now he is seventy, I fifty-one; yet we talked just as of old, and I doubt if we feel much older. He was never a young man, even in those days.

"*7th June.*— To Mark Napier's at Fulham. Mark was in his shirt-sleeves, working at the building of a steam launch he is constructing with his own hands in the upstairs drawing-room of Little Mulgrave House, a beautiful room of the last century, full of china and *bric-à-brac,* perhaps the most incongruous building yard ever chosen. The difficulty will be to get the boat out of the window when finished. A large circular saw stood in the dining-room downstairs. [The boat was safely launched, nevertheless.]

"*20th June.*— Breakfast with George Wyndham and Sibell. George and I discussed the prospects of the General Election. He says the most optimistic Tory calculation is 14 majority, while Loulou Harcourt and the Liberals count on 100 for their majority.

"*5th July.*— At Kelmscott Manor. I came here yesterday. Morris in fine spirits, and inexhaustible energy over his new hobby, the printing press. He is beginning a Chaucer, and there is great discussion whether it is to be printed in single or double column. I am much in favour of the single column. Burne Jones is to do illustrations. I forgot to say that I was at Merton last week with the Morrises, when we saw a brother of his, working in the dye vats there, a dreamy man in workman's clothes, with his shirt sleeves turned up, and his arms blue with indigo to the elbows. I asked Morris about him and, he tells me that having begun life with a good fortune — he had a country place in Herefordshire — he has gradually fallen in the world, and after trying one thing and another to get a living is now glad to be employed on weekly wages. He lives at Merton, and is quite happy, indeed he looked so, dipping wool all day in the vats, in a shed open on to the garden. It is, perhaps, the nearest thing to a conventual life which can be found in the lay world. We walked to-day in the meadows by the river.

"*6th July.*— The elections are going not too well for Gladstone, and though he will probably get a majority, I fear Home Rule is doomed.

Ireland will never have a chance again. On all other grounds I am glad, and so is Morris, but politics are a weary thing. I read him part of 'The Stealing of the Mare,' which he approves, and advises me to publish, though he says nobody will read it; and he read us some of his own Scandinavian translations in return.

"*13th July*.— Mark Napier has got into Parliament, I am glad to see. Gladstone's majority will now be 50 or more. Lord Salisbury, George tells me, will meet Parliament, and will not retire till a vote of want of confidence has been passed. Gladstone's personal majority in Midlothian only 650.

"*19th July*.— Gladstone has now a majority of 46 in the new House of Commons. I have not voted at all in this election, or taken any part.

"*23rd and 24th July*.— Meeting of the Crabbet Club, those present were:

George Wyndham.	Charles Laprimaudaye.
George Curzon.	Harry Cust.
Nigel Kingscote.	Hubert Howard.
Charles Gatty.	George Leveson Gower.
Theobald Mathew.	Dick Grosvenor.
Godfrey Webb.	Mark Napier.
Loulou Harcourt.	

George Wyndham performed a wonderful feat, writing a long poem in a most complicated metre, and full of excellent things in hardly more than an hour, between sets of lawn tennis. Cust wrote another under like conditions, so full of wit that we nearly gave him the prize. George Leveson was also good. The tennis handicap was won by Hubert Howard, the laureateship by Mathew. Hubert won the cup through Grosvenor's magnanimity, who having the last set in hand suddenly found himself lame and retired. Cust is interesting, and of great abilities. George Leveson a delightful butt, and cause of wit in others with untouchable good humour. . These occasions are the salt of life.

"*26th July*.— To Hamilton Aïde's at Ascot to meet Lady Brooke, the Ranee of Borneo. She is, or rather has been, a fine, fair woman, and is now perhaps thirty-seven, living in England away from her husband, Aïde tells me, because he prefers other wives. I have had a good deal of conversation with her about native races and European civilization. I have sent in my proofs of 'Esther,' finally corrected, with five of the sonnet-stanzas cut out. George Wyndham thinks the poem will not greatly suffer, though he regrets it.

"*1st Aug*.— Dined at the Gerald Balfours, Betty charming, and a very gay evening, the other guests being Lady Frances Balfour, clever, but with much of her father's assertive manner, Eustace Balfour, Alfred Lyall, and Margot Tennant, the conversation all the evening very brilliant, but it is useless trying to reproduce it. I sat on a sofa with Margot, she with a fan made of an eagle's wing. I have sent a letter to Sir William Harcourt about Egypt, the moment seeming to have arrived."

There are many other interesting entries of about this date, but they are none of them quite germane to the subject of this volume, unless it is the following, which illustrates the growth among ourselves in England of those doctrines of supermanity and imperial selfishness which we have since ascribed to a German origin, and denounce among the prime causes of our war with Germany in 1914. It was at the time a surprise to me as an avowal by a man of personal amiability of ruthless principles which I found later to be common enough among my ultra imperialist friends.

"*5th Aug.*— To Cromer with Anne and Judith, Betty Balfour also travelling with us with her children. We are staying with Frederick Locker in his wife's villa. Gerald Balfour joined us in the evening.

"*6th Aug.*— Sat in the garden with Betty looking over her father's papers (some of which she has a design to print) and talking about him. Gerald is a very pretty tennis player, and has been at hard exercise all day at it and golf. I like him better now that I know him better.

"*7th Aug. (Sunday)* — Drove with the Balfours and Conny Lytton to Blickling, where we lunched. On the way we had a grand discussion about patriotism, Gerald maintaining that patriotism was the imperial instinct in Englishmen, who should support their country's quarrels even when in the wrong. This of course is not my view. Gerald has all his brother's scientific inhumanity in politics, and it is a school of thought distinctly on the increase, for it flatters the selfish instincts of the strong by proving to them that their selfishness is right. Blickling is a perfect place with a very lovely garden, Lady Lothian doing the honours of it, and showing us all round. There is a small herd still of the wild white cattle, ten cows and a bull, with some calves. They were brought originally, Lady Lothian told us, from a park near Manchester, which became engulfed in the town smoke, a herd then of forty cows (the cowkeeper said twenty), but they were almost all destroyed at the time of the cattle plague, some years since, three cows being at one time all the stock left. Then they got a bull from a herd that had been drafted, and so gradually have restored the breed. Its characteristics are well marked, white with black muzzles, and the ears inside black; the bull was very fine. The herd is tame enough now, being driven in every afternoon to be milked, and the calves are brought up by hand in sheds.

" Constance, Lady Lothian, I knew as a very pretty woman thirty years ago, with her invalid husband (elder brother of my friend Schomberg Kerr), of whom a fine portrait exists by Watts. On our way home we renewed our argument as applied especially to the Irish. ' They ought to have been exterminated long ago,' said Gerald, ' but it is too late now.' He is confident, however, of defeating Home Rule by Constitutional means."

Gerald's argument, I recollect, was based on an application to inter-racial politics of Darwin's law of the selection of the fittest, or rather of what is an exaggerated interpretation of that law. Those who put forward this view forget that Man by the abnormal development of his reasoning powers and his invention of lethal weapons, has put himself outside the unconscious working of the natural law. Darwin is in no way responsible for this application of his doctrine, as is clearly seen in the sympathy he shows with the backward races of mankind, especially in his " Voyage of the Beagle." Though individual strives with individual in the natural world, there is never a combination of a whole species or race to make war with and destroy a feebler race. This was my argument with Gerald. Three years later he was appointed by Lord Salisbury and his brother Arthur, Chief Secretary for Ireland, and proved a kindly ruler while in office there, being by nature an altogether amiable, kind-hearted man, but infected, as so many of our Imperialists were beginning to be at that date, by the politico-scientific doctrines so crudely preached in Germany.

On the 7th of August I started on a driving tour, the first of many such I made in after years, taking the northern road as far as Streatley, then crossing the Berkshire Downs westward, and travelling over grass a quite uninhabited country, " as desolate as parts of Mesopotamia, and in the bright sunlight very beautiful, coveys of young partridges running here and there tamely in front of the carriage, and so as far as Chilton, where I had the good fortune to find entertainment at the rectory house of the parson, Morland, a worthy man, living alone in that lonely place and glad to see a stranger, a hospitality rare of its kind in civilized England, and so on to Kelmscott, where I stayed a couple of nights. I found there my friend John Henry Middleton, the Cambridge Professor, an old ally of Morris's, and intimate in former days with Rossetti. Middleton had been a considerable traveller in out-of-the-way places, and he narrated to me in detail what I had already heard him tell, his experience in Morocco with a Moorish magician. This is his account of the incident:

" He was travelling in 1879 about half way between Tetuan and Morocco, and one evening an old man came to his camp mounted on an ass, with a boy as servant. The man said he was a magician, and proposed to perform three wonders; the first to throw a ball of twine into the air, the second to make a plant grow, and the third to show the face of a person thought of, in a globe of ink. It was already late, and the performance was put off until the following morning — the magician remaining the night in the camp, and in the morning when the tents were struck he was invited to give his performance. It was an open place, uninhabited, and without trees or bushes. Middleton chose the ground at some little distance from where the camp had been. The magician first took from his wallet a large ball of string, large enough to need both hands to lift it, and having made a long incantation he tied the end of the string to one finger of his left hand, and then with a great exertion threw the ball upwards, which unravelled as it went, and, growing less and less, disappeared in the air. He then let go of the string's end, which continued to hang from the sky. The magician and his boy sat at a little distance, and Middleton went to the string and pulled it downwards, as you would pull a bell-rope. It stretched to within about two feet of the ground, but he felt the resistance strongly from above, so much so that he cut his fingers with the string, the mark remaining for several days afterwards. The five men whom he had with him also touched the string, three of these were Moors, one a Berber, and the other an interpreter. It was clear daylight at the time, about half an hour after sunrise. When they had all satisfied themselves that the string was suspended as it appeared to be, the magician came forward, and in his turn pulled it, when it fell down from the sky in coils on the ground; he then rolled it up again into a ball, and put it back into his wallet.

" The magician next took from his wallet a seed, and when Middleton had chosen a bare place, planted it in the ground; he then asked for some palm branches which they had with them, and which had been cut the day before, and he made an arched covering with them over the seed and heaped horse rugs upon the hoops, and then sat apart and made incantations. At the end of a few minutes he invited them to undo the covering, and there, in the ground, a plant was growing, set firmly in the earth, the first time a few inches high, but when he had covered it up again and built the hoops higher, it at last became three feet eight inches high. Middleton measured the plant, found it firmly rooted, and cut off and kept some of the leaves; the nature of the plant seemed to resemble that of the Indian rubber tree, and it had some fifty leaves. It was fresh and healthy though the weather was very hot, it being the month of October. In the third incantation Middleton was made to look into a globe of ink. He desired to see the face of a friend, but instead saw persistently and very vividly a certain landscape he knew well on the river Severn, near Tewkesbury. The magician when asked whether he could climb the string and disappear in the air (like the magician Marco Polo tells of), stated that his grandfather had had the

power, but that he himself was unable. Having been rewarded, he
mounted his ass and rode away. Middleton believes that the manifesta-
tions produced were mesmeric, certainly no trick. The leaves of the
plant he kept for some time, but lost with other things in a shipwreck
on his way home."

Middleton had known Kelmscott Manor in the early days when
Rossetti and Morris first took the house together at a rent of £60 a
year. The Tapestry Room, which is now the sitting-room, used to
be Rossetti's own room, and it was there that he wrote his poetry.
Rossetti, he tells me, was addicted to loves of the most material kind
both before and after his marriage, with women, generally models,
without other soul than their beauty. It was remorse at the contrast
between his ideal and his real loves that preyed on him and destroyed
his mind. It is touching to see still on the table at meals napkins
marked with the initials D. G. R. His ghost seems to me to be present
in all the rooms. From thence I drove on to Stanway, where I found
Arthur Balfour, to whom I narrated Middleton's experience in Morocco, which interested him greatly. We had a pleasant time there,
and I found Balfour most agreeable, glad to be relieved of office, Salisbury having just resigned.

" 16th Aug.— It is announced that Rosebery has taken office after
all as Foreign Secretary under Gladstone. This will neutralise any
good that might have come of a change of Government to Egypt.
Rosebery will continue to represent the Bondholders. Gladstone has
made up his Ministry, every one of them Whigs. Asquith and Lefevre
are the only two who are at all advanced, the rest quite of the old gang,
only one surprise. Houghton is to go as Lord Lieutenant to Ireland,
a triumph for the Crabbet Club!

" From Stanway on to Batsford, which is now Bertie Mitford's. He
inherited it about five years ago from his cousin Lord Redesdale, and
has spent a vast amount of money pulling the old house down and
building a new Victorian Tudor one. He has also laid out the grounds
with elaborate rockeries and a multitude of trees and foreign shrubs,
stabling on a vast scale, a stud of shire cart mares, the most interesting
feature of the place. I remember Bertie as a very good-looking youth,
three or four years older than myself, with a great reputation for
ability, much talent for languages, and a player of the *cornet à piston* —
this was in 1858. We went up for an examination the same day, he
for a clerkship in the Foreign Office, I for the diplomatic service."

Thence (18th Aug.) on to The Glen, where I found John Addington
Symonds staying in the house, and where I stayed ten days with Margot
and a number of young ladies, a very delightful time, of which my
diary is full, but again this is not the place for it.

From Glen I went to Saighton, where one incident occurs which
deserves transcribing:

"*2nd Sept.*— After luncheon we drove, George, Sibell and I, three in
a row, in a dog-cart to Hawarden, George having been especially invited there. We were to meet the G.O.M. at the new library he has
constructed in the village, a terrible building of corrugated iron overlooking the Sands of Dee. Inside it is conveniently arranged, and
must be an advantage to the inhabitants. We were met there by Mrs.
Drew, who told us her father would come presently, and leaving
George and me took Sibell off with her to the castle. While waiting in
the library I was glad to find little Maud Gladstone whom I had known
as Maud Rendel, and with her we whiled away the quarter of an hour
we had to wait. The G.O.M., when he arrived, was very cordial with
George, but not as I think with me. He talked about his books in the
absorbed way he has, going on, without paying the least attention to
the person he is speaking to, especially if it is his wife and she ventures
to interpose a remark. The ladies invited me to go back with them,
and I walked with Maud, leaving George and Mr. G. to follow. She
showed me over the house when we arrived, Mr. G.'s ' Temple of
Peace,' and the rest which I knew from Margot's description. There
were but few old books, and the modern ones were very mixed in
character. I looked through the poetry shelves and found the usual
volumes of Tennyson and Browning, etc. ' In Vinculis ' was there
with the leaves cut open, but not the ' Sonnets of Proteus,' which I
had given him in 1884. Presently Miss Helen Gladstone came in, the
head of Newnham College, and I had some talk with her and found
her agreeable in an austere way. Then the G.O.M. arrived with
George, and we all sat down to tea. I sat by Mrs. Gladstone, good old
soul, who speedily thawed to me, while the G.O.M. still went on talking about books. He had got a rare edition of the Prayer Book and
made it his text, with interludes of discussion, about the various qualities of tea. I asked him what ' N. or M.' meant in the baptismal
service, but he could suggest no explanation. From that he went on
to the revised version of the Bible, which he called ' abominable '; it
was not the first duty of a translator to be accurate but to render the
spirit of the book. This the revisers had missed. ' You see,' inter-
posed Mrs. Gladstone, in the tone of one anxious and apologetic; ' he
is so conservative, and yet people say of him, etc., etc.' ' He has the
spirit of reverence,' I said. ' Ah yes,' she exclaimed, beaming, ' that
is just it; you have said exactly what is true.' But the old man paid
no attention and went prattling on, talking of all things in the same
absorbed way, apparently without sense of their proportion, and for
talking's sake, heedless of our remarks, until at last he settled down into

a ' Quarterly Review ' article and said no more. That, I fancy, is his common domestic life.

" Mary Drew's little girl Dorothy was there, running about without shoes or stockings, and the Spitz dog which Margot had described to me and which had brought in a stick with it to the drawing-room, but I did not notice that Mr. G. paid attention to either. He did not impress me much with the matter of his conversation, impressive as it was in manner. All he said was essentially commonplace. Once he corrected George for pronouncing ' *mythological* ' short as ' *mithological.*' Meanwhile Mrs. Gladstone gave me an account of an adventure Mr. G. had had two days before with a cow in the park. ' It was a strange cow,' she said, ' which had got in by accident and found itself in Mr. G.'s path as he was walking alone, and when he would have driven it out of his way, it turned on him and knocked him down. It stood over him but did not gore him. This,' said Mrs. Gladstone, ' was very unusual in a cow. He tried to rise, but at first he could not, for he had not the breath, but afterwards he managed to get behind a tree and the cow trotted away.' Poor old soul, she touched me with her devotion for him. Of himself I carried away the mixed impression I have had of him before, one of disappointment at finding less than I should have found to worship.

" Hawarden House, the modern castle, is one of the end of last century, very comfortable and nice inside with no great pretension to architecture — outside it is a poor castellated gothic structure. The old castle, which stands in the grounds a little way off, and to which I ran up after tea, is a very interesting ruin. On the whole, we agreed, as we drove home, that we had enjoyed our visit, and that the pilgrimage had been well worth making. The G.O.M. saw Sibell to the door himself, with Mrs. Gladstone and the others. The younger men had been out shooting meanwhile in the Park.

" *3rd Sept.*— Travelled in the train on my way home with Frank Villiers. He has just been made Private Secretary to Rosebery at the Foreign Office, and professes great admiration for him as ' a statesman without personal ambition.' We discussed the Egyptian question pretty thoroughly and the release of Arabi. With regard to evacuation he said that everybody was agreed it would be dangerous and impossible to hold Egypt permanently. Baring had been doing what he could to prepare things for a withdrawal of the troops, but he could find no *men* among the Egyptians capable of carrying on reforms. Baring had told them at the Foreign Office of my idea of having a Fellah Ministry, but could not get capable men. He would be very glad if he could find them, but where were they? I said that I had given Baring the names of suitable Fellah Ministers, but that he had told me the late Khedive would never consent to employ them. I was at one with

Baring as to the kind of reforms wanted, but disagreed with his way
of carrying them out through Englishmen.   It could have no other result but to make evacuation more and more difficult.   ' You may wait
ten years,' I said, ' and you will find no better occasion to evacuate
than the present.   I mean, of course, if you really wish it.'   He assured
me over and over again that that was their policy and their desire.
About Arabi he was not encouraging, but I am to call Rosebery's attention to the matter.

" 15*th Sept.*— At Crabbet.   I have seen Countess Hoyos several
times.   She rode here one morning, and I have been twice to tea at
Paddockhurst (their country place in Sussex, two miles from Crabbet).
Her daughter, just married to Herbert Bismarck, she tells me, is supremely happy, having tamed her Bismarck to a point which could not
have been believed.   He had been a great *coureur de femmes,* women
mainly of the baser sort, and she has touched him to an ideal love.   He
is forty-three, she twenty, a beautiful romance.

" I have had an answer from Rosebery, that is from Villiers, of a
most civil kind, but with the usual official evasion of my questions.   Sir
Wilfrid Lawson has also written.

" 17*th Sept.*— A letter from Margot.   She has been paying visits
with her political admirers, Haldane and Asquith.   She describes all
in a few words as well as such descriptions could possibly be.,

" Lady Lytton was here to-day with her girls to say good-bye before
starting for the Cape.   Meynell also, and his wife.   After dinner he,
Meynell, gave me a most interesting account of Cardinal Manning's
last days.   Meynell was the old man's confidant in his many disappointments and vexations.   The Cardinal's mind had grown large in the
later years of his life, and his view of the Catholic Church, and of
Christianity, comprehensive of all sects and creeds.   He was at odds
with his fellow bishops in England, who looked upon him as unortho-
dox, and worried him a thousand ways, and he had no one of them all
for a friend.   His last hours had been troubled by the worries of his
clergy.   There had been a dispute between two of the Bishops, which
he had referred to Rome, and which caused him great annoyance, and
when he was taken ill the Bishop of Salford (Herbert Vaughan, afterwards Cardinal Vaughan) was unfortunately staying with him, whom
he specially disliked.   His old servant Newman had died, and there
was no one to take care of him.   He refused to believe that he was
dying, and had a strong desire to live, and Vaughan was hard on him
in his insistence on certain formalities demanded of a dying Archbishop,
then having got his way Vaughan left him, and he lay all night alone,
and was found next morning insensible and dying, his fire out in the
grate and no one with him.   Truly death is bitter even to the righteous.

" Meynell told me also of a new movement within the body of the

English Catholic clergy, of the most revolutionary kind, especially among the Capuchins, and that the Cardinal in some measure sympathized with it. A movement of the widest sort, rationalistic and mystic, which embraced all forms of religion and repudiated the finality of any doctrine of the Church, a kind of positivism and creed of humanity in which Plato, and Buddha, and Mohammed were alike canonized as saints, and Christ himself hardly more than these. He assured me that such doctrines were widely held by the younger priests, and that some of their most zealous and able exponents were to be found among our monks at Crawley. It was no heresy, he said, and the General of the Capuchins who had come from Rome to put it down had gone back converted. This sounds to me altogether incredible, but he promised to send me the writings of the new creed in print." [This was the first word I had heard of the Modernist movement, afterwards so notorious.]

Mr. Meynell tells me that I unintentionally misrepresent the views held by Father Cuthbert and his friends. " Not one," he says, " of that fervent group of young Franciscans but fixed all his hope and all his faith on the doctrine, fundamental and final, of the divinity of Christ."

" 18*th Sept. (Sunday)*.— Meynell's talk has done me good. It opens to me a view of a religious position, not absolutely illogical, in which I may still be loyal to all my ideas without quarreling with the Catholic Church. I mean to talk the matter over with Father Cuthbert, the young Capuchin at our Monastery, whom Meynell speaks of as the leading light of the new doctrine.

" *22nd Sept.*-— Lunched at the Travellers' Club with Frank Bertie, whom I had not seen for years, and we had much talk about men and things of a past generation. He tells me Evelyn Baring is seriously ill with eczema in Scotland, one of the plagues with which Moses afflicted Pharaoh. I hope it may determine him to let the Egyptians go. Philip Currie was also there and Sanderson.

" *26th Sept.*— Margot writes that she's starting a paper to be called ' The Petticoat,' in collaboration with Betty Balfour, Mrs. Horner, Mrs. Singleton, and other women friends.

" *27th Sept.*— On a visit to Frampton, a very pretty place with a house of the early eighteenth century, the period I like best for domestic architecture. Our host, Brinsley Sheridan, is a typical country gentleman given to sport; his wife, a Motley, sister of Lady Harcourt, with two nice daughters, and there are sons, but all the boys are at school.

" There is a Miss Fetherstonhaugh staying in the house who showed me letters she had received from young de Winton from Uganda, written in the mixed missionary and fighting language one is familiar

with in Gordon's letters to his sister. These people believe they have
a mission from God to establish the British flag, 'the dear old Union
Jack,' throughout the world and to maintain it there with fire and
sword. Pizarro, no doubt, wrote in the same strain from Peru, when
he destroyed the beautiful old world of the Incas. Truly 'civilization is poison.' Weld Blundell also is staying here, a clever man with
much knowledge and a close reasoner, with whom I have been discussing Eastern questions. His view is the commercial Imperialist one
held by all English civilians who have spent their lives beyond the
Suez Canal, that of seizing and keeping markets. We were to have
gone to Malwood, but Sir William Harcourt has been summoned to
London on the Uganda question and our visit is deferred.

" *1st Oct.*— Lunched with Morris at Hammersmith and his Icelandic
friend Magnusson, with whom he translates his Sagas. It is curious
how much alike the two are physically — short, thick, sturdy men of
the pale-haired, blue-eyed type. Both, too, have the same socialistic
views, only Magnusson is much more professorial in his way of talking and less light in hand than Morris.

" Our ministers have taken courage and Uganda is to be evacuated.
The ' Daily Telegraph ' has a deliciously naïve article in expostulation :
' Uganda,' it says, ' was a few years ago a naked people, now they are
all decently clad . . . but there is a tendency, wherever English authority is relaxed among them, to revert to their old terrible habits.'

" *6th Oct.*— Tennyson died this morning at his house on Blackdown.
Much speculation as to his successor."

On the 12th Oct. I paid my now annual visit to Gros Bois, the party
there being made up of the Gustave Rothschilds, the Comte de Turenne,
Lord and Lady Castletown, and the Talbots, and we had our usual
shootings.

" *14th Oct.*— Coming home Wagram entertained us with episodes
of the French game laws. He remembers three poachers having been
shot dead at various times in the park, two by himself and one by the
keepers. In his own case the man had first fired on him. In the third
case the poacher was unarmed; in none was any inquiry made. He
and the keepers buried the dead men quietly where they fell. The last
of these three events happened as long ago as 1863 and ' Nobody,' he
said, ' knows now where they lie but myself ; the keepers who helped to
bury them are all dead; it has kept poachers most effectually away.
En plaine (meaning the open fields) one does not take justice thus to
oneself, but inside the Park it is best to do so and say nothing.'
Wagram is a fine survival of the old sporting days in France, against
which the revolution declaimed. . . . What is pleasant in the sport
here is Wagram's familiar way with his men; they are all devoted to
him.

" 16th Oct. (Sunday) — An excursion to Ferrières. We drove over all of us in a private omnibus, changing horses on the road. Castletown and I on the top, the ladies inside. I find Castletown a well-informed man, more interesting that I had at first imagined. He saw a great deal of the war of 1870–71, being with the Prussians at the battle of Champigny in this neighbourhood, ' when,' he says, ' if Ducros had only pushed on another two hours he would have broken the Prussian lines and effected his sortie.' Castletown was with the Prussian headquarters staff and knew how anxious they were. He was also with Chanzy in the south, running great risks of being shot as a spy. We talked, too, of *Ireland and Egypt. He is a strong Unionist, but a fair one in his reasoning, and would be a Nationalist if there was hope of a complete separation.

" Ferrières (which is the principal country seat of the Rothschilds in France) stands in splendid woods through which we drove for some two miles before reaching the château. The house itself is disappointing, ' *une commode renversée* ' as Bismark called it when he slept there during the Prussian occupation. It is surrounded with grounds *à l'Anglaise,* a fashion which I like less than the old French gardens. Inside it is like a monstrous Pall Mall Club decorated in the most outrageous Louis Philippe taste, a huge hall lit with a skylight and horribly overdone in its furnishing and upholstery. In the midst, a pathetic little old woman in black, Madame Alphonse Rothschild, in perpetual mourning for her departed beauty. It grieved me to remember her in the days of her glory; and when she picked some carnations from a vase and gave us each one, I asked for a red one and reminded her of how I had seen just such another in her hair nearly thirty years ago (it was in 1863) when I saw her for the first time being dressed in a mantilla for a bull-fight at Madrid. A faint smile illumined her gray face an instant but evidently without recognition of me, and she relapsed into her little old woman's talk about her dogs and birds. Presently we were joined by a pretty little young woman, her daughter, Madame Effrusi, also in black, a very attractive little creature who showed us round the grounds, with the aviaries and menageries, and entertained us with pleasant talk. This gave colour to a rather colourless afternoon and in spite of its architectural monstrosities I have carried away a pretty recollection of Ferrières and the two little quite diminutive gentlewomen living there.

" 17th Oct.— To-day we made another expedition, there being no shooting, to the Château of Vaux le Vicomte. We drove to Brunois, thence by train to Mélun, where we lunched at the Grand Monarque, and on in a fly to Vaux. Vaux is without exception the most splendid dwelling-house it has been my lot to visit. There is nothing in England to compare with it, not Blenheim, not Castle Howard, hardly

Hampton Court. It is what Versailles ought to have been and failed
to be, the ideal of all that is great and sumptuous in the French Renais-
sance style, and at the same time not too vast, a house to live in, not
merely a palace for show. Its present proprietor, one Sommier, a
sugar merchant, bought it a few years back for £100,000, and has spent
another £100,000 on restoring and furnishing it, all fortunately in the
perfection of good taste. His son, a plain youth with yellow hair,
rather ungainly, but with good voice and manner, received us on the
perron, and showed us over everything sensibly and with knowledge.
One feels happy, sugar or no sugar, that this architectural gem has
fallen into such reverent and understanding hands. It had been
offered to the Gustave Rothschilds, who fortunately let it go by. It
is now being carefully put in order, the square mile of garden brought
back from the waste into which it had fallen, statues and vases replaced, and water let in to the ruined *pièces d'eau;* this is real restoration, not a stone has been scraped, not an idea improved on. When
one looks at a creation like this, dating from two hundred and more
years ago, the talk of modern progress in the nineteenth century sounds
childish. From Vaux to Ferrières is as great a descent in the intellectual work of man as from Shakespeare to Mark Twain.

"Coming into the hall this evening for dinner, I saw a grey-headed
man entering at the opposite door, whom for a moment I took to be
Leighton, but it proved to be Carolus Duran, and he tells me he has
been several times taken for Leighton. Duran (or M. Carolus, as he
prefers to be called, Berthe says, on the pretext that he is of Spanish
origin, his real name being Durand, of a cotton-spinning family at
Lille) is an excellent specimen of the French *artiste* and *homme d'esprit.*
An exceedingly good talker on a variety of subjects, art, poetry, languages, music, and his own heart. We drew him out on every one,
and on every one he said things worth remembering. He talked of the
Chicago Exhibition and the prospects of painting in America. Most
American artists, he said, had been his own or Meissonier's pupils.
Art was a matter of education. The Americans would learn it in time.
In poetry he declaimed against Victor Hugo, and exalted Musset, cit-
ing corresponding passages to Musset's advantage. 'All great poets,'
he said, 'are exponents of their own country's genius and ideas, not
of any other country's (see Shakespeare, Molière, Dante, Cervantes),
this, although they are also for all mankind.' He did not think much
of Byron, but quoted Goethe and one or two Italians. He told us he
was Spanish, and had learned Spanish entirely by ear and with a perfect accent, but his quotations hardly bore that out. His Italian accent was better. On music he seemed to talk well, adoring Wagner,
Berlioz, and Beethoven, and he sang snatches of Malageñas in illustration of his ideas on oriental music. Lastly about his own sentiments

and feelings he was very eloquent. 'J'aime la mer comme on aime tout être capricieux et qui vous fait souffrir.' He regretted his 'vingt-cinq ans,' and would have nothing to do with ascetically avoiding pleasure. At the same time he assured us that he now made no more declarations of love, seeing that he was fifty-four. 'You do this,' Lady Castletown said, 'out of timidity?' 'Non,' he answered, 'c'est par pudeur.' That seemed to me a pretty *mot*. On the whole an interesting man.

"*19th Oct.*— To Paris and called on Lord Dufferin at the Embassy, who was in the same room that Lytton used to work in. He was very charming to me, asked me to give him a copy of my new book for his 'Helen's Tower,' a library where he has got together 400 volumes presented by authors, and which is named after his mother. I asked him to help me about Arabi's release, and he spoke nicely of him, and promised to say a word in his favour next time he should have an opportunity. On the general question of Egypt he also volunteered some remarks. He said that on the whole policy of retaining or abandoning a Mediterranean influence no responsible person would be willing to give an opinion uncalled for; but that, if Egypt was to be evacuated, there was only one way, namely, to build up some sort of self-government. He was especially opposed to Turkish rule, and had always intended, in the settlement he made, that the Government should be in the hands of the native Egyptians, not the Turks. He had devised his 'Constitution' for Egypt with that idea. He was not one of those who thought popular government foreign to Eastern ideas. On the contrary the East has been the home of Councils and Mejlisses; and he had always been of opinion that, if you could put Egypt to work *in vacuo,* there was nothing to prevent success. He had been glad to see that Baring recognized the help rendered him by the Councils, and he had written to tell him so. We then discussed how the power of the Councils might be increased, and also the safeguards against interference from Constantinople. He talked with so much interest that his servant had to come in and remind him that he had an appointment to breakfast somewhere, and so it ended. I have written a sonnet for his book, 'Helen's Tower.' Back to London in the evening.

"*24th Oct.*— Lunched with Amir Ali and his English wife. They seem happy together, and have two children. He gave me much Indian news, said that the Hindoos, especially of Patna, were in communication with Russia, and that if Russia took possession of Persia, Asia Minor and Afghanistan, there would certainly be a rising in India; the Mohammedans have separated themselves entirely from the Congress party.

"Dined with Sheffield at the Travellers'. Talking about old times, when he first went with Lyons as private secretary to Paris, the people

at the Foreign Office had told him to note carefully every word of
the Emperor's, as all he said was of political value, but after a few
interviews Lyons perceived the emptiness of the Imperial reputation.
Napoleon III's conversation was that of ' a man threatened with softening of the brain.' Fleury came to them and explained that the Emperor was often in this state, having over indulged himself with women,
remaining helpless in bed for two or three days at a time, incapable of
attending to anything, and with all the affairs of the Empire left in
the hands of his wife. This was in 1867. Claremont (the military
attaché), Sheffield says, sent report after report to the Foreign Office
predicting a collapse of the French army if there should be war, but
nobody paid any attention. He told me that he had been invited by
Frank Lawley to a dinner of reconciliation between Gladstone and
Labouchere. It ought to be amusing, but what an absurdity political
life is! [The Honourable Frank Lawley had been Gladstone's private secretary a good many years before when Gladstone was Chancellor
of the Exchequer, but having been found speculating in Consols his
career was put an end to, and he remained a broken man, not only
politically but socially. Public morality has strangely altered since.]

" *26th Oct.*— Lunched with Labouchere, who was as usual most
amusing. He told me the whole story of his correspondence with Gladstone about their not asking him to join the Cabinet. ' The best of the
joke is,' he said, ' it was not the Queen at all who prevented it. I arranged with Gladstone I should lay it on the Queen, and that he should
then lay it on himself. It really was Rosebery. At the Cabinet
Council about Uganda Rosebery was in a minority of one for retaining Uganda, but Gladstone weakly consented to his putting in the clause
granting a three months' respite, and Rosebery at once got up an
agitation in the press. ' He is an ambitious young man,' Labouchere
said, ' and wants to be Prime Minister, playing the part Palmerston
formerly played with the help of the Tories against his own party. We
shall have to join against him, and get up a cry Delendum est Rosebery.' [This is precisely what happened, and not in Rosebery's case
only, but afterwards in that of his understudy, Sir Edward Grey.]

" *3rd Nov.*— Dined with Esmé Howard, and went afterwards to
hear a lecture by Captain Lugard at the Geographical Society. Lugard,
a little, thin, dark-faced man, not unpleasing, but his lecture terribly
dull. The theatre crammed, for the agitation got up for annexing
Uganda grows daily. Philip Currie was there."

The question of evacuating or retaining Uganda was one of critical
importance with the Liberal party, for it involved the whole question
of extending, or limiting British Imperial responsibilities in Africa.
Our military party was working its hardest, helped by the Tory opposi-

tion in the House of Commons and secretly by Rosebery at the Foreign
Office, against Gladstone and the Radicals for the extension, and
eventually succeeded with the results we have seen.

"*4th Nov.*—'Esther' is out. I have sent copies to Gladstone,
Morley, George Meredith, William Watson, and Knowles.

"To Sir William Harcourt's, whom I went to see in Downing Street.
I found him just going to a Cabinet Council, and in high good humour.
'Well,' he said, 'will you go to Egypt as Commissioner to effect the
evacuation?' I said, 'Yes, if you will recall Baring.' He chuckled,
'It is not Egypt alone they want us to swallow, but the whole of East
Africa. Rhodes was with me yesterday, and showed me this map'
(pointing to one on the table), 'where you will see the territories he
has grabbed. He has put up a telegraph already as far as Niassa
(? Nyanza), and means to carry it on to Uganda, and then to Cairo.
He has offered to run Uganda for £25,000 a year, though he admits
there is nothing to be made of it commercially. You know I am not
much in favour of these things myself, and am for keeping out of
Mediterranean politics, but there are others' (meaning no doubt
Rosebery) 'who won't dance to the music.' I said, 'I think you
ought to make up your minds on the general policy, and either go in
for an African Empire, or leave it alone. If you shilly shally first
one way and then another you will get into just the same mess that
you did in 1882.' Then we talked about Egypt. 'Baring,' he said,
'has sent in a memorandum, in which he says that the whole country
is becoming English, and so it is to remain, the Khedive has lost his
popularity as he has become too European.' *I.* 'Yes, he has brought
back a Viennese woman with him from Vienna.' *He.* 'What, only
one? Baring says everything is going splendidly, and he, Baring
seems to have his horses well in hand, it would be a pity perhaps to
meddle with him.' *I.* 'Yes, I have no doubt Baring has and is driving merrily, but even a timid passenger when he finds the coach is
going to Brighton when it ought to be going to York, may be excused
for taking the reins. He will drive you merrily on to annexation.'
He. 'I would ask you to luncheon, but Waddington (the French Ambassador) is coming, and I am afraid your views are too well known.
Come on Tuesday.' And so it is arranged.

"Later to Hammersmith, where I found Morris at his work, but
pleased to see me. 'It is all a lie,' he said, 'about their having offered
to make me Laureate. Bryce came to see me and talked of it, but it
was only on his own private account. I was fool enough to tell Ellis,
and he told his son, who must needs repeat it at the National Liberal
Club, and so it got into the papers. I fancy from what I heard if they
don't offer it to me they will offer it to Swinburne, but perhaps he won't
take it.' *I.* 'It is five to one he will take it.' *He.* 'That's about

the betting, but Theodore Watts declares he will refuse. That's perhaps all the more reason.'

"*5th Nov.*— A note from Margot, '*au grand galop,*' asking me to
luncheon at her sister Charlotte's. Their paper is to be called 'To-
morrow, a Woman's Journal for Men.' I was shown the title-page.
It is to come out every two months, and they expect it to run for a
year. They are in straits for a political leader writer, and I suggested
Lady Gregory.

"*8th Nov.*— Lunched at 11, Downing Street, with the Harcourts.
Great joking by Sir William about the 'Souls' journal. I suggested
as a motto for it, *solus cum sola,* with an armorial coat,
bearing two flat fish osculant *all proper.* 'Ah,' he said, 'it is their
bodies that I like, and now they are going to show us their souls all
naked in print, I shall not care for them. Isn't that so, Sophy?' (to
his niece, Sophy Sheridan, who sat next to him, pinching her arm.)
He went on to politics: 'We have drawn out a bill this morning," he
said, 'which will destroy all temperance in England for many years to
come. We asked Arch' (the agricultural labour member) 'how many
parishes in England would vote against public-houses, and he said with
conviction "not a single one." '

"*22nd Nov.*— Crabbet. Two young monks of the Capuchins at
Crawley called on me some days ago — Father Cuthbert and Father
Angelo de Barry — to interest me in a project they have of founding
a working order of St. Francis instead of the old begging one. Father
Cuthbert, who had already spoken to me vaguely of his ideas of
Church reform, sent me to-day a note by Father Angelo, setting forth
the scheme, and asking help for them to get to Rome and lay it before
the Pope. I gave them the money they wanted, £50, with pleasure,
for it seems to me a good and timely undertaking which may well lead
to noble things. [The poor young men went to Rome, but, as was to
be expected, came back with a flea in their ears. They were the leaders
of the Modernist Reform Party in their Order but could not get a
hearing at the Vatican. They very honourably returned to me the
journey money.]

"I am leaving England for Sheykh Obeyd. A trouble to me is the
apparent failure of 'Esther.' It is not reviewed, for which I care
little, but even my friends are silent about it, and several of them disapprove. Only from George Meredith has a letter of high approval
come, and one from York Powell at Oxford."

CHAPTER V

Our winter in Egypt of that year, 1892–93, turned out to be full of incident. I found on arriving there, that the trouble I had foreseen between the new Khedive Abbas and Sir Evelyn Baring would speedily come to a head if no attempt were made to carry out Lord Dufferin's promises to the Egyptians of restoring to them their National Government under a constitutional form, and a definite policy adopted for preparing the country for evacuation. Owing to the pre-occupation of our Liberal party in England with the affairs of Ireland and other home politics, the question of Egypt had been allowed to stand over and nothing had been done. Lord Rosebery at the Foreign Office had been left to act, or not to act, as he pleased, and he in turn had left the decision of a policy to Baring, whose idea of Egyptian Government was to retain all power in his own hands, while acting in the Khedive's name.

It was the famous policy of "the Veiled Protectorate," the successful carrying out of which needed two essential conditions, first, that the Khedive should be a consenting party to the make-believe, and, secondly, that its true nature should be concealed from the general Egyptian public. The Khedive was expected to name his own ministers, but the choice of them was to be privately dictated to him by the British Agent. The Government officials were to wear the Ottoman Fez, but the more important of them were to be Englishmen. These were to give advice, not orders, but the advice was always to be obeyed. It was an ingenius plan, adopted from the Government of British India, in its dealing with the native states, while a third condition was equally indispensable, that was the presence behind the British Agent of a sufficient armed force to give emphasis to his advice and enforce his will, the Army of Occupation.

Although not a year had yet passed since Abbas' succession to the Khedivial dignity, he had already rebelled against the position of a mere puppet, and had managed to gather about him the nucleus of a new National party, which consisted of what elements there were in Egypt either of discontent or of such patriotism as was to be found in the country, half political, half religious, which resented the presence of foreign and Christian rule. The Khedive had been greatly aided

84

in this by the publication of Sir Alfred Milner's book, " England in Egypt," which I have described already. It had appeared about the time of the change of Government in England, and had proved an entire success there as a support to Baring's views, but at Cairo it had had an exactly opposite effect. It had too candidly revealed the nature of the Baring policy, unveiling to nakedness the " Veiled Protectorate," and as it had been largely read in an Arabic translation at Cairo, it had caused more alarm than satisfaction there. By the end of the year 1892 the young Khedive was already popular with his native subjects, while even among Englishmen resident at Cairo it was considered that Baring had mismanaged the matter, and there was alarm at the growing ill will that was being manifested between natives and foreigners. There is no doubt that Baring had been at fault through his lack of personal courtesy to the young prince, who, having received his education in Europe, was well aware of what was due to him, and had sufficient wit to know how to assert himself on occasion. These things are alluded to in my diary.

" *1st Dec.*— Landed at Alexandria and lunched at the Consulate, where the Consular chaplain, Davis, gave me some idea of how things were going politically. We had some talk about former Egyptian times, he having been thirty years resident there. What he said bears out what my Egyptian friends have always affirmed, namely, that Said Pasha's reign was the best time the fellahin ever had; he is, however, like all Englishmen here, for a perpetual occupation in order, as they say, ' to keep out the French.' The ladies told stories of the new Khedive Abbas to his disadvantage. He dislikes English soldiers and has made them move farther away from his palace, and he insists upon having his own will in trifles, as on one occasion lately when he made the gate-keepers of the railway open for him, and had forced the Directors to apologize and dismiss the men because, not knowing who he was, they had cursed his father. This happened near Ramleh. We had tea with Sir William and Lady Butler, he being in command of the English garrison. We went on to Sheykh Obeyd next morning.

" *26th Dec.*— To-day, a young fellow, Abderrahman Effendi, was here, a protégé of Abdu's. Talking of Abbas, he told me he was hand in glove with Riaz and Ahmed Pasha Shukri, and that they all belonged to the Hesb el Horiyeh (the Party of Liberty). I told him that if they really wanted Parliamentary Government they must work for it. The Khedive ought to make known his desire for it. He should demand it formally in writing, and I would see that their wishes were represented in the proper quarter. Writing to Loulou Harcourt about the same time, intending it for his father, I said: ' I should be glad to know what is intended at the Foreign Office. I consider that there are elements here of a stronger opposition to the English *régime*

than was the case under Tewfik. For the present the Khedive is young
and Cromer plays with him as with a young bear, humouring him in
small matters and excluding him from all real power, and the young
man amuses himself after the manner of his age, but he is certainly
strongly anti-English.'

" I understand that the Khedive is in accord with the Constitutional
party here. If so there will be less difficulty than last year in carrying
out Lord Dufferin's programme. I really cannot understand how the
Liberal party in England can with any face refuse to do this. It is the
only possible chance of setting the Egyptians on their own legs,

" 31st Dec.— I have been taken up for the last forty-eight hours with
reading Milner's book about Egypt which is just out. It is by far the
ablest defence I have seen of Cromer's policy, and may be considered as
his own apologia, for most of it must have been taken down from his
dictation or at any rate in concert with him; even in form and arrangement of subjects. It is identical with Cromer's report of 1891. There
is a great deal of truth in it and also a great deal of the suppression of
truth.

" 16th Jan. 1893.— Went to Cairo, the first time this winter, on
business with Scott (then at the Ministry of Justice). I found everybody there in a great turmoil, as the Khedive has just dismissed Mustapha Pasha Fehmi and other Ministers from their posts, and has
appointed new ones, with Fakhri Pasha as President of the Council,
without Baring's cognizance. Scott said it was a *coup d'état,* and so it
seems to be.

" 18th Jan.— Baring has refused to recognize the new Ministry until
he has communicated with the English Government. He has given
the Khedive time to reflect, and the Khedive, finding himself insuffic-
iently backed up by the French, has already given in and a compromise
has been come to, Fakhri being replaced by Riaz.

" 20th Jan.— Ismaïl Jowdat [1] has been here and has told me the
whole story of the intrigue of the last few days, thought it dates in its
beginning from much earlier. It is one of those complicated episodes
which make up Egyptian history.

" Abbas, Jowdat says, arriving from Europe a year ago with European notions, readily fell in at first with Baring's plans. He took up
the quarrel with Constantinople Baring led him into, about his firman
of appointment, and for a while was on bad terms with the Sultan.
Mukhtar Pasha, however, and de Reverseaux, the French Consul-
General, have managed latterly to bring him round into opposition,
and he has made up with the Sultan and is strongly anti-English.
They have managed this with the help of the young Sheykh el Bekri,

[1] Ismaïl Bey Jowdat, director of the Cairo police under the Nationalist Government in 1882. See my volumes, " Secret History " and " Gordon at Khartoum."

who was brought up with Abbas and has great influence with him. This young man was at first, like Abbas, under Baring's influence, and Baring sent him to England last summer and introduced him to Gladstone and others, boasting that the Egyptians were becoming English in their sentiments. The young man is of importance from his religious position, which is hereditary. On his way home, however, he passed through Constantinople and there fell under the contrary influence of the Sultan, who gave him high orders and decorations, and of Prince Halim Pasha, whose daughter it has been arranged he shall marry. He returned to Egypt last autumn altogether in the Sultan's interest, and has since received from Mukhtar Pasha a pension of £300 a month out of the Sultan's privy purse. Abbas, disapproving of his visit to Constantinople, refused to see him on his return. Nevertheless, a reconciliation was effected through the mediation of the Khedive's mother, urged thereto by a certain religious Sheykh of Alexandria, entitled Sheykh Tekkiet Gulshani, who desiring to have his title confirmed on his son, which could only be done through the Sheykh el Bekri's firman, interceded on his behalf. The Khedive's mother was this old Sheykh's adopted daughter (god-daughter) and hence his influence. El Bekri then called on the Khedive and was well received, and has since influenced him in favour of the Sultan's policy. Mukhtar and Reverseaux planned between them with Riaz this sudden *coup d' état* which has just taken place, Bekri having got the Khedive to join it. It was Riaz's suggestion putting Fekri forward, and it has ended as planned in his own substitution as Minister. The following are the chief personages concerned in the plot: Mukhtar Pasha, the Sultan's representative, with his Turkish secretary Mohsin Bey, Abd el Salaam Pasha Moelhi, Ibrahim Moelhi and his son Mohammed, Prince Hussein, the Sheykh el Bekri, the Sheykh Gulshani, Mohammed Bey Zoghi and his brother, Rushti Bey, Yussuf Sadyk, son of the old Muffettish, Ahmed Bey el Kharmili, and Ahmed Bey Sofani, of the Legislative Council, Mazlum Pasha, master of ceremonies, Tigrane Pasha, Zekki Pasha, and others. They have made up their ministry thus: Riaz Pasha, Mazlum Pasha, Boutros Pasha Ghali, Tigrane, and Zekki Pasha.

"Later in the day Fenwick Pasha called upon me. He regretted that Lord Cromer had not gained a more certain victory in the crisis. 'Cromer,' he said, 'had offered Mustafa Fehmi to back him if he would remain in office, but Mustafa declined, probably afraid.' The immediate causes of the *coup d'état* were first the publication at Cairo of Milner's book, and second the order issued by Coles Pasha (the English adviser of the Ministry of the Interior) to the Mudirs in his own name instead of that of the Egyptian Minister.

"I have written to Labouchere and to Sir William Harcourt."
This was the Khedive Abbas' first revolt against Cromer. The

ground of the revolt was not ill-chosen, as the Khedive was without question within his constitutional and legal right to name his own Ministers, and it at once dissolved the illusion Cromer had entertained that his and not the Khedive's authority was popular in Egypt. It was everywhere applauded, and it forced Cromer to abandon his make believe and telegraph to London for English troops, a clear admission of his political impotence. It was a first rent made in the famous " Veiled Protectorate," and though Cromer in his book describes it as a victory, it was one of physical force only, not moral force.

" On the 26th of January Hardinge of the Legation [1] was here. He told us that when Riaz was informed of the arrival of reinforcements from England he smiled a blue smile and remarked that they would be welcome, as English regiments had always been well-behaved in the country. ' Riaz,' said Hardinge, ' may not love us, but at least he will be an open enemy.' It appears that Cromer really threatened the Khedive, giving him twenty-four hours to make up his mind, and that the English regiments in garrison had ball cartridges served out. They intended to surround the palace and keep the Khedive prisoner if he refused, but what more does not appear.

" *30th Jan.*— Sir Edgar Vincent and his wife, with Lady Alice Portal and Mr. Eldon Gorst, came to tea. I was glad to find that Vincent took quite my view of the situation. He said: ' They can't go on on the old lines, and must either declare a protectorate or evacuate. The change,' he said, ' in public opinion since I was at Cairo three years ago, is astonishing.' He has been seeing much of Riaz. As to Turkey and the Sultan he confirms all that I have heard of the improvement. ' The resuscitation,' he said, ' of the Ottoman Empire is the most remarkable phenomenon of our day.' And so it is."

Several others have called, all telling the same story, that Riaz has the whole public with him, and that the Khedive is popular everywhere. Only my neighbor, Selim Faraj, being a timid man and a Christian, was frightened when I talked of evacuation as near. He thought it would be followed by a persecution of Christians. ' It is not,' he said, ' as it used to be in Egypt. Ever since the affair of 1882 there has been a growing hatred between Mohammedans and Christians.' This is true, but whose fault is it?

" *5th Feb.*— Parliament has met and Her Majesty has made her speech, to the effect that the sending of troops to Egypt does not indicate a change of policy, also that the Khedive has given her assurances that he will act in co-operation with her representatives.

" *14th Feb.*— Went in to Cairo to see the Sheykh el Bekri. Mohammed Moelhi met me at the station and we drove to a Mowlid [a relig-

---

[1] Sir Arthur Hardinge, then Secretary of Legation at Cairo, afterwards our Minister at Brussels.

ious birthday feast] in the Bab esh Shariyeh, where we found the young Sheykh in a house decorated for the occasion. He arrived as we arrived, and we went in together. There was a great crowd of people, but the Selamlik was empty, and we sat down with El Bekri and talked in French, while religious Sheykhs and others presently came in to pay their respects to him. The Sheykh el Bekri is a young man about twenty-five, of no very imposing appearance, small and pale, very plainly dressed in white turban gombaz and abbo, you might take him for one of the Azhar students, but he has a certain quiet dignity and is most intelligent. He talks French perfectly. I discussed the situation with him both as to the exiles and as to current politics. On the political situation he talked very sensibly, and urged me strongly to call on the Khedive and talk it over with him. I said: ' I will call on leaving Egypt to ask him pardon for the exiles, and then if he chooses to speak to me on other things I will discuss them with him.' But I explained that my situation was rather a delicate one, as I had formerly been exiled and had been put under an obligation not to interfere; still I was in communication with Sir William Harcourt, and any message the Khedive might choose to give me I would deliver. The Sheykh el Bekri told me that when he was in England last summer he had seen Gladstone, and Gladstone had spoken strongly to him in the sense of evacuation and against Lord Cromer's policy. He could not understand that he should now be supporting it. I explained the political intrigues at home and Rosebery's position in the Cabinet. He seemed well acquainted with men and things in England. I gathered from him that the quarrel between the Khedive and Lord Cromer was very much a personal one. At this point music began outside and chanting, and our sofa was turned round to the window and we continued our talk, but with interruptions. I arranged, however, with him that he should speak to the Khedive of my readiness to be of service to him, and that he was to arrange an audience before I left Egypt. This will oblige me to put off my journey (the one I had intended to take) to the Fayum. The thing is interesting, and reminds me not a little of old days. I never thought to become the Khedive's confidant after all that has happened.

"*15th Feb.*— Sir George Bowen came and spent the day. A man of enlightened ideas, and much practical experience in English protectorates, the Ionian Islands, Malta, etc., where he has served officially. We talked out the Egyptian question fully, and were pretty much agreed about it. He says, the Liberal Government at home would willingly evacuate, but fears public opinion. He has talked much since he has been in Egypt with Riaz, and Nubar, and Cromer. Nubar regrets that England did not annex in 1882. Cromer admits that he does not know what to do. There are three possible courses: (1) To annex,

which would cause an European war.   (2) To evacuate, which English opinion would not stand, and (3) To stay on as we are.   This
last is what he (Cromer) intends to do.   Bowen confirms all I have
said of the universality of popular feeling against us here, the desire
that everyone has to see us gone (not personal hatred).   He finds the
Copts quite as much against us as the Mohammedans.   He understands
the feeling as political, and patriotic, not fanatical.   He lays much of
the blame on Cromer, who is not, he thinks, the sort of man to acquire
the confidence of a young Oriental Prince. . . . He asked me my solution, and I told him that I thought the English garrison might be withdrawn to Suez as a compromise, that would satisfy the cry in England
about the route to India.   He is in communication with Lord Kimberley and will write to him, and I trust may do some good, though the
Liberal party seems to have gone in for a thorough debauch of Jingo-
ism.

"*21st Feb.*— Again to see the Sheykh el Bekri, this time in his own
palace, formerly Abbas Pasha's, where I had once been in his father's
time in 1881.   He is certainly a most clever and charming young man,
knowing everything about the politics in Europe and Constantinople
as well as in Egypt.   He sees Riaz constantly, and vouches for Riaz
as a sincere opponent of Cromer, and supporter of Abbas.   Riaz holds
other language to the English here.   I told Sheykh el Bekri that I
thought it very important the Khedive should state in some official
document the exact nature of the promise he made to Cromer as to
his being ' willing to *follow the advice* of Her Majesty's Government
on all important matters,' whereas the Khedive has told deputations
that have waited on him that all he promised was ' to *consult* the British Resident.'   This he ought to make clear.   Sheykh el Bekri assured
me that under present circumstances Abbas could count on the Sultan's
support.   He is advising the Khedive to act in everything through and
with the support and countenance of the Legislative Council.   This is
the right road.

"*23rd Feb.*— To Cairo to order a black coat, the Khedive being
punctilious on the score of clothes.   Fortunately I found one at the
English tailor's ready made.   [It had been ordered for Oliver Montagu
who had just died at Cairo, and had never worn it.]   Had a long talk
with Sackville [1] who thinks things very unsatisfactory, the European
Powers would not allow our annexation, the Turks would come from
Constantinople if we went.

"*24th Feb.*— Sheykh Mohammed Abdu came for lunch and stayed
the afternoon.   I had not seen him since the *coup d'état,* and was anxious for his opinion.   He is strongly in favour of Riaz who, he says,

[1] Lionel Lord Sackville, formerly of the Diplomatic Service, and Her Majesty's
Minister at Washington.

may be depended on, not so Tigrane or Boutros. **Tigrane, Artin, and** the Christians generally do all they can to destroy Moslem education. Riaz is a tyrant, but he is honest. He gave me his opinions of the various Englishmen employed in the country; ' the only good ones,' he said, ' are Scott, Garstein, and Corbett. It has been the introduction of so many inferior Englishmen in the last three years that has ruined English influence.' He laughed much at Wallace and his school of agriculture, and at Willcox with his reforms of the Arabic language. He is very glad I am to see the Khedive, and wants me to impress on him the necessity of keeping well with Riaz, and of taking up young Mohammedans rather than Armenians and Syrians. He would also work in a Constitutional sense. 'We do not mind,' he said, ' the English being here for a year, or two years, or five years, so long as they do not stay altogether. It would be better for the country as giving time for the growth of the Fellah party, but if there is danger of annexation we are quite ready to run the risk of a little tyranny from the Turks, rather than the other greater risk; if you will evacuate to-morrow we shall all rejoice.' Now Abdu is probably the *most* philo-English of the Egyptians.

" On the 25th February an interview with me, which had been published in the ' Pall Mall Gazette,' having been reprinted in the ' Bosphore Egyptien,' I wrote to Lord Cromer to explain that I was not responsible for this, or for joining in any of the attacks made on him in the Egyptian newspapers. ' In England,' I said, ' it is different. There as long as we occupy Egypt without annexing it, the Egyptian question must remain a subject of public discussion, and I am sure you will not think that with the strong views I hold on the injustice of destroying Egyptian Nationality, my expressing myself on the subject was unfair or uncalled for.' In answer he said, while thanking me for my letter, ' I cannot, of course, take the smallest exception to your expressing your views on Egyptian questions in any form you may think fit, neither did I for a moment imagine that you wished to make a personal attack on myself.' I quote this as showing what my relations with Cromer were at this and in subsequent times when we quarrelled politically.

" *28th Feb.*— Went this morning by appointment to see the Khedive at Abdin Palace. I found him in the same room as a year ago, and he came to meet me at the door. He received me very cordially, and talked throughout with a great show of frankness and confidence. His manner is certainly excellent, and he has a wonderful command of words for so young a man, with a very frank, agreeable smile. He began about his farm at Koubbah, which he said interested him far more than anything at Abdin, and we discussed the subject of horse-breeding and the growth of *bersim hejazi*. Then he went on to politics.

He thanked me for having spoken in his favour in the P.M.G. interview. 'The whole English Press,' he said, 'is against me.' I asked him for a history of what had happened. He said: 'As long ago as the end of last summer, when Mustafa Pasha (Fehmy) returned from Europe, Palmer (the Financial Adviser) came to me and complained of my having spoken against him. I asked him how he knew I had done so. He said the people of the Palace were talking. Then Hardinge came with the same complaint, but could not tell me who it was that had spoken. When Lord Cromer arrived he came to me and told me that I was becoming very unpopular (laughter) in the country because I was not cordial with Mustafa Pasha. The fact is Mustafa is an invalid, and has to go in the summer to Europe. He is not fit to be Prime Minister. When he fell ill, Lord Cromer objected to my taking Tigrane, and offered me a choice of several quite incapable persons — Balig Pasha, who is a Cypriote, Affet Pasha, who is one of the worst of men, and Ahmed Shukri, who is quite incapable.'

He then gave me an account of what had happened between him and Cromer as to the promise of following English advice. I asked him to tell me the exact words, and he said: 'We were speaking in French' (to me he was speaking in very good English, and I fancy he keeps his French for his English advisers), 'and what I said was, "Que j'avais tout désir d'agir de concert avec le Gouvernement Anglais et que je ne manquerais pas de le consulter sur toute chose de grande importance."' He denied, however, categorically that he gave any promise of 'following English advice.' I showed him Cromer's despatch published in the Blue Book, which I had in my pocket with the Queen's Speech, and he said the latter was correct enough, not the other. I then told him that I considered it very important since that was so, that he should at once contradict it officially, as afterwards it would be quoted against him, and he promised to make Tigrane write an official despatch in that sense. I then asked him whether he could rely absolutely on Riaz as against Cromer, and he said 'absolutely.' 'If that is so,' I said, 'and you have the Sultan with you, you have nothing whatsoever to fear.' He said, 'Indeed I am not in the smallest degree afraid of any one. I consider that I have a great responsibility here as ruler of the country and a great duty, and I mean to do it. I do not care what happens.' I noticed that he was reticent about the Sultan, but I did not press that matter. About Tigrane he said, 'I know that I can depend better on Riaz than on Tigrane. Tigrane, being a Christian, has no influence in the country, but Riaz has. We must make use of Christian ministers as administrators, not as heads of the Government.' I then asked him about the amnesty for Arabi and the other exiles. I told him I had had letters from Arabi full of loyal expressions towards him, and that I was sure he could count on him to be faithful to them, that Mahmud Sami might be very useful to him, and that I hoped he would allow them to return to Egypt. He received this very favourably, and I went on to say that I had always regretted that his father, Tewfik, had quarrelled with Arabi, and so brought the English into the country — he did not dissent from this — that as a matter of fact, Arabi's policy was precisely the same as his, Abbas' own, namely, to get rid of foreign rule. He said he could not give me a precise answer about the exiles until he had consulted others, but that he would take their case into favourable consideration, and when a proper opportunity occurred he hoped to be able to accede to my request. I said I would not press it on him at the present moment of his strained relations with Cromer. I then advised him strongly to take his Legislative Council into his counsels, and act through it and through the General Assembly, and I told him of Labouchere's view. In all this he cordially agreed. A deputation then appeared in the outer room, and I saw that it was time to go. I took my leave, promising him to state his case in any quarters where I might have influence, and that he could always count on me for the best of my advice. He walked to the door with me, making me promise to come and see him, and his horses at Koubbah. As I was leaving him I said, ' One word more. If Lord Cromer should leave Egypt, and there is any question of appointing an Indian officer in succession to him, I advise Your Highness strongly to object.' He said, ' Oh, certainly. I know them.' And so with great cordiality we parted.

" I am delighted with the young man. He is able, courageous, and self-possessed. He reminds me of his grandfather, Ismaïl, as to wit, *mais en mieux*. He ought to win his game against Cromer.

" Mohammed Moelhi came in the afternoon. I told him all that has passed at the palace and he said: ' Now you must go to Constantinople, the Sultan will wish to see you.' So I shall do if all goes well.

" 1st *March.*— I received a curious visit from one Abdullah El Moughera, an Arab of the Moughera tribe of Aflaj, but born at Shagra, in Nejd. He told me he had left Nejd as servant to Abdullah Ibn Thenneyan Ibn Saoud, who went to Constantinople twelve years ago, wanting to be established in Nejd by the Turkish Government. He had been employed by the Sultan to try and raise troops among the Anazeh and other tribes and had succeeded in getting Sotamm Ibn Shaalan and other chiefs to go to Constantinople. But Sheykhs Ahmed Essaad and Abul Huda had been jealous of him and he had left the Sultan's service and had gone back to Syria. At Jerusalem he had offered his services to the British Consul to raise an insurrection in Syria, and the Consul had sent him on to Lord Cromer. He had seen Cromer and Boyle, but says he could not make them understand him, as Boyle and he talked Turkish, but most probably they would not have anything to do with him, so he came on to me.

"He came again 4th March, and I gave him £10 and advised him to go back to Syria.

"*6th March.*— Abderrahman Ismaïl came and reminded me of what I had advised about the Khedive declaring himself before Parliament met. 'You see,' he said, 'we have taken your advice.' So it is just possible that my words may have had some influence in bringing the crisis on, only I wish they had consulted me as to the way of doing so. I should not have advised this sudden change of Ministers. But perhaps it is best as it is. It was not Ahmed Shukri, but Mohammed Shukri, who, he told me, was working with Riaz. He talked now in the highest spirits of all that was happening. I told him I thought it possible negotiations for evacuation might be begun before the end of the year.

"*7th March.*— To-day I went to see Riaz Pasha. To my astonishment he had written me a most amiable note, asking to see me and signing himself *Votre bien dévoué.* So I called at three at his private house in the Helmiyeh quarter, near the citadel, I suppose the quarter where his old Jew father lived. He received me with the greatest cordiality, a little, wizened, gray old man, with a nervous, twitching face (once Abbas I's dancing boy!) and poured me out his griefs. He began with a long apology for his conduct in past times and of how he would have saved the country if it had not been for Arabi's pushing on too quickly. I did not care to argue that point, as I knew it would take time, and he is sorry enough now for having got the English into the country. He is very angry with Cromer for having humbugged him when he was last in office about evacuation, and on my showing him what Labouchere had written me about Rosebery's intention *never* to evacuate, he threw up his hands in real passion.

"We discussed the necessity of action through the General Assembly, and he quite agreed. But he strikes me as being rather old and infirm, and I doubt if he will hurry on fast enough. Unless they act here, while our Parliament is sitting, they will lose their pains. I talked to him also about getting the Sultan to agree to the neutralization of Egypt in connection with our withdrawal, and he thought it could be managed if the word neutralization was not used to the Sultan. He thought also they might come to an agreement to make over the town of Suez permanently to England, but he begged me not to quote him, also he promised to draw up a programme of reforms. About the Khedive's denial that he had promised to *follow* English advice he did not feel sure, but said that something he thought had already been written about it. He is very Oriental and very vague, but there is something in him that inspires confidence. When I said, 'You must not repeat all I have told you to Lord Cromer,' he exclaimed, 'Ah, could you think it?' Lastly I talked to him about Arabi's return, and he spoke much as the Khedive had spoken, of there being no unwillingness on their part only that the time was inopportune. He complimented me on my constancy to my friend, and we parted on the best possible terms. Coming with me to the head of the stairs he kept repeating: 'Ah, que je suis content de vous avoir vu, que je suis content, que je suis content.'

"*11th March.*— I have written my article, 'Lord Cromer and the Khedive,' for the 'Nineteenth Century,' also letters to Churchill, Labouchere, and Loulou Harcourt, founded on my talk with the Khedive; also 12th March to Mr. Gladstone.

"*22nd March.*— Mohammed Moelhi tells me of a new trouble. A certain Ali Bey, Colonel of a regiment quartered at Koubbah, had made himself conspicuous by his visits to the Khedive, and his congratulations on the issue of the *coup d'état*. This has given offence to Kitchener, the new Sirdar, and they have ordered the regiment back to Suakim, whence it only came six months ago. The Minister of War, Yussuf Shudi, one of the old gang, lets Kitchener do what he likes. [This entry is of more importance than it seems, for this Ali Bey was Ali Bey Kamel, brother to Mustafa Kamel, afterwards leader of the National Party, who began his political career by taking up this quarrel of his brother with Kitchener.]

"*31st March.*— Everard Fielding (he had been staying with us at Sheykh Obeyd) brought the Sultan of Johore to see us, a good old Indian gentleman of very simple manners and much *bonhomie*. He lunched with us, notwithstanding Ramadan, talking pleasantly in *pidgin* English, which did not altogether mar his dignity. With him a young Malay, the general of his army, and his English secretary, Captain Creighton. He complained that though he had been a fortnight at Cairo, he had as yet seen none but English officials, and that Lord Cromer had not encouraged him in his desire to go into Egyptian society. I offered to put him in the way of this, which much delighted him, and as good luck would have it, Mohammed Moelhi called, while we were sitting on the roof, and I introduced him and sent Mohammed back with him to Cairo, to take him, to-day being Friday, to the Mohammed Ali Mosque for prayers, and I am to take him on Sunday to the Sheykh el Bekri and get Mohammed Abdu and other Sheykhs to call on him, and we will put him in the right way to an introduction to Sultan Abdul Hamid when he goes on to Constantinople.

"*2nd April.*— To Cairo, where I took the Sultan of Johore to Sheykh el Bekri, acting for him as interpreter. This was a difficult matter, as the poor old Sultan's English is hardly intelligible, and his ideas are most embroiled, and his manner, too, for an Oriental, is strangely bad, and I fear he shocked el Bekri by a certain *sans-façon* in speaking of holy things, though I was able to smooth down his more unfortunate remarks, as interpreters do. The truth is they were at cross purposes. What el Bekri wanted to find out was whether the Sultan had any panislamic ideas, whether he wanted to see Abdul Hamid at Constantinople for a political purpose, and whether he would encourage panislamic missionaries at Johore. The old man, on the other hand, only wanted a little personal sympathy as a Mohammedan from Mohammedans. He was too humble-minded to expect much notice from Abdul Hamid, and had nothing of any importance to say to him. Thus each misunderstood the other. 'Do the Mohammedan Princes in India,' the Sheykh asked, 'communicate with each other as such, and do they communicate with the Sultan at Constantinople?' To which the other replied that the Malay princes knew each other, but not the others. They had never had the smallest communication with Constantinople, and the Ottomans looked on them as Kaffirs. A Turkish man-of-war had once come and stayed some time at Singapore on her way to Japan, and it was not till just before she sailed that they discovered that Johore was Mohammedan. Then everybody had been delighted. That was the only communication that had ever taken place with the Turks. They saw many Arabs of the Hedjaz at Singapore who came to trade, but they were ignorant men, though some were rich. He would like to go to Constantinople, but he would not put the Sultan to the trouble of receiving him. He was only a small sovereign, and had nothing of importance to say. As to missionaries, he would be delighted if the Sheykh would send them a professor to teach them their religion. They were all Shafaïs at Johore. They said their prayers in Arabic, but did not know the meaning of the words; the Koran was not translated into Malay except some parts of it. He was having a translation made, they were all very ignorant. The young Sheykh el Bekri hardly knew, I think, what to make of it all. The good Sultan of Johore was more successful with other Egyptians whom I took him to. At Abdul Salaam's the Pasha was on all fours to His Highness, and me for bringing him. He described to them his patriarchal way of governing his country with a walking stick —'like the first Caliphs' Abdul Salaam remarked — and how he liked, when he was at home with his wife and his mother, to sit on the floor and eat with his fingers. He wanted to find somebody doing that, but at Cairo there were European chairs and sofas everywhere. We have promised to show him that, too, and he is to go on to Mohammed Abdu.

"Later I went alone with Mohammed to call on Mukhtar Pasha, and had a long talk with him on the political situation, the upshot of which was that he promised no time should be lost in pushing things on. He

would write at once to the Sultan, suggesting that he should take action
in the direction of neutralizing Egypt, and he would urge Riaz to con-
voke the General Assembly here after Ramadan.   It shows how little
these people know of their own affairs, and how entirely Dufferin's
Charter has remained a dead letter, that when I spoke to Mukhtar of
the Assembly, he stoutly denied that there existed such an institution.
' It would be,' he said, ' a most precious instrument in our hands, but I
have never heard of it.'   I exhorted him to consult his papers.   He also
assured me that as long as the Khedive was *dans la bonne voie,* he
could count on the Sultan's support.   Also about Riaz that he was sure
he would work straight now with the Khedive.   Riaz was much
changed in the last two years.   He would jog him on if he was slow,
as he quite saw the necessity for action.   Every year the Occupation
lasted rooted it more firmly.   Lastly, he promised to see the Sultan of
Johore, who I hope will not commit any *inconvenance* when they meet.
It is announced in the papers that Cromer's new yearly Report is published, and that the ' Daily News ' in London supports it, and declares
it must be several years before Egypt can be left to manage its own
Government.

"*5th April.*— Randolph writes me an interesting letter about Egypt.
He says that he is still in favour of evacuation, but at the present time
cannot express his opinion publicly with advantage.   He wishes, me,
however, to tell the Khedive to keep on good terms with Cromer as his
best chance.

"*12th April.*— Lunched with Tigrane (the Armenian Under Secretary for Foreign Affairs).   He is, I think, sound in his Nationalism,
though an Armenian.   We talked about my article in the ' Nineteenth
Century,' with nearly all of which he agreed, objecting only that it
might do harm to the Khedive that I should have stated him to have
denied the promise to follow English advice.   He said he had been
himself the intermediary in arranging the affair between the Khedive
and Lord Cromer, that he had drawn up in writing with Lord Cromer
the form of words the Khedive was to use, namely, ' *Je suiverai volon-
tiers les conseils,*' etc.; that the Khedive had read the Memorandum
and had learnt it by heart, and had promised to use the exact words.
He therefore presumed that the Khedive had done so, and that the
promise was in fact made.   I said there could be no mistake that the
Khedive now denied it, and we both agreed that it was a point of the
utmost importance.   He said that the Legislative Council would be
convened soon after Bairam, when they would introduce a programme
of educational and other reforms.   He would see Mohammed Abdu
as to a reform of the Azhar if I would send him to him.   As to the
General Assembly the country was not yet ready for it.   It would have
to be written about first in the press.   He had himself always been in

that without constant action there was no chance of success. ' Yes,' he said, ' we drift down the stream like a log to the sea.' On the whole I am pleased with Tigrane.

"*13th April.*— Lady H. writes that she has seen Gorst who seemed immensely struck with my article, ' Lord Cromer and the Khedive,' never apparently before having realized what a good case can be made out for the other side.

"*15th April.*— Called again on Mukhtar Pasha, who talked with considerable unreserve. Speaking of the necessity there would be of England's holding Egypt in force, if she were at war with any Great Power, I had remarked we should require 20,000 men —' 50,000,' he exclaimed, ' only to deal with the internal disturbance, and when I come with an army from out there from Damascus you will see how many more you will want.' "

This is the account given by my diary of Abbas' first pitched battle with Cromer, which the latter always claimed as a notable victory, though in reality it was hardly that in any moral sense, Cromer having got his way only by the violent physical measure of calling for British reinforcements and by the unreadiness of the French Government to make it a *casus belli.* Relying on this he succeeded in intimidating the young Khedive to the extent of obtaining from him a compromise in regard to his right of appointing Ministers which he was able to represent in his reports as dictated by himself, but it left him with the Khedive for a persistent enemy, who though many times forced to submit was never reconciled, and who in the end defeated his old enemy, and drove him out of Egypt. I have recorded it here at some length, for it marks the beginning of an obstinate determination on the part of our Foreign Office under the Liberal, no less than under the Conservative administrations in Downing Street, to cling to Egypt right or wrong, wisely or foolishly, to its own hurt twenty years later.

On the 18th April we left Sheykh Obeyd for Athens and Constantinople. At Athens I found my friend Egerton newly appointed Minister, and we lunched at the Legation with him and Arthur Ellis, who was there in attendance on the Princess of Wales on a yachting cruise, and they both talked with a certain sympathy of my Egyptian views, Egerton being still for evacuation as when we had talked of it together in Paris; but we made no stay at Athens more than the few hours allowed by our steamer, and on 23rd April we landed at Galata, and took up our quarters at Myssiris Hotel, where all is unchanged since I was first there thirty-three years before, and where we stayed for a fortnight, an interesting visit, though I failed after all in the chief object of it, that of getting speech of the Sultan.

Our first visitor on arrival was my old ally Ibrahim Moelhi, Moham-

med's father, now a Pasha by favour of the Sultan, and in high favour
at the Imperial court, who put me in the way of seeing various dignitaries, including Munir Pasha, the Sultan's chief intermediary between
Yildiz Palace and strangers of distinction, who promised me an early
audience of His Majesty, but I soon found there were obstacles in the
way of an actual private audience of the kind usual at that time among
the Court officials.   Mukhtar Pasha, from whom I had brought a letter
of introduction to Munir, had described me in it as " a *rich* Englishman
who had for many years defended the cause of the Arabs against the
English Government."   The word " rich " was an unfortunate one as
suggesting ideas of *bakshish* to the official mind, and I soon discovered
that the doors of Yildiz would need more than one golden key to open
for me, a form of blackmail I was not prepared to submit to, for I
have made it a rule in my dealings with Orientals neither to give, nor
to receive, presents.   Neither was I disposed to waste more time than
a few days waiting for this and that arrangement to mature.   Nevertheless I had opportunities given me of seeing a good deal of the
inside machinery of that singular abode, the Sultan's residence and
its surroundings.   I might of course have obtained a formal audience
in the orthodox way by getting the British Ambassador to present me,
but that would not have served my purpose as the conversation of
strangers under such circumstances of introduction was never more with
Abdul Hamid than a polite interchange of compliments.

Our Ambassador at the time was Sir Clare Ford, on whom we all
called, and who received me very cordially as a former member of the
Diplomatic service, and who had for a while worked there in Bulwer's
time as an *attaché,* but we did not talk politics except with Nélidoff, the
Russian Ambassador, who was announced while we were there, and
who had at one time been my intimate friend when he and I were
attachés together at Athens.   Nélidoff always remembered our days
there with pleasure when we met, and so it was on this occasion.   We
talked of old times at Athens when he and I were still almost boys,
he three or four years older than me, and of the paper chases we had
ridden together in the olive woods with Dufferin, he, too, still a young
man, travelling with his mother in the East, and who had spent the
winter with us there.   I found him much intrigued about the Sultan
of Johore, who to his immense surprise found himself an object of
vast curiosity at Constantinople, and who, thanks to Sheykh el Bekri's
introduction, had been received with all ceremonious honour by Abdul
Hamid, though the Court had refused from the first to acknowledge him
as having any claim to calling himself a Sultan.   Nevertheless he was
credited by everyone with a very high position as a Mohammedan
Prince in the Malay States.   Nélidoff told the story of what the Sultan's
chamberlain had said of him when Nélidoff had asked who and what

he was. " Je ne connais pas de Sultan de Johore, mais il y a un prince
de ce nom qui a demandé audience de sa Majesté le Sultan." Nélidoff
was curious to know how many subjects Johore contained, and when I
told him " only half a million " was greatly disappointed. He had been
reckoning on him, I think, as a possible ally for Russia on the borders of
India.

Going on the same afternoon (25th April) to a hotel where he was
staying " I found the Johore suite in the seventh heaven of delight over
their reception last night by the Sultan. Two state carriages had been
sent for them with an escort of cavalry — this had been denied them
in London at the Queen's Jubilee. They had been entertained at a
state banquet, and Sultan Abdul Hamid had embraced his brother
monarch and had bestowed on him the First Class of the Order of
Osmanieh in diamonds, and on the suite correspondingly high decorations. I did not see the old gentleman himself, he being with the
dentist. Mohammed Moelhi alone was not decorated, though as a
matter of fact it was entirely owing to him that Johore had been received at all. The Sultan had refused at first, saying he was only an
Indian Rajah, but Moelhi managed to persuade the palace people
through Jemal ed Din, and the brilliant reception accorded was the
result. Jemal ed Din was at the banquet, and according to Ibrahim's
account, is now in high favour at Yildiz, having succeeded with Abdul
Hamid by his plainspoken audacity. The Sultan has offered him all
kinds of grades and decorations, but Jemal ed Din has wisely refused,
and the other day, on being turned back by the master of ceremonies at
one of the Bairam Court functions, Jemal ed Din pushed his way
through notwithstanding, and so attracted the Sultan's notice, who sent
for him and made him stand close to him behind his chair, nearer even
than the Grand Eunuch. So Jemal ed Din is the man of whom to
solicit favours, and I am to be taken to call on him to-morrow, the
episode of the umbrella in the back room at James Street being con-
signed to oblivion. How foolish Drummond Wolff was to change his
mind at Vienna and not take the Seyyid with him to Constantinople in
1885, as I had arranged he should do. He would have got his Convention ratified and succeeded where he failed.[1]

" *26th April.*— With Judith to luncheon at the Embassy. The German Ambassador was there, with a Swedish Count and Countess and
Carnegie, a cousin of the Ambassador, of a branch of the Southesk
family settled in Prussia, also Nicholson, our Secretary of Embassy,
next to whom I sat. I found both Nicholson and Ford professing
opinions favourable to the evacuation of Egypt; indeed, Ford intro-

[1] For Seyyid Jemal ed Din Afghani's earlier career and his visit to me in London see my volume, " Gordon at Khartoum." See also Professor Browne's account of the Seyyid in his book on Persia.

duced me to the German Ambassador as 'the Englishman most strongly opposed to our Occupation of Egypt.' Nicholson married a sister of Lady Dufferin, and was in Egypt at the time of Dufferin's special mission of 1882–3. He gave me a less rosy-coloured picture of Turkish Finance than Vincent, who is negotiating a new loan, and so makes the best of things here.

" At three on with Judith to Nishantash, in the Musafir Khaneh, an official lodging house for distinguished visitors attached to Yildiz, where Jemal ed Din has rooms. The old Afghan received us with open arms and embraced me on both cheeks in a room filled with reverend Turks, and made Judith sit in the armchair of state, and gave us tea and coffee and entertained us for an hour and a half. Anne had written him a note of excuse in Arabic, which was read out two or three times with great admiration at its style and correctness. Then we had a long talk on politics, partly in Arabic, partly in French, which Jemal ed Din talks pretty fluently. Ibrahim Moelhi was there, but the others did not understand us (very few Turks know Arabic). Jemal ed Din asked my opinion of the various personages in Egypt, the Khedive, Riaz, Mukhtar, Tigrane and I also explained to him the situation in England. He was there some months last year, and had got rather incorrect ideas — for one thing, that the evacuation of Egypt was only prevented by the Khedive's *coup d'état.* He did not understand that the English Liberal party had long before surrendered to Rosebery. About the state of things here we did not talk except that the Sultan would certainly support Abbas as long as he opposed us in Egypt, and that no claim would be put forward by Abdul Hamid of interfering with the Administration there. Altogether a satisfactory visit. There seems a good chance now of my getting my audience at Yildiz, but I told Jemal ed Din that I cannot wait longer than Monday.

" *27th April.*— To the bazaars with Judith and the Walter Blunts (General Walter Blunt Pasha, an A.D.C. of the Sultan, who had called two or three days ago with his wife claiming relationship, though I hardly know on what ground). He talked of his family as connected with Plaw Hatch, in Sussex, a fine-looking old man in a very smart uniform. He has been in the Turkish service since 1878. On our return we found Jemal ed Din and Ibrahim Moelhi calling on Anne, who told us wonderful tales of the system of Palace management. It is arranged that I am to be taken by the superintendent of the Musáfir Khaneh to see Munir Pasha to-morrow during the Selamlik. I am not to ask for an audience, but only to deliver my letter from Mukhtar Pasha. They seem to think, however, that it will require a week or more to prepare the ground for an audience, since nothing here can be done in a hurry. I am determined all the same to leave on Monday, for if I am to do any good I must be back in England before Whitsuntide. The one practical question I want to ask the Sultan is whether, if the English Government were willing to open negotiations on the lines of the Wolff Convention, he also would be willing, but Jemal ed Din thinks it would be impossible at a first audience to go so far as that.

"*28th April.*— To the Selamlik with Judith and the Walter Blunts (Anne being still laid up), a really splendid spectacle. It was held in front of the new mosque at Yildiz, and everything had been done to make it impressive, as there were ninety officers of the French fleet present, brought especially by the Sultan's yachts from the Dardanelles. Sarah Bernhardt, too, was there, to whom the display must have had a special spectacular meaning. What interested me most was the large number of Mohammedan Sheykhs and dignitaries from distant provinces of the empire, who followed the prayer outside the mosque and took part in the procession. This has been the triumph of Abdul Hamid's reign. In one of the tribunes were a couple of old Druse Sheykhs in splendid attire, with whom I exchanged a few words, and one of them recognized me, having been at Salkhat when Anne and I passed through it on our way to Nejd in 1878. They were then, and as late as 1881, at war with the Sultan, now they are his guests, clothed in robes of honour.

"When it was over I went with General Blunt to call on Emin Pasha, the Chamberlain, and got from him permission to visit the Imperial Arab stud at the Sweet Waters; the General would have gone with me also to Munir Pasha, but I explained that perhaps Munir would sooner see me alone; so presently the superintendent came for me and took me to Munir. There was with him an officious little man whom I afterwards found to be Guarracino, the 'Times' correspondent; but Munir sent him away. He then read my letter from Mukhtar and became cordial. We talked a little about the affairs of Egypt, and a little about my travels, and he said he would inform the Sultan of my arrival.

"In the Diplomatic Box which we occupied at the Selamlik, I found our old friend Sabunji,[1] now in fine feather, having a permanent post as translator to the Sultan. He lives at Prinkipo and comes in twice a week to Yildiz. He told me he had had my article 'Lord Cromer and the Khedive' given him to translate, and that the Sultan certainly had read it. He advised me to ask for an audience, but I told him I had no time. General Blunt whispered me that he was 'a palace spy,' which of course he is, and therein lies his value; he may be of great use to us here. The day was lovely, the view splendid, and I enjoyed the pageant as I seldom do things of the sort.

"In the evening we drove to the Sweet Waters and were shown the

[1] See "Secret History."

Sultan's mares. There were, I believe, about 150 of them, all ' mares from the Arabs,' but the greater part of them of very small account. Among the herd, however, one was able to pick out about a dozen really good ones, and two or three of the first class. But there was no mare there at all equal to Ali Pasha Sherif's best, or the best of our own. The best I found had come from Ibn Rashid who, two years ago, sent thirty. But the Egyptian who manages the establishment tells me that they will insist upon tall horses, and I fancy the Bedouins who send the Sultan mares get the big ones on purpose for him, and keep the little ones, which are the best. There was a great hulking mare which Sotamm Ibn Shaalan had brought with him, one I feel sure was never foaled among the Roala. Of horses they showed us seven, the best being without comparison a Seglawi of Ali Pasha Sherif's, an exact match to our Shahwan. This was a really beautiful and perfect horse, but of diminutive size compared with the others, and so less esteemed here, though the Egyptian knew his worth. Next to him was an immensely showy chestnut from Ferhan Jerba, a beautifully topped horse of great quality, but a little overgrown, and, so the manager told me, less good at the stud than the other. Beyond these two there was not one I would have cared to own, two or three of them being quite unfit to breed from. The management of the stud is, I fancy, very defective, as there were certainly four mares out of five barren. There is, however, enough material to make a good stud out of. I should pick out twenty of the best and and sell the others. There were a good many black mares among them, sent as rarities, but I doubt if black is ever a good Arab colour. One of these came from Ibn Rashid and was the best; Sarah Bernhardt was also in the paddock looking on.

" Munir is rather a fine-looking man, with a vigorous, intelligent face, and modern manner — not at all one of the old-fashioned sleepy Pashas — and in all he says he goes straight to the point. He impressed me favourably.

" *29th April.*— Admiral Woods Pasha called on me and talked principally about the Armenian question. He says it has been grossly exaggerated in the London press; that he has seen the text of Newberry, the American Consul's Report, which is entirely favourable to the Sultan's Government, that the ' Times ' refused to publish it, that Sir Clare Ford had sent it home, but that the Foreign Office ignores it. He has written to the ' Daily Telegraph ' a rather weak letter headed, ' Justice to Turkey and the Turks.' But I told him justice was quite out of date now in England, and that he would get a better chance of a hearing if he did not speak of it. To be listened to one must threaten, not plead for mercy.

" To luncheon with the Sultan of Johor and his suite, including Mohammed Moelhi and Ahmed Pasha Ali, A.D.C. to Sultan Abdul

Hamid, who has been attached to Johore for the period of his stay. This Ahmed is the same who was sent to us by the Sultan nine years ago to show us over the palaces and treasury, a good-natured, courtly personage, said to be the most be-decorated of any in Turkey. Our conversation at table was a regular Tower of Babel, for though we were only ten people, we were talking five different languages, English, French, Turkish, Arabic, and Malay.

"In the afternoon we went with the Walter Blunts to see the Sultan's stables at Yildiz — first, however, to call on the director of it, Izzet Pasha, the most European Oriental I have ever met. We found him in trouble, his son having attempted to commit suicide the day before through a love affair. He talked of this quite as a European might. He was sitting in his house near Yildiz, in a rough kind of smoking suit, his hair *en brosse,* and no fez — rather a picturesque looking man, who might have been a French or Italian artist. One certainly would never have guessed him an Oriental. He talked a good deal of heresy about horse-breeding, declared that nine out of ten Arabs had unsound hocks (an absurdity), and they were all unsound one way or the other. He says there is hardly a horse or mare sent by the Bedouins to the Sultan which would pass a veterinary examination. This may perhaps be true, as I daresay they pass on their unsound ones when they are making presents, to say nothing of the horses they send getting changed on their road to Constantinople.

"At the stables, which are inside Yildiz Park wall, we found a splendid collection of stallions arranged in stalls according to their colours, gray, black, or bay — very few chestnuts. Among these the most remarkable were, I think, half-a-dozen brought by Nasr el Ashgar, Sheykh of the Montefik, and several very fine ones from Mohammed Ibn Rashid, and others presented singly by Walys of Bagdad. There were some enormously powerful horses among the bays, and one very fine black horse from Ibn Rashid. But there was unfortunately no intelligent person to explain, nor anybody who knew Arabic, except a black slave. In the first stable there were about sixty horses, nearly all of high quality, but we could not have more than two or three led out, so it was impossible really to judge them. Beyond these were a couple of hundred more, inferior ones, in another stable, and yet a third and fourth stable with European animals. A very old white Arab horse was shown us as the Sultan's favourite for riding, but they say he seldom gets on horseback. Altogether the grandest Arab collection I have seen, and far superior in quality to the mares we saw yesterday.

"Dined at Ahmed Ali's in Stamboul with Johore and his suite; a dull dinner in the modern Turkish style, with music during it — which I hate. Our host showed us with pride some astonishing daubs he had perpetrated at Paris twenty years ago, and some of which he had even exhibited. He had also painted his dining-room walls not badly with representations of orange and lemon trees in tubs.

" On my return I found that Munir had called, but I shall not put off my departure unless I have an audience fixed for a special day and hour. Mohammed is to find this out definitely and bring me word to-morrow.

" 1st *May*.— A dull morning, with a Black Sea fog and cold. Hearing nothing from the Palace, we have taken our places by to-night's Orient express. Called on Ford to say good-bye, also on Woods Pasha. Yesterday I saw Jemal ed Din at Nishantash. He was urgent I should stay on to see the Sultan, and said he would go at once to the Chief Chamberlain to get a definite answer. But no answer has come. I called also on Abdullah Pasha Nejdi (Ibn Thennayan Ibn Saoud) at his house in Yildiz. He lamented being kept a prisoner here and longed to be back in Nejd. But the Sultan is kind to him. I went with Serrur the Soudani.

" To-day Sabunji called. He came here two years ago with some Englishmen to get a railway concession, which came to nothing, but he stayed on till the Sultan, hearing of him through Munif Pasha, sent for him and made him translator. He now has to read and digest all the newspapers of England, France, and Italy, and to write *précis* of their contents in Turkish for the Sultan. He sees the Sultan from time to time and sometimes talks to him about European politics or history or archaeology, of which Abdul Hamid is fond. He gets £40 a month and a house at Prinkipo, and so is in clover. He says the Sultan in afraid to employ good men in high positions for fear they should become too popular. Thus Saïd Pasha was dismissed a year and a half ago because he had become popular with the army by paying the soldiers regularly. Lately, Vincent went to the Sultan with proofs of the roguery of the Minister of Marine. The Sultan gave him in return another paper wherein the same and many more robberies were recorded. He had long known all about it.

" At two Ibrahim Moelhy came to beseech me to stay on a few days till next Thursday, only another twenty-four hours, but I was obdurate. ' I am not a *fakir*,' I said, ' to sit at the Palace door waiting. I am not the Sultan's servant, nor will I dance attendance on any king in the world. If the Sultan wants to see me he must send and say so and I will come, but to-night I go home.' So he went back to Nishantash.

" At five came the Sultan of Johore with Mohammed Moelhi, who has just received the second class of the Mejidieh from Abdul Hamid. So they are all happy. At six Ibrahim and Mohammed returned to see us to the train. All now is satisfactorily settled. We are to go as arranged to England, but Jemal ed Din is so to manage matters that the

Sultan will send for me some time during the summer, and he will obtain for Anne the Chefket Order in diamonds as a sign of extreme favour. In the meantime I am to write to Jemal ed Din letters which he can show to the Sultan on political affairs in England. Thus I shall be his unaccredited Ambassador. The two matters they want principally to be informed about are Armenia and Egypt. And so, much pleased with all that has happened during our week's stay at Constantinople, we are off and away."

Thus ended the eventful spring of 1893 and my part in what happened during it at Cairo. On our way back from Constantinople I note:

" *2nd May.*— In the train all day crossing the great plain of Eastern Roumelia, the Balkans to the north and the Rhodope range to the south, a splendid plain full of storks and large birds of prey, with a few rollers — frogs croaking gaily, bright sunshine. This part of Bulgaria seems very prosperous — the peasants still in their national costume, the villages still with their minarets, though most of the Mohammedan population is gone.

" Mr. Thompson, the U.S. Minister at Constantinople, is in the train. Ford had given me a note of introduction to him. He has told me much about Armenia, having just sent in a report on the subject to his Government. He says that it is proved the Armenians intended a revolt on the 5th January, but were betrayed by one of their own people. The placards inciting the people to rise were printed in England — no Turks were concerned in it. Also he tells me the whole resident Armenian census is under three-quarters of a million as against five millions of Mohammedans. The only province where the Christians outnumber the Moslems is Kaisariyeh, the smallest of the villayets — there they may be three to one. There was some reason for their discontent in the way of injustice, especially through the tyranny of a certain ex-brigand, Kurshid Pasha, chief of the police, but the measures taken by the Government were not very severe. All the prisoners have now been released except 200, and these he had been promised should not be severely punished though reserved for trial. He has been acting in concert with Ford in the matter. He says emphatically that there is not the material in Armenia to make a nation, though the Christian Armenians desire it. Their brethren under Russia would revolt too if they dared. The Catholic Armenians are with the rest in desiring independence. The whole movement has been got up in England and with English help.

" *3rd May.*— Thompson tells me there may be trouble with Russia at Constantinople soon, as the young King of Servia wants to go there and do homage, while the Russian Emperor is opposed to it. The Russians supported the Regency at Belgrade and are angry with the King.

He talked also of American politics and the desire in Canada for annexation to the U.S., the U.S. being unwilling on account of the large half-Indian, half-French population, one million, and 160,000 naturalized Chinese. He says, however, it must come about, through reasons of interest for the Canadians.

"Passed to-day through Hungary — many well bred horses. The gray breed of cattle extends from Constantinople to Pesth. It seems the same as the Roman breed, but with variation. In Turkey the shape is nearer to the Highland Scotch breed.

"*4th May.*— Passing through Germany we got English papers with an account of the debate in Parliament on Dilke's Egyptian motion. The French papers express disappointment. To me it seems most reassuring. Gladstone clearly and emphatically repudiates *indefinite* occupation — talks of convening a European Conference as soon as the condition of things in Egypt returns to the normal. This *must* put a stop to Cromer's annexation policy."

CHAPTER VI

CROMER'S HEAVY HAND

On my return to England after this eventful winter I found myself, a rare thing in my public life, almost popular. I was considered to have got the better of Cromer in our Egyptian battle, and that Cromer had blundered badly in his diplomacy. Labouchere, whom I called on first, promised help about getting up an Egyptian Committee, and that he would consult Dilke about it. "As to Gladstone," he told me, "the question of evacuating Egypt is one merely of his parliamentary majority. 'Can you show me a majority?' the old man says, when questioned about it; he cares nothing any longer for any political question, even Ireland, only to stay in power. His answer to Dilke about Egypt was a mere juggling with words and meant nothing."

I write the same day, *May* 9, "I found George Wyndham, with Henley, the hospital poet (a bitter talker, but a sayer of good things), much pleased with his own parliamentary success, now he is in opposition and free to talk as he pleases. He expressed only a modified disapproval of my doings in Egypt. I gather from him that even the Conservatives think Baring has made a mess of things."

" 11*th May.*— To Downing Street, where Harcourt received me with a slight show of severity at first. 'I hear,' he said, 'you have been raising up no end of trouble in Egypt. Cromer says you have been combining against him with Mukhtar Pasha and the Sultan, and the Khedive, to bring back Arabi, and that you are the instigator of all that happened four months ago.' I said, 'I was an accomplice after the fact, not its instigator,' and gave him in brief what had happened. 'Well,' he said, laughing, 'I suppose we shall have to put in force the old statute, *Ne exeat regno,* to keep you from mischief.' While we were talking, Eddy Hamilton came in, but this did not interrupt the conversation. 'The worst of it is,' said Sir William, 'that it puts your friends into a difficult position. Mr. Gladstone, Morley, and I, are strongly for evacuation, but while there is trouble in Egypt this is impossible.' I asked him, 'Can you really tell me that you would have negotiated for an exacuation if nothing of this had happened? Would you not have argued that while things are going on so well, and we were doing so much good in Egypt, it would be better to let well alone?' 'We should certainly have begun negotiations,' he said. He then asked about the influence of the French in Egypt, and said that if the French were willing to negotiate on the basis of the Drummond Wolff Convention there would be no difficulty, but he had lately asked Waddington (the French Ambassador), and Waddington had answered that the French Government could hardly approve now what it had so strenuously opposed six years ago. Waddington had also maintained that France had been given definite rights in Egypt by England at the Congress of Berlin. Sir William wanted to know about this, and I told him of the terms made between Salisbury and Waddington for the seizure of Tunis, equal rights in Egypt and privileges in Syria. I told him, too, of my conversation with d'Estournelles whom I had met as I crossed over to England on the 5th, and had been introduced to by Alfred Lyall who happened to be on board. I had discussed the whole Egyptian question with him till half way across the Channel, when the sea stopped us, and had found him very sympathetic with my views. 'Well,' said Harcourt, when you write to your friends in Egypt tell them to keep quiet, and we will in a very short time begin negotiations. The difficulty is in the country and in the House of Commons, where we should not have a majority in favour of evacuation, and also with the French Government.' I repeated to him my talk with d'Estournelles, and that I was sure the French Government would agree easily enough after the General Elections. 'Do you authorize me,' I asked, 'to say to my friends at Cairo that if they will work harmoniously with Cromer, we will enter on negotiations for a withdrawal of the troops, say in the autumn?' He said, 'Yes,' But at this Eddy Hamilton made a grimace of dissent and he corrected himself. 'I can authorize you to say what Mr. Gladstone said in the House of Commons the other day.' We parted in all amity, he joking about the possibility of my having been seen in Downing Street at his door. 'Rosebery,' he said, 'has doubtless got his touts on the look out for you, and I must beg you, when you come again, to put on a false nose. I will let you out through the garden gate.' Eddy will, I feel sure, repeat all this to Rosebery, but I do not care if he does.

"Coming home to Wentworth House (where we were staying for the season), I found Lady Lytton, and took a walk with her. She tells me that Lord Salisbury is so angry with Cromer for his mismanagement of affairs at Cairo that he says he is unfit to succeed Lord Lansdowne in India, so no wonder Cromer is angry with me. I am quite satisfied with the way my action has been taken in the official world, and I think Lady Lytton sees that after all I was right.

"*12th May.*— Lunched with George Wyndham, and again found Henley there, and with them a clever young man, Whibley, who writes for him in the 'National Observer.' George gave us some admirable descriptions of battle scenes he had been present at in the Soudan, and set before us the things he had seen and felt as one reads them in Kipling.

"*14th May (Sunday)*.— Spent the morning writing to the Sheykh el Bekri. Then to see Loulou Harcourt who is in bed at a private hospital for some slight operation, but is able to receive friends. He says he expects the Government to win at the General Elections next year, as they will take other bills besides the Home Rule Bill and appeal to the country against the Lords.

"*21st May*.— Lunched with d'Estournelles. He professes the greatest admiration for my politics, but that I suspect is because I oppose English policy in Egypt.

"*1st June*.— Dined at Lady Galloway's in Upper Grosvenor Street, Philip Currie being there with others. She is by birth a Cecil, half sister to Lord Salisbury, an altogether noble soul."

This marks the beginning of a friendship which put me in connection with the Cecil section of the Conservative party and their ideas of foreign policy. Lady Galloway who spent much of her time travelling, was of considerable use to her brother in regard to what was passing on the Continent.

"*5th June*.— Gave a dinner in Mount Street to Margot and Betty Balfour, Harry Cust and d'Estournelles; the latter, who came in full uniform on his way to a State Concert, was very amusing, giving us his ideas about English women and English men.

"*12th June*.— I hear from Lefevre that the despatches exchanged between Rosebery and Cromer are 'most curious.' Cromer was for the wildest violence against the Khedive, but he was given a douche which has brought him to his senses. He is, however, quite out of favour.

"*17th June*.— With Judith and Anne to a garden party at Kew, given by George Lefevre in his official capacity (as Commissioner of the Board of Works). The party was to meet at the pier of the House of Commons, and go up the river in two steamers. As we did not know precisely where the pier was we stopped outside the House of Lords to ask a policeman.

"Dialogue:

"*I.* 'Can you tell me where I shall find the pier of the House of Commons?'

"*Policeman.* 'What peer did you say?'

"*I.* 'The pier of the House of Commons.'

"*Policeman.* 'No, sir, indeed, we have plenty of peers of the House of Lords, but I never yet heard of a peer of the House of Commons.'"

On the boat with us were old Maud Stanley, Carlisle, Maisie Stanley and her daughter, Lord and Lady Denbigh, T. P. O'Connor and his **wife and the Mathew family, Justin McCarthy, Lord Acton and Lady**

Harcourt, a very pleasant party, and a day of tropical heat. The party had been invited to meet the Teck family, who arrived for tea, with the Duke of York and Princess May.

" *21st June.*— To a party at Lady Salisbury's, where I again met Prince George and Princess May.

" *27th June.*— Lunched with Lady Galloway, where I met Mackenzie Wallace; then on to Grosvenor Square, where Margot was entertaining Princess Hélène and a dozen more ladies to see the performance of a Spanish dancer, Candida Lopez.

" *28th June.*— To an open air play at Pope's Villa at Twickenham, where Labouchere was our entertainer, a queer *omnium gatherum,* conspicuous among the guests being Sir William Harcourt, Monty Corry, and numerous Irish members. Most of these last I had not seen since my retirement from Home Rule politics. They were very cordial. ' We treated you very badly,' Healy said, ' in not giving you an Irish seat, we ought to have made an exception in your favour.' ' Indeed,' I said, ' I am very glad you did not.' Dr. Kenny and John Redmond spoke to me in the same sense. I was especially glad to meet Dillon, and had some talk with him about Egypt. He told me the last two years had been the hardest and most thankless work he had ever had to do.

" The play was ' The Tempest,' done with Sullivan's music, pretty but quite inept. Certainly Shakespeare was here at his very worst. What can be stupider than Caliban and the drunken sailors ? The other characters pompous and flat. But beautiful songs. Ariel was wonderfully well acted by Dora Labouchere, a child of ten.

" *30th June.*— With Judith to lunch with Burne-Jones, where he had asked her to sit to him. His wife and son, and sister-in-law, Mrs. Kipling, were there. During the two hours' sitting he had of Judith he was most entertaining, telling us stories of William Morris's oddities. One of the chairs in the studio we observed was rickety. ' Yes,' he said, ' Morris has sat in them all, and he has a muscular movement in his back peculiar to himself, which makes the rungs fly out.' He and Morris are devoted friends, and Morris comes every Sunday to spend the morning with him, and has done so for, I think he said, thirty years. ' I have never taken a fortnight's holiday away from London,' he went on, ' for twenty-three years. That is because I am constitutionally idle. Millais used to say of me, when we were young men, that I was so lazy that when I began to work, I was too lazy to stop. And so it has always been. I have constantly wished to get away to Egypt and to Mount Sinai and to Jerusalem, but I am deterred by the thought that I can get to any of these places in a week. I should like it to take at least six months, travelling slowly through France and Italy, and arriving gradually, so as to be two years away. As this is impossible

I stay on in North End Grove. The garden here is a constant pleasure to me, because I say to myself, my neighbours are calculating how much it is worth a foot for building.' And so on and so on, always with a delightful humour and a voice of sweetest calibre. The drawing meanwhile got rapidly finished, though it seemed as if he had done nothing but talk. It was a lovely sketch in red chalk. [This drawing was to have been given to Judith, but somehow it never reached her, and must have been sold, we think, with the rest of his drawings after his death. We have been unable to trace it.] He was very complimentary about Judith, and was quite affectionate to me at parting. This put us in good spirits, and we rushed away down to Crabbet, Judith's London season being over. She tells me she has enjoyed it immensely.

" *1st July.*— Crabbet. Annual meeting of the Crabbet Club. We sat down over twenty to dinner, and did not leave the table till half-past one. The members present were:

George Curzon.	Hubert Howard.
George Leveson Gore.	Godfrey Webb.
George Wyndham.	Percy Wyndham.
George Peel (the 4 Georges)	Loulou Harcourt.
Morpeth.	Theodore Fry.
Mark Napier.	Theobald Mathew.
Harry Cust.	Charles Laprimaudaye,
Charles Gatty.	and Laurence Currie.

" St. George Lane Fox, and two new men, Esmé Howard and Eddy Tennant.

" George Curzon was, as usual, the most brilliant, he never flags for an instant either in speech or repartee; after him George Wyndham, Mark Napier, and Webber. The next day, Sunday, Harry Cust won the Tennis Cup, and the Laureateship was adjudged to Curzon.

" *16th July.*— The French have been attacking Siam in a way dangerous to the general peace. We were giving a Saturday to Monday party at Crabbet, and George Curzon arrived full of the case. He was to have adjourned the House yesterday, but Rosebery begged him not, as Develle, the French Prime Minister, had explained that he was isolated in his Cabinet in favour of conciliatory measures, all the other Ministers backing up the French Admiral. George asked Rosebery point blank whether he could say that the English Government would resist all attempt on the part of the French to violate the independence of Siam west of the river Mekong, and Rosebery assured him that they would do so. I had some talk also with Philip Currie who is here, about it and about Egypt. He condemned Baring's policy of the last few years, especially as to judicial reforms, and agreed with many of my own views on other points. He said of Dufferin that he had been a failure in Paris. Dufferin had left Paris in a huff at the continued attacks made on him in the French press. George Curzon was very amusing.

"*2nd Aug.*— My news from Paris is (from a source within the Embassy) that Dufferin has been undoubtedly a failure there; he is too fond of paying little insincere compliments, and his wife is too ungenial. There is a very bitter feeling in all classes now against England, and just at this moment it is at fever heat about Siam. After a deal of swagger Rosebery has knuckled down. It is a robbers' quarrel over their spoils.

"*17th Aug.*— Osman Bey Ghaleb was here at luncheon, a very intelligent man. He left Egypt in the middle of June, and stayed a month or more at Constantinople, being there when the Khedive came to do homage. He tells me that great preparations had been made to receive Abbas, but at the last moment the Sultan was frightened and counterordered everything, so that Abbas was received meanly by half-a-dozen inferior officials, none above the rank of Bey. In public this attitude was maintained throughout towards him, but privately, Osman says, it was different, and the Sultan received the Khedive four or five times quite alone and had long talks with him. On going away Abbas declared openly to his suite that his journey had been a failure, but this he thinks was merely to throw dust in English eyes, for he said, ' Abbas is a proud young man, and if he had really been ill received by the Sultan he would never have returned to Cairo, he would have thrown himself overboard first.' It is difficult to understand the Sultan's object in all this. Osman lays it entirely on his timidity. The English Ambassador, he says, bullied him (poor Ford!) on the Armenian question, and frightened him with threats of intervention, but what folly! Even Gladstone could hardly bombard Constantinople or seize the ports of the Hedjaz.[1]

"*23rd Aug.*— We had a private performance this evening of my play, ' The Bride of the Nile,' the Lytton girls acting it, and Lady Clare Feilding and Judith." [N.B. I had written this extravaganza while in Egypt as a relief to my feelings, and to make fun of Baring and the British Occupation, taking as my text an incident narrated by Abulfeda as having happened at the time of the Arab invasion by Amru, when the relations between Egypt and the Roman Empire were not unlike those now existing with the British Empire. The play with our home circle at Crabbet had a considerable success.]

I spent the month of September in Scotland making a family tour of

---

[1] This Osman Ghaleb became afterwards the principal friend and supporter of the National Leader, Mustapha Kamel.

visits; to the Glen, Lochnaw, and Cumloden, but there is nothing in my diary of any public interest. On our way back, I find:

"10*th Oct.*— At Saighton. Spencer Lyttleton came to-day from Hawarden to luncheon and we had a great discussion about the Poet Laureateship. He declares that Gladstone will in all probability not make any appointment to the office. The general sense of the Government is in favour of Swinburne, and it has been ascertained that Swinburne would like to be appointed, but the Queen is opposed on account of the immorality of his early songs, and also on account of his having written against the Russian Emperor (he had suggested his assassination many years before, and the Queen, who regarded the Laureateship as an office in her personal household, considered that this made him absolutely impossible as a candidate). 'The one thing we are afraid of,' Lyttleton said, 'is having Lewis Morris thrust on us. William Morris will not take it, and so no appointment will be made."

"23*rd Oct.*— Once more at Crabbet. Yesterday we had a visit from Baron de Nölde, a Russian traveller, who has just come back from Nejd, where he has seen Ibn Rashid. He carried a letter of introduction with him from the Sultan Abdul Hamid who, he said, made use of him as an informal envoy to bring him word of the exact state of affairs in Arabia. Mohammed Ibn Aruk (our old travelling companion in 1878) went with him, and they followed the same route as we did from Damascus to Haïl except that they crossed the Nefud at a point farther to the east. At Haïl Nölde found Hamoud Ibn Rashid acting as Regent, and was forwarded on by him to the Emir Ibn Rashid by way of Bereyda and Shaggra to his camp near Riad. The Emir entertained him there for ten days, then sent him back with a present of a mare and two deluls to Meshed Ali. Nölde says his journey cost him £6,000, ours cost us about £200. He is a very clever man with a very forbidding face, not unlike Burton's. He stayed the whole day with us and showed some knowledge of Arab horses.

"4*th Nov.*— I have been much occupied during this week about the Matabele War, which has at last come to fighting and much slaughter of black men by white. I took counsel on the subject with the good Evelyn, who was for two nights at Crabbet, and we agreed to make some demonstration of our disapproval. In the meanwhile I have written strongly to T. P. O'Connor on the subject, upbraiding him and the other Irish members for their silence.

"5*th Nov.*— To London early, and called upon Lady Harcourt, with whom was Lord Spencer, a worthy, ponderous man, who complained of the calls made on him at the Admiralty from all parts of the Empire.

"Lady Lytton sends me a letter she received two months ago from Sir Henry Loch (the High Commissioner at the Cape) giving his view of the coming Matabele difficulty. 'It began,' he said, 'by Lobengula, who has not abandoned his rights over the Mashonas, sending a regiment to collect taxes, kill the people, and take cattle.' They did so to some extent in Fort Victoria; then Dr. Jameson ordered a small mounted force to charge — when two chiefs and thirty Matabeles were killed. 'The situation,' he says, 'is somewhat complicated, for while the Company have administrative authority over Mashonaland, they are still, as regards political matters, under my control, and, moreover, the country under my direct administration must be affected by what the Company may do. Probably the Protectorate would be the first to be attacked by Lobengula, should there be war. I have some strong positions and a powerful police force supported, if necessary, by native levies, but still not strong enough to carry the war into the enemy's country and force a battle away from supports. The danger is the Company, as soon as they are a little better prepared, may bring about fighting, as they can't stand long armed and waiting for events with the possible view of committing H.M.'s Government in their quarrel. So I am obliged to watch both friend and enemy, and if fighting once begins, the conduct of it will fall entirely upon me, while if I do anything the Company can lay hold of as causing them commercial loss, either by checking their fighting or by encouraging them to do so, that will enable them to say to Her Majesty's Government: "If it had not been for the action of the High Commissioner we should not have incurred these losses, and they might in consequence endeavour to obtain compensation for these alleged losses out of the Government."'

"This is a good example of the way in which these Colonial wars are begun.

"*9th Nov.*— To Westminster with intent to see Labouchere, who is bringing on the Matabele case in Parliament to-day, but he was out.

"Then to lunch by invitation of Loulou at 11, Downing Street. Sir William was there looking, I thought, older and less healthy than when I saw him last, in less good spirits, too, than is his wont, but he told us some good stories as the meal went on, the other guests being Mildmay and his wife, a sister of Lady Harcourt. When alone with me afterwards in his official room he began complaining of the brutality of the British public, which insisted upon the slaughter of the Matabeles to procure itself markets for its goods. 'It used,' he said, 'to be slaughter for the glory of the thing, but they have given that up now, now it is slaughter for trade.' I asked: 'But why do you do it?' 'Oh,' he said, 'we are all burglars now.' I said: 'If you will allow me to say it, you are in the position of a bishop who burgles a church. Why do you not disapprove?' 'Bishops,' he said, 'are always the first to lay their hands on property when they can do it. I remember Bright telling me that he never knew a bishop express disapproval of a war but once, and that was a war to put down the slave trade.' *I.—*

'You complain of public opinion, but you let the official press, "The Daily News" and the rest, either preach up these wars or sit on silent till it is too late.' *He.*—'The papers are in the hands of the financiers.' I fancy he has done what he could to stop the raid on the Matabeles, but that Rosebery and the commercial Jingoes in the Cabinet have been too strong for him. I asked him whether they were going to do anything in the direction of evacuating Egypt. He said: 'No, nothing at all. The young Khedive has behaved like an ass. He insisted upon going to Constantinople, to get the Sultan to take up his case against us, and the French Government, too, has been absurd. We shall do nothing.' I said, 'I do not see that these are reasons. I hold to my opinion that we shall get into trouble yet about Egypt.' I asked him finally whether Cromer was going to stay on at Cairo. He said, 'Yes, for anything I know to the contrary.' Then he relapsed into his cigar and I went into the inner room to talk with Loulou about Harry Cust's marriage.

"*10th Nov.*— There has been a better debate upon the Matabele case in Parliament than I expected, though the Irish were dumb and the Government justified their Matabele slaughter. Gladstone surpassed himself in the use of his double tongue. He is a shameless old hypocrite as the world has ever seen. I have determined to oppose him what little I can at the next elections. The spectacle of Gladstone, Morley, and the Irish members supporting this anti-human policy in Africa is enough to make dynamiters of us all.

"Baron de Nölde came again in the evening with his cousin, Count de Kreutz. They are projecting a new journey in Central Africa, to start from Zanzibar and go to Khartoum. On their last journey (in Arabia) they took with them 300 bottles of Champagne, 100 of Madeira, and 100 of brandy, and drank them all their two selves.

"I have written to Labouchere offering to help him, if I can, about South Africa.

"*15th Nov.*— Drove over to see Fred'k Locker at Rowfant, and wish him good-bye. He and Evelyn are the only two friends left me in Sussex. Our leave-taking was not a little pathetic for this reason.

"*16th Nov.*— To London, and lunched at Hammersmith. Morris full of the coal war, and the proposed settlement of it by Rosebery. He said the miners had gone the wrong way to work by throwing themselves out of employment and starving. They ought to have refused to work and gone to the workhouse. This would have thrown the whole cost of the war on the masters, 'but,' he said, 'they have an idea of honour in the matter, which I suppose had to be reckoned with.' All I see in it is the strengthening of Rosebery's position, and with it the final disappearance of the ideas of 1880. Evelyn has written to the Committee of the Irish National League at Deptford, to say that he can no longer support Gladstone at the elections. I have been writing to Redmond, but doubt if I shall send my letter. Dined with Lady Gregory."

It was, I think, about this time that I severed my connection with the Arbitration and Peace Society, stating as my reason for doing so that I found the ideas of the Society would be of no profit if realized to the backward races of mankind, or to prevent wars by white men against them, whereas a general war in Europe might possibly give them a time of peace on the principle that when thieves fall out honest men come by their own. " There is talk of Philip Currie going as Ambassador to Constantinople."

"*24th Nov.*— My last visit before leaving London for the winter was to Frederic Harrison, whom I found preparing a lecture he is to deliver to-night. He was glad, however, to see me, and I had half an hour's talk with him. We discussed the Matabele case, on which we are in accord, though neither of us having special knowledge we are unable to take action, nor does he propose to do so, considering that Labouchere has dealt with it as well as it can be dealt with. ' The Government is afraid of Rhodes,' is the whole history of the case. We then talked about Egypt, and I told him of my two conversations with Harcourt in May and again the other day. He told me that as late as June, Morley had told him that he and Gladstone and Asquith and Mundella, and Lefevre were of one mind for evacuation, and that he, Morley, had declared that he intended to have it out with Rosebery, and that if a contrary policy was persisted in one or other would have to leave the Cabinet. I gave him my opinion of the gravity of the Franco-Russian Alliance, of the ferment there was in India shown by the Anti Cow-killing league, and of the position at Cairo.

"He asked me if I knew anything of the reasons why Sir Henry Norman had refused the Viceroyalty of India after accepting it, and he told me a curious story of how Norman had come to him during the Afghan campaign, and while he was a member of the Indian Council, and had given him the most intimate and full information of all that was going on, and how he had come over and over again with details and documents avowedly to help him, Harrison, in his attack on the Indian Government. Norman's appointment to the Viceroyalty would seem to be a late reward by Gladstone for the political service which was no doubt largely instrumental in bringing about Disraeli's overthrow at the elections of 1880. I have agreed to let Harrison know how things stand in Egypt when I get there. I shall also write an article for the ' Nineteenth Century.'

" We left in the evening for Brindisi."

My winter in Egypt of 1893–94 was made noteworthy by a new political crisis, and a new battle between the Khedive and Lord Cromer,

in which Kitchener played a first prominent part, what is known as the
" Frontier Incident." Here again, as in the former instance, though
an accessory after the fact I was not an accomplice, my advice being
taken about it by the Khedive when it was no longer of any use to him.
The entries in my diary show how greatly the facts of the case differ
from those recorded in the Blue Books, and are therefore of interest.

" *28th Nov.*— On board the *Hydaspes*. The only fellow passengers I have made acquaintance with are Lady Waterford and Sir
John Stokes, the latter on his way to the Suez Canal of which he is
Director, to open a new railroad from Port Said to Ismaïlia. With
Stokes I have had much talk about the Suez Canal, British trade and
the Mediterranean route in time of war. He tells me three-quarters
of the tonnage passing through the Canal is British, of which perhaps
half is for English ports, the rest for other ports in Europe. In time
of war with France, this could not continue. The Red Sea was quite
safe, but the whole line of the Mediterranean would be blocked, and
this would continue until the British had broken up the enemy's forces
and confined them to their ports, then convoys could be arranged and
trade resumed. He considers that it would require sixty or seventy
more men-of-war than we have at present to effect this as against the
French navy. He is for making the increase, not for abandoning the
control of the Mediterranean. He considers that the Canal will eventually be internationalized, though by the terms of the concession it will
revert to Egypt in 1959, but ' nobody looks so far as that ahead.'
Stokes reminded me that our first acquaintance dates from the time of
Cave's Mission in 1875, of which he was a member. He is a
stolid old fellow of the out-of-date military type, being a General in
the army.

" *5th Dec.*— My first twenty-four hours at Sheykh Obeyd were a
dream of light-hearted happiness, such as I do not remember since a
child; it was a physical feeling of perfect pleasure, perfect health, and
perfect powers of enjoyment without the least shadow of annoyance.
We arrived at Alexandria on the 1st of December in time to catch the
9 o'clock train to Cairo, and then straight on home in brilliant sparkling weather with just a little freshness in the North wind, the thermometer at 72. Everything on the way was a pleasure, even the new
houses built at Koubbah, and our little railway station at Ezbet el
Nakl, lovely and familiar in its palm grove. Inside the garden all was
paradise. No misadventure this year of any kind, but a blooming look
of extravagant growth, trees, crops, and flowers, the house so shut in
with green we can hardly any longer get a glimpse out into the desert,
hardly even from the house top. Cows prosperous, mares in foal,
every servant happy. Each year decides me more to spend the remnant of my days in the East, where old age is respected, and its repose

respectable. Of news we have as yet heard little; poor Ahmed Bey Sennari (a neighbour) is dead; old Eid Diab, too, gathered to his fathers, and Prince Ibrahim, our neighbour on the other side, gone in an apoplectic fit, or as the fellahin round here say, 'poisoned' by his uncle Ismaïl, whose daughter he recently married, but left behind at Constantinople. 'Ismaïl, I suppose, was angry,' I suggested. 'Oh no,' they said, 'it was on account of the inheritance, three twenty-fourths of which will have come to her. Ismaïl has poisoned very many people for their money '— such is the talk.

"*8th Dec.— Visitors.* Mahmud Bey from Menoufieh, an old fox, formerly Arabist, his object to borrow £30, which he did not get. He tells me Riaz and Mukhtar are now working harmoniously with Cromer.

Selim Bey Faraj, another neighbour, who has let his land at £5 the feddan, etc., etc.

"*9th Dec.—* Mohammed Moelhi called. He tells me the Khedive's reception at Constantinople was as bad as could be. He is now angry with the Sultan, and angry with Mukhtar, who persuaded him to go there; has quarrelled with Tigrane on a personal matter; cannot get Riaz to go fairly with him. Riaz lets things slide as when last in office, giving in to Cromer in all important matters, only from time to time making show of opposition. Nevertheless the English don't like him, and want to get rid of him; so, he says, would the Khedive, too, but he has nobody but Mazlum to put in his place. The Khedive wished the Legislative Council to oppose the estimate for the extra regiments of Occupation this year, but Riaz has yielded the point and nothing will be done. Thus Abbas every day is losing prestige in the country, and the trimmers are making their peace with Cromer.

"The journey to Constantinople was a fatal move. Some strong influence must have been brought to bear on the Sultan, German probably, and Abdul Hamid was partly frightened, partly bought, Mohammed thinks, by financial promises. Edgar Vincent was probably the medium of these. The Khedive has no option now but to keep quiet, maintaining himself as he can at the head of the National party and waiting his opportunity. It would be rash for him to take up the strong position he held in the spring now that he can no longer count on the Sultan. The Sultan was always the dangerous card in his hand.

"*15th Dec.—* Osman Ghaleb and Mohammed Moelhi to breakfast. Osman had an interview with Gladstone in England this autumn or summer. Gladstone asked him two questions: whether the English officials in Egypt were working hard and whether the late Khedive Tewfik was regretted. Osman's answer to the second question was that 'Death was always regretted, but the Egyptians were consoled by having his son Abbas.' Gladstone hoped that Abbas would become friendly to England as his father had been. Gladstone did not ask whether the Egyptians wished the Occupation to be discontinued.

"Colbeck, director of the Bank of Egypt, on whom I called, 15th December, was quite as pessimistic on the English side. He said our position at Cairo was becoming daily more ridiculous. Cromer could get none of his reforms carried through; he was opposed constantly by the Ministry; the Khedive was irreconcilable. Much as he admired Cromer he thought a change was necessary, as Cromer was without power. Cromer was willing to take an Embassy, and wanted Portal named in his place, but Portal was not clever enough, etc., etc. He had heard nothing of a split between Tigrane and the Khedive or with Riaz.

"*17th Dec.*—With Anne and Judith to call on Princesse Hélène and her brother, the Duc d'Orleans, at Shepherd's. The Duke is a fresh-faced, blond young man, good humoured, and good mannered. He has travelled over much wild country, and I talked to him of his experiences, especially in Somaliland, finding him sympathetic as to the advantages of uncivilized life and a contempt of Europe. He and his sister are on very pleasant terms together. On their return from up the Nile in March they will come and see us at Sheykh Obeyd.

"*22nd Dec.*—To Cairo and lunched with Tigrane. I found him very outspoken. He assured me that neither the Khedive nor anyone else at Cairo held me responsible for the use made of the Khedive's name in connection with my 'Nineteenth Century' article of last summer, and he hoped I would write another. As to the Khedive's visit to Constantinople, he declared it had not been otherwise than a success, that precisely the same ceremonial had been observed towards Abbas as formerly towards Ismaïl, that the Khedive had dined several times with the Sultan, who had been most kind to him. I asked him about the Khedive's proposed visit to England, but he told me nothing was yet settled, and I strongly advised that the Khedive should not go, at least as long as Cromer was here, for he would only be paraded as a tame bear, and the thing be counted as a triumph for English policy. If he insisted upon going he should at least go straight from Paris, where he would be fêted, then possibly English people would be polite to him, but it was a risk. He denied there having been any split between him and the Khedive; Riaz and he were on the best of terms. We talked very openly about the prospects of evacuation, and I told him that in my opinion it had been mainly determined by the larger question of peace and war with France, and the military advisability or otherwise of having a garrison in a disaffected Egypt. Tigrane is a clever man and a good talker, modest withal.

"*26th Dec.*—One Ibrahim Shafeï came with a complaint arising out of the Greek drink-shop established in the village of Merj. He was

watering his land near the railway station, and had to construct a
raised channel for the water across the footpath and the Greek objected
to this, as hindering access to his shop, though the land did not belong
to him and the fellah had a right to the waterway. The Greek cut the
channel, the fellah protested, the Greek struck the fellah with a stick,
the fellah took the stick from the Greek, then the Greek ran into his
shop and got out a gun which he pointed at the fellah, and the fellah
ran away but came back ten minutes later to reconstruct his channel,
then the Greek fired at him, fired and struck him, the fellah showed
me his legs and I found twenty-two shot marks in them, he had been
three weeks in hospital and was still weak. The Greek, when arrested,
avowed the deed, but nevertheless, after four days' detention, was let
out on bail, and is back at his shop.

" Nearly every day this month I have seen foxes in the garden when
I have ridden out before sunrise. There are three which I know by
sight, and old dog-fox, a vixen, and a year-old cub. They are very
tame, and I have watched them sometimes within a few yards of me for
ten minutes at a time. It is pretty to see them play and roll each other
over. This month is the breeding season and they are barking very
constantly in the garden (it is a peculiarity of a fox's bark that
whereas nearly all other wild cries seem to be nearer than they really
are, that of the fox sounds at a distance even when close by). I have
also seen one of the large cats called by Hassan Hashem, *kutt berri*
(desert cat). It is exactly like a small lioness, but higher on the leg,
the ears tipped with black and the tail with three black rings, the quarters rather drooping. It is very powerfully built. The Arabs eat these
cats when they can catch them and say they are very fat and good meat.

" *27th Dec.*— To Cairo to see Riaz, who had asked me to come to
him. I found the old man very affectionate and pleased to see me.
He talked in just the same strain as last year about Cromer and the
ill faith of the English government and Mr. Gladstone.

" About the Khedive's visit to Constantinople, he told me most positively first that it had been decided before His Highness went, between
him and his ministers, that he should not make any political proposals
to the Sultan — he said, ' I will swear this to you on the Koran.'
Secondly, that in fact His Highness had not made any, and that his
talk with the palace officials had been confined to his personal complaint
of Lord Cromer's rudeness. Lastly, that the Sultan had been more
than kind to him and had treated him more honourably than a Viceroy
of Egypt had ever been treated, so that the Khedive was perfectly satisfied with all. I asked him whether the Sultan might not have been
won over to the English policy in Egypt, and his face put on the most
expressively incredulous smile. ' You know,' he said, ' as well as I
do that even if in his heart he had such a thought he would not dare

express it.' He told me, too, of an attempt Cromer had made to impose an English doctor on the Khedive's party, which they had refused.

"We talked next about the action of the Legislative Council at Cairo which has refused to approve the expenses this year of the English Occupation, besides making a number of other objections, almost all to my mind very sensible ones. Riaz is clearly in sympathy with them, but he has rather weakly followed English dictation in rejecting most of them. He is doing, however, perhaps as much as is prudent in his opposition to Cromer. ' At least,' he said, ' we have lost no ground this year, if we have not gained as much as we wished.'

"About the Merj case, which I set before him, he amused me immensely by saying in answer to my remark that the Greek would end by killing someone outright, ' Would it not be better if *they* killed *him*?' He promised me to see justice done, and I am sure it will not be for want of his goodwill if nothing results, but Riaz is too old not to be timid in action. He introduced his son Mahmud to me, a little round Circassian whom he has made his under secretary of state [a piece of nepotism which was taken hold of effectively by Cromer, as the young man was quite incapable and was guilty of many stupidities]. He was most cordial in wanting to see me again. Riaz has a wonderful charm of manner, inspiring one with affection as well as respect, badly as he behaved in 1882. For this he is contrite now.

" *31st Dec.*— In answer to a question by Labouchere, Gladstone has said in Parliament that negotiations for evacuating Egypt must be entered into, if at all, with the Sultan, not with the Khedive.

" Mohammed Abdu lunched with us on Friday. He is very well satisfied with the way things are going here; says that Riaz is working well with the Khedive, highly approves the action of the Legislative Council, but as to Constantinople, says the Sultan is mad and there is no doing anything with him. Talking about the Azhar University he tells me there is only one of the Sheykhs there fit to be made Sheykh El Azhar on a Liberal footing, namely, Hassan el Naawi.

" *2nd Jan.* 1894.— My audience of the Khedive. He received me with great cordiality, excusing himself for the mistake about last week's audience, and assuring me that he was not in the smallest degree displeased at what had happened last year, when Knowles announced my article as authorized by him. I said, ' After all it did good '; and he chuckled at the recollection. I found him just as frank and plain-spoken as last year, but more of a man. He is much sunburnt and looks in perfect health. He answered all my questions freely and without hesitation.

" The first was about Constantinople. I asked him whether it was true that he had gone there with the intention of starting an active anti-English campaign? *Abbas.* ' There is no truth in it. I was obliged to go, as it was my duty to the Sultan, but from first to last we did not speak a word of politics.' *I.* ' Then it is not true that Your Highness asked for Turkish troops?' *Abbas.* 'The whole thing is nonsense. It was agreed beforehand that I should say nothing of these things, and nothing at all was said.' *I.* ' But Your Highness was satisfied with the general reception?' *Abbas.* ' Most satisfied. The Sultan showed me all possible kindness. But the question of evacuation was not touched on, nor, indeed, any international politics. I authorize you to repeat this on my part.'

" I told him that I had seen Sir William Harcourt, and what he had said to me about the Khedive's having gone to Constantinople to raise up the Sultan against us. He begged me to contradict this, as nothing of the sort had taken place. I then asked about his intended visit to England. He said he was thinking of it in June. I urged him to decide on nothing in a hurry, as I should be sorry to see him go there without being certain of being received with all the honour due to his position. I feared the visit might be misinterpreted and made use of against him in the Press. He promised to think it over well before deciding. About Riaz he said he was on the best of terms with him, that he was quite satisfied of the sincerity of his opposition to Lord Cromer and that all was going on capitally. He was immensely pleased at the conduct of the Legislative Council, but told me he had had great difficulty in keeping up their courage. They were so timid. One member, Gait Bey Mustafa, had come one day to the Council in a great state of mind because he had been the day before to Kitchener to ask that his son might be received into the military school, and Kitchener had been very rude to him, asking him whether he was not one of those who were wanting to cut down the army estimates, and had shown him the door. This had frightened others, and they had all come to him, and he had made them a little speech on their duty as independent patriots, which had given them heart again.

" He then told me the story of the Sheykh el Bekri. He and the Sheykh had been great friends as boys, and he had had a high opinion of him, but latterly the Sheykh had had his head turned by the desire to play a great political part. He had gone about among the foreign consuls repeating this thing and that. On one occasion Lord Cromer had quoted something the Sheykh had told him which should not have been told, and he had sent for him and asked explanations, and advised him to keep quiet, but he would not be advised. Complaints had also been made to him as to the Sheykh having withheld the payment of certain sums passing through his hands, so that he had sent for the Azhar Sheykhs and warned them to be cautious with Sheykh el Bekri, and the Sheykhs had told Sheykh el Bekri what he had recommended. This had made further mischief. Finally, on the publication in the ' Bosphore' about the two members of the Council having been to Lord Cromer, the Sheykh had gone to Reverseaux, French Minister Resident at Cairo. I had insisted upon its being contradicted, or otherwise 'he would go over to the English.' This Reverseaux had repeated to him, the Khedive — and he had given Bekri a strong piece of his mind about his lack of patriotism. I told the Khedive that I regretted the disagreement, as I had had a high opinion of Sheykh el Bekri's value both for intelligence and courage. But he said he himself was disappointed in him, and things were so.

"Of Lord Cromer he spoke with the same sort of boyish fun as last year. 'When Lord Cromer came back from England,' he said, 'he began to talk to me once more about the details of Government, but I reminded him that last time we had talked of these things it was I who wanted to go into details, and he who found that "it was not my business to trouble myself about them." Since then we only talk about the rain and the fine weather. He comes to see me, but we never talk politics.' He asked me whether I had been to see Cromer, and I told him ' No,' as I did not think he had behaved well to His Highness, and I was unwilling, being opposed to him, to frequent his house. This pleased him very much. He came with me to the door, and on going out I asked him whether I might publish what he had told me, and he said ' Certainly — these are the facts and my opinion, and there is no reason why they should not be made known.' I am immensely impressed with the keenness of his intelligence, and his ready power of expressing himself, also with his frankness and directness. There was no beating at all about the bush, nor use of those vague generalities so common with Eastern statesmen.

"The same day I went to the Sheykh el Bekri, who gave me his own account of what had happened, and on 9th January to Tigrane, who told me more details of the Khedive's reception at Constantinople. It had been most cordial, he said. He was himself in the Khedive's suite on the occasion, as he had been many years before with Ismaïl, and the ceremonial was greater this time, greater than for Mohammed Ali or any of the Viceroys. The Sultan saw Abbas frequently alone. He does not think they talked politics except perhaps, the first time, all that was done by Mukhtar. I asked him if he had any doubt of the Sultan's support if things came to a pinch. He said he had not, the only thing that could tempt the Sultan to intervene against Abbas would be if it were proposed to turn Egypt into a Vilayet of the Empire, but this the Powers would never consent to. His apprehension was not from that side; what he fears is that perhaps the British Government may intervene against the Ministry and appoint men of their own choice without reference to the Khedive. We talked also about the Legislative Council and its discussion of the Budget, and he told me amongst

other things that both Havas and Reuter's Telegraph Agencies get
£1,000 a year each from the Egyptian Government.

"In a letter I wrote at this time to Sir William Harcourt, I gave
him an account of how things were going in Egypt. 'The ideas of the
day,' I wrote, 'are Liberal and modern. The action of the Legislative
Council (in discussing the Budget) is most useful, but everything that
is done here is turned to the native disadvantage by the English officials,
who are angry at having lost much of their power since last year. It
is impossible that the country could be in a more favourable state for
evacuation, but I suppose you will not do it.' And so in truth it was,
it needed a new quarrel and a new crisis at Cairo to prevent what these
considered the danger of its taking place. Lady Gregory, writing to
me on the 16th of January, said: 'From what I hear the Government
in England are most anxious to get out of Egypt, and might make a
volte face at any moment.' This was the danger Cromer and the
English officials at Cairo foresaw. Gladstone might at any moment
take the bit between his teeth and keep his word. It will here be seen
how the crisis was engineered, and Cromer got his way."

I was absent from Cairo on a desert tour when the clash between
Cromer and the Khedive took place. That a new *coup d' état* was in
contemplation by the former had already begun to be rumoured is
shown by an entry in my journal of *January* 21. "Mohammed Abdu
and Mohammed Moelhi called. Moelhi declares that Riaz' Ministry
will not last, that Cromer and Reverseaux have come together, and
that they mean to appoint Nubar in his place. He thinks the Khedive
will consent to this. Tigrane is on bad terms with Nubar and will not
join. It will be practically a renewal of the Dual Control. I think
there is probably something in this, though I doubt the Khedive's consenting." Two days later, 23rd January, we started on our journey,
one of those purely desert journeys on camels in the Western Desert,
where one is absolutely cut off from all communication with the civilized world, as much so as if one were in a different planet, nor did
we return till the 4th of February. It was a pleasant and interesting
tour among the then isolated monasteries of the Natron Valley, and
in the great uninhabited wilderness beyond it. It was Judith's first
experience of a long camel ride, and we had with us Everard Fielding
who was spending the winter in Egypt, and the weather was beautiful,
and all went well, but this is not the place for these out of the world
adventures, and I reserve my description of it for another occasion.
My first informant about what had happened was my friend Osman
Bey Ghaleb who looked in the following day, and gave the exciting
news of what is known in official Egyptian history as "The Frontier
Incident."

To make this understandable it must be explained that Kitchener,

who held the position of Sirdar of the Egyptian army, was already
busying himself with preparing things on the Soudanese frontier for the
advance he had in contemplation beyond Wady Halfa against the
Khalifa (who had succeeded on the Mahdi's death to his power at Omdurman), by endeavouring to obtain the alliance of the various tribal
Sheykhs in Nubia and Upper Egypt. These proceedings were veiled
in extreme military secrecy, the details being carefully withheld from
the Khedive, notwithstanding the fact that Abbas was nominally Commander in Chief of his own Egyptian army. This the young man
resented, among other British encroachments on his Vice-regal power,
and it was a matter that was much discussed between him and his intimates, some of whom were young officers who encouraged him to
assert himself as a reply to Cromer's call a year before for British
reinforcements. Cromer on his side, as has been seen, though unwilling for financial reasons to make any new move in the direction of a
Soudan campaign, kept the necessity of such a campaign in reserve as
a useful argument for deferring the evacuation among those which he
brought forward when the possibility of withdrawing our troops was
under discussion with the home Government. It will be understood
by this, how in the present instance he had a double reason for supporting Kitchener in his not originally serious dispute with the Khedive,
and making it the occasion of a new trial of strength with Abbas, and
a new change of Ministers.

"*5th Feb.*— Osman Ghaleb came and stopped to luncheon, and gave
me the whole history of what had happened in my absence. According
to him the Khedive, while making a tour on the Upper Nile, was determined to find out exactly the state of affairs in regard to the Soudan,
and insisted upon being shown everything and seeing everybody.
Kitchener, who was with him, and had heard of this intention, tried to
prevent it, and to keep him especially away from visiting the prisons,
where a number of political persons were detained, Sheykhs of tribes
and others connected with the Soudanese hostilities. But the Khedive
insisted, and the prisoners appealed to him, and told him their grievances, and he ordered a number of them to be released. It has been
a system on the frontier to pay subsidies to certain Sheykhs of tribes
(friendlies), who are allowed to harry the others, and complaints on
this head were made to Abbas. Kitchener, who does everything up
there in the name of England, being unable to contest the Khedive's
right to pardon, ordered the pardoned prisoners to be released, but in
Queen Victoria's name. There was also some trouble about a hospital which Kitchener did not wish his Highness to see, saying there
were seventy cases of smallpox in it, but the Khedive went and found
there were but sixty patients in all, and no smallpox case.

"Again on the frontier, Abbas insisted on receiving certain Sheykhs who assured him he could travel in safety anywhere with them, even to Khartoum, while Kitchener objected to his going outside the lines, saying there was danger. But the Khedive rode out with the Sheykhs notwithstanding,— Kitchener remaining behind. Lastly, at a review the 2nd battalion of a black regiment officered by Englishmen got into disorder while marching past. Kitchener said it was through the fault of the band, but the Khedive said they had marched disgracefully. At this Kitchener took offence, and offered to resign, but the Khedive refused to accept his resignation, and the thing was explained and settled, and it was agreed that nothing further should be said about it. Kitchener, however, made use of the incident later as a pretext to get the Khedive recalled from the frontier, and telegraphed to Cromer, who telegraphed to Rosebery, who telegraphed to Paris and St. Petersburg to say that he must deal separately with the case (independently of the other Consuls General). The French and Russian Governments agreed to this. Pressure was then put on Riaz, who telegraphed to the Khedive to return.

" The conditions imposed by Cromer were a commendatory order by the Khedive to the troops; the dismissal of Maher Pasha, whom Kitchener accused of having instigated the Khedive's conduct, and as third condition that the English officers in the Khedive's army should have the right to be tried by court martial in England. Abbas is said to have accepted all these conditions. If it is true that he was unsupported by France or the Sultan, he was probably right to do so, but he has reserved to himself the right of explaining the matter in his own way, through Tigrane.

" Osman Bey is far from friendly to Abbas, being a partisan of Prince Halim, and having a grudge against Ismaïl and all his house, because Ismaïl had his brother strangled at Senaar in 1878. He gave us a tragic history of this. He says the Sultan has been bought over to English interests, that he communicated everything that passed at Constantinople between him and Abbas to the English Embassy, and that he has £20,000,000 sterling invested in English securities, especially with the Ottoman Bank.

" *6th Feb.*— Captain Broadwood (afterwards General Broadwood) came. He told me the story of the Khedive's quarrel with Kitchener as he had heard it from Colonel Settle, a good authority. According to this, the Khedive when receiving the officers, native and English, after the review expressed his satisfaction with all, except the infantry, under Colonel Lloyd's command. Kitchener was not present, and coming back a few moments afterwards said to Lloyd, ' Go and tell the men the Khedive is pleased with them,' taking for granted that it had been so. ' I am afraid I can't quite do that,' said Lloyd, ' for His Highness has just expressed disapproval of my part of it.' Thereupon

Kitchener went after the Khedive, and no one knows exactly what took place between them as they were alone. 'It is all the more curious,' said Broadwood, 'because just before the Khedive left for the south, he received us at Abbassieh and spoke in quite a friendly tone.' I have no doubt Kitchener made a quarrel of it purposely to get the Khedive back from the frontier, and that Cromer still further exaggerated it for political reasons. The 'Daily News' has an article anything but unfavourable to my article, though in common with all the English papers it has been full of violent words lately against the Khedive.

"Gerald Portal is dead in England. I am sorry for this on Lady Edmund Talbot's account, as she and her sister had reckoned on his succeeding Cromer here. I see the newspapers make great count of him, but he was a man of very ordinary abilities, pushed on by Cromer, whose faithful pupil and understudy he was. I don't know that he is any loss to us politically here.

"*7th Feb.*— Spent the day wading through nearly a hundred newspapers from England, the arrears of the last fortnight. It is quite astonishing the lies and false arguments they contain about everything Egyptian, only another proof of the fact that the Press is in reality an engine for the concealment of historic truth, the most complete ever invented. There is not a single English paper that treats the recent incident here with even a semblance of fair dealing. Lying hypocrisy and violence are everywhere the order of the day. The French have pushed a military column forward and have occupied Timbuctoo! I am curious to know the exact position here of the Egyptian Government towards the French, and have written to Tigrane proposing a visit.

"*8th Feb.*— Lunched with Tigrane and discussed the 'Frontier incident' with him at length. It would seem that the Khedive did several things while on his journey that were irregular. Maher Pasha, who travelled with him, was formerly Governor of the Frontier Province, and put him into communication with everybody Kitchener least wished him to see. At Luxor he found Minshatti, the Sheykh of the Abdabdeh, who was condemned to death five years ago, but whose sentence had been commuted, and who was made to reside at Luxor. Him Abbas made much of, took on board his *dahabiyah* with him and released. This is the same Minshatti who appealed on one occasion to me, and about whom I wrote to Grenfell. He was at that time specially obnoxious to Kitchener, then head of the Intelligence department on the Upper Nile.

"Again, it is true that His Highness insisted upon making a desert expedition farther than Kitchener approved; and again, that Kitchener had had some Soudanese soldiers, five of them, shot on the plea of desertion without the Khedive's sanction. Tigrane, however, is not very certain of details, and urged my seeing the Khedive.

"As to the final quarrel with Kitchener he says it was a small affair, and the story given me by Ghaleb Bey substantially correct. Kitchener, after resigning and then withdrawing his resignation, had assured the Khedive that it should go no further. Cromer, however, had taken it up beyond all measure, had insisted on Riaz, and then the Ministry, accepting his terms without waiting to hear the Khedive's story, and had threatened consequences which they dared not face. I asked him what these were, but this he said he could not tell me, but it was not merely their own dismissal as Ministers, I fancy it was that the Khedive's army should be put under the English Commander-in-Chief. They had no option but to get the Khedive out of the scrape as they best could. The French Agency had gone entirely against them, owing, he said to *des circonstances personelles* on the part of Reverseaux. This being so, the position is of course a very dangerous one. Tigrane thinks that, if the English Government were to ask the French Government's leave to depose Abbas, the French Government would consider it so distinct a diplomatic gain that it would consent.

"Tigrane told me that the idea of addressing a circular letter explaining the 'Incident' to the Powers had been abandoned, and even that of addressing such a letter to Cromer, though he, Tigrane, was in favour of it. There was danger of a new publication of Blue Books. Cromer has been compiling things against the Khedive all the last year. I asked him if these were things affecting the Khedive's moral character and he said: 'Oh no. But the Khedive has once or twice made complaints against English officers which he had been unable to substantiate, of drunkenness and the like, and it would be sought to prove that he was mendacious and was animated by ill-will.' He thought I might publish an explanation without committing the Khedive. But I cannot do this unless I see him, nor do I think it would be as good a way as officially through the Foreign Office. He assured me there was no truth in the report of a quarrel between the Khedive and his Ministers. 'We got him out of his scrape,' Tigrane said, 'as we best could, and the Khedive knows it.'

"*9th Feb.*— The London papers are really too monstrous. It is evident to me that Cromer and his partisans have determined upon Abbas' removal by fair means or foul, and that do he what he will, nothing now will satisfy them. I am anxious all the same that he should at least put his true conduct on record, and I have written to suggest my seeing him.

"Yesterday coming home I met young Gordon, General Gordon's nephew, who gave me yet another account of the frontier incident. He says that there are eight battalions of native troops on the frontier

under Lloyd, who has local rank as Pasha, and that there is great dislike and jealousy between the black troops and the Egyptian troops.
The blacks, he says, would like nothing better than to have a go in at
the Egyptians, whom they hate and despise. He himself inspected the
troops on the frontier a few weeks ago as head of the Store department,
and found the Egyptian battalions, the 6th and 7th, in a very slovenly
condition. It was just these that the Khedive picked out to praise, and
not the others, of which he said they were a disgrace to the army.
Lloyd, he tells me, has been a great upholder of the Egyptian soldiers,
maintaining, contrary to all other opinion, that they are as good as the
Soudanese, ' but I fancy,' he added, ' he has changed his opinion now.'
Gordon is very severe on the Khedive, but his post, if I mistake not,
is one of those newly-made ones as to which there was an objection
raised (by the Legislative Council).

" 11th Feb.— Brewster Bey called on me this afternoon, having been
sent by the Khedive to thank me for my article in the ' Nineteenth
Century,' and to talk over the situation. He is a little man of about
thirty-five or perhaps more, an Englishman, he told me, born in Devonshire, but who has contracted a slightly foreign accent. He came to
Egypt the same year we did, in 1876, first as a clerk in the customs at
Alexandria, and then at the time of the Suakim campaign for three
years at Suakim, where he served under Kitchener, when Kitchener
was Military Governor there. He did not tell me how he happened to
get the post of private secretary to the Khedive, but he is clearly an
honest man, who, from his sympathy with native Egypt, has fallen
into disfavour with our people. ' I am on the black list,' he said, ' at
the Agency, and beyond leaving cards once a year, I see nothing of any
of them.'

" He spoke in the warmest way of his young master, Abbas, and was
indignant at the treatment he had received in the affair of the frontier.
' Will you believe it,' he said, ' but to the present moment the Khedive
does not know precisely what he has been accused of saying? He has
never been informed.' I urged him very strongly to get the Khedive
to put his own story on paper, and not by word of mouth, to Lord
Cromer, who would repeat it to our Government after his own fashion.
It ought to be done officially through Tigrane and at once. I asked
him exactly what the true story was, and he told me that what the
Khedive had told him was that after the review at Wady Halfa, the
second battalion, which is an Egyptian, not a black one, under English
command, had got out of order in the manœuvres; that when alone
with Kitchener he had expressed himself strongly about it, saying that
it was a disgrace to see good troops so badly handled; that Kitchener
had resigned and then withdrawn his resignation, and had told the
Khedive the matter should remain a secret between them, and that

they travelled back together amicably to Assouan; but that there Kitchener, who seems in the meantime to have telegraphed to Cairo, represented to His Highness that before leaving Upper Egypt he should
issue an order declaring his satisfaction with the frontier force; that
the Khedive had demurred to this, and on being further pressed His
Highness had said, 'You mean, then, to make it a political matter? I
consider this is a question within my limits to decide.' Whereupon
Kitchener replied, 'I am not sure what Your Highness' limits are.'
What more happened Brewster does not know. But he says that,
knowing Kitchener well and knowing the Khedive, he would infinitely
sooner take the latter's word than the former's. I asked him what
sort of man Kitchener was, and he told me he was of no particular
ability, and that he was especially ignorant, for a man who had seen
so much employment here, of native character and native ideas. At
Suakim he had committed the grossest blunders in this way. Kitchener's original quarrel with Maher (this was told me by Kennedy) was
about a large sum of secret service money, as to which Kitchener refused — Maher being Under Secretary at the War Office — to give any
account. This was the beginning of the trouble, as far as Kitchener
was concerned.

"Brewster spoke bitterly of the French and Russian Agents, who
had turned against Abbas in this difficulty, as they had done the year
before. With regard to Constantinople, he also does not trust the
Sultan, 'who will do whatever the English Government tells him.' As
for Mukhtar, he had been against Abbas all through, and was now
playing entirely into Cromer's hands. 'He has not forgotten,' he said,
'the Khedive's telegram to Constantinople at the beginning of his reign,
when he asked who was the Sultan's representative here in Egypt,
himself or Mukhtar?' Brewster considers the situation a very dangerous one for Abbas — in which I agree with him. 'If he goes,' he said
emphatically, 'I shall not stay a day longer in Egypt.' Nevertheless,
the Khedive is full of courage, and Brewster promised to back up my
advice about the note of explanation addressed to our Government.
He thinks I can do no good by explaining matters to the English Press.
A very honest fellow is Brewster, of a kind one would wish to be
served by, but does not often meet.

"*17th Feb.*— I have written a long private letter to the Editor of the
'Daily News' for his instruction, not for publication, explaining the
true state of affairs here.

"*19th Feb.*— Lady Dunmore, who was here with her daughters a
few days ago, gave us a thrilling account of her life and sufferings in
Kashmir, where they were taken, she being an invalid, to spend two
summers, by her husband, but after all it seems to have done her good,
and the girls were enthusiastic about it. She told me to-day a curious

story, which shows how things are done in Russia. When her husband started from India on his journey through the Pamir country, the Emperor of Russia — Dunmore has Russian relations — gave him a private letter which secured him free passage through the Russian lines. On his return the Emperor wrote to him begging that he would come and see him at St. Petersburg and give him an account of what he had seen, the Emperor being very anxious to have unbiassed evidence of the state of things in Central Asia. To this Dunmore responded, and wrote as many as three letters expressing his willingness to come, but never any further message, until quite lately he has learned that none of his letters were received by the Emperor. It appears that the men about the palace exercise an absolute supervision over all the Imperial correspondence, and even the Princess of Wales finds difficulty in communicating with her sister. Now Dunmore has asked at the Foreign Office that his letter of explanation should be presented by the Ambassador, or rather the Chargé d'Affaires, in private audience. The Emperor it appears has been furious at getting no answer, and Lady Dunmore says: 'When he finds out the truth there will be journeys to Siberia for some of those concerned.'

"*22nd Feb.*— Dormer called. He gave us the alarming intelligence that there is a scheme on foot for bringing the Cairo sewage into this neighbourhood. It is indeed the abomination of civilization standing in the Holy Place. We have always looked upon the desert as the one pure, imperishable possession, but if this is to be made a stink-pot for our nostrils we are indeed lost." This plan, which was already in an advanced stage with coloured surveys on a large scale, entitled derisively " Projets d'assainissement," I was the means under Providence of preventing. I wrote to Lord Cromer representing the economical folly of the project which had chosen the only district in the neighbourhood of Cairo suitable for building a rural suburb, seeing that it was the only one which possessed an abundance of good water in a sandy soil, and he yielded to my argument, with the result of what is now the populous suburb of Heliopolis having grown up there. Dormer, who became afterwards Lord Dormer, was at that time employed in the Egyptian Financial Department.

"*23rd Feb.*— Lady Francis Osborne came full of serious advice to me about my ' radical politics,' and the stir my writings were making among the officials here. ' Why do you take pleasure in making your fellow men unhappy?'

"A visit from three little journalists, Sheykh Ali Yusuf, Editor of the ' Mowayad ' (the first Nationalist newspaper at Cairo since Tel el Kebir), Mohammed Mesaoud, and Abderrahman Ismaïl. A worthy man is Ali Yusuf, with nothing of civilization about him. Just a little Azhar student in a turban, clever and sympathetic, but without knowl-

edge of the western world.   The others with a slight veneer of Europe,
but hardly deeper than their clothes." This is the first mention in my
diary of Sheykh Ali Yusuf, who played so important a part later in
Cairo's journalistic history.

"*27th Feb.*— Princesse Hélène and her brother the Duc d'Orléans
spent the afternoon here.   They have been up the river in a *dahabiyah*
to Wady Halfa, and enjoyed themselves immensely.   He is a good
young fellow, manly and intelligent, and extremely nice to her.   He
tells me that in Somaliland he has seen as many as 500 ostriches together.   They go in packs in the autumn and winter months, males and
females separately, but pair in the early spring.   The buffaloes even
there are almost extinct.   It was nearly dark when they left, and I rode
back with them as far as the obelisk.

"*28th Feb.*— Heavy rain, enough to make the spouts on the roof
run, the first time they have done so since the house was finished more
than two years ago.   There is a great deal of nonsense talked about
the increase of rain in Egypt since the Suez Canal was made — and of
fogs since the British occupation.   It is pure rubbish.   Reading old
accounts of travellers two and three hundred years ago, I see that they
generally remark that there is but little rain in Egypt, never that there
is none, and so it is now.   All the change there has been is a certain
increase of morning fogs and dampness through the increased irrigation of the Delta, but I am a sceptic about the increase of rain.   Old
West, our Consul at Suez, told me ten years ago that in his experience
there of forty years he had remarked no change."   I tested this once
later by questioning my chief Bedouin, Suliman, whose home is the
desert between Cairo and Suez, on this head.   "Do you not find, Suliman," I said, " a great change in the climate here in your recollection?"
" Oh, yes," he answered, " there is a great one, and sadly for the worse.
When I was a boy, we had beautiful rains on the upper country with
eshub (green spring herbage) every year for our camels, now not a
single drop, all is burnt up, a sad change certainly."

"*4th March.*— Gladstone has really retired from public life.   He
went to Windsor yesterday, so the telegrams say, and gave in his resignation, recommending Rosebery as his successor.   I suppose now he is
gone there will be a general chorus of praise, but for my part I shall
not join it.   He has betrayed too many good causes not to be an evil
doer in my eyes, and his one remaining cause, Ireland, he leaves in the
lurch to-day by his retirement.   I am glad to see that Labouchere and
twenty more members of Parliament have protested against Rosebery's
succession.

"*6th March.*— It is announced in the ' Bosphore ' and other local
papers that the Sultan has telegraphed his entire approval of the
Khedive's action in the late crisis, and has instructed his Ambassador in

London to protest against the accounts of it published in our newspapers. This, if true, is most important. The Sultan has also presented Abbas with a palace on the Bosphorus, a gift of more doubtful omen.

"*7th March.*— It appears that Rosebery has carried the day and is to be Prime Minister. He is an astute Whig of the Palmerston type, and the Radicals have got what they deserve. The policy in Egypt can hardly long remain unchanged, and I should not be surprised to see Rosebery entering on a scheme for the partition of the Ottoman Empire. It cannot well, however, be carried into effect without war, and so I hope that under Providence it may result in the partition rather of that other Empire for the sake of which we in England have sold our old principles of freedom and respect for International right. The Radical jingo is the ugliest feature of our modern politics." Though Lord Rosebery did not remain in office long enough to carry out this plan in person, it was put in practice later by his Under Secretary at the Foreign Office, and understudy, Sir Edward Grey, with the result we have all witnessed.

"*13th March.*— Young Aldridge called. He tells me he was at the celebrated review at Halfa when the Khedive was supposed to have insulted the officers. He was staying with these officers, and none of them were aware of anything in the way of a crisis having occurred till three days after it. He says the opinion of the officers of the Egyptian army on the spot was that the Khedive had said nothing but what he had a right to. He had praised the Camel Corps and the artillery and the cavalry, but had criticized the infantry, which in fact had been a bit in disorder. The remarks, whatever they were, had been made half a mile away from the men, and the men knew nothing about them, nor ever would have known except for the newspapers. 'What,' says Aldridge, 'was the Khedive there for if not to make remarks?' This doubtless reflects the view of the English officers concerned, as Aldridge is Broadwood's half-brother.

"*15th March.*— Frank Lascelles is made Ambassador at St. Petersburg. It seems but the other day that we were *attachés* together at Madrid, sharing all things in common; he deserves his promotion, for he has worked hard for it in many a dull, forgotten post. Another promotion is Rendell's to the House of Lords. He also deserves it for his great humility.

"*20th March.*— Kitchener has just come back from Suakim from a military promenade in the neighbourhood of Tokar, where the country was found green and well watered with streams running and full of wild creatures, ariels and gazelles. All this because for five years the abominable animal, man, has been excluded. All the world would be a paradise in twenty years if man could be shut out.

" *14th April.*— To Cairo with Anne and Judith, and had luncheon with Riaz Pasha and his son Mahmud. The old man was gay at luncheon, and talked history and poetry apparently without a care on his mind, but when the ladies were gone to pay a visit to his Harem and we were left alone, he suddenly told me that he had just that morning, that very morning, sent in his resignation and that of his fellow ministers to the Khedive. I asked him, ' And did the Khedive accept it? ' He answered, ' *A peu près.*' Then he told me that ever since the affair of the frontier there had been a lack of confidence on the Khedive's part, that he and the Ministers had not been supported, and that the palace paper, the ' Journal Egyptien,' had entered on a campaign against them. It did not suit his dignity, and it injured the public service to remain under those conditions. He had given many years of loyal service to his country, and he was an old man, and he should retire now once and for ever. A tear stood in the poor old Minister's eye, and I grieved with him over his fall with all sincerity. He then talked bitterly of the change that had come over the face of the world since he began his official life. How the English used to be trusted and believed in as the one honest nation the whole East over. But he talked more bitterly still of the French, and yet more of his rival, Nubar, who he thinks is to succeed him. It is doubtless to the French that he owes his present reverse, though Cromer will profit by it to the extent of making a split between Abbas and the National party. Riaz said it was a little of all their doing. He talked kindly of Rivers Wilson. Of Rosebery, he said he had seen him twice at Cairo, once with Cromer, once alone. When alone Rosebery had asked him whether it would not be better to have an English Under Secretary in every department, but that, said he, ' I told him would be putting two captains to a ship, it would go down.' I told him Rosebery was a dangerous man in power as far as Egypt and the East were concerned, that I should not wonder if he solved all difficulties by a partition of the Ottoman Empire, a gloomy view in which the old man shared. ' Poor Egypt,' he said, ' poor Egypt! ' It is a strange chance that has made me, in spite of 1882, the confidant of his political griefs, but in truth our views on most things are identical. He hates Western civilization almost as bitterly as I do myself. He sent us away with benedictions and loaded with roses from his door.

" *15th April (Sunday).*— Mohammed Abdu spent the day with us. He says the National party is in despair at Riaz' resignation, and still more at Nubar's return to power, for Nubar means a reign of money makers and speculators, and the government of Egypt by Europeans and Syrians, strangers from every land.

" *17th April.*— To Koubbah Palace (Abbas' country residence, three miles from Sheykh Obeyd). I was taken to the garden and found

Abbas sitting under some trees near the stables, looking at Arab mares which were being paraded before him. With him was the old Soudanese Mohammed Taher, whom the Khedive introduced to me as a loyal Shaggia. We talked first about the horses, six of them, for which Abbas said he was offering £800. But only two of them were good ones. These were a brown mare, like our Queen of Sheba, and a little grey with a fine shoulder, perfectly level back, and tail grandly carried.

" Presently the young Khedive began on politics. He went through the whole story of the frontier incident and Riaz' resignation, and his appointment of Nubar. As to the first his account was much what I had already heard. He said that it was originally a quarrel between Kitchener and Maher Pasha — that when Maher was appointed Under Secretary at the War Office, Kitchener had tried to persuade him to refuse, but Maher had persisted, though his pay was reduced thereby from £120 to £100 a month. When Abbas started for the frontier, Kitchener had tried to prevent Maher going with him. However, all went well till the famous review at Wady Halfa when he had found fault with the second battalion, and had told the English officer that his battalion had done very badly — this in the presence of Kitchener and eleven officers, some English, some Egyptian. Afterwards he had had a private talk with Kitchener, and had told him it was a shame good Egyptian troops should be so badly handled, and Kitchener had tendered his resignation. But the Khedive had begged him not to take it in so serious a way, and the resignation was withdrawn and the thing ended.

" After this they travelled two days together on excellent terms, till on the third they came to Assouan. There the Khedive wanted to telegraph to Riaz, but found the wires occupied by Kitchener. Nevertheless he sent his telegram to Riaz, telling him what had occurred and that it was of no importance. Later, Kitchener came to him and asked him to send two words of commendation to the officers of the frontier garrison before leaving, as he said the officers were offended and were tendering their resignations. The Khedive asked him whether he wished to make a political question of it, and asserted that it was within his prerogative to send or not to send such a message. To which Kitchener replied that he was not sure whether it was so. Nevertheless the dispute ended in Kitchener's promising to say no more about it. Riaz had been weak in allowing his hand to be forced. As to the change of Ministry, Abbas said that when he had seen Lord Cromer he had consulted him as to whom he should send for, and Lord Cromer had said Nubar. Abbas had objected that he was a Christian, Lord Cromer had advised against a Christian Prime Minister last year. Lord C. then said there was no choice unless the Khedive would like Mustafa Fehmi. The Khedive then proposed Fakri and Mazlum. But Lord

Cromer said they were both insignificant. In the end Abbas had given way about Nubar, and there was a compromise about the rest of the Cabinet. Fakri goes to Public Instruction, Mustafa Fehmi to the War Office, Mazlum to Finance, and Butros, who, Abbas said, had betrayed the secrets of the late Cabinet all through to Lord C., to Foreign Affairs. He asked me what I thought of it. I said that I had no confidence in Nubar, but recommended him as soon as he was tired of Nubar to have back a Nationalist Ministry, strengthening it by adding some European he could trust for Foreign Affairs. He promised to remember my advice.

" The Khedive then talked of his camel ride to Suez, and lastly consulted me about going to England this next summer. I said I would try and find out for him what line would be taken there about his reception, and especially by the Prince of Wales, and let him know. He begged me to write to him. As to publishing anything he would leave that to my discretion. Then he made the old Soudani sit near and talked about Zebeyr, who is evidently out of his favour, and so after about an hour he got up and took me to see his camels, and then with a few more words about my writing to him we said good-bye.

" Although extremely friendly and nice to me personally, I confess that he impressed me less favourably this time than before. He has clearly made a dreadful hash of things, and seems to attach more importance to the getting rid of Kitchener than to the larger political questions. I can see that he is in the hands of the intriguers that surround him, and that he is no match for Cromer, who has won the game against him through the Khedive's own mistakes. Not that Nubar's appointment is much advantage to English policy, for Nubar is in French interests, but Lord Cromer has certainly won a personal victory. The future to me looks very black. The young man has lost something of his frankness, and of his first sublime self-confidence, which was his strength, and I fear he will degenerate into the shifty intriguer his father was before him. Still he is more manly than that, and with honest advice may yet go well. But who is to give it him?

" *18th April.*— Our Mowled of Sheykh Obeyd. A calf was killed for the labourers in the garden, and the girls and those who have been at work on the new house, and a lamb for the Sheykhs, with recitations and chauntings in the evening. [This was a religious festival held annually in our garden at the tomb of Sheykh Obeyd.] "

The Bee Birds have been wonderful this year, three or four hundred roosting every night in the trees near the house. I cannot quite make out what they do in the day-time, for they all disappear from the garden, coming back about half an hour before sunset. Most of these birds travel north at this time of year, but a few stay on during the summer. There are also some of the large spotted cuckoos in the garden just now.

"*20th April.*— Our last day at Sheykh Obeyd. I am grieved to leave it this year more than any year before, and have half made up my mind that this shall be my last visit to England. My true home is more and more in Egypt."

We left the following day, and here I close this chapter. With it ends the episode as far as I was personally concerned in it of the National movement of 1892–1894. It failed through the absence of any strong leader to take direction of it; through the youth and inexperience of the Khedive Abbas; through the unscrupulous determination of Lord Cromer acting in what he considered English Imperial interests, and through the still more unscrupulous money interests worked through Lord Rosebery from London and Paris. Lord Rosebery's family connection with the Rothschilds is a sufficient explanation of this last influence. French diplomacy at Cairo seems to me to have been very weakly managed by M. de Reverseaux, the French Consul General there, though how much of the vacillation between encouragement given to the Nationalists when they made a forward move, and their abandonment when the advance had been made, was due to the French Representative at Cairo or to the Ministers at the Quai d'Orsay, I cannot determine. Be it as it may, the spring of 1894 saw the movement lose its force, and brought to a complete standstill a year later by the retirement in his turn of Nubar Pasha, and Lord Cromer's installation as absolute despot ruling Egypt through a dummy Minister, Mustafa Pasha Fehmi, while the Khedive Abbas, cut off from all legitimate exercise of his viceregal rights, consoled himself with the follies of youth, money speculations, and impotent intrigue.

It was the history repeated a hundred times over of the English manipulation of the native States of India. To me it was a mournful spectacle, a blank period during which, though still maintaining a deep interest in what went on, I held a position entirely of spectator, keeping touch with the local politics of the day during my winter visit to Sheykh Obeyd mainly through Sheykh Mohammed Abdu, whom I established on a corner of my property in a country house within half a mile of my own. He had an advantage for me as historian and diarist of being personally intimate with Mustafa Fehmi who concealed nothing from him, while Abdu concealed nothing from me. It was as an historian only that I followed the development of the Cromerian *régime,* until in 1906 Cromer's astonishing blunders of that year once more gave life to Egyptian Nationalism, and it found a voice in Mustafa Kamel. My diary in the meagreness of its political entries corresponds with my political abstention during this weary interval. Nevertheless there were moments when I said my say with our politicians on Egyptian affairs, and in the London " Times," notably in the year of the new invasion of the Soudan under Kitchener in 1896, of Fashoda, and of the fatal entente with France in 1904. The entries then have a renewed importance, the rebirth of Nationalism in 1906 having lured me once more into the field as an active combatant for Egypt's independence.

CHAPTER VII

A SUMMER IN ENGLAND, 1894

The first news that greeted me on my return to London from Egypt in the Spring of 1894 was the engagement of my friend Margot Tennant to Mr. Asquith, a political event, as it turned out, of the first magnitude, though perhaps not fully appreciated as such at the moment. I find it recorded thus:

"*1st May.*— To Grosvenor Square, where I found Sir Charles Tennant very important over his daughter's approaching marriage. ' It has gone on now,' he said, ' for a year and a half, at first all on Asquith's side, but now Margot is sincerely attached to him. She has smartened him up wonderfully, you would hardly know him.' Upon which in walks Asquith, a little smooth-shaved middle-aged man, with a beatific smile on his face, as of one to whom Heaven's doors have been opened. He reminded me very cordially of our former meetings on Home Rule platforms, and in answer to my congratulations, said, ' Indeed you have reason to congratulate me.' Sir Charles gives his daughter £2,000 a year and a house in Cavendish Square. They are to spend the honeymoon in Caroline Grosvenor's house, 30, Upper Grosvenor Street, which they have rented for the season.

"*4th May.*— George Wyndham came to see me. We discussed Rosebery, and agreed that he was overrated as a statesman, a clever after-dinner speaker, but nothing more. He had been pushed forward by the press and the Jews as a sort of Stock Exchange candidate, but he could not last as leader of a party. George applauded my intention of formally returning to the Conservative fold [a momentary intention never carried out, for I joined no party].

"*7th May.*— Lunched with Sir William Harcourt. In spite of accounts of his ill-health I found him looking better than for a year or two. His budget comes on for second reading to-night (he was still Chancellor of the Exchequer), and Loulou told me in private that it is quite possible the Government may be beaten on it. Sir William was, nevertheless, in high spirits, and I think enjoyed my denunciation of Rosebery as ' Minister of the Stock Exchange.' Alfred Milner came in and we had some chaff, good-naturedly, about Egypt. Nubar has been playing his old games there already, giving a concession to a land company he is interested in. Milner admitted he was an old rogue. Afterwards in private Loulou told me that his father would probably retire from public life at the end of the present Parliament. He himself intends to do so as soon as the Budget is through.

" 10*th May*.— Margot's wedding day, showery and cold, but with occasional gleams of sunshine. St. George's crammed to the ceiling with the gayest world of the gay. It is the only church in London I have the smallest romance about, but to me it is interesting and touching from the vast number of marriages it has seen (including my own). It is old-fashioned, with nice comfortable pews, and none of the tawdry Gothic rubbish they are fond of elsewhere. De Staal was there in the same pew with us, and there were Rosebery and I believe all the Ministers, and Gladstone, who came in late and was cheered outside, and Arthur Balfour. Margot was pale, very pale, but firm and decided, Asquith much smartened up. A great crush in the Tennant house afterwards in Grosvenor Square, Margot surrounded by a crowd of women friends. She drove away in a slatey-blue dress, an apple-green straw hat and dark-blue flowers.

" 18*th May*.— In consequence of a talk I have had with Lady Lytton I have written to Arthur Ellis on the subject of the Khedive's intended visit to England. In it I said: ' When I was leaving Egypt the other day the Khedive, whom I went to take my leave of, spoke to me of his proposed visit to Europe, which was then not quite decided on, and asked me to find out for him confidentially whether if he came to England, his reception would be a really cordial one. By this he meant not so much whether there would be the usual official reception, whatever that might be, due to his rank, as whether he might count upon the kindly feeling of the Court and especially of the Prince of Wales towards him. From what I know of him I feel sure that it is more in the power of the Prince of Wales than of Lord Rosebery or of any of the officials to place things in Egypt, as far as the Khedive is concerned, on a more satisfactory footing than they have lately been. The Khedive is very suspicious of Lord Cromer, not as I think entirely without reason, for the quarrel between them is no doubt largely a personal one, and I think that, if it could be conveyed to him that he could count at least on a friendly reception at Marlborough House, he would be less likely to listen to the advances which are pretty sure to be made to him in Paris on his way through. In my opinion large political interests are involved in the issue of this visit.'

" To-day the tenantry of Crabbet presented Judith with a silver cup on her coming of age. They were most hearty, and recalled the fact of most of them holding their farms from father to son for generations. Judith made an admirable speech in reply, delivered in a clear voice and with a charming manner. Then I showed them some of the family deeds and they all drank champagne in tumblers. The leaders among them were the two Caffins and young Wright of Pryors Farm. The servants, too, at Crabbet are making her a presentation. We have, I think, seven house servants who have been over twenty years with us.

"*21st May.*— An answer has come from Arthur Ellis with an informal message from the Prince of Wales. It is most satisfactory. He says: 'Whilst the Prince of Wales feels some hesitation in sending any message to the Khedive except through the accredited official channel, I may say that should His Highness determine upon a visit to England, he will certainly receive from the Prince of Wales and from society in general every possible attention.' I have written to the Khedive, conveying to him the message."

This little piece of diplomacy I had afterwards reason to regret, successful as it proved in bringing the Khedive to England. The influence of Marlborough House was not a wholesome one for the Khedive's patriotism, and in other ways proved detrimental, as will be seen later.

"*22nd May.*— I see a report in the evening paper that the Sultan has forbidden the Khedive to go to England, but it sounds to me hardly likely.

"*24th May.*— Breakfasted with Sir Henry Loch and had much talk with him about 'civilization' in Africa. He expressed his fear of the spread of Mohammedanism southwards as likely to prove a danger. I wish I could think it. He also asked about Arabia in a way which sounded as if they may have their eye on it, too, in the scramble that is going on. He told me the Chinese were driving the Russians back in Central Asia.

"Anne and Judith have taken rooms at 31, South Street for the season.

"*27th May (Sunday.)* — On Wednesday I called on Randolph Churchill in Grosvenor Square (his mother's house) and had some political talk with him. He is terribly altered, poor fellow, having some disease, paralysis, I suppose, which affects his speech, so that it is painful to listen to him. He makes prodigious efforts to express himself clearly, but these are only too visible. He talked of his election prospects at Bradford and the desire of the Conservatives to delay the turning out of the Rosebery Government. About Egypt he said, 'You know my opinion about evacuation is unchanged, but my tongue is tied.'" This was the last time I saw him. I remember that as he came to the door with me he tried again to explain to me what he wanted to tell me about Egypt, but broke down and said, almost in tears, "I know what I want to say, but damn it, I can't say it."

" *28th May.*— Breakfast with George Wyndham. He is at last bringing out his book of French Lyrics. With any luck it should be a great success.

" *10th June (Sunday).*— To Wotton to see Evelyn, who is in poor health. He wants me to act in concert with him on the question of a new Conservative candidate for East Grinstead. On Thursday I met Frederic Harrison, just back from France. There is great excitement about the Anglo-Belgian Agreement in regard to the Congo and Upper Nile, the last of Rosebery's thieves' treaties, but Harrison says the wirepullers assure him that the French menace will come to nothing. I am not so sure, as it is being taken up in Germany also.

" *11th June.*— Still at Wotton. After luncheon drove to Box Hill to see George Meredith. Found him with his daughter, a pretty little bar maiden just engaged to Russell Sturgis, and another young lady. He is terribly deaf and afflicted with creeping paralysis, so that he staggers from time to time while walking, and once to-day nearly fell. It does not, however, affect his mind, and he has a novel on hand at the present moment which keeps him writing six hours a day. He is a queer, voluble creature, with a play-acting voice, and his conversation like one dictating to a secretary, a constant search for epigrams. I took the bull by the horns at once about his novels, said I never read prose and looked upon him only as a poet. This pleased him, and he gave me two volumes, recommending to me especially the piece called ' Attila.' He told me Tennyson was the first person to discover the merits of ' Love in a Valley.' I asked him to explain sundry obscurities in ' Modern Love,' and he said he would do so if I would come up with him to a little literary den he has at the top of his garden, but the young ladies unfortunately followed us, and he was unwilling to talk about this poem before them, so I missed my chance. During our talk a luncheon was brought to him on a tray, as he said he was too busy to sit down to a regular meal, and could not write after one o'clock, so I left him to his work and drove on. I had driven my four horses in at the front entrance, a difficult feat, and got them out again and went on over the hill to Ockham, where I picked up Judith, and back in the evening again to Wotton over Ranmore Common and down the steep descent of Coombe Bottom. I fancy in all history no team of four horses was ever driven before down that road, not even by Tommy Onslow of happy memory, certainly not by a woman, for Judith had the reins.

" Compare the local rhyme, for Onslow lived close by :

What can Tommy Onslow do?
He can drive a coach and two,
Can Tommy Onslow do no more?

He can drive a coach and four.
Where shall we his merits fix?
He can drive a coach and six.

" 13*th June.*— Dr. Leitner called to talk over Egyptian and Mohammedan affairs. He is gloomy about prospects as I am in the East, where the old sympathy for Eastern things amongst Englishmen is fast dying out, and a reign of Western intolerance is taking its place. There is danger of a partition of the Ottoman dominions, for there is nowhere the smallest wish in Europe to see reform in them, and all Powers alike are in arms in Africa against the Mohammedan Arabs. This is for England and Germany a new feature and a dangerous one for Islam.

" 18*th June.*— Miss Violet Maxse's wedding, an *omnium gatherum,* social, political, and literary. The bridegroom, Lord Salisbury's third son, brought the Tories; Maxse, the Liberal Unionists, with Chamberlain and the rest; the young lady, her friends. I counted six poets in the church, including myself, Alfred Austin, George Meredith, Alfred Lyall, Oscar Wilde, and Edwin Arnold. I found myself next to Lyall, who told me the latest joke about the Laureateship. ' If one must have a Laureate, choose the least of evils, choose Austin.' At the bride's house the crowd was immense, and I found myself for ten minutes flattened like a herring between Lord Salisbury and a tall Dutch clock. Truly matrimony makes strange pew fellows.

" 22*nd June.*— Gave a dinner at Mount Street to Lady Granby, Lucy Smith, d'Estournelles, Alfred Lyall, and Godfrey Webb, all of us more or less poets. After dinner we read and recited poetry, d'Estournelles being by far the most effective, having an admirable manner.

" I hear that Edward Malet is going to resign his Embassy at Berlin because he was not consulted on the Congo arrangement.

" 26*th June.*— Received a visit from M. Ducroix, Editor of the Paris ' Matin.' He asked me my opinion of the situation in Egypt, and I gave it him very frankly, and of French policy there. ' French diplomacy,' I said, ' had made two capital mistakes, first in not supporting native as opposed to European interests, and, secondly, in making the perpetual opposition it does to our English policy without being prepared to fight.' He said they were his own views. Reverseaux had to his own knowledge promised the Khedive to back him in the Spring of 1893 with a French fleet at Alexandria, and then had left him in the lurch. It was the fault of the home Government more than Reverseaux's.

" 30*th June and* 1*st July.*— Our Annual Crabbet Club Meeting. The members present were:

George Wyndham,
George Curzon,
George Peel,
George Leveson Gower,
Esmé Howard,
St. George Lane Fox,
Eddy Tennant,

Hubert Howard,
Godfrey Webb,
Mark Napier,
Theobald Mathew,
Charles Gatty,
Laurence Currie,

with three new members, Lord Cairns, Alfred Douglas, and Basil Blackwood.

" 13*th* July.— Called on Frank Lascelles, who is just starting as Ambassador for St. Pettersburg. We talked over old and new times. He and I were exact contemporaries, both in age and in the diplomatic service, and it is just thirty years ago that we were at Madrid together as *attachés*. Without any very special abilities he has made a rapid career by hard work and good sense. We talked of the Asiatic question and the Egyptian question. He does not believe in the possibility of saving any part of Persia from Russia, who could take it whenever she has a mind to. I walked with him to call on Staal, and left him at the door.

" 16*th* July.— To the Keats memorial meeting at Hampstead with George Wyndham, a curious ceremony. It took place in the parish church, the vicar and his choir assisting in surplices, but the proceedings were entirely mundane. Gosse, who presided, made a dull, platitudinous oration in the tone of a sermon (his father was a Nonconformist lecturer), and the others were even duller. Houghton alone was brief and to the point. The poet's bust was then unveiled, and throughout the only allusion to religion was when one of the speakers enumerated what Keats was not, and included in the list that he was *not* a religious propagandist. When all was over the worthy vicar consoled himself with some prayers and an anthem.

" 17*th* July.— A brilliant luncheon with Margot and her husband at 30, Upper Grosvenor Street, and I took her her Wedding Ode, which I had written for her amusement. The other guests were Mrs. Grenfell, Mrs. Daisy White, Ribblesdale, his brother Reggie Lister, and Oscar Wilde, all immensely talkative, so that it was almost like a breakfast in France. Asquith alone rather out of it. I sat next to him and was rather sorry for him, though he was probably happy enough. Afterwards, when the rest had gone away, Oscar remained, telling stories to me and Margot."

This is a very poor account of an interesting, and in the sequel a tragic, incident which has remained strongly impressed on my mind, as it was one that showed Oscar Wilde at the height of his social glory, and as the last occasion on which I found myself in his company. Of all those present, and they were most of them brilliant talkers, he was without comparison the most brilliant, and in a perverse mood he chose to cross swords with one after the other of them, overpowering each in turn with his wit, and making special fun of Asquith, his host that day, who only a few months later, as Home Secretary, was prosecuting him on the notorious criminal charge which sent him to hard labour in prison.   I remember, too, as a characteristic trait of his dandyism, that when at the end of the half hour we remained on talking, we went away together from the door, I to walk back to my rooms in Mount Street, and he to pay a visit in the same direction, hardly farther.   I said, " We will walk together as far as Grosvenor Square."   " No, no," he said, and called a passing hansom.   " I *never* walk."

This was the end of my London season, and the only extracts I can find in my diary at all of a public character, which was otherwise devoted entirely to the social care of amusement and launching Judith in the world.   It is a record especially of dinners that I gave, and which were for a moment rather the fashion with the Soul society at my rooms in Mount Street.

" *25th July.*— Crabbet.   With Judith on a pilgrimage to see Huxley at Eastbourne.   He lives in a new house he has built near the cliff and with Beachy Head behind it.   He was very cordial and pleasant, and his wife, an excellent old soul, most kind to Judith.   We had only two hours with him but we talked all the time about the origin of the Arabian horse, and I think I got from him all the information he had to give.   He said that in reality nothing was known at all clearly except that horses were unknown in Egypt under the fourth dynasty, that there had been a close connection with Arabia, and that if there had been horses in Arabia there would have been horses also in Egypt, but how they eventually came to Arabia was mere guesswork.   Arabia had doubtless been in former times well watered, and it was possible a wild horse might have been isolated there in the South (this was my suggestion) long after the drying up of the northern plateaux, but the historical evidence, such as there was, was against it.   We might expect something from the cuneiform records when thoroughly examined.   Piétrement's theories were merely speculative.

" Of the human race in Egypt he said that he had long suspected a common origin for them with the Dravidians of India, perhaps a long belt of brown-skinned men from India to Spain in very early days.   Of savage races, he said he had no sympathy with them; he considered there was more difference between the man of the criminal class in London at the present day and the high type of educated thinker, than between the Australian savage and, say, the average man of the time of Elizabeth.   ' Yet,' I objected, ' I suppose you could educate your young criminal into being a bishop.' ' Yes,' he said, ' a bishop would be easy enough because the other bishops would look after him, but not a country parson, that would be a dangerous experiment.' He was surprised to learn that grey Arab horses were not foaled grey.

" *6th Aug.*— A party at Crabbet for Sunday. The Meynells, George Wyndham, Alfred Douglas, and Blanche Wortley. Coventry Patmore, Henley, and Locker could not come. Meynell told us much that was interesting about Francis Thompson, who is the latest discovered of the poets.

" Thompson's history is most curious. He was educated at Ushaw, and his father wanted him to become a doctor, but he had a distaste for it and could not or would not pass his examinations. This led to a quarrel, for the father had married a second time, and Thompson was turned out of the house, or left it in anger. He came to London, where he fell into extreme poverty, walking the streets as a beggar for five years and sleeping under the arches by the Thames. The money he earned he spent on opium, which drugged him to endurance of his life. Nevertheless, he once attempted suicide, spending what remained to him on a large dose of laudanum enough to kill two men. He divided it into two portions and retired to I forget what cemetery in the city and took the first half — whereupon he had a vision in which he saw Chatterton, who took him by the hand and comforted him, and reminded him how the very morning after his suicide a letter had come from a publisher which would have relieved him. So he did not take the second dose, and recovered to find the dream fulfilled by the arrival precisely of a letter from a friend enclosing him the cutting of one of his poems printed by Meynell in ' Merrie England.' Thompson had been in the habit of writing poems on any scraps of paper he could pick up and had sent several of them to Meynell, and among them a paper on Paganism and Christianity, which Meynell had pigeon-holed and forgotten till six months later, when he read them and found them excellent. Then he had tried to get into communication with Thompson, but had lost trace of him and had published the papers in hope of attracting the author's attention. This succeeded, and Thompson, seeing his writings in print, wrote Meynell an angry letter about it, giving the address of a chemist's shop near Charing Cross. Thither Meynell went, and on inquiry was told that Thompson owed a bill there of four shillings for opium, that he had no abode, but might be found at nights in the street in front of Charing Cross Station.

" Through the intervention of the chemist he was eventually discovered and sent to Meynell's house apparently with but few weeks to live, for he was dying of opium. Meynell wanted him to go to a hospital, but at first he refused on account of a girl with whom he had a friendship in the streets. She had been kind to him, just as had been the case with De Quincy, and Thompson refused to go anywhere where he should be unable to see her. But the girl insisted that he should go to the hospital, and when he came out of it cured she had disappeared. I asked Meynell whether it was not a case of love rather than friendship, but he said: ' No. Thompson told me that it was not so, that in his condition there could have been no question of physical love; he was too constantly starved.' Thus Thompson was saved. He has now for the last year been sent to Pantasaph, the Capuchin monastery, where he is taken care of and kept away from drugs. He writes poetry and prose and has no other occupation. Meynell will bring him here one day. He showed us a fine poem of his still in manuscript, entitled ' Amphicypellon,' which he will have printed privately."

This was followed by a pilgrimage to Stratford-on-Avon, which I had long intended, and which I now accomplished, going by road with my four horses, and taking my cousin Alfred Douglas with me, stopping at several friends' 'houses on our way, Lady Hayter's at South Hill, and Dr. Watney's at Buckholt, and Mr. Harvey's at Woodstock. Then across the Wolds by Chipping Norton to Stanway, where we were amongst relations, and so on, two days later, to Stratford. Of this I write:

" 13*th Aug.*— All the way to Stratford there are lovely villages, houses of the seventeenth century built of stone, with stone roofs, people harvesting magnificent crops, but it is a thing to remark that in all this country, north of the Wiltshire and Oxfordshire downs there is no single common, or bit of waste land where a traveller might pitch his tent. Stratford ·itself is a very pretty town, standing on a fine, clear river, with little that is modern about it, marred only by the monstrous Shakespeare memorial, a Victorian building, perhaps the most degraded in architecture of our graceless age. Here Alfred left me in a hurry to return to London, while I stayed on fulfilling the object of my pilgrimage by reading the Sonnets at the poet's tomb.

" Sitting on the chancel steps and in full view of the monument with the poet's portly bust and its inscription, a new light broke on me with regard to his character, and I seemed to see him with less mystery, the full fed prosperous citizen he doubtless was in his later years, affecting gentility and honoured of his neighbours. The truth is there is nothing really more romantic in a poet than in other men when seen at home. The original cast of his face they show in Shakespeare's house, said to have been taken after death, shows him a strong practical man, not over refined, one who at the present day would have been a successful journalist and man of letters. The Shakespeare of the Sonnets does not appear in this bust, rather the playwright and ready writer of dialogue for the stage. I can imagine him in this year of grace, 1894, figuring as a George Augustus Sala, or a Druriolanus in the London literary and dramatic world. Fortunately he was born 300 years ago.[1]

"On my way home I stopped at Kelmscott, where after dinner we played at twenty questions, the things chosen for our guessing being the white horse of White Horse Hill, the pen Chaucer wrote the first line of the Canterbury Tales with, and the American volume of Rossetti's 'House of Life,' which Morris gave his wife. It is always a pleasure to find Rossetti still a living memory in this house.

"*16th Aug.*— Made a late start as I dawdled on talking with Morris, and trying to prove to him that he and Ruskin had done more harm than good by their attempt to make English people love beauty and decorate their architecture. He defended himself good-humouredly, but I think has doubts, nevertheless, for we are engulfed to-day in a slough of ornament. I maintained that the old-fashioned square cardboard box style was less abominable, as were the days when it was considered bad taste to attempt any kind of prettiness. However at noon I got away and drove in floods of rain to Uffington, and up the face of White Horse Hill. There the sun came out, and I pitched my tent under lee of the ancient camp where there was a splendid crop of grass for the horses, and stopped for the night. There was a full moon, and it was bitter cold. Morris declares the White Horse to be a work of the Stone Age, probably 20,000 years old. In the night my horses, which I had tethered to the carriage pole, broke loose and wandered away, and I had a long run after them in the moonlight during which I crossed the old white chalk one, without finding mine, but it is hard to track horses on the grass, and we could do nothing till daylight, and not much then. In the course of the morning they were

---

[1] Not long ago, being asked to write a sonnet for the Shakespeare Tercentenary I embodied my impression gathered on this occasion at Stratford in the following:

"A Tercentenary Sonnet

"Shakespeare, what wisdom shall truth tell of thee,
     More than fame speaks? The world thy playhouse is
     Packed floor to roof to-night with votaries
Shouting thy author's name vociferously.
They call thee to the curtain front. Ah me,
     Hast thou no word for our sublimities,
     No cryptogram of grace to crown our bliss?
Nay speak out all, thou man of mystery.
Tell us the truth.— I seem to hear a voice
     From far-off Stratford, pestered at the call,
     The voice of a hale man of middle age,
Civic, respected: 'Who are these lewd boys
     Would call me back to their fool's festival?
     Truce to all mummings. I have left the stage.'"

25 *February*, 1916.

fortunately brought back by some farm people who had found them grazing two miles away. We then

" *17th Aug.*— Followed the Ridgeway, a rough grass track along the crest of the down as far as near Lyddington Castle, when, striking a high road, we turned left and came to Aldbourne, and so to the Kennet river and Savernake Forest, where just before sunset we camped under one of the beech avenues, a lovely spot, dry and secluded, except for the wandering fallow deer. To-night we bivouacked, there being no sign of rain. It was my birthday of fifty-four, yet I feel little of the cares of age.

" *18th Aug.*— Away before seven driving across the forest, which is splendid. Near its centre stands a column with the following inscription of supreme grandiloquence:

This column was erected
by Thomas Bruce Earl of Ailesbury
as a testimony
of gratitude
to his ever honoured uncle
Charles Earl of Ailesbury and Elgin
who left him these Estates
and procured for him the Barony of Tottenham;
and of loyalty
to his most Gracious Sovereign
George III
who unsolicited conferred upon him
the honour of an Earldom,
but above all
of Piety
To GOD FIRST HIGHEST BEST
whose blessing consecrateth every gift
and fixeth its true value
MDCCLXXXI

" On the other side is a second inscription hardly less amusing:

In commemoration
of
a signal instance of Heaven's protecting Providence
OVER THESE KINGDOMS
in the year 1789
by restoring to perfect health
from a long and afflicting disorder
their excellent and beloved Sovereign
GEORGE THE THIRD
This tablet was inscribed
by
GEORGE BRUCE EARL OF AILESBURY

"After Savernake we came down into the Avon valley at Pewsey, and followed the river on to Amesbury where we baited, and so later to Stonehenge where we camped about half a mile from the stones under lee of a small plantation. The stones I found in possession when I arrived of American tourists, but even these could do little to injure the fine calm of the place, and they were soon gone, and about midnight I returned and went again in full solitude to the stones and spent an hour there alone, making incantations in the hope of raising some ghost of ancient times, but in vain, and though I repeated the Lord's Prayer backwards, nothing would come. Perhaps it was the fact that in order to do so without a book I had first to repeat each sentence in its natural sequence, and this may have neutralized the spell. Then I lay down under one of the fallen blocks and dozed off for an hour or two, but still nothing. Stonehenge has much in common with primitive Egypt.

" *19th Aug.* (*Sunday*).— Moved eight miles on to Quarly Hill, and camped to the west of it. All this plain must once have been heath with scattered juniper bushes, for every here and there on the poorer land, as here and at Stonehenge, there are heath and juniper patches left. It is the modern sheep grazing that has brought the grass.

"Called on Major Poore who lives at Middlecote, close by, and dined with him. He is Urquhart's last disciple and still preaches his doctrines. They have elected him a County Councillor, and he is organizing his district on a system of his own, and teaching the villagers to live according to the Chinese idea of domestic socialism. He is doing good, or at any rate is very happy in the thought that he is doing so. He talked much of Urquhart and his personal charm. We passed to-day close by Wilbury, which is sacred in my recollection on account of Percy and Madeline Wyndham, whose home it was for so many years.

" *20th Aug.*— I am running homewards now, a long day's march, by a grass road to Stockbridge, and thence to Winchester. I was determined to re-visit the scene of my old slave days at Twyford School." This I accomplished, but the account of it in my diary is too long and too personal for insertion here. Another two days, *22nd August,* brought me home to Crabbet, making up 345 miles by road in the fifteen days and a half of my pilgrimage.

Visits to Saighton and Cumloden occupy the rest of my diary of this summer of 1894, but it contains nothing of any political consequence. On *29th September* I write:

"I am preparing for a long departure from England, which may be for years and may be for ever, for I am in the mood for farewells. In public matters there has been the war between Japan and China. My sympathies are with Japan, because her victory will mean a check put to European expansion in that quarter of the globe, and an encouragement to Orientals everywhere to arm themselves and fight against it. Old-fashioned China is a colossus, with feet of clay, interesting, but doomed if it does not put its house in order, somewhat on European lines. The Japanese stand towards China much as Arabi and the Liberal party in Egypt stood towards Turkey twelve years ago. The defeat of Japan by China would have meant immediate European interference in Japan's affairs.

" I am leaving home for Gros Bois, Tunis, and Egypt, and am making arrangements to stay abroad over next summer, but I promise nothing to myself. Anne and Judith will meet me in Egypt in the middle of November, that is far enough ahead for my hopes to look, and so to Crabbet I bid a long good-bye. I shall perhaps never go back to it as my home, for I have plans of making Newbuildings my Sussex home instead. We are so much abroad, that so large a house and establishment are thrown away on us. Newbuildings would fulfil all our purposes."

My usual autumn visit to Gros Bois lasted till 18th October. While there, there is one entry worth transscribing :

" 14*th Oct.* (*Sunday*).— To Paris for the day and breakfasted with General Faverot. He had with him General Descharmes, a young M. de Sivry (a grandson, Wagram tells me, of the Duke of Brunswick), and a son of General Fleury. Descharmes talked much of Japan, where he was military instructor for some years, and in glowing terms of their success in the war with China. He declares them to have *le diable dans le corps* for fighting, and that it would take a European Power all it knew to beat them. ' I would not,' he said, ' undertake to land an army in Japan with less than 60,000 men, all Frenchmen.' "

CHAPTER VIII

A VISIT TO TUNIS AND TRIPOLI

My winter's journey this year began with a visit I had long designed to pay to my cousin, Terence Bourke, in Tunis, where he had bought land in the neighbourhood of Bizerta, and had made his home, having also the position there of unpaid British Vice-Consul. He was a younger brother of my old ally, " Button," who figures so conspicuously in my former volumes, and, like him and all the Bourkes, was gifted with extreme natural ability for dealing with men and generally for affairs. Terence, by this special quality, had made for himself an exceptional position in the regency of Tunis. He had learnt to talk Tunisian Arabic perfectly, and had acquired an influence with the native Tunisians of all classes, unrivalled by any other European. Of all the men I have known who have had dealings with the East, and whom I have seen engaged with them in conversation, I place him first in his power of making friends with them, for he has what Englishmen so seldom possess, an inexhaustible patience equal to the Oriental's own, which enables him to sit as they do, hour after hour, conversing with them, and show no weariness however dull their talk. This is a great power, and through it he has always been successful in acquiring their attentive sympathy, and in obtaining from them their confidence and help. I have often thought that if our Foreign Office had had the wit to name Terence its Ambassador at the Sultan's Court, Abdul Hamid would have remained to this day the ally of England, instead of its obstinate enemy, but that is a kind of intelligence seldom found in Downing Street. This is my diary of my time with him.

" *21st Oct. (Sunday).*— Arrived after a smooth passage at Tunis. The weather still very hot here. Terence met me on the quay, and we came straight up to his house in the Moslem quarter, a lovely old tile-encrusted bit of *bric-à-brac* as one would wish to live in. One enters by a side door in an arched passage, through which the street passes, and by a steep, tortuous stair to the upper floor. One has to stoop to pass into the apartment, and finds oneself in a marble *patio* with four pillars, supporting a dome open from above, the walls partly tiled, partly in white marble, and the woodwork of the roof painted in red and green. From this central hall, which is about 20 feet square, the rooms branch off, the house being roughly speaking, though not exactly, cross-shaped,

with stair and passage leading to the harem at two of the corners.
The furnishing is simple and Oriental, but without pretence. Terence
keeps one young man as house servant, a porter and two women, a
widow and her sister, whom being in poor circumstances, he took into
his house through kindness, Moslems though they are, without offence
in the neighbourhood, and who are his servants, strong, able-bodied
women who go silently about the rooms with arms and legs bare and
unveiled.

"After an excellent breakfast, Terence took me to the bazaars,
which are more beautiful and more purely Oriental than any I have
seen, and then to the Bey's town palace, built, but on a large scale,
in the same style as his own little house, which I have just described.
In contrast to all this we then passed through the French quarter, mean,
noisy, and with stinks beyond description, whereas the Arab town is
sedate and clean and quiet. I have never anywhere seen a contrast so
entirely in favour of Islam. Tunis has recently been made a seaport
by the French, through the device of banking up and dredging a State
canal, across the shallow lagoon which divides Tunis from the sea,
just as the Suez Canal crosses Lake Menzaleh, it is difficult to understand with what commercial object, as there is not sufficient space
inside for many ships to lie. A better plan would have been to make
the port at Goleta, the site of Carthage, which is near the sea, and is
already connected by railway with Tunis.

"*22nd Oct.*—Drove with Terence to the site of Carthage, where
Cardinal Lavigerie has built an unsightly cathedral and monastery, with
a *buvette* attached to it for pilgrims to the shrine of St. Louis. St.
Louis died here on his last unfortunate crusade and, Terence tells me,
is venerated as a saint by the Moslems as well as by the Christians of
the district, who affirm that on his death-bed he made profession of
Islam. He is known to them as Sidi Abu Saïd, and they show his
tomb at a village of that name hard by. The waiting room, nevertheless, of the monastery is adorned with huge cartoons in illustration
of his victories and death as a Christian saint, coloured in the vilest
form of French ecclesiastic art. The gasconading of these pieces is
worthy of Lavigerie, an ambitious prelate who pushed himself into
public notice, with the aid of French Chauvinism, intending to become
Pope. This, however, was not in the decrees of Providence.

"From Carthage we went on to Marta, a summer seaside residence
of rich Tunisians, and lunched with Drummond Hay, our Consul-
General, and his family. They are moving in a few days to Beirout.
With Hay I had much talk on North African affairs. He tells me
the French are trying to work their frontier round by Merzouk to the
south of Tripoli, where they are beginning to open markets, but he
thinks that eventually they will find strong resistance in the Senussi

confraternity. They are making friends, however, with the Tuaregs
and the Negroid inhabitants of the southern oases. As to Egypt, he
professes to share my view of the danger and uselessness of our holding it. He told me that he had recently been given the opinion of one
of our high naval experts, and that it was to the effect that in case
of war with France the garrison in Egypt would have at once to be
withdrawn, and indeed the whole Mediterranean evacuated by our
fleet. To hold Egypt would not be possible.

"I find it very difficult to carry on a conversation in the Tunisian
dialect, even the commonest Arabic words are either unknown here
or so travestied as to be unrecognizable. There is a fondness for
diminutives and for throwing the accent on the last syllable. Amidst
the more educated class a better Arabic is spoken, as also I believe by
the Arabs of the South and the Bedouins generally, but the Berbers
are nearly unintelligible to me. Terence speaks to all with the great-
set fluency, a vile patois but with precisely the native Tunisian accent.
His slightly falsetto voice completing his disguise as no European.

"*23rd Oct.* — Called with Terence on Rifault, the French President
in Charge, who told me nothing interesting, only the common banal-
ities used to strangers on such occasions; and on General Leclerc, the
French commander-in-chief. This done, we took carriage with a pair
of mules for Bizerta, where Terence has a European house, a distance
of some forty miles in less than five hours. A long, dull road with
long stretches of brown fields, at this time of year empty of all life
except that of a few poor tents, with cattle grazing on the stubbles.
It is not till near Bizerta that the hills begin.

"*24th Oct.* — At Bizerta. Terence's house here is less interesting
than the other, being modern and European in style. He has told me
about his domestic life in Tunis. The two women who keep house
for him there lived in his quarter and were very poor, and he has
allowed them to inhabit his house, which they look after in return.
At first, he said, the neighbours objected to these Moslem women living
under the same roof with him, but now they have accepted him in
their quarter and find no fault. Thus he has been able to lead a quite
native life, has learned the language (Tunisian Arabic) thoroughly,
and knows more of the people than any European in Tunis. Here in
Bizerta he manages his large property, takes contracts of all kinds,
speculates in oil, and acts as Her Majesty's unpaid Vice-Consul at an
office in the town. He seems beloved of all, and it is natural, for he
is kindly and quiet and full of intelligent talk, and he has that rare
virtue in an Englishman of being never in a hurry, or bored, or out
of temper, or too busy to see and speak to the poorest man that calls
on him. We went together to see a few details of his management.

"*25th Oct.* — We went round the old town, once a famous pirate's nest, now becoming little by little invaded by Europeans, but still interesting, and stopped to drink coffee with a fat citizen, one of Terence's friends.   In the evening we rode down into the village and talked again, but I am confounded to find that I understand hardly a word of what is said.   Terence is happy and at home with everybody and has a fund of good humour which makes him everywhere *le bienvenu.*   We played chess in the evening.

"*26th Oct.*— We have had much talk all day on Oriental and religious subjects, and I find Terence to have ideas not unlike mine on these matters, and we have made a plan of going in the Spring to visit the Senussi in the Tripolitan desert and perhaps making profession of Islam, at least I hope some day to do so.   I think a hermitage of the kind I have been seeking might be found in the country near Cyrene. In the evening we made a round of the eastern shores of the lake in a steam launch belonging to the Harbour Company.

"*28th October (Sunday).*— Back to Tunis.   Terence tells me the agricultural colonists here are of a superior class to those of Algeria, there being some young Frenchmen of good family among them. These are opposed to annexation, and take the part of the natives as against the encroachments of the officials, but the town colonists are for making Tunis a French province.   The worst of all are some from Algeria, where they are all rabid against '*les Arabes.*'

"*29th Oct.*— Once more in Terence's delightful house in Tunis, Rue des Silots, 41.   A young Tunisian came in to-day to play chess with me and I won two games of him, but he has considerable ideas of play on the Arab lines, which I fancy were once also those of Europe.   The principal differences in rule are that the pawns cannot advance two steps at a time at their first move and that castling is performed in three moves, the king having the right on the second occasion to manœuvre like a knight.   This young man, who is well educated, talked a quite comprehensible Arabic, and I am beginning to understand the others.

"We went in the morning to see the cavalry *remonte* and were shown sixty or seventy stallions, half-a-dozen of them Arab, none good, except one old horse said to be a *Shouey-man* from Nablous. The best were four white barbs from the province of Oran, thick set, short legged, which would be handsome if they had less drooping quarters.   The native Tunisians unfit to breed from in any country.

"*30th Oct.*— Started with Terence for Kerouan by road with four horses abreast in a landau, very like the old *vetturino* travelling in Italy of fifty years ago, very slow but pleasant in fine weather.   We rested two hours at midday on the road under a Carob tree, and stopped for the night at a *fondouk,* a clean airy place the property of a Sherifa, a widow of Tunis, whose husband built it as a speculation forty years

ago. It used to be a paying concern, but the new diligence service has
spoiled its trade, the respectable keeper of it told us. These *fondouks*
are like the *khans* in Turkey, a number of little empty rooms paved
with tiles, where the traveller pays a few piastres for his night's lodging and provides his own food. We paid five francs, which included
a franc for stabling. I should be glad to be always as well lodged in
Europe. The road passes over a series of plains, partly cultivated in
the summer, but all bare now, the hills beyond very beautiful.

" 31*st Oct*.— Another long drive, crossing the Enfida estate. This
caused at one time a political question between England and France,
the facts of the case being these : Kheireddin Pasha (the same who was
afterwards Grand Vizier at Constantinople) having got together this
immense property sold it to a French land company, whereupon a right
of pre-emption was claimed by a Jew, a protected British subject, as
neighbouring proprietor. It was before the French Occupation, and
both governments backed their own clients for political reasons. The
Jew's claim, however, was a rather doubtful one, and as the French
company gave more than the land was worth, he was in fact no loser,
and the British Government gave way. The estate consists of a vast
tract of plain, most of it capable of cultivation, but exposed to the
south winds. The company has planted many hundreds of acres with
vines, but on the whole Terence says it does not pay. The high road
passes for several miles through it, and through the chief farming establishment of which they are trying to make a town of the usual
French kind, with poplars and eucalyptus trees.

" Beyond this there is nothing more in the shape of a house until
one gets to Kerouan. We were so pleased with our night at the *fondouk*
that we determined to go to another at Kerouan instead of to the
French Hôtel. (We were both travelling in Eastern dress.) And so
after some wandering in the streets, it being already dark, we have
taken up our quarters at a house of reception, which is entirely Arab,
and entirely Moslem, about the centre of the town. It is an *okeilah*
or lodging house, where merchants hire rooms by the month in which
to deposit their goods and sleep. We pass in it for an Indian Moslem
merchant and his friend, a Syrian, from Damascus.

" 1*st Nov*.— The *okeilah* is a poor place. We have one little room
between us like a prison cell, opening on to a balcony which runs round
the inner court, open at the top. It is dirty and bug ridden, but decent
and essentially Oriental. The proprietor is a respectable merchant,
originally from Sfax, who sits all day in a room on the ground floor,
which is his shop and counting-house. His trade is to buy wool and
other desert produce from the Bedouins, and to sell them linen cloth.
A number of them have been all the morning in the courtyard, very
noisy in their bargainings, most of them of the Slasi tribe who have a

good robber reputation inherited from past times. Our driver, Rashid, pointed out to us yesterday the sandy passage in the road where caravans used to be attacked by them in the good old days, and even sometimes now of dark nights. This reminds me that about ten miles from the town we came upon a mounted Arab who shouted to us as he passed that a cousin of his had just been killed upon the road, and he was riding for help.

" The proprietor has a son, a simple-minded youth in a white turban, who comes to sit with us and talk, and there are two servants, one a merry man who makes coffee at the door, the other a vague old mendicant who occasionally sweeps out the rooms, and goes on errands. Both these are *hashish* smokers openly, for at Kerouan there is no shame in the drug, and Terence, who went down to spend the evening below after I had gone to sleep, tells me the *kawaji* was most amusing, indeed they were all in roars of laughter through the night.

" Terence is incomparable as a traveller for he has the readiest possible wit and a pleasant word for everyone, and wherever he goes smiles break forth, and a kindly feeling of goodwill from man and maid. He also is an admirable cook, and with Saleh his servant, has given us excellent dishes stewed over a spirit lamp. He can sleep anywhere, and all day long, and never is put out, or bored, or in a hurry, withal of an exceeding good sense and knowledge of the proportion of things, prudent, economical, persistent, the reverse in fact of all that distinguishes Europeans in the East, and astounding at his age (twenty-four).

" We went out last night in the streets, and again this morning, and I think that no one suspects us of a disguise, though they are somewhat puzzled at our affairs. We went to the Mosques directly after breakfast, first to Sidi Okba's of which we entered the outer court only, for the inner shrine was being repaired, and a surly guardian refused us entrance, saying that without order from Sidna el Morákeb the doors could not be opened, so we had to be content with peeping in and complaining of the tyranny. We saw, however, pretty nearly all there was to be seen before we were turned out. At the other Mosque outside the town we were more fortunate. Here we were admitted, and saw all, and made our devotions at the tomb of Sidi Sáhabi unquestioned. It was very hot all day, and we lay stewing in the balcony of the *okeilah* till the *asr* and playing chess, to the wonder of the proprietor's son, whom we told it was an Indian game. Then we went through the bazaars and outside the town to see the walls, all very interesting, and as yet little spoilt by the French invasion, and spent the evening on mats under the city walls, where there was an Arab coffee house, drinking lemonade, and so the long day ended.

" *2nd Nov.*— This morning, being Friday, the Mueddhin chaunted the whole prayer from the Minarets — and there is one just outside the *okeilah* — beginning at four and going on more than half an hour, a fine old-world ceremony, disappearing alas from Islam. Kerouan, however, is a holy city, and preserves some at least of its traditions. We were up with the first light, and having drunk coffee prepared for us by our friend the *hashishi,* and induced his old companion to carry our baggage, which he did with great unwillingness for he was still drowsy with his opium, and paid our two nights' score at the *okeilah,* three francs and a few coppers — it would have been the same if we had taken our rooms for a month, and the proprietor was too sleepy to get up and see to it — we went out through the half awake streets to the Eastern gate, and the office of the new tramway, where we waited an hour and saw the sun rise. Terence employed the time repeating to me a story told in the *okeilah* by the merchant of Sfax, which is as good as most in the Arabian Nights. (It is too long to insert here, and I reserve it for another occasion.) Then we took our places in the tram, and went at a fine gallop across the desolate plains in four hours to the sea at Sus, where we once more put off our Moslem garments and washed and dined at a Frankish restaurant. The tram journey between Kerouan and Sus is a curious mixture of old and new. The coach runs on rails laid across the open fields, drawn by horses running beside it with a long loose trace, so that when it crosses ravines the horses gallop beside it up and down the steep places without checking their pace. The track is all more or less down hill, so that once started the coach goes by its own weight, and the horses have all they can do to keep up with it in certain places, not being harnessed to any pole, the only check on the coach being a brake worked by the conductor in the steepest parts, a most exhilarating way of travelling, and quite practical for that particular journey.

" Sus is a lovely old battlemented town as yet little spoilt, though the usual obscene French houses are springing up outside it. I walked all over and around it and through its bazaars. There is a fine citadel commanding the town on which a French flag is hanging half-mast high. The Emperor of Russia is dead.

" Here we both took ship, Terence to return to Tunis, I to go on to Tripoli, touching at Monastir and Mehadir, two lovely mediæval strongholds by the sea. In the latter I had the good luck to make a friend. Seeing a nice clean Arab coffee-house in front of the mosque, I sat down in it at the same time with a respectable Bedouin, whom I saluted. He ordered at once two cups of coffee, and we talked and made friends, he in good Arabic, a very worthy man, living, he told me, some ten miles from the town, and he has promised, if he passes through Egypt next year on the pilgrimage, to alight at Sheykh Obeyd. I have seldom met a better bred or more kindly man. At Sfax, where we arrived at daylight next morning, *4th Nov.*, I had an odd adventure. Having made acquaintance with a respectable looking man in the boat which took us to the shore, I was glad to accept his invitation that he should show me round the town, which he did with all politeness, and then invited me to his house. This was in a by street of no very reputable appearance, the entrance being by a low door where a donkey stood tied, and on entering I saw at once that it was no Moslem house, as I had supposed my friend to be, for there were women there unveiled, and it flashed on me what was the truth, that they were Jews. This became clearly the case when they set a meal of greasy bread before me, and tried to make me drink absinthe, and I had some difficulty in finding excuse to get away and to explain that I was not myself a Jew, for my conductor had come to the conclusion that I must be one, for my having condescended to speak to him and enter his house, for in these North African towns the Jews are treated as pariahs by the Mohammedans, and he did not understand it as possible that I could be other than one of his own nation treating him with the politeness I had shown. It is no less characteristic of the position Jews hold in Tunis that as soon as I had explained to him the mistake he had made, his manner at once became changed from one of hospitable anxiety to please, to one of undignified begging for a *bakshish,* which I was of course only to glad to give, feeling that the fault had been mine.

" Sfax is an interesting, and except for the Jew quarter, a wholly Moslem town, inhabited mostly by Sherifs, every other man wearing the green turban. It was bombarded and barbarously treated by the French in 1881. The captain of our steamer, the *Ville de Tunis,* tells me that this was in some measure a mistake. When the town was summoned by the French fleet to capitulate, it happened that, being the 14th of July, in the interval before the answer was received, a salute was fired in honour of the day, and the people of Sfax, thinking it an attack and that the shots had fallen short of the town, refused terms of unconditional surrender offered to them. The town was then bombarded in earnest, two breaches were made in the walls, and the place was stormed. The French lost 700 men and gave the Moslem quarter over to sack for twelve hours (this the captain denies, but it is historical), during which the houses were broken into and the women ravished; the broken doors were long left unmended in token against them, and I noticed when I walked through the Moslem quarter in the morning that many doors showed new locks recently put in and new panels not yet painted. The city walls have been mended, but the town inside and the bazaars look poor compared with Sus. The wealth of the town lies outside in the gardens, several hundreds of which surround it, all belonging to the Moslem inhabitants. The

French colonists have tried to buy them out but they will not go. There is a bitter feeling here against the conquerors. According to my Jew acquaintance, Braham ben Gabrail Mazuz, there are a thousand houses of Jews in Sfax, probably an exaggeration. These are divided in opinion about the French occupation, but most are in favour of it, as they were badly treated by the Moors. They are mostly very poor, the richer ones doing trade as middle men between the Moors and Franks. Young Braham came on board again to wish me good-bye, and brought some cake and roast chestnuts and bread for me, but he could not resist asking me for the fare of the steam launch he had taken passage in from the shore, and a franc over.

" Our party on board is reduced to the captain, the doctor, and two cabin passengers, so I have the ship practically to myself. There are very few European colonists in these parts except the small population of drink sellers and restaurateurs. The Arabs refuse to sell their good lands, and the bad are not worth buying, nor has the French Government yet found an excuse in rebellion to confiscate these as has been done in Algeria. The taxes are low, no land tax in coin but the old tenth of the gross produce and a poll tax of, I think, twenty-five francs levied on rich and poor. This last presses on the poor and causes discontent because in the old time it was not levied in extreme cases of poverty, whereas now under the French no one is exempt. Civilized governments always commit this injustice in Eastern lands, falsely pleading immemorial custom.

" *5th Nov.*— Arrived by daylight at Gabez, a palm oasis watered by a small river which rises some five miles inland, they say in several hundred springs. This feeds the gardens, the rest of the country being desert. I found a ramshackle carriage with an Arab driver from Tripoli, who took me round and explained everything. There are but few Europeans here, some warehouses on the shore but nothing inland. The native population is Arab, not Berber. Under conduct of my Tripoli driver I visited the barrage, where there is a run of water about the size of our Mole at Leatherhead, much overgrown with reeds and weeds, an oozy unwholesome haunt of frogs and snakes. Then to the mosque and tomb of Abdul Barber, a pretty place on a hill, and so round. There was a tame gazelle running in the desert outside the villages, for there is no town of Gabez. My driver told me that before the French occupation this was a dangerous neighbourhood, as the Bedouins were always marauding. There is a certain trade here of *halfa* grass, which they bring from two or three days' journey inland, worth, my driver said, five francs the camel load.

" We left at noon and arrived at sunset off Jerba, a long, low island, wooded with olives and palms, the water so shallow that our steamer had to lie six miles from shore, so that we only saw it as an outline on the horizon. This they say is Calypso's Island, a dreamy afternoon place, lying sweltering in a stagnant sea.

"*6th Nov.*— Tripoli. A lovely white town with walls and minarets and an immense growth of palms. Here there is a natural port which could be improved if the Turkish Government would allow Europeans a concession to do it, but it wisely refuses, knowing the consequences. The foreign population consists of some 6,000 or 7,000 Maltese and Italians. There are many Jews, and a large population of Moslems, mostly of Arab race, manly and fanatical. The Tripolitans are not subject to conscription for the Ottoman army, but form a kind of militia having obtained certain terms of independence when the Sultan took possession, in return for their support given against the Bey.

"The palm gardens, which extend for ten miles, are wholly in their hands, and Europeans are discouraged, if not forbidden, from living outside the town. Beyond the gardens all is a sandy desert, and the general character of the place is like our own palm district at Sheykh Obeyd. I called at the British Consulate, and found my old friend Jago officially there, who sent his son with me in a covered cart through the palm groves and to the desert beyond. We stopped to see the Wali's garden, newly reclaimed from the sand. It has all the feature of our own garden in Egypt, but without the *lebbek* trees. He is making a number of such gardens, using the soldiers to do the labour as is the way in Turkey. Then to a place they call the Hahneh, which is a bit of high, stony ground kept bare for the purpose of assemblies and festivities in the centre of the palm gardens. From it one sees nothing but palm tops all round." [The palm district here described was the scene in 1911 of the abominable atrocities committed by the Italian soldiery when, in defiance of all right or even pretext, they made their raid on Tripoli, and massacred the Arabs of the oasis.] "Then to the Suk el Jumaa, and the Suk el Thalatha held on the seashore. Here we found a great concourse of Arabs with camels, horses, asses, and cows for sale, several thousands of them on the beach. Some had brought a load of *halfa,* others sheep, others woollen shawls. I bought a grey and white shawl for fifteen francs, more than their market value, though really beautifully pieces, like the best Scotch or Irish homespun, only better. I should say a good trade might be made by importing these to England.

"After this we went back to a midday meal at the Consulate, a good old Moorish house, but standing unfortunately in the Maltese quarter, which is noisy and filthy in the extreme, contrasting with the Moslem quarters, which are clean, silent and decorous. The Turks keep about 6,000 regular soldiers in Tripoli, but count the native militia at as many more. They have Mudirs and Kaimakams in the principal towns inland as far as Ghadamés, but the policing of the country district is done by the Arabs. They say these inland districts are fairly secure for native travellers, but a great caravan, which started for Wadai in the far south two years ago with £40,000 worth of goods, was plundered there by Rabagh Ibn Zebeyr when he attacked Wadai last year, and none of the merchants have yet returned. This has caused great lamentation and distress in Tripoli.

"We weighed anchor in the afternoon for Malta, there being no direct steam communication between Tripoli and Egypt.

"*7th November.*— We arrived off Malta by daylight, and got inside the harbor at Valetta by nine o'clock, certainly a splendid place. I called at once on Count Strickland, to whom Terence had given me a letter. I was surprised to find him quite a young man, he is thirty-four, and he reminded me that we had met already at Cambridge, when he was an undergraduate and one of the chief officials of the Union and I was down there with John Dillon only seven years ago ; now he has been for six years secretary to the Malta Government, a post of no small political importance, he being half a Maltese, through his mother, a Countess della Catena, and having married De la Warr's eldest daughter, Lady Edeline Sackville. I found him very busy preparing for a debate on the estimates in the Maltese Legislative Council, an annual event, the principal political one of the year.

"The Council was to meet at half-past two, and he took me there with him to attend the debate, an interesting display. The Governor, Sir Arthur Freemantle, was in the chair, the six official members to his left, the fourteen elected members to his right, three or four benches at the end of the chamber being for the public. I was given an arm-chair behind the Governor's. The Council Chamber is a splendid room, and the ceremonial was dignified, but with a certain air of unreality as in a debating club, though it was an important occasion, for politics are running high in Malta just now. The leader of the opposition, Savona, is a man of about fifty, keen-eyed, alert, professional, reminding me a little of Freycinet. He knows English well, and made his attacks sometimes in English, sometimes in Italian, for both languages are used optionally, the more animated speeches being in Italian. There seemed to be a very full liberty of speech, but no applause or dissent of the kind that makes our House of Commons a babel. To me it was most interesting, as the questions treated turned on Constitutional right, and were dealt with ably and with passion. Savona on some previous occasion had been taunted by an official member with having allowed the Estimates to pass untouched, and he was determined now to reduce this year's on certain points in protest against an infringement made three years before by an order of the Colonial Government of the Maltese Constitution. Elected members had been deprived of their right to become members of the Executive. Strickland replied in an able, debating speech, but without, as I thought, having the better argument, or commanding the sense of the Council. One of Savona's proposed reductions was of £10 for the repainting of the Government barge, and this he made fun of. He found, however, support on the point in one of the elected members, Mozu, and Savona lost the amendment, though he carried another reducing the vote by £266 in regard to other items. Freemantle then retired, and a rather noisy discussion followed about his successor in the chair, during which, as it was late, I too went out. On the whole I was pleased with the debate, which was ably conducted by the opposition, there being but one very foolish speaker, a deaf old man, who talked nonsense about *i poveri Maltesi* in and out of season. There was certainly more reality in it than in the Viceregal Council meetings I attended at Calcutta, and must do good as putting a check on the Government's autocratic vagaries, if nothing more.

"Dined with young Sitwell of the Rifles at the Club, and was glad to find him talking sensibly about the exclusion of the Maltese nobility from its membership. This is a notorious scandal and cause of ill-feeling. Looking through the Club list I can find no more than two Maltese names among the English ones, Strickland's and Dingli's. The tone of English society here, Sitwell tells me, is violent about the Maltese and absurd. He and his regiment are off next week for Bombay, where he will find race arrogance more violent still.

"*8th Nov.*— Drove across the island through a series of lovely villages, all of hewn stone, to Hajar Kim, where there is an ancient temple of the Druidical kind, then with Strickland to his country house, on the way to Città Vecchia, a fine villa of the beginning of last century, with courts and fountains and an orange garden. This he inherits from his mother. He tells me there are about twelve families in the island which enjoy a *majorat,* his being one, in the rest property has been divided among all the children, and so has disappeared. This dates from the time of the knights. When the island was given to the Knights of St. John in 1530 by Charles V a proviso was made that it should revert to the Crown; consequently, when the English first occupied Malta it was in the name of the King of Naples that they did so. The French knights had betrayed the island to Bonaparte, who took possession of it as part of the French Republic, ill-treated the inhabitants, robbed the churches, and speedily made the French detested. The Maltese rose against them and invested the fortress for eighteen months and forced a capitulation which the French made, not to them but to Nelson — the annexation to England was an afterthought.

"Strickland explained Savona's attitude of opposition as one caused by disappointment. Savona began life as a soldier in the hospital corps, but having learned English he bought his discharge, set up a school and newspaper, and attacked the Government. He was then taken in the Government to keep him quiet, but left it when the Constitution of 1887 [1] was granted, he having opposed it and recorded in a minute his view that Malta should be governed as a Crown Colony of a severe type. This minute was thrown in his teeth when he seceded from the Government and set up as its violent antagonist. Strickland, of course, is officially prejudiced against him, and will not see in him any patriotic motive, but. he admits that public opinion generally is anti-English among the educated Maltese, while the country people are indifferent. Savona, he assures me, is losing his popularity, but he, Strickland, is tired of the worry and would be glad to change his chief secretaryship for a Colonial appointment. I find him clever and interesting.

"*9th Nov.*— Left Malta for Egypt *via* Brindisi."

The winter that followed that year and the following spring in Egypt was one that has left me few political records, the new National movement headed the last two years by the Khedive Abbas having lost its first impulse through the reasons I have already described, and I stood aside busying myself with other things, and beyond a single visit to the Khedive at Abdin Palace, my diary contains little worth transcribing. I arrived at Sheykh Obeyd on *15th Nov.* and found Anne and Judith already there, and on the 21st Fenwick Pasha, who for the last two years has been English adviser at the Home Office and head of the police, called on me. He had, compared with most Englishmen, been favourable to native self-government, and under the new *régime* had become out of favour:

" Fenwick leaves Egypt immediately to join his regiment in India. He spoke strongly and rather bitterly of the recent change in the administration which has put the police once more under the Mudirs, and thinks it quite uncompensated by the appointment of Gorst as English Adviser at the Ministry of the Interior. He thinks Cromer may have yielded the point from a Macchiavellian motive of allowing the native Government to make mistakes of which he will profit later, but I do not think this.

" *29th Nov.*— To-day being the Khedive's birthday and a whole holiday, Tigrane Pasha came to see us; he is down on his luck politi-

---

[1] Malta had been granted a Constitution of very restricted type by the English Government in 1887, avowedly as an experiment, with the result that many abuses in the government of the island were remedied; but a strong movement having been set on foot by the native Maltese for union with the Italian kingdom the Constitution was subsequently withdrawn.

cally and looks at things as going badly, regarding Gorst's appointment to the Ministry of the Interior as a new encroachment.

"*30th Nov.*— Sheykh Mohammed Abdu to lunch with us. He tells me the Khedive's ideas are unchanged since last year, that he is still bitter against Cromer and the Occupation, that his visit to England was prevented last summer by the Sultan, and much else. The Khedive is very kind to him, Abdu, now, and gave him a private audience of thirty-five minutes, and he has obtained his long-wished for grant of £2,000 a year for the Azhar University. A committee is to be appointed to see to the spending of the sum. We talked over old events and he gave me again the history of the Mufettish Ismaïl Sadyk's murder by Ishak Bey on board the Khedive's steamer. Ishak strangled him with his own hands. He says this was certainly done on the river, immediately after Ismaïl Sadyk's arrest by the Khedive Ismaïl opposite the Jesireh palace. He told us the story of Ali Pasha Sherif's slavery adventure. Ali Pasha Sherif had been recently arrested by our people on a charge of slave dealing, he being the oldest and most respectable personage perhaps in Egypt, and President of the Legislative Council. The Pasha had behaved very foolishly, Abdu said, ' like a child.' The truth was he is in his dotage and has become foolishly attached to a woman on whom he spends his time and money, and it was for her that he had bought the slaves, and he told us also of Nubar's moneymaking schemes now he is in office, and of other scandals that have taken place during the summer.

"*5th Dec.*— Had luncheon with Riaz. He tells me the Khedive's politics have not changed at all since last year. He (Abbas) hates Nubar, and is sorry now, ' poor young man,' for the mistake he made in allowing Cromer to change his Ministry. He would have gone to England in the summer, but was prevented by a French intrigue acting on the Sultan. He lamented the usurpation of new authority by Lord Cromer in the Ministry of the Interior, etc., etc.

"*10th Dec.*— Saw the Khedive at Abdin Palace. He received me cordially, even affectionately, and on my congratulating him on a domestic event expected in his family, and which had been announced, said: ' Yes, it came upon us quite as a surprise. Now I shall marry her. I wished to do so once, but when I consulted our religious authorities they told me I must wait till the child was born. But I will marry her the very day afterwards, this is according to rule.' I said: ' There was no pleasure in life like that of being a father, and hoped that his son would be a blessing to him.' He is evidently in the highest delight. Then he talked of his journey to Europe, and thanked me for my letter about the Prince of Wales. ' I should have liked to go to England,' he said, ' but was prevented at Constantinople. It is impossible to do anything with *him* (meaning the Sultan). Will you

believe it, I was twenty days at Constantinople, and was watched all
the time by spies. He gave me two of his aides-de-camp, who were
constantly with me, even sleeping in my palace at night. Not once did
he discuss any political subject with me, though I several times brought
them forward when we were alone. Each time I did so he jumped
up and shut the windows, lest we should be overheard, but I could
get nothing from him. Even Mukhtar, who was there three months,
got no more than a lecture for not preventing the Cairo newspapers
from writing against him. He told Mukhtar to spend money — he
might pay each newspaper £1,500 a year — but Mukhtar refused to
have anything to do with it. Mukhtar will never be Grand Vizier.
All who serve the Sultan are expected to bow to the ground and say,
" Certainly, your Majesty." We shall never come to any good with him
for our Caliph and Emir el Mumenin.'

Abbas asked me if I had had any news of a new revolt in Arabia, and
I told him I had seen paragraphs in the papers about it, but attached
little importance to them, as such paragraphs always appeared when
diplomatic pressure was being put at Constantinople, and just now the
Armenian question was being pushed forward. The new friendship
between England and Russia boded no good for the Ottoman Empire.
He said: 'I have information that an agreement has been come to
between them by which Russia is to occupy Armenia.' This seems most
improbable, and with it the abandonment of Cyprus by us, as we could
not consent to it without retiring from the Cyprus Convention, which
guarantees the integrity of the Sultan's territory in Asia. As to his
visit to England he said: 'The King of the Belgians invited me to
stay with him, and I asked permission at Constantinople, but was told
I should make pretext to decline, and avoid *all* visits.' He is evidently disgusted with the Sultan's timidity and narrow-mindedness,
but I noticed that he never once mentioned him by name, only as He.

" From this we went on to home matters, and the way in which
Nubar's hand had been forced in the matter of the new arrangement
at the Ministry of the Interior. Nubar was old and stupid, he said,
and had been made to appear to demand it. I am inclined, however,
to suspect that this was merely Nubar's way of excusing himself
to his master. About the slave-trading case brought against Ali Pasha
Sherif, the Khedive told me that it was without doubt a trap laid for
him by Shäffer and the Slave Trade Bureau. Dr. Shafai was an accomplice, and the three slave women had been taught their parts.
When Shafai was condemned to hard labour he was not really sent
to Toura prison, but kept for a month at the caracol in comfortable
rooms upstairs. He, the Khedive, had been asked to pardon him, but
had said the law must take its course. Then they sent him to Toura,
but made him second doctor there. It was all a political intrigue to

discredit Ali Pasha and frighten the Legislative Council. He complained of the timidity and lack of fibre in the native Egyptian members of the Council. 'Look,' he said, 'at Heshmet Pasha, we all looked upon him as a Nationalist and a Riazist, yet directly the trouble came last year he went round at once.' It now being twelve o'clock, after a little talk about Tunis, the Khedive got up and, taking my hand with both his, thanked me and said he knew I was one he could depend on, and who had the welfare of Islam at heart. I am more struck than ever at the frankness of his character and the clearness of his ideas."

The first three months of the New Year, 1895, were devoted by us almost entirely to desert travelling, when we explored the hill country that lies between the Nile and the Red Sea, a piece of desert land almost entirely unknown to Europeans, or indeed to the townspeople of Cairo and the fellahin of the Delta, and as yet unmapped, to me a great additional charm, and except for a few scattered Bedouins quite uninhabited. We had on this occasion my cousin Mary Elcho with us, who was spending the winter in Egypt, and we pushed our explorations as far as the Red Sea, and followed the coast line down it between the high mountain range of Kalála and the Gulf of Suez, a narrow strip of sandy shore seldom or never visited, there being barely room in places for camels to pass, a rugged shore, where the only sign of humanity is the occasional apparition of a distant ocean steamer far away on its road to India or Japan, and at the water's edge a continuous jetsam of empty brandy and rum bottles cast up by the waves, and marking the unholy track of Western civilization. The whole of the precipitous Kalála chain, which runs in places to a height of four and five thousand feet, was in the ancient days before Islam the scattered abode of those early Christian hermits who were so picturesque a feature of the fourth and fifth centuries, and may still, some of them, be identified as former hermitages by the possession of a trickle of water and a palm or two still growing wild, and one monastery, still inhabited, the convent of St. Anthony. It lies in one of the ruggedest and most desolate places in the world, difficult of access for camels, and parted from the Nile Valley by eighty miles of inhospitable desert, and twenty from the seashore on the other side. In all that journey we had met with no inhabitant after our first day's march, and it was with some difficulty that we made out our road to it, for the Bedouins with us had never been there, and we only had knowledge of it by the vaguest hearsay. The convent is hardly ever visited by Europeans, and ours was absolutely the first occasion on which women had been admitted within the Monastery walls since its foundation some 1,500 years ago. All this was intensely interesting, but descriptions of desert journeys lie outside the scope of my present memoirs. It is only here and there that in the interval of these expeditions I find a notice of public events, as for instance:

"*25th Feb.*— The long expected Egyptian crisis seems at last approaching in Europe, if one may judge by the foreign newspapers which are threshing the question of the English Occupation once more out. I fancy Rosebery's escapade with the Congo Company has set up the German Emperor's back, and he is encouraging the French to push us out of Egypt. In spite of our swagger, and it is past all bounds, we shall have one day to go. Our papers repeat the bravado that a great nation like England does not yield to threats. My experience is that it is to threats only of very immediate chastisement that the British public does yield. Soft words never have effect with us."

About the same time the announcement reached me of poor Randolph's death, and on the 30th of March of Princess Hélène's engagement to the Duke of Aosta, and lastly on the 11th of April of the huge scandal in London of Oscar Wilde's arrest and prosecution. Of political events in Egypt there is no further record worth transcribing. The 27th of April saw us back at Crabbet.

This year I saw more than ever of George Wyndham, and spent much of my time with him. He was at the height just then of his literary activity, having become editor of the " New Review," and being pushed forward by Henley as a writer, and at his instigation, and Henley's, my thoughts took a more decidedly literary direction than before. He proposed that I should write for him on Arabian subjects, and this I, being full just then of desert memories, willingly agreed to.

"*12th May.*— Henley proposes to bring out a selected edition of my poems under his auspices, and promises to run me into a more public place as poet than what I now occupy. I am not particularly anxious for this, but he and George may try. George is a good enthusiastic friend, and very dear to me. He has given me a touching description of Pembroke's funeral, at which he was present in the little churchyard near Wilton, where they buried him; the Wilton gardens in their full Spring splendour, the birds singing their hearts out, and many men, the most distinguished in the land, in tears. Pembroke lived a noble, if an unproductive, life, a man of large sympathies and high ideals, but no fixed beliefs, and no results in action. He had at one time an opening in politics which might have led him to any sublimity when Disraeli gave him a place in his Government at the age of twenty-four, but his health was not sufficient for the strain, and he could not go on with it. The rest of his life was spent at Wilton, a paradise on earth, the possession of which I have always thought hinders its possessors, by its beauty, from engaging in the world's ambitions. He lived honoured and beloved by women and by men.

"Sir Robert Peel, too, is dead. I met him on Friday at the St. James' Club and had a talk with him about Japan and China. His death was sudden in the night. He was not a wise man, but interesting, a very good speaker, full of *bonhomie* and sometimes of wit.

"*29th May.*— My poor Locker is dead, not other than a worthy ending to a happy life. His last day was a cheerful one they all say, and he talked more strongly than for some time past. I had called in the evening at Rowfant and had seen him, and was there till seven, and then took his son Godfrey back riding with me, so that he must have died very shortly afterwards, for the announcement is in the 'Times' this morning.

"*Later.* I called again at Rowfant and found to my surprise the family not in mourning. My friend, instead of being dead, is a trifle better, and talks of outliving some of us. It is a mystery how the thing got into the 'Times,' from which it had been copied into all the evening papers with long obituary notices. [It was not till two days later that he died at the age of seventy-four.]

"*22nd June.*— Yesterday when I was in London I called at half-past five on Margot, who is invalided. While we were talking Sir William Harcourt came in, and their talk turned at once to politics, the Cromwell statue debate, and other interests of the moment, but nothing presaged what at that very hour was happening in the House, namely, the defeat of the Ministry on St. John Broderick's amendment in Supply. Poor Margot, as it happened, was in some measure responsible for the Government minority, for as I left her a little after six I found yet another visitor, John Morley, at her door, and she kept him so late giving him good advice that he missed the division! To-day I see the account of it in the papers.

"*24th June.*— Rosebery has resigned, a feeble statesman though a clever man, whom we shall never, I fancy, see Prime Minister again. It seems there is to be a coalition between Lord Salisbury and the Duke of Devonshire, under Lord Salisbury's leadership. I am glad the imposture of Whig Liberalism is defunct.

"Yesterday was my last day at Crabbet, for Crabbet is let for three years, perhaps for four, and we take up our abode at Newbuildings to-morrow. We have no need, with so small a family as ours is, of so large a house, and Newbuildings is enough for all our wants, and I am in a mood to loathe old things and pine for new; nevertheless, it was a melancholy day for me in spite of the brave sun.

"*25th June.*— The day of Princess Hélène's wedding to the Duke of Aosta. The Comtesse de Paris had sent us an invitation, and I drove down to Kingston with Judith, where the wedding was, and then to Orleans House at Twickenham. It was a day of heaven, a brilliant blue sky with a light north wind to freshen the sun's heat. Judith, of course, was late at starting, and so we arrived too late to get inside the church, and the bride and bridegroom were already coming out in procession. The Duke is under-sized, of extremely dusky hue, his features good, but not imposing. Behind them came her brother, the Duke of Orleans, his broken leg still disabling him, and a little after the Prince and Princess of Wales with their daughters, and the Dukes of Coburg and Connaught, Tecks, Fifes, and a number of foreign Princes and Princesses. In the crowd of invited persons there were many French and a few Italians. There were hardly any English. Indeed, all the English I saw were not a dozen. Leighton was there and Lady Burdett Coutts, and a few men connected with the Court, but almost no one belonging to general society. Nor were there any English presents, which is strange, but though living so long in England, they hardly knew any English people. Then we all got into our carriages and drove in procession through Kingston and Twickenham, a really pretty sight, with multitudes of flags and large crowds cheering and every window filled in the old-fashioned houses. There was something Hogarthian in it all. In Orleans House tables were laid for the royal personages and Ambassadors, but we, the less distinguished, had to be content with what we could scramble for at buffets. Then we went into the garden where the bride and bridegroom were making their round of congratulations, and I had the privilege with others of kissing the bride's royal hand. My wedding present of the Kelmscott poems was laid out with the rest. Sweet personage, may she be happy!

" 26th June.— Called on Lady Lytton. She has just been appointed Lady of the Bedchamber to the Queen in the Duchess of Roxborough's place, and she showed me Her Majesty's autograph letter, which was very kindly and even touchingly worded, saying she admired the way she had borne her troubles, recalling Lytton's good services, and in a postscript saying she was glad of Victor's recovery from his recent illness. Certainly the old Queen has the power of conveying her meaning in a few simple, not to say commonplace, words so as to give the impression of a true feeling, more than most women. It affected me to read the letter, I hardly know why.

" 29th June.— Called on Harry Cust at the ' Pall Mall Gazette ' Office. He is much improved since last year and takes his editorship seriously. He told me that when he began with the ' Pall Mall Gazette ' he had a promise of office as soon as the Tories should come into power, but that is now all swept away.

" Then to Newbuildings, where I joined Anne, and we took formal possession. It pleases me much to be there, for it is far more of a hermitage than Crabbet was, and one can forget here the worries of the world.

"*6th July.*— Called on Betty Balfour, whom I found in high spirits at the appointment of her husband as Chief Secretary in Ireland. Gerald is a very able fellow and will doubtless do well on his brother's lines, and I had some talk with him about his prospects there.

"*11th July.*— Pamela's wedding to Eddy Tennant, and afterwards with Judith to a dance at Sibell Grosvenor's in honour of it. George (Wyndham) was in delightful vein and supped with Judith and me, entertaining us with his Epicurean views of life. 'What we want in modern life,' he said, 'is to have more feasting, song, and flowers, and noise, and to sit long and late with beautiful ladies, ourselves crowned with wreaths.' Certainly his own entertainment, the first he has ever given, was perfection. He has just been returned for Dover unopposed, the first member of the new Parliament. His is a happy nature.

"*15th July.*— To my Aunt Caroline Chandler's funeral at Witley, driving there and back from Newbuildings, a full forty-five miles through the oak country of the Weald — an almost entirely uninhabited district. Witley village, with the exception of some half-dozen new cottages, is unchanged from what I remembered it as a boy or for that matter from what my mother knew it, as her drawings of it show thirty years earlier. Only the church is changed, the inside having undergone the modern rage of decoration. The funeral was a shock to me, as it was conducted with cheerful music and a merry peal of bells, which seemed to be absurd. The old English services are all made ridiculous now with pseudo-catholic ' mummeries.' They have lost their dignity of old days, but it is of a piece with the whole English character, which has changed from top to bottom in my short fifty years of recollection. Here was my poor old aunt, who, when she came to Witley first as a pretty bride in 1845, was wedded soberly and in all decorum, now in 1895 at the age of seventy-two launched into a grave piled up with flowers like a birthday cake, to the merriest strains of the organ, strains to which we might with no impropriety have danced. The only old-fashioned thing in the ceremony was that her son's widow, who inherits the property, fainted and was carried out.

"*19th July.*— Lunched with Lady Galloway. There has been a regular rout of the Liberals at the Elections. Harcourt, John Morley, Lefevre, Arnold Morley among the slain. Much talk of all this. Asquith has won or kept his seat.

"*13th Aug.*— A visit from one Oppenheim, a Jew, who has been travelling in Mesopotamia, and wants to go to Nejd. [This Oppenheim was afterwards an agent of the German Government attached to the German Legation in Cairo, much concerned in his Government's intrigues there.]

" 15th Aug.— Lunched with George Curzon at 5, Carlton House Terrace, which he has rented. We talked of things political, and of his own new position in the Government as Under-Secretary for Foreign Affairs. He prefers this to a minor place without power in the Cabinet. About Armenia, in spite of the brave words in the Queen's speech to-day, he agrees with me that they can do nothing. Russia, he says, will never consent to an Armenian buffer State, even if there were the materials to make one, and how can we put pressure on the Sultan? In truth it is impossible, and the sooner they drop it the better, which I fancy they will do. He told me all the same that the horrors were not exaggerated. I told him of Knowles wanting an article of me about Egypt. This he deprecated in due Parliamentary phrase. It was embarrassing the Government and defeating its own end. It would be better to wait a little till the Government had had time to look about it, and the rest which are the common excuses of Under Secretaries. He said that he himself was entirely opposed to evacuation, or change of any kind, that the French were out of court by their having refused the ratification of the Wolff Convention, and that he considered Lord Salisbury would be most unwilling to re-open the question, though as yet Lord Salisbury had said nothing to him on the subject, the matter was not pressing. The Government did not believe the rumours of any joint French and Russian action about Egypt. All this after luncheon.

" Then to Merton to see the new tapestry, Botticelli's Spring, which Morris is making for me there, and on to Coombe where I dined with Bertram and Laurence Currie, Bertram full of old and interesting reminiscences.

" 25th Aug.— A visit to Cromer, Newhaven Court, the Lockers' house.

" Francis Palgrave was here in the afternoon, an interesting man, garrulous, but in a good sense of the word, telling stories, principally of Tennyson, reminiscences of whom he is writing. He talked to me about his brother Gifford (the Arabian traveller), and told me that in the last three years of his life he was reconciled to the Church, and that this had made him much happier and more contented. I asked him how matters had been arranged about the wife and children, seeing that Gifford was a priest and had been a Jesuit. He said his brother had told him that no difficulty had been made, such cases having of course often happened before. He was allowed to continue his domestic life, only not conjugally ; *that* Gifford had told him laughing was no great privation. He was glad to hear me corroborate the accuracy of his brother's account of the politics of Nejd and its social condition. He was anxious I should believe Gifford was never really, or ostensibly' a Moslem.

"Miss Kate Greenaway is also staying in the house.

"*26th Aug.*— I have come to Ockham for a night, where all is much improved since Ralph came into his inheritance. Miss Lawless, the novelist, is staying here, a well-informed, clever woman, and a good talker."

On 8th September I left England once more for abroad.

CHAPTER IX

I left Newbuildings on the 5th, Anne coming up to London to see the last of me (for I was going abroad alone), and as my first stage to Gros Bois.

"*8th Sept.*— Gros Bois. We are much occupied here with a new catalogue Wagram is having made of the family papers. Many of them are most interesting. Wagram's ancestor, the father of Marshal Berthier, seems to have performed on a certain occasion some small service at Versailles — he was in a very subordinate position — helping to put out a fire in the stables and also designing a star and baton for the Marshals of France, and for these was ennobled by Louis XV. The son was therefore not quite a *parvenu* when Bonaparte attached him to his fortunes. He eventually became 'Duc de Neuchâtel et Valangin, par la grace de Dieu et l'acte impérial de Napoléon I, Empereur des Français' (such is the inscription over one of the doors of Gros Bois) and was at one time possessor of Chambord. He died while Napoleon was at Elba, and so avoided the final *débâcle*. But the Marshal's son signed an act of renunciation of the Duchy of Neuchâtel, and restored Chambord to its royal owners, since when the descendants have remained Princes of Wagram at Gros Bois, a far more enjoyable if less splendid possession. M. Jusserand was here last night, and we looked through these papers together, with Duphot the young man who is making the catalogue.

"Jusserand is a very small dark man, with large head of the brachicephalic type — left at the present moment in charge of the Foreign Office, his superiors being away *aux eaux* — a clever talker, and, I should say, a very able official as well as literary man. He was Chauvinist enough to show emotion when reading the original of the capitulation of Ulm signed by Mack, and later the document signed by Ney and others, settling the line of military demarcation in France with the Allies. There are among the documents some interesting letters from Napoleon and one from Marie Louise signed 'Louise.'

"Another interesting man here yesterday was Ludovic Halévy, who gave us reminiscences of the Second Empire when he was Clerk in the Chamber of Deputies, and acted in some sort as temporary Secretary to Morny. His reading of the Empire is that which all who were much

behind the scenes have long known to be the true one, and which History will adopt — namely, that Napoleon III was not by blood really
a Bonaparte, and as little by character, a phlegmatic, good-natured
man, fond of ease and fond of women, with a certain superstitious belief in his star, and ambitious less by natural taste than by position.
Morny, his half brother, was at the beginning his guiding spirit, but
was ousted from favour by the Empress several years before his death
in 1865. The Empress Eugenie was without doubt the cause of Napoleon III's latest misfortunes. A beautiful woman and of good family
in Spain, she was all the same an adventuress, and had had more than
one lover besides the Duke of Sesto, whom she loved before she came
to Paris. The Emperor only married her because she was clever enough
to refuse him on other terms. She led him an unquiet life, making
him constant domestic scenes, from which he fled to Marguerite
Bellanger, at whose apartment he was free from worries. (Marguerite
Bellanger was, if I remember rightly, the daughter of Bellanger, who
kept Voisin's restaurant, and, when I was at Paris, a professional lady
of pleasure.)

"Halévy recounted an incident of which he was witness when
Morny, coming back from the Conseil des Ministres, threw down his
portfolio in a rage, and swore he would never go again while the Empress was allowed to talk nonsense there. 'L'Empereur fera la guerre,'
he exclaimed, 'un de ces jours pour lui eviter une scene de famille,'
and this was precisely the thing that happened. At the time of the
quarrel with Prussia in 1870, she had come suddenly to the Council
Chamber and dismissed the Ministers in her husband's absence, saying: 'Messieurs, il y a congé aujourd'hui. Nous sommes en fête. La
guerre est déclarée.' Halévy is a capital talker — I should imagine of
Hebrew origin, judging by his profile and other signs — a neighbour
of the Prince's here at Gros Bois, and intimate, too, with the Alphonse
Rothschilds. His son, a most interesting young man of the serious
student kind one reads of in French novels but so seldom meets, was
here on Friday — an abler man, I should say, even than his father.
Poor Mme. Alphonse was also here — it being Berthe's wedding-day
— a sad woman, mourning her lost beauty and trying to be gay. There
was, of course, much talk of the attempts made against Alphonse by
the anarchists. He goes about guarded everywhere by detectives. All
complained of the lack of government in France, and all blamed the
Parliamentary *régime*.

"*12th Sept.*— Antonin. I passed through Paris on Sunday afternoon (the 8th) on my way to the Potockis here in Poland, and spent
a couple of hours at the Embassy, or rather in the Embassy garden, to
which Lord Dufferin invited me. I had an hour alone in it, sitting at
the farther end, near the grille — in some sort a sacred spot for me.

Then Dufferin came to fetch me, and took me off to Lady Dufferin, who was holding court for the Lord Mayor of London on the lawn, all sitting on gilded arm-chairs on a red carpet — the Lord Mayor, Sir Francis Reinalls, a ridiculous, pompous little man, who has come over to Paris to make a splash, bringing his gilt coach and four horses with him. Dufferin tells me that at the Elysée Reinalls took upon himself to compliment the President on his *royal* bearing, and to invite him to stay with him at the Mansion House. He seems to have made a fool of himself all round. He told me himself that he had been to the Théâtre Français, and had been so bored that he had gone away to a Café Chantant, and I see the French papers have got hold of the story, while the English ones contain a protest that he has no commission at all to represent the City of London in Paris.

" Dufferin was very kind and pleasant, as he always is to me, and showed me his books. Among them was a volume of Gregory's Memoirs, and he fired up when I noticed it, repudiating with great indignation the story told there of his aunt, Mrs. Norton, having sold the information of Peel's change on the Corn Law question to the ' Times.' He assured me it was entirely false, as he had traced the truth to Peel himself, who desired to clinch the matter. He considered it a cruel libel on his virtuous aunt. But Dufferin is touching in his family fidelity.

" At 6.30 I took train for Vienna, arriving there the night of 9th September. Stayed at Sacher's Hotel, a very excellent inn, and on the morning of the 10th, after calling on Barrington and Clarke at the Embassy, and getting my passport from them, I again took train, and so through the following night and the morning of yesterday, arriving at length somewhat tired and very dirty at Czerny Ostrov, my final station. At the frontier, Voloschitzka, I had some difficulty about my passport, of which the Russian authorities seemed suspicious, but with the help of Count Bielski, a young Pole whom I had met in the train, got through. At Czerny Ostrov a carriage and four was waiting, and I was driven rapidly to Antonin, the last half of the road in Countess Joseph Potocka's four-in-hand of four dark bay Arab mares, very beautiful ones and beautifully matched, going a great pace. The roads were good, there having been no rain for long, and we did the distance of twenty-two miles in about two hours.

" To-day I have been shown the stud. The Arab portion of it is, I am sorry to say, in a lamentable condition compared with what it was eleven years ago when I saw it last. The reason is the want of proper stallions. For one reason or another Potocki has been unable to procure a really first class one, and the horse, ' Euclid,' which he bought in India of Lord William Beresford for, I believe, 500 guineas, has proved an absolute failure at the stud. His stock are coarse, without beauty or action, and are worse than the worst we have ever bred at Crabbet. They have not even the merit, if it is one, of exceptional size. Of the six stallions he showed me there was but one preserving the Arab type, a dark chestnut with four white legs, ' Iflah,' a four-year-old with nice action, bred by a horse he had from the Babolna stud called 'Zarif,' out of a fine old mare, ' Khanjar.' The rest were not worth looking at. ' Euclid ' himself, who has been re-chistened ' Obeyan,' is a horse not unlike ' Kars,' with a fine fore-hand and good points, too, in the quarter, but with a plain head (Kars had a fine one) of the convex type, and lacking distinction all through. It is only another proof of the mistake of breeding from a winner of races if you want to get handsome Arab stock. The fastest horses are, I believe, never, among Arabians, the best sires. The mares, which we looked over in the afternoon, are far better and deserve a better sire. There are a dozen really good ones — the rest inferior — but the dozen are enough to refound the stud, though several of the best are old. I regret immensely having sold ' Shahwan ' to America, as he would have been well employed here, and, except ' Ahmar,' whom I cannot well spare, I have nothing old enough left to give. The mares I admired most were ' Druha ' and her daughter ' Nerissa,' ' Zalotna,' ' Luba,' ' Khiva,' ' Poppeia,' and ' Khalifa,' the dam of ' Iflah.' But most of them had unworthy foals to foot by ' Euclid.' On the whole it was a disappointing spectacle, and I spoke frankly to Potocki, or at least as frankly as it is possible to speak in such cases. I found him well aware of ' Euclid's ' failure. Then Countess Potocka drove me round the oak wood and through the grounds, which have been newly laid out and very well.

" 13*th Sept.*— I have had much interesting talk with Potocki about Polish history, and the great part played in it by his ancestors, who were many of them military leaders. His cousins, the Sangusckos, were independent princes in Lithuania 400 years ago ; and these lands at Antonin and Schepetowka lay on the high road — it is still called the ' black road '— of the Tartar invasions as late as 150 years ago. To come to later times, he talked of the famous Princess Czartoriska, his great-grandmother, who was the beloved of Lauzun, and he has given me Maugras' book to read, which has just come out. It is founded on Lauzun's memoirs, which Potocki assures me are authentic, and the original of which, privately printed, he has had in his hands. I asked him why Maugras, instead of giving a Bowdlerised *rechauffé* of it, had not quoted the original, and he said it entered into quite impossible details, unfit for publication. I would give a great deal to read the original as it stands, for nothing strikes me more strongly than the identity of the highly cultivated society of our day in London with that of Versailles then. Not, I think, that we are so corrupt in money matters, or perhaps quite so open in our love affairs, but still the human nature of it is identical, and the peculiarity of the co-existence of much high ideality in principle with passionate love-making in practice.

"There is much cholera going on in the villages round here. Potocki showed me a village to-day where 100 persons have died, a local outbreak, almost confined to the province of Volhynia.

"*14th Sept.*— Spent the day seeing Prince Sanguscko's stud at Christowka, a really magnificent collection of mares, no English or other than Arab blood having been admitted. The flea-bitten greys were some of them quite wonderful. There is, however, a great lack of promising young stallions, the stallions in stud use being away at Slavuta. Christowka is 20 versts — 16 miles — from Antonin across the black earth of the steppe, now all under cultivation — the few villages much swept by cholera. Christowka itself has lost 160 persons.

"We were received by the manager and his Viennese wife, a young bourgeoise who insisted on entertaining us. The Antonin Director, who was with me, is an intelligent man, a Pole from near Riga, and had been for several years in the service of the Bulgarian Government. On the way home he gave me a long and clear account of Bulgarian politics. According to him (his name is Cherkowski) Prince Alexander of Battenburg, with his many talents, was too young for the position he was given, and made many mistakes. The Russians — though as a Pole he had no desire to praise them — were really governing the country well. Their administration was excellent, and they had carried out in Bulgaria the reforms they only talk of in Russia, the finance being especially good. It has gone down rapidly since their departure. Prince Alexander was sustained by Austrian and English help. Prince Ferdinand he likes better. He, Ferdinand, is a quiet man, much addicted to science, especially botany. He would never have thought of accepting a throne but for his mother. Ferdinand is incapable, Cherkowski says, of having been concerned in Stambuloff's assassination, though Stambuloff treated him with great arrogance. Stambuloff's death was in all probability a private vengeance. He was a man of the most corrupt life, taking advantage of his official position to get women into his power, any who came or whose husbands came to him with petitions. He had violated many women, notoriously a certain singer who was engaged to be married, he and the chief of the police between them. The woman committed suicide on account of it. He was hated for these crimes, and they were probably the reason of his end. He, Cherkowski, was at the head there of the veterinary department. The Bulgarian Government had required of him to become naturalized, but he had refused, so left their service to enter that of Potocki. The Bulgarians were a clever people with much outward polish, but quite corrupt. They disliked all foreigners, but perhaps

Russians less than the rest. He does not believe that Russia will succeed in recovering her lost position in the country."

Slavuta and its stud have acquired a tragic notoriety since this entry was written, having been the scene of one of those hideous outrages which distinguished the Bolshevik revolution of 1917. Prince Sanguscko, the owner of the stud, was in his country house at Slavuta, when a number of disbanded soldiers recently returned from the Russian army broke into his house and took him out of it and brutally ill-treated him, killing him at last with their bayonets, and then pillaging the château and destroying the whole of his Arabian stud. This occurred in the autumn of 1917.

"*16th Sept.*— I was to have left to-day for Kiev, but heavy rain has fallen and the roads are impassable.

"*18th Sept.*— Potocki and I drove last night to Czerny Ostrov and dined at the house there of a certain Countess, once a woman of some fashion at Paris in the days of Napoleon III, still full of gossip, ancient and modern, for she goes yearly to Nice for the winter. At Czerny Ostrov she has a nice villa with gardens and grounds, and a select circle of such fashionable friends as the town affords, with an ancient admirer much dyed and painted.

"Then Joseph and I travelled on through the night and arrived in the morning at Kiev. The country for thirty miles or so south of Kiev is a great oak forest with spaces of cleared land — no very large trees, but growing well, they say, for the first 100 years, till their roots come to the gravel, when their growth is stopped. Oaks and birches are evidently the natural growth of the country, with alders in the swampy places and a few other trees, though there is a certain admixture of Scotch firs, new comers I should say. The Dnieper is the boundary beyond which the great fir forests of the north begin. The cleared land is a wide desolation of stubbles and beetroot, stretching for miles without hedge or landmark.

"Potocki's business in Kiev is connected with the sugar trade, in which he, in common with all the landed proprietors, is interested. The market now is overstocked, and he tells me he is working his factories at a loss. A few years ago they were giving a prodigious income, but the production has become 25 per cent. more than the home consumption, and the general world's sugar market at Odessa has fallen below cost price. He has something like 30,000 acres of land in hand, and his stake in beetroot sugar is a large one. While he went to his sugar conference, I made the round of Kiev with his agent Kosacki, who showed me everything. It is a very beautiful and interesting place with the finest situation, perhaps, of any town in Europe. The view northwards over the Dnieper and beyond over the great forest towards Moscow is splendid, and this evening, with a wonderful effect of light from the setting sun on the gilt cupolas, and a rainbow in the east, was unimaginably grand. Kiev is a very ancient and holy city, with fine churches, undergoing restoration, alas, in view of the Emperor's coming visit. The Petchersk is especially interesting, an immense Convent in the Citadel, thronged just now with pilgrims from distant places in Russia, and beneath it a catacomb to which one descends by a long stair towards the river — a fine old-world place, hardly yet ruined by the villainous modern taste.

" At the inn I made acquaintance with Count Ladislas Branicki, who has arranged that I am to go to stay with his Aunt, Countess Branicka, at Biela-Tzerkov to-morrow, also with Count Pothofski, who has a stud of Arab horses, and other friends of Joseph's. Our inn the Grand Hotel.

" *19th Sept.* — By early train to Biela-Tzerkov, changing at Fastov. There I was met by Prince John Sapieha, who had come with his niece, Mlle. de Branicka, to see another niece away by the train, both the girls very pretty in their different ways. We then drove with four horses, handsome bays, to Alexandrie, Countess Branicka's country house, a very fine place with beautiful woods and pleasure grounds where presently, after I had been entertained with tea and peaches, we went walking to see a pond netted. There is a large family party gathered here for Countess Branicka's birthday. Her married daughter, Princess Radowitz, with her children, her nephew, Prince John Sapieha, and his wife, her unmarried daughter, the pretty one, Sophie, a Countess Zeilern and her daughter, an old Count Diodati, a Swiss in attendance on Princess Radowitz, and a few others whose names I have not quite learned. It is rather perplexing to find oneself so complete a stranger among so many.

" *20th Sept.* — With Sapieha to Uzin, a stud belonging to Count Xavier Branicki, a nephew of the Countess, lying about sixteen miles away. We drove with four common horses, and on the road Sapieha explained to me the Branicki family history. Biela-Tzerkov was the capital of the Ukraine, and in former times the headquarters of Mazeppa. According to tradition the wild horse brought him here from Warsaw. The steppe was then all grass, but hardly anything of this remains now, all being under cultivation. In the latter part of the eighteenth century an immense territory of about a million and a half acres was given to the Branicki of the day — I fancy the same as the Branicki of the Lauzun Memoirs — in lieu of a long-standing claim he had against the Polish Government for the raising and maintenance of troops. He was called the Hetman. The territory was worth very little in those days, but is now a principality, bringing in about 7s. an acre, the current rent. On the death of the late Count, however, it was divided into four. the Countess's share as widow and for her children amounted to 450,000 acres. She is therefore immensely rich. The stud also was divided.

"The history of the stud, of which I have looked over the books, seems to begin authentically in 1813, though Sapieha claims for it forty years or more of antiquity. It can hardly be called a pure Arab stud, as the stallions then imported stand entered as Turk, Turcoman, Anatolian, Persian, Arab, and even in 1828 English, while the mares are equally mixed. It is clear that they have run too much after size; and at Uzin the type is nearly lost. Occasionally, however, they produce a first-class horse, and I saw two such, 'Hamat' and 'Haman,' a bay and a chestnut, of great beauty and ideal action, though 15.2 or more in height. The latter especially is a nearly perfect specimen, and will be retained to breed from. The mares are far inferior in looks to the Sanguscko mares, having coarse heads, long backs, and long legs. They carry their tails, however, generally well. One cannot avoid the conviction about them that they are of mixed origin. I only saw one mare, 'Tamisa,' one would have supposed to be an Arab. They are breeding now largely from an English thoroughbred, which gives more saleable stock. They have, however, a very beautiful imported Arab stallion, 'Heyan,' of which they are proud — a dark, full chestnut, compact, strong, and of the highest quality. I should judge him to be a horse from Nejd, as he is not quite of the Anazeh type. But they know no more about him than that he was brought to Warsaw by a dealer. I strongly advised his use for their stud.

"Countess Branicka is a most amiable woman. Her mother, she tells me, was English, a sister of Colonel Wilson Patten's wife, afterwards Lord Winmarleigh. She is clever and kind, most kind to me, doing everything to make me comfortable, and that I may feel at home. Her daughter Sophie interests me, a strange, original face, with a pretty, delicate figure, and a great look of distinction [afterwards Countess Strozzi]. The other daughter is Princess Radziwill. Sapieha (the Countess's brother) was brought up in England, served in a Dragoon regiment, and talks French with a slight English accent, English with sporting slang of thirty years ago. His father was concerned in the Polish rising of 1830, and had his whole estate in Russia confiscated, worth, Countess Branicka tells me, thirty millions of roubles. His wife, a nice plain woman, had a fortune, and they live in Galicia. He is most amiable to me, showing me all things with great zeal. He is or has been manager of the estate and stud. Altogether a distinguished family, living a large but unpretentious life. The house, Alexandrie, is less than a palace and more than a common country house, and is supplemented with several smaller houses in the grounds, where the guests have their apartments. I should be happy, but that the weather again broke up this evening, and it has become intensely cold.

" *21st Sept.*— Drove another twenty-five versts with Sapieha to see the Countess's own stud — the mares better than those of yesterday. But they are dreadfully in want of good stallions.

" *22nd Sept.* (*Sunday*).— A bad cold, so did no more stud seeing — in bed instead.   But in the afternoon to the oak wood — they call it the park — a delightful place, where we gathered orange-coloured mushrooms.   Mlle. Sophie drove a pair of chestnut mares to-day perfect in shape and type.   All the world drives here.   We went out, three four-in-hands and three pairs — one four-in-hand of ponies being driven by a child of Princess Radziwill of five years old.   There are two very fine teams, chestnuts and bays, and a third of greys, besides the ponies. All is done on a large and bountiful scale, with numbers of old servants, who carry the children about and kiss their mistress's hand or sleeve as in the East.   The park is a sanctuary for wild beasts and birds, and no gun is fired in it.   But they have an English pack of hounds, and go outside with it twice a week fox hunting.   Foxes are plentiful, but get soon to earth.   In the winter there are wolves, and Sapieha told me of a run they had had of forty-two versts after an old one, which they killed.   The hounds were afraid of it, but brought it to bay, and a peasant killed it with a cudgel.

" There has been a race this year at Warsaw, ridden by young Russian officers, of 100 versts or 120 kilometres, say seventy miles.   It was run in the extreme of the hot weather, and, out of forty-one starters, thirty-six horses died.   The race began at eight minutes past two in the afternoon, and the first horse, an English thoroughbred, arrived at a few minutes before eight.   He survived.   The second and third, also English thoroughbreds, died soon after coming in, and the fourth, an Arab from Sanguscko's stud, arrived fresh an hour after the first and took no harm.   The young officers seem to have ridden like lunatics, and I fancy the horses were only half trained.   But I am to have precise details from Potocki.   Most of the horses died actually on the road.

" I took an affectionate leave of Countess Branicka, for she is a really good kind woman, and we have made great friends.   She has a house also at Warsaw, another at Kiev, and another, I think, at Vienna. The rest of the party have also been most friendly to me, and I am glad to have made their acquaintance, where one sees them at their best, in their own country.

" We had some talk about their political misfortunes.   They all say the cause of Poland is lost, and that there is nothing more to hope. The persecution is more religious now than political.   ' I should not be surprised to wake up any morning,' said little Mlle. Sophie, 'and learn that we had to become Greeks or leave the country.' All the peasantry and many of the bourgeoisie have conformed, and the young generation of converted Poles are among the most fanatical Russians. The elder brother of Countess Branicka's husband was concerned in the rebellion of 1863, the last flicker of Polish nationality, and was exiled to Siberia, the property passing, I fancy, to the younger brother.

*   *   *   *

" *26th Sept.*— Constantinople, or, rather, Therapia. I arrived at daylight this morning in the Bosphorus, coming by Russian steamer from Odessa. A lovely morning, with a slight fog or haze, enough to give everything a mysterious look, but brightening into full sunshine later, with fresh north wind rippling the blue water. As we steamed down the Bosphorus the Russian ship's mate, who talked some English he had learned in Japan, described what might be done with such a position in the hands of a European Power, the continuous streets, the railways, the electric light, etc. Thank Heaven, it is still in its old-fashioned way.

" Arrived at Galata I was rowed straight to the bridge, and on board one of the Bosphorus boats, and was so taken back to Therapia, a slow three hours' trip, zigzagging from side to side, and in full enjoyment of the day and place. Breakfasted at Pétala's, unchanged from its condition of thirty-five years ago, when I first saw it on my way home from Athens in this very month of September, 1860. Then, going to the Embassy, I found that I was expected to take up my quarters there, and here I am. It is strange to be here, with Philip for Ambassador and Violet Fane for Ambassadress. Philip is altogether charming, unaffected by his official importance, natural and kind.

" *27th Sept.*— There are staying in the house Pom McDonnell, who is Lord Salisbury's private secretary, come out, I fancy, to gather the Ambassador's innermost thoughts for his master's benefit — a charming fellow — and Henry Yorke and Lady Lilian. I spent the morning answering letters from home, and went riding in the afternoon with Philip and Pom over the heath-covered hills behind Therapia.

" *28th Sept.*— In the Embassy *caïque* to Ruvukdereh to call on Neli-doff (Russian Ambassador) who, as an old friend, received me cordially, but we did not talk politics. He gave me a long and interesting account of a visit he had paid with Ozeroff and Haymerle in 1860 to Cairo, before any of the European innovations began. With Philip and Pom I have had long talks about Egypt, and a little about affairs here.

" *29th Sept. (Sunday)*.— Spent the day on board the *Imogene* (the ambassadorial despatch boat) with Philip, Pom, and Yorke — a perfect summer's day. We steamed down the Bosphorus to the Sea of Marmora, landed on Bulwer's island, circumnavigated Prinkipo, and then crossed to San Stefano, and home about sunset, the walls of Stamboul, the Golden Horn, and the Asiatic shore from Scutari upwards being lit up with the evening glow, a glorious apparition.

"We had much political talk, first about Egypt, which Philip considers to be a danger to us, but which he says can never be evacuated — *never* in the political sense of counting votes at an English election — though we may be driven out of it. He says that the exclusion of France after the war of Tel-el-Kebir, from her position in the Joint Control, was entirely unexpected by him. He was away from the Foreign Office at the time, and nothing surprised him more than to hear it had been decided on. It was contrary to all our declarations and all our policy up to that point. He considers that if the French had declared from the outset their willingness to help in all arrangements and share expenses incurred, it would have been impossible to refuse them a renewal of their position. Lord Salisbury had done what he could to fulfill the promise of evacuation, but the Sultan's refusal to ratify the Drummond Wolff Convention had 'fortunately' prevented its accomplishment. The French policy had throughout been childish. He was inclined to agree with me that it was a pity the attempt of Constitutional Government in Egypt had not been encouraged, as the lack of something of the sort here was what was ruining Turkey.

"Bulwer's island is a barren and not very attractive little rock, of a few acres in extent, with some rubbishy buildings, now ruined, which Bulwer had spent much money on. He had built it for Princess Ypsilanti, a Greek lady whom he loved, and one of the rooms is still decorated with a mirror let into the ceiling, in which she could survey her charms. The Sultan had made him a present of it, and he had eventually sold it at a fancy price, £10,000, to the Khedive Ismaïl. It is occupied by a caretaker who keeps a few lean cows, its only inhabitants. The inner court of the house, overgrown with a yellow rose tree, run wild, and a clematis, would be pretty if the ruined buildings were less mean.

"At San Stefano we inspected the new Russian church, a memorial, not yet finished, of the extreme advance of the Russian army in 1877.

"*30th Sept.*— To-day Philip told me the history of the Armenian trouble, and expressed his opinion distinctly that the Sultan not only knew of the massacres, but had himself given the order for them and approved of them. I think this extremely probable — indeed it is almost inconceivable that, under so strong a despotism as is the present *régime,* any provincial governor or commandant should have dared act thus on his own responsibility. The Sultan's orders probably were to stamp out the rebellion. The mistake Philip seems to me to have made, is that he took the French and Russian Ambassadors into his counsels.

They were sure to play him false. He is now in a very difficult and false position, for they do not back him up fairly at home, and he has used such threats that he cannot well let the whole thing drop, which would have been the wisest course. As far as I understand his thoughts, he intends, in case of the Sultan's continued refusal to accept the English ultimatum, to take some violent action with the fleet, not here nor yet at Smyrna, but elsewhere. He asked me what would be the effect of blockading Jeddah and proclaiming that the Sultan had ceased to be sovereign of the Hejaz. I told him that the Grand Sherif would doubtless succeed to the Sultan's power at Mecca if that power were destroyed, but that he must not count on any portion of the population joining English intervention. Much as they disliked the Turks, they would dislike the English more.

" Communications between the embassy and the palace are all but interrupted at the present moment, nor is Philip in touch with any section of the Turkish Moslem community. His information depends almost entirely upon what he learns from Christians — no Moslem daring to call on him. Now and again he receives a letter in strict confidence, but very seldom, from members of the old Liberal party. He counts on the death or deposition of the Sultan, which he thinks might take place at any moment, and he would favour any attempt to revive a more liberal *régime*. But, until there is a question as between the Sultan and his Mohammedan subjects, he says, he is powerless to take action. It is a misfortune of the position that England has only treaty rights of intervention in favour of the Christian Armenians. I talked all these matters over with Pom as we rode across the wooded hills in the afternoon to Kilia.

" On our return we found Yorke and Lady Lilian and Clara Singleton just returned from Stamboul, where they had witnessed a disturbance, which may prove to be an important one, between a body of Armenians and the authorities. According to the accounts given us ɔy Philip of the affair, it appears that some days ago he received notice from the Armenian Revolutionary Committee that they intended making a demonstration in favour of the prompt settlement of the Armenian case. They were to assemble in Stamboul and present a petition at the Ministry. This seems now to have been forcibly prevented — a number of arrests were made — the Armenians fired shots — a Turkish colonel in full uniform was seen dead in the street — the Turks were allowed by the police to arm themselves with cudgels — some Armenians were beaten to death — and six others were bayonetted at the Zaptieh. But accounts differ greatly. The cavass who escorted the Yorkes declares that his party was menaced, and that he drew his revolver to protect them. But Yorke assures me that nothing of the sort took place as far as his party was concerned. All they saw was the Turks arming themselves with the cudgels — great crowds, and men being carried away in carriages with their arms bound. Still it has produced much excitement, and there is talk of revolution, massacres, and who knows what more.

" *1st Oct.*— The news to-day about the Armenian riot is that the deputation arranged by the Armenian Revolutionary Committee consisted of 2,000 men, who were to meet at Kapu and to march to the Ministry (the Porte), while a deputation of women were to go to Yildiz. On their assembling, however, the police, forewarned of their intention, stopped and arrested the leaders. The Armenians then fired revolvers, and the Bimbashi of the Police was killed. Arrests were then made, the police, it is said, conniving at the Mohammedans of the quarter arming themselves with cudgels and beating the Armenian prisoners. Sixty Armenians are reported killed and fifteen of the police. The last news is that 1,000 Armenians, with some women and children, are being besieged in a church in the Armenian quarter. The revolvers and knives found on the Armenians arrested were all of one pattern, a fact which points to premeditation of defence, if not of attack. All this reminds me much of what took place at Alexandria in 1882 when the fleet was ordered there. I expect to see the programme repeated here. There will be a cry of ' Europeans in danger '; the fleet will be ordered up to the Sea of Marmora; some British sailors will be mobbed on shore; a British Consul will be assaulted; and Stamboul will be bombarded. I am glad I am here to exercise what slight restraining power I can, though I am glad to say Philip shows no sign yet of having lost his head or lost his temper. We drove in the evening to the aqueduct, a very lovely evening.

" *2nd Oct.*— I went in the Embassy launch to Constantinople to-day to lunch with my old relative, Walter Blunt Pasha. We landed at the railway station on Seraglio Point, and drove across the bridge, where all things had returned to their usual quiet. The Pasha tells me the Armenians who formed the deputation had been warned not to come in large numbers, and not to come armed. They therefore divided themselves into groups. One of these was stopped by the police, and, an altercation arising, the Bimbashi struck the leading Armenian with his sword, whereupon the man nearest him drew a revolver and shot the Bimbashi through the head. This led to a general riot; arrests were made and men killed on both sides. There seems no doubt that the Moslems of the quarter were encouraged to arm themselves with staves. He says, however, that the Government is afraid now that the Softas who took part in the riot against the Armenians will continue it against the Government. The Sultan, he says, has become very unpopular in the last two years, and everybody would really be glad to get rid of him. Even the highest officials are kept in a state of tutelage which galls them severely. ' I myself,' he said, ' could not so much as go away for forty-eight hours to Broussa without permission from the Sultan himself. Neither the Minister of War nor the Grand Vizier could give it me.' The Softas, too, are tired of Abdul Hamid, who they think is ruining the country. The army has been unpaid for five months.

" Norman, a newspaper man, came in and told me tales of assaults and assassinations of Armenians last night by the mob. But as yet neither Europeans nor Greeks have been molested. I do not think the matter is likely to go much farther at present. The chief Armenians went to-day to the palace to arrange terms for the men shut up in the churches, and are believed to have been successful. I find Philip very strong on the necessity of getting rid of Abdul Hamid. ' We have come to the conclusion,' he said to-day, ' that it will be necessary to kill him. To depose him would be very difficult, perhaps impossible.' I do not suppose that he would do this by any direct instigation, but he would certainly countenance a revolution which should proceed by this means. The idea is in the air, but twenty years of absolute despotism have weeded out the more venturesome spirits.

" I have written a long letter on the political situation here to Lady Lytton, who will, as likely as not, show it to the Queen, as she is now in waiting at Balmoral. Archibald Lamb has arrived from England, Lady Currie's brother.

" *3rd Oct.*— The Queen's Messenger, old Conway Seymour, was despatched to-day. So I was busy writing letters. Philip went in with him to the Porte to call on the new Grand Vizier, Kiamil Pasha, who is supposed to be more favourable to English policy than the last, Said Pasha. But I fancy there is little real difference. I remember Kiamil at Aleppo in 1877, a little man of Jewish origin, who had once been tutor to the Khedive Tewfik.

" *4th Oct.*— In the launch to the mouth of the Black Sea, and in the afternoon to the Sweet Waters of Asia in the ten-oared *caïque,* a pretty sight. Philip saw the Grand Vizier to-day, having missed him yesterday. He tells me the attacks on Armenians still continue, and the churches are still full of refugees. It is certain, however, that the Armenians are being pushed on by the Revolutionary Committee. It is a Secret Committee prompted, Philip tells me, by Russian Nihilists; and the trouble has been caused by the arrest of Armenians suspected of belonging to it, and their torture in prison. On the other hand murders have been instigated by the Committee, of Armenians suspected of betraying their cause. They seem to count on English help, and talk of an independent Armenia under an English Prince. All this is, of course, impossible, but it is the fault of our people, who have encouraged a rising they are really powerless to assist. On the other hand the Sultan, Philip thinks, has a design of exterminating the Christian

Armenians in the provinces, just as the Emperor of Russia is exterminating the Catholic Poles, and for the same reason, to govern the country more easily.   The delay in settling the Armenian question, raised by
England, has prompted the Committee to more desperate measures.
It is a curious state of things, which Philip says can only end in the
deposition or death of Abdul Hamid.   We discuss these matters daily,
Philip and I and McDonnell and Yorke.

   " On Monday I have arranged to go to Pera to stay with General
Blunt, and on Wednesday I depart for Egypt.

   " *5th Oct.*— A long ride with McDonnell in the forest of Belgrade.
He asked me whether I thought Lady Currie would make a good Ambassadress at Paris.   I had heard from Lady Galloway that Paris had
been promised to Lord Londonderry, and that in any case Philip would
not have it.   McDonnell, however, being Lord Salisbury's private secretary, doubtless knows best, and I trust Philip may have it.   He told
me some interesting particulars about his chief, his many virtues and
his great tolerance for those who had none.   McDonnell is a charming
fellow, with much of the Kerr eccentricity, for he is through his mother
a Kerr.

   " In the evening a large dinner party to the Russian and Austrian
Ambassadors. . . . A sudden change of weather in the night, a violent
thunderstorm with heavy rain, and now a strong north wind.   It is
time I was away in Egypt.

   " *6th Oct. (Sunday).*— A day of wind and rain, no one moving out
of doors till about sunset, when I took Pom out for a walk in the
Embassy garden.   There have been great comings and goings between
Philip and the other Embassies, for they are preparing some joint action on the Sultan to stop the rioting in Constantinople.   Pom is more
communicative now than Philip, and I hope I have been able to in-
doctrinate him a bit in my ideas.

   " *7th Oct.*— The weather has cleared, and I drove in to Pera in an
open carriage, and am now in the house of my ' relative ' at 51 rue
Kabristan, an old-fashioned little box of a place with a bow window
looking over the Golden Horn.   General Blunt has been some twenty
years in the Sultan's service, and received his promotion to the rank of
Ferik, General of Division, only yesterday — a fine-looking old man,
who has no other duty than to attend the Selamlik every Friday, and
wear a handsome uniform.

   " Professor Vambéry came to dinner and Capt. Norman, and we had
a most interesting evening.   The position here at Constantinople, according to these, is this :   The Armenians, having unquestionably begun the disturbance, are now being harried by the joint action of the
police and the mob.   The mob are encouraged, or at any rate allowed,
to break into the khans at night where the Armenians congregate, and

sometimes into private houses, and beat the people they find in them to death with sticks. In some instances the police force admittance at the front door while the Armenian escapes at the back door only to fall into the hands of fellows waiting for him in the street. Thus several hundreds seem to have been killed. The mob is ostensibly headed by Softas, students of the University, but it is probable that these are often police agents in the Softa dress. At any rate it is certain that the police connive. The Armenian churches are full of refugees. Norman has been busy going round to these and to the Patriarch's house, where they also congregate, and told us many tales.

"Vambéry was very communicative. He talked strongly against the Sultan in this business, although he has been a favourite at the palace. He declares that, though superstitious, the Sultan is at heart a free thinker, his religion being with him a matter of policy, and he related several anecdotes bearing on this point. It is the Sultan's brother and heir presumptive, Rashid,[1] who is a true 'fanatic.' The Sultan has a deliberate political purpose, to diminish and drive out the Armenians, imitating in this the Emperor of Russia in his treatment of the Poles and the Jews. Vambéry is of opinion that Abdul Hamid cannot long retain his throne, and agrees with me as to the desirability of renewing the Constitution of 1876. This was the best chance Turkey ever had of putting herself on a level with other European nations. It is the best chance still. But it can hardly be under the present Sultan.

"*8th Oct.*— With Godfrey Webb, Mrs. Horner, Mrs. Crawshay, and Lord Llandaff (Matthews) to see the Museum and St. Sophia's — and with Norman to see the street door of the Armenian church in Pera.

"*9th Oct.*— Left Constantinople for Egypt.

"*12th Oct.*— Arrived at Sheykh Obeyd, *Elhamdu l'Illah.*

Epitome of the Armenian Question, written by me on board ship on my way to Alexandria.

"1. The Sultan, to prevent Armenia being given autonomy, on the ground of its possessing a Christian majority in any one province, encourages the Mohammedans of the Armenian provinces to ill-treat the Christians so as to force them to emigrate.

"2. The Christian Armenians, under the direction of a secret Committee organized by Russian Nihilists, and encouraged by English sympathy, refuse to pay taxes at Samsun.

"3. The Sultan orders their resistance to be crushed at all cost.

"4. The Turkish military Governor crushes it with great barbarity.

"5. The English Government, under Rosebery, urged by its Liberal

---

[1] Mohammed Rashid, afterwards Sultan Mohammed V.

supporters, intervenes. Philip Currie is urged to activity in repeated despatches.

" 6. The ' Times,' seeing in the Armenian question a useful counter-irritant to the Egyptian question, chimes in.

" 7. The English Government invites the French and Russian Governments to join them. This at Philip Currie's initiative.

" 8. These, believing the English Government to be willing to partition Turkey, accept the proposal of joint action. N.B. Rosebery probably is willing to partition Turkey.

" 9. Rosebery goes out of office in England. In Russia Giers dies and is succeeded by Labanov. A change of policy ensues.

" 10. France and Russia, knowing that Lord Salisbury, now at the Foreign Office, will not consent to the partition of Turkey, back out of joint action with England.

" 11. Salisbury, to avoid questions in Parliament and to gain time, professes to go on alone.

" 12. The Sultan, secretly reassured at Paris and St. Petersburg, stiffens his back. The negotiations at Constantinople are dawdled out.

" 13. Gladstone makes his Armenian speech at Chester. Subscriptions are opened in England.

" 14. Salisbury, to make show of being in earnest, orders a British fleet to the Dardanelles.

" 15. The Armenian Committee, encouraged by the approach of the English fleet, and believing Salisbury to be in earnest, and that England will undertake the job of coercing the Sultan single-handed, organizes a demonstration at Constantinople. This is done with Philip's privity.

" 16. The Sultan orders the Armenian demonstration to be crushed.

" 17. The Armenians are crushed at Constantinople with great barbarity.

" 18. ??

" N.B. My impression, gathered from what Philip has told me, strongly is (1) that he was not keen, at the outset of the Samsun affair, to intervene, but took the matter up under Rosebery's orders; (2) that he was responsible for the partnership with France and Russia; (3) that having embarked in the business he has since made it one personal to himself; (4) that for the last six months, at least, he has been in communication with the Revolutionary Committee, probably acting in concert with them; (5) that he was privy to the demonstration of 30th September, probably encouraged it, though perhaps not its being armed. It is he who told me that the Armenian Committee was organized by Russian Nihilists. This Committee has for its object, not union with Russia, but the establishment of an independent Armenia under English protection. They would take annexation to Russia as a *pis-aller*. But that is not their object."

I found out afterwards that on Giers' death the Russian policy towards Armenia underwent an entire change, though Philip Currie was not aware of it at the time. Instead of the old policy of protecting the Christian subjects of the Porte, Labanov's policy was to encourage the Sultan to exterminate the Armenians as allies of Russia's own Nihilists. It is doubtful whether the change was communicated to Nelidoff, a diplomatist of the old school of Christian protection; and I am inclined to think that he was in good faith in continuing his own sympathy with the Armenians, and expressing it to Currie. But of this later.

CHAPTER X

THE ADVANCE ON DONGOLA

" 14th Oct.— I arrived at Sheykh Obeyd and remained there only a
fortnight, going on from Cairo up the Nile to visit Upper Egypt and
Nubia, a part of the Nile Valley still new to me. I travelled on this
occasion alone, my family not having yet arrived, and got as far south
as what was then the extreme frontier of Egypt towards the Soudan.

" 29th Oct.— Left Sheykh Obeyd for the Upper Nile, taking Ali
Suffraji with me as body servant.

" Passing through Cairo called on Gorst, who begged me to inquire
on my journey whether there was any ill-feeling in Upper Egypt between Moslems and Copts, and on other points to get him what information I could. He told me that as to Philæ, the reservoir scheme was
for the time laid by, the finances being not quite safe, and the political
conditions too uncertain.

" At sunset I drove out beyond the Kasr el Nil bridge, to enjoy the
cool breeze and see the villages still partly surrounded by water and at
nine I started by train. I travelled all night, comfortably enough but
for the exceeding dust, with a fine moon in its second quarter, and a
splendid morning star, showing the country still half inundated. People are beginning to sow their beans and wheat in the immense flats of
mud. In other places the plain is covered with sheep feeding on the
new green grass before it is ploughed. Sugar cane is the only growing
crop.

" 30th Oct.— At half-past ten reached Girgeh, where the railway
ends, and took boat in a stern-wheel steamer leaving at one. No first-
class passenger besides myself, except three French engineers connected
with the railway now being constructed to Keneh. With one of them,
Megie, I had some interesting talk. He has been thirty-five years in
the country, having come as a boy with his father, a *protégé* of Linant
Pasha — now for eight years in Upper Egypt — intelligent and kindly.
He tells me there is absolutely no ill-will between Moslems and Copts
— never was any, even in the time of Arabi — knew Arabi — considered him a *brave homme* — had remained at Kaliub till after the bombardment, when he left by the last train for Suez — could have stayed
on, if he had liked, in security at Cairo, though perhaps not in the
villages. I asked him whether the fellahin were better off now or in

Saïd Pasha's time. 'Dans le temps de Saïd,' he answered, 'les œufs se vendaient cent pour une piastre. Voilà ce .que j'appelle la misère. Pour le bien être, oui. Ils etaient à leur aise, et les impôts etaient moins élevés. Mais ils n'etaient pas au courant de la civilisation.' A characteristic French answer. This is a good specimen of the ideas even intelligent foreigners have, and he certainly spoke with sympathy of the fellahin. Stopped for the night at Farshut, where they are making the new railway bridge. It has been sweltering hot all the afternoon, thermometer 85, but cool after sunset.

" *31st Oct.*— Travelling due east, a pleasant wind in our faces — multitudes of birds, not yet scared away by the tourists' guns, herons, pelicans, little white herons, cormorants, pied kingfishers, hoopoes — few signs of European life — immense crops of millet, taller than a camel and rider, this makes the banks green. The Nile has fallen three metres, and the *shadoufs* are at work. This is the season to see the Upper Nile, or any part of it for that matter. I never had a pleasanter fortnight at Sheykh Obeyd than since the 12th, when I returned there — the garden a paradise of birds and beasts, two wolves every evening in the palms at El Kheysheh, and numberless foxes — millions of sparrows roosting nightly in the orange trees (so that the whole garden smelt in the morning like a bird-cage), everything perfection.

" Past Keneh there are splendid reaches of the river, with banks beautifully wooded with *sont* trees in full flower besides *abels, nebuks,* and palms of both sorts — no *lebbeks* nor *gemeysehs,* though I saw a huge dead trunk of a *gemeyseh* by the water side. The *lebbek,* though an old Egyptian tree, seems to have become almost extinct till the present century, when it was reintroduced with the other modern improvements. There can be none in the country older than seventy or eighty years, big trees as they are.

" *1st Nov.*— Luxor. The Luxor Hotel is open, but empty with the exception of an invalid doctor (Dr. Ruffer) and his wife, and Newbury, an archæologist, who comes in for meals, having been here through the summer. Tourists there are none. I went out before sunrise and looked at the temple, and later to Karnak. The ancient Egyptians seem always to have built on the Nile mud, a mean foundation.

" The Consul, Ahmed Eff. Mustafa, called on me and invited me to luncheon, an Egyptian meal served with much hospitality. He is an honest, good man, of the fellah type, very proud of his visitors' book, which dates from 1855, and is a pretty complete history of modern Egypt. I found my brother Francis' name and Alice's, and Lady Herbert's party, and the Mures and Spencers, who were here in *daha-biyahs* in (the autumn of) 1863, and Lady Dufferin's in 1858, with a vast number of others recalling old memories, Strangford's, Beaufort's,

down to ' H. M. Stanley's of the " New York Herald," ' and General
Gordon's in 1884, and Lord Waterford's last year, who shot himself a
month ago — nearly all dead now.

"*2nd Nov.*— Across the river before sunrise to the statue of Mem-
non and the temples of Gournah and Medinet Habou. The latter is
a really fine thing, and I was able to see it alone without guides or fellow sightseers. But I am left with the impression that the Nile itself,
with its great flow of water and its ever green banks and eternal youth
is the really interesting thing, far finer than its monuments. These are
interesting as part of the river's history, not the Nile because of them.
The greatest of human works are a very small matter, after all, and
the world would be hardly poorer if mankind had never been — greatly
richer, indeed, seeing how much beauty we have destroyed. To Karnak
again in the evening, and rode through by the light of the full moon.

" *3rd Nov.*— Again across the river to see some minor monuments
not worth visiting. I was followed by a troop of little girls whom the
tourists have debauched with bakshish. I thought at first they were
Ghazawiyeh, so shameless were they, a sight I have never seen before
in all the lands of Islam. Coming in, I received a visit from Minshatti
Bey the Ababdeh Sheykh to whom I had sent to tell him I was here.
He is a delightful old man, whom our military people have quarrelled
with, suspecting him of Mahdist tendencies. Kitchener deposed him
from the Sheykhat and put in another, Beshir Bey, in his place, who
now lives at Assouan under the eye of the Government, and does their
business with the tribe. But Minshatti is the real Sheykh. The young
Khedive, when he was here, sent for Minshatti, and made much of him,
and gave him a robe of honour. This was made one of the points
of Kitchener's quarrel with the Khedive. The old man tells me that
the Sirdar now treats him better, and he is allowed to go about where
he likes, and is not molested by the police. He promised — but I think
rather doubtingly, for he is probably afraid — to send one of his relations with me if I went travelling, as I intend to do this winter, among
the Ababdeh.

" Had some talk with Dr. Ruffer, who is a distinguished man of
science, a bacteriologist. He had a paralytic stroke six months ago
(it was a case of blood poisoning caused by one of his experiments),
and is here for his health. He is looking for bacteria in the desert
sand.

" Later I went to Minshatti's house, which is just outside the town,
a clean, new building, where he received me with carpets spread on the
mastaba, a nice cool place. I asked him about the Soudan, and the
Mahdi, and the Khalifa, and he told me much that was interesting.
He never saw the Mahdi himself, but several of his relations knew him
when he was a *najar* (carpenter), a boat builder at Dongola. He was

an *alem* and a *faki*; but his political fortunes were the work originally of Jaffir Bey, who had quarrelled with the Government. He said the Mahdi was a good man; and as long as he lived everybody in the Soudan believed in him as the true Mahdi. But the Khalifa had ruined everything. The reason of the Baggara power was that the Khalifa had put forward all the best men of the other tribes to fight, and these had got killed in the wars, while the Baggaras were held in reserve and reaped the profits. The Khalifa had got possession of all the firearms in the country on the pretext of having them in readiness to resist an invasion, and so the Baggaras, his own tribe, were the only ones thus armed. El Nejumi had made his expedition, which ended at Toski [this was the battle won by Grenfell, see later], because an attempt had been made to poison him, and he wanted to get away somewhere where he should be his own master. The chiefs of the tribes when not killed in war had been got rid of on various pretexts by the Khalifa. They had been accused of treason and put into a kind of fetter which Minshatti described to me as being a long tube of iron holding the arms straight out from the shoulder to the wrist. A man with his arms thus fettered was helpless and died in a month. Thus only children were left in the tribes, and the Baggaras, an ignoble tribe with whom the Jaalin and Kababish and Hadendowas and Ababdeh would not in former times intermarry, had got all power into their hands.

"I did not, however, gather from him that the fellahin were ill off. He told me *durra* was at three *reals* the *ardeb,* and all things were plentiful. But the richer people suffered exactions, so that it was the common cry that the Baggaras' rule was worse than the rule of the Turks. He talked a good deal about Salatin (Slatin) and Neufelt. He said that an expedition from the Government would be joined by everyone in the Soudan. I asked him if it would be so if the expedition was an English one. He said that the opinion now in the Soudan had changed, and that the people there no longer regarded the *gufara* (infidels, meaning Christians) as they did ten years ago. Many of them had been wounded and taken prisoners, and had afterwards been released, and had related at home that the *kufara* had treated them well. As Minshatti was certainly suspected of being in league with the Mahdists, and probably was so a few years ago, his evidence is of more value than most. But I expect that the Baggaras are stronger in the country than he quite makes out. The noble tribes are doubtless jealous of them, as there are always jealousies among Arab tribes. Of his own position he said that he was one of the three great Sheykhs of the Ababdeh, the others being Beshir and Saleh Ibn Khalifeh, lately killed at Murad. They each used to received £40 a month from the Government, but Beshir's allowance had been reduced to £32, and his

own to £5. He asked me to try and get his raised. I said I would try
to do so, but fear there is no chance.

" *4th Nov.*— On board the *Ibis*. We passed Erment this morning
where there are many lebbek and gemeyseh trees apparently twenty
years old, also larger factories and some cotton cultivation. I did not
notice any dogs there, though Erment is famous for its large rough
breed. The dogs generally of the Upper Niles are rougher than those
in the north. Matana, a beautifully wooded place, was one of the
Khedive Ismaïl's properties. Esneh in the afternoon, away from the
river with two square masses of ancient stonework on mounds of rubbish. Stopped for the night at Silsilis, the moon very splendid, as red
and bright as a fire lit just under it when it rose.

" My companions on board are three or four English officers of the
Egyptian army, with the limited conversation of their kind. But I
like young Broadwood who commands the cavalry at Wady Halfa.

" *5th Nov.*— Some attractive desert places on the left bank where
cultivation has been abandoned and its place taken by *halfa* grass and
green bushes — the palms gone wild. There are a good many horses
turned out, tethered in the barley to graze, and on the *durra*. Some of
them are bays with white faces and four white legs, probably of the
Dongola breed — tall, with straight shoulders and drooping quarters.
Kom Ombo close to the river, temple and fort on a natural mound.
The river is now generally from a kilometre to a mile broad, a few
mud banks beginning to show in places.

" At 1:30 arrived at Assouan. It has a European appearance. The
approach to it is fine. Having made acquaintance on board with Mustafa Bey Shakir, deputy mamur of Assouan, I inquired of him what
government lands there were for sale — this for Evelyn, who has an
idea of purchasing here — and he sent me on a donkey to look at a
building belonging to the Government known as the Mukhtab el Miri
el Buhari, about two miles down the river. There are well wooded
gardens near it, which the guard said might be bought from the fellahin owners for £10 and £15 the feddan. The Government is asking
£300 for the building. In a few years the railway will be brought near
it, and it might not be a bad purchase.

" Then by train to Shellal, put my things on board the steamer, and
spent the evening sailing about Philæ and the edge of the cataract, one
of the loveliest things I remember of the kind. Indeed, the only recollection I can compare with it is the boating expedition we made on the
great tank at Hyderabad ten years ago. It was a perfect evening, and
the rocks and swirling water in the twilight, and the boat with the
Berber crew singing were everything one could imagine in Philæ.

" *6th Nov.*— Rode on donkey-back before sunrise to see the position
of the proposed dam, which is a mile or so below Philæ. Philæ as it

is, is perhaps the one perfect thing in the world, and anything added to
or taken from it would probably spoil it. So I trust they will leave it
alone. At the same time if they would be content with banking the
river to the natural height of the Nile at flood, I do not see that it
need do a great harm. But of course they want more, and to make it
the biggest engineering thing in the universe. The situation is tempt-
ing to an engineer, as the solid boulders of granite would make it an
heroic bit of stonework.

"At eight we started again up the river. The change of scenery
above the cataract is most sudden and complete, made more so by 'the
as sudden and complete change in the inhabitants, who are here Berbers.
Indeed, Egypt ends abruptly at Assouan. The Soudan begins at Philæ.
These upper reaches, between piled-up granite boulders, are very attractive, as there are many places one might use as hermitages, islands
of rock with a few sont trees and palms, some having the remains on
them of buildings. At Kalabsheh a new and still narrower gate is
passed. This is where the French chose their site for the dam. It
is difficult to say which of the two sites would be the best for the
purpose. Thus, all day long, between endless granite boulders on the
eastern shore, and the same, partly covered with drift sand, on the
western, the cultivation almost nil, a narrow fringe of palms and *sonts*
and *seyyals,* with here and there a patch of vegetables sown at the
river's edge or a field of *durra.*

"*7th Nov.*— We stopped for the night at Dendur, and in the morning light found ourselves outside the narrow gorge, and among drifts
of *nefud* — red sand — on the western bank, apparently encroaching.
Broadwood tells me there is a long line of *nefuds* running north-west
which is impassable for camels. This, as I understand him, west of
the road to the oases. But I doubt if he has been far enough to know.

"I have made friends on board with a military doctor, Mohammed
Eff. Towfik, who began by quarrelling with me as an Englishman
for the occupation of Egypt, but we speedily came to an understanding, and I find him to be a friend of Mohammed Abdu's, and a staunch
Nationalist of the fellah party. Though still a young man, perhaps
thirty-five, he remembers the Russian war of 1877, and knew Arabi.
He told me very frankly that there were people who suspected me of
having stood in with our diplomacy in 1882. It was pleasant to find
a man so fearless and outspoken, especially as much of our conversation was within hearing of the English officers, Broadwood, Lawrie, and
a third, Healy, who understands Arabic. The doctor is a fellah, proprietor of 300 feddans near Benisouef, and declares that the fellahin
are in a worse condition materially than before the rebellion. I doubt
this. But I think it likely he is right about Upper Egypt. Certainly
all this district south of Assouan shows traces of decline; and the

Berber population is lean and hungry. He was eager to know about the Armenian question, and about the condition of India, and I explained both to him. He is a very intelligent, worthy man, of the kind most required. He admitted freely the personal liberty now enjoyed and the liberty of the press, but complained bitterly of there being no self-government, no constitution. I agree with him on all points, except that of the material poverty. He is opposed to 'the reservoirs, but in favour of an advance on the Soudan, at least to Dongola. My own impression is that it would have been best in 1885 to have made Assouan the boundary of Egypt, instead of Wady Halfa. It is a much stronger frontier and far less costly. The only reason for an advance now is to forestall a European one, either Italian or French.

"We stopped for the night at Korosko, and I went ashore with the Commandant, Ibrahim Bey Fathy, a fine looking fellah soldier, who showed us round 'the barracks by starlight. They are making surveys for a railway to Murad, and Broadwood tells me they intend, whenever the advance to Khartoum is made, to take that route. But there is nothing in contemplation at present. The English officers are good fellows, and are very polite and amiable 'to their Egyptian brother officers; but it is easy to see that there is no real intimacy or knowledge of each other's thoughts. Broadwood complains of this; and I should think that, if it came to a pinch, the Egyptian officers could not be implicitly relied on. I fancy they all resent the superior commands being English. They do not mess with the English officers, and live much apart. This is no doubt partly because the English know very little Arabic. Ibrahim Bey spoke excellent English, and dined with us on board. There are two young fellows, Englishmen of the Royal Engineers, who have been sent out here to make the railroad to Murad, excellent ingenuous youths of perhaps 'twenty-three or twenty-four, to whom it is great fun and solid advancement, as they are given the rank of majors in the Egyptian army. This is a sample of what leads to discontent among the native officers, for the work is an absolutely simple one, and could be performed by any of their own engineers. Yet 'these young Englishmen have it. Again, the command of the cavalry at Halfa is left during the summer months to a native officer, but as soon as the winter begins, when there are manœuvres and parades of the kind soldiers love, young Broadwood comes to take his place. My friend the doctor is eloquent on these things, and I have no doubt reflects the general sentiment.

"*8th Nov.*— Passed the battlefields at . . . and Toski, the former fought with an advanced body of the Dervishes, the latter with the main body under Wad el Nejumi. The English officers gave me an account of the two actions. By their showing, it was little more than

a massacre, for the Dervishes were in the last stage of exhaustion from
hunger and thirst, their camels dying, and their women and children.
The way they had come is still marked by the skeletons left on the
sand. They marched some five miles from the river, along the left
bank, sending the women and children at night to get water, the
English-Egyptian army meanwhile cruising comfortably parallel to
them in boats. They had forced the Berber inhabitants of the left
bank to cross over the river and take all eatable things with them, so
that Nejumi's army found nothing. Then, when the Dervishes were
quite worn out, the troops were landed and drove the dervishes into
a gully, where these made their final stand, and were all shot down.
Mohammed Towfik, who was there, says that of all the 4,000 who left
Dongola with Nejumi, only 300 combatants remained to fight at Toski.
The action at . . . was a smaller affair than Toski, and, if I understood rightly, one of cavalry on the Egyptian side. The left bank in
this part is a desolate region of drift sand with a few bushes, but at
Toski there is palm cultivation for a mile or two. The right bank,
where there is no sand, is mostly planted.

" At four we came to Abu Simbel and stopped for a quarter of an
hour, so that we were able to land and look at the temple. Broadwood
showed me a pompous marble tablet let into the rock outside, of which
he was ashamed. It recorded the gallant victory of General Grenfell
over 'the rebels.' The temple is very fine, and has the great merit of
being no ruin, but a perfectly habitable place cut out of the rock, and
very little injured by time. There was a party outside it clearing away
the sand. There is a grave, too, where an English officer is buried who
happened to die on board a passing steamer —'a rotten place,' Laurie
remarked, 'to bury an Englishman in.' The Berbers are a poor,
narrow-chested, feeble, half-starved people, reminding one much of
the natives of Southern India. There can hardly be a greater contrast
than between them and the Egyptian fellahin. The Berbers are exempted from recruiting, and should be exempted from taxation. They
live almost entirely on dates, and are much subject, it is said, to fever.
At night we passed a Government steamer having on board the English
acting commandant of Wady Halfa, Lewis, a little talkative man of
whom Broadwood and Laurie, who are fine young fellows, made light.
We stopped to pay him a visit and then went on in the dark.

" *9th Nov.*— Arrived at Wady Halfa, a beautiful cool morning, with
a strong north wind blowing over the plain. Wady Halfa has the advantage of being placed where the hills are low and stand back from
the river. Otherwise a quite uninteresting place — low military huts
fronting the river, with bits of trees and gardens about them, officers'
quarters and the rest.

" I lunched at the Commandant's quarters with Lewis, who has

returned, and then went with Broadwood to Sarras by train. From
the railway one sees the cataracts well, a wild and pretty country with
plenty of small trees, principally *urdi,* a kind of acacia, on the islands.
The palms have been all cut down by the Dervishes in their hunger.
They occupied Sarras for two years, and, Broadwood tells me, had no
commissariat of any kind, living on anything they could get. They
used to make raids on the villages under Government protection, and
on one occasion cleared out Towfikieh, the civilian quarter of Wady
Halfa, killing some 600, and driving the Greek drink-sellers into the
river, where several were drowned. The country between Wady Halfa
and Sarras has been in part re-peopled, but beyond Sarras it is still
No Man's Land, the Dervish out-post being now at Akasheh, 100 miles
away. We were entertained in the fortified camp by Sellem Bey, an
English officer, who recaptured Sarras from the Dervishes, a good fellow and intelligent.

"*10th Nov. (Sunday).*— Walked round the camp with Broadwood
and then back to Halfa in time to see the camel corps, 275 strong,
marching in from a field day — a really fine sight — the camels mostly
white ones.

"Several Berbers came to seek my intervention with Lewis to get
permission to return to Dongola, their native country. They told me
that there would be *amán* for them there; that the Khalifa was pleased
at the return of refugees, and that they could re-occupy their lands
without hindrance; that there was less oppression than there had been,
and that they would be better off there than here; that the population
of Dongola had been so thinned by the emigration of seven years ago,
and afterwards by the famine, that there was land for all comers, dates
in plenty, *durra* at thirty piastres the *ardeb,* and wheat at fifty. I
asked them about the taxes, and they told me that the Khalifa took a
tithe in kind, but that the Baggaras entrusted with the government did
this in a very arbitrary way, as, for instance, if there was an *ardeb*
of dates, they would count it an *ardeb* and a half; also that nobody
dared make a display of wealth, all superfluity being taken to the *beyt
el mal.* People, however, were not interfered with if they were content to cultivate a few feddans and live on the produce. If they made
money, they must hide it in the ground. As far as I could gather from
them, they considered the independence of the country (*wátani*) from
the Government an advantage, now that there was no longer excessive
oppression. They assured me that, out of 4,000 or 5,000 refugees in
Egypt, most would be glad to return. I promised to talk to Lewis about
it, and, failing his permission, to bring their general case before Cromer.
It seems absurd to keep them starving in Egypt, now they are willing
to return.

"I left Halfa with Lewis in the Government steamer for Assouan —

with us several of the officers who were going as far as Sarras on a shooting excursion. I noticed a pair of *hubaras* (frilled bustards) on the right bank, and had seen one yesterday between Halfa and Sarras. We stopped at four, and they all went shooting except me, bringing back a few ducks, gadwells, shovellers, and teals, also a snipe and a cormorant. Sarras is a very pretty place, with a lake in the sandhills well grown over with tamarisks, unlike anything I have seen north of the Fayum — a village and a little cultivation in the tamarisk scrub, just now beautifully green.

" Much military talk in the evening, my host being a loquacious little man with a crudest of ideas political. According to him, we are to have an English fleet in two years' time which will enable us to do what we like in the world, when we are to annex Egypt and Constantinople too. An empty-headed little fellow, who has been eight years in the Egyptian service and has acquired a certain command of *qui-hi* Arabic most comic, which he imagines to be the purest dialect — all pronounced as written, in a plain English accent. But his servants and men are used to it and make out his meaning. The relations between the English officers and the natives seem to be much what they are in India — that is to say, there is absolutely no community of ideas or sympathy on either side. Broadwood and one or two of them try to be polite and kind, but they know so little Arabic, and have so little knowledge of Eastern good manners that they are unintentionally rude and inspire no affection, only just such respect as their power to reward and punish gives. They would be deserted, I am sure, by their men if it came to any real difficulty. They seem to feel their position rather a precarious one, and would all leave the Khedive's service if the British occupation ceased.

" *11th Nov.*— Arrived at Korosko at four. Walked to the top of the hill overlooking the road to Abu Hamid, the road Gordon took on his last journey. It is a rough bit of country, a wilderness of black wadies and ravines which extends they say for twenty miles, when the open plain or plateau begins. The young engineers pointed out the road of their new railway.

" Dined at the Egyptian officers' mess. Here at Korosko the battalion is wholly Egyptian, a really capital set of fellah officers commanded by Fathy Bey, a big fellah Colonel reminding me not a little of Arabi in 1881. They mess together and live on the friendliest terms; and here, entertaining Lewis and me, and the two young engineers, their demeanour was quite different from what I had noticed at Halfa, and they seemed to be most pleasant in their relations with the English officers. At Halfa they chafe at being under them. Here they are on an equal footing. I sat between Fathy Bey and a captain, Emir Eff. Fowzi, the latter a very good fellow with whom I talked much in Arabic about affairs in Arabia, at Constantinople, and in India, and in Tunis. He had just been on the pilgrimage and complained greatly of the Ottoman misgovernment there. We also talked about Arabi, and I was pleased when Fathy Bey, who joined our conversation, expressed himself warmly about Arabi, and in favour of his being allowed to return to Egypt.

"*12th Nov.*— Arrived early at Shellál, and descended the cataract in a *feluka* — no very hazardous affair. Lunched at Assouan with the English mess and met there Beshir Bey and Ahmed Bey Khalifa of the Ababdeh. Then on board the steamer for Cairo.

" *13th Nov.*— We stopped two hours at Edfu, which gave us time to see the temple, the most perfect in Egypt. Indeed, it might be ' restored to public worship' without the smallest repair. Mere ruins are tiresome, but this is not one. We have half-a-dozen tourists on board, the first of the season — Dr. Ruffer and his wife, a Spanish diplomatist from Constantinople, an old Frenchwoman, and an English geologist. Stopped at Esneh, where there is a temple partly underground, and arrived at Luxor, and for the night, Kus.

"*Nov. 14th.*— A quite cold morning with clouds to the west and a feeling of dampness in the air. There has probably been rain at Alexandria, and very likely a southwest gale in the Mediterranean, where Anne and Judith are to embark to-day. Arrived at Girgeh, where our few passengers got out; but I have decided to go on to Cairo by steamer with the Ruffers. A wonderful sunset, followed by thunder and lightning and some rain — this off Ahmim, a very beautiful part of the river. The night too dark to go on, so after running aground, we stopped for the rest of it.

" *15th Nov.*— I have had much talk with Dr. Ruffer, who is a superior man of science. He was for two years a pupil of Pasteur at Paris, and speaks of him with enthusiasm. He tells me 'that Pasteur had a physical dislike for surgical operations and, he believes, never was present at the experimental ones made on live animals. But he did not hesitate to have them performed by others. I asked him how much truth there was in the accusations made against him of having kept dogs for months under torture, and he said that Pasteur had made a mistake in experimenting on dogs for hydrophobia, as they were much more dangerous to handle; that it had now been found that all the symptoms of hydrophobia could be equally well studied in rabbits; that, after inoculating dogs with the disease, it was necessary to keep them and watch whether or not 'they went mad, and so he had kept some of them for years, but that they were well treated — some twenty-five of them at the time he was there. He said it was a choice between making experiments of this kind and not proceeding with the inquiry. But I gather from him that he is not certain whether 'the object has been obtained. The difficulty of being certain was that only some fifteen per cent. of cases of bites from a certainly mad dog led to hydrophobia. He talked of Pasteur as the one great man of Science France had produced. He described him as a most simple-minded man, entirely destitute of humour, and incapable of thinking about more than one thing at a 'time. If you started him on a conversation he could not change the subject till he had exhausted it. This was the secret of his success. His mind was not a French one.

"Dr. Ruffer is at the head of the Pasteur Institute of London. He tells me he is only thirty-six, though he has grey hair and looks fifty. But he was junior to George Curzon when at Oxford, so I suppose he is of the age he says. More thunder and lightning in 'the evening, away to the north-west. There must have been heavy rain in Jendali and probably on all the hills between the Nile and the Red Sea. It is cold and damp and raw. I am getting weary of the Nile and cannot understand the patience of travellers not invalids who travel on it in *dahabiyahs*. We stopped at Beni Hassan, but I did not go ashore, as I draw the line at tombs. Beni Hassan, however, might, I think, be a good point of departure for our winter's journey. Farther down the river there are impassable places where rocks come down to the water's edge.

"*16th Nov.*— Arrived at Cairo in the afternoon, and glad to get home. The Lower River seems to me vastly superior to the Upper, and has a familiar and pleasant aspect. I had the rare pleasure of seeing a real *seyl* come down into the Nile some forty yards across, and strong and deep enough to carry away a camel — a great turbid flood which had broken through the Nile bank and was rushing some two hundred yards out into the river. It must have come from Wady Senhur, a few miles south of Wasta.

"There has been an earthquake at Rome and a change of Ministry at Cairo. Nubar, the old rogue, has retired, and Mustafa Fehmy is put into his place.

"It was dark before I got to Sheykh Obeyd, and I had some difficulty in making myself heard at the gate, but all is well. *El hamdul illah.*"

The disappearance of Nubar here recorded marks the beginning of the new *régime* in Egypt which was to last for nearly ten years, during which Cromer was to be supreme in every branch of the Egyptian administration, governing through merely dummy native Ministers, with Mustafa Fehmy at their head. Lord Salisbury, now at the head of a strong Unionist Government in England, had made up his mind at all hazards to continue the military Occupation and retain Egypt permanently as a dependency of the British Empire. He also, 'though we did not know it at the time, had a settled design of avenging the death of Gordon and the disgrace of Wolseley's defeat by the Mahdi in 1884 as one of the two matters necessary for England's honour, the other being the defeat at Majuba in South Africa. We know this from his own boast in 1902, shortly before he retired from public life, and we have every reason to be sure that at the back of his determination on both points stood his mistress, Queen Victoria. The present chapter will show the first steps taken in accordance with this policy on the Nile, in its commencement not altogether with Lord Cromer's approval, his objection to it being a financial one, as certain to overburden the Eyptian Budget, and as such premature, but, as will be seen, his opposition on this head was overruled from Downing Street and financial caution, in large measure overcome by the parsimonious ability of Lord Kitchener, to whom the advance up the Nile was entrusted, and who ran it on the cheap.

" Having made this brief explanation I resume my diary.

" 17th Nov.— There have been tremendous *seyls* all round Sheykh Obeyd. Part of our garden wall is broken down by it and the house at El Kheysheh flooded, though no great damage done. Suliman Howeyti had his tent carried away just outside. At Kafr el Jamus eleven houses are ruined, and at Koubba a great *seyl* from the hills broke through the old railway embankment and destroyed fifty houses and a French public garden, threatening even the Palace with flood. The like has never been seen before. Old Deifallah is dying of old age, like Job, on a dung-hill outside Dormer's garden wall.

" Things have gone rapidly in Turkey during the last three weeks. Disturbances everywhere in the provinces, the devil generally let loose.

"20th Nov.— Anne, Judith, and Cowie arrived at Sheykh Obeyd. I dined with Dormer last night.

" 28th Nov.— I wrote yesterday to Lord Cromer about the permission asked by the Dongola people to return to their homes. I said that the story they gave me was that they had emigrated into Egypt after the Mahdi's death to escape the tyranny of the Baggara chiefs who represented the Khalifa's government at Dongola; that they assured me that they would be subject to no vexation now; 'that living there was cheap and land plentiful; that I had mentioned their case to the Commandant at Wady Halfa, who had told me that the chief reason for the prohibition was a fear that the return of the refugees would hamper and endanger the spies sent by the Intelligence Department, but that this seemed hardly a sufficient reason for retaining in Egypt so many persons who were a burden and a trouble. I suggested that perhaps the time was come when 'the question might be reconsidered; there seemed to be no immediate prospect of a military advance and the circumstances of the case had changed since the frontier regulations were enacted.

"Today I went to Cairo and saw Lord Cromer, who told me he had forwarded my letter to Kitchener and would let me know when his answer was received. He then talked of other matters and of the possibility of Mohammed Abdu being named head of the Awkaf. This I, of course, strongly commended. I also saw Gorst.

"*30th Nov.*— Started with Anne for the eastern desert. On our return.

"*3rd Dec.*— Found a letter from George Wyndham with an account of little Percy's accident, touchingly told.

"*7th Dec.*— A visit from Ibrahim ibn Abdallah Thenneyan ibn Saoud el Nejdi who has just escaped from Constantinople. He gave much interesting information. The Sultan is now entirely under the influence of Sheykh Abul Huda; and Jemal ed Din is never received at the palace. Things are going as badly there as possible. He has come to Cairo, hoping through the Khedive's influence to get back to Nejd. His father's grandfather, Thenneyan, was for a couple of years Emir of Nejd, while Feysul was in captivity at Dar el Beyda. But when Feysul escaped and returned to Nejd, he and his family were driven to Bagdad. Speaking of the Ananzeh he assured me their migration North dated from 200 or 300 years ago. The Ibn Saouds are of Anazeh stock.

"*12th Dec.*— I have written another long letter to Cromer about the return of the refugees to Dongola. Kitchener, in reply to my first letter, declared the road to be open to them *via* Assouan and Berber. That would give them a journey of 1,000 miles to accomplish the 100 miles which separate them at Sarras from their homes. He pretends, too, that the Dervishes are threatening the frontier. Our people are humbugs about this almost more than about anything else. The officers when I was there were all complaining that there was nothing for them to do on the frontier if the Dervishes would make no move.

"We went to-day to look at some desert land 280 feddans outside Kafr el Shorafa, for sale by the Government at 50 piastres the feddan, for first price. I would give £2. Ibrahim ibn Saoud came to-day to luncheon. He had been to the palace. He asked me for a letter to Lord Cromer, explaining that his business was to invite English protection for Nejd. He declared that six months ago Fawzi Pasha, Turkish Waly of El Hasa, received orders from the Ottoman Government to send an expedition to take over the Government of Riad and El Haryk. Fawzi was a Syrian, knew Arabic, and would have been able to effect his purpose through the Arab tribes. Correspondence had passed between the Sultan and Ibn Rashid, who had consented to the aggression. Now, however, Ibrahim would wish. the British Government to undertake a protectorate as at Bahreyn and Muscat — at least to forbid the Turkish advance inland. I gave him the

letter, but warned him not to trust too much to English magnanimity.
If we once got our foot into Nejd, it would be difficult to get us out
again.   Perhaps the Turks might be worse, but we were dangerous too.
For that matter the Ottoman Empire was too near its dissolution to
think just now of any forward movement.   Neither was it in the least
probable that England would undertake a protectorate or do anything:
His seeing Cromer cannot do much harm.   So I gave him the letter.

" There is news of a great defeat of the Italians by the Abyssinians.
I am much pleased at this, as their aggression has been one of the
most abominable of our abominable age.   Perhaps now the Dervishes
may drive them out of Kássala."   This was the least excusable of the
many lawless raids made by the Italians in Africa, prompted in part
by the vanity of the parvenu kingdom of Italy to show itself as aggressive as its older neighbours, France and England, partly by mining
speculation.   Unlike most of these raids undertaken by the Christian
nations in our time, it had not even the excuse of calling itself a crusade, seeing that the Abyssinians were themselves Christians, of a
wild, old-fashioned kind, but still just as much Christians as the inhabitants of Calabria, while, compared with the Abyssinian Emperor who
is lineally descended from the Queen of Sheba by King Solomon, the
House of Savoy enthroned at the Quirinal is but a stem of yesterday,
yet not a shadow of reproof was uttered by our statesmen in Downing
Street, and the general remark about the Italian expedition in the
London Press was that the ending of the Abyssinian monarchy would
not be ' felt upon the Stock Exchange.'

" *16th Dec.*— Went in to Cairo to see the Khedive.   He was very
cordial as usual, and made me a number of confidences, some very interesting.   He told me the full story of his visit to Constantinople
this summer.   His object, he says, was not a political one, but to get
permission from the Sultan to build a house on the island of Thasos
where, and at Kavala, he has the direction of the Awkaf.   He wanted
a place to spend the summer in with his wife and child, instead of
going to Europe.   He went to Stamboul in his yacht, and found it so
pleasant there that he stayed two months.   The Sultan was polite to
him, and asked him constantly to dinner, and to hear music, but would
not talk business.   At last he got tired of waiting, and sent word that
he wanted permission to go to Thasos, and also to lay certain papers
before the Sultan connected with the Halim succession and the claim
of the Azhar University to a part of it.   But he got a number of
evasive answers.   At one time he was told ' yes '— at another that
the Sultan had a cold and could not see him — at another that he had
bad eyes and could not read the papers — and other foolish excuses.
In the meantime he had been dogged by spies, and on one occasion
when he had made an arrangement privately to see Sheykh Jemal ed

Din he had been followed so closely that he had turned on the spy and beaten him, and had sent a message to the palace that if he was thus annoyed again he would shoot his persecutors.

"At last a day of audience was fixed with the Sultan for him to say 'good-bye.' But after being kept waiting for an hour, Osman Pasha came to him and began to talk about the Thasos plan, and to try and dissuade him. At this he lost patience, and asked Osman straight whether he had been sent with the message from the Sultan, and, on his admitting it, he spoke his whole mind. 'I told him,' said the Khedive, 'that I was tired of the Sultan's way of treating me, that I had been not yet four years on the throne, and I had come three times to Constantinople to see him, which was more than any of my predecessors had done, and yet he had not spoken to me a reasonable word. My great-great-grandfather, I told him, Mohammed Ali, had never gone to Constantinople, though he was near it once, by way of Nezim and Kóniah. My great-grandfather Ibrahim had never been, though he had a stronger army than the Sultan's. My father was eleven years on the throne, and he never went. I alone went, to do the Sultan pleasure. I even, to please him, gave up last year my visit to England. Her Majesty the Queen, who is Empress of India and 300 millions of subjects, and on whose dominions the sun never sets, had done me the honor of inviting me, and I had accepted the invitation; yet, on account of a miserable bit of paper, a telegram from Constantinople, I broke my engagement and went to the Sultan instead. I am tired of this. You may tell the Sultan that this year I will not go to Thasos, but for the future I shall know how to regulate my conduct towards him. While talking thus — and I never talked so strongly in my life — Nuri Bey joined us, and he and Osman were horror-struck at my words, and shook with fear, and went at once to the Sultan, who sent for me and apologized and loaded me with civilities. But I told him that it was no case for apologies, that I understood now what his diplomacy was, and that I should return to my own country, and forget as far as possible that I stood to him in the relation of a subject. And so it has been. From that day to this I have cut the Sultan's name out of my prayer; I have never been to the mosque where the prayer for the Sultan is made, and, when I pray in my own mosque at Koubba, my chaplain omits the Sultan's name. We pray for "the welfare of Islam and all believers, but not for those (he quoted the words in Arabic) who are bringing Islam to its ruin."'

"I am not sure that I have quoted the Khedive quite verbally, but this is the sense of his words. He spoke with animation, and told the story admirably. He told me also that he had seen Abdallah Nadim [1] at Constantinople, and that he was allowing him to return to Egypt.

---

[1] See "Secret History."

Of the prospects of Constantinople he said he feared the Sultan's subjects would never succeed in getting rid of him, though the European Powers might depose him. He asked me about affairs in Arabia, and told me he had seen Ibrahim ibn Thenneyan, but Sheykh Mohammed Abdu had warned him that he was perhaps a spy of Sheykh Abul Huda's. I told him that I did not think this to be the case, though it might be well to be cautious. Then he talked about the desert, and an expedition he intended to make to El Arish in the Spring, and how he was having the post road repaired to Dar el Beyda. He certainly is a charming young man, and brim full of intelligence.

"I lunched with Gorst and talked to him about the affairs of the Soudan. He told me, as an instance of the humbug that went on at the frontier, of the way in which Wingate had got the credit of Slatin's escape from Khartoum. This has been represented as entirely Wingate's cleverness, whereas in point of fact Wingate was away at the time at Souakim, and the plan was Slatin's own. Maxwell (?), who was in charge of Wady Halfa, received a letter from Slatin, addressed to whoever was in command, asking him to pay the bearer £100, and to promise another £100 in case of success. This Maxwell had done, but nothing more was thought about it till Slatin arrived and embraced Wingate, who had meanwhile returned, calling him his deliverer. Wingate then looked up the papers for the first time, and promptly endorsed them, 'I approve.' There has been a raid quite recently, thirty miles north of Wady Halfa, and sixteen persons have been killed in a village.

"Left a card on the French Minister, M. Cogordan, who sent me a message last summer through Mlle. Lagréné that he would like to see me.

"*19th Dec.*— Eldon Gorst came, with his sister, to spend the day. We took them to the sand hills and set up a shelter and lunched there. I had a good deal of talk with Gorst. He is a worthy young man, very painstaking and desirous to do rightly, but hardly a man of genius. One does not understand why he should have been chosen, out of the many thousand young men whose services are to be had, to be Prime Minister of Egypt. I imagine that he would command at home perhaps £400 or £500 a year. But this is one of the mysteries of Anglo-Egyptian rule. He has a moderate knowledge of Arabic, having served an apprenticeship under Cromer. The fact is, there is no country so easy to govern as Egypt is, given fair intelligence and perfect honesty in the governor.

"*21st Dec.*—M. Cogordan, with his secretary, lunched with us. Cogordan is a man of about forty, of good presence and manners and very amiable. We sat on the roof after luncheon and I took the opportunity of explaining to him something of the history of Arabi's revolution, as to which the French have the absurdest ideas. The origin of my calling on him and of his visit was a message I received in the summer from Mlle. de Lagréné, saying he wished to make my acquaintance. Of current politics we talked little, except as to the Khedive's character, which he praised highly.

"*24th Dec.*— Kitchener gives a final answer about the refugees, refusing on the ground that he does not wish the district re-peopled, for fear it should serve as a basis for Dervish raids. Rubbish!

"There is a fine quarrel on between England and the United States about Venezuela. Lord Salisbury is getting into nice hot water. He has a war with Ashanti of the most causeless kind. His diplomacy at Constantinople has entirely broken down, as the Turks are massacring the Armenians worse than ever — and now he will have to fight or sing small — doubtless sing small — in America. I should not be surprised 'to see the Egyptian question raised at any moment as a European one.

"*29th Dec.*— Went in to Cairo yesterday to see Ali Pasha Sherif's horses. They showed us half-a-dozen which 'were for sale. We shall bid for two, a chestnut colt, two years old, very like Mesaoud, and a grey filly, a Jellabieh, also a two-year-old. We did not see the best mares, but we saw the stallions. They have nothing left now but Aziz, aged nineteen, Ibn Nadir, aged twenty-four, and Ibn Sherara, also an old horse. They are terribly in want of new blood.

"Ali Pasha Sherif has had a decree of interdiction passed on him as incapable of the management of his affairs, and Shakir Pasha is appointed Wakil. He has quarrelled with his seven sons and receives an allowance of £500 a year. Such is the position of the man who a year ago was President of 'the Legislative Council, by favour of the late Khedive Tewfik and Lord Cromer.

"Afterwards to call on Riaz, whom I found with Tigrane, showing him his estate accounts at Melhallet el Roh. These bring him in £10 an acre, gross — expenses of cultivation £4 and tax £1. Net income £5 an acre. He reviewed the state of agricultural things since he had first been in the Government service in 1850. He said that the wars of Mohammed Ali had ruined the country, much of which had gone out of cultivation, but that under Abbas and Saïd the population had nearly doubled. The taxation was then one third what it is now. Everyone was well off. Then Ismaïl ruined it again. The price of land went up after his deposition and stood in 1880 at its highest. It was going down now with the fall in prices of produce. On the other hand the public expenditure had increased since the English occupation by two millions a year, and ten millions capital had been added to the debt."

CHAPTER XI

THE JAMESON RAID

" *5th Jan.*— There is excellent news. Those blackguards of the Chartered Company in South Africa, under Doctor Jameson, have made a filibustering raid on the Transvaal and have been annihilated by the Boers, Jameson a prisoner. I devoutly hope he may be hanged. I have seen this business coming on for some weeks past in articles from the ' Times.' That other high-placed filibuster, Chamberlain, is, I am sure, responsible, or the ' Times ' would never have taken up the matter in the way it has. They seem to have been encouraged in the sort of way these things are encouraged unofficially, by Chamberlain, who would have scored a victory for himself if they had succeeded. As it is he will disavow them. I am much mistaken if Chamberlain, with his three Colonial wars on hand in Ashanti, Venezuela, and now in the Transvaal, involving quarrels with France, America, and Germany, will not upset Lord Salisbury's government, if he does not upset the British Empire.

"Lord and Lady Cromer came here to tea. I had a good deal of talk with him. He says the Jameson episode will do a ' deal of harm ' here, as people will consider it a British defeat (which it is). He added: ' These filibustering enterprises are only justifiable by success. I don't say that they are justifiable at all, but if they don't succeed the actors in them should pay the penalty.' I think he is rather uneasy in his mind. We talked also about Egyptian affairs. He told me the Khedive was spending money very foolishly and would soon, at the present rate, be bankrupt, also that complaints had been made to him by fellahin in the neighbourhood of Koubbah, whose land he had been attempting to take, reviving obsolete claims against squatters on abandoned land, but he was not sure the complaints were true, the complainants refusing to come forward openly. They stated that they had been bullied by the palace people and beaten with *kurbajs.* He asked me if I had received complaints on the subject, but it is new to me. He told me that Ibrahim Bey Ibn Saoud had been to him twice, the first time to evoke his protection against the Sultan, to which he had replied that, as long as he, Ibrahim Bey, remained unamenable to Egyptian law he had nothing to fear. The second time he had brought him a ' ridiculous paper,' the copy of one he had submitted to the Khedive, charging the Sultan with all sorts of crimes, and appealing to the Khedive to occupy Nejd. He had had to give him ' a piece of his mind' and tell him that if he meddled with politics and the Sultan heard of it and demanded his extradition, he should not interfere to protect him; if he wanted to talk Arabian politics he had better go to Bagdad.

"We also discussed the appointment of Alfred Austin to the post of Poet Laureate. He, Cromer, thought William Watson would have been better. The Empress Frederick had 'tried to get Rennell Rodd appointed. He had never heard of Austin. Indeed, Austin's appointment is a ridiculous one, for, with the exception of three sonnets, Austin has never written anything in the smallest degree good. His sole claim is that he has been a solid supporter of the Conservative party in the press. I remember him well as a young man about thirty-eight years ago, when he first came up to London and published his earliest verses, ' The Season, a Satire,' and the rest. Some of them rather smart. He was a Catholic and moved in a small way in Catholic society, but later married an Irish Protestant and, I believe, joined the English church. He was the most absurd little cock sparrow of a man ever seen, and childishly vain of his talents. He has improved with years, but not in his verses. His principal poem, ' Madonna's Child,' is about the dullest and silliest tale in meagre blank verse ever produced. He has floated in at last to the Laureateship on the success of a prose volume about his garden in Kent. There really was no choice, however, for the post. William Morris refused, the Queen objected to Swinburne, old Patmore was a Catholic, the rest were, if possible, worse than Austin. He is better anyhow 'than Lewis Morris, the Liberal candidate, or than Watson, Dobson, Davidson, and the rest of the sons of their own penny trumpets.

"*9th Jan.*—The German Emperor has telegraphed his congratulations to Kruger, and this seems to have produced great anger in England. We have now managed in the last six months to quarrel violently with China, Turkey, Belgium, Ashanti, France, Venezuela, America, and Germany. This is a record performance, and if it does not break up the British Empire nothing will. For myself I am glad of it all, for the British Empire is the great engine of evil for the weak races now existing in the world — not that we are worse than the French or Italians or Americans — indeed, we are less actively destructive — but we do it over a far wider area and more successfully. I should be delighted to see England stripped of her whole foreign possessions. We were better off and more respected in Queen Elizabeth's time, the ' spacious days,' when we had not a stick of territory outside the British Islands, than now, and infinitely more respectable. The gangrene of colonial rowdyism is infecting us, and the habit of repressing liberty in weak nations is endangering our own. I should be glad to see the end.

"My old woodreeve, Bates, at Crabbet has hanged himself in his cart shed — a man of genius in his way of life, who, beginning as a day labourer, rose to be the best judge of timber in Sussex, as well as a successful farmer and churchwarden of the parish. Having completed eighty-four years of life and fifty of honest service in the Crabbet Estate, and having entertained his friends the night before, he went out in the early morning to his shed and was found there dead hanging from a beam. I can imagine the old man carefully tying the noose, as his manner was, without mistake. It was noticed by those who had been with him at dinner the night before that during the meal he had a hank of rope on his knees with which he was playing. In the morning he had got up by candlelight, asked his old wife ' How are you, old girl? ' and had gone out to the cart shed, where he was found hanging.

" 11th Jan.—Took Anne and Judith to Koubbah to see the Khedive. He received us with great *empressement,* talked a good deal about the petty vexations and the affronts put upon him by the English officials, and showed us his stud. He has got 'together some nice mares, but nothing quite first class, except two of Ali Pasha Sherif's, one of which is our horse Mesaoud's dam, a very splendid mare, with the finest head in the world. He has bred some promising colts and altogether the thing is well done. He invited us to go out with him some day on a desert expedition, and sent us to the station in his barouche.

" There seems a good chance now of the Egyptian question being re-opened as a European one, for the feeling against us in Germany is very strong over the Transvaal affair, and Egypt is the point where they can best put on the screw. I am sorry it should come in this way, though it is what I have always foreseen, for Egypt internationalized to the profit of Europe is not a pleasant prospect. It comes of Cromer's wrong-headed adminstration, where the one object has been to Anglicize, not to establish a National Government. Egypt, too, has been scandalously used for the creation of highly paid posts for not very capable Englishmen. I foresaw all this and protested years ago, but it was of no use. Now we shall evacuate the country not for the benefit of the Egyptians, but for that of the scoundrel European Colonies.

" Yesterday Dawkins and his wife were here — he a new man sent in Milner's place, and a friend of Milner's. I talked to him a good deal about Cromer's policy, in which I think he partially agreed with me, as they all do when it is plainly put before them that we *cannot* stay on for ever in Egypt. But, when things are quiet, and they see a chance of holding on, then they harden their hearts.

" 15*th Jan.*— I see in the papers that negotiations are likely to come on between our Government and the French about Egypt. I have therefore put my ideas about a possible agreement for evacuation on paper, and shall probably send it to Lord Salisbury through Pom McDonnell. It ought to be a quite easy thing to arrange if only Lord Salisbury was willing. His great necessities just now should be our occasion.

" 16*th Jan.*— Mohammed Abdu and M. Arminjan to luncheon. I talked the matter of evacuation over thoroughly with Abdu. He tells me that, much as he is attached to the Khedive, it would not do to trust him with power — the Ministry should be independent of him as far as possible, and supported by some sort of Constitution. He thinks this essential. There are good men to be found who would hold their own as ministers against Khedivial encroachment, but not the men now in office, who are mere dummies. The ministers ought to be irremovable as long as they have the support of the Chamber of Deputies. If we could get the French to agree to this, evacuation would be quite simple. It really looks as if it might come. Lord Salisbury has quarrelled with everybody, and it is about time he should patch up matters with some of them — and France is the most dangerous. I should prefer, myself, to see the British Empire break up. It has become a curse to the world, but, for Egypt's sake, an arrangement with France would be better at the present moment.

" 23*rd Jan.*— The English papers are sickening about the Transvaal, a mixture of swagger and poltroonery. One would have thought the less said about Jameson's ignominious defeat by the Boers the better, but our blessed public must needs make a hero of him, a man who fought for thirty-six hours, and had only fifteen men killed and then surrendered, not a pretence of its being in any better cause than moneymaking and land-grabbing. The 'Times' prints a poem in praise of him by the new Poet Laureate. Austin has managed to turn off some spirited doggerel, and to get it recited at a music hall, so low are we sunk. I have been busy writing my letter to McDonnell, and also finishing my article about the evacuation of Egypt for the 'Nineteenth Century.'

" We have had several visitors here. Madame d'Hautpoul and her cousin, Miss Pereira, Lady Decies and a pretty daughter, and Mr. Douglas Murray. The latter told me one or two new things about Egyptian history. Lesseps had told him that it was he who dissuaded the French Government from joining in the bombardment of Alexandria or occupying the Suez Canal, thinking that the English would get into military difficulties; also that when our fleet entered the Canal, Admiral Hoskins threatened Victor Lesseps to hang him from the yard-

arm if he interfered with the operations. Lesseps was a vain old
fool.

"*25th Jan.*— Lady Galloway has arrived at Cairo. I went in to see
her at the Legation, where she is staying with the Cromers. She told
me that it was out of the question to think of our evacuating Egypt,
that if we went out the French would come in, or there would be massacres and a lot more rubbish, which I fear represents Lord Salisbury's
view. She also blamed Rosebery for the Armenian policy, but excused
Lord Salisbury for continuing it on the ground that he had a real sympathy for Armenia, and real hatred for the Turks. The Russo-Turkish
alliance is announced by the ' Pall Mall,' it cannot but be true. I fancy
the Russian Government is glad to ally itself with a fellow suppressor
of Nihilism, whether Russian or Armenian. The Armenians seem
likely now 'to be exterminated between them, our Government playing
the most foolish figure imaginable. Lady Galloway is coming to
Sheykh Obeyd on Monday.

"*27th Jan.*— Lady Galloway was here for luncheon to-day. I have
written my memorandum on the evacuation of Egypt, and am sending
it to Lord Salisbury through Pom McDonnell. In my letter to Pom I
say: ' I have drawn it up very carefully, and after consultation with
some of my Egyptian friends, who best know the situation, and in whom
I have most confidence as honest and patriotic men. I have also some
reason to believe that Monsieur Cogordan, the present French Minister, would enter into some such plan were it suggested to him. He
is a far fairer and more intelligent man than any of his predecessors
here. I have said nothing of it, however, directly to him, as I only
know him very slightly. You know how anxious I am that Egypt
should be allowed to work out her political destiny in peace, and I foresee that if Lord Salisbury does nothing 'towards a solution of the question now, it will be forced upon him later in a way which will lead to
the sacrifice of all Egyptian hopes. With the support of Germany
withdrawn from our occupation, it is impossible that Europe should
long delay making the question its own. This sensible Egyptians fear
as a worse evil than anything in their present condition, for it would
mean Egypt for all the speculators of Europe.'

" Our policy at Constantinople has certainly gone an absolute smash,
and Philip must be feeling small. A treaty is announced between
Russia and Turkey, which, whether quite true or not, must be very near
the truth. I strongly suspect that the famous incident of Saïd Pasha
taking refuge at the British Embassy was an ingenious trick to spy
out the real ideas of the Ambassador. Saïd may very well have gone
there with the knowledge and privity of the Sultan, and the result may
have convinced the Sultan that England was his bitterest personal en-

emy.   Certainly from the day of Saïd's return to his own house things
have altered at Constantinople, and the Sultan has gone his own way
without seeking any more to be on 'terms with us.[1]

"*30th Jan.*— Anne and I start on Monday for a considerable journey
in the southern desert beyond Kalala.   Judith goes up the Nile with
Lady Decies, and Sheykh Obeyd will be shut up.   I feel better and in
better spirits, though the future is dark for me.   If this next summer
brings me nothing of value to my life I shall not return to England
again.   Perhaps I may find my hermitage this Spring in truth and
reality, but I must go to England once again first, to solve one or 'two
questions and complete my memoirs.

"*3rd Feb.*— Our party at Sheykh Obeyd is broken up.   Judith went
this morning to Cairo, and will stay there till she starts up the Nile.
Anne and I leave to-morrow for our long desert journey, it ought to
be an interesting one.   I went to-day to the War Office, and saw
Wingate, and looked over maps with him.   I find that almost nothing is
known of the country south of Kalala, so that we shall be exploring a
new region.   I have taken tracings of such maps as they have in 'the
Intelligence Department, and they are not much.   Floyer has also sent
me tracings.   I had some talk with Slatin, a commonplace little German, quite unworthy of ever having served the Mahdi.   He talked a
great deal about the prospects of reconquering the Soudan.   I have
been reading Kipling's new ' Jungle Book,' and the story of the Indian
Minister who became a fakir.   It seems to me the only worthy ending
of a public, perhaps of a private life ; but it wants great physical courage to endure."

February 4th to 26th in my journal is taken up with 'the diary of a
camel journey made by Anne and me, with Suliman Howeyti and two
other Bedouins of the Howeytat, under the guidance of Sobeyeh Ibn
Zeydan of the Maaze tribe, through the Maaze country south of the
Kalala mountains to the granite range of Jebel Ghâreb southwards to
Kúfra, Dokhán, and Kitár, regaining the Nile at Keneh, a journey of
400 miles of uninhabited desert, made in twenty days, of the greatest
possible interest.   My diary, however, is little more than an itinerary of
each day's march, suited rather for a paper in the Royal Geographical
Society than for the present volume, and I do not transcribe it here.
It was for the most part through an entirely unexplored and unmapped
region.   We returned from Keneh by steamer to Cairo.   All that I
will say of it here is that it was the last and perhaps the hardest of all
'the many desert journeys Lady Anne and I undertook alone together,
and as such stands out in my memory as one of the most delightful.   I
made a rough map of our route for private use, not for the Geographical
Society (of which I am almost the oldest member), because I have

---

[1] Compare Dr. Dillon's "Eclipse of Russia."

long convinced myself that it makes itself the precursor and instrument
of Europe's penetrations and conquests against the wild races of mankind.

"*7th March.*— Back at Sheykh Obeyd. Great things have happened
since we were away. First and foremost the Italians have been
smashed in Abyssinia, thoroughly and I hope finally. They have most
richly deserved it. The whole history of their doings on the Red Sea
has been a disgrace even to this graceless nineteenth century. They
went there at our bidding in 1884, a job of Lord Northbrook's when
we were in straits with the Mahdi and thought they might help us. We
gave them Massowa, which did not belong to us, but to Egypt, Egypt,
of which we said we were acting as guardians and trustees. At first
they occupied the island only, then little by little they encroached upon
the mainland on the plea of wanting a hill station, then they made
leonine treaties with the king and encroached more and more, and then
they put forward pretensions for a protectorate. Next they made a
dash at Kassala and captured it from the Soudanese. This turned their
vanitous heads, and nothing would serve them but they must make war
again with Menelik, wanting to grab the whole country. Menelik pretended to yield, for the Abyssinians are cunning, but let loose an army
of Chouans upon them. The Italians were defeated and shut up in a
fortress. The fortress was invested and at last capitulated on good
terms granted them by Menelik, who, though victorious, asked for
peace. His magnanimity, however, was put down at once in Italy to
cowardice, the 'heroic' Italian defenders of the fortress were treated
.as if they had been conquerors, and pretensions were put forward of
annexing the whole of Abyssinia. Menelik, however, calmly went on,
all sections of the Abyssinians joining him, and proposed as an alternative condition of peace, that the Italians should return to their original
quarters at Massowa; and war was renewed. The Italians then sent
50,000 men from Italy, but their General would not wait for the supports, fearing to be superseded, and with 15,000 men gave battle, and
has now been entirely destroyed. The Italians have lost 60 cannons
and 10,000 men, all most probably killed, and are being swept into the
sea. This is a righteous ending to their iniquities. It is enough to
make one repent of ever having wasted sympathy on liberty, to see
these Italians, hardly released from their Austrian bondage, counting
it a glory for their mushroom kingdom of Italy to attack and enslave the
oldest free people and kingdom in the world — for the Abyssinian monarchy dates from before the time of King Solomon — and there was
not a voice in Europe to cry shame! All the English papers applauded.
'The wiping out of the little kingdom of Abyssinia won't make much
difference,' they said, 'on the Stock Exchange.' But for once Providence has answered 'No.' Crispi, the Italian minister, formerly a

revolutionist, now a renegade tyrant, has fallen. He will be lucky if he does not get torn to pieces in the streets, and it will fare hard with the Italian monarchy. The Duke of Sermoneta, who was at Cairo amusing himself, has been sent for to Rome. He has always been an opponent of 'the Colonial policy, but he will be too late even if they make him minister.

"Next the Transvaal business has developed. Jameson and his band have been fêted in London, and old Kruger must, I think, be sorry he did not hang them. It would have been the best policy, for Englishmen are cowards in the face of hanging, and we should have had no more filibustering for at least a generation. Rhodes, too, has been to England, and seems to have squared 'the Opposition. The inquiry is to be put off, and, if possible, shirked, and I fancy Chamberlain has saved his bacon. It is more obvious, however, than ever that he was in with Rhodes and Jameson, though possibly they acted without his exact knowledge at the last moment. But the British public is easily gulled, and Chamberlain's protestations of innocence have been swallowed even by the opposition papers and Sir William Harcourt. It is a base world and will not prosper — but it tries one's patience to have 'to wait to see the end of it.

"T. P. Gill has been here twice this week. He has come here for his health and to pick up ideas about evacuation, and I have got him an audience of the Khedive. He saw Cromer on Thursday, who told him all the usual story about the wickedness of Abbas and his unfitness to reign. Gill's impression is that he will try to get him deposed. Cromer also fancies the French will come to terms which will leave him, Cromer, still in power here, but this will not be. It seems, however, certain that negotiations are going on between 'the French and English governments relative to the evacuation. McDonnell has acknowledged the memorandum I sent to Lord Salisbury, who 'thinks I will understand that he cannot write just now on 'the subject of it '— which is the case. At any rate Lord Salisbury has read it, and that is something.

"Gill was very interesting in his account of Parnell's last days. He saw much of him in all the time, both before the divorce trial and during 'the party split which followed. It was he who carried on the negotiations with Dillon and O'Brien when they were at Paris, and he left the party when these failed. He tells me that Parnell had a complete case in defence against O'Shea, O'Shea having connived throughout and profited in a money way. The house at Eltham was really Parnell's, and O'Shea went there to blackmail him. He showed his whole defence to Gill before the trial. But Mrs. O'Shea would not allow him to defend himself as she wanted a divorce so as to marry him. She was a woman quite unworthy of him, who neither sympathized with his politics nor at all appreciated 'the height of his position. Later again when Parnell would have agreed to retire for a while from the party, and was quite willing to make peace, she always stood in the way of it — and he used to come back from Brighton changed and uncompromising. Lastly his devotion 'to her and the worry of his public life was too much for him, and she really hastened his end by her exigencies. I asked him whether he committed suicide. But he was emphatic that it was not so. ' Parnell,' he said, ' was the last man in the world to do it. He was a fighter to his last breath, and would not give in. It was the worry and the strain of fighting that ended him.'

" Evelyn has come and is staying with us.

" 12*th March.*— Evelyn and Gill have gone. The Armenian Blue Books are published. They show, as far as I can judge by the extracts given, 'that our Government has made a complete diplomatic fiasco. Philip seems to have had really nothing to go upon for his trust in Russian and French co-operation, and it has been exactly the old game of taking a threat to be as good as a blow, which Lord Granville was so fond of. Of course the whole truth is not given in the Blue Book. The reason for taking up the question in 1895, rather than at any other time was, I have no doubt, to make a diversion for the Egyptian question. It was probably the reason, too, why Lord Salisbury was so foolish as to continue his predecessor's error. Nothing can excuse his having put the threat to Turkey into 'the Queen's speech if he was not prepared to act up to it.

" 13*th March.*— The English papers have come, telling of the Italian defeat at Adowa, no trace in any of them of the smallest sympathy with the Abyssinians or of disapproval of the wanton invasion of their country. All sense of the rights of weaker nations is lost in Europe even among the best and most generous of nations.

" 14*th March.*— Mohammed Abdu was here 'to-day and tells me there is some prospect now of Arabi's being allowed to return first to Cyprus, then to Egypt. Mustapha Fehmy, the Prime Minister, has spoken to him about it, and says that Lord Cromer is willing if the Khedive consents. If 'this is so the thing ought to be managed.

" 15*th March.*— Sheykh Saleh, the Sheykh of the *muhajjerin,* the refugees from Dongola, called to-day. He says that Kitchener has told him the Government intends to advance to Abu Hamad and Berber as soon as the railway is finished to Wady Halfa. This can hardly be, however, for several years. He assures me the people of Berber would be willing, and of Abu Hamad, but the Khalifa is still powerful. Berber he declares to be the key of the Soudan, as all roads converge there.

" 16*th March.*— It is announced that an advance is to be made immediately to Dongola by arrangement with the German and Austrian

Governments, so as to make a diversion in favour of the Italians at Kassala. There is no doubt that troops have been forwarded up the river for some time past, as long ago as when we were on our way down from Keneh (a fortnight ago), but the final decision to advance must have been come to suddenly. Even now I can hardly believe it, it would be a most flagrant sacrifice of Egyptian for European interests, although there would probably be little resistance at Dongola; it must entail a re-opening of the war with the Soudan, and what has Italy done for Egypt to deserve Egyptian help?

"*20th March.*— I wrote to the ' Times ' in the sense of my first impression of the affair, but I find that the facts are even more damning to our government than I had supposed, and for once I have done Cromer an injustice. Anne saw Lady Cromer on Thursday and she complained bitterly to her of the thing having been decided by Lord Salisbury ' over Lord Cromer's head,' who had strongly disapproved of it. Moreover, Mohammed Abdu, who was here yesterday, tells me that the Egyptian Ministry was also opposed, Mustapha Fehmy saying that they had no money, and that it was impossible. Even the Khedive, who was keen on an advance to Dongola two years ago, objected to fighting for Italy, though I hear from Hadji Mahmoud that His Highness is to start up the river 'the day after to-morrow. Hadji Mahmoud got the news from Ali Pasha Lalla, and the vice-regal camels have already been despatched by train to Girgeh. I am sorry he should intend this, as he will get into trouble if he has done it off his own bat, and if at the suggestion of Kitchener or Cromer they will turn it to his disadvantage. Mohammed Abdu, however, was to see him to-morrow, and I hope will give him good advice.

" I sit most of the day at Sheykh Obeyd's tomb, watching the birds through a glass. There are half-a-dozen kinds nesting in the *sont* bushes there : the Nubian shrike, a kind of blackcap with a black throat, the Palestine redstart, and two small warblers. There are also the thrush, the Egyptian dove, the crow, a pair of spotted cuckoos, a hoopoo, and a chat.

"*22nd March.*— A large party of visitors. Lady Galloway, who has come back from a journey up the Nile, which she has made with Lady Jersey. Then the Potocki party, Joseph and his wife, Zamoyski and his wife, Prince Radziwill and two other Poles. We had tea at the tomb and showed off the horses.

" It is certain now that Cromer had nothing to do with the new Soudan campaign, the thing having been arranged between the Emperor of Germany and Frank Lascelles (this was 'the account given me by our Polish friends). The Emperor, I imagine, has promised to support our staying on in Egypt in return for the help given by us vicariously to his ally the King of Italy. I notice already an announcement that Germany does not intend to be otherwise than friendly to Japan, which is also probably part of the arrangement. It means in any case that we are to have a new lease of occupation here. About the advantage or disadvantage to Egypt nobody seems to have thought or cared. I have written to John Morley, giving him my view of what is going on, as I see he has brought the matter forward in Parliament. It was through him that we stopped the Soudan war eleven years ago.

"24th March.— Sheykh Mohammed Abdu called to tell me what is going on at the palace. He sees the Khedive now twice a week, and leads the prayer on Fridays at Koubbah, omitting the Sultan's name. He was with the Khedive some little time ago, and while he was there, a letter came from Lord Cromer, complaining of the Khedive's having privately expressed disapproval of the Dongola campaign. The Khedive was very angry at this, and afterwards saw Lord Cromer, who repeated the complaint. The Khedive answered that upon this point he was in agreement with his Lordship, to which Lord Cromer did not dissent, but said that now that the thing was resolved on, it was necessary to put a good face on it, and hoped that the Khedive would speak in that sense to the soldiers. The Khedive has done so since. Lord Cromer, too, has brought him a message from Lord Salisbury, apologizing for an 'error of form' on the part of the English Government in ordering an advance on Dongola without first informing His Highness. Lord Salisbury explained that the advance was decided on 'to satisfy Egyptian opinion.' The Khedive narrated all this to Mohammed Abdu, and I have no doubt it is true.

"25th March.— The English papers of the 17th and 18th came to-day. Lord Salisbury's statement in the House of Lords is amazing. He has made no such deliberate misstatement of an important truth since the Congress of Berlin.

"A large party to spend the afternoon, brought over by Lady Galloway; Lord Yarborough, Benson, the author of 'Dodo,' and others. She brought with her Arthur Balfour's speech and Lord Salisbury's declaration.

"26th March.— Sheykh Hassan Abu Towil called to tell me that the Government had assembled the Sheykhs of the tribes between Assouan and the Mediterranean Sea, to confer with them as to the raising of 7,000 horsemen for the Soudan war. Their answer so far has been that they have neither horses nor arms. He asked my advice. I advised him strongly to get out of the matter if he could, as the war will prove a bad business for Bedouins engaged in it. I doubted if one in five would return. He told me that in former wars the Bedouins had never been called to go out of their own district where they had acted

as guards. It would be better to say at once 'the men were unwilling
to go to a distance. He promised to bring Abu Shedid (head Sheykh
of the Howeytat) with him to-morrow to consult.

"*27th March.*— A letter from Lady Lytton. She tells me: ' Rhodes
knew about Jameson's advance on the Transvaal, but certainly *not*
Chamberlain, though he may have encouraged Rhodes too much.' Just
so. It means that Chamberlain told Rhodes not to tell him the details,
but gave him to understand that he would be pleased at the *fait ac-
compli.* About the Soudan expedition she had great confidence in Lord
Salisbury, though ' one knows that what comes out in Parliament is all
arranged.'

"*30th March.*— Received a note from Abdin, granting me audience
of the Khedive for to-day, so to-day I went there. He asked me first
about our journey to Ghareb and Keneh, which interested him much,
but we soon got to politics. He gave me a full account of what happened regarding the advance on Dongola. The question was begun
soon after the battle of Adowa by the arrival in Egypt of our military
attaché at Rome (Slade?), when a council was held,[1] consisting of
Knollys, Kitchener, the attaché, and Cromer. At this they decided to
send a force from Tokar 'to Kassala to take over that town from the
Italians and garrison it with Egyptian troops — this with the consent
of Italy, and Cromer telegraphed their decision to Lord Salisbury.
The Egyptian Government were not consulted, only *informed* of this,
and gave consent. After 'this they knew nothing till, on the 13th
March, Lord Cromer received a telegram from London, saying an immediate advance on Dongola had been ordered. Kitchener was in bed,
and not at all expecting it. Neither he nor Cromer had recommended
it; and, in fact, they disapproved. The next day was Beiram, and
after the mosque, Mustapha Fehmy was informed of it by Cromer or
Kitchener, I am not sure which, and it was not till 7.30 that the Khedive
learnt it from Mustapha Fehmy. He refused his consent until a Council of Ministers had been called, especially because of a demand made
that Suakim should be handed over to England. He disapproved of the
expedition on account of the hot time of year and the suffering of the
men and the increased cost of land transport at Low Nile, also because
it was made in no Egyptian interest. At the Council Kitchener withdrew the demand for Suakim. When asked about it, he said that it
was not in question. Consent was then formally given to the rest of
plan. Cromer had since come to complain of his, Abbas', having
talked against the war, and had threatened to write against him in the
Blue Books. Abbas had answered that he objected on account of the
'time of year and the cost, not in itself to the re-occupation of Dongola.
' Oh,' said Cromer, ' in that I am with you, but you ought to be glad

---

[1] A fortnight or three weeks before Beiram.

to help the King of Italy. He gave hospitality to your grandfather for many years at Naples.' 'Yes,' answered Abbas, 'and made him pay pretty heavily for it too.' (Ismaïl lent a very large sum to the King, which I believe was never repaid.) Cromer asked the Khedive to write for publication an address 'to the Army approving the objects of the campaign; but Abbas declined, saying it was not necessary to talk politics to soldiers. He promised, however, to exhort them to obey orders and do their duty. This he has repeatedly done. I asked him whether Kitchener had recommended 'the Dongola campaign, and he said 'No; he knew nothing of it till he woke up out of his bed.' Also as to the Duke of Cambridge, whom I suspected of having arranged it, 'No, he is an old man, too old to conceal anything, and as we had a deal of talk together I should have found out.'

"The Khedive also told me the detail of letters written to the Queen and to himself by King Mangasheh of Abyssinia, complaining, to the first, that he, being an old ally of England, England had nevertheless supplied arms to the Italians. Mangasheh is a son of King John, whom we put on the throne. His letter to the Egyptian Government was to propose joint action against the Khalifa, in order to recover his crown, which had been taken from him and carried away to Omdurman. In his letter to the Queen he asked England's good offices with Italy for a peace. Both these letters were written before the battle of Adowa, and were conveyed to Cairo by a cousin of Mangasheh. They were translated at the Cairo War Office. The Queen's answer was in general terms, hoping that peace would be made. The answer sent by Lord Cromer, in the name of the Egyptian Government, was a proposal that Mangasheh should advance on Omdurman, when they would together get back the crown, and Mangasheh should be recognized King of Abyssinia. Mangasheh, however, Abbas said, would never go against Menelik, as his father John had specially recommended him to recognize Menelik as Emperor. Mangasheh's envoy went away dissatisfied, especially with the presents given him, which had been supplied by 'the Secret Service Fund of the Egyptian War Office, namely, a gold watch, a musical box, a red umbrella, and some dresses, which he told the Khedive he should be ashamed to deliver to the King, as they were the same as those worn by prostitutes in Abyssinia. They were chosen by Kitchener. The Khedive said it would be a good thing if I wrote an article in conformity with what he had told me; and I promised to do so, but without compromising him. In going away I asked him to allow Arabi to return to Egypt; and he questioned me about him, and I told him what an honest patriot he was, and that I would make myself answerable for his loyalty. He promised me that he would speak to Mustapha Fehmy about it, and I think he means it. He said: 'What you tell me about him I must believe, for nobody who knows you can doubt that you are the best friend that Egypt has.' And so we parted. I was again much struck with his great intelligence and power of expressing his thoughts.

" *3rd April.*— I have been writing an article, ' The Truth of the Dongola Adventure,' for the ' Ninteenth Century.'

" I see they have been pushing George Curzon with questions in the House of Commons about Cromer's approval of the campaign — this I doubt not in consequence of a letter I wrote to Morley, telling him that Cromer had certainly not recommended it.

" *7th April.*— Dawkins (the new financial adviser) was here 'to-day, and tells me that the half million sterling taken from the Caisse de la Dette has been spent already. The whole savings of Egypt will have been used up before the campaign seriously begins.

" Young Somerset and his bride, Lady Katherine, came on Saturday, a pleasing pair, who propose going to the Natron lakes on camels. I tried to dissuade her, as she has never yet been on a camel, and there was the chance of great heat so late in the year, but on Sunday, Easter night, there was a thunder shower, and the weather has become almost cold.

" *10th April.*— Gorst and his sister came to luncheon. He, like Dawkins, evidently disapproves of the war. He says that it will end in England's having to make the campaign at her own cost, as Egypt has neither the money nor the men. I am, however convinced that it will be put a stop to as soon as a convenient pretext occurs. There is a report that the Italians have evacuated Kassala. Also the Matabeles have risen and killed a number of the Chartered Company's people, and are besieging Bulawayo. The Chartered Company have no troops, and English regiments will have to be sent to the Cape, and there will be none to spare for a Soudanese campaign. I wish the Matabeles all possible good fortune, and trust they may capture Rhodes, who is said to be on his way from Fort Salisbury to Bulawayo. The man, however, is too sly, I fancy, to be caught, or to run any personal risks, and a telegram to-day says he is laid up with a fever, and unable to move! The Dongola expedition, therefore, will, in my opinion, get very little farther than Akasheh. Gorst tells me it is true that Rhodes took away with him 200 negroes from Cairo. He says they ' volunteered.' But the grounds of his belief seem slight. ' I inquired,' he said, ' whether they were going willingly, and was told that they were.' He is much averse 'to the seizure of black men, as practised by the Sirdar Kitchener, for the Egyptian army, and told me confidentially that he had had the intention of putting a stop to it, as it is quite illegal. But the campaign had interfered with his project. There has been a general raid on all negroes in Egypt. They are seized and forced to serve in the army on very small pay — I think thirty piastres a month, twopence halfpenny a day — and are there practically slaves for life — or rather for as long as they are able to serve — for when past work in the army, they are pitilessly cast adrift without pension or provision of any kind. Yet we English pretend that our mission in Africa is to put down slave-raiding and slavery. The English officers at Wady Halfa told me last autumn that it was as precisely slavery as any existing in the world.

" We are leaving for England on the 17th. I am glad to go, having been seven months away.

" *12th April.*— Young Gordon (General Gordon's nephew, Bill) is here with his wife. He confirms about the spending of the half million by Kitchener, but says the expedition is being done very cheaply. He has the ordering and arranging of the supplies, and says that the new equipments, saddles, arms, etc., have only cost £20,000. He, like Gorst and Dawkins, considers the Intelligence Department absurdly over-rated and overpaid. Wingate and Slatin between them get £1,700 a year. Gordon has had some experience of the department, having been employed under it at Souakim, and he knows how the information brought in is cooked, and how the spies suit their news to 'the demand. I asked him about the negroes taken away by Rhodes. He thinks it likely that they were handed over by the agent of the Zanzibar Government (which had been recruiting in Egypt). He himself supplied Rhodes with uniforms for them out of the public stores ' at a good price.' He saw a great deal of Rhodes during the few days Rhodes was at Cairo.

" *15th April.*— They are apparently at a deadlock on the frontier, the Finance Ministry being angry with Kitchener for spending all the money. It must eventually fall on the English exchequer, if persisted in. But I still hope Lord Salisbury will be satisfied with the demonstration and go no farther.

" *17th April.*— We leave to-morrow morning for England. Mohammed Abdu was here yesterday with a young Turk of the Liberal party from Constantinople. He was employed till lately in the Ottoman bank. He seems not very hopeful of things on 'the Bosphorus, there being too many persons in high places interested in keeping the present system going. The army, though no better affected than the rest to the Sultan, is without any leader for a revolt, and as long as it can be paid it will do nothing. The civilian population has no power to move.

" Mohammed Abdu gave me particulars about the raid there has been made on the negroes in Egypt. Over 800 have been seized by the police for Kitchener and put into the army. In some of the provinces every black man of whatever age was taken and sent to Cairo, where the valid ones were retained, the rest turned adrift in the streets. Yet our Government talks of putting down the Slave Trade as one of its objects in this Soudanese war. There seems to be no doubt that the 200 negroes taken by Rhodes to South Africa were practically purchased from the Government of Zanzibar, which has 'recruited' them here. In the recent raid negroes holding respectable positions were seized, among them a son of the Khedive's porter, the servant of El Abbasi, Sheykh of the Azhar, and a writer employed at £7 a month in the Native Courts at Cairo. These were rescued, but very many others were driven off.

"I spent my last day, a very lovely one, in the garden — the roses well in bloom, the nightingales singing, bee birds flying about, a roller sitting near the tomb, and in the evening a jackal. I lit two candles there for Sheykh Obeyd to get us a good passage home. We had our Mowled there on Monday. Old Sheykh Abderrahman Faki promises to say prayers for me in my absence, but expostulates that I do not go 'to his mosque. I prefer to recite my Fatha at the tomb."

We reached London on the evening of the 24th, and slept there.

"*25th April.*— Breakfasted with George Wyndham. We are to go together on a pilgrimage to Stratford in connection with a monograph he is writing on Shakespeare. He has the practical editorship now of the 'New Review,' and in Parliament is making a cave against Chamberlain, whom he agrees with me in considering as at the bottom of all the Government mischief. He says there is no doubt in the world that Chamberlain was in with Rhodes and Jameson in 'their attack on the Transvaal, and he is angry with him for having backed out of it, and ruined the plot at the last moment to save his own bacon. He has been seeing much of Jameson, whom he likes, and of the gang that have been running the Transvaal business, about a dozen of them, with Buckle, the 'Times' editor, and Miss Flora Shaw who, he told me confidentially, is really the prime mover in the whole thing, and who takes the lead in all their private meetings, a very clever middle-aged woman. George made, it appears, a good speech in the House ten days ago, attacking the Government on the line of their having disarmed 'the Outlanders, and left the Chartered Company defenceless. Chamberlain has since been making overtures to him of friendship, and has been walking about with him ostentatiously in the Lobby; but, seeing this did not stop George's mouth, he has since shown animosity. I warned George that Chamberlain was a man who would do him a mischief if he could. George is very happy with all this busy work.

"My article will be out on the 1st duly corrected in the 'Nineteenth Century,' and George has asked me to write him another for his June number of the 'New Review.' I shall give him one on the Moallakát with my translation of Antar's Ode.

"Old Alfred Montgomery is dead, and buried with a wreath from

the Prince of Wales 'to our dear friend.'   So he ought to sleep happy
to the Judgment Day.   He was quite the last of the old D'Orsay set
in London, and remained a ' man of fashion,' dining out to the end,
though he died actually away from London at Burley, with his daughter, Edith Finch.

" *28th April.*— To London with Anne.   Ralph came to luncheon in
Mount Street, and I afterwards dined with him.   He showed me the
whole existing correspondence between Byron and Mrs. Leigh.

" *14th May.*— I have been down, for the most part alone, at Newbuildings, enjoying a wonderful fortnight, the woods lovely in green
and gold, nightingales singing night and day from every hedge, quite
a dozen close to the house so that one can hear them at any hour of
the night chorussing when one opens a window.   I have finished my
article on the ' Poetry of the Ignorance,' and am half way through
another on the ' Origin of the Arabian Horse,' for the June and July
numbers of the ' New Review.'   George and I and Sibell, and one of
the girls, are to go to Stratford on Saturday.   I lunched to-day with
them and young Rosslyn, a pleasant specimen of the golden youth of
the day.

" Then to Hammersmith, where I found my poor old Morris looking
very ill and aged, toddling feebly in front of his house.   We went in
together, and he brightened up, and told me of his maladies in a cheerful
not too desponding way, and I stayed on an hour or more and had tea
with him.   My new tapestry, the Botticelli, is finished, and I am to
go with Mrs. Morris on Saturday to see it in Oxford Street.   Morris
showed me the title-page of his Chaucer, which is about the finest
thing he has done, the whole has been subscribed for, a matter of
some £9,000.

" Gill, whom I saw in Mount Street, repeated to me more of what
Cromer had told him about the Soudan.   He asked Cromer whether
he should be in favour of an advance to re-occupy the lost provinces.
In reply to this Cromer had told him that some time or other the Soudan
would have to be reconquered from the Khalifa, but the question was
by whom.   As for imposing such a task on Egypt he was most emphatic.   ' I should never think,' he said, ' of proposing that the poor
fellahin in their blue shirts should be charged with it.'   This, it is as
well to remember, was as late as the beginning of March, and within
a week of the expedition being ordered from England.

" *15th May.*— Had tea with Lady Lytton at her house in Sloane
Street.   She thinks it a pity I should have written what I have about
the Dongola campaign, which has set people against me just as I was
coming home.   By ' people,' I suppose she means the Court, and I
strongly suspect that Her Majesty has been the determining cause of
the forward policy in Africa.   Lady Lytton was at pains to persuade

me that it was entirely Lord Salisbury, and that nobody else had been consulted about it.

" 16*th May.*— Lunched with George and Sibell, and found Madeline, his mother, there, looking fresh and well and younger than I have seen her for years, and came on with them in the afternoon to Stratford, where we now are. We have already been to the Church and the Grammar School. George is a capital companion for a visit of this kind, as he enjoys sightseeing, and besides knows all about Shakespeare, and has his theories about everything. We are at the Shakespeare Hotel, a pleasant inn of the old kind. We have spent the evening reading ' Venus and Adonis ' and ' Lucrece.' I have always been a great admirer of these two pieces, which are the most elaborate and sustained of their kind, and splendidly rhetorical. I did most of the reading as George has a cold.

" 17*th May.*— A beautiful hot day which we spent driving round the country with a jibbing horse. We went to Charlcote and wandered about the park, and then to Mary Arden's cottage, and to Anne Hatha- way's. Both cottages are interesting, and quite untouched and un- restored, the latter inhabited still by a descendant of the Hathaways. It is after all no such long way back to Shakespeare's time, seven gen- erations in my own family, and I think people largely exaggerate the changes that have taken place. Remote country villages can have hardly at all changed. In the evening I read them translations from the Moallakát, about which George is enthusiastic. My article for the ' New Review ' has put him upon the track of discovery as to certain features of chivalry in the Middle Ages in Europe, a subject not yet properly traced to its origin in Arabia. We have had a thoroughly literary two days, to me of much profit.

" 18*th May.*— Mary joined us from Stanway with Miss Balfour, and we all went to see the church and the tomb, then back to London in the afternoon.

" 20*th May.*— Dined with Pamela, and then went to the Foreign Office party in honour of Her Majesty's birthday, an immense crush, but as always a fine sight, and many people one knows.

" 29*th May.*— The Morrises have been here at Newbuildings since Tuesday. He, poor man, very feeble and aged. I fear from the look of things that it is some form of consumption, and that he will not recover. But his spirits are fairly good, and he talks at times as bril- liantly as ever. The new piece of tapestry he has made me, Botticelli's Spring, is up and is very decorative and brilliant in the drawing-room, though the faces are hardly as good as they ought to be. It has been a great difficulty to execute it, he says, and has turned out better than he expected. We think the three figures with the flowers are March, April, and May. We have had many interesting talks on art, politics, and religion. As to the last he does not believe in any God the Creator of the World, or any Providence, or, I think, any future life. But he is not a pessimist, and thinks mankind the 'crown of things,' in spite of man's destructive action and his modern craze of ugliness. His illness does not make him gloomy; only it troubles him in his work.

"Swinburne's new poem was reviewed yesterday in all the papers. Morris thinks it poor stuff and not worth doing, as the story, 'Balin and Balan,' was quite perfect in its prose form in the 'Morte d'Arthur.' 'It would not do, however,' he said, 'for Swinburne to hear me saying this, for he would never forgive me.' Swinburne, it appears, is the most sensitive and jealous of men, and cannot bear the smallest criticism. But he and Morris have not met for some years, though Mrs. Morris goes now and then to see Swinburne. Tennyson, Morris says, was the same, and never forgave him and Burne-Jones for having disapproved of his bowdlerization of the 'Morte d'Arthur' in the 'Idylls of the King.' I drove Morris yesterday to Crookhorn and a little way round. He is, I think, happy here. The oak woods are new to him, though he was born in Epping Forest, and he likes the multitude of birds. He creeps about a little among them in the sun.

"*31st May (Sunday)*.— The Morrises left yesterday. I think he enjoyed himself while he was here, and he talks of coming back for another week later, and of our making a drive together in Epping Forest, where he was born. But I fear he is very ill. He has told me something of his origin. His father was a bill broker in the City, and he himself was destined for that trade. 'If I had gone on with it,' he said, 'I should have broken the bills into very small bits. We had some mining shares in Cornwall, and when I succeeded to them I sold them. My relations thought me both wicked and mad, but the shares are worth nothing now.' I took him yesterday to see Shipley Church, a fine old Norman tower, injured with restoration. He was very indignant, swearing at the parsons as we walked up the nave: 'Beasts! Pigs! Damn their souls!' We had a long discussion whether the love of beauty was natural or acquired. 'As for me,' he said, 'I have it naturally, for neither my father, nor my mother, nor any of my relations had the least idea of it. I remember as a boy going into Canterbury Cathedral and thinking that the gates of heaven had been opened to me, also when I first saw an illuminated manuscript. These first pleasures which I discovered for myself were stronger than anything else I have had in life.' He talked much about his Iceland journey, as he often does, and has a sick man's fancy to go there again, for it would do him good. 'I am a man of the North,' he said. 'I am disappointed at the fine weather we are having here. I had hoped it would rain, so that I could sit indoors and watch it beating on the windows.'

"*1st June.*— Went up to London to take Anne to a Geographical meeting, where Theodore Bent gave some account of his travels south of where we were last winter. Like all our geographers nowadays he is an arch Jingo, and talked of opening up the country by gold digging as if it would be a work of piety. The Geographical Society has lent itself to this sort of thing in Africa for the last thirty years.

"*2nd June.*— To lunch with Judith at Margot's; a great treat. Margot was delightful and most amusing. We found her with Lady Greville, who had come to interview her, on 'the subject of women cross country riders, for some magazine. Margot was splendid in her description of the various styles of riding, and of the falls and smashes she had had and witnessed. ' There are only three women,' she said, ' who really have the nerve to ride a line of their own, and I am one of them.' Her baby of last year has in no way spoilt her nerve, and she had seventy days' hunting during the past winter. Two of her step-children were with her at luncheon, and the governess, which gave her a somewhat matronly appearance, but she is otherwise unchanged from the days of her hoyden maidenhood — affectionate, and nice, and cleverer than any one else, with a pretty colour in her cheeks, but very thin. ' I have lost two stone,' she said, ' since you were with me at the Glen. I only weigh 7 stone 6, but I like to ride big horses. The best I ever had was 16.2.

"*3rd June.*— Newbuildings. I have sent the following to Morley:

' As the debate on the Soudan campaign is coming on I write a line to say that I think you will find the action of the Italian Government explainable on the supposition put forward in my article in the " Nineteenth Century " of May, viz., that the arrangement made with the German Emperor was due not to the Italian Government, but to the King of Italy personally through his appealing to the Emperor. The Italian Government, and especially the Duke of Sermoneta, whom I know well, are or were when they came into office opposed altogether to the Italian Colonial policy. The Duke's hobby (if one may call it so) is financial economy, and he would have liked to see the whole of Erythrya with Kassala, and even Massówah, given up. I am sure, therefore, that it has been the King's influence that has been at work overruling that of his Ministers. The Italian Government's object now, I imagine, is to get their expenses in Erythrya, or at any rate at Kassala, paid for by the Egyptian Government or ours, on the plea that they have been *pacifying* the country in Egyptian interests. It is all nonsense of course, but our Government, by inviting the Italians twelve years ago to take Massówah, has put itself under some obligations to Italy, which will be made the most of.

'P.S. I am convinced that the whole of this business was worked in the first instance by Royal personages, including our own, much more than by the various F.O's.'[1]

"*8th June.*— There is news of a 'victory' in the Soudan at Ferkeh, come, however, just too late to serve as an answer by the Government in Parliament. Labouchere rushed this debate on Friday, and it came off most successfully, whereas the battle, which I have little doubt was fought by order from Downing Street, was only fought on Sunday.

"Coming up to London in the morning I stopped at 90, Sloane Street, to see Frank Lascelles. We had some talk about Egypt and the Soudan, and he admitted to me that there had been a conversation between him and the Emperor William, such as I allude to in my 'Nineteenth Century' article. But he professed ignorance as to the real reasons of the decision come to, to advance to Dongola, also surprise at its having been made.

"*10th June.*— Mrs. Morris writes that Morris is less well, losing weight daily and growing weaker. But the doctors will have it that it is nervous exhaustion only, and recommend a sea voyage and rest. I do not believe them. She is to take rooms for him at Folkestone meanwhile, a sad prospect.

"*13th June.*—My good friend, J. H. Middleton, is dead.[2]

"*15th June.*— An inquest has been held on poor Middleton. The jury have returned a verdict of 'death from misadventure.' What is curious is that it now appears that for twenty years he has been a morphia taker, and his long illness has been entirely due to that cause. I have so often talked over with him his friend Rossetti's death from chloral, which he used to deplore! He is a great loss, or rather, one should say, has been a great loss, for he has been dead to the world and to his friends for something like two years.

"Margot came to dinner with George Wyndham and Harry Cust, a merry *parti de quatre,* and George stayed on talking with me after the others were gone.

"*16th June.*—Lunched with Philip Currie and his wife, just back from Constantinople. There seems little chance now of their being transferred to Paris. Afterwards to Lady Galloway's.

"*24th June.*—Yesterday to Folkestone to the Morrises. He is distinctly better, and I hope may yet come round, as the doctors declare he will. He talked a great deal about his boyhood, said he had read the whole of Scott's novels before he was seven, and had gone through the phase of 'Marmion' and the 'Lady of the Lake.' At his school,

---

[1] Compare Dr. Dillon's "Eclipse of Russia."

[2] John Henry Middleton, director of the South Kensington Museum.

Marlborough, he was neither high nor low in his form, but always last in arithmetic [in this like me] ; hated Cicero and Latin generally, but anything in the way of history had attracted him; he knew English history better than Greek history, though only the latter was taught; he had learned nearly everything he knew of architecture and mediæval things running about the country round Marlborough as a schoolboy. The Morrises are at the Norfolk Hotel.

"*26th June.*— With Everard Fielding to see Tissot's pictures, not really good either in drawing or in taste, and rather sham in their Oriental realism.

"Breakfasted with George, who was in the highest of his high spirits, having been up at a ball till five at Grosvenor House, and then out at nine to try a new bicycle on Hampstead Heath, which is to run forty miles an hour. His triumphs are my triumphs, and I delight in his happiness.

"*1st July.*— Lunched with Harry Cust, who is starting in a few days for South Africa.

"*10th July.*— Went with George Wyndham to a dinner given by Henley to the 'New Review' contributors, a deadly dull affair, as all men's dinners are — the most interesting person I met there was the Dane Brandes, who has the honour of having invented Ibsen. Whibley also was there, with whom I talked.

"Things are going badly in South Africa for the Chartered Company. The black are in arms, and it seems doubtful whether they can be put down. Rhodes is now quite discredited.

"*11th July.*— Lunched with Lady Galloway, and down by the afternoon train to Canterbury to stay with Guy Wyndham and his wife, who are quartered there. They have a very beautiful child, a boy called George.

"*12th July.*— With Guy to see the Cathedral. I am disappointed with it, after all Morris told me — that is, with the inside, which has been scraped out of most of its interest. Only the tombs are splendid, especially that of the Black Prince. The tower outside, seen from the cloisters, is grand, and I have arrived just in time to see these and the chapter house unspoiled. 'If you had come a week later,' said the verger, ' you would have found the whole a mass of scaffolding.' Dean Farrar, who wants, Morris says, to be made a Bishop, is bent on scraping and destroying all that has hitherto escaped, a hideous madness of destruction nothing can prevent.

"In the evening back to London, and dined with the Morrises, to wish him good-bye, as he sails for Norway next week. The garden at Kelmscott House is lovely with hollyhocks.

"*15th July.*— To the Horse Show at the Crystal Palace, where

Mesaoud has taken first Arab Prize, Meijliss second. This is satisfactory, though in truth no great triumph, seeing what a poor competition it was.

"17th July.— Went to see Bowles and consult him about Egyptian affairs, and as to bringing forward the case of Rhodes' 220 Soudanese, which certainly ought to be done. Bowles has made for himself by his cleverness a certain position in the House of Commons, and I would rather he took the case up than the Radicals.

"18th July.— I have written to the 'Times' about Cecil Rhodes and his 220 Soudanese recruited at Cairo, and never since heard of.

"In the afternoon I started for Blackdown, going by way of Petworth, where I left cards, nobody being at home. Then on by Lodsworth Common. This is, I think, the easiest, though the longest road, and may be about twenty-one miles. I found Harrison at cricket with his boys, now grown-up young men, but they came in presently, and I played a set of lawn tennis with the philosopher, and spent a pleasant evening discussing his creed of Humanity and mine of anti-Humanity. It seems to be pretty much the same thing as far as politics are concerned, for the principal wish of both of us is to see the break-up of the British Empire. He has some right to believe in Humanity, as he has never had a pain or ache or a sleepless night in his life, and he is past sixty. Thus in half serious humour we passed the evening. There is nobody in the world less like a philosopher or a religious leader than the good Harrison.

"19th July (Sunday).— Off at five in the morning, having said good-bye overnight, going by Lodsworth and Ebenhoe, Kirdford and Wisborough Green, an old-fashioned bit of country as any in Sussex, belonging, I think, all to Leconfield. Long may it so remain.

"3rd Aug.— Dr. Jameson has been sentenced to fifteen months imprisonment, a sentence at once too much and too little. The Government has made him a first-class misdemeanant, so as a punishment it is very little. At the same time if the sentence had been carried out it would have been a savage one. He ought to have been hanged at Pretoria. The 'Times' has refused to publish my letter about Rhodes' Soudanese.

"6th Aug.— There has been heavy cholera up the Nile. Captain Fenwick dead, and one of the young engineer officers I saw at Korosko last November. He was under twenty-four, and was receiving £1,000 a year from the Egyptian Government, and thought himself a lucky fellow to be there. They are to advance on Dongola at the end of the month. What our Jingoes want is to wait till the Egyptian army is exhausted by heat, hard fighting, and cholera, and then to send an English army to Khartoum in cool weather to reap the profits of the campaign in English interests. This is being advocated unblushingly in the ' Pall Mall ' and elsewhere. I wrote to expose the scandalous intention, but they would not print my letter.

"10th Aug.— Started on a driving tour in the New Forest, stopping the first day for luncheon at Lavington with Reginald Wilberforce and his family. I have known Reginald all my life, that is to say, from the year 1845, when we lived for a while at Alverstoke after my father's death, and when his father, the Rev. Samuel Wilberforce, afterwards Bishop of Oxford, was Rector of the parish. There were three boys then — Reginald, at that time called Garton; Ernest, now Bishop of Chichester; and Basil, Chaplain of the House of Commons. They were all three as bad boys as could be wished, and my mother nicknamed them 'the sons of Eli.' Ernest, with whom I was in 'the same class at school, an especially wicked boy, which is saying a good deal, but now just as justly respected, and a Right Reverend Father in God. The only good boy of the family was an older brother Herbert, but he had died at sea, while the wicked ones lived on to adorn the Church of England with 'their virtues. Thus is the child father to the man. I went over the little parish church after luncheon with Reginald, who is an amusing talker.

He showed me the grave of his Aunt Caroline, who had been Cardinal Manning's wife. It remains without inscription of any kind. The old Cardinal visited it in 1876 and talked of putting up a stone, but he was probably perplexed as to the wording of the inscription. ' Wife of Cardinal Manning ' would have looked strange. Reginald, however, thinks now of doing this, and suggests ' Wife of Henry Edward, afterwards Cardinal Manning.' Reginald told me much else that was interesting about Cardinal Manning's visit. He had come down for the consecration of the Catholic church at Burton Park, and asked to be allowed to lunch at Lavington, so they entertained him there, and he saw all the old parishioners and was much affected. Afterwards he walked to the top of 'the down with Reginald and discoursed to him' about his soul, exhorting him to conversion — thus for two hours. Their last words were: ' Think, my dear Reginald, if God should require your soul of you to-night, where should you be?' To which Reginald, ' Why, my dear Uncle Henry, I should be in the hands of God.' As his Eminence was leaving, the parishioners all came to wish him good-bye, and he blessed them each in turn. When Reginald had put his uncle into the carriage, he said: ' And is 'there no blessing, no little blessing for me?' They never met again, and ' he never cared for me after this,' Reginald said, ' though he used to see my wife and children and was always most affectionate to them.' He tells me the way Purcell, his biographer, got hold of the Cardinal's diaries and letters was this. He had had several conversations with Manning on the subject of his biography, and Manning had given him some sort of verbal promise about it and had shown him where his diaries were kept, and one day he came to the house when the Cardinal was out and persuaded the servant to let him have them, saying that the Cardinal had told him to call and take them away, he knew where they were, and had authority, etc. But it was a pure theft and Manning had begun legal proceedings for their recovery when he died."

I went on the same afternoon and camped on Goodwood Down, and on the next day through Chichester to Fareham and Southampton, and camped again in the evening at the edge of the New Forest, the immediate object of my journey being to pay Auberon Herbert a visit at Oldhouse. Of this I write:

" 12th Aug.— Oldhouse lies pretty well in the heart of the Forest. One descends to it from the high road by a grass track of a mile and a half. It is a freehold of half-a-dozen acres, recently purchased by Auberon of its owner, and there he has made his hermitage. The old cottage he has pulled down and in its place has built up a number of cheap buildings of brick and wood devoid of architecture. Fortunately they lie in a hollow and so are invisible until one is close by. Auberon has done so much for the Forest, and fought so many battles to preserve it from the Crown officers, that he must be forgiven this one lapse. I found him with Stafford Howard, the Crown Commissioner, and Esdale, a local squire and verderer of the Forest, Auberon's ally in the Forest battle. I had much talk with them about this. The chief difficulty is what to do with the great fir enclosures, the firs ought to be cut down, but there is nobody to buy them, and an ugly growth of them is creeping over the open spaces, self-sown. It ought to be put a stop to, or in fifty years' time the Forest will be like Woking cemetery.

" Auberon is much aged since I saw him last, and more flighty than he used to be. He is beset with a double mania, a craving for fresh air and in contradiction a terror of draughts, so that he is always shifting from in to out of doors and putting on or taking off extra clothing. His two children, Bron and Nan, wait on him with angelic devotion. They do all the work of the house. When I arrived Nan was in the kitchen up to her elbows in flour, making bread. She is a great strong girl of sixteen, the picture of health, with limbs like a boy's, great honest grey eyes, good complexion, and good teeth. Auberon and I have talked a great deal on politics, Eastern and Western, he, as his way is, asking innumerable questions. We agree on most subjects, but he is too tender to his countrymen's sins, excusing them and comparing them favourably with the French. He has become an entire vegetarian, as is his daughter, and for the most part his son. Their way of life is the most uncomfortable imaginable. They have no fixed hours for meals, or for getting up in the morning, or for going to bed. The first

regular meal is said to be at half-past two in the afternoon, and there
is another at twilight in the evening, but they do not sit down to either
meal.   Auberon sits in a summer house during part of his meal, while
the children run in and out, and he has constantly to get up to arrange
and re-arrange his clothing, which is of Shetland wool shawls and
jerseys, and the children are called to put up and take down wooden
screens on this side and that as the wind may seem to blow or not to
blow.   Nan, with inexhaustible patience, humours and serves her father, and Bron is almost equally good to him.   This is the best tribute
that can be paid to Auberon's system of education, but it is clear there
must be a breaking point somewhere.   I don't know which child to ad-
mire the most, the boy or the girl.

" 13*th Aug.*— Spent the morning alone writing, for Auberon has his
occupations.   He is a wonderful man, with a certain ethereal beauty
of the Shelley kind, which has increased with years.   His theories are,
I believe, essentially true, and he is true to them in practice, but without
his children it would be a desolate, impossible life.   He took me for
a walk at luncheon time, discoursing as he went, his daughter following,
us, all ears for our talk.   She is very nice and pleasant, as girls
of sixteen always are, still wearing short petticoats, and with
hair cut short, enthusiastic at the thought of going, perhaps this winter,
to Egypt.

" 14*th Aug.*— On by Ringwood and up the Avon valley to Salisbury,
where we baited at the White Hart, an excellent inn, but vitiated by a
German waiter.   I went over the Cathedral, which has been scraped
inside and garnished from end to end.   In another hundred years it
may perhaps tone down again to beauty, but at present the black pillar
stems, newly polished, have the effect of so many tall stove pipes.   It
was infinitely finer under the old whitewash, but the deans will have
their way.   Then on to Wilton and George Pembroke's grave.   The
house is shut up, as Sidney finds himself too poor to live in it, and the
days of their joyous youth are a vanished dream.   Then on across the
Down through Groveley Wood, the biggest mere wood in England,
where I remember riding with Pembroke and his brothers and sisters
thirty years ago, when they were children, playing a game of Puss in
the Corner, with wild galloping down the rides.   There at nightfall I
camped.

" 15*th Aug.*— Another short morning's drive brought us to Stockton
where I spent the Sunday with my cousins Pamela and Eddy Tennant.

" George has been appointed to the South African Committee, and is
to sail for the Cape to-day."

From Stockton I went on through Warminster and Longleat Park
to Mells.   "Longleat is very fine approached from this side, but the
house disappointed me.   It is very perfect, too perfect, and, large as it

is, it is lost in the size of the park. What makes it look dull is the uniform plate-glass which has been put in every window. It is astonishing how this destroys the beauty of old buildings. It is as though the eyes in a beautiful face had been put out and replaced with spectacles. I prefer Mells, where I now am, a really fascinating little place, a comfortable eighteenth-century house, remote and shut in, which gives a sense of immemorial quiet screened from the world's view. I arrived late at half-past seven, but they had not yet gone to dress for dinner, and presently out rushed the whole family. Mrs. Horner, with her children, very pretty ones, and Godfrey Webb, who is staying there, and Horner, who went out to help me choose a camping place, and invited me in to dinner. I was not expected, but travelling in this way calls out the latent hospitality of the countryside almost as much as if one were in the East, and Horner gave himself endless trouble about my road to Wells next morning.

" *17th Aug.*— My day's drive to-day was along the Mendlip Hills to Wells, where I baited the horses at the Swan Inn, near the Cathedral. Wells Cathedral is the most perfect in England. The inside has been scraped, but not much spoiled, while the outside is quite intact. Its surroundings are unique — the Bishop's palace, the famous wells in the Episcopal garden, and the moat. While in the Cathedral I got shut in behind the choir, and sat on a stone bench listening, not unedified, to the chaunting of a service. It is an interesting thing to have witnessed, as I have, from its beginning, the revival of the Church of England, which fifty years ago seemed almost dead. In those days a Cathedral like this was left almost without ceremonial from Sunday to Sunday, and the officiating canon, if he read the church service to his clerk, would begin with ' Dearly beloved brother,' for want of other congregation. Now all is elaborately ordered, yet I confess I like the old godless way best, it was more honest and marked the fact, which was a fact, that the continuity of church worship had been broken at the Reformation. Now all is sham mediævalism, sham seventeenth century, sham eighteenth century. We shall get back presently, I hope, to our pews on eclectic principles, and a new Georgian era of ecclesiastical wigs and gowns. Then I ran down by train to Glastonbury and back, and camped for the night in a beautiful coombe belonging to a Mr. Tudway, a local banker to whom Horner had given me a letter, dining with him in a beautiful Georgian house belonging to his family since 1760. Here my driving journey ended, for we were overtaken with heavy rains.

" *30th Aug.*— We have had three public events during the week, first Cecil Rhodes has patched up a peace with the Matabeles, heralded in all the daily papers as an heroic act of courage, because he went personally to the Matabele camp to treat. Secondly, our gallant fleet has bombarded Zanzibar. The Sultan had died suddenly, and Khalid, one of his relations, son of the former Sultan Bargash, had seized the throne and got the native soldiery to join him. These held the palace against the fleet, which bombarded them from close quarters, killed five hundred of them, and burnt out the remainder. Our papers are again exultant, and raise a cry for annexation on the plea for abolishing slavery in Zanzibar. Yet I remember fifteen years ago Sultan Bargash applying to me to get the Indian Government to allow him coolie labour as a substitute for the slaves. Zanzibar was a model Arab State, a hundred times more liberal in its ideas than the Government of India, which would not hear of helping the Sultan. I know this, having brought the case before Lytton. Thirdly, there has been a new great slaying of Armenians at Constantinople, the companion of what took place last year, but on a larger scale. It was begun, as in the first instance, by the Armenian Committee, which seized the Ottoman bank and threw bombs into the street, their object being to force on a crisis. To this the Moslems retorted with a massacre.

"*2nd Sept.*— The Nile expedition has been stopped by floods, great *seyls* from the hills, which have swept away the new railway just as they have finished it. The talk is now of having hardly time to get to Dongola before the river goes down. If the expedition fails, all I have said about the abdication of Providence has been blasphemy. The good Egyptian troops have been worn out by hard work in a thankless labour. They are said now to be ' tired.' Broadwood wrote me this some time ago.

"*3rd Sept.*— To Wotton to dine and sleep. The good old Evelyn is packing up his trunks to go on pilgrimage to Jerusalem. Next day to London to see Morris, whom the doctors now declare to be in a pulmonary consumption. Mrs. de Morgan was there and Cockerell, and while I was sitting with them in came Madeline Wyndham, beautiful in her old age. She took me away with her to see some enamel work she is learning to do at the studio of one Fisher, and I was shown all the process of mixing the colours, ground glass with water, arranging them on a silver plate and burning 'them on a small oven. Fisher has done a beautiful triptych of a Crucifixion, and a very pretty classic bit called ' Love's Chase,' but the best thing there was one of Madeline's own, two peacocks.

"*8th Sept.*— Started on a series of visits 'to Scotland, and, on my way north, I find the following:

"*12th Sept.*— Met Lord Loch in the train, and had much interesting talk with him on South African affairs and the intrigues of Germany. He 'told me that when he was at Pretoria some of the Boers explained these to him. Also that the opposition of Germany in South Africa dated from 1886, when Bismarck began it, as against the Empress Frederick. We also discussed the possible deposition of the Sultan. He thought this could only be done by Russia, as our fleet could not get through the Dardanelles without heavy loss."

While in one of the country houses I found in an anonymous book, dated 1722, the following admirable epitaph of a Duke of Buckingham, which I cannot help transcribing here, so suitable is it for the agnosticisms of our day.

> " Pro rege sæpe, pro Republica semper.
> Dubius sed non improbus vixi.
> Incertus morior sed inturbatus.
> Humanum est errare et nescire.
> Christum adveneror. Deo confido,
> Omnipotenti benevolentissimo.
> Ens entium, miserere mei."

> Often for the King, always for the Commonweal.
> Doubting but not wickedly have I lived.
> I die uncertain but unperturbed.
> It is human to err and not to know.
> I venerate Christ. I trust in God
> The omnipotent the most kind
> Being of beings, have pity on me!

Back to London, where we found " great preparations being made for the Emperor and Empress of Russia, who are being fêted in the middle of an agitation against Russian policy at Constantinople. All our English world has gone mad with self-righteousness.

" *26th Sept.*— Gladstone has fired off his powder against the Sultan at Liverpool, but there was no shot in his Armenian gun. All he can think of as a means of coercion at Constantinople is to break off diplomatic relations, summon the Sultan to take action of some kind and go no further. It is too foolish. All the time he was in office the old man lifted not so much as a finger for the Armenians, and now that he cannot help them he would play their champion against Abdul Hamid, who owes the strength of his position mainly to English diplomacy, as he should remember. In 1882 Gladstone called on Abdul Hamid to help him to put down liberty in Egypt by proclaiming Arabi a rebel and, as he explained to an Indian Mohammedan deputation at the time of Tel-el-Kebir, sent troops to Egypt ' to establish the Sultan's rights there.' In all this he made the Sultan his accomplice against the liberal Mohammedan party, and by doing so set Islamic patriotism on reactionary lines and gave the Sultan his present triumph over his reforming enemies. If liberal Islam is powerless to-day in the Sultan's grasp it is distinctly Gladstone who has made it so, yet now he comes forward shocked at the result. I should like to write these things, but who would listen?

"*28th Sept.*— Dined with the Morrises. He came in like a man risen from the grave, and sat a few minutes at the table, but seemed dazed and unable to follow the conversation. Miss de Morgan was there, and his wife waiting on him, and a young man who had charitably come in to sit up with him at night. He seemed absorbed in his misery.

"*4th Oct. (Sunday).*— Morris is dead. I got a letter telling it from Lady Burne-Jones this morning. She says, ' Our dear friend Morris died at twenty minutes past eleven this morning, as quietly as ever a babe went to sleep in its mother's arms.'

"It has come sooner than I expected, though I knew his case was hopeless. It is better as it is. He is the most wonderful man I have known, unique in this, that he had no thought for anything or person, including himself, but only for the work he had in hand. He was not selfish in the sense of seeking his own advantage or pleasure or comfort, but he was too absorbed in his own thoughts to be either openly affectionate or actively kind. I suppose he had a real affection for Burne-Jones, they saw each other constantly and spent their Sunday mornings, always together, and I have seen him tender to his daughter Jenny and nice with her and with his wife, but I doubt if he thought of them much when he did not see them, and his life was not arranged in reference to them. To the rest of the world he seemed quite indifferent, and he never, I am sure, returned the affection I gave him. He liked to talk to me because I knew how to talk to him, and our fence of words furbished his wit, but I doubt if he would have crossed the street to speak to me. He was generous and open-handed in his dealings, and I fancy did many kindnesses in a money way for people in distress, but he fashed himself for no man and no woman. The truth is he would not give an hour of his *time* to anyone, he held it to be too valuable. Thus, while all the world admired and respected him, I doubt whether he had many friends; they got too little in return to continue their affection. I should say half-a-dozen were all the friends he had. I do not doubt myself among that number, intimate as I was with him and much as I loved him. It will be a great grief for Jenny, a great break-up for Janey, and a great loss for the world at large, for he was really our greatest man.

"*5th Oct.*— I came up to London to see if I could be of any use at Kelmscott House, and first I called on Burne-Jones and had luncheon with him and his son. He said that his interest in life had come to an end with Morris, as all their ideas and plans and work had been together all their lives. Phil, with whom I had a private talk, gave me curiously enough the exact same impression of Morris as that which

I wrote in this diary yesterday. His impersonality, his lack of personal affection for anyone except, perhaps, for his, Phil's, father. Then I went on to Hammersmith. The coffin, a very plain box, lay in the little room downstairs, with a beautiful old embroidered cloth over it and a small wreath of leaves and sad-coloured flowers. It was the room which was his bedroom, and where he died, with his best and favourite books around him. The morning after the day I dined with him, Tuesday, was a fine one and he was taken out for an airing in his chair, and he enjoyed it thoroughly and said he felt well. On coming in he insisted on going upstairs, but the exertion was too much; he broke a blood vessel and lay after that for the most part insensible till he died on Saturday.

"*8th Oct.*— Rosebery has resigned his leadership of the Liberal party. I wrote at once to Loulou Harcourt to congratulate his father.

"*15th Oct.*— I am leaving home this afternoon for Egypt, stopping as usual for three nights at Gros Bois on my way. Jusserand and his wife there, and Giovanni Borghese and young Norton, Mrs. Norton's grandson, now at the Paris Embassy."

CHAPTER XII

SIWAH

"*24th Oct.* 1896.—

"I have been reading Slatin's 'Fire and Sword in the Soudan,' a sensational volume written with a purpose, the style obviously Wingate's, as it is identical with his 'Ohrwalder' book. Slatin is a mean wretch to have published it, and the Mahdi made a mistake in not cutting off his head at once when he surrendered, and sending him straight to Paradise. His professions of loyalty to the Khedive and to our gracious Queen are fulsome, and those of disloyalty to the people whose religion he adopted to save his miserable life, disgusting. Gordon's judgment of him is justified when he distrusted him as a traitor and despised him as a renegade, for he shows himself here doubly both.

"With regard to the Mahdi, Slatin declares him to have been a hypocrite and an impostor, but his opinion rests upon no evidence given and seems to me wholly improbable. Slatin only saw him a few times and was never at all in his confidence, and on the few occasions that 'the Mahdi spoke to him he seems to have done so kindly and reasonably. Slatin is himself a witness that the whole of the Mahdi's followers believed in him to the very end, and it is quite incredible that they should have done so if, while preaching self-denial to others, he had really been the monster of depravity Slatin affirms him to have been in his private life. Such a discrepancy could not have been hidden from the Soudanese world and could not but have destroyed the popular belief in him. With regard to the Khalifa Abdullah the position is different, as Slatin *was* intimate with him and Abdullah had no pretensions to high sanctity, nor did his followers believe in him as a saint. Slatin talks about his own military honour, but how does the case stand? When he surrendered to the Mahdi he was put in reality on parole, that is to say, he promised and swore fidelity to the Mahdi, in return for which he was allowed his freedom and an honourable position in the Mahdi's army. He used this position to betray the Mahdi by writing letters to Gordon in a sense contrary to his orders. For his treachery he might justly have been shot, but after a short imprisonment, and on his giving a new parole, he was reinstated only to escape and betray again.   We shall see this honourable soldier made a K.C.B.   [And so he was].

" 27th Oct.— Arrived at Sheykh Obeyd to-day, the garden very green and beautiful.   The Nile is at its full, and everything is drinking deeply in the hot sun.   I am surprised, as I am every year surprised, at the quality of the loveliness, the vivid colours, the depths of shade, the brilliancy of the light.   It is an absurdity to waste one's life elsewhere.   I am too idle to write, I can only enjoy.

"9th Nov.— Sheykh Mohammed Abdu called to-day, and we had a long talk about the Khedive.   Abdu is dissatisfied with certain things His Highness has done, and especially with a dispute about land he has had with Hassan Musa el Akkád.   He calls the Khedive's conduct puerile, which it doubtless is.   He says that his marriage was entirely his mother's doing.   When Abbas first came back from Europe, he wished to have a bachelor's establishment without women, but his mother forced half-a-dozen slaves on him, and eventually he chose the one he has married.   He has had a new disappointment this year in the birth of a second daughter instead of a son.

" 19th Nov.— To Cairo to see the Khedive.   He received me in the same friendly way as always, and talked, as always, without reserve. He asked me if I had been to Constantinople, and we discussed the situation there and the probability of European intervention, which must come with the Sultan's increasing financial difficulties.   The power of the Porte will then be re-established and a financial control set up.

" He talked much about Dongola and the unfairness that had been exercised towards his own Egyptian soldiers as contrasted with the English soldiers, only one baggage camel was allowed to every five Egyptian officers, while Kitchener took as many as 150 camels for himself and his mess.   The Egyptian soldiers had to do all the work, the English got all the credit.   As to the English battalion it did next to no work, and did not even march on foot, but was sent by rail while all the Egyptians marched.   The fellah soldiers, too, had never a hot meal given them, nor more than ten hours rest in the twenty-four. They had insufficient water, and only two loaves instead of the three they gave them at Cairo, the third loaf they could have, but they must pay for it.   I asked him how much the expedition had cost.   He said first a half million taken from the Caisse, then several hundred thousands taken for the railway.   He did not know when the expedition would be renewed, but not till next autumn.

" He also told me the whole history of Rhodes and the Soudanese he took from Cairo.   He, the Khedive, had seen them himself being embarked for Suez.   There were 200 of then, men got together by Kitchener, and made over to Rhodes in a lump.   Kitchener had told him they were not good enough for service in the Egyptian army. They had gone with Cromer's consent but without his, the Khedive's, permission. Their exportation was quite illegal. Cromer had apologized for the informality of not asking permission. The Khedive knew nothing of what had become of the men, except that he had been told they had been disembarked at Mombaza. Rhodes gave the men a month's pay in advance and took their women and children with them. The women were given a shilling each as bakshish. ' But this is not all. A little before this happened a negro came to me and told me of a case of slave dealing, of a man and woman who had been bought by the sons of Prince Ibrahim for their harem. To prevent a scandal I told the young men they must get rid of them. Whereupon they went to Lord Cromer and threw themselves at his feet and begged forgiveness. Cromer then took the two slaves and married the woman to one of the soldiers who was given to Rhodes, and the man was sent with the rest to Suez. Also they took one of my Shaggias (soldiers of his bodyguard) who went away taking my uniform with him, but I had him stopped and brought back.'

"We stayed talking for three-quarters of an hour, and he made me a number of pretty speeches when I went away,. He was rather inquisitive about a journey I had arranged to Siwah, which he had heard of and seemed anxious to dissuade me from. I suppose he had heard of it from his camel men. I also called on Riaz and Tigrane.

"*29th Nov.*— A long letter from George Wyndham from South Africa where he has been with Rhodes getting up a case for him for the Parliamentary Committee. His letter is an interesting one written at intervals of a long ride from Buluwayo to the Transvaal frontier. The work done in South Africa is sickening, and seems likely to lead to the destruction of the whole black race south of the tropics. The Rinderpest has destroyed all wild animals, and is destroying their cattle. The ' rebels' are being blown up by dynamite in the caves of the Matoppo hills, and their chiefs shot in cold blood, and while all this is going on we are having meetings the whole of England over to denounce the Sultan because he is destroying the Armenians. Was there ever a nation like ours? Never, since the world began.

"I had a long talk with Mohammed Abdu a few days since. He has read my ' Nineteenth Century' article about Armenia, and approves all I have said against Abdul Hamid. He looks upon him as mad and to be deposed. He gave me an interesting account of his own persecution at the Azhar by the old-fashioned Sheykhs of the Ulema in the days of Ismaïl, especially by Sheykh Aleysh. He had, he says, at one time, as many as 4,000 students who attended his lectures, but the Conservative opposition was too strong for him. Still there was a good deal of liberty of thought and speech at Cairo even in those days, it never was as bad here as it is now at Constantinople, but all the old-fashioned ideas of liberty and humanity are fast disappearing from the world. Abdu and I find ourselves almost alone in our views. The best effect my article has had in England has been to make John Morley pronounce himself in favour of coming to terms about evacuating Egypt. His speech on this head is a paraphrase of my article.

" Mrs. Morris and her daughter May have been staying with us here at Sheykh Obeyd for the last ten days.

" 13*th Dec.*— We went in yesterday to Cairo to see Ali Pasha Sherif's horses which, with the rest of his property, are to be sold by auction on Thursday. We shall probably bid for three or four of the brood mares, and so save a remnant from extinction, sold to us privately before the auction.

" 17*th Dec.*— The luck of the thing is that Ali Pasha's affairs, being in the hands of trustees, it is to spite them that the old man is willing to sell privately to us. He insists on his right to dispose of them as he pleases. When he had received our cheque he sent the mares off in the dark at four in the morning. Now there has been a row between the old man and the trustees. Ali Pasha declares that not another horse shall go out of the stable without his permission. Mutlak, who arranged the whole thing for us, found him this morning sitting at his window which overlooks the yard of his palace and the stables, with a Winchester rifle loaded at his side, with which he swears he will shoot anyone who ventures to come near these. The old man is considered mad by his relations, and his sons have had him interdicted and his affairs placed in Sabit Pasha's hands as trustee, but we have got the mares and they are beautiful. The mere name of having purchased them will be worth much to our stud, for they are celebrated the whole East over, and I don't think the trustees will care really to dispute our purchase. Abdu tells me that according to the terms of the interdiction, Ali Pasha may do what he likes with his moveable property, and Carton de Wiart, the leading lawyer here whom I have consulted, gives me a curious account of the reason of the interdiction. It was a little political job of which there are so many done at Cairo. When Ali Sherif, two years ago, was involved in the slave trade prosecution, feeling ran high between the Khedive and Cromer about it, for in reality our people took advantage of the old man's age and infirmities to force on him an apology which he might perfectly well have refused, for he had done nothing illegal. Cromer, seeing he had been in the wrong, agreed therefore to the following arrangement by mutual concession. On his side he consented to the dismissal of Shäfer, the anti slave-trade official who had brought the action against Ali Sherif; and the Khedive on his side agreed to Ali Sherif's being interdicted as incapable of managing his affairs. But Ali Sherif was not really mad, only extravagant and old.

"*22nd Dec.*— Anne and I called on Princess Nazli yesterday. She is looking an old woman now, but is still full of life and conversation. She has thrown herself lately into the Young Turkey movement at Constantinople and has written a letter to the Sultan which she asked Anne to translate for her into English, though she speaks English perfectly. She told us she considered Abdul Hamid very near his end now, and she only hoped that he would be assassinated and not simply deposed, as it would be a good lesson for his successor. Hitherto the Young Turks had been averse from this extreme measure, but according to the latest news they are now determined on it. In 'this I should not be surprised if they were following a hint from our Embassy. Murad, she said, is quite sane, and would be Abdul Hamid's successor. About politics in Egypt she also talked, praising Cromer and the English Occupation and in virulent abuse of the Khedive. A good deal of this I know to be nonsense, but she is a clever woman, and I fancy has done much towards converting travelling Englishmen to a belief in their ' great and noble work ' in Egypt. Cromer intervened with the late Khedive to prevent his cutting off her allowance as princess of the vice-regal family.

"*30th Dec.*— Mohammed Abdu came yesterday and told me the news. There has been a great row on account of 'the confirmation by the native appeal court of Sheykh Ali Yusuf's acquittal. Ali Yusuf had been prosecuted for publishing in his newspaper, the ' Moayyad,' a telegram relating to military events during the Dongola campaign, which it was asserted he had got from a telegraph clerk of the name of Kirillos. The evidence against Ali Yusuf was of the slightest kind; that against Kirillos only presumptive. The latter had on one occasion been seen copying a 'telegram, not the one in question, presumably for the press. Against Ali Yusuf there was no evidence at all. Nevertheless Cromer seems to have determined on fighting a battle with the native press, and when the case came before the Appeal Court, Cameron, the English judge, informed his two native colleagues that they were expected to find the accused guilty, or they would involve the Native Appeal Court in strong measures of ' reform ' which would be taken against it. He also accused 'them of having been tampered with by the Khedive, and when they indignantly refused to find the accused guilty, Cameron refused at first to sit with them in delivering judgment of acquittal. Now Cromer has announced that a number of English councillors would be added to the court so as to swamp the native members. Abdu assures me that as a matter of fact the Khedive had nothing to do with the matter, and that the judges could not have decided otherwise on the evidence before them.

Nothing so scandalous has happened here since the Kitchener affair, and this is really worse, as it is an attack on 'the integrity of the law. Carton de Wiart, the Belgian lawyer, who is at the head of his profession here, confirms the story to me, and there seems to be no doubt about it. Abdu declares that Lord Cromer is led by the nose by certain Syrians, of whom the editor of the ' Mokattam ' and one Shakur are the principal agents. Certainly he appears to be under unfortunate inspiration. It has become very much a personal struggle and quarrel between Cromer and the Khedive. Lord Salisbury allows Cromer to carry matters with a high hand. The Khedive, on the other hand, is also led by intriguers, so that there is really no rational authority at the head of things." This was the beginning of Lord Cromer's interference with the operation of the law in Egypt for political purposes, an intervention which he carried afterwards to extreme results.

" *28th Jan., 1897.*— I am preparing for a long journey to Siwah, and perhaps to Jebel Akdar and Benghazi. This should take forty days at least, and there is just a little risk in it, especially as I am far from well, but it is a thing I want to do and I feel if I put it off till another year it will never be accomplished. Possibly I may be able to go as far as to visit the Sheykh el Senussi, but this is doubtful, as the Sheykh has disappeared within the last year, and it is not known exactly where he is, but I shall learn all about that from my friend Abdullah el Jibali, in the Fayoum, to whom, in the first instance, I intend to go. I hope all the same to accomplish my journey successfully and be back in time for our annual migration to England.

" *2nd Feb.*— I have arranged to start on my journey on the 5th, having by good luck met Abdullah el Jibali yesterday, when I was in Cairo, and have arranged that he is to send me on to Siwah and Benghazi. I am looking forward immensely to this trip, and only wish Anne was going with me, but she will not leave Judith, so I must go alone. There is just a little danger in the journey, principally of my falling ill, so I have signed a codicil to my will. All my preparations are made, and I am away on Friday with a good prospect of getting through to Tripoli or Benghazi. If only Anne were going too ! "

The journey to Siwah proved much more difficult and dangerous than I imagined, and is of sufficient political interest to make me include the whole of my travelling diary in 'this volume contrary to my general rule about desert expeditions. I started in ill health and in a frame of mind of unusual recklessness and depression as well, feeling that it would be the last I should make of any serious kind. I had, too, at the back of my mind, the 'thought that perhaps I might find among the Senussis something of the better tradition of Islam I had been so often disappointed of in the more civilized Mohammedan lands, and possibly that true desert hermitage I had so often dreamed of. Something of this will be found noted in my diary, and I give it hardly at all abridged as it stands there.

"5th Feb.— Left Sheykh Obeyd at half-past seven. Our travelling party consists of Suliman Howeyti, Owde his cousin, and Eid, all Bedouins of the Howeytat, and Salem, my Egyptian body servant for cook, with Abd-el-Salaam of the Oulad Ali Bedouins, my own six camels, one with foal at foot, and my mare Yemama. Anne and Judith rode the first few miles with me. We passed the Obelisk of Heliopolis and followed the Towfikiyeh Canal to Mustórod where Anne and Judith turned back. They saw a blue kingfisher on the way but I missed seeing it, which I take for an ill omen. From Mustórod we followed the Helwa, the sweet water canal — overtaking many people on their way to market at Cairo with loads of *bersim*. A few white herons were about, and by the cactus gardens we saw tracks of jackals, nothing European, till we reached the railway station of Pont Limon at Cairo, then on through the town to Kasr el Nil Bridge, mixed up with carriages, people on bicycles, and the usual mongrel crowd; and on to within half a mile of Mena (nobody recognizing me) when we turned to the left and camped beyond it on the sand. I have with me the following moneys for my journey, £40 in English gold, £5 in silver dollars, and £8 in small silver, £1 in half piastres — total £54 13s.

"6th Feb.— To-day we followed up the Nile valley passing to the right of Sakkara — many tracks of foxes and jackals on the desert edge. Great fields of lupins (*termès*) — the Delta very green — desert larks but few other birds, except wagtails. Camped at half-past two by the *birkeh,* where the road branches off to Tumiya — teals, coots, pochards, pintails, and other small waterfowl. The water brackish. A very beautiful evening.

"Abd-el-Salaam tells me he went campaigning with 1,500 of his tribe, in the first year of Ismaïl's reign, to the Soudan, taking the outer road of the Oases, and as far as Darfur and Kordofan. He told me also much about Jebel Akhdar (the Cyrenaica). There are five springs in it, he says, with streams running from them, all well wooded with trees, *zeytoun* (olive) and *karub,* with much grass and crops watered by rain. It is held by the Harabi tribe with whom the Oulad Ali had been *goum* (enemies) from the time of Saïd Pasha. But he, Abd-el-Salaam, has friends amongst them. He has travelled to Benghazi and to all the Oases, but not to Tarablus (Tripoli) or Tunis. He boasts that the Oulad Ali are of Anazeh blood; as to the Harabi they are of Harb blood. He is fasting for Ramadan, which no one else of us is, and is rather cross and obstinate. I am not sure about taking him beyond Kasr-el-Jibali. There is beautiful sweet camomile here for our camels.

"*7th Feb.* (*Sunday*).— Off at half-past seven. A plain desert march, following a track made by sheep and cattle the whole way. Sighted a fox in the early morning on his way home to some limestone cliffs. Also passed two cattle droves. No other incident. I remember twenty-one years ago travelling this way and having a tussle with a young Arab horseman, who had jeered at us for our European dresses. He pointed his gun at us, and I took hold of it and pulled him off his horse, his girths giving way, and he came a tumble, much to his discomfiture. This was in 1876. We are encamped under the tamarisks, where formerly Fraser, who was travelling with us, and I shot hares.

" Abd-el-Salaam has gone on with his recollections. The expedition he tells me was six months away on their Soudan campaign, each horseman receiving 200 piastres a month and all found, including camels and horses; also their families received from £13 to £14 while they were gone. There was no fighting, ' victorious without fighting.' In all this Western desert southwards there is no pasture, except a little *nossi* that comes up after the rain, or northwards till you come near the Mediterranean.

" *8th Feb.*— A continuous march of eleven hours through the Fayoum, passing by Toumiyeh, Senuris, Fidimin, Senhur, Abuxeh, and Bisheh. Then, having crossed the river, a branch of the Bahar Yusuf, we camped on the other side, at nightfall, a couple of miles short of Kasr-el-Jibali. I preferred taking excuse of the night to stop, for I was tired, and I knew that going on to the castle would mean sitting up till midnight waiting for a sheep to be killed and cooked. The Fayoum is a bad country to camp in, all black mud and crops, with hardly an open spot; and we were lucky, after travelling five or six miles looking in vain, at last to pitch upon a dry unoccupied field on the edge of the cliff above the river.

" At Toumiyeh the land has been taken possession of and cultivated by some Jews, who got a concession from the Government. Otherwise the town is much as it was in 1876, when I remember going to see a poor notable of the town who was dying, they told us, of love. The Mamur of the district in those days had taken from him forcibly one of his wives, the youngest, last, and best beloved of them; and we found him lying on his death-bed, surrounded by his friends lamenting his loss, and he smelling an onion which he held in his hand.

" *9th Feb.*— I was already asleep last night when Abdallah Minjo-war, hearing of my being in camp so near him, rode out to see me; and I had to get up to receive him. We drank tea together and made all the arrangements necessary for my onward journey. He will send two men with me, Minshawi and another, with camels to El Wah (the small Oasis), Siwah, Jerabub, and Jebel Akhdar, and will write letters to the various Sheykhs, and see me through to Benhazi or Dernah.

Abdallah is by position a great man. He has an immense territory and
lives in a castle, which if not mediæval belongs to the age of Mohammed Ali, and has a really beautiful stone gateway worthy of any century. He tells me his father and his tribe came into Egypt first in
Mohammed Ali's time, having been invited here from Jebel Akhdar
in Tripoli. He was once there with his father, Minjowar, as a boy.
In appearance he reminds me of the Emir Abd el Kader, and is in
truth a man of high and generous character, a great personage here
on the desert edge. The Government has recently made a high road
for him to Medinet el Fayoum, of which he is proud. I rode in to see
him after breakfast, and we are camped now inside his wall. Many
poor people, particularly boys and women, have run up to kiss my hand
yesterday and to-day. Expenses besides *bersim,* 10 piastres. Yesterday we passed an immense swarm of bees covering the rocks in a
ravine by the river.

"All is satisfactorily arranged. Abdallah will send Minshawi with
us, and a second man with two camels, and a head man, Beseys, on a
delul. He is to carry letters of credence for us to the chief persons
at Siwah and Jerabub, and to the two principal Harabi Sheykhs of the
Jebel Akhdar, at whose tents I am promised to alight within twenty,
say thirty days. I shall not be able to see Senussi as he has left Jerabub,
but I shall see the head of the Zaghwiyeh, the Monastery there, and
be well received. We are to start on Thursday, 11th, with four *ardebs*
of beans for the camels and barley for the mare. Salem is to go into
Medinet el Fayoum to-morrow, to get what things are still required,
as nothing will be procurable anywhere beyond. I have spent the day
slugging in my tent — very hot, with many flies, an object of attention for the villagers, and of attentions from Abdallah, his relations and
friends. Beseys, who is to go with me, is an oldish man, with a
rugged, ugly face, but I think that he will do. Minshawi we know
already. Abd-el-Salaam has left us. He was too old for the journey,
and required too much in the way of comfort, and did too little in
the way of work. Also Abdallah objected to him, and he himself
was inclined to leave, so I paid him his five days, and he is gone.

"We spent the evening talking, principally with a very intelligent man
of fellah origin, and of good education, who had been an Arabist, and
now is living here, cultivating a few feddans, which Abdallah has let
him have more or less as a charity. He gave us his views of Egyptian
politics, which are exactly Arabi's old ones. It is refreshing to hear
them in these days. Old Beseys listened with an occasional word of
approval, but Abdallah was sent to sleep by it and retired.

"Kasr-el-Jibali is a place of religion, and it being Ramadan, prayer
goes on nearly all day long, from an hour before sunrise, when a kind
of matins is chanted by a select few, till sunset, when there is a general

service attended by everybody. The singing is far from good, as
each worshipper intones in his own key, and the effect is not unlike that
of the old village hymn-singing of fifty years ago in England. There
is even a certain non-conformist popular character about it, which is
different from anything I have heard elsewhere. The mosque is a
new one, built close to the castle, in excellent taste. It might be a
hundred or two hundred years old for all one can tell from its architecture. It has no minaret, and is a plain square buttressed building,
with a slight ornament on the top and lancet windows. We are
camped too near it for quiet, and have been exposed all day to 'the
curiosity of prayer-goers. Also the ground is very dirty, and life is
made difficult with flies. Indoors, in the castle, it is hardly better, for
the guest rooms are built for the summer, and are cold to sit in, being
away from the sun. So I am obliged to wait on in my tent till the
hospitable pleasure of Abdallah is exhausted, and I have his permission
to begin my march. These days of hospitable waiting in towns and
villages are a heavy price one has to pay for 'the joys of desert travelling. But my departure is promised for to-morrow at noon. Suliman's expenditure in provisions for the journey comes to 275 piastres,
something under £3.

" 11th Feb.— Away at last in the highest of spirits, with a cool westerly wind blowing in our faces. The camels arrived early, and I obtained Abdallah's permission, dear good man, 'to mount and go. When
all was settled I told him I wished to have a few words with him alone;
and we went into the great room of the castle, and I told him I was
very anxious to see, if not the Sheykh el Senussi, who has gone south
to Kufra, at least one of the principal Sheykhs of the *tarik* (the religious order) at Jerabub, and I begged him to give me a letter for one
of them. ' You know,' I said, ' that I have for a long time been with
you at heart, of the *mumenin,* but I have not borne witness for
reasons you will understand. I wish to ask certain questions of the
Sheykhs of the Senussia, and to understand their teaching, and it
seems to me that the members of the *tarik* are the only good Moslems
in the world, or at any rate are the best.' The good man readily as-
sented, and showed me much affection, and told me that he had already written to the head of the community at Jerabub, introducing
me as the son of Hajji Batran of Aleppo, for he 'thought that would
give me a favourable reception. But I begged him to write again and
tell the Sheykh the truth of the case, that I was an Englishman who
desired instruction, and he has accordingly done so, though he has
left the other letters, those written to the Harabi Sheykhs of the Jebel
Akhdar, as they were with my name as Ibn Batran. Fortunately I
knew Hajji Batran when at Aleppo, or rather I knew his son, Hajji
Mahmud, and may, perhaps, be able to personate a grandson from

so far away. A cousin of Abdallah's, one Ali, who accompanied me on horseback as far as this camp, has given me particulars of the arrangement made and tells me that it is necessary, inasmuch as the Arabs of the Jebel Akhdar bitterly hate all of European race, whereas, if presented as a relation of Hajji Batran, who had married a *hatherieh,* townswoman, of Dernah, I should be accepted as a relation. The Hannádi, he explained, were of the Beraza clan, the same as the Harabi. There was a son Naïf born to Batran; and I must personate him. I do not like this. But Ali said there was real danger in going among people so wild as his mountain kinsmen; and he besought me to be content with Siwah, and to turn back from there by the sea-coast route to Mariut. I am, however, in 'the mood for an adventure, dangerous or not." [N.B. It will be seen that these letters of Abdallah, whatever their precise nature, were unfortunately conceived, and brought about the misunderstanding which led to the attack made on me at Siwah.]

" We are encamped five miles from Kasr-el-Jibali in a bit of tamarisk underwood well screened from the wind, at the outmost edge of Nile irrigation in the direction of the Oases — how happy to be at last alone! The Nile water reaches no farther westwards. A little run of it feeds the last fields, which are of wheat, barley, and *helbeh* (a sort of clover). On the *helbeh* Yemama is turned out to graze, and the camels eat it brought in to them. The two new camels have arrived, sturdy little beasts of the Western type, brown both, and rough haired — not beautiful, but good. The men, too, are of a wholly other type from that east of the Nile. Suliman and his two Howeytat companions have almost a look of breeding contrasted with them, while Ali's mare, of which he is proud, as being of western blood, is a plain barb, honestly shaped, but of no distinctive type. Beauty is the natural gift, to desert man and desert beast, only of peninsular Arabia.

" *12th Feb.*— Abdallah appeared again last night, having been preceded by his younger son, a pleasant youth of mixed 'type — the son of his *jari* (concubine) Salem said — who had dined with me. Though grown up, the young man has never seen more of the world than Medinet el Fayoum and El Wah, not even Cairo or the Nile. Abdallah has a separate establishment with the boy's mother close by here. He and I embraced affectionately at parting. He has done everything in his power to further my wishes about the journey and has brought seven or eight letters which he has written to various persons on my route, including the most important of all, one to Sidi Abu Seyf, the head prior of the Jerabub monastery, Senussi's right hand. He has entrusted me to old Beseys, who is one of the confraternity, and who is to explain to Abu Seyf how matters stand with me religiously. ' Abu Seyf,' Abdallah said, ' is as my own heart to me, and he will treat you

as myself.' Letters, too, have been written for the two principal
Bedouin Sheykhs of the Harabi in Jebel Akhdar, and I am to go on to
Benghazi if I like or return by Dernah and the sea route to Skanderia.

" We started to-day at sunrise and I walked an hour or more on foot,
it being cold, before mounting my *delul*. Our course south by west,
then turning more westward. At eleven we came to the edge of Wady
Rayyan, a great chaotic depression from 50 to 150 feet below the Nile.
It is absolutely barren, and there is no trace in it of Nile mud or clay
of any kind, most of the surface soil being drift-sand and grit, with
the bare limestone rocks showing here and there. This effectually
disproves the theory that Rayyan was the Lake Mæris of Herodotus.
it is nothing but a dried up *sebkha,* like the Jôf and many another
desert depression. There are curious rocks in it set in lines, which
look exactly like the remains of buildings; but they are all, I think,
natural. Nor do I believe that any part of the Valley was ever inhabited except perhaps by hermits, who planted the palm tress which
still struggle to live on near the springs. Descending into the belly of
the wady, we quickly found ourselves among *nefuds* (sandhills) which
run across it here and there in lines from north-west to south-east,
and make effective fortifications against camels. Here Suliman's desert
craft became of service (for the three Harabis with us were useless
for anything but pottering along a track) and he and I went forward
to look out the easiest places for the camels to cross, while in the
steepest Suliman and Eid made paths for them slantwise in the deep
sand. The old camel man, Haj Abd-el-Rahman, not choosing to follow us, was left behind, and we consequently had to camp some four
miles short of the main spring, but in a nice spot, a deep hollow under
sand hillocks and *tarfa* clumps. This part of the wady has vegetation,
tarfa, ghurkud, erta — none, however, in green leaf — much of it
dead, firewood abundant. Barom. 50 feet below the Nile water at
Kasr-el-Jibali.

" 13*th Feb.*— At sunrise we started, after a good night's rest for
me under my *hejeyra* (my carpet shelter, the one with a scorpion
worked on it), and on to the spring. This lies due south of the *khusm*
(snout) of Rayyan, at the extreme edge of the vegetation, a number
of bush palms together, with a lovely spring welling up in a sand-
bottomed basin, the water running in a little stream for twenty yards,
when it disappears. The two Harabis, Beseys and Minshawi, attribute
to it miraculous virtues. The water only runs, they say, when travellers come to drink, and it varies in volume with the number of their
camels. When there are many camels you have only to encourage it
by calling to it ' Ha, ha, ha, ha, ha!' and it comes bubbling up so fast
that you can water 200 camels in the afternoon. It is hot by night,
cold by day. To-day, the wind being cold, it was lukewarm, rather

flat water, ill-tasted but not salt, 'therefore ' sweet,' as desert waters
go. Yemama drank well of it, and we took away two *girbehs* full, in
addition to our two of Nile water, as this is the last water until we
come to El Wah. Some ' sons of dog who have no fear of God ' had
fired the palms and left some of them in ruins, but the palm immediately
over the spring was untouched in flower. We found tracks of
gazelles, hares, jerboas, and foxes there, but no recent traces of men
or camels. The wady is little frequented.

" From 'the spring we turned south-west and mounted by an even
slope to the top of the *nukbeh* (pass), which we found barred by a
complete rampart of *nefud,* which we had some difficulty in surmount-
ing — then on and on through a desolate land wholly barren, a cliff on
our left hand, until at the *asr* we came to a singular rock, exquisitely
poised, about twenty feet high, of friable lime stone worn away on
every side, below. A mile or two beyond this we descried a little
pasture *shgáa* with a *seyyal* tree. Here at 4.15 we encamped.

" Beseys gave me some information this afternoon as we rode together. The elder Senussi, he tells me, came from Fez and died at Jerabub in the year A.H. 1271. Beseys saw him, an ancient man with a
small white beard, regular features ' like your own.' He was 110 or
120 years old when he died. He left two sons, Mohammed Sidi el
Mahdi and Sherif. The latter died last year. The elder left Jerabub
in anger with the Sultan of Turkey after this, and has gone with a
few disciples to form a new Zaghwiyeh in the South. I understood him
to say that the quarrel was in consequence of the stopping of a subsidy,
but I may have heard him incorrectly as he has lost his front teeth and
is hardly intelligible. He told me that from Fez 'to the Hejaz there
were about 150 Zaghwiyehs containing each from twenty to thirty
brethren *akhwan.* People exaggerated the numbers because there were
many lay servitors, who cultivated the crops and bought or sold for
the brothers. There is no brotherhood at Kasr-el-Jibali. Abdallah's
grandfather was the first who came to Egypt. He became *awely* (saint)
and is buried in the koubbah at Kasr-el-Jibali. He left four sons,
of whom Minjowar was the eldest.

" *14th Feb.*— A long monotonous tramp from sunrise to sunset across
a gravelly *hamad* (plain), no leafy thing all day. Camped in the
plain about 400 feet above the sea — 30 miles.

" *15th Feb.*— Again from sunrise to sunset. Passed a beautiful
wady with *seyyal* trees — *gholam, shgáa, nossi* — Khabra Balbal — then
the *Bahr bela ma* (river without water), whose height is 350 feet above
the sea. A long day's tracking of the road obliterated with *nefuds* —
hyæna, wolf, and fox tracks. We camped in the *nefud.*

" *16th Feb.*— We are encamped at last in the basin of the Wahat
(oases), barom. 315 feet above the sea and 300 below the sand-ridge

at the top of the pass, where we first caught sight of 'the valley. This was a happy spectacle, a break in the brown rags of the desert foreground, dipping down and showing blue hills beyond. From this pass we went down by a gradual descent for a couple of hours. We are still some miles from the two villages of the oasis, with 'their palm groves showing blackly against the rocks beyond them. We are enjoying an afternoon's rest quietly in the shadow of a great rock half a mile from a spring. The sandy ground is pleasant, with hillocks tufted with green rough grass, *ékresh* and *rukeyb,* tamarisk, *ithel,* and dwarf palm. There are two springs, one on a mound 20 feet high, but the water was flat and bad — the other sweet, which runs for a few yards in open ground, with a little greenness round it — no trees.

" It is agreed 'that from this point I am to adopt a Syrian identity as Sakr ibn Zeydun el Helali, related by marriage to Sidi Abd el Kader at Damascus, and to Hajji Batran at Aleppo, with a title of Bey from the Dowlah, travelling to see his relations at Dernah and Benghazi. I shall not go into the villages here, so that no questions may be asked by officials. Beseys, too, is anxious to keep clear of them.

" I like Beseys. As we rode ahead of our party yesterday on our *deluls,* I talked to him about religion and about my wish for a hermit's life in the desert, and he much applauded the idea and promised to take me 'to a spiritual father of his own, Sidi Maymum, who lived just such a life in the Jebel Akhdar. The wely would put me in the way of a true vocation and give me all the advice I wanted. I asked him about Jerabub and the Zaghwiyeh there. He assures me the whole of the Akhwan have left it. Sherif, the second son of Senussi, followed his brother Sidi el Mahdi in his flight southwards, but came back to die at Jerabub, and is buried there with his father. Abu Seyf upon this left Jerabub with the rest of his following, and now there are only lay brothers and poor people there who look after the palms. Beseys is very pious himself, and prays every morning for some time as he rides. While we were talking earnestly on these pious matters we missed our track in the *nefuds,* and were some time finding it again. It is exciting work picking out the cold scent of an old track by odds and ends of camel *jelleh* and doubtful landmarks, as exciting as following hounds, and we became keen and jealous. But Beseys is a really good old man, and I think takes a true interest in my conversion. It is forty-three years since he travelled the road before, being then a boy of an age young enough to need being told not to lag behind, or get separated from the rest. That would make him no older than I am, but in appearance he is quite an ' ancient of days.' We got back eventually into the right road by following a hyæna track. Hyænas, jackals and foxes in the desert are fond of frequenting caravan routes for what they may chance to pick up, and know them well — the first

for the hap of a dead beast, the foxes for dropped dates. We passed
a place where foxes had been gathering scraps at the site of an encampment. At Balbal yesterday there were fresh gazelle tracks, besides
larks singing and wagtails quite at home. There are no Bedouins in
these deserts as there is no water and little pasturage. The thorn trees
are consequently uncut, and the *nossi* grass of last spring stands un-
eaten. Balbal is a beautiful spot. The Bahr is much less interesting,
being merely one of those long serpentine depressions so common in
the desert. This one being 350 feet above sea level cannot have ever
been a mouth of the Nile. Its bottom is of limestone without a trace
of Nile mud. A caravan carrying dates was just setting out from
the spring as we arrived.

"*17th Feb.*— We have moved camp to a spring just north of Bawiti,
which is the last village of the Little Oasis westwards.

"Last night I had a long ride alone to get a look at the Oasis, climb-
ing on Yemama to the top of the Harra which stands like an island in
its midst. The top of it is level ground, smooth enough to canter on
from end to end, one of the loneliest places I ever saw, for I crossed no
single track of beast or bird or reptile, nor was there trace of men having ever been there, though so near the villages. It is apparently vol-
canic. One gets a good bird's-eye view from it of the palm groves and
the four villages, Sabu, Mandija and the double village of Kasr and
Bawiti. It is clear that much more land was cultivated formerly. The
ithel and tamarisk clumps must have been private property. They are
being fast destroyed now. There is a deal of rough camel pasture in
the Oasis, so that we grazed as we went.

"I met a man cutting palm leaves to-day to make matting and asked
him to get us a guide to Siwah, as neither Beseys nor Haj Abderrahman, nor yet Minshawi know the road any farther. I was riding alone
in front on Udeyha, and having stopped was sleeping under a palm
tree outside Bawiti when I was wakened by a man greeting me. He
was a Berber from Farafra who offered to be of use and showed us
the spring hard by. Now we have sent Minshawi and Salem in to
market and are camped in the sand hills.

"In the evening I rode round the Oasis with Minshawi, but did not
enter the village, as the Government Chiauss has been inquisitive about
me, and I think it prudent to run no risks. There is nice *halfa* grazing
here. Everywhere there are bunches of palms with springs more or
less in use for gardens, some of which are beautiful with large olive
trees, *esshaar, sont,* and *safsaf* (willow). The palms are the most
vigorous I ever saw, having, as the saying is, 'their feet in the water,
their heads in the fire.' We passed the ruins of a building, probably
Roman.

"*18th Feb.*— Haj Abderrahman has left us to go home. He would have taken the two camels back with him but I would not allow it, as they are Abdallah's, not his, and I told him I would be answerable for the price of the beasts. He was unwilling to go farther. Now Minshawi has brought us a tall Soudani, Osman, from Siwah who will travel with us, and we hope to be off not later than noon. There are many tracks of foxes and jackals about, and I heard an owl at dawn.

"Off at 10.30, and marched till sunset. The nukbe lies due north, and is steep. There was no marked track till we crossed the caravan road and turned west. The plain on the upper ground is an absolutely barren hamad, gravel and sand grit, quite devoid of life — 500 to 600 feet above the sea. No sign of recent travellers on the road. A very cold north-west wind. Camped under lee of a low tell.

"*19th Feb.*— Thermom. 42° and a bitter wind. I find that Osman the Soudani has only been this way once before, and that twenty-five years ago, and travelling by night, and in the opposite direction to what we are now going. He is a Falata from Bornu, which he left when seventeen years old ' on account of a war.' [He had been taken as a slave, and had been carried by his captors to Merzouk, the northern oasis, and ultimately to Siwah, whence he had escaped to El Wah, travelling by night, and hiding in the daytime. For this reason he knew almost nothing of the road, except the general direction. He did not tell me this till afterwards.] He has been astray in the oases ever since, and may now be about fifty. I like him as he is plain spoken, and with an agreeable black face, nearly pure negro blood, though he boasts of the Falata as Arabs. The Falata have a Sultan of their own, he says, and know nothing of the Dowlah.

"Eleven hours' march to-day — thirty-two miles. Camped amid driving sand, barely protected from the wind.

"*20th Feb.*— Crossed several *nefuds* to-day all running north-west and south-east, which obliged us to travel far south, and then north-west again — then came to another deep depression where the caravan track disappeared for fully ten miles. We had much trouble following it, but by the help of skeleton camels recovered it at the nukbe beyond. At one place we came across an old *menzil* (encampment) with a dead camel, and the wooden frame of a *hedajeh* (camel saddle) all at least two years old. But Eid and Minshawi collected the *jelleh* (camel dung) finding it still good for firing, and Suliman made prize of the saddletree. Beyond the nukbe at four o'clock we came for the first time since leaving El Wah, on a bit of camel pasture, *sreygá* and camomile and *nossi*. The *nossi,* though a year old, had not been grazed, but I found the hole and track of a desert mouse. Yemama eagerly devoured the *nossi*. Osman surprised me by saying of her, ' Her sire is perhaps *koheyl.*' I find that he knows all about the horse breeds, Duheym, Jilfa, and the rest. He assures me that in Bornou and Wadi they have thoroughbred *koheyls,* the great people as many as ten of them, besides great multitudes of camels. We are encamped in a pleasing spot, with just enough of the pasture to feed our ten camels.

" *21st Feb.*— To-day has been full of excitement for us. After about four miles from our start we came to the edge of another great depression, the nukbe being well marked with stone heaps pointing to a corresponding nukbe beyond, about eight miles off. We went down, therefore, confidently, though the track quickly disappeared. The depression was choked with *nefuds* to our right, but to our left was clear, the loose soil being composed mostly of old shells. Its height above the sea at the lowest point was 100 feet. It soon, however, became plain that we were out of the track, though the westerly direction was good, and we had to cross a *sebkha* (salt swamp) with a treacherous bottom, and climb a very steep gradient to the nukbe. Osman, nevertheless, maintained that all was right, but soon we found ourselves in a wilderness of *nefuds.* Here Osman's knowledge came to an end, and after floundering over ridge after ridge for some time, he acknowledged that he knew not where he was. We therefore sat down and called a council, and having watered Yemama from the skins, somewhat solemnly, for we felt that it was the last we could spare her, it was agreed that Suliman and I should go forward alone scouting, either to come across the track or find some height from which we might get sight of a landmark. It seemed an equal chance to try right or left for the track. At starting we crossed the tracks of a gazelle, an ariel Suliman said, and it seemed to me a good omen. After a while, bearing somewhat to the right, we got out of the *nefud,* and on to a hard gravel, and I sent Yemama along at a good pace in the direction of some hills to the west north west, saying all the prayers I knew to my saints, Mohammedan and Christian, for a good issue. Nor had I long to wait. At first it seemed a very hopeless quest, with a brown horizon all round me and low brown hills each like the other. But it was nice cantering with the fresh wind in my face, and as I got on to higher ground the view opened and I saw the hill I was following rise higher and higher apparently about five miles off. At a point of the plain where there was a little mound I stopped and looked all round me. Far away to the west there seemed to be a little break in the horizon, and examining through my glasses I felt sure it was a wady, the wady of Sittarah (where the water was said to be which we were looking for). Still it might be a mistake, an effect of mirage, and I galloped back to Suliman, who was following on my *delul,* to ask his opinion. We then both agreed that we saw a wady with mounds of tarfa, perhaps palms, and that this was our wady. So I sent him back with the good news and to bring the camels on, and cantered on to the hill to get a better view. From the top of it I saw everything, as I thought, clearly, the tarfa mounds, the dark green wady, and the hill, blue beyond — almost like the Nile valley.

"We were, therefore, in the highest spirits, and Suliman and the camels having joined me at the foot of the hill, and he having also climbed up and convinced himself, we went on singing with joy. Two more hours, I thought, and we should be at the spring, and I led the way over the intervening *nefuds* gaily. The sun was in our faces as we topped the last of them, and saw at last the plain of our hopes before us. Suliman and I looked in each other's faces blankly. There was nothing at all of what we were expecting — only another long, low, shining plain. The tarfa clumps had resolved themselves into as many bare black stones, and nothing to break the horizon but a single pyramidal hill far away, a full day's journey off. It was a bitter disappointment. We asked Osman when he arrived with the camels whether he recognized the valley as Síttarah, and he said 'no.' We were worse lost than before. Nevertheless, we were convinced that the valley must be still before us, and like an old hound Suliman ran off to the left casting for some sign of it, and presently came, by extraordinary good fortune, on a track, and then a mile or two still farther on, at the very place where the black stones were which we had taken for tarfa clumps, to our exceeding joy, lay the great caravan road — we had not seen it for two days — running with at least a hundred parallel camel paths bearing due westward. This, 'if not the work of the *ján*,' we know *must* be our road. It led straight to the pyramidal hill, and '*there*,' said Suliman, 'the water will be.' So now we are camped at sunset, once more praising God for his bounty, and in good heart and hope. Old Beseys and all of them had given themselves up for lost. They had made no complaint, but also had made no effort to find the road, but had ridden silently — Beseys saying his prayers at intervals. Perhaps they were heard in heaven." [N.B. What is very remarkable in this adventure is that both Suliman and I, he being a master in desert craft, having been deceived by the mirage, were so not to our own hurt but to our advantage, for the apparent vegetation lay precisely where the caravan road was emerging from the sand. The mirage in our case saved us. Not that we were yet in great straits for water, except for the mare, for we still had skins enough for our own drinking, and the weather was cold. But, if we had failed to hit off Síttarah next day, we should have soon been in sorry plight, for Síttarah is the only water between El Wah and Siwah. What makes travelling without guides so dangerous in the western desert is that the oases are mere cup-like hollows in the plains, which one may pass to right or left of without sign of their being near. There are almost no landmarks visible from the plain, and the sands have encroached, obliterating the ancient roads, which are most of them now abandoned. In former days the oases must have been all inhabited, but are not so now. The sand drifts are gradually overwhelming them. To pass by one of these and so miss the water is for a caravan a terrible disaster.]

"*22nd Feb.*— Close to our encampment we found the skeletons of two donkeys, which Osman recognizes as connected with a gruesome tale. Last year at El Wah, a witness being wanted in the affairs of a certain khawajeh, probably a Greek, who had died there, the Egyptian authorities, urged on by an officer of the Inglis, sent to Siwah for the man, who was brought to El Wah with his wife and his two boys. These, when the inquiry was over, wanted to return, and, notwithstanding that it was summer, the man set out for Siwah with his family, and his two donkeys carrying jars of water for the road. The donkeys, however, broke down near Sittarah, doubtless here; the water was finished, and the father sent the elder of the two boys forward with a jar to Sittarah to bring them water. On his return the boy found his mother and his brother already dead of thirst, while the father was still alive. But having drunk, he too died, and the boy was left alone to bury them and tell the tale. We found the graves by the roadside near the donkey skeletons. These, Osman says, were the last who travelled here, and it was two years ago.

"As I walked with Osman this morning he told me the story, and also much about Burnou and Wadai. There are there, he assures me, wild *koheyl*. The Arabs catch them at their watering places in pitfalls or traps which catch them by the leg. They keep these horses tied up fast for three days, then put bits into their mouths and ride them. They can go ten days without water. This he told me in almost the same words as those used by Leo Africanus 400 years ago. I asked about their colours, and he said they were bay, white, and dark; they had long manes and tails; some Arabs ate them, calling them *halal*. I asked him about the *lant* (mentioned by Leo Africanus), and he said, 'Oh, yes *el ant*,' and described it as red (bay) above with a white belly and dark markings between the red and the white, like a gazelle — the male alone with horns, big like a cow. I am convinced this is the Eland of natural history. There are also elephants, lions, and giraffes. The elephant is half *halal* (permitted food), half *haram* (forbidden food), the fore toes *halal*. He has eaten the flesh. He described the giraffe as a tall camel with two small horns. The Falata, he said, hunt all these — and the gazelle with hawks. They ride *koheyl*s after the ostrich and the *lant*. All this is most interesting. There are also wild asses.

"All this time we were following the caravan road, and at about eleven we sighted bushes — this time real bushes — and I galloped on some three or four miles to the dry edge of the Lake of Sittarah. It lay exactly as Suliman had said, under the pyramidal hill. This eastern

end of the lake (which is a salt lake and quite undrinkable) is clearly a
paradise of wild beasts. The tracks of the ariel gazelle were like those
of a flock of sheep, and of the hares, like those of rabbits at Newbuildings in the snow, round every bush. And there were jackal tracks, and
the track of a wolf and of a wild boar quite fresh. I was surprised to
find the jackal tracks, as I had never seen them before far from inhabited places. But their being here was later explained by the dates,
which they doubtless feed on. Of bushes I found *ghurkhud* and *aghur,*
the latter always a sign of former cultivation, tamarisks on a mound or
two, and a single palm bush. I should have liked to encamp here on
the chance of seeing an ariel; but it was necessary to find the water
first. Osman could not recollect where the spring was, except that it
was under palms, and about two miles farther on palms were visible.
So I once more cantered on. The first palms stood in a swamp near the
lake, just opposite the pyramidal hill, with blue water beyond them for
quite a mile. The swamp, too, was a main home of the wild beasts,
but as yet I saw no birds. I was driven out of it by the midges and
mosquitoes, which assailed me in battalions from the reeds, and I was
glad to get back to the desert and wait there for the camels. When
they arrived we all dispersed in search of the spring, which Osman
could not find, examining palm clump after palm clump. At the western edge of the lake there is no marsh, and the *nefuds* come down to
the water's edge with only a fringe of reeds and tufts of palms, which
we found covered with good fruit. Of these we plucked and ate. The
first hopeful sign of water was when with a rush and a scream out of a
palm clump flew a blackbird, a real English blackbird. I had never
seen one in the desert, or in Egypt, except in my own garden of Sheykh
Obeyd. This was a proof there must be good water, and soon after
Suliman discovered good water by digging in the sand to his elbow
at a place which seemed frequented, and Osman found more under the
very last palm of the Oasis westwards. The springs had been choked
with sand drift, but were easily dug out.

" Minshawi, meanwhile, had got another supply from the shore of
the lake. The lake itself is salt, like all desert lakes, but by digging a
few yards away from the edge, drinkable, though brackish, water can
be had; and of this Yemama drank her fill. She was very thirsty, as
yesterday she had been on half rations. We all felt very happy, and
agreed to spend two nights and enjoy the water. There is all here a
man with a few she-camels can require to live on, good pasture, good
water, and good dates. The lake is covered with flamingos, and I saw
a heron and heard wild geese. I think I saw pelicans. I also saw one
chrysippus butterfly, but no land bird except the one blackbird. It
would be a paradise for a hermit, but for the gnats. These came out
in swarms at sunset, and drove me out of camp, and a mile away into the

nefud, where I spent the night alone with Suliman and our two *nagas.*
Of all the hermitages I have yet found this is the best. It is *never*
visited by man. There are no Arabs anywhere within a hundred miles,
and it is very beautiful — a winter hermitage, I mean, for in summer
it must be a furnace. It is hot even now.

"23rd Feb.— After a delightful night I walked at sunrise to the top
of the highest *nefud,* from which the whole lake can be seen. It is
very interesting. Clearly the Oasis has been inhabited, but has been
overwhelmed by the *nefuds* advancing on it from the south and west.
The lake may be seven miles long, and is very beautiful. The northern
shore is bounded by low cliffs, the ancient limit doubtless of the lake,
which is shrinking, and will some day be a mere chaos of *nefud,* as so
many others are. It was somewhere in this desert, they say, that
Cambyses disappeared with his army. I can well believe it, for we
were within a little of such a misfortune two days ago. If the weather
had been less clear and cool I could not have seen the valley, and with
a sand wind we might easily have perished. Now all seems easy and
delightful. In the afternoon I went out for a ride, intending to visit
the pyramidal hill, but got into a quicksand, crossing over a half dry
arm of the lake, out of which I had some difficulty in dragging my
mare. The blackbird I saw again at the same place, and a kestrel. It
is so hot to-day that I had the tent pitched for a shade — the first time
we have used it, as I sleep under my carpet shelter. The barometer
shows the lake to be 120 feet below sea level.

"24th Feb.— Started at sunrise, believing our difficulties to be now
over, but we took a wrong track, which led us south-west instead of
farther north, towards some distant palms we had sighted an hour after
leaving. This took us to what I believe to be the oasis of Bahreyn —
at least such an Oasis is marked on my map. [N.B. A very excellent
German map.] This Oasis is very like Sittarah, though with two lakes
instead of one — whence its name. Osman pronounced this to be
Araj, and said we were now close to Zeytoun and Siwah, which I knew
could not be the case, and was sure when we came to the second lake
it could only be Bahreyn. The road, too, westwards, we found blocked
by a great *sebkha* (a dry salt marsh), and we were obliged to turn
north and travel several hours to recover the right road. Fortunately
we fell in soon with the track of a donkey, and two men who had been
to the oasis, we think, to gather dates, a track of about ten days old,
which we followed. The barometer at Bahreyn showed exactly 0°
above the sea. The donkey track led us to a *nukbeh,* where we fell
in with a well-marked road bearing north-west by north over a plateau
of limestone hillocks, each about ten feet high, like the crested waves
of the British Channel in rough weather, with the space between them
sand. The road was carefully marked with *rijms* (cairns), and easy

to follow, and I cantered gaily on to find a camping place, where we now snugly are, screened from the north-east wind. It is fortunate we found the donkey track, or we might not have hit off the road. Yemama is now in excellent condition, and ate up her two *melwas* of corn during the night. The camels were all watered before starting. At Bahreyn to-day I saw a kite and a raven.

"I find Beseys is very unwilling now to go to Jerabub, being afraid, I think, of displeasing the Akhwan. We have agreed to find out at Zeytoun or Siwah whether Abu Seyf is at Jerabub or not, and to pass by without alighting if he should be absent.

"*25th Feb.*— To-day we are in a worse plight than ever. We started very early, taking up our path of yesterday, which brought us in a couple of hours to the end of the limestone plain, and to my great delight to the edge of a new and very deep oasis which I knew must be the Araj we were looking for. Araj has no lake, only a little standing water and a tamarisk marsh. But a vast number of palms are scattered over a wide basin with many isolated clumps, very beautiful, in the sand. It was no case here of the *nefud* having destroyed the villages, as in the other oases, but of abandonment, one cannot say why. There are palms enough left to support many villages. The cliffs here are on the south and west sides, the sand slopes on the north and east. Still on the track of the donkey and the two men we chevied along the edge of the jungle north westwards, the ground covered with the tracks of gazelles, hares, and jackals. Of birds I saw only three, mourning chats, black with white beaks and rumps — nothing else alive. The depth of the oasis puzzled my barometer. It must be about 150 feet below the sea. From the bottom the track led up by some clumps of palms, where I am sure there must be water underground, across deep *nefuds* to the opposite *nukbe* marked by some wonderful rocks — one quite square, white as marble, and with curious architectural markings, another like a tall chessman, both 100 feet high at least, their tops level with the plain above, a splendid hermitage where one might find shade and shelter at all hours and in every weather. They are geologically of limestone, with layers of shells, their tops black, like lava. One layer of the chessman, one of those round white flakes, Suliman calls *dirahem* (money). This place was the wildest, the most romantic, the most supernatural in its natural structure I have ever seen, an abode of all the *jan*.

"I cantered up the sand slope to the top of the pass, elated at having found Araj corresponding so well with my map, and being in front forgot to give orders for water to be looked for, and the girbehs filled. Hence our present trouble. For on gaining the upper plain, instead of the well-marked track we had expected, we found nothing but a wind-swept plateau of *nefud* interspersed with mounds of stone, where the donkey track speedily disappeared or was lost, nor could we ever again find it. We were left now to our sole wits and the mercy of God, for the wind was blowing hard from the north-east and was drifting the sand hopelessly. Suliman, now in command, recommended descending towards some hills to the north-west, and this brought us to a new formation of limestone ground, arranged in flat masses with sharp edges, the most abominable imaginable interspersed with sand. Across this we floundered with our camels for several hours, when Suliman, having climbed to the top of a low tell, announced that he had seen a valley with palms, and it was resolved, much against old Osman's wish, that we should cross the whole valley on the chance of striking a track near the hills. The trend of the valley was westwards, and if it was the beginning of the Siwah valley, Suliman argued, it must have a road passing up it. So Suliman and I went scouting with the tall buttresses of a crag to west-north-west for our object. Now we have almost reached these, but have found no sign of road or life — only a poor wagtail lost in the strong wind. We have camped for the night, feeling ourselves to be out of all reckoning (for this according to the map should have been the Siwah valley, yet it is absolutely without trace of human passage, old or new). We are camped in a hollow near two *seyyal* trees, ill screened from the wind, and in very miserable plight.

"*26th Feb.*— I spent a restless, uncomfortable night, disturbed at finding that of our five water skins three were already empty, and reproaching myself with having let the men pass Araj without replenishing. I felt myself responsible, too, from having taken the direction of our route out of Osman's hands. Old Beseys and the rest, except my own Bedouins, were clearly of opinion that I was wrong. The wind, too, raged furiously, and kept me waking, and in the darkness I imagined all kinds of disaster, more especially when I found the stars overhead obscured with drifting sand. I said prayers to all my saints and repented of my sins, and so I think did all the party. Once in the night the sky cleared and I got a sight of the Pole Star and made a line on the ground with my camel stick as a guide in the morning, for my pocket compass is out of order and cannot be relied on. There were even moments when I thought gloomily of ordering a retreat to Araj.

"In the morning, however, more courageous counsels prevailed, and we took our due course west towards the *khusm* (the headland) determined to go straight forward and solve the question of this being the Siwah valley or no. Nor were we long in suspense. We had hardly gone a mile when, riding in front, I came upon a little single path leading to some *seyyal* trees which had been pollarded by Bedouins, a sign of human neighbourhood, and presently, to my delight, to the old caravan road, reappearing plain and unmistakable. It relieved us from all anxiety, and following it we found ourselves by mid-day at the first bushes of the Siwah oasis." [N.B. It is well here to note, as a general rule of travelling in the desert without guides that, when looking for a lost camel track or road, there is more chance of finding it at the point of a headland in the wady than elsewhere, for the reason that it is there that the shortest cut would be made in rounding a trend of the hills. This justified Suliman in making for the *khusm* yesterday.] " Soon afterwards we came to *sebkhas,* where there were tracks of many pasturing camels, and then within sight of the oasis of Zeytoun and the Senussi Zaghwiyeh standing on high ground a mile or more from its palm trees. As it was near sunset we resolved to rest here and have made a pleasant camp under some *ghurkhud* bushes. *El hamdul Illah.*

" *27th Feb.*— In half an hour from leaving camp we came to the Zaghwiyeh, and Yemama started at the sight of strange human beings, the first she had seen since leaving El Wah, who came out to receive us. These were servants and slaves of the monastery, and we were shown by them the well where we watered mare and camels — a small well just outside the buildings. These were not different from an ordinary small village, a score of low square houses with a mosque attached. The servants may have been half-a-dozen or more, an unhandsome set of men, especially those of the Siwah type, which is one of the ugliest in the world, yellow skinned, brown haired, snub nosed, hare-lipped and light eyed (such one imagines the Huns to have been). In marked contrast to them was the ' brother,' who came out presently to entertain us, an Arab of the Western type, not unlike my friend Abdallah Mijower, with a singularly pleasant smile. One could imagine him having great influence with the people. He had a look of goodness which could not be mistaken. His name, he told us, was Sidi Hamid of the Mujábara tribe of Aujla. He has with him only one fellow brother, a Siwan, inferior to him in every way. He gave us all the news of the brotherhood, how that, after Sidi Sherif's death, Sidi Abu Seyf had also died, leaving Sidi el Médani head of the community at Jerabúb. He said we should have no difficulty in our journey to Benghazi. It was four easy days to Jerabúb, and from thence we could go straight to Bir Menús in nine days, with one water on the sixth day. He would like to go with us himself. He was very kind to me, and though he did not eat with us, it being Ramadan, he gave me some good *gazali* dates and some pomegranates, and milk and dates to the servants, who were not fasting. Then he called his fellow brother Mohammed, and they recited a *fatha* for our safe journey, all standing together outside the monastery, and we went much pleased on our way.

" Old Beseys tells me it is their practice to entertain all comers for two nights with milk and dates — otherwise to occupy themselves only with prayer and the superintending of the palm cultivation. (Cardinal

Lavigerie's White Fathers imitated in this their way of life.)   One might do worse in the world than be a Senussi brother.   Every difficulty seems now to be in the way of solution.   Beseys is confident of accomplishing our journey by Jerabúb to Benghazi.

" Thus we travelled till four o'clock, when we reached the first isolated garden outside Siwah, where Beseys found a friend, who invited us to stay with him, and we should have done well to accept, and presently we encamped for the night just outside the Eastern town, of the two of which Siwah is composed, half a mile away south of it in the sand among some groups of palms.

" *28th Feb.*— A day of disaster.   Last night after dark, Mohammed Saïd, Omdeh of the Eastern town, came out to see us; a fat, well-dressed, dark-faced man whom Suliman pronounced to be ' a splendid prince.'   We had bought a lamb (for Sheykh Obeyd), and Suliman cooked it for us, and Mohammed Saïd ate of it largely with a friend and he had just got up to say good-night and go, having promised us a guide and all we wanted for next day, when we saw lights coming, and a number of persons, horse and foot, and the word passed that it was the *hákim* (government representative), a *maown* (police officer), the chief man being away at Skanderia.   He was polite and amiable, a slender man with no palate to his mouth, speaking almost in a whisper, and with him a number of Siwans who, as I understand now, were Sheykhs of the Western town.   These all sat down, and I, too, was obliged to stay out their visit while coffee was being made.   Old Beseys, as his way is, made most of the conversation, and he began very imprudently to tell them we intended going to Benghazi.   The sheykhs, upon this, became curious and inquisitive.   Old Beseys strung tales of my being from Nejd, and I was obliged to join in to the extent of saying that I was from beyond Sham (Damascus), between Sham and Bagdad, and my name Sakr.   They were curious to know my business, but I answered vaguely, also as to our road.   I did not for a moment suppose there was anything hostile in their intention, and they drank their coffee and said good night amiably enough, the only disagreeable incident being that during the night a thief came to my tent and stole away my carpet shelter, which I had used to seat my visitors upon outside.   It had been carelessly put back at the door of the tent, and the night was one for thieves, being without ·a moon.   I was awoke out of my sleep by Suliman's shout, who had seen the thief stealing away between the palms, but too late to stop him with his prize.   I was put out at this and all the more resolved to move away early — Mohammed Saïd had suggested it — to another place ' near his castle.'   This castle was barely half a mile away (to the west), a country house built upon a rock, and we accordingly moved camp by daylight and pitched the tent a hundred yards from the house on open ground.

"I had just settled that the servants were to go to town to buy what we wanted when Suliman came to my tent to tell me of an armed party approaching from the town towards us, and that we ought to get our guns ready. I loaded my gun, and then looked through my glass, and saw in fact a little army, some 200 men, on horse and on foot (and with camels), advancing from the Western town, which, though evidently armed, I could not believe had any intention hostile to ourselves. The servants were for flight with the camels, and old Beseys and Salem and the younger Arabs disappeared. Only Suliman and the good old slave Osman stayed with me, and, seeing it was absurd to think of defence, I told them to put up their weapons, and sat down again in my tent waiting the event. Presently the Siwans arrived, and I heard them call out 'Salaam aleykum,' and 'amán,' and supposed it to be all right. But half a minute after I found myself surrounded by a number of men, mostly Soudanis, who were pulling the tent over my ears. On seeing me sitting there, they rushed forward and caught hold of me by the wrists and pulled me to my feet. I expostulated with them, and they became more violent, and though I made no defence except in words one of them struck me a blow on the side of the neck and others began to try and pull my clothes off me, others pointed guns and pistols at me, and there was a vast hubbub and confusion, one dragging me one way and another another. I received several blows on the head and one from some weapon on the cheek. All I could make out of their cries (for there was an immense uproar and they were shouting the most part in a language — Berberi — I did not understand), was something about Sidi-el-Mahdi.

"There were half-a-dozen sheykhs on horseback, with an old white-bearded man brandishing a drawn sword, others with blunderbusses and every kind of impossible weapon. I recognized in them several of those who had drunk coffee with us the night before. My captors hustled me towards the town, tearing me nearly in pieces in their desire to get my pistol from my belt, which at last they tore away. The sheykhs on horseback were evidently in direction of the whole affair. I had lost sight of Suliman and the slave Osman, but I heard afterwards that they, too, were considerably knocked about. I received a rather nasty blow on the nape of the neck and another with some weapon on my cheek bone, but neither very serious, and, not being really hurt, I managed to keep my temper. The sheykhs made no effort to protect me in any way; but, when they had got my pistol, my assailants left me more or less alone, as there was a general rush to pillage the baggage. Fortunately the leather bags with spring locks were a puzzle to them, and they could not tear them open. But I had no leisure to attend to this, and my captors marched me off towards the town, every now and then having a drag at my cloak or my *hezam*

(girdle); 'el dirahem, el dirahem!' ('the drachmas, the money!')
they shouted; 'you have a thousand? you have two thousand?'

"At last a man, with a better face than most, came up to me, and I
made myself his *dahil* (according to the Arab formula, '*ana dahilak,*'
by seizing his cloak, an act of surrender), and he took me to join a
second body which had been waiting behind the first, and some of these
threw their cloaks over my head to protect me from further blows. It
was a rabble rout as ever was seen, and they marched me to the town,
where the women were all shrilling their triumph (*ulu-lu-lu-lu*) from
every housetop. I did not know in the least what it was about or what
they intended, but they seemed all very angry, and at times I thought
they meant to kill me. But, strangely enough, I was not at all frightened, and felt interested in it all almost as a spectator." [The truth
is it was a very lovely morning, the air sparkling and clear, and the
whole thing, with its almost mediæval and quite barbaric costuming and
staging, was more like a pageant than a reality, so that it seemed difficult to realize that it was quite in earnest; nor had I time to think much
or consider what it meant.]

"Arrived inside the town, I was marched to an open space where
there were two erections not unlike gallows, and for a moment I
thought that I was perhaps to be hanged. All I could imagine in explanation of the affair was that some revolution had broken out in
which I was accidentally involved. But we did not stop at the gallows,
and presently I was bidden inside a house and up a stair which led to a
nice open room with *mastabahs* (seats) and a pleasant outlook to the
north. This proved to be the *mejliss* (council chamber) of the Sheykhs
of the Gharbieh (western town), and there we sat down. I took the
best place, and called for water, which was brought; and a great talk
began among the Sheykhs, who were now by way of protecting me.
Having drunk and recovered my breath, I asked them the reason of all
their wrath, and of the attack made on me, but could get no intelligible
answer except that the Maown was coming. I explained that I was a
person well known at Cairo and a friend of Effendina's (the Khedive's). But they said they knew nothing of Effendina — they had a
government of their own, and that I should go to the diwan (government house). Soon after the Maown arrived. He had made me the
kindly offer of his services last night, and I now whispered to him that
I was an Englishman. This made him still more courteous, and I think,
poor man, he did all he could to set things right, with considerable tact,
too. And, as things went on better, I whispered the same intelligence
also to one of the sheykhs who sat next me, and with the same good
effect. There was now a great hurry to restore the plunder, and most
of the things taken were by degrees brought in, the chief losses being
two of my three guns, and my good Persian sword (the sword Moham-

med Ibn Aruk of Tadmor had given me), also my little store of gold
— £29 had been abstracted from my small red bag, which must have
been done by the sheykhs themselves, for the silver had been left, and
certainly the common plunderers would have left nothing. And so,
little by little, matters cleared. The Maown brought water, and himself washed my cheeks from the blood, and a *katib* (scribe) having arrived, I dictated a statement of the case, though I don't think it was
signed by any one.

   " After this, my servants one by one appeared all with tales of the
losses, and Suliman and Osman of their bruises — and we were escorted
by the Maown to the diwan, which is the general Government House of
Siwah. Here we now are, in not uncomfortable quarters upstairs, with
several mud-built rooms and a nice roof top. The camels are below
in a great yard; and after all the trouble nothing serious has really happened. Only it is clear our onward journey is stopped. Our money
and our arms are gone, and there is a general demoralization among the
servants. Salem is thoroughly frightened and has given warning, and
the others all declare for an immediate return by Alexandria. So here
my expedition ends. The timid Beseys, it turns out, ran away to his
friend Mohammed Saïd at the first news of the approaching army, and
came late, on the Maown's summons, to the *mejliss,* where the Sheykhs
set upon him, excusing themselves for the attack by laying it on Beseys'
assurance to them that I was this that and the other; and, indeed, I
think it has been mainly his fault. It was quite unnecessary for him
to talk about my going to Benghazi to anybody but Mohammed Saïd;
and I am not sure he had not talked also about the road to Jerabūb.
Still we must be thankful for small mercies, and it has all been in the
way of the adventure I was seeking. None of us is hurt, and for the
small losses I shall make the Egyptian Government responsible. They
should either give up holding Siwah or keep order here. As it is, the
Maown, poor man, is powerless. He told me his sorrows to-night. He
has been twelve years here, on £7 a month, and has but six men under
him for the preservation of the peace, four of whom are disabled by
fever, and he himself suffers from it. His second in command is dying
of consumption, and spits blood continually. His superior, the Mamur,
at £25 a month, has just been recalled, and I think he cannot read or
write. His *bashkatib,* chief secretary, is down with fever, and the
second, too, is sick.

   " 1st *March.*— Things look pleasanter this morning. It is arranged
that we are to leave to-morrow with a messenger the Maown is sending
to Alexandria with the news of our adventure. We shall take the
northern road by Akabah and the sea coast. Last night was a noisy
one, of chaunting and processions, as Ramadan is ending. [N.B. The
diwan overlooked the great square of the mosque, which was crowded

all night with a multitude of devotees, and a wild concourse of Oulad
Ali Bedouins who had come in to Siwah from the north and west to buy
dates and attend the coming festival. The Oulad Ali are all more or
less adherents of the Senussia, and what may truly be called 'fanatic-
ism,' was rampant among them. It was a curious and impressive sight,
and cannot have been very different from the condition of things at
Omdurman and el Obeyd in the time of the Mahdi. At midnight and
again at the hour of the morning prayer a gong was sounded, apparently
by the blows repeated singly of an iron hammer, with the effect of a
series of sharp reports like those of a rifle, sharp and penetrating, followed by the call to prayer splendidly chaunted by the *mueddhin,* and
then a general chaunting maintained for an hour or more, wild and
menacing as anything to be heard in the world.] The best explanation
of the attack made on me is Ramadan. The Siwans are mad with it.
Beseys tells me the Akhwan took part in yesterday's affair. It is quite
likely. Others say it is on account of our having gone on arrival to
Mohammed Saïd, who is at the head of the opposite faction, that of the
Eastern town. But I think plunder had not a little to do with it, and
the recklessness which Ramadan brings. Certainly the whole of the
Gharbieh town was concerned in the attack. I regret it as upsetting my
plans for the Jebel Akhdar, but it cannot be helped. It may serve as a
useful instruction as to this western Islam of which I had hoped something. If the condition of Siwah is all the fruit the Senussia has to
show, the tree can be but little worth.

" *2nd March.*— The day has passed in going to and fro on the part
of the Maown to arrange matters for our start to-morrow. They have
imposed two *khabirs* (guides) on us, one from each village, for whom
I am to pay £4 each. This will leave me with only fifteen reals and a
piastre, all counted. The Sheykh of the Gharbieh, who is chief guar-
antor in the transaction, is the same who led the attack on us yesterday.
There is little doubt that the prime movers in the affair were the Akhwan. Some say that Mohammed, the Siwahi brother who recited the
prayer with us at Zeytoun, followed us on his white donkey, and that
he was the cause of the night visit paid us, and the questions asked of
us as to our projected journey. The Sheykh of the Western town led
the *ghazu,* but the men who first attacked me were, I am sure, slaves
of the Akhwan. I remember among their cries when they struck me
with the gun, '*ya kelb, la te fut and Sidi el Mahdi.*' Indeed it was all
done in the name of Sidi el Mahdi. Now old Beseys says he recognized
one of the Akhwan as leader in the attack.

" Of the Sheykhs there were three prominent leaders, Othman Habbun, the old man with the naked sword (this I believe to have been
Hassuna), and the young dark man with the prominent eyes, who afterwards sat next me at the *mejliss,* Mohammed Kuli. All these three

were on horseback. I am certain, too, that the gold stolen from the red bag was taken, not in the general plunder, but afterwards — this because the bag, though not locked, was shut with a spring, and if the plunderers had got it open they would not have left the silver or the pistol, both of which were inside. I suspect it was Othman took it. Beseys says that the arms are in his hands and in those of the Akhwan. The name of the man who first protected me is Abu Bekr Mohammed Daoud, and another was Mohammed Mansur, Hassan Mansur's brother, on whom they now lay all the blame. Mohammed Kuli was among the advanced riders. I consider Abdallah Homeydeh among the most responsible of the second division. The three commanders of the advanced party are then — Othman Habbun, the worst, Hassuna, and Mohammed Kuli. It was Mohammed Kuli, I think, who pointed the pistol at my head. They lay all the blame on Hassuna now, who they say is *asi* (in rebellion) against the Government, and has possession of my sword and guns.

" Othman has been to see me and has brought back the money, or rather its equivalent of ten sovereigns and twenty-five *bintos*. The Sheykhs of the Gharbieh have all been with me, talking, and are now polite enough and anxious their quarrel with me should be settled; and I have used a little *siasa* with them, acquiescing in their view of Hassuna's sole guilt. They have asked me to get him removed by the Government as a mischief maker. It was Abdallah Homeydeh who made the remark in the *mejliss* ' We know nothing of Effendina. We have a government of our own.' " [N.B. I am sorry not to have noted more in my journal of these Sheykhs' conversation, for much of it was interesting as connected with the affairs of the Senussia. I found Othman Habbun by far the most able man among them, a strong, capable rogue. The rest were very poor creatures, some of them of the most degraded physical type I have ever come across, and apparently without those sentiments of honour most Arabs pretend to even if they are without them. The Siwahi are, however, no real Arabs, but men of very mixed origin with much negro blood, and apparently some northern blood too, for there were individuals with yellow faces, pale eyes, and tow-coloured hair. They are probably descended from the criminals formerly sent here in Roman and later times, for Siwah was a convict settlement.]

" 3.30. — I have had a last talk with Huseyn Effendi, the Maown, and have learned several things from him. Othman Habbun is no other, he tells me, than the Wakil of the Akhwan at Siwah. This explains the whole affair, and it is on him and the Akhwan that the whole responsibility of the attack rests. He is now anxious not to compromise the Senussia with the Government, and represents Hassuna as the dangerous man, making him scapegoat in his place. Hassuna is Sidi el Mahdi's strongest adherent in Siwah, an⌐ if the Government attempts to arrest him, he will doubtless fly and take refuge with the Sidi, as he did once before in the Khedive Tewfik's time. I am tired of waiting here, but the delay has been fruitful in the knowledge I have acquired. It is an experience not, I think, bought too dear.

"*3rd March.*— Got away at last from Siwah, accompanied by the Maown on his white donkey and our four chief adversaries on horse-bask, Othman Habbun (Wakil Sidi el Mahdi), Mohammed Mansur (Hassuna's brother), Mohammed Kuli, and Abdallah Homeydeh. They were riding wretched underbred mares of which they professed themselves proud. But Othman cast envious eyes on Yemama, who was fresh with her rest and full of spirits.

" I have promised the Maown to try and get him named Mamur. He says that with twenty-five men and a small cannon he could manage the town — and I think he could if Othman were removed. He is the only dangerous one of the lot, as he is intelligent, unscrupulous, and bold. The Senussia in these oasis towns is a mere madness and ought to be suppressed. It is, all the same, picturesque and interesting. I have slept the last two nights on the housetop, and the midnight call to prayer is the most impressive thing I ever heard. The town guards call their watchword, which is answered all over the town. Then the drum is struck, in sound like the sharp crack of a rifle, 1 — 2, 3 — 1 — 2, 3 — 1 — 2, 3. Then, after an interval, the *mueddhin* chaunts. Till midnight the whole town is silent — dead silent — there are no dogs at Siwah except those brought in by the Bedouins. But afterwards there are intervals of watch calling and prayers till daybreak.

" The four Sheykhs got off their horses at the outskirts of the oasis gardens and were wishing us good-bye, when Mohammed Saïd appeared in the distance. ' I think he is not of your friends,' I said. ' We are all friends here,' they answered, laughing. ' Fi aman Illah,' said Othman. ' Salaam aleykum,' I answered, and he, ' Aleykum es salaam.' Mohammed Saïd then rode up. He talked of riding farther with us, but I would not allow it. He proved useless to us at the pinch, and he only compromises us now. The little Maown I parted from with real regret. He has been very kind and very clever. I am to deliver a letter he has written to the Mudirieh (Damanhur, of which Siwah is an annex), and to send him my pistol and a donkey's bridle by one of our guides when these return. Mohammed Saïd handed me a list of those who had been concerned in the attack on me, and then he too departed. When all were gone and we were once more in the open desert we all breathed more freely, and have pushed quickly on and are stopping now at the last *hattieh* (palm clump) of the oasis, some twenty-five miles from Siwah.

" *4th March.*— A long march from 5.50 a.m. to 5.20 p.m. over hard *hamad* (gravel plain) at best pace — say thirty-five miles — and camped at the first sheltered place on descending towards Garah.   A hot march, as the wind was behind us, followed by a bitter cold night.

"The two guides are Kheydr, an old man, tall and big-nosed, a Senusite — he was one of those who rode against us on the 28th at what I call the battle of Jupiter Ammon, for the ruins were within half a mile of the fight.   The other, a great strong blackguard of the opposite faction.   They are both amiable now, and made me a present of Siwah bread and date cake, very good, in a pretty basket.   The old man I like.   He said to-day, 'I have been inquiring about you from your servants, and I find we made a great mistake about you.   It will ruin Siwah.'

"*5th March.*— There are three factions at Siwah: 1. The Senussia, comprising 950 out of the 1000 male inhabitants.   2. The followers of one Abd es Salaam of Tuggurt, and 3. The followers of Mohammed Dhaffir el Médani of Constantinople.   Of this last Mohammed Saïd is a member, and so is our guide Khalaf.   Mohammed Dhaffir it was that made the mischief at Yildiz against Sidi el Mahdi, and caused the Sultan to cut his subsidy.   It is therefore pretty plain that our arriving with letters to Mohammed Saïd was a first cause of suspicion.   They seem to have jumped at once to the conclusion that I was a spy, from Mohammed Dhaffir or another, with plans against their chief."   [N.B. This Mohammed Dhaffir el Médani is doubtless the same Sheykh Zaffir who corresponded with Arabi on behalf of the Sultan in 1882.   See my "Secret History."]

"This morning we descended to Garah, a pretty little oasis, with a quaint village perched on a mushroom rock, inhabited by negroes. There are two springs and a well, the western spring called Ain Makhluf, the eastern Ain Faris.   Makhluf has a deep hole in the middle of the spring like that at Wells.   We found the inhabitants of Garah *en fête,* for to-day is the Id (festival) and their Sheykh, an old negro, came out to greet us and ask us to alight, but I would not stop, and we have come on to the far end of the oasis, and are camped under some wild palms.   Some fifteen miles to-day.   According to the barometer we are here 250 feet below the sea level.   It was 400 above yesterday on the high plateau.

"In all this time of trial I have been reading Doughty — certainly the best prose written in the last two centuries.   He is of excellent counsel for such straits as we have been in; and I think it was in great measure due to his influence that I took the passive line I did the day of the attack.   Any other would have cost me my life.

"*6th March.*— Thirteen hours' march without a halt, perhaps forty miles.   Our course was north-east by east, to the *khusm* of Abdel Nebbi.   Thence there are two roads which part company to join again at Lebbakh. We chose the northern way. We are camped at the first palms of a new oasis.

"*7th March.*— All day till three skirting a great *sebkha* with cliff to our left, and camped at a spring. Found a dead pratincole and saw two falcons. Barometer shows 165 below sea level. The name of our camp, Gatara. Water pretty good, an open spring with a run of water from under palms. Chats with white heads and tails, as at Siwah. A yellow wagtail with black head. Twenty-five miles.

"*8th March.*— Rounded the point of Gatara and on to El Haj, six hours. El Haj, an open spring in a sandy ravine, water salt. At 2.50 crossed a bay of the *sebkha,* and camped at a *hattieh* — perhaps twenty-eight miles. Saw a gazelle on the *sebkha,* and flushed a quail. We are camped 1½. miles east of the pyramidal peak of El Tartur. Good *guttáf* pasture for the camels.

"*9th March.*— Took water from an open pit under Abu Tartur. It might be easily passed unnoticed, being marked only by some burnt palms. A great bird of prey, brown, grey, and black (?), and some pippits. All day coasting the *sebkha,* with lines of hill still in front. Eleven hours' march, thirty miles. We have now travelled, according to my calculation, 198 miles from Siwah in seven days.

"*10th March.*— To Lebbakh well, eleven hours, say thirty miles, good *nossi* and *sgaa* pasture. The well is about three-quarters of a mile south of the headland, the last of the range eastwards. It is marked by a low *tel.* I am tired, and Yemama is tired. The *sebkha* ends here.

"Later. I was premature about the well. After three hours' absence Kheydr and Eid have returned, having failed to find it. So we are without water. I have given what remained in my *girbeh* to the general stock. Yemama had a *jerdel,* and there is now absolutely no drop in camp, except one quart bottle I keep always in reserve. Kheydr promises water to-morrow at noon at Maghara, 'sweet as the Nile.' We are now, I calculate, 160 miles from the Nile valley.

"*11th March.*— A long forced march of thirty miles. I did not ride Yemama, as she is suffering from thirst, and is looking thin and tucked up. They found the well this morning, but it was salt, and the mare would not drink. To-day we passed through herds of wandering camels. There is pasture, *erta, nossi, adr.* At half-past two crossed a party of Oulad Ali, who told us we were going wrong, and took us to Maghara water — most fortunate. Maghara is a small oasis three miles south-west of the first *step* of the hill.

"*12th March.*— The Bedouin who showed us the water, Abu Bekr, lives in the neighbourhood. Every ten days he visits Maghara, and fetches ten *girbehs* of water on donkeys for his household, a bright, good Bedouin, who was really unwilling to take the present I offered

him. I said, 'For the water.' He answered, 'It was not worth it.'
(If we had not chanced to meet him it would have fared ill with us.)
From this point I took command, as Kheydr had no clear idea of the
direction. Abu Bekr had told us, 'go towards that star,' pointing to
one rising in the east. I made my course a point north of west, and
made a nine hours' march, perhaps twenty-three miles, letting the
camels feed, and am camped in a good wady, with *erta* and *eshub.*
Yemama eats the *erta,* and several kinds of *eshub,* besides the *nossi.*
We have our six *girbehs* full, to last us till the Nile or the Wady Natron.

"13th *March.*— Another nine hours' march due east. I insisted
upon this, as they wanted, all of them but Suliman, to go south-east,
which I knew must be wrong. So across country we went, taking careful bearings at every height to keep our line true. It was all open
ground. Some camel herders we passed told us the Wady (Natron)
was in front of us, thus confirming my judgment. At 2.45 we camped
in a bit of pasture, whence we disturbed gazelles. These are now once
more of the smaller Eastern kind. (They are larger in the west).
Came on a vulture on a dead camel. Saw cranes passing northwards
overhead. Three days more should see us now at home. Twenty-
seven miles' march.

"14th *March*— Held doggedly on my course due east, passing much
petrified wood. There is a general discontent at my persisting in my
own direction over hill and dale, all good going on gravel. At noon
we crossed a well-marked caravan road, bearing north-east, but I held
on by compass, and presently we got glimpses of a yellow wady about
three miles off I knew must be Natron, and at four found ourselves
within two miles of the westernmost convent straight in front of us
(a good bit of navigation). Here we are camped. Some thirty miles
to-day.

" 15th *March.*— This morning our party broke up, Beseys and Minshawi making a line for their home in the Fayoum, our two khabirs also
leaving us to visit friends in the Rif, and we down the Natron Valley,
passing four convents on our way to Sheykh Ahmed and Fum el Bahr.
We camped in the plain between Natron and the Rif. Twenty-eight
miles.

" 16th *March.*— This morning we saw a strange sight. The moon
was setting, and we saw three moons, and the sun was rising, and we
saw two suns. At noon we reached the Nile Valley and rested awhile,
feasting our eyes on the greenness and the water near Sheykh Ahmed.
Then on, and camped at Fum el Bahr. Thirty miles.

" 17th *March.*— Reached Sheykh Obeyd on St. Patrick's day, at
11.15, a weary crew, having travelled 413 miles in fourteen and a half
days, the fortieth day from our leaving it. *El Hamdul Illah*!

" 24th *March.*— Sheykh Obeyd. I returned from my Siwah journey on the 17th at a quarter past eleven, meeting Anne accidentally on her way through the palm grove from the station. I could hardly speak for tears of joy. I had been away the forty days, during which she was to expect no news of me, and this was the forty-first, and during the whole of that time I had not spoken a word of any language but Arabic, till I had come even to think in Arabic, and I was weak and worn out, and famished in mind and body. Our last run from Siwah, 413 miles, had been accomplished in fourteen days and a half.

"Since then I have been resting, except that on the 20th I went into Cairo and lunched with Gorst, and at his suggestion drew up a memorandum in writing for him of the circumstances of my journey. There have been two political events during my absence, the war in Crete and Rodd's mission to Abyssinia. I hardly know what to say yet on either case. Personally I have come back from my journey with my mind cleared on one point important to my life. It is as to religion. My experience of the Senussia at Siwah has convinced me that there is *no* hope anywhere to be found in Islam. I had made myself a romance about these reformers, but I see that it has no substantial basis, and I shall never go farther now than I am in the Mohammedan direction. The less religion in the world, perhaps, after all, the better."

CHAPTER XIII

OMDURMAN AND FASHODA

From this point my more violent activities in life may be said to have ended. My health had suffered seriously from the extreme hardships of my journeys, hardships which hitherto I had borne with easily, but which now at my age of fifty-six had taken their revenge on me. The next two years were for this reason an unhappy period of my life, and this, though I do not often make mention in it of my sufferings, is reflected in my diary.

We left Sheykh Obeyd on the 19th April. Four days before, on 15th April, I had gone to wish the Khedive good-bye. He received me pleasantly, as always, with pretty speeches about my friendship for him, and the good report of me he heard from everyone. He asked about my journey to Siwah and the attack made on me. I made rather light of it with him as a *ghazu* (an accident of travel), but he said he had heard it was the doing of the Senussia. About the state of affairs between Greece and Turkey he said things could not be going worse. The Sultan was ruining the Empire, the end could not be far distant. "But where can we look," he asked, "for another chief? In Arabia there is only your friend Ibn Rashid, and he is little more than a Bedouin." With Sheykh Mohammed Abdu too I had a farewell talk.

"*17th April.*— Abdu brought me news that war was declared between Greece and Turkey. We agreed that it was better things had come to actual war. Personally I think that it would be no loss for the Ottoman Empire if the Greeks should be able to hold their own in Macedonia, though I do not expect it, for a defeat of the Turkish army would bring about a revolution at Constantinople, and even a European war would do no harm. 'When thieves fall out, honest men come by their own.' The Ottoman Empire cannot be made to last in Europe, and as soon as the remnant of the provinces there are lost the better it will be. I expect, however, to see the Turks advance on Athens, when the Powers would doubtless intervene to stop the fighting, which they could do by pressure at Constantinople. Then there may be a second chance for the establishment of a better order of things on the Bosphorous, for it would be too great a scandal to allow the Sultan and his palace clique to go on for another twenty years on a new lease of absolute power; possibly the victorious general might become the leader of a constitutional change in Turkey, but we shall see."

"*1st May*.— Back in England, where we arrived at the end of the month. The Greeks have been smashed badly by Edhem Pasha in Thessaly; they seem to have run away rather than fought, which would be more creditable to them if they had not been the aggressors in the quarrel. I am sorry, on the whole, as the Turkish victory is strengthening the Sultan's hand at Constantinople, and will put back the clock of reform. There is little chance, I fear, of Edhem's coming forward as a revolutionist, but I am nearly dead to politics as, indeed, to all else but the horses and the sunshine.

"*8th May*.— The Greeks are again beaten and in retreat, and the Turkish army will now advance on Athens and dictate its terms of peace. The Sultan is entirely rehabilitated in public opinion, for the world adores military success, and he will probably now go on in triumph till he dies.

"*18th May*.— Newbuildings. On the 13th George Wyndham came to spend the day with me and stopped the night. He was full of his journey to South Africa and of his South African Commission, where he has played the part of advocate for Rhodes and his gang, and is still playing it. With this I am of course in little sympathy, but George and I know how to differ without quarrelling. He told me much of the inner working of the great intrigue and promised more some day. We also talked about the Henley edition of my poems, and about his own ' New Review.'

"*3rd June*.— George was here yesterday. The South African Committee is virtually, not virtuously, over, and no one in his senses can doubt that Chamberlain was privy to the raid, not indeed at the last moment but in its initial stages. I asked George whether it was not so. ' Chamberlain has denied it,' he answered diplomatically.

"*15th June*.— Drove to Bramber and dined with Button in his newly purchased old house there, St. Mary's, which he has furnished with bric-à-brac, and had the little meadow behind it laid out in miniature avenues. We talked of old political times. He tells me that at the time Wolseley started for Egypt in 1882, the Rothschilds had the *whole* of their working capital in Egyptian securities, and were in such a fright about the Domains lest Arabi should flood the country and destroy the property pledged to them, that they got Wolseley to hurry on the campaign at all costs to prevent his cutting the canals. Button had this from Wolseley himself at the time, and it agrees with what he (Button) told me then.

"*17th June*.— Hyndman came to breakfast with me in Mount Street, and we discussed the state of Europe, Africa and Asia. He knows a great deal and told me many curious things, among others the genesis of the English connection with the Suez canal. He assures me that it was not Beaconsfield's idea, but Greenwood's, who was at that time Editor of the 'Pall Mall Gazette,' and on whose staff Hyndman was. Greenwood conceived the plan of the Government buying the shares, and after consulting with his colleagues on the paper went to Lord Derby to suggest it. Derby approved and sent him on to Beaconsfield, who at first was much disinclined, but eventually agreed, giving the job to the Rothschilds, a quite unnecessary waste of commission as the shares could have been bought with Treasury Bonds in the ordinary way. He told me much, too, of his dealings with Lord Salisbury at election times, and about French and German socialism. He stayed two hours with me.

"*20th June* (*Jubilee Sunday*).— The streets decked out with scaffolding and red cloth. London architecture lends itself to these disguisements, as there is nothing to lose by being hidden.

"*21st June*.— Alfred Austin's 'Jubilee Ode' is published in the 'Times,' and as good as a thing of the kind can be, and I have written to tell him so. When he was first made Laureate I did not write, because I really could not have said anything about his poetry that would have pleased him, but to-day I am able to do so with a good conscience. We are old acquaintances of something like forty years' standing, and personally I am pleased at his success.

"*22nd June*.— The Queen's Jubilee Day — the evening and night of which I spent on Chanclebury Down, camped among the thorn bushes near the top of the Ridge, a beautiful but rather hazy evening, quite warm, no moon, little parties of country people out on foot, others in vans, but not enough of them to injure the solitude. At half-past nine rockets began to be fired away at Shoreham, and a light appeared on Leith Hill, then illuminations at Shoreham and Brighton, and precisely at ten bonfires were lit up. I counted ninety-seven of them, and there were probably more, for the clump hid part of the horizon. It was an inspiriting sight, and we tried to make out our own bonfire at Newbuildings, which lies in a straight line between Chanclebury and Leith Hill.

"*26th June*.— The day of the Jubilee Review at Portsmouth. A Jingo apotheosis which contrasts strangely with my recollection of Portsmouth seventeen years ago, when our military and naval glory was at so low an ebb that even I felt humiliated.

"*27th June* (*Sunday*).— I am at Swinford on a visit to Austin. Austin is naïve about his position and dignity as Poet Laureate. He assured me that he had made it a condition in accepting the post that he was not to write Odes to order. I asked him how he had written his Jubilee performance, suggesting that it must have been troublesome

to manage. On the contrary, he told me, he had done it without more
effort than just to fix his mind determinedly and reverently on Her
Majesty, waiting till the inspiration came, 'and (after a pause) it
came.' He showed me a letter from the Queen's private secretary,
thanking him for the verses, and saying that Her Majesty thought
them very pretty, but when he went to present them at Windsor, she did
not ask him to recite them. A letter from Lord Salisbury was in
the same sense; however, Austin is so loyal that he even apologized
for depreciating Victorian architecture. In the afternoon we all sat
talking on the lawn, Lady Paget and Lady Windsor being of the
party, and it was suggested that each of us should give his idea of
Heaven. Mine was to be laid out to sleep in a garden, with running
water near, and so to sleep for a hundred thousand years, then to be
woke by a bird singing, and to call out to the person one loved best,
'Are you there?' and for her to answer, 'Yes, are you?' and so turn
round and go to sleep again for another hundred thousand years.
Austin's idea was to sit also in a garden, and while he sat to receive
constant telegrams announcing alternately a British victory by sea,
and a British victory by land. He talked to us a good deal about Irving, and told us that Irving had begun life as a boy of all work in
the family of a solicitor in Cornwall, where his father and mother
were butler and cook. The solicitor put the boy into his law office as
a junior clerk, but dismissed him because he paid no attention to business, only to play-acting in office hours.

"6th July.— A letter from Joseph Potocki telling the ugly news of
the burning of the Countess Branicka's stud and stables; one hundred
and thirty horses perished, including two colts they bought from us
last year. It is said to be the vengeance of an English groom dismissed
for theft. Her daughter Sophie is engaged to marry Prince Strozzi.

"12th July.— My new room at Newbuildings which I call the 'Jubilee Room' is finished, and looks already part of the old house. It was
built without plan, elevation, or sketch of any kind, Thorpe and I
working it out together as we went on." [The Jubilee Room was
more than a room, being a separate building with two stories. Thorpe,
a plain stone and bricklayer born and bred in the parish, a painstaking,
conscientious man working slowly, but with a complete knowledge of
his trade and its older traditions. The panelling inside was done by
my estate carpenter, Dench.]

"15th July.— The South African committee has published a report,
certainly the most scandalous ever jobbed. It absolves Chamberlain
in these words: 'Neither the Secretary of State for the Colonies nor
any of the officials of the Colonial office received any information
which made or should have made them or any of them aware of the plot
during its development.' It may be noticed that this pronouncement

carefully avoids what undoubtedly happened, namely that Chamberlain's attitude to Rhodes and Beit was practically this: ' Manage the matter your own way, but remember I am to know nothing about it.' Rhodes is condemned publicly in the report, but will be let off all punishment. He will not even be struck off the list of the Queen's Privy Councillors. I hear that the Queen personally assured the Emperor William when the raid happened that none of her Ministers were cognisant of the affair, and this assurance given by the Queen accounts for the strange attitude of Sir William Harcourt and other Radicals on the Committee who have signed the report. The whole of our public life is rotten, and will remain so till we have received a serious defeat in war. The Queen is at the bottom of half the Imperialistic mischief we do abroad. She is pleased at the title of Empress, and likes to enlarge her borders. I should not be at all surprised if she was really in the Jameson affair with her Ministers, indeed this is the best explanation of the extraordinary manœuvres of the Government, and the connivance of the official opposition.

"*24th July.*— Our annual Arab stud sale at Crabbet. Brilliant weather; an immense gathering; 320 persons sat down to lunch; a good many of these, foreigners and colonials; a successful but tiring day.

"*27th July.*— To London and lunched with George, whom I found triumphant over the issue of the debate on South Africa last night. He considers the triumph of the Rhodes group, which is his own triumph, due to superior ability in the Parliamentary management, the skill with which they split the Liberal opposition, the capture of old Harcourt, the forcing of Chamberlain's hand into open support of Rhodes and the bamboozling of the stupid M.P.'s. With regard to Chamberlain, George admires him as the grandest specimen of the courageous, unscrupulous schemer our politics have ever seen. He says that Chamberlain was not an accomplice of the actual armed raid made by Jameson — though he certainly was in the political intrigue — and he (Chamberlain) would not deny it — against the independence of the Transvaal. He described Chamberlain's speech and the menace he (Chamberlain) threw out to Dilke if any one should dare propose the cancelling of Rhodes' position in the Privy Council. Chamberlain did not name Dilke, but his eye, while speaking, travelled along the benches of the Opposition, so that it was clear to all what his meaning was. It was a base threat, and he would certainly have followed it up if the Radicals had dared accept his challenge. George triumphs in all this, but to me it is pitiful to see a young man like him, the heir of all the ages, connecting himself with such a scoundrel crew. The whole Cabinet is now the duumvirate of Balfour and Chamberlain, but I told George he would find one day that Arthur would be the victim of some base trick in order that the other might reign alone."

In August I made a driving tour through the West of England and South Wales. The day before starting I received a letter from Edward Malet breaking the silence of fifteen years. It was very cordial and expressed regret for our troubled relations in the past. I have answered it in a way which I hope may bring about a renewal of our friendship. The occasion of his letter was the discovery among his mother's papers of a number of MS. poems he thought were mine. In reality they were Lothian's as I can see by the handwriting, and also by internal evidence — poems of dates between 1861 and 1864, the time Schomberg and I were most together and most with Lady Malet. I need not give a full account of this journey. We passed through Petworth and Rogate, where I found Hugh Wyndham, just retired from diplomatic work after his forty years' career. Then by Bishop's Waltham to Salisbury and Stockton, stopping for a couple of hours at Wilton on my way. This time I found Sidney, now Lord Pembroke, at home with his family of boys at cricket, much as I found the former generation thirty years ago. " Wilton is the paradise of England with its three rivers, eternally beautiful and unchanged while its owners change and perish. One passes by and finds Herberts living there, happily idling their lives away, as one finds swallows year after year nesting in a village, and one imagines them to be the same Herberts, as one imagines the others to be the same swallows. At Warminster next day I stopped to bait and dined at the ordinary at the Anchor Inn, it being market day among the farmers with whom I talked agriculture and the price of mutton. But when they found I was not there to buy lambs they lost interest in me. I found to my surprise that of the ten farmers dining with me five drank water only, the rest cider. Our meat was roast ducks carved by a chairman at the head of the table, and at one moment I was half afraid they were going to make speeches." I spent my Sunday, 8th August, at Mells, where I found a company of " Souls," then on to Bristol where I put up for the night at an odd place of entertainment called " The Bath," kept by a Dr. Shaw and his wife, a pretty woman, who had been long in India, and who was the attraction evidently of the guests, mostly retired Anglo-Indians, patients as well as guests, as indicated by the menu cards, which were marked with medicines as well as wines. Bristol is the refuge of such broken-down officials, who live at its cheap lodging-houses. The next day, crossing the Severn Channel by the tunnel to Cardiff and St. Fagan's, where I spent the inside of a week delightfully with the Windsors in their romantic castle, which is such a perfect thing, an old Carolan house set in the *enceinte* of an older castle wall, spoilt by nothing modern, the object of my pilgrimage, and back, still driving through the romantic

country of King Arthur and the Knights of the Round Table, Caer-
philly, Caerleon, Chepstow, and the Forest of Dean, where I camped
close to what is called the Devil's Chapel, and thence by Berkeley Castle,
Easton Grey, Broad Hinton, and Savernake, Hurstbourne, Minley, and
so home. It had been a journey of 385 miles, made in nineteen days
with my four Arab mares, not one of which had tired or been off her
feed for a single day, and trotted in gamely, eager to be at home. The
journey had done me good. My journal of this tour is extremely interesting, but once more it is impossible to give it a place here, as it
would lead me too far along the pleasant byways of social life and
away from the prescribed high road of public things.

" *4th Sept.*— For the last three weeks there have been high doings in
India on the Afghan frontier, and to-day expeditions on a large scale
are announced. This is closely connected with our absurd policy at
Constantinople. The position to-day with Russia protecting the Cali-
phate at Constantinople, France in alliance with Russia and Germany
also in the coalition against us, justifies all I wrote and did in Egypt
sixteen years ago. Dined at my club and had some talk with Nicholas
O'Conor who, heaven help us! is now Her Majesty's ambassador to
the Emperor of all the Russias.

" *25th Sept.*— To Saighton, where I find a house full of friends and
acquaintance, Dick Grosvenor, Edward Clifford, Gatty, Henry Milner
and Lady Clifden, etc., with nothing for a vegetarian to eat [Lady
Windsor had persuaded me to become a vegetarian], and I dined off
two mushrooms and a raisin; nevertheless a pleasant evening, George
laying down the law about Shakespeare, Ronsard, Brantôme, and a
number more.

" *27th Sept.*— At Saighton. Played lawn tennis with George.
Spent the evening with him, arguing with some heat the eternal question of the right of savage nations to existence. George, who represents the general sense of modern Imperial England, denies them
any such right at all. I am sick of their arguments from Darwin and
the survival of the fittest.

" *29th Sept.*— Back to London and wrote going up in the train a
piece of verse for Gatty's translations, the hymn beginning:

> If this dark valley of distress and tears
> So green appears.

" *1st Oct.*— Shooting at Newbuildings with Charles Wyndham,
Scrope, and Evershed. Scrope is a nice young Yorkshireman, very
understanding about horses, but in poor health. He gave us a naïve
account of the Jameson raid as narrated to him by his brother, who
took part in it. It seems to have been a regular drunken frolic.
Jameson had up I forget how many wagon-loads of drink the week

before he started, including, I remember, thirty-six cases of champagne which he distributed to his men, with leave to get drunk for three days. There were among the men a number of loafers brought up from Cape Town, some of them waiters from the restaurants, who had never been on horseback before, and the whole force was more or less drunk when it started. Jameson had told off three men to cut the telegraph wires, but they were in such a condition that they mistook a barbed wire fence for the telegraph and cut off a hundred yards of it and carefully buried it instead of the other. When they got near Johannesburg, Jameson could not find the way and picked up Boers to show it them, who of course led them wrong. Scrope's brother and others knew the road but were not listened to. As to drunkenness, I can well believe the story, for I remember how, on a journey in South America in 1868, some English men of the party riding with me took for all provision on the road, a gigantic demi-john of spirits, which they strapped to the back of a horse and drove in front of them."

I left England in October once more for Egypt, still in bad health, indeed in worse, for I had foolishly allowed myself to be persuaded into becoming a vegetarian as well as the teetotaler I had been for fifteen years, and the life at Sheykh Obeyd, delightful to those in health, was too primitive to be suited to an invalid. On board the ship that took us to Alexandria I found Walter Harris, the "Times" correspondent in Morocco, who told me a good deal about his life at Tangiers where he has a garden four miles from the town. He talked also about the war in Thessaly where his brother was killed last summer while helping the Greeks. The Greeks had abandoned the brother when wounded, after robbing him of everything. They had behaved abominably during the war. The Crown Prince of Greece himself told Harris that he had seen the Evzoni throw paraffin on the Turkish wounded and set them on fire.

I found all well at Sheykh Obeyd, except that the desert round us was beginning to be cultivated and enclosed. The day will come when we shall be caught in a network of gardens and country houses, though so far no great harm has been done. People argue with me and say, "But your property must be increasing in value," as if that was any consolation for losing the solitude. Foxes are still plentiful in the garden and I have twice seen a very large wolf, old and grey, who, they tell me, has been here all the summer, frightening the boys who cut the grass for the horses. Salem says the wolf pursued him one evening and tore his shirt and Suliman that he had taken two of his lambs from his tent outside our wall. He comes and howls under our window after nightfall. There are certainly two sorts of wolves here besides jackals, unless, indeed, the intermediate size is a cross between wolf and jackal. Our present guest is of the big desert kind.

" *23rd Nov.*— I have been reading Froissart's ' Chronicles.' He must have lived a happy life, if what his biographers tell of him is true.   The age of chivalry, brutal as it was in its fighting aspect, seems to have been sweetened by a good deal of romance, but to this Froissart hardly alludes, and, tells only of battles and sieges, which were most of them ignoble proceedings.   Edward III's idea of war seems to have been to raid the French towns everywhere, except just where the French army was.   Both Cressy and Poitiers were fought by the English because they could not get away from the pursuing French, and the victory in both cases was won by the skill of the English archers on the one side and foolish generalship on the other.   As a rule, it was only the unarmed fighters on foot that were killed, the knights and squires surrendered to ransom as soon as they were knocked off their horses.   This was all their chivalry of war.

" *26th Nov.*— Sheykh Mohammed Abdu came to see me, and told me the political and court gossip.   The latest is about a trial in which a young man is being prosecuted for insulting and libelling the Khedive in verse.   The true movers in the matter, Abdu assures me are Moharram Pasha Shahin and Sheykh el Bekri in conjunction with Sheykh Abul Huda at Constantinople, and it was done to please the Sultan. Cromer, however, has mixed himself up in it, and in order to obtain a verdict, or rather to screen some persons implicated who are favourable to English policy, has had the Egyptian Procureur of the native courts replaced by Corbet, an Englishman.   The Khedive is still on bad terms with the Sultan, and the poem was written to please his Majesty, but by an unfortunate mistake in the printing, one of the insulting epithets applied to the Khedive is ' Turk,' so that it has given almost equal offence at Yildiz.

" In India, the Afridis I am glad to see are still gallantly maintaining themselves against General Lockhart, and our troops are getting nicely ' punished' in their turn.   It is clear from their accounts that but for the superior fighting qualities of the Sikhs and Ghurkas the white regiments could not be got to continue the campaign.   Lockhart has had to encourage them publicly not to be ' downhearted.'   There is talk in England of conscription for the army, and our people will soon begin to understand that they can't have the amusement of empire without paying the price.   The British Empire is a structure that might crumble at any moment, the sooner the better, say I.

" *29th Nov.*— We have a guest with us, Nasr el Mizrab, nephew of that Mijuel el Mizrab, who was Lady Ellenborough's last husband. He is a well-spoken man and has travelled more than once with Frankish explorers in the Syrian desert, Russians and Germans, buying horses for them of his Anazeh kindred.

" *9th Dec.*— Young John Evelyn has come to stay with us.   His father sent him to me on his way up the Nile, saying that he wished him 'to learn Arabic, to keep a diary, to acquire habits of observation and self-reliance and not to imbibe Jingo principles, also to marry early.' I find the young man excellently disposed to all these things except the last.

"*21st Dec.*— I am starting on Christmas Eve for Jebel Attaka near Suez, as I think I am well enough now for desert travelling. Eid, Suliman's young Howeyti cousin, who travelled with us last March to Siwah, and was so good a desert man, is dead. He had joined in a ghazu in the summer beyond Akabah, and, on his way home, being parched with thirst, drank of a well whose property it is to kill the drinker in fourteen days. He reached home alive, but died soon after.

"*23rd Dec.*— Had an audience with the Khedive and took Walter Harris with me. The talk was principally about the Turco-Greek war, as to which Harris gave us some curious details. The King of Greece himself told him that the reason that he left Vasos in Crete was so as to bring about a blockade of the Piræus. 'I should then,' the King said, 'have been able to tell my people that but for the intervention of the Powers I would have marched with a hundred thousand Greeks to Constantinople. As it turned out, we were not prevented by the Powers and so had to make a war, for which none of us had bargained."

Abbas afterwards told us of his cousin Prince Aziz's attempt to go to Nejd. The Prince had got as far as Sherm, a small port in the Sinai Peninsula, intending to cross over from there to Moelhi, and then on to visit Ibn Rashid, but the Khedive had stopped him by telegram. He was afraid of being compromised in Constantinople by the visit, and was also unwilling that so light-headed a member of the Khedivial family should be the first to visit Nejd after the conquests of old days. Aziz is now at Nakhl, where he is being detained by the Egyptian governor of the fort.

"Lunched with Rennell Rodd, and called afterwards on Riaz Pasha and on Gorst. Harris was to have started with me to-morrow on my desert trip, but has been prevented."

The desert trip was a bit of exploration connected with a map I was making of the country between Cairo and the Red Sea. I returned from it on the last day of the year.

"*12th Jan.* 1898.— News has come of the death of Mohammed Ibn Rashid at Haïl, 'in his bed,' they say after a seven days' illness. If truly in his bed, he may rank as one of the most uniformly successful of Arabian monarchs. For five and twenty years he has reigned in Nejd, warring every spring upon his neighbours and always victoriously. He has not once been defeated in the field, and has reduced every tribe in succession to his obedience. His only misfortune has been that he has left no son, and his inheritance will probably be disputed between

Abdul Hamid, son of Hamoud, his first cousin once removed, and Hamoud Mattaab, his nephew. Both, they say, claim 'the seat,' and are appealing to Constantinople for support. This may bring the Turk into Nejd, for the Sultan was never so powerful in the desert as now. Still, it is a far cry to Haïl.

" The Soudan campaign is being pushed on, and British soldiers are being sent up the Nile, on a pretext of defence against an attack by the Khalifa. How anybody can be green enough to believe these official tales I cannot understand. The true reason is the advance of the French expedition [under Marchand] to the Upper Nile at Fashoda, and so the desire to be beforehand with them at Khartoum. The sending of British troops is not at all because they are needed, for our English regiments are inferior in every way to the Egyptian ones for such work, but to gratify the English Government, and especially the Queen, who considers the glory of her reign tarnished by the death of Gordon and who wants it avenged. If Egyptian troops alone recaptured Khartoum it would be a reproach to the British army, which was defeated in its attempts to relieve Gordon there. They like, too, to be able to say that the British military Occupation is necessary to Egypt for its frontier defence — only another false excuse in the long list of false excuses for staying in Egypt begun twenty years ago.

" *21st January.*— Gorst and his two sisters and Captain Fitzclarence lunched with us. Gorst has given me a list of the people reported to have been killed at Siwah on the 20th April of last year in a local fight. It includes several of my friends there, including Hassuna, but I feel sceptical about the whole story.

" *22nd January.*— A visit from Cogordan, the French Minister here. We talked about the Soudan expedition. He tells me Kitchener will be in command of forty thousand troops including those recently taken over from the Italians at Kassala, and the ten thousand English who were in Egypt. Of the Marchand expedition he disclaimed its importance, and laughted at the talk that a French flag will be found flying at Khartoum.

" *26th January.*— Old Charles Villiers is dead, the father of the House of Commons. I remember him at Frankfort as long ago as the winter of 1860–61, dining at our Legation with the Malets. He impressed me at the time as the most wonderful and delightful talker I had listened to. He seemed to take an interest in me too, and drew me out till I talked a deal of boyish nonsense. The recollection of his wit and charm is strong with me still."

Here follows another six days' journey in the Eastern desert on *deluls,* travelling fast and map-making as we went, as I was anxious to complete my survey of the country north of the Kalala range. It was bitter cold on the upper plateaux, and the hard life nearly finished me, and hastened my return to England.

" 15*th February*.— The papers report the Queen's speech on the opening of Parliament. It contains, perhaps, more than the usual number of insincerities. Politics in England are in a hopeless condition, and will remain so until the Empire begins to break up, when it will be too late to say or do anything. I shall not be sorry if I live to see it. The British Empire has done so much harm to so many nations and peoples that it deserves to perish, and we English will be better off as a Nation shorn of our dependencies than now. It will hurt our pride, but injure no true interest.

" Prince Osman is dead. He was riding to the Pyramids on his camel, and fell off suddenly ; they say apoplexy. He was the cleverest and most amusing of the Khedivial family, if not the most reputable ; a brother of Princess Nazli, and first cousin, once removed, of the Khedive. He had been brought up at Paris, and was always a bit of a *boulevardier,* very pleasant and good-natured, and with an extraordinary knowledge of the events, political and social, of his time, a fat Falstaff in appearance, but like the others of the Khedivial family, with a certain bodily hardihood and endurance on camel back ; my oldest friend among them, and I am sorry to lose him.

" 25*th February*.— Anne and Judith lunched a few days ago with Bill Gordon, who told them that the real reason for his uncle's resigning his post as private secretary to Lord Ripon in India was as follows. When Ripon was appointed to India it was resolved by the Cabinet that he should break up the gang of permanent officials who form the Simla ring, and it was on this understanding that Gordon accepted the post. A special point to be attacked was the treatment of Ayub Khan (the Emir of Afghanistan) as to which Government had evidence showing our English officials to have acted unjustly and tyrannically. Gordon had drawn up a special memoir on the subject which was to be acted on immediately upon Ripon's landing at Bombay, but Ripon was no sooner on shore than the officials got hold of him and persuaded him to let the matter rest. Gordon, upon this, threw up the appointment, for he saw his chief was too weak to carry the policy through. A Viceroy of India needs to be a man of iron to hold his own and Ripon was every good thing except that.

" There is talk of Cromer's going to the Foreign Office. What the Tories want now is a strong man to carry out their policy of violence, and Cromer will suit them. I care little how things go, for the time of reasoning is past. There will be no change till the Empire breaks up and Cromer may as well sit on the Imperial safety valve as another. I had a long talk to-day with Mohammed Abdu about this and other matters.

" In Paris Zola has been condemned to a year's imprisonment for bringing forward the Dreyfus case. This is an event of great significance, for it means that in France as in Germany and Russia, militarism reigns supreme. It will be so in England, too, before many years are over, and then good-bye to liberty of any kind. If the nations of Europe will only cut each other's throats in a Thirty Years' War there might be some hope for the world, but they are too cowardly for that. All they dare do is to swagger hideously, and talk about their honour. It will be with them as it is with the Spaniards who are ruled by military pronunciamentos. With regard to the Dreyfus case, when I was at Gros Bois last autumn, I asked Wagram the truth of it. He told me that it was to please the Austrian Government that the case had been tried privately, that justly or unjustly condemned, Dreyfus was an *affreux canaille,* and had made some confession of guilt, but I see little difference in point of canailledom between these wretched military spies and their wretched military superiors, who employ and pay them. Spying, whether by a paid agent or a paying agent, demoralises those that indulge in it, and the military code of to-day recognizes every treachery and every baseness as lawful. What nonsense to talk about military honour! There is no such thing. Can one conceive any greater blackguard than the *soi-disant* Esterhazy unless it be his military backers, Pellieux and the rest? On our side the Channel, too, we have some pretty blackguards to show lately.

" *9th March.*— Left for England. Mohammed Abdu came to wish me good-bye. I was suffering with great pain so that I felt almost dying. Two years ago under like circumstances I should have made him my profession of faith, but to-day no, though I was moved at parting with him as though I were saying last words to a dearest friend, but I feel now there is no reality in it all. The Moslems of to-day who believe are mere wild beasts like the men of Siwah, the rest have lost their faith. Still less does Christianity appeal to me. I do not wish to live again. I only wish for the extinction of the grave. I am going home alone, Anne staying on for another six weeks in Egypt. I have telegraphed to my servant, David, to meet me at Venice and see me slowly home. My sole idea now is to be for a week with George in Mount Street, and then to be nursed by Cowie at Newbuildings. It was fortunately quite calm weather on my voyage up the Adriatic, and at Venice I found an invitation waiting me from Lady Paget at Bellosguardo in Florence where I stayed two nights, and then on, arriving in London on the 23rd March, where I found George Wyndham established in my rooms in Mount Street, which I had lent him; there was room for us both there, and his cheerful influence did me good.

"*24th March.*— George is taking a less practical part now in politics, being up to his eyes in literature, but he walks home most nights with Arthur Balfour from the House and hears a good deal of what is going on. He tells me Lord Salisbury does not intend resigning, and though he has made over the Foreign Office temporarily to Balfour, he still keeps interfering with affairs there not altogether to Arthur's pleasure. In talking about the scramble for China, I had remarked that I should have thought an alliance with Japan was the obvious English policy. He said, ' Yes, but it looks as if Japan had been squared by Russia.' [This is the first mention I can find in my diary of what was afterwards to develop into the Anglo-Japanese alliance.]

"George's new edition of Shákespeare's poems is just out, and he is busy editing a new weekly paper, ' The Outlook,' started as a ' raft ' on which to save the fortunes of Henley and the other writers wrecked in the ' New Review.' Gladstone is dying of cancer, poor old soul, and it has been agreed to soothe his last days with morphia as he cannot live long.

"*29th March.*— Lady Gregory came to see me and talked much about Ireland. She has now become a strong Nationalist, and has been busying herself about the demonstrations for ' '98.' If I were well enough I would go over for them in May.

"George is much put out at the inaction of our Government in China, where there is a combination of Russia, France, and Germany against us, and at the general failure of Lord Salisbury's policy as a check to the British Empire. He asked me why I wished ill to the British Empire. I said, ' because we had done too much harm in the world, and though the other nations of Europe also do harm, they are not able to do it so effectively as we do through their lack of knowledge, and of those qualities that make of Englishmen an administrating race, also because the *Empire* is a poor cockney affair invented hardly twenty years ago to the ruin of our position as an honest *Kingdom* at home.' I remember well the disgust of George's father and of other old-fashioned Tories, when Disraeli first foisted on them the Queen's brummagem Imperial title.'

"*31st March.*—' The Chronicle ' has a sensational but probably true account of an ultimatum sent by the American President to Spain on account of Cuba. It seems likely to lead to war. If so I hope that Spain may be able to hold her own, not that Cuban independence lacks my sympathy, but because between Spain and the United States I am obliged to be on the side of the older and more barbarous country. The Yankees as the coming race of the world would be worse even than ourselves.

"*1st April.*— At five to-day Lady Gregory brought me the poet Yeats, an Irish mystic of an interesting type. He is tall, lean, dark, good looking, of the same type of countenance as John Dillon's, very narrow between the eyes and short-sighted. We talked much about the ''98' demonstrationes of which he is organizer, and of the coming doom of England, and we talked also of another mystical poet and patriot, Russell, (A. E.), with whom Yeats was a fellow student at Dublin. Russell, in order to subdue his will, became cashier in a haberdasher's shop, where he acquired repute as an accountant, but always spent his Sundays and holidays in the Wicklow Hills, writing poetry and seeing visions. Russell has now been removed to a higher sphere as political organizer. Both believe in ghosts and fairies and in the transmigration of souls, and have magic powers of seeing the future and of prophecy.

"Yeats experimented magically on me. He first took out a note-book and made what he called a pyramid in it which was a square of figures, then he bade me think of and see a square of yellow as it might be a door, and walk through it and tell him what I saw beyond. All that I could see at all clearly was that I seemed to be standing on a piece of green, rushy grass, in front of me a small pool from which issued two streams of very blue water to right and to left of me. He then bade me turn and go back through the door, and told me I should see either a man or woman who would give me something. I failed to see anything but darkness, but at last with some effort I made out the indistinct figure of a child, which offered me with its left hand some withered flowers. I could not see its face. Lastly he bade me thank the person to whose intervention the vision was due, and read from his notebook some vague sentences prefiguring this vision. The performance was very imperfect, not to say null.

"*5th April.*— Arthur Balfour made his statement in the House to-day of the Government's China policy. George tells me the speech was 'statesmanlike,' but I gather from him that it was no very pronounced success. Indeed, how should it be? The British Government has leased Wei-hai-wei, which seems to be a sort of second best to Port Arthur, but of no very practical value for coercing Pekin as it cannot easily be connected with it by land. I should have thought it would have been wiser either to make an alliance with Japan and war with Russia, or else to let the whole thing severely alone, but George thinks Japan has already been squared by Russia.

"*6th April.*— I had a bad return of pain which lasted all night until twelve to-day when I took an infinitesimal dose of morphia, which at once stopped it and raised me from the depths of misery to the state of happiness of a schoolboy just loosed from school.

"*9th April.*— There is an announcement in the papers of 'A great British victory in the Soudan — Gordon avenged.'

"*11th April.*— Saighton. I came here for the Easter holiday, arriving in a miserable plight of pain, but to-morrow Sibell (Lady Grosvenor) is to take me to Holywell to be bathed by the miraculous fountain there for my cure. Some Vandals, calling themselves the Town Council, are claiming the well which they want to let to a soda water company at £500 a year, but George intends to oppose this in Parliament. There is nobody here but the family, including little Percy and Bendor, the latter grown into a very nice young man. George has been entertaining Mr. Cecil Rhodes at my rooms in Mount Street while I was away, using them, I fancy, as a place of secret communication between the Government and Rhodes, whom they dare not publicly avow.

"I see the old Tichborne claimant is dead, asserting his rights to the last. Certainly there was something about the man not wholly vulgar. I saw a good deal of him at Buenos Ayres in 1868, and, though a mountain of flesh and of no very refined clay, he seemed to me a gentleman born, gone down in the world, rather than a mere plebeian. Richard Burton, who was there at the same time, and who travelled across the Pampas with him in the Mendoza diligence, believed in him as authentic at the time, and so we all did. I remember seeing him once involved in some vulgar dispute in a café, while playing billiards, and he seemed to me to behave as a gentleman would have done under somewhat trying circumstances, and now they have buried him with considerable pomp and a coffin plate recording his baronetcy, attended by the licensed victuallers who supported him as a show in his last days.

"*12th April.*— I have been to St. Winifred's well at Holywell. After a very bad night of pain I nevertheless made up my mind not to put off the visit. Fortified with a dose of morphia I set out with Sibell and George. We went by train from Chester, passing not far from Hawarden, where the G.O.M. lies dying, and the sands of Dee. We were fortunate in our day, which, though wild at starting, turned into a perfect spring afternoon. Sibell had written to Father Beauclerk, the Jesuit at Holywell, to expect us, but he was away. I was glad of it, as thus I was free to bathe as a plain pilgrim without religious supervision. I suppose no pilgrim ever washed there with less Christian faith and at the same time with so little of the mocking spirit. I have a belief in holy places and holy people quite apart from all religious creeds, and I felt a great confidence in the Saint that she would do me good. We arrived at the best moment of the day, at one o'clock when everybody was away at dinner, so that we were alone and there was no difficulty in that sweet old place in supposing ourselves back in the fifteenth century. The girl in charge of the gate gave me two towels, and I had brought a nightgown with me, and so plunged in. It was cold work, though the water, they say, is 52

degrees, but I did the traditional three journeys through the water up
to my armpits, going down into it by steps and up the opposite side,
and then took a complete dip over my head in the outer tank and knelt
on St. Bruno's stone.   I was quite alone while doing this, except for
George.   Then, when I had dressed, we sat awhile together in the
sun, and went on to the inn for luncheon, where Sibell was, and so
home in the afternoon to Saighton.   The buildings of the well are
still almost perfect, the shrine just as it was put up in Henry VII's
time, not a stone of the pavement renewed nor anything of the modern
kind except some wooden dressing sheds and a few stupid scrolls with
texts hung up inside the shrine.

" 13*th April.*— I have had no pain all day, thanks to St. Winifred,
a long night of sleep and to-day no pain.   I spent the afternoon with
Sibell, talking about the chances of life and death and of a world beyond.   The longer I live, the less I believe in any such, at least as
far as my own living again goes.   I feel that I have worn out my vital
force and that eternity can bring me nothing but a dreamless sleep.
All the same, I believe in St. Winifred and her Well, and include her
in my canon prayer as my patron saint, which I have a right to do,
seeing that I was named after my great-grandmother, Winifred
Scawen."

My miraculous cure thus wrought did not last long.   I had no sooner
turned my back to St. Winifred and Saighton than my pains began
again, and I began to think that the Saint had made a fool of me.   I
saw new doctors in London, but they were unable to help me, and
after lingering on there until the 6th of May I went down to Newbuildings to bear my troubles alone.   " The world," I wrote, " is only
meant for those who are in health, and the maxim of our forefathers
was a sound one, that a dying man should keep wholly out of sight."
This was the last entry in my diary before the crisis came.   On the
following Sunday, after a night of great suffering, I broke a blood-
vessel, and for a week or more lay in danger of death, nursed by the
careful hands of the good Cowie, our housekeeper, and of Sydney
Cockerell, who had just entered on his duties with me as my private
secretary.   Between them and my hospital nurse, Miss Lawrence, who
then first undertook my charge, they saved my life.   Then I recognized
that St. Winifred had only deferred her benefits, and that, as in the
case of most miracles, she had chosen a natural road of cure.   However that might be, the cure, though it nearly killed me, was an in-
disputable one.   The pain from which I had been suffering so long
had left me desperately weak, it is true, in body but clear in mind,
and able once more to take an interest in life, and at the end of three
weeks to resume my diary.   The first entry I find in it contains the
following:

"*28th May.*— To-day Mr. Gladstone is being buried in Westminster Abbey.

"*6th June.*— Cockerell is a treasure, arranging my books and getting me others. He is full of interesting recollections of Morris. *Apropos* of the lovely little Kelmscott volume, containing ' The Nightingale and the Cuckoo,' he assures me that Morris had never heard the nightingale sing, and that he used to complain of it; also what seems even more incredible, that he had not read the poem through, and was waiting to do so for it to be in print. The proof-sheets came the day he died, and he never read them. We are putting the new bookplate into our Kelmscott books, where it looks a natural part of the volumes as the bookplate was cut by the man Morris employed for his armorial designs. Cockerell has been of the greatest use to me, arranging my papers and giving me new interests in life. I have written several Sonnets and an inscription in verse for the table Mrs. Morris gave me; my mind is vigorous and clear." [The table here referred to was the dining-table used by Morris and his family when they lived at the Red House, and given to me by Mrs. Morris when she was dispersing her furniture on leaving her house in Hammersmith.]

In the meantime Anne and Judith had returned from Egypt. They had been lingering on at Paris, but had been hastened back by my illness, and were now in London, having taken a house there for Judith's London season.

"*19th June.*— Burne-Jones is dead. This is a vast misfortune. He was to have painted Judith as one of the figures for his last picture, ' The Vale of Avalon,' but that will never now be. According to his wish he is to be cremated, and then buried at Rottingdean. It is an honour for Sussex that it should hold his ashes.

"*5th July.*— Percy Wyndham, who has been down to see me, tells me that he had spent the afternoon with Burne-Jones two days before he died. Burne-Jones was in the highest possible spirits, playing at ' Bear ' with Pamela's children. Later, however, a friend had dined with him, to whom he had talked gloomily of the prospects of the world and of the human race. The friend had remarked that no one should have such pessimistic views who was not an atheist. To which Burne-Jones had exclaimed, ' Thank God, we are not that.' He had been taken ill suddenly in the night, and had died in half-an-hour. With Madeline, too, I have had much conversation about Burne-Jones. She had written me a beautiful letter about him and Morris, and had asked me to write a sonnet for her about them. ' I should like it better,' she says in it, ' than anything else you could possibly do for me, and you are the only person almost who could, if even you can, and I will wait no matter how long for it, and if I depart from this life from pure old age while waiting, well, I shall hope that then I shall be even better able to appreciate it in my future and next development than now. But, for the sake of the world, a sonnet, something beautiful about them, ought to be written. Such writings act as beautiful reflectors to the divine light (that immortals such as those two were) have left to the world, in the beauty of their work, it directs the eyes of those that knew them not, to see and know them, for the world in some ways is so dark that even the Divine Light needs a reflector or glasses to guide the eyes, the spiritual eyes, darkened eyes I had rather say, for it is the darkened eyes in the human race, not the darkened world that prevents them seeing and knowing the glorious divine light and beauty that is in this world, only few see it, either in Nature or Art. Some are blind, hopelessly blind, others have films on their eyes, but they can be removed. At first they only see trees as men walking, but finally they can see, see and so live, but they at first require glasses and reflectors, and artificial means of help, and, to my mind, Poetry can be and is the art of all others that helps us most in this world to see. Each divine art acts as a guide and reflector to the other; Poetry helps Music, Music Poetry, both cast light and concentrate it on the other arts.' This suggested the sonnet I have since published, and which begins; ' Mad are we all, maids, men, young fools alike and old.'

"*15th July.*—Wotton. I find Evelyn with strong Spanish sympathies in the war that is going on, on the same grounds with mine. The papers announce the news of the surrender of Santiago de Cuba on honourable terms, and there is great talk of peace being made, but I doubt its being near. Spain has less to lose than America by going on with the war, her colonies being practically already gone, and Europe being almost certain to prevent a Yankee invasion of Spain. The financiers who inspire the Press call out however, for it, and would have it made at any price, as it is injuring trade.

"*2nd August.*—Bismarck is dead. My only personal recollection of him is of meeting him at old Lord Brougham's in Grafton Street. Lady Malet, who was Brougham's stepdaughter, some say his natural daughter, asked me to tea alone, to meet him, and he came and stopped talking with us very pleasantly for an hour. He had been an old admirer of Lady Malet's when they had been together diplomatically at Frankfort, and they were still on very intimate terms. This may have been in 1862. My memory of him is of a tall rather thin man, with agreeable manners, and talking English perfectly. At that time somewhat of an Anglomane, he was still unrecognized by the general public of Europe as a great statesman. Indeed, he was laughed at in Germany for his reactionary, out-of-date opinions, and was not a little unpopular with the masses. If he had failed to win at Sadowa, he would certainly have been torn to pieces by the Berlin mob. Lady Malet had always the fullest faith in his genius.

"*9th September.*— On Monday the 6th news came of the defeat of the Khalifa and the taking of Omdurman, and with it of Hubert Howard's death, my only friend there and almost the only one on our side to lose his life. The slaughter of the Dervishes seems to have been premeditated and ruthlessly carried out. When I was at Bramber the other day Button told me that 'a heavy butcher's bill' had been ordered, as it was intended to make the avenging of Gordon a chief feature of the business. Telegraphic communication with England was on this account stopped (the excuse being that the wires had been broken by a storm) lest any order of moderation should come, and as far as I can read the despatches since received, there must have been a wholesale massacre of the wounded and fugitives. The figures given to-day are ten thousand counted corpses, sixteen thousand wounded, who have crawled away to the river or the desert, and three hundred or four hundred more killed in the town of Omdurman after the fight, and only three thousand to four thousand prisoners!!! As Button told me, 'the performances of Tommy Atkins in the way of killing at At-bara (a few days before the fight at Omdurman), passed everything ever heard of. He was like a raging wild beast.' One may be pretty sure that orders were given to spare none.

"All this has moved my bile to the point that I have written in pro-test to the 'Times,' but I doubt if they will print my letter. The whole country, if one may judge by the Press, has gone mad with the lust of fighting glory, and there is no moral sense left in England to which to appeal. It is hideous but unmistakable.

"Hubert's death is pitiful. There was nothing in the world to take him there, for he was not in the army, nothing but a boyish whim. He dined with Anne and Judith in London almost the night before he started, and told them he was determined to fight. He was a delightful boy, with a ringing, merry laugh it did one good to hear, and he had considerable abilities, and the best of hearts, and he ends in a blind alley of Omdurman a paid servant of the 'Times.'

"*10th September.*— My letter to the 'Times' is printed, which is more than I expected. I am curious to see whether it raises an echo anywhere, but as yet no voice has spoken in any London paper, except that Miss Gordon protests in her brother's name against his being 'revenged.' A queer Christian country ours! On the other hand there has been an outbreak in Crete, a Moslem mob has risen against a party of English marines sent by the Admiral to raise the custom dues, and some have been killed, and the British Vice-Consulate has been burnt, and Cretan Christians massacred, Edhem Pasha and the Turkish garrison looking on."

One characteristic letter was written to me at this time, apparently by a parson; it says, "By a curious coincidence an answer to your let-

ter in the 'Times' of yesterday is given in one of the Psalms for this
morning's service, viz., Psalm lviii, verses 10–11: 'The righteous
shall rejoice when he seeth the vengeance; he shall wash his footsteps
in the blood of the ungodly, so that a man shall say, Verily, there is a
reward for the righteous, doubtless there is a God that judgeth the
earth." A more important letter, however, was to follow from no less
a personage than Herbert Spencer. Spencer was not at the time known
to me personally, nor had I at that time ranked myself among his disciples, and the letter came to me as a surprise. It reached me 4th
October.

"*4th Oct.*— A most interesting letter has come to me from Herbert
Spencer on the subject of my letter about Omdurman, and mentioning
also an article on my poem, 'The Wind and the Whirlwind.' [This
article, I afterwards learned, was by Francis Thompson.] Spencer
has long looked out, he says, for a poet who should write a poem, the
main lines of which he sketches in his letter and he asks me to undertake
it. (It was to be a dialogue in Heaven after the manner of Goethe's
'Faust,' between God and Satan. Satan complaining that mankind has
surpassed him in wickedness, sacrificing to Thor and Odin while
nominally sacrificing to Jehovah.) I wish I could think myself capable
of doing this with any effect, but I am too hopeless of getting such a
subject listened to at the present moment and too little believing in the
divine government of the world."

This led to a correspondence between me and the philosopher and
eventually to my undertaking to write a poem, " Satan Absolved," more
or less on the lines suggested. In a second letter, dated 6th October,
Spencer writes: " My beliefs are pretty much as pessimistic as those
you express. . . . Did I think that men would remain in the far future
anything like what they now are I should contemplate with equanimity
the sweeping away of the whole human race." [For the first letter see
Appendix III.]

"*12th Oct.*— A visit from Mrs. Meynell and her husband, and
Francis Thompson at Newbuildings. I had invited them to come for
the night, but Meynell had explained that this was impossible, 'the poet
(Thompson), having an inconvenient habit of setting his bed on fire.'
They came down, however, for the day. I met them at the station, a
very lovely day, and as we drove through the woods Meynell pointed
out to me that 'the poet of nature' was wholly absorbed in the 'Globe'
newspaper he had brought down with him in the train, such being the
way with London poets. Thompson, though born in Lancashire and
speaking English with a broad provincial accent, is a true Cockney.
He is a little weak-eyed, red-nosed young man of the degenerate London type, with a complete absence of virility and a look of raptured
dependence on Mrs. Meynell which is most touching. He is very shy,

but was able to talk a little when the general conversation was not too loud, and he seems good-hearted and quite unpretending. He has written no poetry, Meynell tells me, now for some years, being cured of his morphia. But Meynell thinks the fountain may some day break forth again. Meanwhile, he gets a living by literary criticism in the ' Academy ' and other journals. When we all went out after luncheon to the woods, I found him quite ignorant of the names of the commonest trees, even the elm, which he must have seen every day in London. I pointed one out to him, and he said, ' I think, a maple.' On the whole, however, I liked him, for he was quite simple and straightforward. Only, it was difficult to think of him as capable of any kind of strength in rhyme or prose. Meynell has greatly improved conversationally with years, and has become a most agreeable man. Thanks to him, the visit was a pleasant one and they all went home in spirits.

" 15*th* Oct.— All this week has been one of excitement over the quarrel with France about Fashoda. A Blue Book has been published giving the English case, and, imperial plunder being in question, all parties, Tories, Whig, Radical, Churchmen, and Nonconformist have joined in publicly extolling English virtue and denouncing the French. For myself I see nothing in it more respectable than the wrangle of two highwaymen over a captured purse, morally both sides are on a level. The English position in the case is that there has long been a scheme of appropriating the Soudan with all the Upper Nile to the Lakes — this, in anticipation of the event which must some day happen, of the British occupation of Egypt proper coming to an end, through European intervention. The scheme has so far been disguised, and whenever objection has been raised, the Egyptian claim to the old Soudan provinces has been put forward and, as we have seen, the Egyptian army has been made use of to do the rough work of re-conquest, only now and then have there been indications given of the truth. In the present Blue Book there is one where Lord Salisbury instructs Monson to declare at Paris that ' By the military events of last week all the territories which were subject to the Khalifa passed, *by right of conquest,* to the British and Egyptian Government.' Yet all the *gobemouche* press is ringing the changes on our ' legality.' And what a strange plea of legality as towards Egypt! What would be said in private life if a guardian and trustee who had undertaken to manage the estate of a minor, as we forced the Egyptian Government in 1884 to abandon the Soudan and leave it derelict, and then, the opportunity having occurred, should take possession of those derelict farms as belonging to nobody and should do this with the approval of the whole world, moral and religious! Yesterday, there was a great public meeting in favour of universal peace, and our leading Nonconformists on the platform applauded Lord Salisbury for having thus swindled Egypt and defied France. We live in an odd age.

"Judith's engagement to Neville Lytton was announced to-day.

"*16th Oct.*— I think very seriously of the crisis between England and France. It will likely enough lead to a war, for both sides being in the wrong each naturally sees the other's wickedness and so believes itself right. The best road to an agreement between them would be that each should give up its preposterous claim to the Nile Provinces. Lord Salisbury, among his many reasons for renewing the Soudan campaign three years ago, said that the destruction of the Khalifa's power would make it easier for England to evacuate Egypt. Let him keep that part of his programme and France will be satisfied. Our people, however, want war, fancying it is a favourable moment for dealing single-handed with France. I hope we shall not be invaded in Sussex.

"*17th Oct.*— To Saighton. Things look very warlike with France, and war would certainly happen if the position in Europe were at all less unfavourable to the French, but as it is their Government will certainly not risk a fight if they can help it. The danger lies in the weakness of their Government, in the long discredit into which France has fallen, and in the ascendancy of the army. There may be a revolution any day and representatives of the Bourbons and of the Bonapartes are announced as being on the frontier.

"Arrived at Saighton. I have had it out with George about Fashoda. He states the English case with brutal frankness. ' The day of talking,' he says, ' about legality in Africa is over, all the international law there is there consists of interests and understandings. It is generally agreed by all the Powers that the end of African operations is to " civilize " it in the interests of Europe, and that to gain that end all means are good. The only difference between England and France is which of them is to do it in which particular districts. England intends to do it on the Nile, and it makes no difference what the precise legal position is. We may put forward the Khedive's rights if it is convenient or we may put forward a right of conquest, or a right of simply declaring our intentions. One is as good as another to get our end, which is the railway from Cairo to the Cape. We don't care whether the Nile is called English or Egyptian or what it is called, but we mean to have it and we don't mean the French to have it. The Khedive may be kept on for some years as a sort of Indian Maharajah, but it will end in a partition of the Ottoman Empire between England, Germany, and Russia, France will be allowed North-western Africa. It is not worth while drawing distinctions of right and wrong in the matter, it is a matter entirely of interest.'

" This of course is the true thought of our Government, and has been for at least ten years, but for the first time to-day it is beginning to be avowed. George represents all that is most extreme, most outrageous, in modern English politics, and it marks the decline of the higher traditions to find one like him proclaiming and defending it. I shall not write again to the ' Times,' I should only mar the effect of my last letter, which has certainly been great, and do no good. The dispute between France and England is a dispute between rival card sharpers, and the very best thing that can happen is that they should beat in each other's heads.

" 18*th Oct*.— Worked all the morning at ' Satan in Heaven ' [' Satan Absolved ']. George has gone up to London.

" 19*th Oct*.— Made my pilgrimage of thanksgiving to Holywell in drizzle and fog, taking my nurse, Miss Lawrence, with me, and my crutches, which I deposited at the Shrine, bound up with a nightgown and a label thus inscribed :

" ' Set here in thankful token of a cure from long sickness after bathing in St. Winifred's Well. By her servant W. S. B. October 19, 1898.'

" The scene inside the shrine was the most interesting I ever saw in Europe. Three men were being passed through the water stark naked, but for a slight bathing drawer round the loins, and each time after passing they knelt on the pavement, dripping wet and prayed aloud. A priest was reciting ' Hail Marys,' and at the end of each ' Hail Mary,' ' Holy Winifred, still in an unbelieving age, miraculous.' There were lighted candles and flowers, and the fervour of these naked men, one a mere bag of skin and bones, was tremendous. In the dim light of a foggy day nothing at all congruous to the nineteenth century was visible. It was a thing wholly of the middle ages, the dark ages, the darkest of the dark ages, magnificent, touching — it brought tears to my eyes. I hung up my crutches in a corner with other relics, and placed Sibell's flowers which she had sent as a thank offering on the altar, and knelt for some ten minutes reciting the Penitential Psalms.

" Outside the shrine I found Father Beauclerk, a young, good-looking Jesuit, but deaf and afflicted with some ailment, perhaps paralytic. He told me that the Town Council of Holywell was about to try its power of closing the Well, and so of preventing the bathing, which has gone on here precisely as it is to-day since the rebuilding of the Shrine in the reign of Henry VII, and doubtless for many hundred years before it. The true legal ownership of the water seems in doubt. The Duke of Westminster is Lord of the Manor, and granted some thirty years ago a long lease to the Town Council, but by some accident never signed it. The Town Council in its turn leased it to the Jesuits, who put up a railing and established a charge of twopence a head for maintenance of the place. This charge the Town Council holds to have barred the free access of the public to the water. Otherwise the public right would seem absolutely clear. Certainly no bather has been refused admission since before the Norman Conquest. Father Beauclerk took me to see one Lambert, an innkeeper, who gave me further particulars, and who agreed if guaranteed in costs to contest the matter as a Holywell rate-payer and habitual bather. He tells me religious feud is at the bottom of the mischief. Father Beauclerk has been imprudent in making use of the Well for purposes of conversion, and in running it as a religious show. This has enraged the Nonconformists, who have determined to put down the pilgrimage as a Popish nuisance. In order more completely to desecrate the Shrine they propose to lease it to a Soda Water Company at £500 a year, and close the Well on a plea of sanitation. Lambert himself is a Protestant, but having been cured of sciatica by bathing there, is a partisan of the Well. As an innkeeper, too, his interests are affected, for the town depends largely on pilgrims for its prosperity. It is clear that steps must at once be taken to save the Shrine, and I gave Father Beauclerk a cheque for £20 towards legal expenses. He seems, however, to be sadly unpractical, and we must put the conduct of the case into other hands.

"*20th Oct.*—.Back to London, where I saw Treherne, the Anti-Scrape lawyer, about St. Winifred's, and also Cockerell. In the evening a telegram came from George to say that the Duke of Westminster would take action in the matter, so that relieves us of a great difficulty."

CHAPTER XIV

"SATAN ABSOLVED"— THE BOER WAR

" George is in high spirits, as he has just been appointed Under-Secretary for War, a less interesting place than the Foreign Office, but still important, especially at the present moment. Things look more and more warlike, as Russia seems to be backing France, and I suspect most of the Continental Powers are against us. It is impossible Lord Salisbury should maintain the full ground he has chosen, that of refusing to negotiate without a war. The French will not give in like that. The way out of the mess would seem to lie in the direction of a European Congress, or at least of European intervention in the interests of peace. George says that the British fleet has its programme ready, and the French fleet would be shut up in their ports in a few days. He and the ultra Jingo section of the party are all for war. He gets £1,500 a year by this appointment.

" *22nd Oct.*— To Paris, by Newhaven and Dieppe, much the pleasantest route. I have not travelled by it since I landed at Newhaven in a storm with a shipload of frightened refugees flying from Paris after Sedan.

" *23rd Oct.*— Neville came to breakfast with me, and later old Julienne, Francis Currie's *bonne,* who amused us with her view of the political situation. The government of France, she said, was in the hands of ' un tas de gueux, passez-moi le mot,' who were pillaging the country, and there must be a new *régime* — Orleanist, Bonapartist, or what ever else, she did not care, so long as it was not Dreyfusist. As to the Fashoda trouble, it was all the rapacity of ' la grosse Victoire,' meaning our own gracious Majesty, who wanted all the earth for herself and would leave nothing to poor France. ' Nous sommes bien bas, allez.' I fancy this represents pretty fairly the general opinion at Paris.

" At 3 to Gros Bois, where I found our hostess entertaining two Parisian ladies, dressed up like Parisian dolls, a ci-devant Russian beauty, the Comtesse de Talleyrand, and Mme. Chevreau, her neighbours. We were a party of six at dinner, lively in the usual French way, which means all talking at once. I had some quiet conversation, however, with Wagram before the guests arrived. He refuses to believe in a war and thinks the thing will be arranged. Russia, if it came

to war, would fight too, and we should be attacked in India. I see that
Redmond is openly declaring himself at Dublin in favour of the French,
but I doubt if either Ireland or India is really attackable.

"*24th Oct.*— Wagram was away all day shooting at Chantilly with
the Duc de Chartres.   Prince Henri d'Orléans was there and showed
him a number of abusive letters he had received, mostly from Germans, in connection with the Dreyfus case, he being a violent anti-re-
visionist.   Wagram brought back with him in the evening the Fashoda
Yellow Book just published.

"*25th Oct.*— The new Yellow Book gives a much more dignified
form to the French argument than it has received in our Blue Book,
and I consider that, logic for logic, M. de Courcel has the best of it.
It is also clear that, as I suspected, Lord Salisbury *has* been negotiating,
though it is equally clear that he has allowed his back to be stiffened by
the London Press and his colleagues' speeches and Lord Rosebery's.
The French terms are now pretty fairly formulated.   They will evacuate Fashoda on being allowed to keep the Bahr el Gazal with access to
the White Nile.   A Cabinet has been called in London for to-morrow,
when a final decision will be come to.   In face of the extraordinary out-
burst of Jingo violence in England I doubt such terms being accepted
and war seems probable; nobody, however, here seems of that opinion.

"M. Hanotaux, late Minister of Foreign Affairs, and M. Vandal
were here to-day and I had much conversation with both.   Neither
would hear of war for such a trifle as Fashoda.   M. Hanotaux maintained that no war would be popular in France, that nobody knew where
Fashoda was, or cared three straws about the Marchand Mission.   He
even considered the Egyptian question itself one of small importance for
France.   As for the Bahr el Gazal, it was 'a country inhabited by
monkeys and by black men worse than monkeys.'   A war with England
over such a dispute would be worse than a crime, a folly.   He was of
opinion that such a war would ruin both countries.   It would last two
years; it would be carried on interminably because neither could vitally
attack the other.   'I admit,' he said, 'that your fleet may destroy ours,
that you may blockade our ports, and that we could not land troops in
England, but what then?   You could not touch us in France, or even
in Algeria or Tunis; it would ruin your trade and leave you at the end
worse off than ourselves.   You would find yourselves faced by a triple
coalition.   I do not believe in the possibility of war.'   I told him of the
military fever we were suffering from in England, but he refused to
believe that Lord Salisbury, who was 'un homme d'Etat,' who looked
at the future, would quarrel to this extent with France, England's only
possible ally, for any such cause.

"I asked him about the Army, what its feeling was, what line it would
take? 'The French Army,' he said, 'is always ready to fight when the

word is given, but it does not busy itself with politics, and will not intervene to force on any policy. It can be counted on absolutely to
obey its orders, whether for peace or war. No war would be popular
now in France, and there was no such military fever now here as I
had described in England.' He added, however, that if the Army at
any time found a leader in any popular general who should become
Minister of War, the situation might change, the public might easily
become excited. If an appeal were made to it by the Government
against England then the Army would, doubtless, show its readiness to
fight. The Dreyfus case was also discussed. Vandal and Wagram
were against revision, Berthe and, cautiously, Hanotaux for it. This
was continued between Berthe and Wagram to the point of violence
all the evening, Wagram maintaining that there were secret pieces of
evidence which if made public would ruin the Army and ruin France,
Berthe that no conceivable evidence could have such effect, the only
people to be ruined being the General Staff. Personally I am much
charmed by Hanotaux, who talks well on many subjects and without
display of vanity. He has a pleasant *regard* and a sympathetic voice.
He gave me his views on architecture and art and talked to me, as
knowing him, of Herbert Spencer. Vandal also talked well, but is less
interesting. Both are academicians.

"*26th Oct.*— The Brisson Ministry has resigned and all is confusion
in Paris. This will probably ease the tension towards England and
make a peaceful solution more possible.

"M. et Mme. Sommier, the owners of Vaux, and a Mme. de Brie
came to luncheon. Sommier is a man of cultivation and intelligence,
who has taken in the 'Times' newspaper for years so as to get news
of the outside world, a rare circumstance in France. Like all the rest
he says war is impossible for such a trifle as Fashoda, that France is
not prepared for war, and that nobody wants to fight.

"*27th Oct.*— Three men arrived to shoot pheasants, M. Chevreau,
Comte de Gontaut Biron, and Comte de Kergoulet, all men of great
intelligence and good talkers as well as good fellows. We shot in the
forest beyond the park, but had no great sport. In the evening there
was an excellent political discussion, turning principally on the overthrow of the Brisson Ministry and the chances of their succession.
They think it probable that Delcassé will remain at the Affaires
Etrangères. None of them will hear of a war with England, in which
they say they would be beaten. My neighbour at dinner, M. de Kergoulet, a young Breton gentleman of old family, did not scruple to say
they would withdraw from the Nile and apologize rather than that.
None of the party, except Wagram, expressed any very different sentiment. I proposed as a bridge of escape from an impossible situation
that the French Government should express its willingness to acknowl-

edge Egypt's right to the whole of the Nile provinces, but not the right
of England. I believe that this would practically save them from their
dilemma without loss of honour, and would leave the Nile question for
a more favourable moment for raising it in conjunction with the whole
Egyptian question. The question of Alsace-Lorraine was also debated, and it was generally admitted that there must be sooner or later
prescription, a limit of time beyond which resentment could not be continued, though that time had not yet come. But for this the German
alliance was what would be most advantageous to France and a coalition
against England. I asked them whether they thought it true that the
Emperor William had proposed such a coalition two years ago, and
they said it was most probable, but not certain. Such a coalition was
impossible at present on account of the sentiment about the lost provinces, and nations live by sentiment, it was the mainstay of their
patriotism. I had it on the tip of my tongue to say patriotism is the
virtue of nations in decay, but I felt that that would be hardly civil,
though the aphorism would be a good one. [A better one would be,
'patriotism is the virtue of weak nations, it is the vice of the strong.']

"M. de la Siseranne was also of our party, an excellent talker like
the rest, but with more pose, as one would expect from his position as
conférencier and dogmatic art critic, a shock-headed man *taillé en
brosse,* less attractive than the others. He was strong on the point of
the time being nearly come when the animosity about Alsace-Lorraine
could be decently buried. 'There is,' he said, 'prescription for all
things, one does not now refuse one's hand to the descendant of him
who guillotined one's ancestors in 1793,' meaning, no doubt, Carnot.

"*28th Oct.*— To Paris on my way home. Called on Abu Naddara,
who gave me some details of the Marchand mission. Marchand had
come to him three years ago to ask his advice about penetrating to the
Upper Nile, and how to make friends with the Khalifa, and he (Sanua)
had given him papers inscribed with texts from the Koran, and as I
understood him, introductions from one or two persons at Omdurman.
Marchand's idea was to go and make friends with the Mahdists and
help them against England. He was certainly sent by the French
Government. Sanua is severe on the stupidity of French diplomacy,
and considers France very low down in the scale of European nations.
He told me a good deal about his visit to the Sultan Abdul Hamid,
who had received him with all honour, and allowed him to speak frankly
and openly about affairs. He says the Sultan is acquiring an immense
prestige from the Emperor Wilhelm's visit, which is everywhere in the
East regarded as an act of homage. It was Abdul Hamid who first
suggested to the Emperor to get rid of Bismarck. On his first visit to
Constantinople they were talking about Bismarck's great power in
Europe, and the Sultan said, 'I should not like to have so powerful a

servant, would your Majesty like to see how I treat mine?' William
said, 'Yes.' Abdul Hamid then touched a bell, and when the attendant
entered said, 'Send for Kiamil,' the then Grand Vizier. Instantly
horsemen were despatched at a gallop through the city seeking the
Minister, who presently appeared and stood, with head bowed and
folded hands, before them. The Sultan for awhile took no notice, and
let him stand, then casually 'You need not wait, it is of no consequence,
go,' and the Grand Vizier went. William took this lesson to heart, and
dismissed his Chancellor hardly less brusquely.

"Dined with Neville and his friend Geoffroi, a young fellow art
student of a modest serious kind at the hôtel where I was their entertainer. We discussed art, literature, and politics. The young man is
rather socialistic, hates the army, in which he is just about to be obliged
to serve, and is a Dreyfusard. He assures me military service is most
unpopular, and war still more so. It is clear nobody in France will
take up the quarrel thrust on them by us over Fashoda.

"*29th Oct.*— Back to England. To-day it is announced that
Marchand has left for Cairo, so the quarrel *solvitor ambulando*.

"*3rd Nov.*— Newbuildings. Knowles has agreed to my writing on
the Fashoda affair in the 'Nineteenth Century,' but says he hopes I
will not forget the motto which is his, 'my country right or wrong.'
What absurdity! One would think that England was a poor struggling
nationality, oppressed by a strong neighbour, and in need of the help
of all her sons, not what she is, the mill in which all the nations are
being ground.

"*4th Nov.*— Anne and Judith left for Egypt, I staying on in England for the winter. Lunched with George Wyndham at Willis's
Rooms, where he is near his work at the War Office. We discussed
the Fashoda business about which there will certainly not be war,
George said. Also that our Government had squared the Emperor
William. The Duke of Devonshire and Henry Chaplin were lunching
at another table, and greeted George as 'dear George.' Of Chamberlain, George said, 'He is for war at any price.' He (Chamberlain)
has just come back from America, where they are going through the
same absurd military fever that we are here.

"*7th Nov.*— At Newbuildings with Cockerell. Delcassé has made
his climb down about Fashoda, certainly a pitiful one, which reduces
France almost to the level of a second-class Power. The Emperor William meanwhile has been touring it in Syria, and making speeches at
Jerusalem. I fancy his concurrence with English policy has been
bought by some promise of recognizing him as the Sultan's protector
with a future reversion of the Holy Land. Our Jingo papers, especially
the 'Chronicle,' have been clamouring for the annexation of Egypt, or
at least the declaration of an English Protectorate, but that is probably

not within the limits of Lord Salisbury's present agreement with Wilhelm.

"*9th Nov.*— Left Newbuildings for Gorsey End, near Lyndhurst, for the winter, driving in beautiful weather by Rogate, where we are being entertained by Hugh Wyndham and his daughter Florence, stopping also to call on Charles Wyndham at Midhurst. Hugh, talking of the agreement with Waddington made in 1878 at the Berlin Congress in regard to Tunis, told me that he had had it from Odo Russell that the thing was transacted at the British Embassy. Odo Russell had said to him, ' You must be prepared for some startling moves,' and told him what had happened. This was soon after the agreement." [Sir Hugh Wyndham had been Secretary of the Berlin Embassy at the time.]

The whole of this winter I spent in the New Forest, having been advised to go there for my health, as I could get easy hunting there, and so be much out of doors. My principal friend in the neighbourhood was Sir William Harcourt at Malwood, whom I saw frequently, but otherwise I was much cut off from political society, though I went up now and then to London. At Lyndhurst I was busy writing my poem, " Satan Absolved."

"*20th Nov. (Sunday)*.— To luncheon at Malwood. Sir William in excellent form, principally about the bishops, with whom he is now in violent conflict. He narrated to us a conversation he had had with the Duke of Devonshire as to the nomination to a bishopric. The Duke's account of it was this: ' He had written two letters to Salisbury, recommending a fellow, he couldn't remember the fellow's name, and Salisbury hadn't even answered. He had written because Courtney and another fellow, he couldn't remember his name either, had wanted it.' On inquiry it had turned out that the proposed nominee was Page Roberts, and Sir William had taken an opportuniy of asking Lord Salisbury why he hadn't made Page Roberts a Bishop. ' The fact is,' said Salisbury, ' I thought they were talking of Page Hopps, and we gave it to some one else.' ' That,' said Sir William, ' is the way they make bishops.' Our luncheon was quite a feast, as Lady Harcourt has a very good cook. Rawnsley and his wife were there.

"*22nd Nov.*— Knowles has returned me my article on ' Fashoda,' on the plea of its being too late, and that, besides, it would not be wise to publish it, doubtless the true reason.

"*28th Nov.*— Cromer has consented to give Judith away at her wedding if I am prevented from being present. This is as it should be, for personally I have always been on pleasant terms with Cromer, much as we may tilt politically.

"*3rd Dec.*— To London, where I saw George Wyndham. He tells me they had a tremendous dinner a few nights ago, all the Under-Secretaries, at which, after the consumption of much champagne, they toasted each other as ' the youth of the day and the future Cabinet of 1910.'   All were present except Austin Chamberlain, who had been run over by a cab.

"*8th Dec.*— Basil Blackwood came to breakfast with me in Mount Street, just back from a shooting expedition in East Africa.   He gave me an account of it, as well as of Hubert Howard's death.   He and Hubert had been very close friends.   Basil is a nice youth, not a little like what his father was when he was young.

"*10th Dec.*— I have been buying books with Cockerell's help at Morris's sale, his ' Gerarde's Herbal,' a Berner's ' Froissart,' and Malory's ' King Arthur,' the Copland edition of 1557, the last a book to lie always on one's table.

"Last night there was given a great private dinner to George Curzon, at which most of the ladies who are our friends were present.   [This was a farewell dinner to Lord Curzon of Kedleston on his departure for India as Viceroy.   I have an amusing letter from Curzon of that date, as member of the Crabbet Club, excusing himself for accepting an office which, according to our Rules, entailed a resignation of membership, but I cannot print it here.]   Both George Wyndham and Sibell gave me an account of the feast.   He, George Wyndham, recited a poem he had written for the occasion.   Hugo (Elcho) proposed Curzon's health in a speech which George declared beat even his (Hugo's) record, and Curzon's reply was also most amusing.   No pressmen were invited except Harry Cust, if he can still be called one. It is described in the evening papers as a ' congregation of the Order of the Souls.'

"*16th Dec.*— The event of the day is Harcourt's retirement from the leadership of the Liberal party.   The true reason of his retirement is the conversion of the whole party, or at least the whole Liberal Press, to Jingo Imperialism.   I wrote yesterday to congratulate him on his published letter.   To-day I have a line from him in answer.   He says: ' *Anche io* have escaped out of gaol and am a free man.'   I hope now that his tongue and Morley's will be let loose to attack the militarism of the day, of which Rosebery is the most outrageous champion.   They will have plenty to say and will give dissentients heart.   There must be a few lovers of liberty left in England, but for the moment they have no voice more powerful than Labouchere's.   I consider Harcourt's retirement a distinct gain for liberty, if not for Liberalism.

"*17th Dec.*— To London on business, and dined at the ' Travellers,' where I was introduced by d'Estournelles to his new Ambassador, Cambon.   I had a long talk with the latter about desert travelling, and my adventure at Siwah.   Having mentioned that I was at Paris at the time of the late crisis they asked me ' which crisis,' and I without think-

ing said 'the crisis of Fashoda.' Cambon's countenance fell at the
word, and he changed the conversation, though heaven knows I meant
no harm.   It is arranged between d'Estournelles and me that I should
get up a little dinner at Mount Street for the Ambassador after the
Jour de l'An, but I fear I should disappoint d'Estournelles' expecta-
tions.   He counts, among other inducements, upon my inviting Lady
Galloway, who, being Lord Salisbury's sister, he thinks would interest
Cambon.   He wants Cambon to make a good impression in English
society.   When he finds out how little I am a *persona grata* with the
Government he will probably be less keen for my assistance; however,
that is their affair.   [N.B. Cambon had been sent to England after
the Fashoda affair and the change of Ministry at Paris, expressly to
bring about a good understanding between France and England, and in
this he succeeded admirably.   I believe it to have been due to him more
than to any other Frenchman, except perhaps Delcassé, that the Entente Cordiale was come to four years later with the withdrawal of all
French opposition to England in Egypt.   It is probable that at the
time of Fashoda an understanding was come to between Lord Salisbury
and Delcassé for the partition of North Africa.   England to have the
East, France the West, Germany and Russia to be eventually allowed
the spoil of Turkey and Persia.   The full development of the plan
being put off till the death, when it should happen, of Sultan Abdul
Hamid.]

"   *19th Dec.*— Old Lord Napier and Ettrick, Mark's father, is dead.
He was a man of distinction, and no small ability.   He was for many
years in diplomacy, and was then sent as Governor to Madras.   The
last I saw of him was six or seven years ago, when I was at the Glen.
His chief achievement in life was the making of Mark.

"   *26th Dec.*— I have been staying at the Danes for Christmas, a
family party.   To-day we drove over to North Mimms, to make acquaintance with Loulou's *financée.* North Mimms, a beautiful old
place, but turned inside out by a Victorian architect, who has been let
loose on it regardless of expense.   Loulou's new relations are Americans, the young lady simple and unaffected, and tenderly attached to
Loulou."

I ended the year 1898 at Ockham with Ralph and Mary, more happily
than was its beginning.   "The first four months were of exceeding
physical pain with the final breakdown, followed by a great contentment
of mind and body.   That great act of abdication, 'the taking to one's
deathbed,' teaches one the value of the smaller pleasures of life.   Intellectually I still feel growth, and while growth continues one is not
yet old.   Judith's marriage has been an event of supreme satisfaction.

"   *1st Jan.,* 1899.— I am back at Lyndhurst.   Lady Lytton tells me
that the Queen was greatly opposed to Neville's marrying before he

came of age, and that her Majesty is constantly inquiring about the date of the wedding, and has been soothed by being told that Neville will at least be twenty on his wedding day.

" *4th Jan.*— To Malwood, where I had a long talk with Sir William Harcourt about the line he ought to take as an independent member of the Opposition. He told me that he intended to bring forward the whole anti-Imperial case on grounds of economy. I told him that I did not think he would get much following that way. Nobody cared enough about economy to be enthusiastic over it. I thought he would have more success if he gave his opposition a moral basis, exposing the demoralization of England through the violence and bloodshed Imperialism entailed, the fraud, lying, and hypocrisy, and the growth of militarism. Carried away by my argument I pressed him so closely that he almost lost his temper, and as a final word said : ' Well, what you say may be true, but this is my plan, and I mean to stick to it.' Lady Harcourt, however, who was there, took my side, and afterwards made me go with her upstairs to see her boy Bobby, and repeat to him my argument. ' It will do him good,' she said, ' for he is just at a moment of crisis when a very little may turn his ideas one way or the other.' I found the boy in bed with a cold, writing his views on politics in a copy-book, and I turned my eloquence on him. Old Sir William's ill-humour was almost pathetic, and did not last long, and Lady Harcourt said to me as we went upstairs, ' He will not really mind, and he will remember what you said when you are gone.' Really there never was a moment, when a man with convictions and some knowledge of foreign affairs, could do more in England.

" Bennett, one of the military correspondents in the Soudan, has written a powerful article in the ' Contemporary,' exposing the barbarity of the war, about which all the country has been shouting triumph, and about Gordon College at Khartoum. The British public are paying to ease their consciences for the incredible slaughter of Omdurman.

" *6th Jan.*— The run of the season with the New Forest deer hounds, in pursuit of an old roebuck from Lady Cross Lodge right across the open heath of Beaulieu plain, very fast to the far side, when he turned back and again faced the open. About the middle of the plain, on his second journey, he lay down, and jumped up in the middle of the hounds, racing away for two miles in view with the pack at his heels to Hackett Pond, where he took the water and swam for ten minutes with the pack after him, and out again, and was run into and killed in the open. They say they never had so good a run before. It lasted seventy-five minutes. I was riding Mahruss, who carried me in the front rank all the way, the only heavy weight that went fairly with the hounds.

" *7th Jan.*— Cromer has made a speech to the Soudanese Sheykhs at

Khartoum, declaring they will now be ruled by the Queen of England and the Khedive of Egypt. This lets the cat out of the bag. I was quite sure the thing was in contemplation from the reticence of Lord Salisbury. All these weeks he has been allowing the rest of his Cabinet to make altruistic speeches about the Soudan having been 'reconquered for Egypt,' but has been mute himself, remaining by his telegram to Monson. The high moral nature of the transaction has been appealed to by every newspaper in England notwithstanding Bennett's exposure of the atrocities of the campaign. I have written to congratulate Bennett on his courage.

" 13*th Jan.*— Indoors all day writing about the new settlement in the Soudan. It is ludicrous to follow the antics of the so-called Liberal papers, the 'Chronicle,' the 'Westminster Gazette,' and the rest, in their endeavour to make the seizure of the Upper Nile for England fit in with their moral heroics about England's duty of 'reconquering it for Egypt.' What they don't understand is that Lord Salisbury was very quietly playing with them. He was delighted at the time of his ultimatum to France to get the support of the Radical Press, and he let them run on to their hearts' content about England being Egypt's trustee and the Nile being Egypt and Egypt being the Nile — that was Rosebery's phrase — and it pleased him that the Nonconformist conscience should call heaven and earth to witness what a moral and unselfish nation we were, and how abominable were the French, who would pilfer Egypt's inheritance. He was glad to get the support of the Exeter Hall people and the bishops and the clergy by letting them boast of the evangelical missions they were going to start at Khartoum, all the while having up his sleeve this card of Kitchener's, English Viceroyalty of the Soudan in the name of Her Gracious Majesty and a strictly Mohammedan Protectorate. The world are fools, or rather, they ask to be deceived, and deceived they are. The 'Chronicle' will very soon come fully into line with the 'Telegraph,' and find it an exceedingly clever trick to have made a cat's-paw of the Egyptian Government in English interests. What can be more amusing than to add the Upper Nile to the British Empire, and make the Egyptian fellah pay for his conquest and maintenance, the profit being wholly for England. Meynell tells me that when Sir William Butler (who is his brother-in-law) met Kitchener on his arrival at Dover, he said to him, 'Well, if you do not bring down a curse upon the British Empire for what you have been doing, there is no truth in Christianity.' Kitchener only stared.

" 14*th Jan.*— Drove to Abbotsworthy to stay with George Lefevre,[1] where we have had a deal of talk about politics. Lefevre is of opinion that Rosebery's retirement from the Leadership of the Liberal party

[1] Now Lord Eversley.

was resolved on by him with the idea that he could get Lord Salisbury's succession, if not as Unionist Prime Minister, at least as Unionist Foreign Secretary. This is likely enough. We went to look at St. Cross and the Cathedral at Winchester. The old 'brother' at St. Cross, one Joyce, who acted as showman, was describing to us the mechanism of an ancient confessional in the wall of a church there, and I asked him, 'Do you hold, sir, with the modern practice of confession?' His answer was amusing. 'Modern confession, sir. I was taking a lady round the church last week, and when we came to this 'ole in the wall, I invited her inside. "Now, Madam," I said, "have you nothing to confess to me?" And she was a pretty woman, sir. "I confess," said she, "that I 'ave been in 'ere alone with you quite long enough." That's my idea of modern confession and you may let Sir William 'Arcourt know it with my compliments.'

"*15th Jan.*— Back to Lyndhurst, stopping on the way at Malwood for luncheon. Sir William is immensely pleased with my confessional story, which exactly hits his humour. Loulou was there, and Bobby, the younger boy, and we had a great discussion about poetry and poets. I expounded to them the glories of Malory's 'Morte d'Arthur.'

"*20th Jan.*— The papers give the text of a convention made between Cromer and Boutros Pasha — a leonine convention indeed. The text, however, shows it less of an annexation than Cromer's speech suggested. As far as I can read its meaning it would become legally inoperative if England evacuated Egypt, for it provides only 'a system for the administration and making of laws . . . giving effect to the claims which have accrued to Her Britannic Majesty's Government by right of conquest to share in the present settlement and future working and development of the said system of legislation.' This can hardly be construed into sovereign rights. Nevertheless, it is practically as bad as possible for Egypt, for it will saddle on her the whole cost and labour of the war of reconquest not yet completed and make her budget responsible for Soudan deficits.

"*21st to 23rd January.*— At Hewell. I have made friends here with Rowton and have talked Egyptian and other matters over with him. He is, of course, a Jingo of the Jingoes, as becomes a courtier of the Queen and Disraeli's once private secretary, but he can talk without asperity even on the delicate subject of the British flag at Khartoum.

"*2nd Feb.*— To-day is Judith's wedding day. I came up to London and joined Edith Lytton and the family dinner party, where we drank the health of bride and bridegroom. Edith had with her a telegram from Her Majesty expressing sympathy, and later another saying that she had telegraphed to Lord Cromer asking for news of the wedding and giving his reply, '*marriage duly performed.*' This Her Majesty had underlined to show, Edith explained, her disappointment at the baldness of the answer. The Queen, she said, would have liked something gushing, but, of course, Lord Cromer treated it merely in an official way and would go to no expense. Both telegrams were signed ' V.R.I.,' which, Edith says, is always Her Majesty's signature now. I thought the ' I ' had been reserved for communications east of Suez, but the Queen is pleased with her title of Empress and uses it always. She has shown great interest in the marriage all through.

" *7th Feb.*— The ' Times ' publishes my Soudan letter in a prominent place, and as to-day is the opening of Parliament it may perhaps do good. Nubar Pasha is dead, and they are giving him a public funeral at Alexandria, while all the English papers are full of his praises, yet this wily Armenian arrived penniless in Egypt fifty years ago and has made four millions out of his various tenures of office. For this he is applauded by the London Press as an Egyptian patriot and statesman. He was unable, I believe, so much as to talk Arabic.

" *12th Feb.*— Lord Salisbury has given certain explanations in the House of Lords about the Soudan which are better than nothing, but the Opposition is too flabby to push him farther than he condescends to go.

" *16th Feb.*— Called at 44, Belgrave Square, where Mary, Pamela and Madeline are sitting for their portraits in a group to Sargent. It is being painted in the drawing-room. In the background there will be their mother's portrait by Watts.

" *19th Feb. (Sunday).*— Faure, the French President, is dead, and there is a good deal of excitement over the event, but I do not anticipate anything final at present. The chiefs of the Army would like to overthrow the Republic, but in the absence of any popular candidate for the throne, they are afraid to move. The rank-and-file, especially the conscripts, would not follow them.

" *22nd Feb.*— I have been helping to get up an agitation against the Parliamentary grant of £30,000 to Kitchener, and questions have been asked in the Commons. Brodrick admits the digging up of the Mahdi's body and the throwing it into the Nile, and they are bringing further questions about the mutilation, that is to say, about young Bill Gordon's having cut the head off to keep as a ' curio.' The whole thing is revolting — a piece of military revenge for the death of Gordon and the defeat of Wolseley and excused now on the absurd plea of its having been ' a necessity in view of the possibility of a fanatical revival.' What makes the desecration worse is that Sir Herbert Stewart's grave had remained all these years untouched in the desert where he fell, but the Liberal front bench is ready to condone every horror, being more Jingo than the Jingoes.

" *24th Feb.*— To the House of Commons for the Soudan debate which was led by Morley, ably and courageously. I heard Grey speak in good parliamentary style, but without eloquence, the Tories applauding him. [He had become Under-Secretary for Foreign Affairs under Rosebery.]

"*26th Feb.*— Morley's speech reads well in the 'Times,' and is founded for the most part on my letter published a fortnight ago. There is to be a separate debate about the desecration of the Mahdi's tomb.

"*1st March.*— Gave a dinner to the two Ambassadors, Cambon and Staal — with Margot, Lady Windsor, and Mrs. Benson for other guests; it was very gay, thanks to Margot, who talked imperfect French with great courage and volubility, and amused us all. Staal was as usual witty and charming, and after dinner Cambon, who is a bit of a *poseur,* sat on a sofa between two of the ladies, telling stories of Pierre Loti and his fabulous love adventures. Loti, when at Constantinople, had made the acquaintance of an Armenian lady of the half world, and on that slender foundation of romance built up his tale of an intrigue with the Turkish inmate of a harem of the Eyub quarter who died of jealousy for his sake. So successfully had he done it that he had convinced himself of its truth, and to the point that when he returned to Constantinople, and was staying at the French Embassy, he came in one day from a walk, and assured Cambon, who knew the true story, and Loti knew that he knew it, that he had just been to weep in the spot in the Eyub quarter where he had been so happy. He had found the quarter burnt, and the house reduced to ashes. Cambon assured us that Loti did this in all good faith, having been able to persuade himself to believe in these *bonnes fortunes* as things that had actually happened.

"*8th March.*— Lunched at the French Embassy. Staal, Maxse and his daughter, Margot and others. I asked Staal, who sat next to me, how it was that Tolstoy managed to remain on in Russia, untroubled by the Government. He said it was entirely due to the great literary position he held in Europe. It was thought wiser to tolerate him at home than to send him away to exile.

"*9th March.*— George Wyndham came to see me this morning, and I lunched with him and Madeline Adeane later at Belgrave Square, where we saw the first sketching in of Pamela's head which Sargent had just done in a couple of hours' work. It is wonderful as a likeness and as a bit of rapid execution, giving just her playful prettiness, and the peculiar wave of her hair, a sketch in the manner of Velasquez, with exactly his strong touches, unintelligible when looked close into, but alive when seen at a distance. Mary, too, has been sketched in not unsuccessfully, and Madeline less well. It should make a remarkable picture, probably Sargent's best. He is to be allowed no licence with the magentas and mauves he loves. I met him on the doorstep as he was going out, a rather good looking fellow in a pot hat, whom at my first sight I took to be a superior mechanic.

" 10*th March.*— By early train to Guildford to sit to Watts. (It had been arranged for me by Madeline Wyndham that Watts should do my portrait, a special favour he accorded her in deference to their long friendship.) The sittings were to be at his house, about three miles off by the Hogsback, an ornamental, not too ornamented cottage of the usual Victorian kind, which he has christened 'Limnerslease,' much to his friends' amusement, Cockerel tells me. Burne-Jones used to call it 'Dauber's Den,' 'Painter's Palette,' and other nicknames. The old man, well and alert, went to work at once on me, talking without interruption the whole time, and sometimes, finding me a good listener, with eloquence, though he complained of having been unable all his life to hit the right word in conversation, or even in writing. He is by nature, he says, a poet, but without the gift of expressing himself in any form of words. That is why he has worked all his life to express himself in colour, which after all he can only do imperfectly. He cares for his art, and desires to do it well, but principally as a means to his end of giving form to his ideas. He also wished to make these ideas intelligible to the widest circle of disciples, and for this reason he has refused to connect his art with any special epoch or any special creed. His figures are ideal figures, which will suit all ages and all beliefs. He once received a letter from a woman in Australia, who wrote to tell him that as a girl in Manchester she had found life so hard, she had intended to die, but by accident had seen a photograph of his 'Love and Death,' which had consoled her, and now she was married, and prosperous, and happy. She kept the photograph always hanging in front of her bed. This he said was a greater satisfaction to him than any success he had had merely as a painter.

" To some extent he blames Burne-Jones for being too much a man of one age. He (Burne-Jones) had locked himself up in the fourteenth century and had stayed there. Except for this he spoke warmly of him and of his charming qualities. He told how he had set Burne-Jones once on horseback at Little Holland House, starting him to canter round a ride he had made there, but he forgot some hurdles which had been put up and poor Burne-Jones fell off, nor would he ever be persuaded to mount again. Of Morris, he spoke with less enthusiasm, and I fancy there was a coolness between them in later years, though formerly he had seen much of them both. His heroes are Ruskin, Carlyle, and Rossetti, and he quoted ' The lost days of my Life ' as the finest of all Sonnets, an opinion which has long been mine. He does not think very highly of Rossetti as a painter, rather as a poet. Millais and Leighton were his two special friends among artists, and how many charming and beautiful women! He spoke more than once of

Lady de Vesci. The handsomest head he had ever painteu was Sir
Henry Taylor's, but his best man's portrait he considers to be Burne-
Jones', his best woman's portrait, Madeline Wyndham's. He
sets greater store, however, on his allegorical subjects than on his
portraits.

"11*th March*.— To Limnerslease again, having slept the night at
Milford. To-day we talked much on the subject of the destruction of
the weak races by the strong, and, like so many people nowadays,
while deploring it Watts excused it as inevitable, a law of nature and
the fulfilment of destiny. I thought he must have been talking about
this to Gerald Balfour, whose portrait he has just been painting, but
he told me how he had hardly had any conversation with Gerald during their sittings. With me he has talked uninterruptedly, sometimes
leaving his work for five minutes altogether to explain and illustrate
his arguments. Two of his illustrations I remember. Speaking of the
ritualistic controversy and the necessity of ceremony in all religions,
' Ceremony,' he said, ' is the substance of religious belief, it is what
outline is in a picture, it ought not to be required, indeed it does not
exist in nature, but it is often impossible to understand what is meant
without it.' This seemed to me a particularly good illustration. Again,
speaking of the part reason plays in our religious ideas, ' Here,' he said,
pointing to his forefinger, ' is sentiment, here is faith, here is charity,
here is hope, all four fingers stand together on more or less equal terms,
yet they can grasp nothing without this,' bending down his thumb,
' which is reason.' He was intensely pleased when I applauded and
said he had always thought it good.

"12*th March (Sunday)*.— At Newbuildings, gathering the first
spring flowers, which I am going to colour in my Gerarde's Herbal,
the one bought at Morris's Sale.

" I have concluded the purchase of Fernycroft in the New Forest
from Lord Montagu, 31 acres of woodland. It formed part of the
hereditary lands of Beaulieu Abbey, an outlying croft where the monks
kept their cows.

"14*th March*.— Entertained York Powell with others at dinner.
I have known him since 1863, when he was a boy, and I a quite young
man, travelling in the Pyrenees, but we have hardly met since, though
in correspondence now and then on literary and political subjects, where
we mostly agree. He was made Professor of History at Oxford, some
years ago, and is a good fellow, with a larger mind than Dons usually
possess.

"17*th March*.— Again at Limnerslease. Mrs. Watts took me to
see Mrs. Hichens' house close by, where there is a portrait of old
Prinsep, the finest Watts ever did. Indeed, I think it almost the
finest portrait ever painted in England. The house is set under a chalk

pit looking south, and screened from all cold winds.   Princess Christian
came in, but seeing strangers, decamped.

"*24th March.*— The Government has published a meagre parliamentary paper upon the doings at Omdurman, and the desecration of the
Mahdi's tomb.   Of course everything is denied, or made to appear to
be denied, except the fact, which could not be concealed, of the throwing of the Mahdi's body into the Nile.   As to the killing of the
wounded, the denial does not include the general order which, without
doubt, was given of killing men lying on the ground in battle after
they had fallen.   This is thought to be excused by the story, much exaggerated, of wounded men getting up and firing at our soldiers, but
the true reason of the slaughter is that Kitchener was campaigning on
the cheap, and did not wish to be encumbered with prisoners, and
especially wounded prisoners.   This, and the desire to have 'a record
bag' as a revenge for Gordon.   The destruction of the tomb is a crime
of which Kitchener meanly excuses himself by saying he was away
when it was done, though he had given the order, and for the political
reason of preventing the tomb's becoming a centre of pilgrimage, and
so of fanatical feeling.   This is mere fustian.   The thing was done to
emphasize the revenge taken, young Gordon, Gordon's nephew, having
been sent for from Cairo expressly for the job, and given command
of the bombardment during the battle, with orders to fire at the tomb.
Afterwards he was intrusted with the blowing-up of the ruins and the
violation of the grave.   Kitchener admits that 'the skull was preserved
and handed over to me for disposal,' which leaves it to be implied
that young Gordon performed the act of mutilation.

"*27th March.*— To Brighton to see old Herbert Spencer at his
house in Percival Terrace.   I found him lying on a sofa in a dressing-
gown, with slippers on of an ornamental feminine kind.   He began by
talking for ten minutes about his health, and explaining that his fresh,
rosy colour was no sign of health; then he got round to the subject of
my visit, the militarisms and brutalities of the day, the idealization of
football and all games of force, the rehabilitation of Napoleon and other
war-making scoundrels who had long been condemned as such, with
the rewriting of history to suit the agressive ideas now in fashion.
He repeated what he had said in his first letter to me, that if he did not
believe there would be a return to humane doctrines, it might be in a
hundred, it might be in two hundred or three hundred years, he would
not move a hand to prevent the destruction of the whole human race.
He applauded what I had said in writing to him of its being probably
necessary that we should be first beaten and invaded here in England
by a foreign enemy, and he thought it would be the best thing that
could happen.   'I am quite as pessimistic,' he said, 'as you are about
the present, only I foresee a change in the remote future.'   'In the

remote future,' I replied, ' it will be too late, everything that is interesting and beautiful and happy in the world will have been destroyed.
The world will be inhabited then only by the ugly and dull, and miserable white races.' This made him talk of the South Sea Islanders,
the Burmese, and other unspoiled people. He said he had intended
writing to William Watson to suggest a poem on the gradual degradation
of a South Sea Island community by the missionary and the trader.
Watson had not much backbone in his poetry, but he thought he could
do this. Trade competition was only another form of war waged by
the strong against the weak, less abominable, perhaps, than fire and
sword. For this reason the Czar's peace proposals should be supported, though they would not result in any real cessation of civilized
aggression. We talked also about race hatred and the influence women
had in fostering it, and I told him about India. He showed me some
beautiful photographs he had had sent him from Burmah, of the
happy poor people there, and contrasted them with the faces of our
own poor. Then complaining of being tired, for he had been talking
very energetically, he sent me down to have my luncheon with the two
ladies who look after him, a housekeeper and a young lady who plays
the piano to him. They are both new in the house, and he seems to
have no relations or belongings except these two, and they are strangers.
After luncheon I went upstairs again, but Spencer soon tired of talk,
and, ringing the bell, he sent for the young pianist, whom he directed
to play Masaniello and a piece by Purcell, which she did for twenty
minutes. She did this very nervously, as he was continually interrupt-
ing her, begging her to play either a little faster or a little slower.
This done, we fell to talk again about the domestication of animals.
While talking he occasionally gets excited, and jumps up from his
sofa and walks hurriedly about the room, until suddenly recollecting
himself and his health, he stops. He explained to me that he had been
an invalid since he was a young man, and he will be seventy-nine next
Tuesday, and has a right to be careful.

" On the whole I am rather disappointed with Spencer. He is so
very dry, and so much wrapped up in himself, his ailments, his work
and his ideas, to the exclusion, it seems to me, of individual sympathies.
His mind is clear and logical, he expresses himself well, but without
eloquence or such power as compels attention; not once was I able to
feel myself in the presence of a *great* man, only of a very well-informed
one, a pedagogue and able reasoner. There was nothing in him of
the softening character which old age so often gives, and which is
so touching. Still I am glad to have spent this day with him, for his
is one of the great names of our time, and his work has been great.
His rooms in Perceval Terrace are cheerful, facing the sea, and he
seldom moves out, the ladies tell me, except for a drive in the after-

noon, nor does he often see people, so I may take his asking me to visit him as a very high compliment. He has promised to send me a copy of his volume on Sociology. At three I left him and walked back to the station, and so home to Newbuildings, glad not to be a philosopher.

" *12th April.*— Yesterday and the day before I have been entertaining Prince and Princess Sherbatoff, showing them the stud, with her brother, Count Strogonoff, both highly intelligent Russians, and breeders of Arab horses." [Sherbatoff had travelled in our footsteps in Mesopotamia, and had started an Arab stud on his estate somewhere between Moscow and the Ural mountains, on the same principle of thorough breeding as our own.]

" Sir Wilfrid Lawson sends me the heads of a speech he intends making on the Soudan vote. It reads like the speech of Balaam, and I have answered him: ' If English Liberals and humanitarians leave it to the Irish to express disapproval of Kitchener's ways with the wounded and his treatment of the Mahdi's head, I can only say that they had better vote in silence. You praise Kitchener for his deeds as a soldier. It is all the argument needed to justify the parliamentary grant. Kitchener did not make the policy of the war, for that he is not responsible, but he was responsible for the brutal way he conducted it, a brutality which makes his success, no very great one, a disgrace.'

" My final sitting to Watts. The old man was more agreeable and interesting than ever, and we parted on terms of real affection. The portrait is a fine one, the best, he said, he ever painted, but this is more than the truth, for it cannot compare with his great achievements of thirty and forty years ago. Our talk has never flagged for a moment during the sittings. I told him of my visit to Herbert Spencer, and asked whether he had ever painted him? ' How could you expect me,' he said, ' to paint a man with such an upper lip?' He has no opinion of the philosopher as a man, and declares him to be wholly selfish.

" *18th April.*— The first nightingale.

" Young Oliver Howard came to dine and sleep, and to consult me about a hare-brained expedition he was bent on to Jerabúb and Kufra. I strongly advised him to turn his thoughts elsewhere. It is quite enough that his brother Hubert should have got killed in Africa without his doing the same, and for even a stupider reason. Neither he nor any of his proposed companions have had the smallest experience of the North African desert or know a word of Arabic, though one of the party has been in Somaliland shooting lions. For his father's and mother's sake I dissuaded him.

" *22nd April.*— Anne returned from Egypt, having left Judith and Neville at Paris.

" *27th April.*— With Cockerel to see the new mosaics at St. Paul's about which there has been angry correspondence in the ' Times.'

They are not in the best style of decoration, but the over brilliancy of the mosaics will soon blacken in the London smoke and tone down to the rest.

" On my way back from London in the evening we travelled by accident with D ——, who as usual was full of interesting talk. He told us, with a little pressing and on promise not to give him away, the true history of the Mahdi's head. The mutilation of the body seems all to have come of a mere bit of rowdy nonsense on the part of certain young English officers. He says it has long been a custom with the members of White's Club who are in the Army to bring back trophies from any wars they may be engaged in and present them to the club. He, D ——, had jokingly proposed to E —— W —— to bring back the Mahdi's toe-nails from the coming campaign. Kitchener, on this hint, seems to have fancied having the Mahdi's head for himself to make an inkstand of, and gave Gordon the order to dig the body up and keep the head for him. This accordingly was done, and at the same time finger-nails were taken by some of the young officers, but they got talking about it at Cairo and hence the trouble. He says he had the whole account of the thing in detail from W ——, and that Kitchener received the head from Gordon, who was charged with the destruction of the tomb, and he actually had it (he, Kitchener) as an inkstand until Cromer wrote about it, when he ' put it behind the fire.' D —— was quite incredulous about its having been buried at Wady Halfa, or anywhere else. It was just put ' behind the fire.'

' He gave an interesting account of Kitchener, whom he had known, he said, ever since they were both together at Woolwich, before the French war. He, D ——, was at a preparatory military school, reading for the military college, but Kitchener had passed in. Kitchener was ' a rough young devil,' and he and another cadet got into a row, partly about a woman, partly about money, and Kitchener's father, who was poor, refused to pay up for his son. The son, consequently, ran away with the other boy, and was tried by court-martial as a deserter. The two went to France and enlisted in the French army and fought in the war in the Army of the North, and Kitchener got some credit for his handling of a mitrailleuse on one occasion, and eventually, when the war was over, came back to England and got old Linthorn Simmons, then the head of Woolwich School, to forgive and take him back, and he got his commission. ' But,' said D ——, ' he always was what I have said, and did not know how to behave.' His conduct afterwards to the Khedive proved this. He was, however, a wonderful organizer, though a bad general. He had very nearly lost a battle at Atbara by his clumsy handling of the troops, and again at Omdurman, when he had wheeled the Egyptian army in such a manner as to place it between the Dervishes and the English contingent, so that

these last were unable to take any part in the firing.   Now he had been
given absolute power in the Soudan, and was using it in the most arbitrary way.   When Carlisle went up to Khartoum to visit the grave
of his son Hubert, Kitchener ordered him back immediately he had
performed this duty.   He would not hear of Carlisle's staying longer
than the second day.

" *3rd May.*— Dined at the Centenary of the Sussex Club, a piece
of local patriotism out of my usual way; indeed, it is twenty-five years
since I dined with the Club.   There were ninety-three members present, the Duke of Norfolk presiding, who did the duties simply and
well.   I sat between Henry Campion of Danny and Brown of Holm-
bush.   They asked me to take the Chair at their next dinner, a thing
which would have entailed a speech on me at this one, but I managed
to get out of it.   My father was one of the first members, having been
elected in 1808.

" *18th May.*— Yesterday I was in London and met my friend Harry
Brand,[1] just back from Australia, where he has been Governor of a
colony.   He found it dull work among people without literature, art,
or culture of any kind, except a taste for bad music.   He was offered
to stay on as Governor-General, but wisely refused.   Harry and I are
contemporaries and we swore, long ago, the oath of brotherhood, so
I have invited him to take up his residence in Mount Street with me
till his country place, The Hoo, becomes vacant in August.

" *19th May.*— Lunched with George Wyndham at Willis's Rooms.
He told me of a book young Winston Churchill is publishing, blurting
out all kinds of inconvenient truths about the Soudan campaign.   The
desecration of the Mahdi's tomb Winston calls ' a foul deed,' as indeed it
was.

" *26th May.*— I have written to Morley on the Kitchener case, as
he is taking it up publicly and has made a speech on it at Lydney.   The
Liberal newspapers, however, are afraid of touching the matter, and
the ' Daily News ' burks this portion of his speech.

" *27th May.*— I have finished my poem, ' Satan Absolved,' and feel
more content with life in consequence, having the sense of having done
all I could, and having made my individual protest against the abominations of the Victorian Age.   The 24th was the Queen's birthday, Her
Majesty being now eighty.   There is a foolish letter in the ' Times '
pointing out the wonderful fulfilment of a prophecy of Sidney Smith's,
who, sixty years ago, exhorted her Majesty to make it the boast of her
life to avoid war and to have it on her conscience to say, ' I have made
no orphans or widows.'   This for one whose reign has seen whole races
of beings exterminated under her rule, and only the other day thanked
God that her troops had destroyed 30,000 Dervishes!

[1] Lord Hampden.

"*28th May.*— George Wyndham came down last night to dine and sleep, and to-day I drove him to Worthing, where we lunched with Henley. On our way over the Downs we stopped and walked up to Chanclebury Ring, which George had never done, and found some white dog-violets nearly at the highest point. George has told me a good deal about the internal rivalries in the Cabinet, which may well break out if anything happens to Lord Salisbury. What he calls the reactionary Tories are headed by Hicks Beach, but the young Tories, including himself, would not serve under Beach. As long as Arthur Balfour is there they will follow him, but if any accident sent him too out of the leadership they would revolt from the main Tory body and form a third party of ultra-imperialists with Chamberlain. About foreign politics George says that it is now simply a triangular battle between the Anglo-Saxon race, the German race, and the Russian, which shall have the hegemony of the whole world. France he considers gone as a great Power, as much gone as Spain or Austria, but the Emperor William means to be supreme overlord. He is holding his hand for the moment till he can get an efficient navy, but as soon as this is ready there will be a coalition against England. He, George and the young Imperialists are going in for England's overlordship and they won't stand half-measures or economy in pushing it on.

"*3rd June.*— Young Winston Churchill has made a speech in which, while condemning the desecration of the Mahdi's tomb, he excuses Kitchener on the ground that it was done in his absence and that he was keeping silence in order not to incriminate his subordinates. This throws the odium of the deed on young Gordon, a quite innocent person, for both Anne and Judith, who have been seeing Gordon and his wife at Cairo all through the winter, assure me that he repudiates the deed with absolute disgust. I have consequently written to the 'Daily News' telling the truth about it.

"*4th June (Sunday).*— Lunched at Sir Wilfrid Lawson's where I found John Morley. We had a long two hours' talk about the Kitchener vote which is to come off to-morrow. Morley is very fierce against Kitchener, and I gave him what help I could, besides what I wrote to him on the subject. But he is hampered by all sorts of conditions. I urged him not to admit the capture of Omdurman as a great feat of arms. It was a trumpery affair for which to give a peerage, but he would not take this line, though it really invalidates his whole argument. He is already in a depressed frame of mind, for Campbell Bannerman is to second the vote, and he thinks the result of the debate will be to make a further cleavage between the two sections of the Liberal party, his own anti-military section being left with a small minority. Even Harcourt's vote he thought was doubtful. I proposed to go and see Harcourt and try and persuade him to vote against the grant, but

Morley said, 'If you do, for God's sake don't tell him you have seen me,' which shows how little confidence in each other there is among the chiefs, even of the Anti-Jingo section. He ended, however, by saying I might as well go to Harcourt without mentioning him. I found Sir William at the Avondale Hotel in capital spirits, but when, after some talk about the New Forest, I mentioned the Mahdi's head, I saw his countenance fall, and he changed the subject to the Transvaal, where he thinks trouble is coming, and then while we were talking about it he was suddenly called out, and I did not see him again. I asked Lady Harcourt when we were alone to try and get him to support Morley, but she said, 'I have given up trying to get him to do anything but what he chooses,' which I take to mean he will do nothing.

"*5th June.*— Again to London where I found a note from Lady Harcourt, telling me that what had interrupted my talk with Sir William yesterday was the news brought him of Loulou having been taken seriously ill, so that his wedding, which was fixed for to-morrow, has had to be put off.

"My letter about Kitchener is in the 'Daily News' neutralized according to an editorial dodge by printing next to it what is headed as 'The true story' in contradiction to mine. At first I was alarmed lest young Gordon might have confessed, in spite of his denial, that he was the real culprit, so I went down to Chelsea and lunched with my kinsman, Gerald Blunt, at the Rectory (whose son's wife was a sister of Gordon's), and he reassured me on this point. He says that Gordon's family are furious at the slur cast on him. Then at four to the House of Commons. George had got me a good seat in the special gallery, and I found myself among friends, Rennel Rodd, George Peel, Canon Wilberforce, and others. Kitchener, who returned to England last night, was sitting with Roberts in the Peers' gallery. After the usual irrelevancies, Arthur Balfour opened the debate in a brief speech recounting Kitchener's services, for the Opposition was quite unequal to the occasion. Kitchener's name had not been very warmly received, and it would have been easy to appeal to the better feeling of the House, though the result of the vote could not have been altered, but Campbell Bannerman's rising to second the vote, though he expressed himself pretty strongly on the 'vulgarity' of the desecration of the tomb, put things at once into a false position, and Morley who followed to oppose it, with the strongest of possible cases, proved feeble beyond all recorded feebleness. His arguments were weak to fatuity, and he gave himself away over and over again till the House laughed at him. So much was this the case that Balfour already found himself in sympathy with the House before he rose to reply. He did this in a speech of great skill and eloquence, which, as mere oratory, it was a relief to listen to, and he succeeded even to taking a high moral line with the wretched Morley, and in proving to him conclusively that Kitchener was absolutely justified, indeed bound by every principle of right feeling to blow up the tomb, dig up the body, chuck it into the Nile, and what he called 'disperse the remains.' Absurd as his argument was it was conclusive with the House, and Morley had not even the wit to ask what became of the poor head, or who was entrusted with the various operations. I doubt if Morley will ever make a speech again in the House, I should not if I were he.

"Personally I am not altogether dissatisfied with the result. We have gained at least this, that we have forced Balfour and the Government and the House of Commons to declare themselves in favour of the extreme abominations of war, and have in so far exposed the hypocrisy of modern England. It is better so than that the country should have it in its power to boast that it did not approve, although it did the deed. Kitchener got his £30,000, his money perish with him! I was glad to notice that, except old Roberts, who came with him to the House, none of his brother Peers in the gallery offered him a congratulation, or spoke a word to him.

"*7th June.*— In all the newspaper articles on the Kitchener Debate, not one has the wit to see the flaw in Balfour's argument. It rests entirely on Kitchener's assertion that he had the Mahdi's tomb profaned, and the body dispersed deliberately with a political intention, that of publicly showing the Mohammedan world of Africa that the Mahdi was an impostor. The untruth, however, of this is easily discoverable even in the meagre Blue Book published. If it had been true it is certain Kitchener would have reported the fact with the reasons to Cromer *at the time,* and that Cromer would have reported them *at the time* to the Foreign Office. But though the thing happened in September, and though Kitchener in the meanwhile had been back in London, and in personal communication with everybody, including her gracious Majesty the Queen, the Government professed to be ignorant of the facts until the month of February, the earliest document in the Blue Book being one of February 17, when Cromer sent home a communication of February 1 from Kitchener. Kitchener then for the first time gives his explanation thus: ' I would add,' he says, ' that my action regarding the tomb of Mohammed Achmet, the so-called Mahdi, was taken after due deliberation, and prompted solely by political considerations.' How anybody at all conversant with the way in which Blue Books are edited can be simple enough to believe in face of this comparison of dates, that the ' political considerations ' were not an afterthought passes my understanding, yet is clear that Morley and even the Irish overlooked the absurdity. The whole discussion in Parliament was unreal, nobody wanted to believe, except perhaps Morley. The Irish look on Kitchener with a sneaking regard. as in some measure an Irishman, while Dillon has Catholic sympathies which prevent his quite disapproving the crusade. In this way Balfour's absurd argument held its ground, and I suppose will hold it in history.

" 15*th June.*— The plot for annexing the Transvaal has taken a new development. Chamberlain, to force the hand of the Government, has published a despatch of Milner's written on the 4th of May of the most aggressive kind, and the newspapers are full of flame and fury, the ' Daily News ' leading the chorus. They talk about Milner's ' cool and impartial judgment' just as if Milner had not been specially selected by Chamberlain to put the job through. Milner was sent to Egypt ten years ago to convert English Liberal opinion to the plan of remaining on there instead of withdrawing the garrison, and having succeeded in that mission he has been sent to the Cape to convert English Liberal opinion to the idea of reannexing the Transvaal. Milner, though an excellent fellow personally, is quite an extremist as an imperial agent, and his journalistic experience on the ' Pall Mall Gazette ' has given him the length of John Bull's foot very accurately, so that he is invaluable to the Empire builders. Now there will certainly be war in South Africa. They have tried every kind of fraud to get their way, but old Kruger has been too astute for them, so they will try force. They seem to have squared the German Emperor, France is in chaos, they think their opportunity come. Chamberlain will not rest until he has Kruger's head on a charger. The Boers, however, will fight, and there is some chance of a general war between the Dutch and the English in South Africa, which may alleviate the condition of the only people there whose interests I really care for in the quarrel, namely the blacks. It will also be a beautiful exposure of our English sham philanthropy, if at the very moment the Peace Congress is sitting at The Hague, we flout its mediation and launch into an aggressive war. Anything is better than the general hand-shaking of the great white thieves and their amicable division of the spoils.

" I am now staying at Oxford with York Powell at Christ-Church. Powell is an excellent good fellow, and seems to be much liked at Oxford in spite of his somewhat heterodox views on politics, for he has a certain Socialistic tendency enough to have widened his mind. We had a deal of talk to-day, principally on poetry and literature, of which he has a large knowledge. I told him, among other things, of my having consulted Jowett fifteen years ago half seriously about the possibility of my entering the University as an Undergraduate, and how he had answered me. ' You could never pass the examination for Balliol, but might try Christ-Church.' ' Insolent dog ! ' said Powell, resenting the slur on his College. It is lovely weather, the Christ-Church Meadow looking its best, and while we sat on a bench in the Elm Avenue talking, a little redstart was watching us. Then we went into the Cathedral to see the Burne-Jones Morris windows. Prayers were going on for the Queen, the Prince of Wales, and the Houses of Parliament, and they were intoning, ' Give peace in our time, O Lord.' Then we dined in the hall, and talked with two Dons, Myers and another, about Eastern travel and horses, till I got away to bed.

" *21st June.*— Lane will publish ' Satan Absolved.'

" *28th June.*— Herbert Spencer consents to have ' Satan Absolved ' dedicated to him, but is in a terrible fright lest it should be found out that he gave the idea of the poem, ' on account,' he says, ' of the *odium theologicum* and the injury it might do to the spread of his philosophy,' so I have written a preface without exactly saying this, though it is not very courageous of him to leave me alone in the coming battle.

" *29th June.*— Breakfasted with George and Sibell, who showed me two very interesting letters from her son Bendor, describing the interview between Kruger and his chief, Milner (whose private secretary he is) at Bloemfontein. The letters were written actually during the conference, and contained sketches of old Kruger, whom he described as very old and infirm, and also very sly. He talked of Kruger as ' bluffing.' He writes with a boy's enthusiasm for his chief, and seems to be enjoying himself greatly. I showed George my preface to ' Satan Absolved,' which he thinks cannot fail to attract attention.

" On my way home by the late train I travelled as far as Dorking with Harry Cust. I gave him my view of the way the Transvaal quarrel had been engineered by Chamberlain and Milner. He professed to regard this as the extreme of political scepticism. ' A poet,' he said, ' should not be so unbelieving in honesty.' He was on his way down to Admiral Maxse's, where he was to meet Meredith and others.

" *8th July.*— Our annual Arab Sale, an immense concourse of people, 380 sitting down for luncheon in the tent. Colonel Sdanovitch our principal buyer for the Russian Government.

" *8th Aug.*— I have been staying for the last few weeks at Fernycroft, but to-day I went to London, where I found Hampden at my rooms in Mount Street. He has been living there all the last month. We went in the evening to see the Savage South African Show. It is a return to the shows of Imperial Rome, minus the bloodshed, and is worth seeing as a spectacle, though it is monstrous to look on at these captives brought to London to make a Roman holiday. The white swaggerers who are given the *beau rôle* to play in the exhibition are of course disgusting, but the black men managed to preserve their dignity and make the others look foolish. The superiority of the black man over the white was throughout conspicuous, and it did not need the patter of the whites on the stage to explain that it was only their maxim guns that gave the latter their victory."

From 9th August to 16th August I was at Fernycroft, my new acquisition in the New Forest, and after that on my annual summer driving tour once more visiting St. Fagans, where, amongst others, I found Lord Rowton and Sanderson, of the Foreign Office.

"*21st Aug.*— Both are good company, and we have had much friendly discussion of politics. Rowton tells me that never with his consent will Dizzy's Memoirs be published. He is light in hand and eminently reasonable, full of amusing anecdotes, especially of his old master, and of his lodging-house plans, an odd hobby, for it is not altogether a charity, paying, he tells me, 4 per cent. on the capital, but it doubtless does much good. Sanderson has talked freely on the Transvaal quarrel, and expresses very moderate opinions. He believes in a pacific arrangement. This in contradistinction to Windsor our host who, though the quietest and most moderate of men on other topics, takes fire about the Transvaal almost as a personal matter.

"*29th Aug.*— Back at Fernycroft. Chamberlain has made another violent speech, and it is clear now, as, indeed, it has been all through, that he is forcing on a war with the Boers. The Liberal press is childish, and there is practically no opposition. The Liberal party has swallowed so many violences and so many diplomatic frauds in the last twenty years that it may as well make up its mind to swallow this too. I, as an enemy of Empire, shall say not a word.

"*1st Sept.*— Partridge shooting with Mark Napier and Terence Bourke. I shot well, the first time since my illness, killing twelve birds in as many shots, but I am no longer keen for sport of any kind, and go out principally as an old custom and to justify the expense of game preserving. My logic about shooting here in England is, that it is the only way of preventing the destruction of wild animals. If there was no shooting, no one would be at the expense of paying gamekeepers, nor would it be possible to prevent the rag-tag and bobtail of the towns from snaring and netting. The abolition of the game laws would mean the extinction not only of all game, but of the small wild birds and beasts, too, which enjoy the peace of the protected covers, while, if I did not go out shooting myself, my gamekeepers would take no trouble to prevent poaching, so I kill my few brace of partridges and pheasants, that the rest may live in peace. In Egypt, where there are no game laws and no birdsnesting, I never fire a gun.

"*3rd Sept. (Sunday).*— I have written a long letter to Frederic Harrison about the Transvaal, apropos of his open letter to Lord Salisbury, which has just been published. It is principally to explain to him that he is mistaken if he really relies on Lord Salisbury to control Chamberlain, or to do anything to prevent a war which he and the Queen desire. Also to let him know what Milner's position is in the affair.

"*11th Sept.*— The world has gone mad over the verdict of guilty given in the Dreyfus case. Of course it is abominable, but what did anyone expect? It was clear from the time that Gallifet took office that there would be a compromise of the case, and that the compromise would only be that Dreyfus should be found guilty and then pardoned, and that be the end of it. As to our virtuous selves, we are of course in a state of splendid denunciation of our neighbour's sin, this at the very moment that we are pushing forward a new raid on the Boers, certainly no smaller public iniquity, huge though the other may be. I drove to-day to Malwood, but Sir William was away. Lady Harcourt would not hear of war with the Transvaal.

" *16th Sept.*— I have written again to Harrison about the Transvaal. He answered me a week ago, urging me to write to the 'Times' in the same sense as I had to him, and as to Salisbury saying, 'It is well to attribute virtue to a powerful man, even if he has it not. It must make him doubt of it.' This I cannot do, as I am certain the 'Times' would not publish such a letter. I have explained to him how Buckle is one of the gang acting with Rhodes, and how the Jameson Raid was concocted, so to say, in the 'Times' office, and how there is no true peace party in England. The only difference between Liberals and Conservatives in these cases is, that while both rob with the cry of 'your money or your life,' the Liberals would like the money given up peaceably, the others after a fight. I have told him that I do not believe in the possibility of any change of opinion until we have got a good beating ourselves, and that it is by no means impossible the Boers may make a formidable stand. In any case it would be better for the world that they should be destroyed fighting for their independence, than that they should be bullied or cheated out of it.

" *18th Sept.*— Fernycroft. A telegram came from Madeline Wyndham to say she was coming to spend the day here. I accordingly met her at Southampton. On the way there I read in the papers the Boers' refusal of Chamberlain's ultimatum. A very dignified document it is, and one very difficult for our people to answer. Morley had already a day or two ago at a meeting in Manchester given away the whole Liberal case against the war, publicly approving the Franchise demand, made by our Government on the Transvaal, a mere red herring which the Radicals have run to in full cry. The consequence is that the whole English press to-day is with the Government and war is certain." [N.B. The pretext of demanding the franchise for the Outlanders in the Transvaal was a trap laid by Milner especially for Morley and the Radicals who stepped into it precisely as was intended. Once having approved the demand it was impossible for these with any logic to disapprove the military steps taken to enforce the demand on Kruger, and war became a necessity.]

" *21st Sept.*— The news is all very ominous, indeed it will be a miracle if war does not break out of itself on the frontier without further waiting, and so give our Government the pretext it wants. Under the circumstances I have resolved to publish my letter of the 2nd to Harrison.

"Dreyfus has been pardoned; and so the case ends according to programme. Our papers are in a righteous fury and Dreyfus swears he will continue the struggle. But it will not end here. It has cost France dear — her position on the Nile, her position as a great European Power, and her good name in the world. Gallifet deserves well of his country for the courage he has shown and the wisdom in ending it.

"*26th Sept.*— Frederic Harrison writes that he wishes to see me about the Transvaal. He warns me that I should have to modify my letter to him if I sent it to the 'Times.' It was 'violently actionable,' he said, and as I should have no defence, it would cost me £10,000 to have it printed as it stood. But he hoped I will publish something. He also tells me as a secret that, at his suggestion, the Queen of Holland has, he believes, written to our gracious Majesty, begging her to intervene to stop the war, which otherwise is inevitable. This would seem the best chance, though nothing is more certain than that Queen Victoria has been a prime mover in the Government policy. These military blood sheddings are not displeasing to Her Majesty, and she has just allowed Kitchener to make her a present of a white ass from Omdurman.

"On receipt of this letter I went to London and at Mount Street found Hampden. He tells me Lord Salisbury has arranged with Portugal to take immediate possession of Delagoa Bay.[1] This he has learned confidentially from the Colonial Office. I then went down to Sutton Place, in which delightful old house I now am staying with Frederic Harrison and his brother.

"*27th Sept.*— Sutton Place. I have had a long talk with Harrison about the Transvaal, which we both think must fight unless indeed there is royal interference in Holland. We have decided not to publish my letter as being too libellous, also the time is a little gone by for it to do much good. I read him my 'Satan Absolved.' He thinks it should be the sensation of the year. He will write a review of it in the 'Nineteenth Century,' refuting its attack on humanity and giving me an opportunity of defending my ideas in prose. This will make it almost certainly a success.

"The Harrisons, or rather, Sidney Harrison and his mother, have been tenants of Sutton for twenty-five years. The house is much dilapidated as to doors and windows, and is a fearfully cold house to inhabit even in September, having, unlike most old houses, ridiculously small fireplaces, which seem to have been always there. I slept in the west wing, the only spare bedroom, big as the house is. I have known

[1] Compare Dr. Dillon's book, "The Eclipse of Russia."

Sutton Place as long ago as the year 1855, when it was occupied by
my cousins, the Lefevres. In those days there was a Catholic chapel
in the east wing to which we used to be sent on Sundays from West
Horsley. The east wing was then uninhabited, a melancholy romantic
vacancy with a great staircase, hung with family portraits mouldering
on the walls. The chapel was in an upper room used for mass on
Sundays, according to an old endowment. Now the wing has been
restored and is occupied and the chapel placed elsewhere.

" *29th Sept.*—Back to London. Lady Lytton tells me that Kitchener
is a great favourite at Court. She was with the Queen and Kitchener
when they went to Natley Hospital, and was impressed with Kitchener's
manner to the wounded soldiers. ' What these Royal personages ad-
mire,' she said, ' is that he is such a stern man.'

" *30th Sept.*— My cousin, Gerald Henry Blunt and his wife (she is
General Gordon's niece and sister to Colonel Bill Gordon) is here at
Newbuildings to dine and sleep, and I have heard from her the whole
story of the digging up of the Mahdi at first hand, or rather, as her
brother told it her. ' Bill,' she said, ' was entrusted with the bombardment of the tomb from the gunboat on the river during the battle of
Omdurman, and after it he was ordered to blow up the ruined remains
of the dome, as being already shattered and unsafe. This he did, but
it was no part of his orders to interfere with the body of the Mahdi.
It was left untouched under the ruins until Kitchener's return from
Fashoda, when Kitchener had it dug up and thrown into the river.
Bill was not present at this, nor was the job assigned to him, but Kitchener and most of his staff were present, and Kitchener ordered the
head to be kept, intending to send it to the College of Surgeons, as the
head was a very large and remarkable one. It was sent on board the
steamer in a kerosene tin and taken down to Cairo, but was never in
Bill's charge, and he disapproved of the whole business. Eventually
when the scandal was made about it, the head was entrusted to two
English officers to take up the river again to Wady Halfa.' These reported that they ' buried it at night, somewhere in the desert,' they
don't know where, so very possibly D——'s account of its having been
' put behind the fire ' is correct. Mrs. Gerald Blunt thanked me pro-
fusely for the letter I had written to the ' Daily News ' in her brother's
defence, and said that Bill considered that Kitchener had treated him
unfairly in the affair. They had all made a scapegoat of him because
he did not stand in with them in certain not very straightforward
things. She is a nice, cheerful little woman, enthusiastic about her
' Uncle Charlie,' and not at all conventional about the military nonsense
of the day.

" *30th Sept.*— To the Hoo, where I found a family party. Hampden
and his wife, and sons and daughters. Nothing is talked of but the

Boer war. I notice that Harry, who was quite moderate about it when
he first came home from Australia, has now imbibed all the violent
Liberal-Unionist views regarding it. His eldest son is ordered to the
war, and the younger ones talked loudly about 'exterminating the
Boers.' We expect hourly now to hear of guns gone off on the
frontier.

"*2nd Oct.*— Back to Newbuildings. The 'Chronicle' is running
a new red herring to-day, and has proposed sending the Duke of Devonshire out to South Africa, of all men in the world, to arrange a peace.
They are ready, however, to follow every false scent thrown in their
way. The Government's present plan is to try and make people think
they don't want war, and don't want to wipe out Majuba, and don't
want to annex the Transvaal. We shall see when it is over. If, after
a successful campaign, the Transvaal is not annexed, and Milner is not
made a peer, they may claim not to have intended it; but both these
things will happen.

"*7th Oct.*— We have been expecting the Boers to advance on Natal
all the week, but something has delayed them. Perhaps the abortive
attempt by the Queen of Holland to intervene with our Queen. The
Boers seem to be losing their chance by this delay, but I fancy old
Kruger knows what he is about. He has, I think, to consult his friends
in Europe, at Berlin and elsewhere, before each important move. He
has managed to get the whole sympathy of the Continent with him,
indeed, of the whole world except ourselves and the Americans. These
last are backing us, as we backed them in their iniquity against the
Filipinos. The Transvaal Committee, too, in Manchester, has been
telegraphing absurd messages to Kruger, telling him that the Duke of
Devonshire may be trusted. If this has at all influenced the old man,
the Transvaal Committee deserves hanging, for the delay of the week
may cost him dear.

"*9th Oct.*— The men at the Clubs now mock at Kruger, saying he
won't fight, never meant to fight, and the rest. Reginald Carew, whom
I met at the Travellers, talked in this sense. He leaves for South
Africa with Buller's staff on Saturday, but I told him not to be discouraged, that the Boers would certainly not cave in. He thinks they
have lost what chance they had by waiting. Perhaps so. Still they
will fight." [N.B. This was General Pole Carew, who went on Buller's Staff. I remember him lamenting his bad luck in the belief he had
that what little fighting there might be would have been over long before Buller's arrival. He distinguished himself during the war principally, I think, as being the first to burn down the Boer farms. He
is a connection of mine through the Glanvilles. I have known him in
India when he was Lytton's A.D.C. It had been arranged at that time
that he was to go with me as representing Lytton on the journey we

proposed taking that year in Arabia, but which Cavagnari's death at Kabul and Lytton's recall from India prevented. (See 'India under Ripon.')]

" 10*th Oct.*— The streets are placarded with the Boer ultimatum, so I hope the end has come.

" To the British Museum with Cockerell, and saw Dr. Budge, of the Egyptian Department. He gave us a deal of information about the Hyksos and Assyrians in connection with Horse History. But all these authorities differ so much from each other in what they tell you, that one cannot have much confidence in their knowledge. As Huxley said, it is still all ' guess work.'

" 12*th Oct.*— Dined with Sibell and George, and Lady Windsor in Park Lane, and went with them to see ' King John ' at Her Majesty's theatre, an egregious performance. I never cared about ' King John,' and, as acted by Tree, it was a violent piece of ranting. George, with whom I walked home after it, told me that Tree had chosen the play as being full of Jingo tags and no Popery talk. But the audience was too dull to seize the points.

" We talked much about the war, which is declared to-day. George's brother Guy is on White's Staff at Ladysmith, and he expects them to advance. White's orders from England have been generally to stand on the defensive, but George is sure he will not remain quiet, and ' of course we must leave all liberty to the men on the spot.' Baden Powell is at Mafeking, and there will be fighting there. He told me a good story of a certain J ——, who is notorious for keeping clear of danger. He has just telegraphed to his wife from Kimberley, seven hundred miles away from Mafeking, ' War declared. Mafeking will be attacked by Boers to-morrow — probably destroyed. No cause for anxiety.' About the general prospects of the war, George still believes in the theory that Kruger is ' bluffing,' and that after a bit of a fight he will knock under to Buller and make terms, otherwise he thinks it will be a very long and tough job. He says that the Cabinet would really have come to an arrangement with Kruger but for the bitterness of the feeling against Chamberlain. There was a moment when they would have accepted terms which, while giving Chamberlain an appearance of a diplomatic success, would have left the real advantage to Kruger. Kruger, he thinks, ought to have accepted the proposal of inquiry and discussion, have agreed to go himself to Cape Town, and then have delayed and put off till everybody was tired of it. He had himself heard Chamberlain say when they expected such acceptance by Kruger, ' It seems my failure has been changed into a *pæan.*' Now, however, there is no way but to fight it out. I told him I, too, was glad it was to be so. My chief fear had been lest the Boers should be jockeyed out of their independence without fighting. Besides, I look upon the war as perhaps the first nail driven into the coffin of the British Empire. I believe that if the Boers can hold out six months Europe will intervene.

"17th Oct.— In South Africa the Boers are advancing steadily southward, and have invested Mafeking and Kimberley. Their plan is doubtless to get the Dutch in Cape Colony to rise and join them. It seems their best chance. Buller went off on Saturday to take command of the British Army. They gave him what is called a 'send off' at Southampton by crying a bogus victory in the streets.

"Swinburne has published a ridiculous sonnet in favour of the war, and Kipling has also been in the 'Times.' My 'Satan Absolved' must stand for poetry on the other side. I got an advance copy of it to-day.

"19th Oct.— Newbuildings. Hampden and Neville are here. Much argument about the Transvaal war. Hampden very fierce in defence of the Government. We shot to-day, Mark Napier joining us as fourth gun. Violent discussions again in the evening, Mark maintaining that, while the English officers are good, the rank and file are worthless, and that in a long campaign the English regiments would go to pieces; Hampden annoyed, as having a son in the army. But all ended pleasantly.

"21st Oct.— The Boers have been beaten in an attack they have made upon White's Camp. George had the happy task in Parliament, as Under-Secretary for War, of announcing the victory.

"23rd Oct.— More victories. The 'Chronicle,' after championing the Boer cause all the summer, has now gone clean round, and shouts triumph with the rest. It is a dastardly world.

"27th Oct.— To London. People are not so pleased now with the war in Natal, as, in spite of the reported victories at Glencoe and Elandslaagte, Dundee has had to be evacuated, the guns and wounded being left behind. They say Ladysmith will now be invested. Guy Wyndham is there, with White's staff in the threatened position.

"29th Oct.— Herbert Spencer has written again about 'Satan Absolved.' He is disappointed at my not having stuck to his idea in the poem, but on the whole he approves. 'Unquestionably,' he says, 'Satan's description of man and his doings is given with great power, and ought to bring to their senses millions of hypocrites who profess the current religion. I wish you would emphasize more strongly the gigantic lie daily enacted, the contrast between the Christian professions and the Pagan actions, and the perpetual insult to One they call Omniscient in thinking they can compound for atrocious deeds by laudatory words.'

"1st Nov.— News of a great defeat of the British army before Ladysmith. Two of Her Majesty's best regiments, the Royal Dublin and the Gloucester, laid down their arms to the Boers, 2,000 men of our most veteran troops. There seems now a chance of the whole British army capitulating before Buller and his men can relieve them from England. Letters from old Watts and Kegan Paul, both in sympathy about ' Satan Absolved.'

" *2nd Nov.*— To Malwood with Anne and stopped to lunch. After it, old Sir William took me into his smoking room, and we talked over the whole South African case. The old man is, I think, secretly just as pleased as I am with the success of the Boers, though, when I said I should like to see the Boers established in Cape Town, he protested he could not go with me as far as that. However, he spoke strongly enough, and told me a number of most interesting things about Rhodes and Milner. When he was Chancellor of the Exchequer in 1893, Rhodes came to him about his railway project and humbugged him not a little. Sir William showed me a map on which Rhodes had marked his schemes, and he came again, when he was in England after the Raid, ' to face the music.' Sir William says he is an astonishing rogue and liar, but occasionally blurted out truths other rogues would hide, and he had boasted how he bought up everybody by putting them into good things on the Stock Exchange. He said that, though he, Rhodes, was certainly privy to the projected revolution at Johannesburg, he did not think he knew precisely of the Jameson Raid. The reason the Outlanders at the last moment would not rise was that they found out that Jameson intended to hoist the British Flag, and that did not suit them. They wanted to continue the Republic and run it themselves. As to Milner, Sir William said he was certain he was sent out on purpose to pick a quarrel with Kruger. He had seen a great deal of Milner while he was Chancellor of the Exchequer, and Milner came to wish him good-bye — and he had told him he knew why he was going. He knew, too, that Milner had told Lady Cowper at Panshanger before he left for the Cape, ' If I come back without having made war I shall consider my mission has failed.' Milner was an enthusiastic Jingo, but knew nothing of Statesmanship. Sir William also told me he had seen a good deal this year of Cromer, and had been charmed with him. He had found Cromer very moderate, hating Rhodes and hating Kitchener, and doing his best to keep them within bounds. He told me that if the Liberal Government had remained another fortnight in office they would have made Redvers Buller Commander-in-Chief, instead of Wolseley. Altogether my visit was a most interesting one. I wish I could remember a tithe of what he told me.

" *3rd Nov.*— A violent wind and rain, but we are snug here in our wood. Ladysmith is invested and isolated. There are reports of another defeat of White. I hope nothing will happen to Guy.

" *10th Nov.*— There is a severe article on ' Satan Absolved ' in the

'Chronicle' quoting Newman, and complaining of my profanity. I have nice letters, however, from York Powell and Mallock.

"*20th Nov.*— At Inchmery. The Belgian Minister, who was here yesterday, tells me the Queen of Holland wrote to Queen Victoria to beg her to make peace with the Transvaal, as so many of her subjects were engaged in it. He says the Queen did not like the use of the word 'subjects,' and did not answer the letter. He considers that the war, as far as it has gone, has much damaged England's prestige abroad. It has shown people specially that English officers, though brave, are without science. They all play too much instead of learning their work. He has been nineteen years in England, and is an Anglophile, but like all the rest he disapproves this war, and thinks it will result badly for us, even if in the end successful. We have suffered defeats which will encourage our enemies next time they quarrel with us.

"*23rd Nov.*— Fernycroft is shut up for the winter, and I have gone to Newbuildings, and am to start for Egypt on Wednesday. Fernycroft stripped of its leaves looks melancholy enough, and the thought of Egypt with its birds and butterflies is irresistible.

"They are making an immense fuss in the papers about the Emperor William's visit to Windsor. He has come in spite of the disgust of his own people, who are furious against us on account of the Boer war. But I fancy he knows his own game, and hating us at heart has come to spy out the nakedness of the land with a fresh military eye. Our newspaper people, however, would go down on their bellies to him and lick his feet if they were allowed.

"*24th Nov.*— To Wotton to dine and sleep. They have fought a new battle in South Africa, and another in the Soudan, and announced them as two British victories — victories I suspect to order for the German Emperor's benefit. The South African one seems nothing much to boast of besides 200 of our men lost, mostly of the Guards. The other is probably less bogus. Dear old Evelyn still sticks religiously to his political principles with me. We are the last of the anti-imperialist Conservatives.

"My poem is getting fearfully maltreated in the newspapers where I have no friend, as it attacks the country and Christianity alike, and what is worst, the newspapers themselves. This, however, was to be expected, and it is not the first time I have had the world on my back.

"*25th Nov.*— Back to Newbuildings and shot rabbits with Neville. I am closing my accounts of all kinds for the year, and shut up this journal in no sanguine mood of having anything happier to relate in the diaries of another year. The only thing I love now is my cat, and I am obliged, alas! to leave it behind."

CHAPTER XV

LAST YEAR OF THE NINETEENTH CENTURY

" 1st Dec.— On board the Messageries ship *Niger* off Corsica on my way to Egypt, having for the twentieth time shaken the dust of Europe from my feet. The day I started, Tuesday morning, I lunched with George Wyndham. He gave me the latest news of the war. They hope at the War Office to relieve Ladysmith in the course of the next eight days, but not without battles, one or two. They acknowledge now that the Boers are immensely stronger than they thought, that they are fighting according to the latest new scientific rules, and are armed with the newest of new weapons — they are officered in a large measure by Germans, and are holding their own determinedly. George does not make too much of the latest victories, Belmont and Graspan. But it seems to be part of the Boer tactics to invite attack on strong positions, and to hold these as long as they can inflict loss on their enemies — then at the last moment to run, so that, although the position is taken, the victor suffers most, and the Boers reassembling at a preconcerted rendezvous are not much the worse for their defeat. ' We could not let our men act like this,' said George, ' for if they once began to run there would be no stopping them.' So he by no means considers the matter over, sanguine as he naturally is. Guy Wyndham is still shut up with White at Ladysmith — and he showed me a most interesting letter from him written a month ago, immediately after the defeat of Nicholson's Nek, or whatever it is they call it. The letter described excellently an attack in three columns delivered by White, all of which failed in the presence of superior numbers, and it seemed to suggest of superior generalship. Guy had been with a detachment of a few hundred men pushed forward into an exposed situation from which it was more by luck than skill that they managed to extricate themselves. One of the officers had suddenly observed that the rest of the column seemed to be in retreat, and after pooh-poohing him at first they observed it too, and Guy volunteered to ride across the open hill under a heavy fire to ascertain the truth. This he did and discovered that the General in command had entirely forgotten the detachment, and sent it no order of retreat with the rest. So Guy had to ride back over the same rough ground with bullets and shells striking the earth all about him. The detachment was not brought in without considerable loss.

The letter, very simply written, gave a powerful picture of the hap-hazard character of modern warfare, and of the extreme helplessness of the units of an army while in action. The letter said nothing of the surrender of the third column, which was perhaps not known at the time by the writer, or it may have been purposely omitted, for what George showed me was a typewritten copy of the letter made for family reading. He was going down with it to his mother at Clouds in the afternoon, where there is naturally a great anxiety. Of the victory in the Soudan, and the death of the Khalifa, he seemed to admit that it, like Methuen's victories, had been timed to coincide with the Emperor William's visit to Windsor, just as the Dundee victory was for the Parliamentary vote. Personally, George was in the highest spirits, amply consoled for his disappointment at his not getting the Foreign Office instead of the War Office last summer.

"I have been reading Kegan Paul's Memoirs, which are extremely interesting. His description of his first school at Ilminster might stand for my own experience at Twyford, a mere hell upon earth — and I notice that the Ilminster master had been a Twyford boy, under Bed-ford, whom I remember as a very old man living on in retirement, near the school, when I first went there in 1847. The caning cupboards, on either side the head master's throne at Ilminster, were clearly modelled on the Twyford ones. I received a letter only the day before I left home from old Roberts who used to cane me in them, begging piteously for pheasants to eat in his old age. Now I am reading Aubrey De Vere's Memoirs. The two books are much on the same lines, and both interest me greatly, recalling memories of people I have known, and phases of thought gone through. Nevertheless Kegan Paul's is by far the best, being simpler and less literary. De Vere bores one a little with his poems, and his explanations of them. I remember him well when we lived at Mortlake for a year in 1853. He used to come and see my mother while he was staying with the Taylors at Shene. Mrs. Cameron was another of his friends, but Taylor was the central figure. For Taylor, Mrs. Cameron affected a great devotion, and had a portrait of him by Watts hung in a recess of her drawing-room before which a lamp continually burned. De Vere posed as a poet, and we children thought him a bore. All the same I have a very high respect for him now. An *homme de bien,* if ever one was in the world. Many years later, I came into communication with him regarding the letters of 'Proteus and Amadeus,' which he edited at Newman's sugges-tion. At one time Newman had almost consented himself to do the editing, for Dr. Meynell, the 'Amadeus' of the letters, was much at Edgbaston just then. But for one reason or another the old man changed his mind, and De Vere undertook the thing for him and wrote the preface.

"It was in connection with this that, in 1876 or 1877, I went to Edgbaston and stayed three days at the Oratory. I do not remember if at that time I kept a journal. I think not — and I may as well write here my recollection of the visit. I had stopped at Edgbaston on my way back from the west of Ireland, where I had been staying with Laprimaudaye at Treenlawr, and I had caught a toothache fishing on the Lough which worried me greatly, and I remember distinctly feeling as I knocked at the door that I should be thus *hors de combat* at the moment of my coming to consult the great man. Nevertheless my distress was vain, for I was shown up to him at once, and, at the instant of touching his hand when he received me, my pains vanished, nor did they return while I was staying in the house. Newman's was a wonderful hand, soft, nervous, emotional, electric; and I felt that a miracle had been wrought. I told Father Ryder of it at the time, but he charged me that I should tell no man, and I said no word of it to the Saint himself. Newman, though he knew well that I had come to consult him for the good of my soul, and though I had much conversation indirectly with him upon spiritual things, did not attempt to argue out any of the fundamental principles of religious thought, and sought to influence me rather through the heart by his great kindness, and by the confidence with which I was admitted to all the life of the community. It was a touching sight, indeed, to see the old man taking his turn with the rest to wait on us at table in the Refectory — and living his simple life of piety and cheerful unselfishness. The lives of monks and nuns are alone in some accordance with the life of Jesus. All the rest of Christianity is an imposture and an impudent negation of Christ.

"*5th Dec.*— Arrived at Sheykh Obeyd after nearly two years' absence. At Alexandria I had to wait some hours, and spent them in the company of Hewatt and his family at Ramleh. I found the Hewatts, to my surprise, very anti-Jingo about the war. There has been another 'victory' on the Modder — and another heavy loss of officers and men. I am sorry to see among the killed one of Mrs. Earle's two 'splendid sons,' about whom she wrote to me a month ago. She did not deserve this misfortune, for she was very humane in her ideas, and hated soldiering and all its ways.

"Anne met me at Cairo, and we went on home at once, having the good luck to travel in the same carriage with Sheykh Mohammed Abdu. Of all Easterns, perhaps I might say of all men, my dearest friend, Mohammed Abdu, after having been imprisoned for his Liberal opinions, and exiled by the Anglo-Khedivial restoration of 1882, has gradually become recognized for what he is, by far the ablest and most honest man in Egypt — and they have made him our Grand Mufti, the highest religious authority in the vice kingdom. I gave him an acre of land two years ago, and he has built himself a country house on it, and so is now our nearest neighbour.   When we said good-bye on my leaving Egypt last I little thought we should meet again.

" *6th Dec.*— Coming back here is like rising again from the dead. Everybody connected with the place clearly took it for granted I should be seen in it no more, and acted on the supposition.   Nothing very bad has been done, and some changes are for the better, but still they have been made.   My gazelles have been sent to the Zoölogical Garden, some of the horses have been sold, the house has been re-arranged. I feel like a guest in it — the *revenant* — the ghost who has returned. Perhaps it is all the more delightful, for the garden is in splendid leaf, and the trees never had a thicker shade in a more brilliant sunshine. Encroachments in the way of new wells and cultivated fields have been made all round us in the desert, and we are already almost completely cut off from the open plain.   But it is the least of the evils that threatened us four years ago.   First the sewage farm, and then the building operations.   So that the new corn fields may be looked upon as a comparative blessing in an age of unscrupulous progress.

" *15th Dec.*— Two new Boer victories, or rather British defeats. One at Stormberg, the other at Spytfontein.   People will soon be getting angry in London, and perhaps leave off some of their music hall songs.   There is a ridiculous swaggering one in the papers, promising Uncle Paul to dine with him on Christmas Day.   It reminds me of the Paris cry, ' à Berlin,' which became historic.

THE NEW PATRIOTIC SONG

Now Sung at the Music Halls and Theatres with immense success.

KRUGER'S DINNER PARTY; Dec. 7, 1899

or,

We'll be There.

Written by Fred C. Smale.   Composed by Geo. Le Brunn.

Oh, Uncle's giving a party and he's asked us all to come,
    We'll be there!
We're marching up from Durban town, behind the fife and drum
    And we'll be there!
There's some from Dublin City, there's some from out the West,
The Devon lads " be vitty," there's Gordons with the rest;
Oh, Uncle, don't you trouble, there is time enough to spare —
    We'll be there!

(Chorus) So please you, Uncle Paul, light the Lantern in the Hall
    (We know we're welcome as the flow'rs in May),
Just keep the pudding hot for the lively little lot
    Who are coming up to dinner Christmas Day.

We've got some little sailor men, we thought you wouldn't mind,
    They'll be there!
We are bringing them to see our Uncle Paul so good and kind,
    They'll be there!
They have come across the ocean, they would like some tea and buns,
Then they'll just give you a notion how they work their little guns.
    No, Uncle, dear, they are not at sea — they travel everywhere.
    They'll be there!

(Chorus) So please you, Uncle Paul, just arrange a little ball
    (They're having one or two upon the way);
Majuba some went through, and they want to speak to you,
    So they're coming up to dinner Chrismas Day.

Pretoria's a place we've often wanted for to see,
    We'll be there!
The air with us, there is no doubt, will splendidly agree,
    We'll be there!
Perhaps I may just mention, we are coming up in style,
And with the firm intention of remaining for a while;
Still, Uncle, don't you worry, for mother's paid the fare.
    We'll be there!

(Chorus) So please you, Uncle Paul, see that there's enough for all.
    There's fifty thousand Tommies on the way,
And somewhere in a bag they have got a little flag
    To stick up in the pudding Christmas Day!

————

KEITH, PROWSE and CO., Cheapside, E.C.

[N, B. Several of our regiments *did* dine with Uncle Paul that Christmas Day, but it was as prisoners of war.]

"A torrent of newspaper abuse has fallen on my ' Satan Absolved.' The first notices were fairly moderate, but as the war has gone more and more against our Army, they have become more and more vindictive. They began by admitting that the poetry had some eloquence; then it was found clever, but vulgar; then blasphemous, vulgar, and stupid. Now the condemnation is extended to all my poems. It has been discovered that the ' Songs of Proteus ' were a plagiarism on Meredith's ' Modern Love ': and that in the rest of my works I have been ever sinking deeper in the mire.

" *17th Dec.*— The third and main British army is badly beaten on the Tugela River. MacDonald (John Murray MacDonald), Anne's cousin by marriage, who is staying with us, declares he shall go off himself to fight. He is a mild semi-Jingo Radical of the school that believes the British Empire has a divine mission to subdue and occupy the waste places of the earth. I have been arguing the Boer case with him for

the last ten days.   To me it is incredible how any reasonable creature
should believe such trash.   His wife and her niece Irene Noel are
generally on my side.   But to-day when I say, 'Now we ought to make
peace with the Boers' they are all against me.   Even Anne thinks that
the rights of the blood feud forbid *that*.   Yet what absurdity!   War,
when it is a war of aggression, as they all admit that this is, is mere
murder, and though it is humiliating to make peace on a defeat, it can't
be surely *right* to go on.

"As to the wisdom of persisting, the Boers are really better soldiers
than ours.   We had a few good regiments to begin with, but they are
pretty well used up now, and the rest is of a feeble kind.   Our army,
if it can fight, cannot march, and has to stick to the lines of railway.
Our superior numbers are consequently of little advantage.   The Boers
are making a splendid fight for their freedom, and are winning all
along the line.   Every honest man, English or not, ought to rejoice.
Instead of this, we English are in league with the Americans, we, who
were the two peoples who have posed as champions of freedom in the
world, to subdue two small, weak nations, the Boers and the Filipinos,
fighting for their independence, and not a word of disapproval is heard
amongst us.

"Young Walter Gaisford, Talbot's A.D.C., was here the other day,
lamenting that the Khalifa and his dervishes had all been killed, so
that there would be nobody left to shoot, he complained, even in the
Soudan.   'There is hope, however, that, when the Boers are polished
off, we may go on to a war with Abyssinia when more sport will be to
be had.'   This is the way our young fellows look at war ('a high old
rabbit shoot').   It is good for them and the world that they have at
last met their match.   War will be unpopular enough in England soon
if it goes on as at present, and there will be a chance then for the weak
nations to remain unmolested.

"*20th Dec.*— Prince Aziz was here yesterday and told me things
that were interesting.   He was once a lieutenant in the 16th Lancers,
and talks intelligently about the war.   Gatacre, he says, was always a
fool, violent and abusive to the natives in India.   He had been certain
he would get into trouble when it came to fighting.   The Prince holds
the British Army cheap.   They would never have been able to get to
Omdurman but for the Egyptian troops, who did all the work and all
the fighting, and in South Africa they were inferior in everything to
the Boers.   Things have come to a pretty pass when this fat Egyptian
Prince can hold such opinions.   But they are perfectly justified.   Kitchener, as a last hope of saving the situation, has been named Chief of
the Staff to Roberts, and is to start at once for the Cape.   The Dutch
in Cape Colony are in revolt.   The English newspapers say there has
not been such a position of things since the Indian Mutiny.   It is

thought old Roberts, who is popular with our rank-and-file, will be able to restore confidence. But he is too old for serious work, and they have shoved Kitchener forward to the real command. I don't believe either of them is a bit better than our beaten Generals. I had long talks with Roberts in India years ago, and he gave me a poor notion of his intelligence, good old fellow as he is. As for Kitchener, he knows nothing of European war, and his Soudanese experience will serve him little. He has the curse on him of the Mahdi's head, and deserves to fail. There is a paragraph in the papers this week giving an account of the Khalifa's end, and how courageously he met it. This man has been uniformly represented as a contemptible coward. Yet he met death as nobly as any of Plutarch's heroes.

"*25th Dec.*— Christmas Day. Kitchener has left Egypt. Though he sailed from Alexandria he had not the grace to go to Montaza, where the Khedive was, to bid him good-bye. Yet he has been drawing £6,000 a year latterly from the Egyptian Treasury, and high pay for the last fifteen years. A bearer of the white man's burden at £6,000 a year!

"*29th Dec.*— I have received a nice letter from old Herbert Spencer about the attacks made on my poem by the critics, and saying he thinks I was probably right when I told him I thought it would need a foreign army landed on our shores to bring us quite to our sober senses. There is at present a lull in the South African fighting, the Boers waiting to be attacked again and the English not having got their second wind.

"Margaret Talbot came to-day and spent the afternoon. Her husband is in command here of the English garrison, and is, of course, much grieved at the way the Boer War is going. He would like to be there, but at the same time would dread the responsibility of failure where so many others have failed. She described Kitchener's departure. He was only half an hour at Cairo — the time between one train and another, and said hardly a word to anyone. No one here regrets him, for he has made no friends.

"*31st Dec.*— The last year of the 1800's ends disastrously for England, or rather for the British Empire. For England can only gain by the break-up of that imposture. I think now there really is some chance of such a consummation, for we are sending the whole of our armed force into South Africa, where it is likely to become engulfed, and we have got the whole sentiment of the world, civilized and uncivilized, against us.

> Thou hast deserved men's hatred — they shall hate thee;
> Thou hast deserved men's fear — their fear shall kill;
> Thou hast thy foot upon the weak, the weakest
> With his armed head shall bite thee on the heel.

" Percy Wyndham writes : ' In this terrible struggle in South Africa we see a picture in little of what will be the close of the present dispensation, to use the language of those who believe in prophecy, when the survivors of Teutonic blood will fight for the mastery of the world — in that struggle the Dutch, South African or Native, will have a look in.'

" Two young British officers were here this afternoon. They are both agog to join the fighting, looking at the whole thing entirely from the professional point of view. ' If we are not in this show,' they said, emphatically, ' we may as well hang up our hats.'

" *1st Jan.,* 1900.— The Emperor William, the papers say, has issued a rescript, ordaining that the new Christian Century is to begin in Germany to-day. This, if true, goes one better than Carlyle's Emperor, who was *super grammaticam.* I find the Moslem centuries go down to the end of the hundreds, and begin again with the year one.

" Mohammed Abdu, our Mufti, was here this afternoon. And to him I read Herbert Spencer's letter, which immensely interested him, and afterwards described to him my poem. He considers Spencer the first of living philosophers, and has translated his book on Education into Arabic. I also explained to his brother Hamouda my views of the rights of animals, which was one absolutely new to him. Though on reflection he said that it was strictly in accordance with the Koran and Moslem teaching, which enjoins respect to animals, and even to inanimate objects. So that it is forbidden wantonly to deface so much as a stone. In truth, it is Christianity that is really responsible for the brutal attitude of modern man towards animals. No other religion that can be called a religion tolerates it, but our Christian doctors have laid down the atrocious doctrine that beasts and birds were made solely for man's use and pleasure, and that he has no duties towards them. It is only in the last hundred years that Europeans, having partly freed themselves from Christian teaching, have begun to take a humaner view. The doctrine of evolution has pushed it a bit forwarder, for though it has injured the cause of savage or coloured man as having equal rights with the white man, it has established our far away kinship with the beasts, which was formerly denied. So that there are a few amongst us who begin to doubt our right to bird and beast slaughter. My own view is that wild birds and beasts who do no harm to man have a right to be left in absolute peace. But that those whom we help to breed by giving them protection may fairly pay a certain tribute, just as our tame beasts are made to do, though the higher law would be to let all live. We argue these things nightly at dinner.

" *5th to 10th Jan.*— We were occupied with a desert excursion to within sight of Ismalia on the Suez Canal and back, our furthermost point being a prominent dark brown rock, which stands some hundred feet above the plain overlooking the Bitter Lake. From this point we marched north north-west to the Sand-hills and the Wady Tumey-lat. The following day, the 9th January, Anne and I made a long camel trot of six hours across the gravel plain, crossing Wady Jaffra to another conspicuous rock south of Belbeis, and so on the 10th back to Sheykh Obeyd. It was a pleasant excursion, but contains little worth recording.

" 10th Jan.— Mohammed Abdu was here to-day, and confirms to the full the accounts of Kitchener's dealings with the Mahdi's head as I gave it last summer in the ' Daily News,' especially as to Cromer's dis-approval of it and his dislike of Kitchener. We agreed that at last God's Providence was moved to anger against these abominations, and that England's Empire would go the way of all the rest.

" There is a letter in the ' Times ' just come which I think caps every-thing yet written for absurd bombast. Its author is old Reid, the naval constructor, a former Gladstonian Radical, and still M.P. It shows to what a pass of self-glorification we English have come, for the Radicals are worse now than the extremest Tories, and I have had to write home to tell them to cease sending me the ' Daily Chronicle ' and the ' Man-chester Guardian,' and replace them with the ' Daily Mail ' and ' Morn-ing Post.' The only London paper that speaks a word of sense is the ' Westminster Gazette.' Here is the concluding paragraph :

" ' May I add, Sir, that my thoughts search history in vain for any spectacle of national heroism greater than, or equal to, that which Great Britain and her truly noble colonies are presenting to the world at this moment. The crafty and foreigner-aided enemy lies in our territory and across our path, with shell guns on every available hill, and trenches dug between; with barbed wire stretched to protect their cunningly de-vised lairs, and cover spread to conceal their more or less rebellious persons. Their power to deal out death and mutilation is their delight; their skill in doing so is their pride; and it is known that the flag which they most hate is the Union Jack, the very symbol of freedom and equality throughout the world. They have done their level and their unlevel best to slay our men and lower our flag on our own soil. They are difficult to tackle, for they fight lurking, and fly alike from cold steel and the open field. All that human heroism combined with ani-mal cunning can perform they will do against us, and they will add to these such prayers as even ignoble lips oft dare to address to the God of battles. But have they alarmed us? Have they " frightened the isle from its propriety? " Have they detached one colony from the mother-land? Have they caused young or old, citizen or noble, poor or rich, small or great, worldling or worshipful, in any part of this Imperial Realm to shrink or hold back from the encounters, however deadly, to which they have challenged us? No, Sir, there has sprung from every

part of the Empire a flame of patriotism and of heroism so high that
the whole world is, so to speak, alight with it, and, depend upon it, while
we rejoice, the world wonders and admires.' "[1]

N.B. The total Boer population thus described as menacing the
British Empire, with its 200,000,000 souls, is exactly that of Brighton.

" 15th Jan.— I have been reading Mivart's article on the ' Continuity
of Catholicism,' which has raised a tempest against him.   It is certainly
the most daring declaration ever made *in articulo mortis,* for poor
Mivart is, I believe, dying. If, forty years ago, I had found a Catholic
writer equally bold, I should have been saved from much infidelity, but
now it is too late.   Mivart is clinging desperately to his faith, but it is
at bottom an impossible thing to reconcile science with any form of
Christianity.

" 21st Jan.— A letter in verse about ' Satan Absolved,' from Sir
Wilfrid Lawson, which is bad verse but amusing:

> Brayton, 9th Jan. 1900
>
> Your work on the Devil, dear Blunt, I have read.
> What a curious fancy to enter your head!
> The World, I admit, is as bad as can be;
> But how *he'*ll make it better I scarcely can see.
> I fancy if matters were right understood
> There's a Spirit of bad and a spirit of good,
> They're continually fighting in battle array
> Each pulling like mad in a different way,
> The one is Jehovah, Jove, Lord, Names like these,
> The other is the Devil as bad as you please.
> Then between these two powers comes man on the scene,
> Where he comes from there's no one can tell us, I ween;
> But still here he is with a body and soul
> Designed, I imagine, for filling some rôle.
> His rudder is conscience by which he should steer,
> But at present it seems to be quite out of gear.
> But come, my dear Blunt, do not let us despair.
> Even yet we may make something of him with care,
> At present he is — you and I never flatter —
> At present he is just as mad as a hatter.
> His brain has undoubtedly met with a shock,
> Which has sent him through Africa running amock.
> The nobility, gentry, and clergy of course,
> His madness by all in their power enforce,
> And all in this country are cutting their capers
> At the murders recorded each day in the papers.
> Well, in trying my best to hunt these matters out
> That the Devil is in it I haven't a doubt
> Well, I will resist him, as long as I can,

[1] " Times," 1900.

And so do my best to emancipate man.
Some good yet we may see when there comes to the front
The excellent doctrine of Lawson and Blunt.

" 28*th Jan.* (*Sunday*).— A long talk with Mohammed Abdu on the
whole subject of mankind and the dealings of the strong with the weak.
I find he is as pessimistic as myself.   He has been reading the *Towra,*
the Old Testament Pentateuch, lately, and attributes the brutalities of
Christianity largely to its connecion with Judaism.   As to the treatment
of dumb animals he quoted to me several of the *Hawadith* enjoining
kindness, and it is certain that wanton destruction of these is contrary
to the sentiment of Moslems.   Wanton destruction is indeed peculiar
to Christendom.   Abdu believes in no good future for the human race,
and I fear he has as little faith in Islam, Grand Mufti though he be, as
I have in the Catholic Church.

" Buller has had another reverse before Ladysmith at Spion Kop.
This time it is General Warren who has suffered defeat.   I am glad of
it.   It was he that hanged the Bedouins for the Palmer affair after
Tel-el-Kebir.   I have written to Leonard Courtney to say I will join
the ' Stop the War Committee,' and am sending £50.   This though with
some qualms of conscience, for if the war goes on another six months
it really may smash up the British Empire.

" My once dearest friend Lothian is dead.   What a grief this would
have been to me five-and-thirty years ago!   He was the lightest of all
light-hearted companions, yet serious too.   We made our storm and
stress together at Frankfort when Darwinism was a novelty, and solved
the riddle of the universe together gazing at the stars.   We have gone
different roads since then.   He to lead an uneventful life of high and
various dignities in Scotland, I to adventure in what devious ways.   It
is only casually that we have met for years.

" 29*th Jan.*— I have written the following in answer to one who had
criticized my ' Satan Absolved ' on the ground that though splendid if
intended as a *reductio ad absurdum* of Christianity, it stopped short of
accepting Nietsche's doctrine of Force.   ' Of course the poem was a
reductio ad absurdum.   The thing that seemed to me supremely in
need of being shown ridiculous was the worship of humanity in any
form.   I am not a disciple of Tolstoy.   He believes in the possibility
of improvement, in moral progress, and in a far away Christian civilization.   I do not.   At the same time I do not mock at Christian ideals.
If Man were not the ludicrous, vicious ape he is, but were capable of
being converted to a quiet, harmless life without thought for the morrow
— or ambition or desire more than to praise God and enjoy himself in
the sun like the lilies of the field, the world would be a very happy place,
as it was before Man came to disturb it.   But of course this will never

come to pass. It never even really began. That, however, is no reason for adoring as you say you do Force even tempered by Fraud. There is nothing in the smallest degree admirable in either. If it is true that your worship of Force is to be the creed of the future, and very likely it will be so, it is only another proof of the innate vulgarity of man. Nietsche is an ass. The law of the strongest, as we see it in Modern Civilization, is not the law of Nature, only the law of *human* nature, which is a very different thing. The oak tree does not monopolize the forest, nor are the flowers which grow there trash. If Nietsche had been as many years as I have in the East he would not talk of the Christian ideal as being a creed of a slave for slaves. He would know it was far more truly the creed of the dervish, of the poor, happy vagrant who scorns property and scorns what we Europeans absurdly call the " dignity of labour," and who is as free as the birds of the air. It needs Oriental experience to understand this. The place for European civilization is the Paris boulevard; south of the Mediterranean a white skin is only a form of leprosy, and from an æsthetic point of view you might as well plant the New Forest with cabbages as have anything to do with applying the doctrine of Force to the world at large.'

"Mivart has been formally excommunicated by Cardinal Vaughan. It seems to me that if Catholics are really called upon to believe that the first man was the Adam of the Garden of Eden, and that all the books of the Old and New Testaments not merely ' contain Revelation with no admixture of error,' but were also ' written by the inspiration of the Holy Ghost and have God for their Author,' we may abandon the idea of any possible reconciliation between religion and science. Of course one knew the thing was hopeless, but still there were many Catholics, even priests, who pretended it was not.

"I have had several more talks with Mohammed Abdu. He tells me that several of the high English officials here make money in illicit ways. He is, however, as little in favour of internationalizing Egypt as I am, for that would merely be to exchange one wolf for a pack of wolves. He is bitter against Cromer, whom otherwise he likes, for having established nothing that can survive of indigenous Government when the English Occupation ends — nothing, that is, that can be counted on to work on Liberal and honest lines. There has been a general proscription of the patriotic and enlightened element in the country, and the men pushed forward have been those who had least self-respect and could most surely be counted on for their pliancy.

" 5*th Feb.*— Parliament has met, and the Queen's Speech has been telegraphed. Pharaoh has hardened her heart, and declares that she will carry the war on to a successful end. Buller has, however, clearly been badly beaten again at Spion Kop and Ladysmith must fall. The famine in India is a new ' judgment of God ' upon the Empire, and, just as in old times, the stress of the punishment falls on the innocent. There are three and a half millions of people now on daily relief. Yet I suppose not a single official of all that have fattened upon India will forgo a third of his income — or a fourth or a tenth part of it to feed the people — this although they are subscribing and making the natives subscribe to the South African War. It is the ' divine mission ' we are carrying out of making the world happy!

" Osman Digna has been captured at last and brought in chains to Cairo. ' A large crowd pressed forward eager to see the dark, long face, brilliant eyes, large mouth, and long grey beard, of a frightened and dignified old man who sat with chains round his sore ankles and swollen, bare feet.' I quote ' Our own correspondent.' This is how the British Empire makes its ' Roman holiday '! But the hour of vengeance is, I hope, now very near.

" *8th Feb.*— George Wyndham has made a very able speech in defence of the War Office and his political fortune is made. I am glad of this, though his principles in politics have been up to now abominable. He is no Philistine at heart, and will be sobered both by the defeat of his policy and his personal success, and may end as a great and large-minded statesman. He was wise enough to confine his speech strictly to the War Office, and did not attempt to explain the policy of the war: being a subordinate of very short standing in the Government he will not be held responsible, and people will only see in him what they most appreciate, a very clever parliamentarian defending a bad party cause in the best possible way. The only speech that was sound on the Opposition side was Sir Robert Reed's, which stated the whole case against the war fully and fairly.

" 14*th Feb.*— I have written as follows to John Dillon in honour of the reunion of the Irish Parliamentary Party:

Sheykh Obeyd, *Feb.* 14, 1900.

" DEAR DILLON,

" I write to congratulate you and the rest of my old friends of the Irish Parliamentary Party on the reunion of the Party, and your resolution to be once more independent of English ones. You know that for the last ten years I have held aloof from politics and have been mute about Ireland. But I cannot help saying now how much I sympathize with you all. The moment certainly has come for a new departure — for Ireland's one chance lies in the check given to our English plan of a world-wide Empire which has been accepted equally by both parties and which leaves no room anywhere for Nationalism. I think, too, that the iniquity of the war we are carrying on in South Africa, and which both Parties almost equally approve, should make it intolerable for an honest man to remain any longer allied with either.

I don't know which is the more despicable, the boasting Tory who made the war openly for the fun of the thing and to fill his pockets, or the Radical, who has allowed himself to be persuaded that he might bully the Boers cheaply and in accordance with Liberal principles. At any rate I am glad to see Ireland free from both of them. There was always to my mind a certain danger to her high ideal in her connection, however temporary, with our ambitions. Imperialism is very contagious, and Scotch, as well as English Radicalism, has been entirely perverted by it. I have often thought that the ' union of hearts ' we talked so much about in 1887 might, if it had become a reality, have only led to the perversion of Ireland too. It is best as it is — at least until we English are humbled to entire sanity.

"I shall be glad if you will show this letter to Harrington and Healy and Redmond, as well as to Davitt and O'Brien, as I intend it equally for all. It is a great pleasure to me to be able to think of you fighting once more well together for Liberty as in the days of our old campaign."

" 15*th Feb.*— Cockerell arrived last night from London very keen for sight-seeing, and to-day Evelyn also came; he is strong for stopping the war, and also approves of my letter to Dillon.

" Mohammed Abdu was here in the afternoon and told me the true story of the military trouble at Khartoum. Kitchener has long been hated by the Egyptian Officers, whom he has throughout ill-treated, allowing the English Officers to behave arrogantly to them, and paying no attention to their complaints. The Egyptian troops have been made to do all the hard work, and have been given no credit, while the black troops have been petted and spoiled. When things began to go badly at the Cape Kitchener got alarmed, and tried to prevent any news of the English defeats reaching the Soudan, but he could not hinder it leaking through. Then fearing a revolt he ordered the ammunition to be taken away on the pretence that it was old and would be renewed, but the Soudanese regiments refused to give up the old till the new was supplied; the Egyptian Officers were suspected of encouraging the refusal and some were arrested. In the middle of it all Kitchener was recalled to go to South Africa, and the thing was patched up by Wingate who is less unpopular, though it is not wholly settled yet. Abdu tells me that the idea now is in the event of the Egyptian Question being brought on by the European Powers to call in Turkish troops to replace our English garrison. This would be a lesser evil than the advent of French or Italian troops, which would only mean the Internationalization of Egypt. Mohammed Abdu knows that it has been talked over among the Ministers and with Lord Cromer. I am inclined to hope that it may really end thus for there seems to be no chance of a simple evacuation in favour of a native Egyptian Government. Abdu has a good opinion of Cromer personally. But says there are a number of shady things done by his subordinates.

"*16th Feb.*— Buller's third attack on the Boers and his attempt to cross the Tugela has failed as abjectly as the other two, and we may hear any day now of the fall of Ladysmith; a final attempt I fancy to capture a victory in view of the vote in Parliament for which it has served its purpose, though later it turned into a defeat.

"*17th Feb.*— To Cairo with Cockerell. The first time I have been there this winter, after seventy-four days at Sheykh Obeyd, so that I felt strange and naked in European clothes. On the road we met Prince Aziz who talked with much intelligence about the management of his property. These Khedivial Princes are all of them shrewd men of business. He also gave us news of the relief of Kimberley, a telegram having come last night. This will have the practical effect of putting that sad villain Rhodes once more on the scene of the world's intrigues. I am sorry for it.

"I called on various necessary people, including Margaret Talbot in her new official house as the General's Lady, and on Cromer, who talked to me for half an hour about Nile irrigation, the debts of the fellahin, the famine in India, and such administrative subjects as he talks best on. He is certainly a great man in his official way. We did not touch on any dangerous matters, nor allude in any sort to past differences. Personally I like him much. Amongst the plans he discussed with me was one in connection with the National Bank of advancing small sums of £5 and £10 to the fellahin at 9 per cent., to enable them to get out of the hands of the Greek usurers, who charge them thirty and forty per cent. This is precisely the scheme the Nationalists of 1881 had, and its adoption by Cromer is another proof of the foresight of those poor patriots whom we cannoned into silence. With the single exception of constitutional government, I believe every article now of the National Programme has been adopted by us.

"*24th Feb.*— The MacDonalds and Irene, and her brother are gone to Greece, after staying here three months. She is an attractive child, clever and pretty — and her brother, Byron, interesting, because quite uneducated, with a good heart and much sense. Young Ward was here yesterday, who is acting as correspondent to the 'Times.' He gave us news that Roberts, having raised the siege of Kimberley, has now got Kranje's army in such a position that it seems likely to surrender. This is important, and I fear will rehabilitate Chamberlain and the Rhodes gang. Lady Lytton writes to me after her waiting at Osborne: 'I enjoyed my three quiet weeks at Osborne, and the Queen is such a splendid example of wisdom over the war and all the sorrow and things that follow from it, and she always judges rightly without too

much emotion. . . . You say you wish they would stop the fighting.
Every one wishes it also, but we must get to Pretoria first, and be
able to get equal justice for all our people there, and for
which reason the war has been brought on England, and it
will be a very long business of years — so let us try and be
patient, and good will come out of it in the end. The spirit of wishing to help is quite splendid everywhere in England, and the soldiers
must be allowed to do better than they have done as yet before they
stop fighting.' This no doubt is her Majesty's sentiment. Milner who
arranged the ' equal justice' *casus belli* will now doubtless get his peerage. Sibell writes in the same strain about the unselfishness of the
war, and the noble qualities of all concerned. One might think it was
a crusade, instead of being the Stock Exchange swindle it is. The art
of governing the world has become the art of deceiving, not only the
people, but if possible one's own high-minded conscience.

"*1st March.*— I went into Cairo with Cockerell, and learned the
relief of Ladysmith. Kronje capitulated a few days ago at Paardeburg,
and the Boer army has evacuated Natal, and seems to be concentrating
for a final stand on the Drakensburg line. One thing is satisfactory in
it, the release of Guy Wyndham from his captivity. There have been
debates in the House of Commons about Chamberlain's part of the
Raid. He now says that his white-washing of Rhodes after the Committee Report only concerned Rhodes' money transactions. I remember George telling me at the time (and he was in the thick of the plot)
that they had played a trick on the opposition in getting Harcourt and
the rest of them to agree to the Report on an understanding that Rhodes
was to be thrown over, and also, if I remember rightly, in forcing
Chamberlain's hand to support Rhodes. This one thing is certain,
Rhodes remained, and is still a Privy Councillor.

"*5th March.*— I have been very busy getting ready for our long
intended pilgrimage to Mount Sinai. Anne is unable to go as Judith
has written hurrying her departure for the expected baby, but Cockerell goes with me and my nurse, Miss Lawrence. We are to start
on the 7th, and take steamer to Tor on the 8th, and be met there by
our camels.

"*6th March.*— Evelyn spent the day with us having come to Egypt
with his daughters. He is in trouble having just received a telegram
from his son to say that he has joined the Imperial Yeomanry and is
going to South Africa. It is the smart thing to do just now, and all
the world is mad for fighting.

"*7th March.*— To Suez by train, a hot, disagreeable journey, and
put up at the ' Bel Air,' next the station. Suez full of pilgrims, the
streets crowded and gay.

"*8th March.*— Occupied in taking our places by the Khedivial steamer for Tor, and getting passports for Suliman and Hassan at the Moudirieh. The people there very friendly, as the Governor was formerly an Arabist and the Katib had been secretary to Mahmoud Fehmy. The place was being besieged by pilgrims come for their passports, which cost them 150 piastres, to the Hedjaz. In the afternoon went on board the *Chibine* with the agent Beyts, whom I remember twenty years ago at Jeddah, where he had a house of business with one Wild. He did what he could to make us comfortable, but the *Chibine* is crowded with pilgrims, 350 of them, they say.

"*9th March.*— I went to my berth early and woke about half-past one, and opened the cabin window as it was very hot below, and so was lying awake thinking over the lapse of years since I was last at Mount Sinai and the poor issue of our short lives, when I felt as it were a blow received by the vessel, and immediately after a second blow. At the first moment I thought it was an earthquake shock — we had had one last Tuesday at Sheykh Obeyd — and called out to Cockerel, who shared my cabin, to that effect; but looking out of the window I saw a line of breakers close before us on the port side, and the ship began to be knocked about by the waves. It was very dark, but the breakers were plain enough, and I said to Cockerel, ' No. We are on a Coral Reef.' I had not undressed and had nothing but my shoes to put on to be ready for all events. And I went to Miss Lawrence's cabin and told her to get up and dress as we were aground. Then on Cockerel's confirming what had happened I went on the upper deck where Suliman and Hassan were, and got the life-belt I always carry out of the bullock trunk in which it was and put it on Miss Lawrence. She was not at all frightened, nor indeed was anybody else as far as I know — though the Pilgrims began reciting their prayers aloud. The wind was blowing pretty strong, and I could make out the line of the shore not far off and the breakers, though the night was dark. There did not seem to be any immediate danger, but we prepared ourselves for whatever might happen, and in the darkness, of course, there was room to imagine the worst. I did not stay long, however, on deck, but after some talk with Suliman went below and lay down again, for it was clear there was nothing to be done till daylight. I had looked at my watch as soon as the vessel struck, and found it was seven minutes past three. Cockerell and Miss Lawrence stayed on deck, I believe, till morning. After a bit I got to sleep again, for the ship was steady enough, and there was nothing very tragic in the appearance of things.

" By daylight we were able to make out where we were. Suliman thought at first the hills in front of us were the Hamam Faraoun. But later we made out Serbal and the mouth of Wady Feiran, so it is now agreed that we are ashore north of Ras Jehan. The Captain, Ross,

did not seem to know much about it. He told us he had only left the
deck ten minutes when the thing happened. [This turned out afterwards to have been quite untrue. He had come on board late, having
been at some entertainment at Suez, and gone to bed early without giving any proper instructions as to the course. No watch was kept, and we
drove straight on a coral reef, without so much as slackening speed
or with a cry of breakers ahead! We must be clear eight miles out of
our course, and it looks like bad seamanship. Here we are, anyhow,
stuck fast on a line of sand banks (they proved to be a reef about
a mile from the shore) and with small chance of getting off to-day or
any other day. The steamer is miserably ill supplied with boats,
and still more miserably with seamen, there are only four boats capable
of taking off at most a dozen passengers each, and of these one is
already lost. They launched it, the Captain says, in order to put
out a hawser for an anchor to windward, but it was swamped by a
breaker, and at least one man has been drowned. I saw another
holding on to the hawser for some minutes, and we thought he would
be swept away too, but at last he got hold of a rope and hitched it
round him, and was pulled up the ship side, but it was a near shave.
The boat drifted away, and is now on the sandbank (reef) bottom
upwards, and five lifebuoys, which were thrown to the drowning men,
are drifting on shore. The captain asked me about the nature of the
country on which we had run, the shore of the Sinai penisula, and I
offered to let my Bedouin, Suliman, go in a boat if they could put
him safely on shore when the wind drops; he would then take a message to Tor, which is not more than forty miles away, asking help.
Suliman, however, is very unwilling to go, now that he has seen
the *feluca* swamped and the man drowned, nor will I let him attempt
it until the wind goes down. [It was Suliman's first experience of
being at sea, and, like most Bedouins, he was frightened at being off
his own element.] Should it become calm I shall propose that we are
all sent on shore here with our baggage, as we are the only passengers
for Tor, and we have provisions enough with us for a fortnight. I
am writing this at 9.45 a.m.

   " 1.30 p.m.— Things look worse than they did. The tide going down
has shown that we are on a coral reef, which may be half a mile
in width, with, perhaps, three miles of comparatively still water
beyond it to the shore. Also the wind has become stronger, and, though
the waves do not break over the deck, we are beginning to heel over
in rather an alarming way. I finished Tolstoy's ' Resurrection ' this
morning. It is a most depressing book, and makes one as willing as
one can easily be to leave a life so miserable as Tolstoy shows it.
I don't know which is the more hopeless, the picture of polite society
en décomposition, or that of his convicts and political prisoners who

find a dreary satisfaction in helping each other in ways which human nature cannot really be satisfied with. All the same, one clings a bit to life. There is a certain physical menace in death which it is ill to face, and I feel it more strongly this afternoon than I did last night when the danger was vaguer and newer. The poor man drowned has saddened us, and made the danger seem more real, but as yet we have not even begun to feel discomfort. No water has reached the cabins, or even the decks, except now and then the spray of a wave, and the sun is shining brightly, and we are surrounded by flights of happy seagulls. The shore is romantic and beautiful between Serbal, in front to the north-east and Ghareb to the south-west, both mountains which I love and on which I could be content to die. It is the physical repulsion that one has, that of being knocked to pieces on the reef, or drowned in one's cabin. Two ships have been sighted far off, but they took no notice of our signals, and we are fully ten miles away from the usual Red Sea course. My own only satisfaction is to think Anne did not come with us. She has a terror of water, though of nothing else, and would have been unhappy. Both Cockerell and Miss Lawrence are cheerful and undisturbed; indeed, every one is behaving well. We are all three sitting on the upper deck now, on a carpet with one of the pilgrims next us, a man from Mitgamr. At every blow of a wave which shakes the ship he ejaculates, 'Ya robb! Ya róbbina'! (From God are all things. Yes, all. Our Lord is merciful. Ya, Robb!) Below there is an old lady who puts her head out of the cabin and calls to her son, 'Ya, Yusuf! Ya, Yusuf!' The rest are devout and quiet, and there is none of the affectation of merriment one would see under like circumstances on board a P. and O.

"*10th March (Friday)*. [N.B. This part of my Diary is splashed with sea water, but still legible.] We have had a very bad night and things this morning look almost hopeless. With the rise of the tide at sunset the wind increased in violence, blowing still from the north-west, and the waves swept the upper deck. I went up to try and persuade Suliman and Hassan to come below, but they would not move. The whole night through the ship was banged upon the reef — raised by each wave, and let down with a thundering bang upon her keel, which prevented much sleeping. At times it seemed as if she must break her back. At midnight it was quieter, but it is worse than ever this morning, and the ship has settled lower into the water. There is only one comfort, she is now wholly aground, and cannot sink lower. It depends all on the wind. If it goes on like this for another night she will break up, and there is no chance of a rescue. There are practically no boats and no sailors. The captain would not risk trying to land the passengers except in a calm. Even the arrival of another ship would be of no use, as we could not be got off. If the wind does not fall, it will not be our pilgrims' fault, for they pray strenuously, with a fine male devotion. The women have been drilled to silence, or at any rate to pray instead of complaining, even the little boys shout, ' Alláhu Akbar. Ya latif ' ! and the women add prayers to Seyd el Bédawi of Tantah. For my own part I say my usual prayers to the dead and to St. Winifred, who may help me, as she did three years ago, a superstition which quiets the mind. I have been reading the Gospels, too, in an edition Cockerell got me for our journey to Sinai, parts of Mathew, Mark, and Luke, the doctrinal parts of which are splendid, and as little like our English nineteenth-century Christianity as it is possible to conceive. How foolish my Nietsche correspondent's talk about it is. The water is coming into the cabin, so I must leave off. Miss Lawrence has been altogether admirable through all this, doing her duty to me as a nurse just as if at home, and cheerful and courageous as I never saw anyone. I have just been on deck and got wet through. It has made me feel more indifferent to what may happen, and I contemplate the water filling up the cabin and drowning us without much repugnance. It is the getting wet that one really dislikes. It is now 7.30 a.m., and we hope the wind is lulling, otherwise our prospects are poor.

" 11 a.m.— Though things remain precisely as yesterday, and with rather less chance of a good issue, for the wind blows as hard as ever, everybody on board has settled down to the situation. There are no more querulous plaints of the women, and the prayers are less incessant. The children are playing merrily in the saloon, the little boy pretending to bastinado the little girl on the soles of her feet, and there is a group of women on the ground gossiping as if at market. This, I suppose, is in all human nature. People go about their affairs, however much there may be an earthquake or any other catastrophe impending. I have settled down to a novel, which I brought with me in case of accidents causing delay anywhere. There is no sign yet of succour from any quarter, and I expect to-night will be critical. The thumping and banging on the reef goes on, and all of our cabins are in a leaky state at the portholes; fortunately the ship stands pretty steady on her keel, with only a slight list to port. This has kept us fairly dry, though on the main deck the pilgrims must be suffering terribly. There has been no cooking done to-day, as the fires are out. Also salt water has got into the fresh water tanks, and we may be soon short of water to drink.

" Later. In the afternoon, at Cockerell's suggestion, we moved our quarters from the after-cabin, which is being much battered by the sea, to the upper platform in the centre of the ship. There we are sheltered by a bit of awning from the wind and spray, and the waves do not wash quite so high. Suliman had already established himself there, and it is pleasant to have our little camp with him altogether as if we were in the desert. The sight of the waves breaking over the reef is interesting, and there are seagulls to watch and floating seaweed, and one can mark the variations in strength of the wind; the centre of the ship, too, is free from the thumping of the stern, and we have a feeling here that even if she breaks in two, the fore half where we are would remain firm on the reef. Nor is it a small advantage to be free from the incessant prayers of the rich pilgrims in the cabin, who shout in chorus all day long, and of the children who, in imitation of them, make treble invocations of their own. In the forecastle, which we overlook, the pilgrims, mostly Persians, confine themselves to an ' Alahu Akbar,' when any specially big wave breaks over them. There is one of them stationed on purpose to look out for the big waves and announce their coming. Here we are settling ourselves for the night.

" 11*th March.*— The sunset last night was less yellow than the day had been, for there had been a thick haze, and the stars and the moon came out, but the wind blew all night as hard as ever, the waves running up to within a couple of feet of our platform, making one wonder whether the afterpart of the ship had not been carried away. We made ourselves as comfortable as circumstances would permit under our awning, and I took a little dose of morphia to keep me warm through the night. I had got wet through in my European clothes, and have now got on my Arab things, and so dozed through the night, trying to fancy myself in Jendali or on Kalala. Miss Lawrence and Cockerell too, none of us in much comfort, for we could not lie down. Still things might mave been worse, and we were able to keep dry, and the wind is not a cold one. The pilgrims, among whom we are now established, began by being not quite friendly, one or two thought I was masquerading as a pilgrim, and asked me why I wore the *akhram*, and whether I had a passport from Constantinople, nor could I altogether satisfy them, as they did not understand Arabic, being mostly Turks or Bokharists. But the feeling amongst them has quite changed now. This is owing to my having taken their side against the captain, and decided him at last to send off a boat to the shore. [The captain, since the ship had struck, had shut himself up almost entirely in his cabin, refusing to do anything or take any measures.] The pilgrims had insisted upon his sending off a boat, and had come to the cabin door in a body, under the leadership of an old sea-captain, a Moslem from the Caspian, a rugged fellow in an Astrakhan cap, who declared he could easily steer a boat on shore at high tide across the reef, and so carry the news of our shipwreck to Tor. This seemed to me a sensible plan; and I went with them to

the cabin, and got the captain to consent, though there was a difficulty
in finding men to man the boat, as all the ship's crew (there were only
five of them), odd men picked up at Suez, were frightened at the
drowning of the sailor on Thursday, and I volunteered myself, if
necessary, to go, and with me Suliman to run on with the news to
Tor; and Cockerell also would have gone and Miss Lawrence, but
there was no boat large enough for us all, and at last it was decided
that Suliman alone should go, with five of the ship's crew. He was
very unwilling, as he is terribly afraid of the sea, but I persuaded
him there was really no great danger. He bid me a solemn farewell,
taking off most of his clothes and handing over to me his money and
his passport. Then the ship's crew would have nothing to do with the
Caspian sea-dog as their commander, and at one time the whole plan
seemed as if it would break down, for Captain Ross was without
resource or power of command. At last, however, just on the turn of
the high tide, they got the boat launched and across the reef, and so to
the shore in safety. We were able to watch them till they landed. So
Suliman at least is out of danger, and may bring us help from Tor.
The boat was the last one left, as one was lost on Thursday, and the
two others were destroyed last night by the sea. Some of the ship's
company are making a raft, in case things come to the worst. Except
the lack of drinking water, however, I don't think there is much immediate danger, as the wind has moderated and the sky has become
clear. The difficulty is that there is no means now of getting the
pilgrims on shore, even if it is calm, as we have not a boat left, and
are without water. We ourselves fortunately have with us three
quart bottles of water, which are still intact, and a large number of
oranges, but unless help comes to-morrow or next day, it will fare
badly with all of us. One of the pilgrims, though very amiable to us,
has told me the captain's throat ought to be cut. They all think he
is hiding water, though that is not the case. There never was a ship,
however, sent to sea worse found, or with a more incapable captain.

"We have made special friends with two of the pilgrims, Russian
subjects, one a Tartar, living at St. Petersburgh, formerly an Alem
of Bokhara, who has spoken to me in high praise of Sheykh Jemal
el Din. He is a very superior man, in a snuff-coloured robe. The
other, a Mongol from the Crimea, who has been a student for the last
fourteen years at the Azhar at Cairo. This one is a thick-set heavy
man of the true Chinese type, or rather of the Mongol type, from
which Chinamen derive their features. These have taken up their
quarters next to us, and they are very polite to us — with them most
of their friends. We have distributed a few of our oranges among
them; all complain of thirst. The most interesting of all, however, is
an Arab from Medina, a *Muhajjer* who affects the character of a wely.

He is the most beautiful human being I ever saw, going bareheaded, with an immense shock of black hair in ringlets; his face is very dark, and brilliant as a hawk's, his teeth splendidly white, and his eyes of womanish, gazelle-like lustre. His beard, too, like his hair, is a whole mass of ringlets, and his hands and feet are of perfect form. With all he is kindly and friendly, with a peculiar, inconsequent way, as becomes a saint. [He was fantastically dressed when he came on board, with gorgeous muslin robes, but these got soon draggled with the sea water, without thereby affecting his gay spirits or pleasant smile. He would go about from one to other of the pilgrims with a pleasant word to each, and gave away at once the oranges we gave him. His exact position in life, except that he was a *Muhajjer,* I never ascertained, but he invited me cordially to his house if I visited Medina, and was especially polite to all of us. Most of those that I have mentioned talked Arabic, but many knew no word of it, having come from distant parts of Asia.] They are evidently good, pious people, and it is a relief to find ourselves among them at a solemn moment like the present, when we have death, so to say, staring us in the face, and away from the few ungodly Englishmen who frequent the bar of the first class cabin. I never marked the contrast more, and it consoles me not a little for the rest.

" Miss Lawrence is wonderful in her simple courage and good sense. She makes us all as comfortable as the small space we have will admit, and has not said a complaining word. When I said to her half in fun, ' Your poor patient has almost come to the end of his tether,' she answered simply, ' I cannot think we shall be drowned. God would not allow all these good people who call on him to perish.' Cockerell, too, is full of help. He has made friends with a young Belgian and a young English accountant, who are better than the rest, and gathers a deal of information about all that is going on.

" It came on blowing terribly again in the afternoon, and the sea has put on the pale green look it has in the northern seas — each wave capped with foam. The waves are pouring over the lower decks, and the ship is sinking a bit in her bed. A great ship was seen just at sunset, and wild hopes were indulged. The sailors hoisted a torch at the mast-head, but the vessel was too far away and soon disappeared. Nor could she have helped us had she come to us for no captain would put out a boat in such a sea. Notwithstanding all this we under our awning on the bridge have passed (*12th March*) a not quite uncomfortable night. Only one woke every few minutes with a start, and thoughts forced themselves on one's mind of things beyond the world. There were signs of lightning in the hills in the direction of Mount Sinai, and one seemed to see in them God's anger in his dwelling place, perhaps at one's impiety at seeking to set foot on it, and for the attitude I have taken of having complained or his dereliction of his duty and neglect of the World and Man. Towards morning just in front of us stood the Scorpion, for the sky was clear, and it reminded me of many things. It was then that Miss Lawrence used the words that I have recorded. This is the worst night that we have passed, and there seems little left to hope.

" 12th March.— Our fourth day on the reef, which is whiter than ever with foam — the wind stronger and the waves higher. The cabins aft are flooded, and the people are leaving them, and crowding on to the bridge. Nevertheless there is a more cheerful feeling, for at eight o'clock a vessel approached which was recognized as one of the Khedivial Line Steamers, the *Misr,* evidently sent out to look for us. We could not, however, communicate with her, as there is no system of signalling on board, and the sea is far too big for them to launch a boat; they have therefore gone back in the direction of Tor, waiting we suppose for the wind to moderate. This gives us something to hope for, and all agree that the gale cannot last much longer, and that the ship is too fast on the reef to be in immediate danger — only that the pilgrims are in straits for water, and I hear that a woman and child have died. The stewards, meanwhile (for the government of the vessel and the administration of the supplies are abominable) are selling soda at exorbitant prices to the richer people. We dare not give away our water yet, as it would be drunk up at once, but we give oranges. Personally I have not drunk a tumbler of water in the last three days and have eaten nothing but half-a-dozen oranges. The morphia I have taken does away with both thirst and hunger, there is much dampness too in the air, and the pilgrims I think suffer much less from thirst itself than the thought of it, knowing there is no water. Most of them come from the northern countries where water abounds, and the thought of being without it frightens them, as it does not frighten the Arabs. They make very little complaint, however, considering how hardly they are treated. I go on writing my journal and reading and dozing between times. The sun is shining brilliantly, and we are not so uncomfortable for the waves do not reach us, and the spray here and on the forecastle is not very wetting. It is at night that the gloomy thoughts come.

" There is a Greek boatswain or second officer who tells me that he has been eight times wrecked, and twice in this same *Chibine.* If I get safe on shore this time,' he said, ' I go to sea no more. I sell oranges for a living, it is better.' He is certainly right. They have finished two rafts, or rather punts, unseaworthy looking craft, which I should be loath to embark in. The thought of the Red Sea sharks has been, I fancy, with all of us, though we say nothing about it. The still water inside the reef must be full of them — here it is too rough, and there is only drifting seaweed and a multitude of gulls.

"Later. The weather shows signs of improvement, though the sea is as high as ever, and the wind is hardly less, but the sky is clearing, and the line of hills on the west coast is beginning to show again. We can see Ghareb and the rest. I feel confident the wind will fall at sunset. And the *Misr* should return and take us off to-morrow — but everything depends upon the fall of the wind.

"Evening. Our troubles, I hope, are over. At 4 p.m., behold as a *coup de théatre,* H.M.S. *Hebe,* a gunboat, arriving from Suez to our rescue. The sea was still very heavy, and the wind as strong as ever, but Commander Taylor in command of her, gallantly put off in a whale-boat, and has himself come on board our wreck. His arrival has relieved us entirely from our anxiety, for though he cannot land us to-night he is satisfied our ship is in no immediate danger of breaking up. He will return in the morning and take us all across the reef at high tide, if it is still rough, or directly to Tor if the wind has gone down. He is a good, clean-shaven, grey-eyed little British officer of the best type. To us personally he offered, if we wished, to take us all three off with him at once to-night, but as he seemed to think it would be rather a risk, especially with Miss Lawrence, we elected to stay on the wreck yet another night — and it is well we did — for the whale-boat as we could see it had a narrow shave of being capsized, and was unable to get taken on board the *Hebe* on her return until the *Hebe* had moved down a mile or two to leeward of the reef. What has caused Taylor coming is this. As long ago as Saturday the people at Suez became uneasy at getting no telegram about us from Tor, but imagined the *Chibine* must have neglected to call there and gone on to Jeddah, then rumours came that something was wrong, and the *Misr* was sent out to look for us, and later Cromer, having been referred to, ordered the *Hebe* out. The *Hebe* was to have looked for us on the West Coast of the Red Sea, but fortunately just as she was getting up steam our telegram, carried by Suliman and despatched from Tor, arrived, telling them where we were, otherwise they would have searched the Western Coast in vain, and might not have found us for some days. However, as our friend the Crimean pilgrim says, ' El hamdu l'Illah ' (God has not forgotten his slaves). We are all congratulating each other now, and the pilgrims are showing their good-will to us, and thanks for having helped to get Suleyman sent ashore, in a number of agreeable ways.

" 13*th March* (*Tuesday*).— Our last night on the wreck was a peaceful and a joyful one. At sunset the wind, as was expected, dropped — and it is now nearly a dead calm. I slept profoundly. With the first light we got our traps together, and distributed all our remaining provisions among the pilgrims who were ravenous for our oranges. These were rescued at last from the water which had been sweeping over them on the after deck. They had been well packed and were not much spoiled. The best of them went to our friends, Sheykh Abdul Hamid, and the gallant sea-dog of the Caspian, Suleyman Ismailoff of Astrakhan, the rest I took with Hassan in a bundle to the forecastle where they were eagerly grabbed for by the Persian pilgrims, especially the women. Here are the names of our chief friends on board, Sheikh Abdul Hamid of St. Petersburgh, one of the Ulema, and his friend, Suleyman Ali from Crimea, a Crim Tartar Student of the Azhar, Captain Suleyman Ismailoff of Astrakhan; our friend the *Muhajjer*, whose name I have unfortunately forgotten, Mohammed Ali, aged nine, a gay boy who was the captain's servant. Gilroy, an English accountant going to Jeddah, Dr. Edward Rist of the Sanitary Board of Alexandria (an Alsacian Frenchman, of whom we afterwards saw much).

" 3 P.M. We are on board H.M.S. *Hebe*. At eight o'clock we were taken off among the first of those rescued by Captain Taylor, and are once more on the clean deck of a British man-of-war, feeling that after all the British Fleet has its beneficent uses and was intended for other things than only the bombardment of Eastern towns. Taylor tells me that but for the telegram sent by Suliman, we must have been several days longer on the reef — we might well have been overlooked till it was too late. All is ended now, however, and we can say ' El hamdu l'Illah.' In the course of the morning other ships arrived, and all the pilgrims having been taken from the wreck and placed on board them, they went on their way to Jeddah, while we returned to Suez on the *Hebe*.

" Names of the Officers of the *Hebe* are: Commander Taylor, Lieutenant Frederick Loder Symonds, Lieutenant James Kirkness, Surgeon Herbert Gill, Chief Engineer George Pascoe.

" The officers of the *Hebe* are an excellent set of men; they have entertained us all last night on board, feasting our hunger, and giving us stretchers for beds. Remembering the navy as I knew it forty years ago at Athens, these young officers seem to me superior in intelligence and manners to what they then were. The *Hebe* is one of the new and highly scientific gunboats which require men of head and education to work them, and they took pleasure in explaining to us everything, more indeed than I did in listening, for machinery is the least interesting of novelties. We might have been taken on to Tor if we had wished it, but I decided against this, seeing the peril we had escaped, and I have a superstition against continuing a journey in face of a strong warning; indeed to me this is more than a warning.

I see in it a menace forbidding me to approach the Holy Mountain. Perhaps another year I may return, but not now.

"In the early morning as we arrived at Suez I was awoke from sleep by a very terrible dream or imagination, for I was between waking and sleeping. The screws of the gunboat had been reversed, and there was a fearful vibration on board, so loud that it sounded like a storm. I thought that we had come to the head of the gulf to that place where Pharoah and the Egyptians were overwhelmed in the sea, and that an immense wind had struck us from the west, so that the gunboat was being driven on to the eastern shore. It was a storm so terrible that nothing could live in it, and I knew that it had been sent by God, and I heard a voice saying: 'There are no pilgrims here to save you again by their prayers,' and I was terror struck and I made my profession of faith —'La Allah ila Allah, wa Mohammed rasul Allah,' nor was I relieved of my fear until I had looked out of the scuttle and seen the lights of Suez, and smooth water, and the Scorpion in a quite clear sky. [I think the extreme vividness of this dream was probably due to the morphia I had been taking during the wreck.] I remember Captain Taylor, whose cabin I was sharing, asking me what o'clock it was, and I told him a quarter to three. He was surprised at my knowing this when, having struck a match, he found that I was exactly right. I had calculated it by the stars in the Scorpion's tail, which are an excellent clock at this time of year, but sailors have forgotten these old-fashioned observations of the stars."

The next fortnight of my journal is defective. The excitement of the shipwreck over, I felt the effect of it, and was once more suffering in health. My last days in Egypt before returning to Europe were occupied in laying before Lord Cromer the circumstances of the pilgrim case, and urging him to take up the defence of these Moslems, whose safety had been so jeopardized by the disgraceful mismanagement of the Khedivial Government, the lack of all proper provision for them on board, and the incompetence of the captain. I also wrote a strong letter in the same sense to the " Times," with the effect that a naval court of inquiry was appointed to be held at Suez on board H.M.S. *Halycon*. Consul Cameron presiding. This Court Cockerell and I and Dr. Rist attended, and we gave evidence with the result that on the 28th of March, the Court found against the Company, and Rist and I were publicly thanked for our " public spirited action," while it eventually led to new regulations being issued with regard to the pilgrim traffic in the Red Sea, which to some extent alleviated the evils of the system so long pursued. All that I find of importance in my journal is the following account of my final visit to the Khedive.

"*2nd April.*— To see the Khedive at Abdin, where I found Moham-

med Abdu also waiting for an audience. He introduced me to Mohammed Pasha Shukri, the Khedive's Turkish secretary, and other
functionaries, all very amiable, as they had heard of the shipwreck
and how I had brought the pilgrim case forward.

"Abbas received me with affection, and we had a most intimate
and interesting conversation. It began about the pilgrim traffic, as to
the better regulation of which he promised help. Then he went on
to talk of his journey to the Western oasis. He told me that he had
been extremely well received by the Senussia, and had found out
everything he wanted to know about them. Their principle of conduct, he said, was to obey the law in all countries where they resided.
In the Zaghwiyahs nothing was permitted to be done which could bring
them into conflict with the Government. Although they imported arms
and ammunition, largely from Egypt, these never passed through the
Zaghwiyahs, but through individuals, generally poor men, so that if
discovered it would not bring them discredit. In the Zaghwiyahs
nothing compromising would be found. He assured me, however, that
the Arabs of the Western tribes, all of whom belonged to the brotherhood, were well armed with Martini rifles; the brothers were very
particular whom they would talk to; they would trust no Christian,
and no Moslem who served a Christian, as, for instance, no Egyptian
soldier, because the Sirdar and officers were Christians, also no Moslem who did not pray and openly show himself such. He was evidently much impressed by their strength and their organization, and by
the instruction and high character of their leading men. All this seems
to tally with what Mohammed Abdu told me lately of the Khedive's
having become ' superstitious and opposing Liberal reform in the Azhar on the ground that he feared to lose the prayers of the old-fashioned
faithful.'

"He then talked of his intended visit to England. I advised him
to talk frankly to everybody, and promised to do what little I could
personally to dispose people in his favour. Lastly, he told me Lord
Cromer had spoken to him about allowing Arabi to return to Egypt,
but he had a grief on this head against Lord Cromer, inasmuch as
Cromer had refused to allow his grandfather, Ismaïl, to come back
and die in Egypt. Ismaïl was suffering from cancer, and only asked
to see Cairo before he died, but Cromer had refused, why then should
he now come to him and say, ' Let Arabi return.' We stood together
discussing this matter for some time, as I was going out, and it ended
by his promising or half promising to grant Arabi's pardon. Another
farewell visit was to my old friend and neighbour, Sheykh Hassan
Abu Tawil, now very near his end. I found him (*5th April*) like
Job upon his bed, surrounded with comforters, a mere skeleton, too
feeble to rise. I asked him whether he had had the doctor to see him,

but he said ' No, he preferred to be doctored by God,' and this is probably best even scientically. I told him the tale of our shipwreck, and he besought me to have a lamb slain for Sheykh Obeyd, and I promised him so to do, though I have a quarrel with our local saint for the little good he did me two years ago. I shall be grieved to lose old Hassan, for he is good, and much beloved by his tribes-people. We leave Sheykh Obeyd for Italy to-morrow."

My journey home was made with Cockerell and Miss Lawrence, Lady Anne having preceded us, and at Brindisi I received a telegram from her, announcing the birth of a grandson. Another fellow-travel-ler was M. Cogordan, the French Minister at Cairo, a man of great intelligence and knowledge of art and archæology. We stopped the night at Ancona and several days at Florence, where we found Lady Paget and Lady Windsor, and where I made acquaintance with Mrs. Ross, Lady Duff Gordon's daughter, who was so long in Egypt, as to which she had pleasant recollections of things that happened thirty and more years ago. Our next halting place was Lucca, which I had not visited since 1852, when, as a boy of eleven, I spent the summer at the Lucca Baths. I remember having been taken to see the Holy Coat, and of having beheld in the streets the Grand Duke and Duchess of Tuscany, with the fat grand ducal children, pass in their carriage in days before the invention of the Kingdom of Italy.

The next day I went with Cockerell to call on Ouida at her villa at S. Alessio, some three miles from Pisa. I had been in correspon-dence with her on literary matters, and took the opportunity of pay-ing her a visit. " Our driver did not know the house or who we wanted, until he suggested ' the lady with the many dogs.' We said, ' Oh, yes, the lady with the dogs,' and so it was. Ouida's house proved to be a nice old villa with a high garden wall and an eighteenth century iron gate, towards which from inside seven or eight dogs, poodles mostly and nondescripts, came at us, open-mouthed, when we rang. It was some time before we could make our ringing heard, and the bell was answered at last by a portly man-cook in cap and apron, who, after some further delay, on my sending in my card, admitted us. We were shown into the front hall, and there found the lady of the house seated at a small table, as one sees in the opening scene of a play, arranged apparently for the occasion. She was a little old lady, dressed in white, who rose to meet us and reprove her dogs, still yelp-ing at us in chorus. A mild reproof it was, nor did it save us from their caresses. The largest poodle placed himself upon my knees, and another took my hat in his mouth. ' They do not often bite,' she ex-plained, ' except beggars.' I had been prepared by the violence of her writings and anecdotes I had heard of her from Lady Paget and others, to find a person somewhat loud and masculine, but Ouida proved the reverse of this. In face she is much more French than English (her father, she told us, was French, M. de la Ramée, and her mother an Englishwoman), small featured, soft, and distinguished, with a high forehead, rather prominent blue eyes, dulled and watery with age, almost white hair, and that milk and roses complexion old people sometimes acquire, and which gives them a beatified look. It was difficult to believe her capable of such a malevolence as her novel, 'Friendship.' She can never have been a sensual woman, whatever passions she may have revelled in in her writings. Her conversation is good, intellectual, without being affected, or the talk of a blue stocking. It gives you the impression of a woman who has thought out her ideas, and has the courage of her opinions. We talked about the inhumanity of modern Europe, especially modern England, and the rage for slaughter, which is its chief feature. Also about Italy and Crispi, who is her *bête noir* there, as Chamberlain is in England. She talks English perfectly, as she says she does also French and Italian, and complained to us of the slipshod writing of the day. It was evidently a pleasure to her to talk, and to find us such good listeners. With Cockerell she was immensely taken, and was curious to know who he could be, for I had not introduced him, and persisted in thinking him a personage in disguise. At the end of a couple of hours we moved to go, but she would have detained us, and made us promise to come again. She cannot, she says, now go to England, on her dogs' account, and, indeed, they monopolize her life. Altogether she is a pathetic figure, condemned to solitude, not by choice, but by necessity, and regretting the cheerful society of Florence, an exile imposed on her, I fancy, by poverty and her bitter pen. 'The world,' she said, 'takes its revenge on us for having despised it.' We both left her with feelings of respect, almost of affection, certainly of sympathy and pity.'' [With Cockerell Ouida corresponded to the day of her death, though I believe they never met again.]

Yet another visit in Italy was to Princess Hélène, now Duchess of Aosta, at her palace in Turin, where I had luncheon with her and her husband, who struck me as a kind of understudy of the Emperor William, a good talker but somewhat brusque. As fourth at luncheon there was his stepmother, the Dowager Duchess Letitia Bonaparte, daughter of old Plon Plon, who is much with them. I was introduced to both as a revolutionary character in connection with my adventures in Ireland. There was talk also of the Transvaal War, which they, in common with all foreigners, consider an unfortunate, not to say ridiculous, affair for England. The meal was a pleasant one, and in the afternoon Cockerell and I went on by the night train to Paris. My companion in the sleeping car was Colonel Needham, military secretary at the Rome Embassy, who told me that Kitchener, who had been the best hated man in the British army, is now becoming almost popular in South Africa. A visit to Gros Bois followed where, as usual, there was much interesting talk. Among other things told me was this, that the seriousness of the anti-Semitic rage in France was due to Alphonse Rothschild's neglect to buy up Drumont. He might have done it for a small sum early in the day, but did not recognize Drumont's power sufficiently and now it is too late. The Jews are put in Coventry by all the great French world. There, as elsewhere abroad, I found it considered that we had made ourselves ridiculous in South Africa and that the war ought to be stopped.

We arrived at home in England 25th April.

"*1st May.*— To the Danes to see Lady Lytton, travelling there with Betty Balfour, who told amusing stories about Ireland, one being of a voyage the Queen had made in her yacht. The Queen used to be a good sailor, but is disturbed now if it is at all rough and likes the doctor to sit with her in the cabin and look after her. It came on to blow and a wave struck the ship rather roughly, which alarmed and made her indignant. ' Go up at once,' she said, ' Sir James, and give the Admiral my compliments and tell him the thing must not occur again.'

"I talked to Lady Lytton about the Khedive's intended visit. She said the Queen would certainly see him if she was at Windsor, but would most probably be away at Balmoral, and there was nobody else who could be depended on to be polite. Lord Salisbury, now Lady Salisbury was dead, would give himself no trouble, no more would the Duke of Devonshire. Broderick and Lady Hilda were worse than useless and the rest would not think it their business. She knew nothing about the Prince of Wales. There never was a time when it was more difficult to get the duties of politeness done to foreign princes.

"*2nd May.*—Lunched with George Wyndham at Willis's Rooms, he in high feather with his parliamentary success, though things are not going as smoothly as they might at the War Office. They are in trouble there about despatches they have published blaming Buller, and George will have to defend the Government on Friday. Evan Charteris was lunching with us, which prevented any very intimate talk.

"*17th May.*— Button spent the day with me at Newbuildings, his mother having come with him. He tells me the relief of Mafeking is being carried out by Kitchener, though his name has not been mentioned in the newspapers in connection with it. He went on to describe the different systems of slavery and forced labour of the blacks in South Africa. One of the great grievances of the Johannesburg people was that they were not allowed by Kruger to have compounds in which to keep their ' labourers.' Kruger was afraid they would arm and drill their blacks, and consequently forbade it, leaving them to hire labour as they could, which cost them a good deal more. The 'compound' system of 'free labour,' as practised at Kimberly and elsewhere in Rhodesia is an ingenious substitute for slavery. The negroes are recruited with promises of very high wages, and the wages are actually paid, but once inside the walls of the compound they are permanently prisoners and have to spend their wages there. To prevent their leaving with a show of legality, a rule is enforced that each negro before going out must be dosed. This has the double motive of preventing them from swallowing and carrying away diamonds and, as the dose is an immense one, of frightening them from undergoing it. The dose plan was invented by the Jew Porgés, who is now a millionaire at Paris. Such negroes as, having saved money, face the dose and are allowed to depart, are waylaid on their way back to the Zambezi, from beyond which many are recruited by Boers in league with the mining authorities, and stripped of all they have. The Government, he says, is making itself very unpopular in Ireland and he thinks also in England, but I cannot agree with him that there is the least chance of their being turned out at the General Elections.

"*21st May.*— The streets of London are decked with flags for a foolish victory, the relief of Mafeking, and even the cottages in Sussex flew their Union Jacks. This war has been so little glorious that our patriots are thankful for the smallest of small mercies. One would think that Napoleon and all the armies of Europe had been defeated by the British arms.

22nd May.— The Poet Laureate has published an absurd effusion in the 'Times' about the relief of Mafeking.

" Called in the afternoon on Keegan Paul, who is still confined to his room and chair, and learned the details of Mivart's death, which are dramatically terrible.

"*23rd May.*— Called on Father Tyrrel, the Jesuit, at Farm Street. Keegan Paul had shown me a letter from him about my poem, ' Satan Absolved,' in which he had said, amongst other approving things, that my account of the Incarnation was precisely the one he had always had in his mind and he had suggested my calling on him, so I went. I found Father Tyrrel very sympathetic, a thin, somewhat ascetic figure, with a nervous, imaginative face, his age perhaps forty-eight. We talked of Mivart, for whose ideas he clearly had much sympathy, but he blamed him for having lost his temper in the quarrel. He spoke strongly against the Roman Congregations, thought Vaughan had been unfair in denying to Mivart an answer to his questions, but all the same he was severe on Mivart for the final quarrel. It could only be excused by the failure of his mental balance through ill health. I asked him what really was the theology of Mivart's position, especially with regard to the inspiration of the Holy Scriptures. Was Mivart bound to accept the Pope's Encyclical? He said the Pope's Encyclical, though an interesting pronouncement as being made by the Pope, was in no way binding, though the extreme theologians maintained that it was. Vaughan had no right to demand of Mivart adhesion to it, an adhesion which was beyond what was ever demanded of converts before their reception into the Church. Mivart's fault was one of temper. He should have held his tongue and let the Congregation say what they would. I asked him whether he knew Meynell, but he said, 'No, not personally,' and added that as to his Liberalism of thought, he did not mind how liberal a man was so long as he retained a definite basis for his ideas. By this I suppose he meant that there must be a certain bed-rock of faith in the Church, however ill-defined. We talked of Stonyhurst, and he was surprised when I praised his system of protecting boys from all contact with evil. I said it had been good for me if not for everybody. He called it a French system, not peculiar to the Jesuits, and said it was much altered now at Stonyhurst. Certainly, Father Tyrrel is as enlightened a priest as I have ever met. He agreed with me that it was impossible not to believe in Evolution, whatever might be pronounced at Rome. 'Rome,' he said, 'is two hundred years behind-hand. They never read any modern work of criticism there, and do not take the trouble to understand the opinions they condemn.' Forty years ago a priest so outspoken would have saved my faith.

"Herbert Vivian looked in on me, fresh from Abyssinia. He tells me the Abyssinian army has just been beaten by the Mohammedans of the Southern Province. He gave a curious account of the French colonists at Zeila, who sleep, he says, naked in the streets with the native women, and who do every kind of violence, without restraint, against the natives.

"*26th May.*— Old Philip Webb came down for the day with Cockerell, a worthy old fellow, who is leaving off work at his trade of architect, and is searching for a hermitage in which to end his days. He has been too honest to make his fortune, and talks of living in a £10 cottage. I shall try and find him one.

"*28th May.*— All is satisfactorily settled about the Khedive's visit to England, Lady Lytton writes from Balmoral that he is to be lodged at Buckingham Palace and the Queen will give him private audience.

"*9th June.*— Roberts is now in Pretoria. Our country fools have been in ecstasies again over this, though it is quite manifest that both Bloemfontein and Pretoria have been purposely evacuated by the Boers who have not lost a gun or hardly a man in their retreat. The papers are all saying the war is over, but I think it may well last till next year. The Boers' campaigning season begins in October, and if they can manage to hold out in their mountains till then, they may turn the tables yet.

"*26th June.*— I have moved to-day from my rooms in Mount Street to 37, Chapel Street, Belgrave Square, having taken the whole of that house, a small one, with Hampden, as Mount Street was too small for us both.

"*27th June.*— Dined with Godfrey Webb and Hugh Wyndham at the Travellers. The excitement of the moment is the trouble in China, where the Foreign Embassies are in danger from the mob. The Chinese, after a long course of bullying by the Powers, worrying by missionaries, and robbing by merchants and speculators have risen, and are, very properly, knocking the foreign invasion on the head. Admiral Seymour, with two thousand men, mostly English, who was sent up to relieve the Embassy, is himself blockaded, as is Tientsin behind him, and the rumpus is general.

"*28th June.*— The Khedive has arrived at last in London at Buckingham Palace.

"*3rd July.*— To London and lunched with Wilfrid Lawson, who told me a number of splendid new stories, and took me to an Aborigines Protection Conference. Dined with Charles Russell and his wife.

"*7th July.*— Our Arab Sale Day. An immense concourse of guests but few buyers, some five hundred sitting down to luncheon. Hampden proposed my health as a poet, politician, and horse-breeder, which, in my reply, I said was unkind, seeing that in the first two characters I had been a failure, and I then gave them my idea of how to breed horses for war. Many were prevented from coming by the news from China, where all the European Ambassadors, they say, have been murdered by the mob. People are shrieking against the Chinese, as inhuman barbarians, and there is wild talk about the Yellow Terror. I wish I could believe that Europe stood in the smallest danger from it. [This tale about the murder of the Ambassadors turned out to be a Stock Exchange scare invented by the 'Daily Mail.']

"*13th July.*— Drove with Anne to Wotton, stopping on the way at Holmwood to lunch with William Gibson and his wife, a pleasant Frenchwoman. He is an odd creature, much engrossed in ecclesiasticism and the Irish Celtic revival, in honour of which he wears a drab kilt, being by birth a Dublin Irishman of the Castle persuasion.

"*15th July (Sunday).*— At Newbuildings. Alfred Austin is staying here. We put him on a horse, but he was not happy on it, and made ingenious excuses for ending the ride. We have had long talks and discussions on theology, philosophy, and the Catholic church. He is an acute and ready reasoner, and is well read in theology and science. It is strange his poetry should be such poor stuff, and stranger still that he should imagine it immortal.

" 17*th July.*— It is certain now that the Europeans in Pekin have all been massacred.   [Nevertheless it turned out that the whole story was a fable invented by the halfpenny press.]

" 31*st July.*— The King of Italy has been assassinated.   The wonder is that he has not long ago fallen a victim to his subjects whom he has led into miserable poverty and ground down with taxes for his political ambition.   He wanted to be an Emperor like the rest of them, Emperor of Ethiopia, and this is the end.

" 13*th Aug.*— Started on my summer driving tour, going by Old-house, where I had a long talk with Auberon Herbert about the great affairs of the world.   His son Bron has gone as correspondent to the ' Times ' in South Africa, not much to Auberon's contentment.   Then on to St. Giles', where I dined and slept at the Shaftesburys'.   The next day by Rushmore to Clouds, where I stayed a week or more.

" 4*th Sept.*— Arrived by the night train in Paris, and drove straight to the Horse Show at Vincennes, where I am exhibiting a number of Arabs, but the feeling just now is too strong against everything English for much hope of our getting prizes.   The judges are French military men, of the same class that sat in court-martial on Dreyfus.   Also the Sultan has a number of horses at the show which he has entered in the names of various Turkish Generals, so as to elude the rule making Government studs ineligible for competition.   There were some *saises* looking after them, whom I cross-questioned in Arabic, and they let out to me that all really belonged to the Sultan.   The handsomest Arab mare is one sent by Prince Sanguscko, a very great beauty with a flea-bitten coat.   Then on to Gros Bois.

" 5*th Sept.*— Gros Bois.   There is nobody here but the family.   Alexandre, the boy, is a good talker and a good fellow, very superior in intelligence to most young fellows of his age, which is seventeen, while the two girls are charming and begin to make a feature in the conversation and amusement for the house.

" 6*th Sept.*— To Paris to see the International Exhibition, a fatiguing affair.   I went through the Pavillons Etrangers, of which incomparably the best is the Spanish, most of the others are cluttered up with the rubbish of modern manufactures, and even the English Pavilion, which represents a Victorian Gothic country-house, has a certain vulgarity, but here in the Spanish section there is an incomparable dignity.   By a stroke of genius worthy of her days of splendour, Spain, ignoring altogether the nineteenth century, even to its bric-à-brac, shows us a mere empty house with tapestries on the walls, tapestries the most magnificent ever shown, and in two small glass cases in the centre of the room, the armour of Charles V, and the dress worn by Boabdil el Chico — absolutely nothing more.   The beautiful Morris tapestries in the English House looked tawdry after these.

"*7th Sept.*— To Vincennes with Wagram where we breakfasted, and saw the horses paraded before President Loubet. A Fourth Prize of 1,000 francs has been awarded to us for Mesaoud, and one of 500 francs for Bozra. All the superior prizes, however, have been got hold of by the Sultan, under the name of Muzaffer Pasha, and with the help of his own Inspector of Studs, Fuad Bey, and of one Hector Passega, manager of the Ottoman Horse Show, both of them being judges here, has manipulated the jury and swept the board. There was only one first-class stallion in the Ottoman show, sent from Bagdad, and that has been left out of the prize list. The others are rather ordinary beasts, the First Prize being taken by a small black stallion, whose colour is his chief recommendation. Only one is fit to show at all with ours; however, it does not much matter, as we have had many admirers of a serious kind, and have already sold one mare, Makbula, to Count Strogonoff for 10,000 francs.

" To-day is Berthe's wedding-day, and I have written her a sonnet. Giovanni Borghese and Madame de Jaucourt, a friend of the Prince of Wales, have come. After dinner, there were fireworks in the park, and a crowd of people from the neighbourhood.

"*8th Sept.*— With Berthe in her new automobile to Paris for the day, going at about fifteen miles an hour. It is certainly an exhilarating experience, quite new to me, and if the machine could be made cheaper (hers cost £800, and an ordinary one £400) would doubtless take the place of horses and carriages. In France it is already much used, but in England, where the roads are neither so broad nor so straight, I doubt whether they will become popular until the mechanism has been simplified and cheapened very considerably. We went a round of the Colonial shows of the popular kind, representing March- and setting fire to African villages, and French generals bombarding the Madagascans. Then to the Petit Palais with its splendid bric-à-brac, and alongside it the Grand Palais, a modern monstrosity forming together a caricature of the nineteenth century. On the one side a huge show of everything hideous the century has produced; on the other, giving its eclectic fancy for ages gone by.

"*9th Sept.*— Paid a last visit to the Horse Show, where we have taken four medals and prizes, 1,000 francs, 800 francs, 600 francs, and 500 francs. The printed list calls them *recompenses* it being not even pretended that the judging is according to merit, the medals being awarded to the exhibitors rather than to the beasts. As a rule those who sent most animals got most prizes.

"*10th Sept.*— Back to Newbuildings, taking Alexandre with me for some English shooting. He is a nice young man, extremely well educated and full of ideas, which he expresses fluently in somewhat imperfect English. 'In France,' he said to-day, talking of duels, 'when men quarrel and one receives a *gifle,* he is expected to beat himself.'

"*22nd Sept.*— Politically much has happened in the last week. Kruger has abandoned the Transvaal, and the Boer army, though never yet beaten in battle, seems to have broken up into small bands, so that our Government has some ground for saying the war is over. On this, Parliament has been dissolved. I shall take no part whatever in the new elections, as neither political party has the slightest claim on my sympathy. It is difficult to say between Rosebery and Chamberlain which would be the more dangerous in power.

"*1st Nov.*— I left home on Monday for Egypt, this being Thursday. London, when I passed through, was in an absurd uproar on account of the return of the City Volunteers from South Africa. People have become idiotic over this war, to the extent that they really think something chivalrous and noble has been achieved, while we have been making ourselves not only detested, but a laughing-stock the whole world over. I found George getting ready for a speech he is to make at Dover. He talked very scornfully of Rosebery and the Imperial Radicals, who had dished the chances of their party by supporting the war, and had put his own party in power for another fifteen years. ' There will be a reaction, of course, some day,' he said, ' but they won't profit by it. Rosebery will have to join us altogether, as Burke did Pitt, or be left out permanently in the cold. He talked of his own prospects of promotion, which he said had been a little injured by his candour in admitting defects in the conduct of the war, though he had saved the Government by the line he took last Spring. ' But it does not matter,' he said, ' politics are a long game, and I shall not lose in the end by telling the truth.' As it was, he had some chance, he said, of being shifted to Ireland, and he said I must write and tell him what I thought of it if it came to pass. I said the Irish remembered he was Lord Edward Fitzgerald's great-grandson, and it would be something to start on, but would not carry him far. George's political hard work has aged him and he is much greyer than I am, though only thirty-seven. Hampden, who expresses Chamberlain's ideas about the war, said to-day, ' It looks as if the only way of ending it will be to deport all the Boer women and hang all the Boer men. Roberts will come home and leave Kitchener behind him to do the butcher work.' He argued quite seriously that this was not only necessary but implied nothing disgraceful to us as a nation, yet Hampden was a Gladstonian Radical M.P. of the most advanced non-intervention type twenty years ago, and is now a respected Liberal nobleman and ex-Governor of a Colony.

"*6th Nov.*— On board the P. and O. *Valetta.* Among the passengers is a Mr. Seton Karr, a lion shooter, who showed me photographs of his victims in various parts of the world. These amateur killers for killing's sake, who compass the four continents of the earth at vast labour and expense only to destroy, are a pitiful feature of the age we live in. What have the lions and elephants in Africa done to Seton Karr that he should travel 20,000 miles, and spend a fortune to extinguish their race? Men of his stamp, though he seems a very worthy man, need to be put under restraint, far more than half the lunatics in our asylums. They do a thousand times more harm. There is no pretence with him of science, missionary work, or Imperial politics, and in so far he is respectably sincere. His work of destruction does not injure his moral nature, but he is a dangerous criminal all the same, and ought to be straight-waistcoated. I see that my letter to the 'Times' of last winter has had the effect of causing regulations to be issued in Egypt which, if carried out, will do something towards saving the small wild birds there from extinction at the hand of European gunners. If this succeeds, the British occupation will have done something to justify itself in the eye of whatever force rules the world.

"I have been reading Mrs. Browning's letters. They are interesting in many ways, but on the whole poor literature, lacking, as they do, all wit. They are gossiping, too, in not the best sense, and commonplace, far inferior to her poems, for which I have the highest admiration. There is nothing in them which makes one love the writer, and very few of them would be worth preserving if not written by so famous a poet. Browning stands out well in the volume, and the few scraps that are given of his writing show the superiority of the man, as an intellectual power, over his wife. Her enthusiasms are poor stuff in prose. There are a few meagre allusions in them to Robert Lytton, and one, a pretty one, to Anne, but the whole series written in Italy is infected with the sentimental vulgarity of the Anglo-American colony, which had its headquarters in Storey's rooms in the Palazzo Barberini, and which so nauseated me thirty and more years ago at Rome. Browning himself was not exempt from it, though this does not appear in the volume, for I remember him in his later years, a gossipy diner-out in London and teller of second-rate funny stories. He did not on these occasions show to advantage, though beyond question he was a thinker of a very high order, the most intellectual poet we have perhaps ever had.

"Another volume I have skimmed is Watts Dunton's absurd romance, 'Aylwin,' a thing of the lowest order of childish melodrama. Kipling's 'Stalky' is the third volume. Here, at least, we have vigour and wit, though it is brutal in its realism and displays the seamy side of our British schoolboy life without mercy. It needed courage to print it. Kitchener, I fancy, has served in some sort as his model. Lastly, I have read Tourgueneff's 'Smoke,' which is excellent.

"*7th Nov.*— A day of great enjoyment. We landed at Alexandria and came on by special train to Cairo, arriving at sunset, a light wind blowing from the north, which puts one in the gayest of spirits. There are few things more beautiful than the Delta at this time of year, or where one sees more life from a railway carriage window. The appearance of plenty and happiness does one good after the squalor of Europe. The country districts are still quite untouched by our Western ugliness. On the whole journey from Alexandria I did not see a European or a European dress, yet the fields were full of people, with their buffaloes and donkeys and camels crowding the country roads, men, women, and children gathering cotton in manifest enjoyment of their lives. How different from our own agricultural England, where one may travel for miles without seeing a living being and where all labour is done silently, except at hay and harvest times. The splendid wealth, too, of the crops, especially the maize, delights one. Then there are the birds, I counted nine kingfishers, some blue, some pied, and as many hoopoes, besides numbers of spur-winged plovers, which are far more brilliant than our English ones, and kestrels, kites, hen harriers and other large birds, to say nothing of the flocks of smaller ones. I was met by my mare and Mutlak at the station, and rode through the moonlit garden, which was alive with cicalas and so enjoyed its whole beauty. Then, after a drink of fresh milk with Mutlak and a cup of his scented coffee, we got on our mares again, and rode out into the desert. It was as light as day with the full moon, and we were able to canter our mares with their unshod feet noiselessly on for some miles till we came in hearing of dogs barking, which showed us where Suliman's tent was. It was set behind a little hillock surrounded by sheep and camels, and we had some difficulty in waking them, but Aïda (his favourite wife) heard us, and looked out and then Suliman. Here, too, seemed an abode of happiness as good as is to be found in the world. It was eleven before we got back to Sheykh Obeyd, and we must have ridden ten miles.

"There are three bits of news. Aared has revolted from Ibn Rashid in Nejd; the Sultan is building a railway from Damascus to Medina, and a French company has bought up a tract of land beyond Kafr Jamus to build a new town near us like Helwan, Heaven forbid! There are three fox earths in our stable yard, and I heard the jackals cry outside my window between one and two.

"*9th Nov.*— Mohammed Abdu called to-day. He has seen the Khedive, who came back from England highly pleased with the civility shown him by the Queen, the Prince of Wales, and the Government, but as I had told him would be the case, there had been no talk of Egyptian politics, though those at Constantinople had been mentioned. He sent me messages of thanks through Abdu, and said he had intended going to Crabbet according to my invitation, if his illness had not prevented him. Mohammed Abdu praised him for his power of making himself agreeable when he chose, as he had done in England, but said he had been most indiscreet afterwards, having told everything that had happened there to the editor of the ' Mokattam,' who had straightway published it.

" George, according to a telegram, has got the Chief Secretaryship of Ireland. I am glad of it for him as a step in his ambition, but it is a thankless task, if he thinks to reconcile Ireland to English rule."

During the rest of the month my diary is mostly filled with an account of explorations made in the eastern desert, interesting in themselves, but not of sufficient importance to be here transcribed. We were back at Sheykh Obeyd the first week of the month.

" *10th Dec.*— Oscar Wilde is reported dead. He was without exception the most brilliant talker I have ever come across, the most ready, the most witty, the most audacious. Nobody could pretend to outshine him, or even to shine at all in his company. Something of his wit is reflected in his plays, but very little. The fine society of London and especially the ' Souls ' ran after him because they knew he could always amuse them, and the pretty women allowed him great familiarities, though there was no question of love-making. Physically, he was repellant, though with a certain sort of fat good looks. There was a kind of freckled coarseness in his colouring I have seen at times in other Irishmen. I was never intimate with him, though on superficially cordial terms when we met. He had been two or three times at our Crabbet parties and was a member of our Club, but only attended one regular meeting. The last time I saw him was at that brilliant luncheon party at Asquith's in Upper Grosvenor Street which I have already described. His poetry, though nothing very wonderful, was good, especially his ' Ballad of Reading Gaol,' as was also a protest he wrote on leaving prison against prison treatment, and if he had then begun a decent life people would have forgiven him, but he returned to Paris and to his dog's vomit and this is the end. I see it said in the papers that he was received into the Catholic Church on his deathbed, a strange ending, and yet not strange !

" *22nd Dec.*— The old century is very nearly out, and leaves the world in a pretty pass, and the British Empire is playing the devil in it as never an empire before on so large a scale. We may live to see its fall. All the nations of Europe are making the same hell upon earth in China, massacring and pillaging and raping in the captured cities as outrageously as in the Middle Ages. The Emperor of Germany gives the word for slaughter and the Pope looks on and approves. In South Africa our troops are burning farms under Kitchener's command, and the Queen and the two Houses of Parliament, and the bench of bishops thank God publicly and vote money for the work. The Americans are spending fifty millions a year on slaughtering the Filipinos; the King of the Belgians has invested his whole fortune on the Congo, where he is brutalizing the negroes to fill his pockets. The French and Italians for the moment are playing a less prominent part in the slaughter, but their inactivity grieves them. The whole white race is revelling openly in violence, as though it had never pretended to be Christian. God's equal curse be on them all! So ends the famous nineteenth century into which we were so proud to have been born.

"*25th Dec.*— Christmas Day. I have embodied some part of my feeling in a letter to the ' Times,' if they will print it (' The Shame of the Nineteenth Century '). The Boers have shown themselves alive within the last week and have won two battles, capturing over 500 men, and are now in full march forward into Cape Colony. The railroads are cut behind them and Kitchener seems pretty well bewildered. There is something like a panic in London for the last week of the old century.

My old friend and neighbour here, Sheykh Hassan Abu Tawil, at last is dead. I went to see him four days ago and found him lying speechless with his eyes closed, in the little closet he used as his sleeping room. He looked the picture of frail, worn-out humanity, with a Job-like Eastern patience on his fine old countenance, over which the flies were crawling as they doubtless crawled in his childhood in the tent where he was born. He died last night at midnight, and we heard the women wailing a short mile away at daybreak, while we were breakfasting on the roof. Now they have buried him, walking in beautiful procession, men and women, past our gates to his grave in the desert. These country funerals are touching things, with the flags flying and the chaunting and the wailing, dignified, and with something in them of triumph as well as grief, which mitigates the ugliness of death. Old Sheykh Hassan has gone to his grave, full of years, the last of the old-world Arab Sheykhs of Lower Egypt. His tribe, the Aiaidé, were all tent-dwellers when he was young, a wicked, turbulent lot, whom he has controlled with a mild humanity much to his credit. With me he has always been on more than friendly, on affectionate terms, and I grieve for him as sincerely as his own people. It is a link broken for me with a pleasant past which will not be joined again, for the fashion of the old world passeth fast away at Sheykh Obeyd and we shall soon be engulfed in the town.

"*31st Dec.*— I bid good-bye to the old century, may it rest in peace as it has lived in war. Of the new century I prophesy nothing except that it will see the decline of the British Empire. Other worse Empires will rise perhaps in its place, but I shall not live to see the day. It all seems a very little matter here in Egypt, with the Pyramids watching us as they watched Joseph, when, as a young man four thousand years ago, perhaps in this very garden, he walked and gazed at the sunset behind them, wondering about the future just as I did this evening.   And so, poor wicked nineteenth century, farewell!

END OF PART I

APPENDICES

APPENDIX I

My Paris Diary of 1870

The fragment of Diary here printed was begun by me at Paris in the early summer of 1870, a few weeks only before the rupture of relations between France and Prussia. I already knew Paris well, having been a member of the British Embassy there in Lord Cowley's time, and I had remained in pleasant personal relations with my successors on the Embassy staff, and so found myself in close touch with all that was going on diplomatically. There were few days when I did not see one or other of my Embassy friends. I had only just left the diplomatic service, and now on my marriage I had come to Paris with my wife, meaning to make our temporary home there, before settling down finally to country life in Sussex. I had a romantic feeling about the great capital of the world's pleasure and was deeply interested in all that concerned France when the war broke out, and was fired with a corresponding sympathy when it resulted in her unlooked for overthrow.

Of Germany, too, her adversary, I had had experience. Among the many posts I had filled as attaché and secretary I had been twice at Frankfort, a place at that time of first diplomatic importance as capital of the Germanic Confederation and seat of the Diet, and had made there my apprenticeship in Central European politics. When I was first appointed to Frankfort in 1860, Bismarck, though already noticed as leader of the Junker party at Berlin, was still at the outset of his political career. The old King Frederick William was still King of Prussia, and Bismarck was not much in his good graces. His place at Frankfort had just been taken by his rival, Count d'Usedom, who was in better favour at Court. Usedom was a highly intellectual man, a leading member of the Liberal party in Prussia, and his sympathies were with the movement for a United Germany, then a Liberal movement having for its acknowledged head the Duke of Saxe Coburg, elder brother of our English Prince Consort, nor was it till Frederick William's death that Bismarck's power with the Hohenzollerns found its opportunity.

With Usedom I was intimate, spending most of my time at the Prussian Legation, where I held in some sort the position of child of the house through the favour of Madame d'Usedom, the good-natured Scotchwoman who figures in Bismarck's memoirs under the name of Olympia as his *bête noire,* the subject of his unsparing jests. Both she and Usedom were too outspoken to please the Bismarckian ideas of diplomacy; and in their society, though I took little interest as yet in the great world's politics, I learned much that I have not forgotten of Berlin policy and of the hopes and fears of German patriotism in which the Hohenzollerns under the old King had as yet refused to play a part. I remember a visit paid to Frankfort by the Crown Prince of Prussia, afterwards Emperor William I, and his accession a little later to the Prussian throne, which set Bismarck securely in the saddle and began that intrigue which resulted in the war with Denmark over Sleswig Holstein, as to which Usedom was daily eloquent.

I have dreamlike memories, too, of many hours — some pleasant, some wearisome — spent in attendance on the Princes and Princesses of the Royal and Electoral Houses to whom we at the English Legation were accredited, including Princess Alice of Hesse Darmstadt, our Queen Victoria's daughter, and a vast number of cousinly allied royalties assembled one summer at the family château of Rumpenheim, where I had the privilege of paying an early court to our future Queen Alexandra while she was still a girl of seventeen, and her sister, afterwards Empress of Russia, pretty but plainly dressed maidens of no acknowledged importance, though we at the Legation had been secretly apprised of the intended marriage of the elder with our Prince of Wales.

All these incidents were unconscious elements in my diplomatic education. My thoughts, however, at the time ran more on poetry than politics, and what interest I took in German thought lay rather in the direction of science which was beginning to perplex me, for Darwin's "Origin of Species" had only just been published.

My second appointment in Frankfort found the Bismarckian policy in full swing. After three years' absence at other posts — Madrid, Paris, and Lisbon — I had returned in 1866 in time to witness the great duel in the Diet between Prussia and Austria shortly after to be decided at Sadowa, which displayed Bismarck as the leading force of his generation.

Of the great man himself I have but a single personal recollection, that of a couple of hours spent in his society at tea alone with Lady Malet. He was then still an object of dislike and even ridicule at Frankfort, but already recognized by Lady Malet, a very clever woman, to whom he had paid a certain court while at the Frankfort Legation, and who already saw in him the man of genius he was soon to show himself. My memory of him is of a tall, distinguished personage, still slight in figure, who, having been told about me by our hostess favourably as having some faculty of verse, talked pleasantly and well on literature and science in excellent English for a couple of hours, affecting a certain Anglomania, where he touched on politics. He showed himself thus at his best, and left me with a feeling of the heroic such as a young man gives to one already beginning to be famous and who had been kind to him.

All this, however, had failed to give me when I left Frankfort after Sadowa any enthusiasm for Germany, and when the war of 1870 broke out I was strongly anti-Prussian. My connection with the Paris Embassy in the days of the Napoleonic glory had made me a partisan of France, and I had come to look upon Germany as intellectually the home of barbarism given up to the grosser forms of social life and clumsy in its politics as in all else.

With these few words I leave my diary to tell its own story.

"*Paris, 27th May,* 1870.— I have taken the first floor of No. 204, Rue de Rivoli, at 8,000 francs rent. My proprietor is M. Desfontaines, one of Louis Philippe's councillors. He is an old man who lives at Noissy, and his house is managed by his concierge, whom we call the *faux bon homme*. He sits with his wife all day under the arcade, and the people of the quarter dislike him because he has made 100,000 francs. Every Monday morning he brings us from the country a country bunch of flowers.

" To-day I went with my cousin Francis Currie to the other side of the Seine for furniture. We went to one Recapet's, a bric-à-brac dealer, and having to ask the way I inquired of a shopwoman in the faubourg, a dealer in religious prints, the road to the 'Passage Marie.' 'The Passage Ste Marie,' she answered, correcting me. There is still religion in France! Yesterday Francis Currie saw a dead man fished out of the river near the Pont Royal. A woman in the crowd asked what it was all about. 'A naked man,' my cousin answered. 'If it is only that!' said the woman. I afterwards drove with my wife to the Jardin des Plantes, and back through the Faubourg St. Antoine. Coming home we saw the carriages of 'Le Singe' as they call their Sovereign.

" *30th May.*—We drove down on Saturday to Chantilly by the old Royal Road passing through St. Denis and Luzarches. There are some fine views on the way, but the road is still paved nearly the whole distance. In the Forest we noticed two large oaks on the boundary between Oise and Seine. These are the only trees more than twenty [*sic*] years old. The races on Sunday were pleasant and the weather fine. A horse called Bigarreau won the principal stakes.

" *2nd June.*— To Fontainebleau to play tennis. Our party was Frank Lascelles and his wife, Henry Wodehouse and Mr. and Mrs. Fred Ricardo. Lascelles and I played from two till half-past six. The *paumier,* Garcin, is eighty-three years old. In his time he has played tennis with Wellington and others of the Waterloo heroes. 'Napoleon Bonaparte,' he told us, 'played in the tennis court at Fontainebleau, but did not show much aptitude. Il n'avait pas même des dispositions. Quant a Wellington, il ne faisait que s'y amuser, il venait de gagner la bataille de Waterloo.' (The old man hobbled into the court to play us a *chouette,* supported by a granddaughter, who picked up and handed him the balls. He pretended at first not to be able to send the ball over the net, but with five francs on the set he soon recovered his skill and won his money. Anne made an excellent drawing of the court while we were playing.)

" *3rd June.*— Two great fires have taken place, the one at Fontainebleau, which destroyed a large part of the Forest, the other at Constantinople, a thousand houses burnt at Pera, including the English Embassy.

" People in Paris seem to be becoming aware how grossly they have been cajoled in the matter of Liberal reform. I myself thought three months ago that it was sincere, and I was only surprised that so long-sighted a policy should have been adopted by the Bonapartes, who have always held by small expedients. For the future of the dynasty there could have been no greater folly than a sham conversion to constitutionalism and a repetition of the old trick of the plebiscite. Another such victory and the dynasty is lost. They complain already that Ollivier is nothing else than Rouère over again, and that personal government is precisely what it was last year. I care nothing for all this, not being one of the Singe's subjects.

"*8th June.*— We dined last night at the British Embassy, thirty covers. Amongst the guests were some of the new French Ministry — Grammont, Mège, Richard, also Monsaud, Under Secretary at the Affaires Etrangères. Lord Lyons keeps great state at the Embassy, with Sheffield managing the household, and Edward Malet for Private Secretary. They all three go out driving in a barouche every afternoon in the Bois de Boulogne, with a dog named Toby on the fourth seat. The Parisians mock at it calling Malet 'le petit brun,' and Sheffield 'le petit blond.' The Duke and Duchess of Montmorency were at the dinner. He is the hero of a rather mean adventure. Being by birth a Perigord, he solicited through his wife, who was an Aguado and partly Spanish, one of Empress Eugénie's set, a grant of the Duchy of Montmorency, the direct line of the Ducs de Montmorency having failed, though there were still collaterals. One of these, the Comte de Montmorency, who now represents the family, scratched out the new Duke's arms from the panel of his carriage the first time he drove up in it to the Jockey Club. It led to a duel in which the Comte was slightly wounded, and the Club, indignant at the affair, expelled the Duke from their house. On this the Duke appealed to the Court, the Empress happening to be Regent at the time, and the police received orders to close the doors of the Jockey Club if they persisted in the expulsion. The Club succumbed, and so the matter ended. [I was constantly in and out of the Chancery at our Embassy during all this time, having through my former official connection with the Embassy still many friends there, Lascelles, Malet, Saumarez, Claremont, and Atlee, thus I heard the news pretty regularly as the Embassy heard it.]

" The ' Figaro ' has published a *charge*. Villemessent, the editor, begins by announcing that he has sold his paper to the Irreconcilables, and articles and letters follow, signed by the chiefs of the revolution. The best is a piece in verse, purporting to be by Victor Hugo in which his style is well imitated. Half the town has been taken in by the hoax.

"*11th June.*— There is news from Lisbon of disturbances, Saldanha being the hero of these. I used to see this curious old Field Marshal very frequently during the summer I spent at Cintra in 1865. He was a *poseur* of the first water, and nature had given him a head and figure exactly suited to the part of *ancien militaire,* which he had been playing ever since the day of the Peninsular War. He is now eighty-five. Twenty years ago he made a revolution in Portugal very like the present one. He got a few regiments together, and when the King marched out against him with the rest of the Portuguese army these at once joined the Marshal, and the King had to gallop back alone with his A.D.C.'s to Lisbon. Saldanha had no political principles, but being a restless, vain old man, could not bear to be forgotten. I saw him again at Rome in 1867, on his way in uniform to the Jesuit church in Easter week, his whole coat, front and back, a mass of stars and orders. He is the most completely decorated personage in Europe. Also he has the pretension of universal knowledge, and has written a book or pamphlet on every possible subject from Pisciculture to the Immaculate Conception. At Cintra he had a garden of acclimatisation. His wife, the widow of a British navy surgeon, was a worthy Englishwoman on whom he imposed absolute silence in society so as to conceal her defects of education.

"Another revolution is an absurd one at Monaco, where the *Prince héritier,* who married Lady Mary Hamilton last spring, has slapped his wife's face, and asks for a divorce. The late Duke of Hamilton, her' father, so well known here at Paris as the Empress's cousin and intimate friend, with many faults of conduct, was a grand seigneur. His worst folly was his marriage with a Baden Princess who despised his Scotch nobility and gave him a heavy set of German heirs. He met his death by slipping down the narrow stairs of the Maison Doreé where he had been supping with Henry Howard and a couple of women after an opera ball. The Empress learning what had happened hurried to his rooms and was with him till he died.

"Déjazet is retiring from the stage on which she has been popular for nearly seventy years, having begun as an infant prodigy at the age of five.

"Yet another scandal has been one in the Spanish Royal Family. The ex-King's pension has been left unpaid, and he sues the ex-Queen Ysabel for arrears.

"I have bought a pair of horses of Mrs. Lyne Stevens for 4,000 francs. She was on the stage, and her husband dying left her an immense fortune which Claremont, our military attaché here, manages for her at a salary of £1,000 a year.

"*26th June.*— The Orleans princes have addressed a letter to the French Parliament demanding their readmission into France. Courbet, the painter, has refused the legion of honour. The Paris papers consider the refusal a miracle of virtue.

"*28th June.*— The claim of the Orleans princes has been refused through fear, probably, that they should go on to demand their property in France confiscated by the Republic. The Chantilly Estate is said to be worth 280,000,000 francs. Among the wills and bequests I see that this Estate, bought of the Duc de Nemours, has just been left by Sir Edmund Antrobus to his son, held I suppose fictitiously for the Orleans family.

"Yesterday morning died Lord Clarendon, our Secretary for Foreign Affairs. I met him four years ago when I was staying with the Usedoms in the Villa Capponi at Florence, a sleek white little old man, with a pulse, it was said for some years at forty, and an agreeable old-fashioned manner. His brother, Charles Villiers, I met several times at the Malet's at Frankfort in 1860, a very brilliant talker, who was kind to me, and interested in my young man's chatter. Their mother was the Mrs. Villiers of the Byron correspondence.

"*1st July.*— To Versailles to see whether the historic tennis court there was in a fit state for play. A nice litle girl in charge of the place told us that an order had just come from the Ministry for its restoration. The court is miserably out of repair, the floor chipped, and the plaster falling from the walls, the brass plate commemorating the oath of 1789 was taken down by Dalmand the *paumier* some years ago, and *remise à neuf*. The court had not been used for four years, and there are but a few rotten old balls to play with, but the court was played in this summer.

"Queen Ysabel has signed her abdication publicly of the Crown of Spain, and the Prince of Asturias, her son, becomes King Alphonso XII. On the same day a rival Prince of Asturias was born to Don Carlos at Geneva. The Pope has sent his blessing to them both. I well remember the Court of Queen Ysabel, and the *besa manos* ceremonies in which the little Prince Alfonso figured with his parents, set in a tall gilt chair, having his hand kissed fast asleep. He had in those days a most beautiful little Andalusian pony, a miniature horse, but only twelve hands high, with silky mane and tail sweeping the grounds, legs fine as a gazelle's. When the revolution came which drove the Bourbons from Spain, Prim gave the pony to his son. I met General Prim in the summer of 1863 at the baths of Panticosa, a pale, ugly little man, with no kind of distinction, suffering from an internal disease which gave him constant pain, half his political energy, they said, was caused by this. General Prim was the leader then of the Progresista Party. He was at the baths for his health with his aide-de-camp, General Milans del Bosch."

The abdication here mentioned of the exiled Queen of Spain was the occasion of the quarrel between France and Prussia a week or two later, which resulted in the disastrous war, the capitulation of Sedan and the overthrow of the Napoleonic dynasty. I was, at the time of writing, strongly anti-Bonapartist, a reader of the "Lanterne" and other journals of that type, more than my diary shows. In this I shared the general view of the Parisian mob, and even of the *bourgeoisie* who were sick of the Empire. The gossip of the Paris streets was retailed to me daily by my old *bonne* Julie, who had a curious faculty for gathering news as she was constantly wandering about the streets where she had become a well-known character by reason of her kindness to birds and beasts, and sufferers of all kinds. With the sergeants-de-ville of the Tuileries quarter she was a favourite, for she was always ready to help in cases of sickness, or accident, coming within their province. A Bretonne peasant by birth, (she had had an uncle a priest, massacred during the great Revolution on the steps of the altar, while he was celebrating mass). Her political prepossessons were strongly Orleanist, as became one who had been in their domestic service, for she had been housemaid in her young days under Louis Philippe in the Château, as she called the Tuileries, and knew every room in it from cellar to garret. Another informant of the same class was my cousin, Francis Currie's *bonne* Julienne, a pendant of my Julie. She had a German husband, waiter in a restaurant, and brought us gossip from the German point of view, also an amusing woman. To these two may be added our man-servant Desiré who appears from time to time in the diaries.

"*4th July.*— The 'Constitutionel' publishes the news that Prim has offered the Crown of Spain to one of the Hohenzollerns, a brother of Prince Charles of Roumania, and that the candidature is accepted. On this a general outcry from all sides. A Hohenzollern, it is said, at the Escurial will complete the wild beast show of Europe. We have already seen a Bonaparte at Fontainebleau, a Savoy at Venice, a Hapsburg in Mexico, to-day the rage is for German Kings, the most wonderful phenomenon of the age. Yesterday we drove to St. Germain with a mixed company of Americans, French, Jews, and Brazilians, to dine there on the terrace. The event of the day was Grammont's speech in the Chambers. He declared that if the candidature of Prince Leopold of Hohenzollern was not withdrawn ' France would know how to act without hesitation and without weakness.' This being considered a declaration of war with Prussia was tumultuously applauded by all parties in the House. The move is considered an excellent one for the Bonapartists, who need a show of energy to cover their humiliations of the past four years, for the first place in Europe is every day becoming more plainly Prussian. Whether the Germans are beat in the war, or the Emperor Napoleon, I shall feel some satisfaction. St. Germain looked lovely as it always does."

Though my diary does not record it, I remember well the excitement there was among us that evening at the news which had been brought down by Frank Lascelles, or some other diplomatist of our party, and how in the beautiful summer's night we walked upon the terrace after dinner, and looked across the river towards Paris, and how someone suggested, though we none of us had much misgiving as to the fortunate issue of the war, the possible trouble there might be for the fair city which we loved. Our imagination for a moment encircled it with a girdle of armed men, and a gulf seemed opened suddenly at our feet of unknown adversity. Yet, as I have said, none of us, not even those who ought to have known it, had a suspicion of the unreadiness of France for a serious campaign. There had been a comparative lack of interest in the Paris newspapers at the first announcement of the Hohenzollern candidature, which was treated by them as only another rebuff for the Imperial diplomacy, and it was not till Grammont made his valorous speech, and after him Ollivier that a cry, *à Berlin*, began to be raised.

"*8th July.*—There has been a report that Prim has abandoned his Hohenzollern, but this is not true. The German papers affect not to treat the French menace as serious. At Madrid the Cortes are to assemble for the vote on the 20th. If the present candidature is not withdrawn before that date the position of France will become less simple.

"To-night I start for Southampton to meet my brother Francis, leaving Anne here. He is returning from Australia via the Cape and Madeira."

[A fortnight's break occurs here in my diary caused by my absence from Paris.]

"*27th July.*— I have been more than a fortnight in England, and my journal has been interrupted, but I will recapitulate the events which have led to the declaration of war. In answer to the French demand of a withdrawal of Prince Leopold's candidature Prim denied the right of France to interfere. At first all previous knowledge of the candidature was denied in Prussia, but it soon appeared that King William had given his assent to the Prince's acceptance. But on the matter being pressed by the French

Government William withdrew his consent, not as King, but as head of the Hohenzollerns, saying at the same time that if Spain still chose to elect the Prince he would not as King of Prussia interfere. Nevertheless France insisted on a formal disavowal of the plan by the Prussian Government. Things being in this position, to the astonishment of all, Prince Anthony, Leopold's father, writes to the Spanish Government withdrawing his son's candidature, Leopold himself remaining silent, and the Prussian Government professing not to know even where he is. In France Leopold is thought to have gone incognito to Madrid, as his brother Charles in like circumstances went incognito to Roumania. I have no doubt in my mind that some such stroke was contemplated by Bismarck, as Usedom has often told me that Prince Charles' expedition was sanctioned by the Prussian Government, and that it was Bismarck's policy to raise up anti-French influences in every corner of Europe, in Greece, in Italy, and in the Turkish Provinces. In England it was very generally believed that Prince Anthony had settled the matter, and the 'Times' sang a Te Deum of peace, the stocks rose prodigiously in London, and two days after, Sunday the 16th of July, as I was sitting in the balcony after dinner in Belgrave Square (number 44, my cousin Percy Wyndham's house), I heard the news hawkers bawling out, 'Declaration of War.' A story had appeared in the 'Times' that morning, relating that M. Benedetti the French Ambassador at Berlin had accosted King William contrary to etiquette in the Public Garden at Ems, and had there again urged the claims of France, and that the King turning on his heel had told his aide-de-camp to inform the Ambassador that he had no more to say to him. This story has since been denied, but it has been made use of both in France and Germany to inflame popular passions. On Monday morning the 'Times' announced the war, and declared that the French Emperor had committed the greatest crime Europe had witnessed for thirty years. The 'Times' has since persisted that the war is one of aggression on the part of France with the Rhine Provinces for object, but I have never met for years past a Frenchman who has not laughed at the idea of taking possession of the Rhine, or who would have given a fig to annex. People expected a battle would be fought at once, but ten days have passed, and no blow has been struck.

"This morning the 'Times' gives us a new surprise, the draft of a treaty between France and Prussia (undated) in which the annexation of Belgium and Luxemburg by France is agreed on if necessary by force of arms. The draft has no appearance of authenticity, its style being unlike that usual in treaties, and the French used is poor. Some such scheme may have been talked over between the French Emperor and Bismarck, soon after the late war (the war of Sadowa), but I cannot conceive its having been thus put on paper. I expect the French Government to deny the authenticity of the document, and perhaps ultimately they make make a counter-charge against Prussia of designs on Holland. Feeling in England is pretty well balanced between France and Prussia, but people fail to see that France is in reality fighting for her existence. This is no war of Government against Government, but of race against race, of France the last of the great Latin nations against Germany. If Germany

is beaten she will recover, if France she will go the way of the other
Latins. The Radical Party in England side with Prussia because they see
in it a triumph of atheism and socialism in Europe. France after many
years goes forth to the Rhine singing the Marseillaise in the cause of
order and religion. It is strange.

"*28th July.*— We drove this morning to St. Cloud to see the Emperor
and his son start for the war. He went off by the back door, and nobody
saw him go. The flag was pulled down exactly at ten o'clock. The
Emperor has his headquarters at Metz.

"*29th July.*— It is decided that the French garrison is to leave Rome.
M. Visconti Venosta, the Italian Foreign Minister, has engaged to protect
the Holy See from the Garibaldians; the Pope, however, is I am sure quite
able to take care of himself at Rome. The Foreign Legion is, or was,
when I saw it in 1866 as fine a body of men as any in the south of Europe,
they did not need the French *chassepots* to beat the Garibaldians at
Montana; however, we shall see. The announcement of the new dogma
of Papal infallibility has passed almost unnoticed after all, though there
are rumours of a schism in Germany.

"*30th July.*— To-day we have a full explanation of the projected treaty
[that published in the 'Times' of the 27th, about Belgium and the Rhine
provinces]. Benedetti writes to the official journal, stating that soon after
the war of 1866, being one day with Bismarck at Berlin, and talking as
they had often talked of proposed territorial changes in Europe, Bismarck
said: 'What is the good of always talking, why not put our ideas in
writing.' Thereupon giving Benedetti a pen and paper, he dictated the
famous draft and kept it, as he said, to show the King, a stroke worthy of
the golden age of diplomacy. I know positively from Usedom, who was in
the thick of affairs in Prussia during the war of 1866, that Bismarck
promised the Rhine provinces, or, at least, those south of the Moselle, to
France as the price of her neutrality, but never with the intention of
keeping the promise. Benedetti must have been a great donkey to be
gulled by Bismarck in this way, but the story he gives of the transaction
bears the impress of truth. It explains what was so odd in the draft,
namely, that in quoting the names and titles of the high contracting parties
the King of Prussia's name stands first. Bismarck is the most wonderful
man of his age, but he has outwitted himself as well as Benedetti here.
Public opinion in England is veering round from Prussia; and Belgium,
which is most interested, acquits France in the matter.

"A skirmish has taken place on the frontier, where strangely enough
an Englishman in the Baden service was killed, the first victim of the war,
his name Winslow. The addresses of the Emperor and the King to their
troops are both published. The King appeals to God the Emperor to
Glory, quite in the old style.

"Yesterday we drove to Versailles through the Forest of Meudon, a
lovely old deserted road, never used apparently since Versailles became a
royal residence and the new high road was carried through Sèvres.

"Lascelles tells me the true history of the message sent by King William
to M. Benedetti 'Allez trouvez son Excellence,' the King said to his aide-

de-camp, 'et priez le de venir baiser mon c—l.' He also related an anecdote of Bismarck illustrative of his equally Rabelaisian style of humour."
[This anecdote is omitted as unprintable.]

"*Aug. 2nd.*— Went last night to the Opera to hear 'Masaniello.' Between the third and fourth acts the stage represented the French camp,
and Faure in the uniform of the Garde Mobile sang the 'Rhin Allemand' :
Nous l'avons eu votre Rhin Allemand. The Marseillaise was then called
for and Marie Sasse came forward with the tricolor and gave it amid great
enthusiasm. It was the most emotional thing I ever saw on the stage.
Faure afterwards was called for and sang the Marseillaise in his turn,
kneeling down at the last verse, and wrapping himself in the flag. All
the house stood up while it was being sung. The effect was lessened to
me by the uniform and by the tricolour having on it a little gilt eagle, but
in spite of this I have seldom been so touched. [The Marseillaise was
then being sung for the first time in Paris, after having been proscribed
there for twenty years.]

"*3rd Aug.*— It is officially announced that a division of the French army
has captured the heights above Saarbruck and driven the Prussians out of
the town, Saarbruck being just over the frontier. The Emperor and the
Prince Imperial were present and under fire.

"*5th, Aug.*, 9 *p.m.*— Learned at the Embassay that the Prussians had
taken Vissembourg yesterday and that General Douai had been killed, one
gun captured. They told me a battle was being fought to-day, the news
hitherto rather unfavourable to the French. MacMahon had 80,000 men
under his command, so it should be a great battle. [This proved to be the
battle of Worth.] I have arranged in case of a defeat to send my wife
and Miss Noel [her cousin Alice Noel who was staying with us] to Havre
with the carriage and horses. I shall stay here myself. Paris has been
very silent this evening. I told Julie at dinner that the Emperor had been
killed. 'Quant à cela,' she said, 'si je vois aujourd'hui passer son enterre-
ment je ne dirai que tant mieux.' The weather since noon has been sultry
with an attempt at thunder. There is a heavy black cloud over the sky
to-night.

"*6th Aug.*— Last night at half-past ten, hearing that something was
happening on the boulevard I went out. Bands of men were marching up
and down singing patriotic songs, the boulevard crowded, people talking in
knots. There was the rumour of a defeat. (According to the 'Times'
the French had been driven out of Vissemberg, one gun taken and 500
unwounded prisoners, also the French camp taken. Vissembourg is a few
miles from Rastadt, where the Prussian Crown Prince has his headquarters.) I sat down outside Bignon's to read the 'National,' and was joined
there by Malet and Lascelles. They are both staunch Frenchmen. They
considered it looked very bad there being no news. They knew a severe
battle was being fought that afternoon. I dreamed all night of Prussians
and their victories. God rot them !

"This morning I went to the Embassy to volunteer my services to the
Chancery, as they have more work there than they can do. They seemed
to think that after all there had been no fighting yesterday. At half-past

two Julie rushed into the room telling me that a great victory had been won, the Prince of Prussia and 20,000 prisoners taken. It was too good to be true, but flags were being put up everywhere in the streets. I ordered out the carriage and drove down the Rue de Rivoli eastwards and on round the boulevards. The Faubourg St. Antoine and all the east end of Paris was a mass of flags and excitement. After the Boulevard des Italiens, however, on our way back these thinned and at the Madeleine all was bare as on ordinary days, till on arriving at the Embassy, we found that the whole thing was a gigantic *canard*. Somebody had posted up a telegram with this news at the Bourse, and in a couple of hours the excitement had reached every corner of Paris. In the afternoon an attack was made by the mob on the Bourse and its frequenters. The man who had posted up the telegram was nearly torn to pieces, and the Jews and other rascals who were there had the coats torn off their backs.

"*7th Aug.*— This morning the news seems bad. The 'Figaro' says that it is a time for calm and dignity.

"*4 o'clock* — MacMahon has been defeated in a great battle at Reichshoffen [Worth]. He has retreated on Nancy; his communications with Metz were cut, but seem now to be restored. On the same day yesterday General Frossart was driven out of Saarbruck. The Emperor in his bulletin says that great sacrifices must be made by the country. There is great depression in Paris. A band of respectable people came past our house shouting '*La patrie en danger! Des fusils! A la frontière!*' At this moment a great crowd is collecting round the Tuileries. Julie has gone out to see what the news is. Claremont says the French have been outnumbered, that they had not 200,000 men in the field. The Empress is at the Tuileries. People begin to talk ominously about the present dynasty. Dalmand at the Tennis Court [he was third *paumier* to the tennis court of which I was a member close by in the north-east corner of the Tuileries Gardens] says he has only one wish, to die by a Prussian bullet!

"Yesterday a mob assembled at the Place Vendôme and forced Ollivier to make a speech from his balcony. He promised the news should be placarded every two hours. Paris is declared in a state of siege. I have ordered the carriage for ten o'clock to-morrow to drive to Nantes, whence Anne and Miss Noel will go on to Deauville. I shall return by train. I am afraid of the horses being seized for the war.

"*5 o'clock.*— Julie has come back to say that the Emperor's despatch was that he did not know where MacMahon was. This looks very bad.

"The battle where Frossart was beaten was Forbach. MacMahon's they call Freshvillers. If MacMahon has been cut off we may expect the French centre to be attacked on both sides and probably beaten somewhere in front of Metz.

"*8th August.*— No news this morning. MacMahon seems to have joined the main army before Metz. The Parisians are rapidly becoming demoralized, the Bonapartists blaming the Republicans, the Republicans the Bonapartists, and both blaming Fortune. All parties seem inclined to lay down their arms directly the army is beaten. I was not wrong in believing that twenty years of Cæsarism had destroyed virtue in France.

It is well to talk of 1792, but the Republicans then were other men than now, and when their army was beaten the people fought on. To-day French patriotism is limited to killing the enemy. Nobody cares to be killed. Paris will probably open her gates to the Germans, and having consented to a disgraceful peace she will then settle matters with her rulers. I have sent Anne, Miss Noel, and the horses to Deauville to wait till events declare themselves. There were no particular disturbances last night. The English are flying from Paris. I believe Paris to be impregnable if held by a sufficient force. It is also too large to invest. If the remains of the army after a defeat were to throw itself into the capital it might form a nucleus for the whole nation. Let them proclaim a Republic if they will or take one of the Orleans princes for king, but let them continue the war. France can never make peace on her defeat or she must perish. The windows of the Tuileries were lighted all last night. It is remarkable that not a word of sympathy with the Empress Eugénie can be heard.

"*7 o'clock.*— It is reported, but not officially, that King William crossed the Rhine last night with 120,000 men at Colmar. I have been playing tennis with Lascelles. He takes a brighter view of things than I do. He thinks that a defeat would not end the war, but that a Republic will be proclaimed under Gambetta or Jules Simon and the war be carried on. He thinks that if the Prussians enter Paris they will find a Republic there, and will place the Comte de Paris on the throne, but I am certain no Orleans Prince would accept the Crown at such hands. Perhaps Napoleon will put himself in the hands of the Prussians. Who knows, perhaps Bismarck might re-seat him on his throne. All the foreign Ministers have been to Lord Lyons to ask what they shall do in case a Republic is proclaimed. Metternich (the Austrian Ambassador) has sent his Pauline (Mme. de Metternich) to Calais. As we came out of the tennis court we saw Persigny driving past in his Victoria towards the Tuileries.

"*12 o'clock (midnight).*— Dined on the Boulevard. Great crowds of people. Saw a carriage attacked by twenty or thirty people, a man standing up in it looking very pale and waving his arms. A troop of dragoons came down the Boulevard and people cried, '*A la frontière!*' This is because they think no troops should remain at Paris. The dragoons trotted on to the Louvre and are now in the Carrousel.

"The Prince Imperial has come back and it is said the Emperor was also there (in the Tuileries); some think he is there now. Ollivier is also supposed to be in hiding at the Palace, though a cordon of police guards his house in the Place Vendôme at night. Julienne's husband, who is head waiter at the Hôtel Meurice, told Julie that the Comte de Paris was there five days ago. I believe he will be in Paris again as President or King before a month is out. Sedition is talked openly and by respectable persons of all sorts. The 'Soir' used guarded but very plain language to-night and I believe it is certain that the deputies of the Left signed a document requesting the Bonaparte family to withdraw from France. If the French can get rid of this incubus they may find heart to fight their battle out. The Emperor has shown himself in this crisis what I have always held him to be, an irresolute man, incapable of any great sustained policy. I believe him to have permitted Grammont's original speech on the Hohenzollern question with the intention and full expectation of the matter being compromised, but the country carried him away and he was obliged to follow. He has been carried fairly off his legs; even a great victory could now hardly keep him on his throne. *Il a gêné la patrie."* [What I did not know at the time of writing this was that Napoleon III was incapacitated from playing the difficult part demanded of him in the crisis by an attack of the stone, which caused him great suffering. The decision, therefore, between peace and war had been left practically in the Empress's hands, to whom the blame of the decision rightly belongs.]

" I am more hopeful of the National honour to-night. The army beaten, the French ought still to have heart to win the campaign, holding as they do the sea [Prussia at that time had almost no navy]. They can in time starve the enemy out. As I sat at dinner the poet Morin came to speak to me. He was very earnest in asking my candid opinion on the state of France. He seemed much *émotioné,* but I noticed that he ate a capital dinner.

"*9th August,* 12 *o'clock (noon).*— At the Embassy they talk of a Republic under the dictatorship of General Trochu. I confess I never heard of him before. The Chamber opens to-day. Great bands of blouses have marched there, and a great band also of police. They say the Opposition will demand the immediate arming of all the citizens of Paris inscribed on the Electoral Roll. This morning Julie came in to me with my little dog Rachael dying in her arms.

" Something must have happened to the Emperor; he has either run away or abdicated or been shot. These ideas pass through one's mind. No one ever mentions him.

"*2 p.m.*— They are shutting the Tuileries garden gates.

"*6 p.m.*— I ran out and found the gates shut, but at the Tennis Court gate by saying I was a *sociétaire* they let me in, and looking over the balustrade of the terrace, saw some thousands of people collected in the Place de la Concorde and on the Bridge in front of the Corps Législatif. Biboche and Sérafin and Dalmand, the three *paumiers,* are absurdly impressioned by the course of events. Biboche is a Bonapartist, Dalmand a patriot without colour, Etienne, the marker, fancies the Republic, and Sérafin has *tout simplement* a wife at home with the scarlet fever. All look upon France as lost. At three o'clock we were turned out of the Tennis Court, and the garden was cleared of nurses and lovers. I went and sat in the Place de la Concorde for an hour, till driven in by a thunderstorm, which stopped any revolution, if such was intended.

" A band came by our house just now, singing, with a ridiculous young negro marching in front flourishing a wooden sword. I am beginning to tire of the crisis. General Lebœuf has resigned his command, Bazaine becomes Commander-in-Chief. [It was Lebœuf who, when the Emperor asked him whether the army was completely ready for war, answered *' Jusqu'au dernier bouton.'*]

"12 *p.m. (midnight).*— On a motion by Jules Favre for the organization and arming of the National Guard throughout France the Government have been beaten by 243 to 21. A second proposal for the formation of a Committee of National Defence in the House was also thrown out. In consequence of the first vote the Ministry has resigned. Count Palikao (General Montauban) is charged with the formation of a new Ministry. This is considered as being virtually an overthrow of the Empire. It is expected that the new Ministry will declare the House the supreme authority, and that the Imperial Family will be invited to leave France. Marshal Bazaine has accepted the command in chief. General Changarnier the Republican has been received by the Emperor at Metz and has appeared in public with him. [Changarnier had been a rival candidate to Louis Napoleon when they stood for the Presidentship of the Republic in 1850.]

"I dined with Lascelles and met M. de Hübner (the Austrian). He is a violent hater of Prussia, but declares that she must crush France. I cannot think that if only Frenchmen will be true to themselves, if the army can throw itself into Paris, all may yet be well. Austria, Denmark, and even England may think it the moment to intervene; Prussia cannot support a long war with all her ports blockaded. But if the French accept the terms offered on a defeat they will be lost for ever. Imperial France has no virtue to fall back upon; a Republic is their best chance; it is the only name that has a power to rouse.

"When I came home Julie talked of her recollections of the Emperor. She remembered seeing him when he came back to Paris in 1852, and, when kneeling on the steps of the Madeleine, he was blessed by the curé. As he rode from the church and entered the gate leading from the Place de la Concorde into the Tuileries garden, a crown of flowers was let down from the upper part of the grille upon his head, and the people called out for the first time, 'Vive l'Empereur!' Three weeks later he was crowned at Notre Dame. She also talked of his marriage, and Julie knew the details because she was in Henry Howard's service, and he was Mrs. Gould's lover.[1] Mademoiselle Montijo was taken to Compiègne by Mrs. Gould, though she was not invited, and there the Emperor saw her out riding. She was very beautiful, and had a wonderfully fair complexion. The Emperor, although he knew she was the Marquis d'Aguado's mistress, had a caprice for her, and wanted to make her leave Aguado, but she said he must marry her and he did so, in spite of his friends and Ministers. He said in his excuse that having, as they told him, done so much for France, France must do this for him. According to Julie, Napoleon and Eugénie made *mauvais ménage* at first, but the Empress had never been reproached for misconduct since the marriage. The child, the Prince Imperial, was certainly hers, as any one could see by comparing her photograph with the boy's. People had said that he was not, but this was untrue. Julie has often been with letters from Howard to Mademoiselle Montijo, when she lived with her mother in the Place Vendôme, *un misérable entresol sur la cour.* The house is No. 4, I think she said, in the south-east corner of the square. She and her mother kept two women

[1] The Honble. Henry Howard, Secretary at Paris.

servants, a cook and a *bonne*. Julie cited as a sign of the *misère* in which they lived, that these women wore handkerchiefs on their heads instead of caps. Aguado, elder brother of the Comte and Vicomte, kept a one-horse *remise* for her, and provided for them in other ways. Julie declares that, Eugénie had other worshippers, too, ' *même des Allemands*.' Aguado was married to an Englishwoman, who is now remarried to his brother, the Vicomte. He went mad when Mademoiselle Montijo married the Emperor, and afterwards died. She lived on in the Place Vendôme till the week before her marriage, when she was taken to the Tuileries to be married from there at Notre Dame. Such is Julie's account. Julie and M. Perrier, Howard's valent, used to talk these over together, ' *Ce pauvre M. Perrier qui est mort*.' History is written from such intimate talk.

"My own recollections of the Emperor are not very many. I saw him for the first time in 1851, on the day of his *coup d'état*, when he became President for life. We, my brother Francis and I, with our mother, were passing through Paris on our way to Italy, and we were staying at the Hotel Wagram, only two doors from my present apartment here in the Rue de Rivoli. Francis and I went out with our tutor, Edmund Coffin, to see what was going on in the streets. The Rue de Rivoli was full of people, and there was a cordon of gendarmes between it and the Place de la Concorde. ' *Liberté, Egalité, et Fraternité* ' was still written up everywhere on the walls. The President rode by close to us with his Staff, and passed up the Rue Royale. This was a very early recollection, before he was Emperor. When I next saw him it was at Biarritz in 1863. He used to walk about there leaning on the arm of his Chamberlain, Tascher de la Pagerie, moving slowly like an old man. I went one evening to a ball at the Pavillon, and was presented to him and the Empress. The Empress reminded me that she had seen me at Madrid some months before, which was true, for I had been to an audience of the Corps Diplomatique when she was paying her visit to Queen Isabella. At the ball the Emperor walked about looking bored, not at all as if he was in his own house. He is a thick-set, coarsely made man (with legs too short for his body), and in his uniform might be taken for a sergeant. He has nothing remarkable in his face, except his cold green eyes, which have a strangely fascinating, but repellent power. They give him a certain distinction. I have since, while at the Embassy, been to balls at the Tuileries, but have never had personal speech with him. I have listened to him, however, talking once for twenty minues at a time with Lord Cowley, at one of the receptions while the Empress was finishing her *cercle*. They were discussing on that occasion a review there had been of the English and French fleets, and his remarks were the essence of commonplace. He has none of the ease of manner, the lightness of thought, the *esprit Gaulois* which go so far in France, a heavy, slow-thinking man, talking French with a provincial accent. It is strange that such a man should have ruled the French for twenty years. If he had died a month ago he would have left a great name in history. Now who knows? He may be ranked on a level with Louis Philippe. Such are the chances of a man's glory.

" *10th Aug.*— I have drawn £40 in five-franc pieces for the siege. It is already difficult to change bank notes. The town is quieter to-day. No news from the army. A list of the new Ministry is published, Palikao, La Tour d'Auvergne, Magne, Rigault, Girardin — more Bonapartist than ever. The Chamber supports them for the present. Paris is full of troops, 500 Marines marched past our house this morning on their way to the war, all stout, smart fellows. I take it no troops have ever fought better than the French have done.

"I have been reading Prévost Paradol's last book, 'La France Nouvelle,' published last year. The concluding chapter reads prophetically now. He gives the future of the world to the English race, true enough if it includes our off-shoots, American and Colonial, but he hardly foresees what must happen, the extinction of England herself. England's political life will be over the day that Holland is annexed to Germany. There is also little sign of the continuance of the intellectual eminence of our race. Literature never long survives a nation's decline, and in the English speaking off-shoots no sign of intellectual life has yet been given, though America has had a hundred years of independence. The English language, however, is never likely to become a dead one. Her literature will still live, even if it ceases to be productive; in France it is otherwise. French will be a dead language, as dead at least as Spanish is. As for German, which is to become the language of Europe, it shows no sign of producing a readable literature. The only German I can read is Goethe's, who took the best of his inspiration from Rousseau. Where he is purely German, he is pedantic and wearisome. Germany possesses some good lyric poetry, but romance, tragedy, history, all are dull. What is really meritorious is the scientific writing, but that is owing to the matter rather than the manner. The Volkslieder have the melancholy charm of barbarous poetry, but the serious poets are without humour. German is bourgeois and its literature bourgeois. [This is a poor diagnosis. I ought to have at least excepted Heine, but I left him out, I suppose, as being a Jew living at Paris, and more of a Frenchman than of a German.]

"*14th Aug.*— Deauville. I came here on the night of the 11th, as there was no special news at Paris. The day I left, old Barre (the doyen of the Paris Tennis Court) came to breakfast with me and after it we played tennis, Brinquant making us a *chouette*. Barre was playing in better form that I can remember him. Brinquant has just been called out to join the army, being between the ages of twenty-five and thirty-five. He will have to go as a '*simple pioupiou.*' Substitutes are still to be had at 8,000 francs, but it is considered dishonourable not to march in person. In the middle of our game a company of grenadiers marched in through the door by the net, and took formal possession of the Court, turning us out. The officer in command saluting us politely from the net with his drawn sword, saying, 'Messieurs, vous êtes priés d'évacuer le jeu.' [This proved to be absolutely the last game old Barre, the champion *paumier* of his day, ever played, for he died of the hardships of the siege, though not till 1872. He was a wonderful player, especially on the floor of the Court, so that though I was then young and active, he could still give me the walls. In private life he was excellent company, and some of us used to invite him to restaurant dinners, where his stories were of the best of an extreme *grivois* kind, for he had led the gayest of gay lives.] In the train, as I came down here from Paris, I got into conversation with two deputies from Mantes. One narrated his having asked Grammont how it was that the army had been caught unprepared? Grammont had answered that before making his declaration to the Chamber he had inquired of Le Bœuf, 'Are you ready?' and Le Bœuf had replied, 'I can put 600,000 men on the Rhine in a fortnight.' Everybody is angry with Le Bœuf.

"A letter is published from the Prince de Joinville offering his services to the Emperor. Changarnier has been made Commandant de place at Metz. He is seventy-two years old. On Friday the 12th, Anne, Alice Noel, and I drove to Glanville, from which village the Glanvilles of Catchfrench claim originally to have come. There is a château there, which we visited, of the time of Louis XIII, undergoing restoration by its propretor, M. de Glanville, a man of sixty, whom we found at work weeding in his grounds. I noticed that the coat of arms over the door was not our English Glanville coat, and he told me that he had not the pretension of descending from the original family. It must have been a picturesque old place before the restoration, the avenues and the park round it good, the elms just like the Cornish elms at Catchfrench, the country about it beautiful and very English. We then drove on to Pont l'Evèque, a charming, sleepy old town full of cats, and dined at the Bras d'or, a drum was beating there, and a crier calling out all men from twenty-five to thirty-five for the war. Later we saw the mayor posting up a notice announcing the capture of Nancy by a detachment of the enemy's cavalry.

"16*th, Aug.*— Paris. I came up yesterday morning by train from Deauville, and on my way to the station read a telegram announcing that the French army had crossed to the left bank of the Moselle, and meeting the Prussians in force had repulsed them. The telegram is dated Longueville and signed Napoleon. The Emperor seems to have left Metz on the 14th at two o'clock intending to go to Châlons. Nancy, which is in the hands of the Prussians, is a town of 30,000 inhabitants. It is quite open, and was occupied by them without resistance. The advance posts of the enemy have been pushed on to Toul and S. Mihiel.

"Yesterday was the festival of S. Napoleon, probably the last which will be ever celebrated in France. Paris was silent as the grave, and when I first arrived I thought a disaster must have happened. Bands of men were at work on the fortifications. There is much to do before Paris can resist a siege, houses to be razed and trees cut down. There were no illuminations and scarcely a flag. I remember the fête of the 15th of August in 1864 when I had just joined the Embassy as attaché. The Emperor was then still popular, believed to be the longest head in Europe. The Place de la Concorde, the Quays and the Invalides were one great crowd, theatres open to the public gratis, shows and entertainments at every corner. A balloon was being sent up from the Champ de Mars. Carriages were forbidden to circulate in the too crowded streets, all but those of the foreign Ambassadors. I had only that morning arrived, and Lady Cowley took me with her and her daughter, Lady Feodore, and

Sudley in her own barouche, and we drove up the Champs Elysées at a foot's pace, a conspicuous figure in the good-natured Parisian crowd for the illuminations. Now *quel degringolage!*

"The night before last there was an *émeute* in the Villette, a band of men crying 'Vive la Republique,' attacked some unfortunate *pompiers* in their guard house, killed two or three, and then fired into the mob who were coming to the rescue. They were some fifty or sixty armed with daggers and revolvers, but after a show of fight they ran away, some being caught and almost torn to pieces. The incident has been put down to 'the gold of Bismarck,' just as in former days there was talk of 'the gold of Pitt.' Paris is still full of Germans; there will be a general massacre of these if it comes to a siege, perhaps of us English too. At this end of the town everything is quiet. Count d'Aquila who arrived at Deauville with eighteen of his favourite horses the day before I left, has made over his house in the Avenue de l'Impératrice for an ambulance, so I hear has Evans the American dentist.

"5 *p.m.*—A letter has been posted officially from the sous-prefet of Verdun, stating that cannonading was heard the whole of yesterday, and that it was reported the Prussians had lost 40,000 men the day before near Metz. On the other hand the 'Independence Belge' gives a despatch from Berlin from King William to the Queen of Prussia announcing a glorious victory. Edmond About writes in the 'Soir' describing the entry of the Prussians into Saverne and MacMahon's retreat. The French, he says, were ridiculously commanded. The Prussians are levying contributions in France just as they did in Frankfort and Homburg in the war of 1866.

"17th *Aug.*—This is my birthday of thirty, it finds me healthy, wealthy, and wise, three things I never thought to be. Anne has made me a birthday present of a silver coffee pot, I have long coveted, a Louis XVI one of very beautiful French design. I have nothing left to wish for as a birthday gift, except the destruction of the German army.

"I went last night to the Gymnase theatre, where they gave 'Diane de Lys,' the moral of which is, 'Il a voulu garder sa femme et il l'a gardée.' The French pieces now generally give the *beau rôle* to the husband on the stage as is also the case sometimes in real life, such as in that of Beaumont who wounded his wife's three lovers one after the other. One of the three duels was with Metternich. Metternich has, as all the world knows, been Mme. de Persigny's lover, and then made court to Mme. de Beaumont. She taxed him one day with his former devotion, and to prove to her that it was at an end he made over to her Mme. de Persigny's letters to him. These were found by Beaumont in his wife's drawer along with letters to her from Metternich. The Ambassador, who is no Palladin, refused to fight. Beaumont threatened to expose his treachery to Mme. de Persigny. The matter was laid before the Emperor, and Metternich, it being decided he must fight, was run through the body, but soon recovered. Beaumont also wounded du Hallay and another, whose letters also had been found. Now nobody dares approach Mme. de Beaumont. Metternich is what is called a *gros fat,* who likes to be called Monseigneur.

I have played tennis with him, but he is a poor performer. Du Hallay is a fat, funny young man, fond of a joke, but one would think innocuous in a virtuous household.

"De Voguë, MacMahon's aide-de-camp, was killed at Worth, a good-looking, very charming man of about thirty-five, bald, but the ideal of the *beau militaire.* I used to know him in 1865, meeting him often at Madame Arcos' (the Empress Eugénie's lady in waiting). He was at that time Princess Poniatowska's lover — she a very pretty woman, tall, blonde, and amusing.

"The Orleans Princes have been refused service in the army.

"18th *Aug.*— Yesterday at half-past five Blount, the Banker, came to the Embassy, and announced that a great victory had been won the day before, the 16th. He stated that he had seen press copies of the despatches, and that the details were most complete. Schneider, President of the Chamber, fully believed the news, and Ministers were only waiting to announce it till written accounts should come. All the result was a telegram published 'hier 16. Il y a eu une affaire très sérieuse du côté de Gravelotte. Nous avons eu l'avantage dans le combat, mais nos pertes sont grandes. Comte de Palikao.' And this morning the 'Figaro' gives an account of the battle of Borny fought under the walls of Metz, otherwise called of Longueville. Gallifet is reported to have charged the enemy. Gallifet is a brave man, and I always liked him in spite of his swagger. It used to be a fine thing to see him play tennis with Smijthe of our Embassy, who is a cool-headed man with one shoulder higher than the other, an accident which gave him an extraordinarily heavy cut stroke on the floor, most exasperating to Gallifet, who is a wild hitter. Gallifet plays well, but was overmatched by Smijthe, who was the best player in the tennis court three years ago. Gallifet used to call out, 'Ah dites donc, M. Smijthe, vous m'exasperez avec votre damnée patience; tappez donc, M. Smijthe.'

"I have been talking with Julie. She tells me her father was maire of a village in Brittany and her uncle a bishop murdered at the altar during the revolution. She had a brother older than herself killed in the campaign of Russia under Bonaparte, and her father died of grief. He left her a *dot* of 40,000 francs, but her worthless husband ate it all. She tells me that we have a *mouchard* here on the fifth floor, whose wife is a chatterbox. She has let out to Julie that the Empress has just sent the husband to England with her jewels.

"19th *Aug.*— General Trochu is named Commandant of Paris. I went yesterday to look at the fortifications. The guns on the walls are ridiculous old pieces such as my Uncle Toby might have mounted on his horn work. I was sent about my business by the sergent-de-ville. Carriages still pass into the Bois de Boulogne over a narrow plank bridge. The Germans describe the battles of Borny and Gravelotte as victories, and say the French army has been driven back into Metz.

"21st *Aug.*— Caen. I went down on the 19th to Deauville by train, where I found Anne much better, and the next day, yesterday, we drove here, stopping at Dives for half an hour to see the church. This is interesting on account of the list of names kept there of those knights who followed William of Normandy to England in 1066. I counted some seventy names of families still existing in England, among them the Byrons, de Buron. Here at Caen we are at the Hôtel d'Angleterre. The town is full of conscripts, some in blouses, some in coats, all in red trousers, young and happy. I have heard more singing in the streets here these two nights than during all the last fortnight at Paris.

"With difficulty I procured a copy of the Paris 'Journal.' Things seem drifting towards a quarrel with England. The 'Times,' which has taken a violent side for Prussia in the war is now exasperating the French with its good advice. Now, it says, is the moment for the neutral powers to insist on peace. I expect to see proposals made for an armistice, to be followed by peace on the principle of the *status quo ante bellum,* France to retain Alsace and Lorraine, but with the condition of immediate disarmament. If such be accepted *tout serait sauvé fort l'honneur.* I consider the position so critical that, instead of going to Brittany as we intended, we start to-morrow for the north. France, if she quarrels with England, will be virtually outlawed and fighting for her life, and we cannot expect any but the laws of necessity to rule her. Already the days are being recalled to mind when France threw defiance in the face of all Europe in the shape of 10,000 heads upon her scaffolds. She will scarcely stop to distinguish between friend and foe, but I trust my precautions may not be needed. The French army may yet be victorious, and the 'Times' is not England, but who can say? In the case of a rupture my sympathies must be with France, but I am bound in form at least to my own country.

"*22nd Aug.*— Pont l'Evèque. We left Caen at ten, and driving on got here at five, having stopped three hours for breakfast at Dozulé, our inn there the White Horse, rustic, but good. Another capital country inn here, the Bras d'or.

"The news to-night is bad, none for two days from Bazaine, who is shut up in Metz. A letter has come from Lytton in Vienna, who expects nothing but disaster for the French army. I still believe the Prussians will be driven out of France. Prussia is blockaded and nearly bankrupt.

"*25th Aug.*— On the night of the 23rd we slept at La Bouille, a village on the Seine to which Rouen merchants go out to dine on summer evenings, and yesterday to Rouen, Hôtel de France. We shall have to wait here two days until our carriage wheels have been new tyred.

"The news to-day is better. Communication with Bazaine restored. Bazaine declares that if he is still in Metz it is that he chooses to stay there. The news from Prussian head-quarters absolutely contradicts this. In England they choose to believe the Prussian account. I do not. Neither Bazaine nor Palikao would dare in the present state of France to publish news directly false. The position of Englishmen in France is becoming precarious, indeed of any person without visible occupation. Prince Lubomirsky was arrested two days ago as a spy, and many quite innocent people have been mal-treated by the mob. I shall go back to Paris for a night to see how things are going on, and then drive to Dieppe and send Anne and Miss Noel to England.

" Strassburg is being besieged. There was a report yesterday that Phals-bourg had been taken. The King of Prussia has appointed Governors of Alsace and Lorraine as Prussian provinces.

"*27th Aug.*— Rouen. I have been again to Paris. Going up in the train I heard another spy story. The man who told it seemed to be a Rouen merchant and the victim a friend from the country, a Normand, a *bel homme* of fifty years. He had asked some questions about the mobiles in front of the barracks, had been arrested by a sergent-de-ville, and got his clothes torn by the mob. In Paris a decree has been issued expelling ' *les bouches inutiles.*' A letter in the ' Figaro ' asks whether the ladies of pleasure may be properly so styled. The Government has answered the question seriously by sending 2,000 of these women to the Conciergerie, ready to be packed off at a moment's notice.

" At the Embassy I found them in little anxiety. Brinquant is not yet ordered off. Webster, the old Queen's messenger and Philip Currie's boon companion, is dead. Lord Hertford has also chosen the moment to die at Bagatelle, his house in the Bois de Boulogne. He also was a type, the original of Thackeray's Lord Steyne. He remained to the day of his death a patron of the half world, and has left illegitimate children and no will they say. He was fond of jokes, *à la Regence.* The most amusing of them was connected with a young clergyman he had engaged as chaplain [but I forbear transcribing it]. His Lordship has long been *légendaire* in Paris, yet such is the disturbance in the public mind, his death is mentioned without special comment in the papers.

" The Prussians are at Châlons, and in a few days, unless great events happen, must be in front of Paris. The city will be summoned to surrender and threatened with destruction on refusal. The army is far away and the garrison insufficient for defence. The Prussians will hardly postpone a bombardment, and it is possible Paris may be taken by storm and burnt. The Crown Prince, who is believed to be marching in advance, probably counts on an insurrection as soon as he shall make his appearance at the gates, or he would hardly risk so desperate an adventure with two French armies in his rear. The Chamber is in an uproar, Gambetta calling for news of the army, but the town is quiet and cheerful and the Parisians seem ready to do their duty. Trochu has command of the place. Edmond About, in the ' Soir,' croaks ominously. He has been in the jaws of the lion and dreads its teeth. The ' Gaulois ' says that the Emperor is in such a state that a surprising announcement might be any day made. How strange it is to remember the early days of the war a month ago when the Empress told her son ' Va donc mon enfant et sois digne du sang des Bonapartes et des Guzmans,' and when the train was out of sight, ' Sa Majesté redevint femme.' At the first engagement at Saarbruck we were told: ' Le Prince Imperiale ne se laissa nullement impressioner; les vieux soldats le voyant si calm fondirent en larmes . . . Quand commenca la canonade le Prince demanda a l'Empereur " Dites donc papa c'est une balle qui siffle auprès de nous, ou bien un boulet." " On ne peut jamais savior au juste mon fils," repondit l'Empereur. . . . Après la defaite de l'ennemi le Prince Imperiale presenta au jeune Conneau [his favourite playfellow] une balle qu'il avait ramassée sur le champ de bataille.' This is what the 'Gaulois' used to tell us.

"I left Paris last night, looking sorrowfully on the Tuileries and its garden, with the trees brown in it like autumn. The sergent-de-ville and the sentinel stood as usual at the garden gate, the fountain played, the sun shone, and the children and *bonnes* chattered as though the world were not already crumbling about their ears. Julie is left with orders to bring away the plate and pictures in case of the worst, and I shall take Anne over to England and then come back if the siege is not begun, but one cannot foresee. I dream every night of armies and victories and defeats."

This was my last visit to Paris before the city was invested by the German armies and the siege began.

There is not much in my diary worth quoting after this. Having had our carriage wheels new tyred we drove on to Dieppe, arriving there 29th August, in heavy rain, to find the whole place full of refugees. "There are a thousand men drilling here on the beach in blouses with a red cross on their left sleeves. I am struck with the number of able-bodied men one sees everywhere idle, although the whole country has been called to arms. Perhaps there is a want of weapons. Dieppe is full of English who affect sympathy with Prussia. General Trochu has at the eleventh hour ordered all the Germans out of Paris within three days, one would have expected within three hours. The bombardment of Strassburg has done great damage. Kehl has been burnt. A shell burst in a Pensionnat at Strassburg where the young ladies were at their history lesson. Seven were killed. Phalsbourg holds out bravely.

"*30th Aug.*— Julie has just arrived from Paris; very amusing about her troubles in getting away. The Hôtel Meyerbeer, where I used in former days to lodge, has been sacked. Some Frenchmen came to dine there, and the landlord (a German), seeing them out at elbows, thought fit to remark, 'You are too poor to dine here. I have just got an order from the King of Prussia for a dinner of ninety covers for this day week.' The men, upon this, fell on him and wrecked his house. There are said to be 40,000 Germans in Paris. Our Proprietaire, M. Desfontaines, has come into No. 204 from Noissy, through fear of the invasion.

"*31st Aug.*— The Embassies are to remain at Paris, the Empress Regent having declared her intention of remaining. Princess Mathilde has sent away her valuables, as have probably most others who are rich. The heroism of non-combatants in Paris will be shown mainly in their purses. I go to England to-morrow to see Francis [my elder brother], who starts shortly on his way back to Madeira.

"*2nd Sept.*— At Worth Forest Cottage. The 'Daily News' announces in large capitals, 'Decisive Battle, MacMahon totally routed,' and prints a telegram from William to Augusta: 'May God, who has hitherto be-friended us, continue his protection to our arms.' I felt very sick and angry, the more so because I have found everybody here at home crowing over this final result of the war. Awake half the night, thinking bitter things There was a great battle before Sedan yesterday.

"*3rd Sept.*— Spent the morning fishing at Cinderbanks. On coming in I heard the news of the surrender of the remains of the French army by General Wimpfen, MacMahon's second in command, and of the Emperor. Great numbers of French and many German soldiers, driven on to Belgian soil, have laid down their arms. Count Flahault, one of the last men of the First Empire, died yesterday. Many years ago he eloped to Gretna Green with the heiress of the Keith Barony, and always after Madame de Flahault came to England for her *couches,* so that her children should be British subjects, and her son have a right to his seat in the House of Lords.

"*5th Sept.*— To London for the day, and saw Philip Currie at the Foreign Office, who gave me an alarming account of the disturbed state of France. He showed me a letter just come from a girl who was governess at a French château in the south. She wrote that the peasantry were surrounding the house.

"*6th Sept.*— Back to Dieppe.

"*8th Sept.*— Crossed back again with Anne to Newhaven in a gale of wind. We were thirteen hours at sea, and ran some risk of being driven on to Beachy Head. At Newhaven we found our Swiss horses, and drove on to Worth Forest. Before leaving Dieppe I sent Julie a box containing 100 lb. of ship's biscuits, with a letter of instructions as to her conduct during the siege. I also offered my apartment to the *maire* as an ambulance, but my proprietor refused his consent. [The biscuits fortunately reached Julie just before communication with Paris ceased, and proved a Godsend to her during the four months the siege lasted. My cousin, Francis Currie, whom, though I have said nothing about him in my diary, I had seen constantly during my last weeks at Paris, making our speculations on the course of events together, remained on quietly in his rooms in the Palais Royal right through both siege and Commune, continuing his philosophic occupation, the pursuit of pleasure, without disturbance or much hardship. I should have stayed on with him, but for my wife's expected confinement, and seen the drama out. It was an opportunity missed I still regret.]

"*25th Sept.*— Since my return to England I have not read a newspaper, nor shall till peace is made."

A few extracts from letters, written me just then by my friend Robert Lytton, dealing with public events, may here be added. He was at the time first Secretary of Embassy at Vienna, but on leave in England, and in close touch with all our chief diplomatists.

"*11th Sept.,* 1870.— Knebworth. I am very doubtful as to the Germans claiming Alsace and Lorraine, but if they do claim it, it will be baseless, abominable, unprecedented, and irredeemable should England stand by quiescent while her boasted ally of yesterday is being dismembered. Yet a colleague whom I met yesterday, fresh from the Foreign Office, told me the Government is firmly resolved to do nothing, and does not seem to think the situation worth a Cabinet Council. We shall pay dearly and perhaps more than we can afford by and by for the excessive prudence of our present policy, which is, I am told, strongly recommended by Lyons, who is afraid of burning his fingers and losing his reputation as a safe man. France will, of course, be thrown into the arms of Russia, and sell her support in the East for a European alliance of vengeance on her faithless friend across the Channel."

I remember that my own feeling at the time about Alsace Lorraine was one of rejoicing that the Germans, whom I hated, should have let slip an opportunity of high-minded moderation which would have redoubled the glory of their victories. While at Worth Forest with my brother Francis, we used to argue the French and the German case, he strongly maintaining against me that the French defeat had delivered Europe from its chief danger. Germany, he thought, could never be a serious menace.

"*3rd, Oct.,* 1870.— Ormeskirk. Odo Russell [our Ambassador at Berlin] who sees all the despatches now as soon as they arrive, and is therefore a good authority, writes to his wife, who is here, that Bismarck has intimated to us his intention of eventually, after taking Paris I suppose, sending the Emperor back to France with a slice of Belgium by way of a letter of recommendation to the French people. You may fancy how this has fluttered our Downing Street dovecote. I can myself hardly believe the story, but if Bismarck really does play off this practical joke on us what a *reductio ad absurdum* it will be of the lauded prudence of the Gladstone Cabinet in regard to that absurd Belgian treaty. Odo adds that Bismarck wishes to keep Bazaine locked up in Metz with the whole garrison till the end of the war, but not to attack them or destroy them, because it is his wish to hand over to the Emperor at the end as large a remnant as can yet be saved of the Imperial army. Meanwhile Russia is certainly arming fast, and the Russian merchants in the city have already created a panic there by their expressed apprehension, which seems to me perfectly well founded that she is about to attack Turkey. I take it that whenever she pleases Russia can do this with perfect impunity and success."

"*7th Oct.,* 1870.— Knebworth. In connection with the story I mentioned in my last, Odo says that Bismarck avers that, although it is necessary to keep Bazaine safe in Metz, he is anxious, if possible, not to starve or otherwise destroy the army shut up in that town, in order that at the end of the war he may hand over to the Emperor as much as can be spared of the Imperial forces for the preservation of order in France. However, I still disbelieve the story. In a letter which Lady Emily received from her husband the day I left Lathom, he said: 'The French Government has again for the third, and it says for the last time made a most earnest and pathetic appeal to us as the old friends and allies of France to come to the rescue, to which we have replied by a long despatch to the effect that we pity France, but can't help her. This document is a very painful one to read, and it is one which I am certain your dear father [Lord Clarendon] would never have written.'

"Lady Cowley, who did not go to see the Emperor at the request of the Empress but on her own hook from Frankfort, said he was looking in much better health than she expected to find him, that he seemed deeply mortified by the abuse of the French Press, but maintained that he was still the favourite of the French people, and seemed to count on returning to the Tuileries. The Empress wrote him a most insulting and heartless letter calling him a '*lâche*,' the receipt of which was the occasion of that fainting fit which gave rise to the rumour of his attempted suicide. He told Lady Cowley that he was literally without a sixpence. Grammont, who has been staying with Lord Malmesbury, declares this to be perfectly true, and that the utmost the Emperor's few remaining friends hope to be able to make up for him is £1,200 a year. The Empress, I believe, has some fortune of her own, but they are on the worst possible terms. I hope I shall soon be able to invite myself to 'Worth as Lady Cowley invited herself to Wilhelmshöhe.

" Did you see that the French papers, learning from the English Press that the Prussians were supplied with the best information from their general staff, exclaimed in chorus: ' Nous savons maintenant qui est cet espion qui a fourni aux Prussiens tant de précieux renseignements; c'est M. le General Staff, homme d'une astuce remarquable.' "

END OF MY PARIS DIARY OF 1870

APPENDIX II

Memorandum as to the Evacuation of Egypt

The evacuation of Egypt is a question partly of honour, partly of prudence. Of honour, in view of the pledges given; of prudence on military grounds.

If Egypt could be held honourably and without risk of war, there is much to be said in favour of continuing the English protectorate. It secures our Mediterranean route to India at a small cost. Its prestige to us is of value, and we should be spared the discredit of a withdrawal under French pressure. We owe it, too, to the Egyptians, whose army and political aspirations we destroyed in 1882, to continue to them our assistance in their weakness as against other Powers.

Nevertheless the risks appear to me great. Egypt's position on the Suez Isthmus is too important geographically to be allowed permanently to any one European Power by the rest of the Powers. It stands marked out for neutrality as between them, and France will certainly not consent to our holding it permanently without a war. As a question of near danger I have reason to feel sure that a complete agreement has been come to between France and the Sultan (probably, too, the Czar) regarding it, and that the return of the Liberal Party to office in England will determine their joint action.

It is therefore of some urgency to consider whether we are strong enough by land and sea to refuse at all hazards.

I agree entirely with Mr. Gladstone when he hopes that Lord Salisbury rather than himself may negotiate the evacuation. Mr. Gladstone's position abroad will be weak, as he will be without cordial support from the Central Powers, while his position in honour towards France will be hampered by his many pledges. Lord Salisbury could get better terms for the Egyptians, and would be less likely to sacrifice them to the exigencies of European diplomacy.

I believe an evacuation might be effected on one or other of the following lines:

(1) The simplest and most expeditious plan would probably be to hand over the military responsibility to the Sultan. This would have the advantage of postponing the ultimate question. It would place Egypt, as regards European ambitions, under whatever degree of integrity the Ottoman Empire enjoys. Ottoman troops could certainly guard her southern frontier and prevent surprise from other quarters. England, this quarrel about Egypt settled, would then revert to her former friendly relations with Turkey, and in the event of a break-up of the Empire would be free to take

406

whatever steps her interests required. As regards Egyptian opinion, I believe that on the whole it would be not unfavourable to such a solution. There is no love for the Turks among the fellahin, but the Sultan's authority would be accepted by them as natural and legal, while it must be remembered that the Khedivial rule is also Turkish. The Sultan, indeed, might be expected to protect in some measure the Arabic-speaking population against a renewal of oppression by the Turkish Circassian Pashas, and, in any case, he would be jealous in their favour of European aggression.

No administrative interference, however, need be conceded if the transfer of military protection be made under agreement. It is probable that, if the right claimed for England in the Wolff Convention of ultimate intervention were withdrawn, France and Russia would not oppose such a solution.

(2) A better plan, if honestly attempted by England, and as honestly accepted by the Powers, would be to re-establish the National Government on liberal and progressive lines, under guarantee of neutrality.

Although much time and opportunity have been wasted during our nine years of occupation in repressing political life among the Egyptians, I am still of opinion that something in the shape of Constitutional Government would give them their best chance of permanent independence and progress as a race. It must not be forgotten that in 1882 a Constitution on a European model (decree of March, 1882) was obtained by the Egyptian National Party, which gave considerable promise of efficiency as a means of asserting native right against both the Turkish ruling caste and the European colonists. If it had not been put down by England's armed intervention, it would in all likelihood have given a new impulse of progress not only to Egypt, but to the surrounding Mohammedan lands. I am of opinion that even yet its restoration at Cairo would have this effect, and is not impossible. The National Constitutional Party, though broken as an organization, exists in the individuals who composed it, and in younger men of a new generation holding similar ideas. From among these a Ministry could be formed to set the Constitutional machine in motion under sympathetic English auspices, nor do I doubt that within a couple of years it would be found competent to conduct the business of the country without further military aid. It is by men of this party alone that Sir Evelyn Baring's better work in Egypt is appreciated, and it is only to their hands that the work of continuing it could be reasonably entrusted.

Unfortunately for such a solution, the Constitutional idea finds many adverse influences under present conditions. The Khedive and the Turkish Party, which we have replaced in office, are wholly opposed to it. The European officials representing financial interests consider any form of popular government less manageable by them than the present absolute *régime*. And Sir Evelyn Baring would as little approve. Lastly — and this is perhaps the greatest obstacle — the French and foreign policy generally in the East desires nothing so little as to see a genuine resuscitation of political vitality among the native races. Under the present despotic yet feeble *régime*, France counts on succeeding England in controlling a weak prince and weaker people until such time as Egypt may fall to her share of the Ottoman spoils.

The attempt, therefore, if made at all, must be made honestly and with the thoroughgoing support of a sympathetic English representative, otherwise it cannot but fail.

(3) The third solution of placing Egypt under joint European guardianship and political control, is one against which, however it may recommend itself as a settlement of European differences, I feel bound to protest in native Egyptian interests.

Under English rule the native populations have been carefully protected, and their rights maintained against the encroachment of foreign colonists. But under any other European rule than England's the reverse would certainly be the case. Egypt under French or Italian or joint European control would be exploited in whatever direction it was thought that revenue could be best increased. The fellahin now enjoying their hereditary lands would be speedily dispossessed and reduced to a practical slavery worse than any they have hitherto known, and as a race would probably be little by little displaced, the demoralized, and extirpated.

As already remarked, the fellahin in 1882, alarmed at this very danger under the Anglo-French control, had asserted themselves politically and forced their rulers to grant them a means of self-defence in the form of a Constitutional Government. They had acquired the support of a large army with sufficient prestige to deter attack from more than one of the Powers, and they were backed by much sympathy east and west in their attempted reforms. Having for our own reasons suppressed all these possibilities of good for them, it would be a supreme injustice to overlook their interests now in the settlement to be made. To Mr. Gladstone especially, who is so largely responsible for the intervention, it should be a matter of honourable concern that this race and people should not perish.

(4) To withdraw the British garrison under present conditions and without a political settlement would be to court future difficulties.

Sir Evelyn Baring's policy of the last five years, based as it has been on the view that Egypt was to remain a permanent annex of the Indian Empire, has practically destroyed all authority there but that of the English Occupation. Egypt's present government is a mixed European, Armenian, and native bureaucracy controlled by half-a-dozen Englishmen with the British garrison at their back. No native government in any sense of authority exists. The Khedive, indolent and without initiative, is a mere dummy Prince. His Ministers, most of them Turks of advanced years, have been chosen for their pliancy rather than their ability. Their names have no weight, and their duties are little more than to sign without reading the documents placed before them. The great departments of Finance, Irrigation, War, and latterly Justice, are directed by Englishmen. The army and police have English superior officers; and even the Interior is, I believe, in process of being taken over by us.

This Anglicized condition of the Government could not long survive a withdrawal of the English troops. Even were it consented to by France, it would rapidly lose its authority. English control, though not unpopular with the fellahin, is disliked by every class in Cairo and the towns, and would at once be the object of attack, open or secret.

It is a mistake to suppose the Khedive attached to English influence, or to be depended on in any way to support it. On the contrary, while leaning on English support these last ten years he has deeply resented the usurpation of his authority, and the many indignities he has been made to accept. It is more than probable that seeing French influence in the ascendant, he would secretly favour the intrigues which would be begun against the English commands in the Army and the English Civil officials. A couple of years would thus see the downfall of the whole structure of English influence so elaborately reared. In the absence of any native political organization in the country its government would then become practically French; and this is doubtless what the French Foreign Office counts upon. I deprecate such a result both for English interests, and especially for the Egyptians for the reasons already given.

Such, I take it, are the various lines on which evacuation could be effected. If the Liberal Party is prepared with a definite plan by which Egypt could be provided with a satisfactory Government preparatory to withdrawing our troops under settlement with the Sultan and Powers, I think its leaders do well to press evacuation on public attention. But it is idle for them to entertain the idea that any such Government has been already formed, or even that a first step in that direction has been already taken. Sir Evelyn Baring's policy is entirely one of remaining in Egypt, and each year sees more and more authority placed in English hands. Otherwise I see no alternative but to re-establish the Sultan's military authority, or to brave the danger of European complications, as Lord Salisbury will doubtless do, and remain. An English protectorate would be a lesser evil to the Egyptians than any form of European Joint Control.

WILFRID SCAWEN BLUNT.

Paris, *Nov.* 5, 1891.

N.B. This memorandum was written for Lytton while staying at the Paris Embassy, but I am not sure whether he ever read it, for he was lying on his death bed. Edwin Egerton, however, then first Secretary and *chargé d'affaires* of the Embassy, highly approved of it — so much so that he gave a copy of it to Blowitz, who sent it to the "Times," where it may be found, though not quite in its full text.

W. S. B.

APPENDIX III

Mr. Herbert Spencer to Mr. Blunt

[Recd. *October* 4, 1898]

5, Percival Terrace,
Brighton.

DEAR SIR,

For some years I have been casting about for a poet who might fitly undertake a subject I very much want to see efficiently dealt with. At one time I thought of proposing it to Mr. Robert Buchanan, who, in respect of vigour of expression and strength of moral indignation seemed appropriate, but I concluded that the general feeling with regard to him would prevent a favourable reception — would, in fact, tend very much to cancel the effect produced. Afterwards the name of Mr. William Watson occurred to me as one who had shown feelings of the kind I wished to see expressed. But admirable as much of his poetry is, the element of power is not marked; he does not display a due amount of burning sarcasm. Your recent letter in " The Times," and since then a review in " The Academy," in which there were quotations from your poem, " The Wind and the Whirlwind," lead me to hope that you may work out the idea I refer to.

This idea is suggested by the first part of Goethe's " Faust "—" The Prologue in Heaven," I think it is called. In this, if I remember rightly (it is now some fifty years since I read it), Mephistopheles obtains permission to tempt Faust: the drama being thereupon initiated. Instead of this I suggest an interview and dialogue in which Satan seeks authority to find some being more wicked than himself, with the understanding that if he succeeds this being shall take his place. The test of wickedness is to be the degree of disloyalty — the degree of rebellion against divine government.

Satan gives proof that his rebellion has been less flagitious than that of men.

He confesses to having been a rebel, but an avowed one.

He has not, like men, professed to worship the Christian God while perpetually worshipping the pagan gods; he has not day by day sacrificed with zeal to Thor and Odin, while nominally sacrificing to Jehova.

He is not like men who, tepidly joining in praises of Christ as a model on one day in the week, on the other six days bring up their sons in glowing admiration of blood-stained Homeric heroes.

He is not like men who, nominally admitting on Sunday that forgiveness is a virtue, emphatically insist on and practice on all other days the duty of blood-revenge.

He has never done like men who, professing the Christian principle of submitting to injuries, ridicule as idiots the few Christians who propose to act on that principle.

He has not, while professing to relinquish the savage law of retaliation — a life for a life — adopted the far more savage law — for one life many lives.

Satan goes on to urge that he has never with rebellion joined perpetual insults as men have done.

I have never turned your churches of mercy into pagan temples by hanging up in them the torn flags of conquered peoples.

I have never blasphemed by thanking you for aiding in mowing down tens of thousands of men who worshipped you under another name.

I have never blasphemed by calling you Omniscient while ascribing to you unutterable stupidity — the stupidity of being ready to accept perpetual professions of obedience as sufficient to cancel perpetual acts of absolute disobedience: being so pleased with laudations, prayers, and obeisances as to overlook the contemptuous disregard of peremptory commands.

THE REPLY

If while sacrificing to me in name men have sacrificed to Pagan gods in act, it is your doing. You have betrayed them into this rebellion. Only by your delusions has it been possible to make them think that I should accept words in place of deeds. Joined though it is with lying and hypocrisy, the rebellion of these beings is not worse than your rebellion, because you have prompted it.

SATAN

But if I deceived them it was only because they wished to be deceived. They wished to gratify their revenge while having the blessings promised to those who forgive.

REPLY

You cannot be pardoned.

SATAN

But may I mete out their punishments according to their own measure? They ask to be forgiven their sins as they forgive the sins of others. May I torture them in proportion to their unforgiveness? For every time they have professed the religion of love and practised the religion of hate, may I thrust them a step lower down in hell?

Might not some such ideas as these, presented with power, produce considerable effects upon a few men, though not perhaps on many?

I am faithfully yours,

HERBERT SPENCER.

END OF APPENDICES

INDEX TO VOLUME I